Science under Scarcity

Food Systems and Agrarian Change

Edited by Frederick H. Buttel, Billie R. DeWalt,
and Per Pinstrup-Andersen

A complete list of titles in the series appears at the end of this book.

SCIENCE UNDER SCARCITY

Principles and Practice for Agricultural Research Evaluation and Priority Setting

Julian M. Alston
George W. Norton
Philip G. Pardey

Published in cooperation with the International Service for National Agricultural Research

Cornell University Press

ITHACA AND LONDON

This book was printed from camera-ready pages provided by the authors.

First published 1995 by Cornell University Press.

Printed in the United States of America

⊚ The paper in this book meets the minimum requirements
of the American National Standard for Information Sciences—
Permanence of Paper for Printed Library Materials, ANSI Z39.48-1984.

Library of Congress Cataloging-in-Publication Data

Alston, Julian M.
   Science under scarcity : principles and practice for agricultural research evaluation
and priority setting / Julian M. Alston, George W. Norton, Philip G. Pardey.
      p.   cm. — (Food systems and agrarian change)
   "Published in cooperation with the International Service for National Agricultural
Research."
   Includes bibliographical references (p.   ) and indexes.
   ISBN 0-8014-2937-4
   1. Agriculture—Research—Evaluation.   2. Agriculture—Research—Cost
effectiveness.   I. Norton, George W.   II. Pardey, Philip G.   III. International Service
for National Agricultural Research.   IV. Title.   V. Series.
S540.E92A58   1995
338.4′363072—dc20   94-40637

To

Cameron, Deborah, John, Louisa, Marj, Michelle, Sydney, and Toby

Contents

Illustrations

Tables

Foreword

This book represents the culmination of a research agenda that extends back to the late 1940s. The agenda was initiated by a group of scholars at the U.S. Department of Agriculture and the University of Chicago who began to explore quantitatively the sources of growth in agricultural production.

This initial research revealed that the growth of agricultural production in the United States could only be partially explained by growth in conventional inputs — in land, labor, capital, and operating inputs — as traditionally measured.

But what was the source of the newly discovered growth in the productivity of the factors used in agricultural production? An initial step was to associate productivity growth with technical change and to attribute technical change to agricultural research. This set off an extended debate that lasted well into the late 1960s about the relative significance of technical change embodied in physical inputs as well as new knowledge arising out of education and experience, embodied in the human agent.

By the early 1970s the methodology that had been developed to measure rates of return to agricultural research and to human capital was being extended to the process of research planning and to allocating research resources. Alternatives to the more intuitive approaches, such as scoring methods or the congruence between research expenditures and the value of production, were being explored. The growth of international support for agricultural research in developing countries added impetus to this effort in the 1970s. And the decline in research support in the more constrained economic environment of the 1980s represented one additional source of demand for more effective research planning and management.

This volume by Alston, Norton and Pardey is the culmination of both the rate of return and the research resource allocation studies. It is impressive both in its comprehensiveness and in its depth. It will hardly be possible in the future to contribute to either research or practice in the fields of research evaluation and research resource allocation without referring to this book.

VERNON W. RUTTAN
Regents Professor
University of Minnesota

Preface

Resources for agricultural science are scarce. Worldwide, public agricultural research systems are being asked to do more with less. As government budgets tighten generally, agricultural research administrators face ever-sharper pressures to justify their budgets and to economize. Increasingly, research administrators are being asked to provide evidence that the costs of their operations are justified by the benefits. At the same time, the demands placed on agricultural science are also changing. Agricultural science is being asked to contribute to knowledge and technology and to satisfy demands for information on many new issues — environmental problems, food safety and quality, and rural development — without foresaking traditional work.

Closer scrutiny and tighter resources imply a greater need for evaluation of public-sector research and for economically effective allocation of resources to it. All research is planned and evaluated to some degree. The relevant questions are how much planning and evaluating to do, who should do it, and what form it should take. Some say there should be little formal planning and evaluating — that too much planning and evaluation can stifle the generation of new ideas, the heart of any research program. Others say planning and evaluation are necessary for accountability in the use of scarce public funds. The former group would argue that relatively unstructured planning and evaluation in the past have produced results with high rates of return: "If it ain't broke don't fix it." The latter group point to the slowness of research systems to adjust to the changing needs of society and to the realities of scarce public resources.

It is important to distinguish the economic problem of research priority setting from the related scientific, technical, and management issues that arise in implementing priorities, getting the research done, and getting the results adopted. It is tempting for many, in the pursuit of accountability, to take the process of evaluation and priority setting too far. Our view is that processes for planning and evaluating research can be helpful at every stage in the research system but that structured quantitative methods are most beneficial for making strategic decisions when research priorities are being set across broad commodity programs, disciplinary (and multidisciplinary) programs, and research problems.

The formal analytical apparatus and priority-setting approaches that are developed and described in this book are most useful when they are applied at an aggregative, program level. They are less useful at a detailed, disaggregated, project level for at least three reasons. First, the costs of fine-tuning might not justify the benefits in terms of improved allocation of resources to research. Second, measurement problems become increasingly important as the degree of disaggregation increases.[1] Third, micromanaging creative endeavors such as research can be counterproductive; more detailed allocation decisions are probably best guided by well-structured incentive systems instead of interventionist, "hands-on" allocative mechanisms. The last is perhaps the most important consideration. Formal evaluation and priority-setting procedures should not be used as a basis for replacing ingenuity, serendipity, and scientific entrepreneurship with bureaucratic procedures. There is a wealth of informal evidence that a successful research program rests heavily on the spirit, imagination, judgment, and integrity of agricultural scientists who are allowed freedom of enquiry. The role of research evaluation and priority setting is to help determine the boundaries within which free scientific enquiry occurs.

Once decisions have been made about the numbers and types of scientists to employ and broad parameters have been placed on operating budgets, highly structured evaluation and priority-setting procedures can reduce the efficiency of the research system. A balance must be struck between the use of formal evaluation and priority-setting procedures and informal alternatives at any level of decision-making. The trick is to ensure that the relevant economizing principles are involved in decisions regarding resource allocation, without overly managing individual scientists. Personal and professional incentives for scientists must be built into the system so that they respond to the demands of clients, generate new ideas, and produce high-quality products. Occasional quantitative, economic, and social evaluations

---

1. A major difficulty when assessing research impact at the project level involves apportioning observed or predicted changes in yields or reductions in unit costs to research-induced changes in particular components of a technology package *while holding other components of that technology unchanged.* Given the interrelationships inherent in many new technological packages, it is likely that spurious attribution, double counting, or both will result.

of individual projects or programs of research can be useful, but not whole-sale, costly, quantitative evaluation of all potential and completed research projects.

Some say that research evaluation and priority setting should be left to the scientists themselves. However, scientific merit alone is not sufficient to justify maintaining budgetary support for research or for setting strategic research priorities. Research administrators recognize that assessing the social value of research is useful for justifying budgets and is essential for making strategic decisions on research investments.

Without economic analysis, it is difficult to assess the social value of scientific knowledge or new technologies and to make informed judgments about the trade-offs in allocating scarce scientific resources. This means there is a growing role for economists in research evaluation and priority setting, because biological scientists are no more capable of providing reliable answers to questions of economic value than economists are of evaluating the scientific potential of biological experiments. The roles of economists and other scientists are complementary. Scientists' opinions are needed to help define the possibilities of advancing knowledge or providing new technologies and information if resources are allocated to particular programs. The input of economic analysts is useful in estimating the economic value of the research, including the distribution of benefits and costs, and in advising decision makers on procedures for incorporating economic principles when setting priorities and allocating research resources. Economists have made significant progress in developing methods for research evaluation and priority setting, but many research analysts and administrators do not have a working knowledge or appreciation of them. *Science under Scarcity* has been written, in response to the demand from research administrators and the analysts working for them, to fill that knowledge gap.

The title *Science under Scarcity* was chosen partly to convey the view that the increased current scarcity of resources for agricultural science implies an enhanced demand for methods that will help research administrators justify continuing budgetary support and economize within the constraints of their budgets. Of course, research resources are always scarce, and there is always potential for economizing in the allocation of those resources, but many budgets for agricultural research are increasingly tight and the likelihood of impact is greater at a time when people are being pressed to look for alternatives.

If we are successful in assisting research administrators in making better decisions on research resource allocation, there is another sense in which scarcity might be alleviated through better information. In a world in which more than a third of the population live in poverty, the title *Science under*

Scarcity graphically expresses the important role that agricultural science has always played as the mainspring of economic progress in developing economies, and as an engine for lifting the technological constraints that limit the capacity of the global food and fiber system to produce more within ever-tighter natural resource constraints. We hope that by helping agricultural scientists make better choices in their *research* resource allocations, this book can contribute in an economically meaningful way to a reduction in the problems that are associated with global scarcity of *other, nonresearch* resources.

Objectives

We were motivated to begin writing this book in the mid-1980s, when the International Service for National Agricultural Research (ISNAR) was faced with ever-increasing demands by national agricultural research systems (NARSs) to provide workable research-evaluation and priority-setting procedures. A substantial body of literature had developed on ex post research evaluation, and a more disparate, gray literature on priority setting was emerging. We had been involved in several studies ourselves and were aware of the need for cost-effective and practical methods for evaluating and prioritizing research, but we were also conscious of the importance of having methods that could be defended at a conceptual level as being consistent with the relevant economic theory. Priority-setting methods that do not appeal to a consistent conceptual framework are likely to be ad hoc and to produce recommendations that are difficult to defend and, therefore, more easily dismissed by decision makers. An integrated treatment of research evaluation and priority-setting procedures was needed, one that would relate procedures to theory and provide guidance for when and how to apply particular methods.

The overriding goal of this book is to lower the cost of implementing conceptually sound research evaluation and priority-setting procedures. Research administrators want procedures that
- are cost-effective
- can incorporate multiple research programs (defined by commodity, problem area, or spatial focus)
- can assess trade-offs among multiple objectives

Our premise in writing this book is that any method or procedure adopted should draw from a consistent conceptual framework. A range of approaches have been suggested and used, but they have not always been theoretically sound or consistent or appropriate. The specific objectives with respect to

research evaluation and priority-setting methods are
- to place them in a policy and scientific context
- to describe their key theoretical or conceptual elements
- to review, synthesize, and assess alternative procedures
- to provide insights into issues associated with implementing these procedures

To accomplish these objectives, we review appropriate theory, assess the literature, and draw on previous experience in implementing research evaluation and priority-setting procedures. Procedures are assessed with respect to their consistency with economic theory, their ease of implementation, and their appropriateness for the problem at hand.

Previous Work

The methods and lines of enquiry described in this volume trace back several decades. Willis Peterson, Vernon Ruttan, Burt Sundquist, and others at the University of Minnesota have addressed issues of research policy and evaluation in both developed and developing countries for many years. Vernon Ruttan's (1982) *Agricultural Research Policy* book raised many of the issues that we attempt to deal with in *Science under Scarcity*. The Minnesota work on research policy and evaluation had intellectual ties to the University of Chicago where studies by Schultz (1953a) and Griliches (1958, 1964) spurred a flurry of activity by graduate students such as Robert Evenson, Willis Peterson, and others, who evaluated the economic impact of agricultural research and extension. Work on research evaluation and priority setting spawned several conferences, beginning with one at Minnesota in 1969 that resulted in the book edited by Fishel (1971), *Resource Allocation in Agricultural Research*. An Airlie House Conference in 1975 led to the book edited by Arndt, Dalrymple and Ruttan (1977), *Resource Allocation and Productivity,* that took an international focus. An interregional project (IR-6) funded by the U.S. Department of Agriculture from 1979 to 1991 resulted in three sets of symposium proceedings (Norton et al. 1981; Sundquist 1987, 1991) and numerous papers on research evaluation.

Since the early 1970s, there has also been a broadening of the base of work in this area. Several major studies have been carried out in Australia, supported by the Australian government (including the Industries Assistance Commission report on *Rural Research in Australia* in 1976 and the monograph by Edwards and Freebairn on *Measuring a Country's Gains from Research* in 1981), and a large number of smaller studies have dealt with particular institutions or industries. Similar developments have taken place in Canada and the U.K., with major studies reported by Klein and Furtan (1985) and Thirtle and Ruttan (1987) and a host of monographs and journal articles. In relation to less-developed countries, economists working at or for the international agricultural research centers, particularly CIAT, CIMMYT, ICRISAT, IRRI, and ISNAR, have been involved in numerous efforts to evaluate the effects of research and assist with setting priorities for research in their own centers or for their clients. Beginning in the mid-1980s, the Australian agency ACIAR supported a series of research priority-setting projects in several Asian NARSs and also undertook an ex ante evaluation study at the global level (Davis, Oram and Ryan 1987). In addition many studies have been conducted by developing-country governments on their own behalf. There have been several reviews of parts of this literature, including Schuh and Tollini (1979), Norton and Davis (1981), Greig (1981), Scobie (1984), Parton, Anderson and Makeham (1984), Fox (1987), Scobie and Jardine (1988), and Schultz (1990).

Most of the ideas in this book were borrowed from this general literature. It would take too much space to list all of the people to whom we owe an intellectual debt or to enunciate the size of the debt in any detail. We hope that those who read this book will think that it does a fair job of communicating the ideas that have been developed by the work of those who have inspired us.

Acknowledgments

We have drawn on the patience, counsel, guidance, and collaboration of a good many people in preparing this book. We would especially like to thank Jock Anderson, Barbara Craig, Howard Elliott, John Freebairn, Grant Scobie, and Vince Smith, as well as Jim Chalfant, Matt Dagg, Cesar Falconi, James Houck, John Mullen, Vernon Ruttan, and Helio Tollini for reviewing and commenting on all or major parts of the manuscript. During the course of writing this book we benefited from the advice of Randy Barker, Doug Beach, Fred Buttel, Derek Byerlee, Jeff Davis, Klaus Deininger, Paul Driscoll, Wilhelmina Eveleens, Shenggen Fan, Bob Herdt, Bob Lindner, Luis Macagno, Will Martin, Alex McCalla, Bruce McCarl, and Brad Mills, and our NARS colleagues in several country studies, especially Modan Dey, Patricio Espinosa, Gustavo Ferreira, Melania Lima, Wilfredo Moscoso, Julio Palomino, and Stanley Wood. The institutional support we received from ISNAR, the University of California at Davis, the University of Minnesota, Virginia Tech, Cornell University, and the University of Saskatchewan is also gratefully acknowledged.

We are particularly thankful to Fionnuala Hawes who gave generously of her good humor, word processing, and desk-top publishing skills, to Kathleen Sheridan for outstanding editorial work, and to Nienke Beintema for proofing the manuscript: *groetjes* and *bedankt*. The final production assistance of Leta Kelley and the design inputs of Richard Claase are also gratefully acknowledged.

JULIAN M. ALSTON
Professor
University of California at
Davis

GEORGE W. NORTON
Senior Fellow
International Service for
National Agricultural Research
Professor
Virginia Polytechnic Institute
and State University

PHILIP G. PARDEY
Senior Research Officer
International Service for
National Agricultural Research
Associate Professor
University of Minnesota

Introduction

Governments have to decide what resources to make available for public-sector research. In turn, research administrators have to allocate resources across research problems, programs, people, and places. In order to make these decisions effectively, decision makers have to evaluate alternatives and set priorities. This book reviews, synthesizes, and assesses research evaluation and priority-setting procedures. The term *research evaluation*, as used in the book, refers to assessing the economic effects of research.[1] The value of research evaluation is both as a means of accounting for the effectiveness of past research investments (i.e., ex post evaluation) and, looking forward, as a basis for setting priorities and allocating research resources (i.e., ex ante evaluation).

Applying the principles and procedures identified in this book will provide new knowledge and help decision makers achieve their objectives. Even when the procedures described here are not adopted explicitly, incorporating the underlying economic way of thinking about research investments will help structure decision-making processes and improve their outcome. At the same time, the principles and practices described here should not substitute for the best judgments of scientists and policymakers in the research–priority-setting process. They provide a unifying framework within which to synthesize a wide range of scientific and economic data that would otherwise be difficult to reconcile and use. Thus, good judgments can be made even better, and poor judgments may be exposed.

The evaluation procedures outlined in this book enable the various productivity-related, distributional, and environmental consequences of re-

1. See Horton et al. (1993) for alternative approaches to research evaluation.

search to be reported using a comparable money measure. By so doing, they can reveal research opportunities and consequences that at first sight may not be so obvious. The systematic approaches to research evaluation and priority setting described here pay due regard to the economic context in which research is funded, conducted, and adopted without abandoning the scientific basis of the research process. This book provides a set of basic principles and procedures that are differentiated primarily by their degree of detail and complexity, and it gives guidance to the application of methods judged most appropriate for different representative situations.

Intended Audience

The primary audience for this book are analysts working for agricultural research systems who have at least Master's-level training in economics. Most agricultural research systems have access to such expertise. Parts of the book should be of direct interest to research administrators as well, although much of the material (especially in chapters 3, 4, and 6) is fairly technical. Where possible, we have put the more difficult material in footnotes or appendices. However, the bulk of the book is targeted toward economists who will be carrying out and interpreting research evaluation or priority-setting analyses for administrators. Some degree of technical sophistication is inevitable in a book of this kind. In presenting these evaluation methods and priority-setting procedures, we have been sensitive to the data and resource constraints that commonly confront analysts and decision makers in less-developed countries. Nevertheless, most of the material presented here is also directly applicable in a developed-country context.

The principles and practices described in this book are also relevant to those concerned with research evaluation and priority-setting problems in sciences beyond agriculture and beyond the public sector. While the primary focus is public-sector agricultural research, the approaches described here are equally applicable (or with small modifications) to nonagricultural research and to some private-sector situations. In particular, the ideas and methods in this book apply directly to the allocation of public-sector R&D resources between agricultural and nonagricultural research. Also, most of the evaluation and priority-setting methods are directly applicable to the decisions about research undertaken by producer organizations (e.g., using funds collected by a levy) and could be extended to consider choices about funding R&D versus product promotion and so on.

Science under Scarcity is most likely to be used as a reference book by economists doing applied studies on the economics of research. For that reason considerable use has been made of headings and subheadings, and an extensive subject index is appended. The book can also be used as a supplementary text in graduate-level courses on agricultural development, applied production economics, and welfare economics. A basic understanding of economic principles is required for most of the chapters, and for some, competence in statistics and mathematics is needed. A companion set of training materials for research evaluation and priority setting has been produced at the International Service for National Agricultural Research (ISNAR), including additional details to facilitate the application of the suggested methods. An interactive computer program *Dream©*, developed at ISNAR, that applies the economic surplus methods described in this book is included in the training materials.

Topical Outline

This book contains four major sections. In the first section, the institutional framework and conceptual issues associated with research evaluation and priority setting are addressed. Chapter 1 considers the institutional, scientific, and policy contexts of agricultural research. It discusses the influence of the type of organizational structure and the scientific context for research, on research evaluation and priority-setting procedures. It addresses research as an instrument of social policy and discusses the reasons for public-sector involvement in research and the need for research to improve institutions as well as technologies.

Chapter 2 presents the theoretical and conceptual issues in research evaluation and priority setting in a relatively nontechnical fashion. It introduces the concept of a research production function and the key factors influencing the economic consequences of research. The concept of economic surplus as a welfare measure is fundamental to the work in this book. Therefore, in chapter 2, the foundations of economic surplus measures are described, and criticisms of economic surplus as a welfare measure are reviewed and evaluated. Critical assumptions in the economic surplus model are also discussed and evaluated. Then we introduce a range of extensions of the model.

In the second major section, econometric and economic surplus measures are reviewed and synthesized. This section is significantly more technically demanding for the reader than the others; it contains the theoretical and conceptual underpinnings for all of the approaches being discussed in the other sections of the book. Chapter 3 presents parametric, nonparametric, and index-number approaches to the measurement of agricultural productivity. Primal and dual approaches to measuring the structure of production and (research-induced) technical change are considered, and measures of output, conventional inputs, and research and extension variables are detailed. Statistical issues related to specification error, multicollinearity, and simultaneity are briefly reviewed. Chapter 3 concludes with a discussion of the use of results from econometric models for measuring the effects of research directly.

Chapter 4 presents a comprehensive treatment of the measurement of research-induced changes in economic surplus. Horizontal and vertical market relationships are modeled, in large part to enable the benefits from research to be disaggregated among different groups of producers, consumers, or input suppliers. Such disaggregations are important when there is an interest in the impact on particular groups (such as domestic producers and consumers for a traded good, or suppliers of labor). It is suggested that this multimarket approach can also be used to explore the impact of research-induced quality change. Also in this chapter, the effects of market-distorting policies on the size and distribution of benefits are given some attention. Sustainability and other externalities are discussed briefly. Several of the more common variants of economic surplus models are presented in graphical and mathematical forms, and a fairly general method for calculating benefits from research is described.

In the third major section, implementation issues associated with research evaluation and priority-setting methods are presented. Chapter 5 builds directly on chapter 4 and focuses on the measurement of economic surplus with an emphasis on practical issues and using the results to make decisions. It addresses the different types of information required for different types of decisions and the implications of varying the degree of detail. Practical approaches are suggested for defining objectives, obtaining basic data and other information needs, developing the information base (including tables and questionnaires), data processing, and presenting and interpreting results. Step-by-step procedures for implementing the evaluation methods provided in the previous chapter are included in an appendix. Chapter 6 identifies mathematical-programming methods that can be used for analyzing the trade-offs involved in allocating scarce research resources across competing programs. It discusses the rationale for applying these optimizing methods and the modeling options available, and it identifies requirements for making these procedures operational. Chapter 7 presents the scoring approach that has been used as a shortcut method for evaluating alternatives and trading off multiple objectives. We review the use of scoring models in practice and contrast them with the methods described in chapters 5 and 6 in terms of consistency with the basic principles presented in earlier chapters. To conclude this chapter, we provide practical guidance on shortcut procedures and rules of thumb that can be applied when a more formal analysis is not warranted.

The fourth and final major section of the book provides an overview and assessment of research-evaluation and priority-setting procedures. Chapter 8 gives a perspective on when each type of method is likely to be most useful. It highlights some of the difficult methodological issues that are yet to be resolved, suggests potentially fruitful areas of future model development, and concludes the book.

The following conventions of style and nomenclature were adopted in the presentation of mathematical symbols in the text in general, but some exceptions were unavoidable (e.g., the use of s to denote shares of producer revenue and S to denote shares of consumer cost):

	Convention	*Used for*	*Example*
1.	base font	functions and operators	
		natural logarithms	ln
		functions	f(.)
		relative change in X (dX/X)	$E(X)$
2.	italics	all variables	
3.	upper-case italics	scalar variables	
		output price	P
		output quantity	Q
		variable input price	W
		variable input quantity	X
		fixed factors	Z
		relative supply shift *down* in the price direction	K
		relative shift of supply to the *right*	J
		relative reduction in producer price	Z
4.	lower-case italics	rate of change of a scalar variable	z
		absolute supply shift *down* in the price direction	k
5.	bold italics	vectors and matrices	$\boldsymbol{Z}$
6.	Greek letters	parameters	
		supply elasticities	ε
		demand elasticities (usually absolute values)	η
		elasticities of substitution	σ
		percentage tax (negative subsidy)	τ
		per unit tax (negative subsidy)	T
		technology index	τ
		first difference operator	Δ
7.	italic t	time index	t

Part I

Institutional and Conceptual
Framework

1

The Institutional, Scientific, and Policy Contexts

Worldwide, public-sector agricultural research is big business. By the mid-1980s public-sector agricultural research systems were spending $9.2 billion (1980 dollars) annually: $4.4 billion in developing countries and $4.8 billion in developed countries (Anderson, Pardey and Roseboom 1994). This global investment in public agricultural research represents a 2.6-fold increase in real (i.e., inflation-adjusted) terms over the amount that was invested just two decades earlier.[1]

It may be big business, but "business as usual" may not be sustainable. Questions are being increasingly asked about public-sector agricultural research: How much should be spent? How should it be spent? Who should spend it? Who should pay for it? What is the role for the private sector? How can the resources be used more effectively? The questions being asked are similar around the world, but the answers might differ depending on the institutional, political, and scientific environment in which public-sector agricultural research is being conducted. For instance, in most countries agricultural research is funded and administered independently from tertiary education, but in the United States and India, for example, they are intimately connected. Even among countries with similar institutional arrangements, there can be considerable differences in the objectives of the agricultural research system as well as important constraints imposed by other policies or other aspects of the economic and cultural environment.

1. Notably, the public research system in developed countries grew by 2.2-fold while the systems in developing countries spent 3.4 times more in the mid-1980s than they did in the early 1960s.

3

In this chapter we consider the implications of three aspects of the agricultural research environment. First, there is the "institutional setting" for research: the nature of funding arrangements, the legal and other considerations, the general objectives, the organizational culture, and the system of incentives and rewards. Section 1.1 discusses the implications of different executing agencies that carry out research, their organizational structures, and the funding arrangements. Second, there is the "scientific" context of research, including the general biological and physical sciences and the nature of the systems being studied. That context also includes research and adoption lags, as well as differing mixtures of basic and applied research. The importance of these factors for research evaluation and priority setting is addressed in section 1.2. Third, there is a "policy" context: agricultural research is only one of many policy instruments and its economic impact is conditioned by other policies. In section 1.3 we consider the economic reasons for government intervention in research, the implications for the appropriate forms of intervention, and the objectives for it. To conclude, we discuss research as an instrument of social policy, considering the availability of other policy instruments to pursue different social goals.

1.1   Institutional Setting

Agricultural research is conducted in a variety of institutional settings that may influence the procedures for allocating research resources. Three key features of the institutional setting are (a) the form of the "executing agencies" that carry out the research, (b) the "structure" within those agencies, and (c) the "funding arrangements" for R&D.

1.1.1   Executing Agencies

There is a wide range of organizational structures for public agricultural research systems. Typical systems include (a) those based in a university, (b) those based in a ministry of agriculture, (c) autonomous or semiautonomous research institutes, and (d) agricultural research councils. Mixtures of these systems are common, and public systems usually coexist with private ones.

The best organizational structure for research will vary, depending on the size and resources of the economy and its stage of development, the nature of the government bureaucracy, the objectives for the research system, and other factors. Each type of research system brings with it special characteristics. For example, a university system may consider the complementarity between research and education when setting priorities, while an institute system may not. A system based in a ministry of agriculture may give less budget autonomy to its agricultural research director than the autonomous-institute system does, but it may have its goals tied more explicitly to the government's goals for the agricultural sector and less directly to those of particular commodity groups. The choice of priority-setting procedures for research may be affected too. For example, a value is placed on educational output when setting priorities in a university-based system but not when setting priorities in a ministry-of-agriculture system.

The ministry-of-agriculture model has been the most common system for research on food crops in smaller countries and an important part of integrated federal-state systems in large countries (Trigo 1986). The autonomous or semiautonomous research institutes have been most common in countries with a significant amount of plantation agriculture or other large-scale forms of production. Several countries, particularly in Latin America, have recently attempted to increase the degree of budget and management autonomy for systems that have historically followed the ministry-of-agriculture model (Sarles 1990). The agricultural-research-council model is found primarily in Asian countries such as India, Bangladesh, and the Philippines. Council structures are often justified on the grounds that they improve the coordination of a system in which two or more of the other models are present (Jain 1989).

1.1.2   Structure within Agencies

Most university-based agricultural research is organized within discipline-based departmental units. This structure evolved in part because it facilitates teaching. The university-based systems are often the most difficult to evaluate because the units are neither strongly linked to commodities (in some cases they research issues that span both the agricultural and nonagricultural sectors) nor solely focused on research.

Nonuniversity-based systems have tended to include a combination of commodity-based, multidisciplinary units, as well as disciplinary units such as soil science, plant pathology, and agricultural economics. Research systems in developing countries most often follow this combined commodity-discipline structure. Particular commodities or disciplinary units are then frequently assigned to individual stations or institutes within the system.[2]

The implication of the commodity-discipline structure is that research evaluation and strategic priority setting involves evaluating the benefits from

---

2. Sometimes these systems contain multidisciplinary, noncommodity-based units as well, such as natural resource management research units.

commodity-based research programs, ranking them, and suggesting resource allocations, as well as evaluating, ranking, and suggesting allocations to disciplinary programs. As mentioned above, it is often easier to evaluate and prioritize commodity programs and the disciplinary components of commodity programs than it is to evaluate disciplinary programs that cut across several commodities or multidisciplinary programs that are not commodity-based (e.g., natural resource conservation).

Superimposed on the commodity and disciplinary foci in most countries is a spatial structure; programs are evaluated both regionally and nationally. Sometimes regional and commodity foci are correlated, but not always. One implication of the spatial structure is the need to assess regional as well as national priorities and the consequences of research results spilling over from one region to the next. These may involve spillovers of technologies themselves or the spillover effects of induced price changes. Some research agencies have a mandate that applies specifically to a subnational geopolitical region or a particular agroecological zone, and some agencies have mandates that are multinational as well as multiregional. In all of these cases, the technological and price spillovers may have significant consequences.

1.1.3   Types of Decisions

Resources are allocated to research at different stages in the system, at differing degrees of aggregation, and they have an impact in several dimensions. Research priorities are set across commodity programs, disciplinary (and multidisciplinary) programs, and research problems. Decisions on program emphasis affect the locational emphasis of research, the focus on particular factors of production (e.g., land, labor, and water), and the distributional effects of research (e.g., on different farm sizes, on producers versus consumers, and on people at different income levels and at different points in time). These are strategic decisions that guide a research system over several years. The generation of information to support such decisions is at the heart of this book.

Decisions about allocating resources within research programs involve the selection of specific projects and experiments within projects. These are generally tactical or shorter-term decisions that affect the relative emphasis *within* commodity and disciplinary (multidisciplinary) programs. There is a danger of stifling the ingenuity and entrepreneurship of scientists by over-formalizing this allocation process. However, it is desirable to have a process in place so that given suitable guidance, researchers can properly screen alternatives. In some situations, even for such tactical decisions, a full-scale formal evaluation and priority-setting study will be warranted.

Cutting across strategic and tactical decisions are allocative decisions made with respect to operating funds versus human and physical capital. To a large extent these day-to-day operational decisions are the province of research management and beyond the scope of the formal procedures outlined in this book, although of course they ought to be consistent with the same underlying principles.

1.1.4   Funding Arrangements

Funding for public agricultural research is provided by a variety of public and private sources. The federal-state (national-provincial) and public-private sharing of funding responsibilities is justified in large measure on the notion that research benefits spill across geographical boundaries and across firms and, hence, a mix of funding sources will generate the optimal amount of overall research investment. Such spillovers may mean that federal funding of state research can also be justified normatively on distributional grounds.

Funding of research in developing countries by more-developed countries can also be justified, in part, by the direct impact on the economic self-interest of the donors or by distributional (moral) considerations. Strategic political self-interest undoubtedly plays a major role (Ruttan 1989). Whether the motivation of the donors is to "do good" or to "do well," for many countries, particularly in Africa, external sources of support (grants and loans) can constitute the largest share of the budget (often more than 60%). The influence of these various factors on domestic research priorities can be substantial.

The specific mechanisms for collecting financial resources and funnelling them to public agricultural research are also quite diverse. Money may be collected through targeted agricultural taxes, general export taxes or import tariffs, income or land taxes, or commodity check-off schemes, among other means. Most often the funds are derived primarily from the general revenues of the government. These public-sector resources may then pass through the ministry of agriculture in whole or in part, or they may be combined with private and external support provided to a semi-private foundation which then channels support to the public research system. The specific funding mechanism has implications for the incidence of research costs and the rate of return (Alston and Mullen 1992) and can influence the processes for evaluating the effects of research, setting research priorities, and allocating research resources.

1.2 Scientific Context

General developments in biological and physical sciences have dramatically changed the opportunities and requirements for successful R&D and the nature of the systems being studied. Such changes and other factors define the scientific context in which agricultural research is conducted, which, in turn, has implications for research benefits and costs and for procedures for evaluating R&D and setting priorities. In this section we consider three elements of the scientific context of research: (a) the varying nature of research itself (i.e., relatively basic as well as more applied and adaptive research), (b) the role of the linkages that transfer information and research results, and (c) dynamics — the fact that agricultural research is a time-intensive process (taking time to produce results that require more time for adoption and that may eventually depreciate).

1.2.1 Basic, Applied, and Adaptive Research

Not all research results are intended to be applied directly by farmers, policymakers, or other decision makers. Some research is intended to generate fundamental knowledge that other scientists can use when conducting more applied research and developing specific technologies or institutions. For example, applied plant-breeding research makes use of research results in genetics, molecular biology, and statistical theory. Molecular biology and statistical theory make use of even more basic research in mathematics. Therefore, agricultural research can be viewed along a continuum from very basic research in scientific disciplines to very applied and adaptive research with farm-level and policy-level applications (Huffman and Evenson 1993; Seaton 1986). Basic research provides the foundation for more applied research, and some applied research results may be further adapted or tested before being used in the field. Advances in biotechnology have influenced research at several locations along the continuum in recent years and have served to strengthen linkages between basic and applied research. In some important respects, modern biotechnology methods have changed the nature of the research process itself (Persley 1990).

Because basic research does not directly result in changes in production or cost, it is relatively difficult to quantify the benefits arising from such research.[3] Smaller NARSs tend to concentrate on applied and adaptive re-

---

3.   This is not to say that benefits from basic or pretechnology research cannot be quantified using the conventional apparatus. To do so it is necessary to infer implications for changes in particular technologies affecting commodity markets arising from a particular pretechnology innovation.

search;[4] however, even large, resource-abundant NARSs conduct a good deal of applied and adaptive research. The different types of research are complementary.

This highlights the point that the *users* of research results are not necessarily the economic *beneficiaries* of the research. Scientists in applied research may use the results produced by scientists in basic research. Producers may use the results of applied and adaptive research. The ultimate beneficiaries, however, may be producers, consumers, and scientists who perhaps do not live in the same state, region, or country where the research takes place or where the research results are adopted, and who perhaps are not even living at the time when the research is undertaken or its results are adopted, in the case of work on sustainable agricultural systems. Sometimes the principal users of research results may be nonfarm producers in the private sector (e.g., suppliers of farm machinery, plant material, or chemical inputs), but even in these cases, the ultimate beneficiaries may be farmers or consumers rather than agribusiness firms.

1.2.2 Research and Technology-Transfer Linkages

Some agricultural research systems have a mandate to transfer information and technology to producers and policymakers. Even when the provision of extension services is not part of its mandate, a research institution has to obtain information on the current and potential problems facing producers and other clients and has to test new technologies under actual production conditions. Decisions about research investments must consider farm-level problems and the constraints on technology adoption, as well as the problems facing other users of research products.

The role of on-farm research in relation to on-station research has been examined in recent years (Tripp 1991). Not all research can be done at the experiment station because too many factors are held constant, thereby reducing the applicability of the results. Likewise, not all research can be conducted on-farm because there are many factors that must be held constant at some stage in the research process, which is difficult to do at the farm level. Many agricultural research systems now contain a significant on-farm research component, which, among other things, is intended to keep scientists aware of current and emerging problems and to help them understand how their research fits into the farm system.

---

4. Adaptive research involves bringing in and modifying technologies and institutions produced elsewhere. The smaller the country, the more economic it will likely be to focus on testing and adapting research results from other countries, particularly if results are available from regions or countries with similar agroecological, economic, and social environments.

Extension systems and on-farm research link research investments to current problems. Ideally, research and extension systems involve a two-way continuum of communication from basic research to transfer and adoption of information and technology, but in many instances the reality falls far short of this ideal.

Farmers and ranchers are not the only users of the knowledge generated by agricultural research systems. Input suppliers, processors, policymakers, community development planners, and many others have become more significant clients for public agricultural research systems than they were a few years ago. Technology- and information-transfer mechanisms for these groups are often less formal than the farm-to-station linkages.

Technology- and information-transfer issues are also linked to questions of location, size, and scope in agricultural research within a country and to questions of international spillovers of research results. However, there has been relatively little formal analysis of the optimal location, size, and scope of research facilities and programs (Ruttan 1982; Pardey 1986).[5] A variety of factors influence the location, size, and scope of within-country transfers of agricultural research technology as well as international transfers. These include (a) the sensitivity of the applicability of research results to environmental conditions — the similarity of climate, topography, farm size, and so on within the country, (b) the relative costs of site-specific research versus transfer and adaptation of technologies, (c) the complementarity with and availability of research results from other countries or international research centers, and (d) economies or diseconomies of size and scope (Evenson and Binswanger 1978; Pardey, Roseboom and Anderson 1991).

1.2.3 Dynamics

The current stock of usable knowledge is the result of previous investment. It can grow as new research investments are made and diminish as current technologies, institutions, and pretechnology information depreciates. Utilization of this stock has not only a spatial but also a time dimension.

It often takes a long time for research knowledge to be developed and adopted, typically one to 10 years between the initiation of a research project and the dissemination of results. Borrowing research results (e.g., plant lines or varieties) from other countries can shorten research time in some cases, but many high-payoff research projects still cannot be completed in less than a year. Therefore, part of the purpose of research priority-setting activities is

---

5. Analysis of spillovers has received somewhat more attention. For example, see Edwards and Freebairn (1982), Brennan (1986), Davis, Oram and Ryan (1987), Evenson (1989), Griliches (1992), and Wood and Pardey (1993).

to make longer-run strategic decisions that, once made, can insulate certain types of research for long enough to allow successful completion.

The length of time needed for research as well as for adoption is important for another reason. The sooner research results are achieved, the greater the potential economic returns. Benefits received today are worth more than the same received tomorrow (because those received today could be reinvested sooner to earn additional returns); so, research evaluation and priority-setting procedures must recognize the need to discount future research costs and benefits.

Not all applied research is intended to raise agricultural productivity from current levels. Significant research investments, particularly in entomology, plant pathology, and plant breeding are required just to maintain current levels of productivity. Estimates indicate that 35% to 70% of U.S. agricultural research is needed to maintain previous research gains (Heim and Blakeslee 1986; Adusei 1988; Adusei and Norton 1990). Several developing countries have found that, with insufficient research support, productivity not only ceases to grow, but actually declines. Therefore both research evaluation and decisions on allocations of resources to research must consider research depreciation and the fact that it may vary by commodity.

1.3   The Policy Context

The institutional and scientific contexts interact with government policy to define the environment in which agricultural research takes place. Together they determine the economic impact of R&D and they have implications for research evaluation, priority setting, and resource allocation. These separate elements of the research environment are not independent: for example, the institutional arrangements arise in part from a consideration of the objectives and the scientific context.

The main (normative) economic argument for government intervention is a "market failure" argument. In this section we lay out that argument and related arguments, and we discuss the use of research to pursue objectives other than economic efficiency. Other factors that might *explain* public-sector agricultural R&D are discussed as well. Finally, social science research is presented both as a comparatively neglected component of agricultural research and as a complement to other types of agricultural research — such as when an economic way of thinking about R&D is integrated into the institutions where research is evaluated and prioritized, and research resources are allocated.

1.3.1 The Economic Justification for Government Intervention

The primary justification for public-sector investment in agricultural research, from an economic-efficiency standpoint, rests on the assumption that there is a "market failure" in the private production and funding of R&D. That is, the market does not provide the private sector with incentives to support the quantity and mix of research that would be best from society's point of view. Such market failures arise when individuals cannot appropriate all of the benefits from their R&D investments.[6] Other individuals can "free-ride" on the investment. The ability of the private sector to capture the gains from research varies from industry to industry and from country to country because of differences in technologies and laws governing property rights, among other things (Evenson and Putnam 1990). When private benefits are less than social benefits from an incremental investment in R&D, there will an underinvestment in R&D from society's point of view and it will become appropriate for the government to intervene.

One typical intervention is to make public funds available to support R&D that may be carried out in either the private or public sector — most often the latter. However, taxpayer funding of public-sector R&D is not the only way to correct a private-sector underinvestment. When the underinvestment is due to free-riding by producers on one another, it might be fairer and more efficient for the government to create an institution to carry out research on behalf of producers using funds collected by taxing output, for example (Alston and Mullen 1992).

Because public resources are limited, when the objective is to correct a market failure, the public sector ought to focus its support more heavily on types of research that have a high social payoff but which the private sector has relatively little incentive to support. Historically, the private sector has concentrated much of its own research efforts in the areas of seed, machinery, and chemicals, where patents and licenses have generally been more easily obtained and enforced, thus avoiding or reducing many of the free-rider problems that arise in other settings. Private firms also undertake R&D to develop new technologies for processing, typically post-harvest processing, storage, and transportation technologies, where secrecy enables firms to capture the cost savings arising from such innovations. Because gains from more basic research may be difficult to capture privately, the public sector often supports research that cannot be transferred immediately into new technologies and institutions. In some cases, the private sector conducts this

---

6. Information and technologies developed from research have, to some extent, the characteristics of "public goods" (e.g., public defense or radio broadcasts), for which one person's use does not diminish their availability to others.

research, in some cases it is done by the public sector, and in some cases the two sectors jointly complete the research.

Farmers and ranchers have little incentive to conduct much of their own research. Their large numbers and relatively small firm sizes (and the fact that many of the products from research have the characteristics of public goods) typically mean that individual firms would not be able to capture much of the total benefits. In addition, there are often economies of size and scope in research, which means that a large, diversified organization is often able to do the same research at lower cost than a number of smaller ones could.

The fact that, in some cases, research is most efficiently carried out by a large (public) organization does not necessarily mean that it should be paid for out of general government revenues. Spending and funding decisions are separable. In many countries, producers provide financial support to the public research system. This support may be generated through self-imposed levies by producer groups or through export taxes. For example, rice producers in Uruguay directly support rice research, and Colombia funds its research on coffee through a tax on exports. The relevant question may be what the cost-sharing arrangements should be between the different arms of government and producer levies in supporting particular research programs. And the answers may be expected to vary among programs.

It has also been suggested that because there are economies of size and scope in research, small firms (i.e., firms that produce only a small fraction of total production) might not be able to undertake large-scale research programs and therefore may be at a disadvantage compared with very large firms in generating their own research. Thus, public research may provide knowledge that enhances the competitive structure of the market (Ruttan 1982).

An additional reason sometimes offered for public-sector involvement in agricultural research is that research, higher education, and extension are complementary (Ruttan 1982). The U.S. land-grant university system of integrated agricultural research, teaching, and extension takes explicit advantage of these complementarities. However, R&D institutes, particularly in developing countries, are often totally divorced from teaching universities and are less well structured to take advantage of complementarities with teaching and, sometimes, extension.

Finally, some say that, from society's viewpoint, the private sector will underinvest in R&D simply because research is risky — the payoff is uncertain because the scientific outcome is unknown and, even if the research is successful, its economic impact depends on things that cannot be known with certainty. However, most economists would disagree. All economic activity is risky and the justification for government intervention must go beyond the presence of risk to show that the private sector is unable to spread its risk economically. It is not obvious on the face of it that research risk is special compared with other business risk.[7]

A further implication of the economic arguments used to justify government intervention in R&D is that public resources for research should not be allocated in a manner that competes with or crowds out actual or potential private-sector research. Government intervention is warranted only if (a) incentives are such that markets fail to produce the socially optimal amount of research, (b) economies of size and scope in research threaten the competitive structure of markets, or (c) opportunities exist for exploiting the complementarities between research, education, and extension. Even when government intervention is warranted, the form of intervention might not involve using the general revenues of government to fund the research or doing the research in a public-sector institution. Thus, the predominant form of agricultural research, public-sector research funded by the government, is economically justified only in a limited set of conditions.

It might be expected that those necessary conditions will be fulfilled more often in poorer countries than in richer ones. In less-developed countries there might be a greater chance of market failures in research associated with transaction costs, problems with property rights, or other distortions (e.g., capital market imperfections). In counterpoint, however, for similar reasons, in less-developed countries the opportunity cost of the general revenues of the government can be expected to be relatively high — the taxation system is likely to be relatively inefficient and there are many competing uses for the funds for health, education, rural infrastructure, and other capital investments that also have high rates of return. Thus, while there might be grounds for a greater role for the government in research in less-developed countries, the potential for public-sector research funded by general revenues might be smaller than in more-developed countries.

1.3.2   Research as an Instrument of Social Policy

Agricultural research is conducted in the context of other economic and agricultural policies, but research is only one instrument of social policy, and most nonefficiency-related objectives are more effectively pursued using other policy instruments. Thus, public-sector research should be treated as one of several available instruments for attaining agricultural-sector goals,

---

7.   There is no doubt about the riskiness of research. The argument is that such riskiness is not pertinent to the social evaluation of such investments (Arrow and Lind 1970).

and decisions on research resources should reflect the reasons behind public-sector involvement in research. In many places, stated objectives for the agricultural research system include economic growth, income distribution, and food security.[8]

Growth in agricultural production is important for improved welfare and overall economic development in many countries. Even in wealthy countries, production growth can help keep food prices down, generate foreign exchange, and improve competitiveness in world markets. Agricultural research, through its influence on productivity, is a major source of growth in agricultural production and income; however, research is just one of many activities that can contribute to growth.

Some policies focus on income distribution among different income classes, geographic regions, different types of producers, and between producers and consumers. Research can have significant distributional implications, but this need not mean that research should be directed to pursue distributional objectives.

Food security, the long-run sustainability of agricultural production systems, and the quality of the natural resource base are becoming more important objectives. Population pressures, outdated and inappropriate institutional structures, and a variety of other factors have created a series of problems with deforestation, soil erosion, desertification, and pollution. Agricultural research can either reduce or worsen these problems through its impact on technology and institutions.

We mentioned earlier the question of whether the riskiness of research justifies government intervention. A separate idea is the impact of research on the risk associated with agricultural production. Statements of national goals and objectives often refer to desires to improve security and make incomes more stable. Alternative agricultural research portfolios may have different implications for the variability of agricultural production and hence for food security or income variability. Priority-setting exercises in research might consider its effectiveness as a risk-reducing strategy but ought to do so with due regard to the effectiveness of other public interventions designed to stabilize output, prices, and incomes.

More generally, the use of public-sector agricultural research to pursue nonefficiency objectives can be questioned on two grounds. First, considering more than one objective adds greatly to the cost of decision-making, and second, there are usually better instruments for pursuing nonefficiency goals.

---

8. Environmental objectives are frequently voiced as well but can be thought of as falling under growth, distributional, and security objectives. For example, environmental concerns often arise when measures of growth fail to include the external costs associated with environmental damage or when the distribution of benefits to future generations may be jeopardized.

Research administrators have a difficult enough time evaluating research programs or choosing a research portfolio when increasing total net benefits (sometimes referred to as *growth* or *efficiency*) alone is the objective. It is even more difficult when two or more objectives are involved. When multiple objectives are considered, the evaluation involves not only identifying specific objectives and measuring the contributions of alternative research programs to each of them, but it also requires trading off or weighting the alternative objectives. Attaching weights is problematic because the subjective value judgments of individuals are required and decisions must be made about whose judgments are relevant.

In addition, when multiple objectives are being pursued, it is important to assess the comparative advantage of research relative to other policy instruments for meeting social objectives. Many economists view agricultural research as a blunt instrument for achieving nonefficiency objectives. Research directors often agree, but other agricultural policymakers and interest groups sometimes make their support for research conditional on a consideration of its distributional, security, and environmental consequences. These latter groups argue that (a) agricultural research has distributional consequences and (b) the transactions or political costs associated with using research to meet particular objectives are lower than those associated with alternative policies.[9]

The economic arguments support a singular objective of economic efficiency. On the other hand, it appears that public-sector agricultural R&D is often driven, in fact, by its impact on particular groups. Thus, distributional objectives may be a fact of life in public-sector agricultural R&D. An important role for analysts evaluating research programs is to inform decision makers about the costs of biasing the research portfolio in pursuit of particular objectives.

1.3.3   Political Economy Perspective on the Demand for Research

The discussion above provides a normative perspective on the circumstances under which government *should* be involved in funding or executing agricultural research. It does not consider explicitly, however, the underlying political and economic forces that affect the demand for particular levels and types of research. Decisions on allocating resources to research are made in the context of these forces. The incidence of benefits and costs of research generates political pressures that influence the size and direction of research

9.   Some economists (e.g., Gardner 1988; de Gorter, Nielson and Rausser 1992) have suggested that policymakers may even use research to try to offset the negative distributional effects of other policies.

funding. Hence, this incidence must be understood by analysts attempting to inform decision makers. Furthermore, research policies and pricing policies may be jointly determined (Gardner 1988), and each set of policies can affect the economic costs and benefits of the other (Alston, Edwards and Freebairn 1988; Alston and Pardey 1991, 1993).

The potential beneficiaries of research include producers, consumers, owners of factors of production, and even scientists and administrators themselves. Who benefits depends on many factors, including, among other things, the nature of the research-induced technological change, the nature of the market for the commodity being affected by it, and the incentive structure in the research system. The country's trade status in the commodity (i.e., whether it is an exporter or an importer, whether it is able to influence world prices), its price policies, the nature of the research, government regulations, and other factors also have an influence.

The possible joint determination of research and price policies, combined with the unequal ability among producer groups and others to influence the direction of technical and institutional change (Ulrich, Furtan and Schmitz 1986; Roe and Pardey 1991), lends particular importance to analyses that demonstrate the trade-offs associated with alternative research portfolios.

1.3.4   Roles for Social Science Research

Private incentives for research are especially lacking in the social sciences. Socioeconomic research develops marketing and management tools, provides information to improve efficiency in the farm and marketing sectors, aids in the design of new technologies, and supports improved policy decisions. Much of this work, especially market information and policy analysis, has a large public-good component. Agricultural research, particularly in developing countries, is often viewed as synonymous with developing improved technologies (e.g., new crop varieties, methods of pest control, and livestock management practices). Socioeconomic research tends to receive little attention in agricultural research institutions, although it can enhance the benefits from technological innovations (Byerlee and Franzel 1993), as well as being valuable in its own right.[10]

Research evaluation and priority-setting methods should be able to take advantage of the types of outputs produced by socioeconomic research. However, as we will see later in this book, the methods of analysis presently

---

10.   Within research institutions that focus on technology development, economists and other social scientists are often involved in planning, monitoring, and evaluating research. In addition, they can coordinate with the socioeconomic units in the planning and policy sections of the ministries of agriculture and finance to help design policies that facilitate rather than hinder the adoption of new technologies.

available are much better developed for evaluating the impact of R&D leading to *embodied* technological changes (where the effects are reflected fairly directly in commodity or factor markets) rather than *disembodied* technological changes (such as those commonly produced by social science research).[11] Our ability to evaluate the impact of R&D varies directly with the nature of R&D. Basic or pretechnology research is more difficult to evaluate from an economic perspective than applied or adaptive research and extension. Structuring research programs to encourage interactions between social and technical scientists can be beneficial, in part as a way of developing an institutionalized "economic way of thinking" about the role of the R&D effort in the economy, what R&D should be done, or any other questions about the economics of public-sector agricultural R&D, such as those posed at the beginning of this chapter.

11. One exception may be social science research directed at policy reform, which, if successful in leading to a policy change, is directly reflected in commodity and factor markets. Evaluating the contribution of social science research is much more difficult than evaluating the benefits of the policy change since understanding why policies change is so difficult.

2

Research Evaluation and
Priority-Setting Principles

Agricultural research is an investment in the production of knowledge that must compete with other activities for scarce resources. Like any investment, it involves a choice either to reduce current consumption or to forego alternative investments. Evaluating past investments, assessing alternatives, and setting priorities for future investments are all the subject of economics. Hence, agricultural research evaluation and priority setting are economic problems. This chapter presents the theoretical and conceptual issues involved in applying the principles of economics to the economic problem of evaluation and priority setting in agricultural research.

The economic problem of setting research priorities contains several elements: (a) identifying the objectives of the research, (b) defining the relevant alternatives to be assessed, (c) assessing the effects of the alternatives and evaluating those effects in relation to the objectives, and based on the evaluation, (d) comparing the alternatives and making selections. The main focus here is on the economic assessment of the effects of a given research program or set of program options and the evaluation of those effects as a basis for priority setting.

This chapter presents a conceptual model of how agricultural research and extension affect agricultural production and, through markets, how they affect prices and the value of agricultural production. Other conceptual issues (about putting an economic value on the consequences of research) are also introduced in this chapter in a nontechnical, summary fashion, leaving technical issues and detailed aspects to be covered in later chapters.

19

We begin by presenting an overview of the nature of research and technical change from an economic investment perspective. The core of this analysis is a partial-equilibrium framework that uses consumer and producer surplus to measure economic benefits. This model is central to the work in this book and is discussed here in detail. In the latter part of the chapter we consider a range of extensions to the basic model (such as allowing for market distortions or incorporating international trade or the general-equilibrium effects of research) as well as approaches to measuring the distribution of benefits and costs among groups and over time.

The chapter comprises five main sections. The first (section 2.1) introduces the notion of an agricultural production function in which "knowledge" is a factor. Knowledge, in turn, is produced by research according to the research (knowledge) production function.[1] In a supply-and-demand framework changes in agricultural production arising from research-induced changes in knowledge are reflected as a shift in commodity supply. Because changes in knowledge have impact over many years, there is a dynamic relationship between today's research investment and future production, supply, and prices. In turn, there is a stream of benefits associated with a particular investment in research, and this stream can be evaluated using economic surplus measures and summarized using cost-benefit techniques. Other issues, such as how to deal with uncertainty and adjustment costs, are touched upon at the end of the section. In later chapters, we return to some of these topics. In chapter 3, in particular, we look at different types of technical changes in different econometric representations of production and technologies; in chapter 4 we look in much more detail at the translation of research-induced market displacements into measures of economic benefit.

The second section of this chapter (section 2.2) presents economic surplus measures of research benefits. The concepts are introduced and criticisms of the use of economic surplus are reviewed — and essentially dismissed. So-called "alternatives" to economic surplus, for research evaluation, are discussed and found not really to be alternatives. Section 2.3 lays out the key determinants of the size of total benefits and their distribution among different groups. This discussion summarizes the main ideas that are developed formally and in detail in chapter 4. The most critical point raised in this discussion is the pivotal role of the size and nature of the research-induced supply shift as a determinant of benefits. Other factors — such as elasticities of supply and demand and market-distorting policies — have their main effects on the distribution of benefits. Section 2.4 provides a heuristic treat-

---

1. One way to look at the impact of research is in the context of a model of the supply and demand for knowledge rather than a model of the supply and demand for commodities. The former has conceptual appeal but is less attractive for practical problems. See Perrin (1972).

ment of some general-equilibrium implications of research (chapter 4 examines some of the more technical aspects). Finally, section 2.5 discusses the critical issues that arise when agricultural research is used as an instrument of social policy, as well as the implications of multiple research objectives. It concludes that other policies are better suited for pursuing nonefficiency objectives (e.g., security, income distribution) and research priorities in general ought not to be biased away from the efficiency objective.

2.1   Investing in Research and Technical Change[2]

We have said that agricultural research is an economic activity that involves the investment of scarce resources in the production of knowledge. This is done with a view to increasing future agricultural productivity and, thereby, contributing to a range of economic and social objectives. Although there are many interesting and important research problems, they cannot all be undertaken because research resources, including capital, skilled labor, and other inputs, are scarce. Inevitably choices must be made about the total resources available for research and the allocation of those resources among (and within) research programs. This problem of deciding on the allocation of research resources is part of the broader problem of research management and policy-making. The application of economic principles can assist this activity. In addition, economic techniques can be used to measure the economic effects of agricultural research in order to provide estimates that can be used in the logical decision-making framework provided by economic theory.

In most instances the main objectives of agricultural research are economic, especially economic efficiency and equity (or total national income and its distribution). The efficiency objective relates to whether the investment is an efficient use of resources — could the resources earn a higher rate of return in an alternative investment? The equity issue concerns how the benefits and costs are distributed among different groups in society. In many cases, even when there are great benefits to society as a whole, some people are made worse off by changes in technology. The question arises whether the change in the distribution of well-being associated with a particular research program is compatible with social objectives or whether some alternative research program, with different distributional implications, would be preferable. The *positive* (as opposed to normative) economic aspects of these questions — regarding the likely effects of alternative

2. This section is inspired by and draws heavily on both Griliches (1979) and the more recent discussion and review provided by Scobie and Jardine (1988).

research investments on the size and distribution of national income — can be addressed using economic analysis. The evaluation of these economic effects of agricultural research — either in retrospect or in prospect — involves three central elements: (a) the relationship between the size of the investment in research and output or productivity, (b) the relationship between increases in productivity and flows of economic benefits, and (c) a procedure to account for the timing of streams of benefits (and costs).

One concern is that economic analysis only provides a partial assessment of the consequences of investment in research. It is true that economic analysis cannot entirely answer the *normative* question of whether one particular research program is better or worse than another without information about the relative value to be placed on the different objectives of the research, including total benefits, their distribution, security, and other effects. In our view, all research effects are susceptible to economic analysis and there are few (if any) aspects of research that are truly "noneconomic." However, some effects are surely difficult to incorporate directly into an economic analysis. For example, an economic analysis can shed light on the consequences of research and technical change for food self-sufficiency, total employment or unemployment, environmental concerns (such as land degradation, sustainability, and air and water pollution), and even on the maintenance of excellence in disciplinary or program areas.

The "noneconomic" aspect is that these effects are not directly pecuniary and in many cases they are difficult to value. But this concern applies with perhaps equal force to the "economic" effects of research on total welfare and its distribution through changes in agricultural productivity. Economists have tackled similar problems of valuation in other contexts, such as measuring the value of human life, the costs of pollution, or the value of pristine wilderness, using contingent valuation or willingness-to-pay methods and other related techniques (OECD 1989).

2.1.1 Relating Research, Knowledge, and Production

To address the effects of agricultural research, several important questions must be answered: (a) What is the probability that the research will be successful? (b) If the research is successful, how soon will the results be available for adoption, how widely applicable will the results be, how quickly will they be adopted, and how long will they be used? (c) Once adopted, how much will the results of research contribute to changes in productivity and output and for how long? (d) What are the costs of the research and how are they distributed over time? Once these questions have been answered, the net benefits can be estimated. But that process is seldom straightforward. For the most part, the difficulties are measurement problems. Some problems, however, are conceptual.

Knowledge in the Agricultural Production Function

Successful investment in agricultural research leads, among other things, to increases in agricultural productivity so that either more measured output can be produced with the same amount of inputs or the same amount of output can be produced with a smaller quantity of measured inputs. These increases in productivity stem from the development of new or improved outputs, or of new, better, or cheaper inputs, or through other changes in knowledge that enable producers to choose and combine inputs more effectively. In more concrete terms, the types of benefits from research-induced changes in knowledge include the following:

- more output (for a given expenditure on inputs)
- cost savings (for a given quantity of output)
- new and better products
- better organization and quicker response to changing circumstances

We can think of current knowledge as a capital stock that has been created by past investment, that depreciates over time, that can be augmented by new investment, and that yields a service flow as an input into agricultural production. An investment in agricultural research is an investment in maintaining or increasing this capital stock. While the stock of knowledge may be expanded as a result of research, the new knowledge might not be used immediately. The extent to which the stock of knowledge is utilized — the rate of adoption of research results — depends principally on its applicability as determined by the expected profitability of using the innovation and the user costs of acquiring the information. Benefits arise only if knowledge is utilized. Knowledge, per se, is of limited value.

These ideas can be represented algebraically in terms of a production function in which agricultural output in time t, Q_t, depends on quantities of conventional inputs, X_t, various infrastructural variables such as public investment in roads, communications, irrigation and education, Z_t, uncontrolled factors such as weather, W_t, and the flow of services, F_t, deriving from the stock of knowledge, K_t.

$$Q_t = q(X_t, Z_t, W_t, F_t)$$

(2.1)

Research investments can lead to a change in productivity (output per unit of conventional inputs, Q/X) by changing the quality of conventional inputs or their prices (i.e., through a change in the technology used to produce those inputs), through an increase in the stock of knowledge, or by increasing the utilization of the existing stock of knowledge. The service flow, F_t, is endogenous: the extent of *utilization* of available knowledge depends upon relative factor prices, P_t, the stock of human capital in agriculture, H_t, and the extent and quality of extension services, E_t, among other things.

$$F_t = f(K_t, P_t, H_t, E_t) \tag{2.2}$$

The stock of useful knowledge on the one hand depreciates by an amount D_t as it is replaced by better information or when circumstances change to make it less useful. On the other hand it increases by an amount I_t because of the incorporation of results from past investments in research.[3]

$$K_t = K_{t-1} + I_t - D_t \tag{2.3}$$

Through repeated substitution for K_{t-1} in equation 2.3 it can be seen that the current knowledge stock, K_t, is defined by the entire history of *changes* in this knowledge stock, implying an infinite lag structure for research.

The Research (Knowledge) Production Function

The increment to useful knowledge arising from a particular research investment is likely to depend upon a number of factors, including, for instance, the existing stock of knowledge and the available research capital.[4] That increment will also vary among commodities,[5] scientific disciplines, and research problems, and it is influenced by a host of institutional variables related to the management and deployment of research staff and the resources with which they work.[6] All of these additional influences are repre-

3. In addition, technology may become obsolete because of the invention of new, better technology or as a result of changes in prices or other incentives leading to its abandonment in favor of some other existing technology. In some cases obsolescence may be seen as an extreme form of depreciation (e.g., where the build-up of specific pests means a particular variety becomes progressively less profitable until it eventually ceases to be grown).

4. When the stock of fundamental knowledge needed for applied agricultural research is readily available, the productivity of agricultural research will be greater. In a related but opposite fashion, the quantity and quality of previous applied agricultural research can lower the marginal productivity of new agricultural research because of diminishing returns. Of course, additional fundamental research could then be used to shift the agricultural research production function upward, reducing the effect of diminishing returns (Evenson and Kislev 1975).

5. The research required to cause a given shift in the corresponding commodity production functions typically costs less for certain field crops such as wheat, maize, and rice than for livestock or horticultural crops (Scobie 1984). It is often asserted that livestock research is costlier than crop research to obtain the same shift in the knowledge production function because of differences in the reproductive lives of plants and animals and the extra cost in maintaining (e.g., feeding and housing) an individual animal compared with an individual plant. Certain perennial crops are also costlier to research than annual grain crops that may produce two or three generations in a year.

6. Factors such as the timing of disbursement of research funds, spatial location and availability

sented here by the vector of variables, $\tilde{Z}_t$. In addition, because the production of useful knowledge takes time, there are time lags between the investment in research and the yield of results. The dynamics of the relationship between past investments in research, R_{t-k}, and increments to useful knowledge, I_t, are complicated and uncertain. A general form of the relationship is

$$I_t = i(R_t , \ldots , R_{t-L_R} ; K_{t,} \tilde{Z}_t) \tag{2.4}$$

where L_R is the maximum research lag that keeps earlier research investments from affecting the current research-induced increment to knowledge, and $\tilde{Z}_t$ represents other factors that affect the productivity of a given amount of research resources such as the commodity, technology, or problem focus of the research as well as the institutional and management environment within which these resources are deployed.

This relationship between research investments and changes in the stock of useful knowledge is sometimes termed a *research production function* or a *knowledge production function*. The research production function is a central component in relating agricultural output to research inputs. While this relationship sometimes may be left implicit, it usually must be addressed explicitly in some way. Assumptions about the properties of the research production function — such as diminishing returns to research expenditures or economies of size and economies of scope — imply restrictions on the relationship between research investments and productivity and, therefore, between research investments and shifts in the market-level output supply and input demand functions.

Several interpretations of the model in equation 2.4 are possible, depending on the purpose at hand. It might be interpreted as representing the accumulation of knowledge by society as a whole or it might instead represent the accumulation of knowledge used by agricultural producers. In the latter case, measures of the resources spent on transferring information to farmers by the public sector (extension) and by the private sector (including merchandising by input suppliers and others and efforts by farmers themselves), as well as factors influencing the costs of information transfer (e.g., searching for, screening, and selecting technologies) would be included. Reflecting this idea, the following model augments the previous one with current and lagged values of extension expenditures, broadly defined.[7]

of research facilities, ratios of numbers of researchers to numbers of technical and support staff, incentives facing researchers, and the like, all play a role here (e.g., Pardey 1986).

7. If the increments to useful knowledge are defined in relation to society as a whole, extension would still be involved either (a) as a determinant of useful knowledge (knowledge not being useful until it is in appropriate hands) in equation 2.4 or (b) in the production function, as in equation 2.2, as a determinant of the flow of services from the stock of knowledge in society as a whole. Either

$$I_t = i(R_t, \ldots, R_{t-L_R}, E_t, \ldots, E_{t-L_E}, K_t, \tilde{Z}_t) \qquad (2.5)$$

where L_E is the maximum extension lag, which is likely to be shorter than the maximum research lag, L_R.

This model includes general research investment variables, R_t, and extension variables, E_t, indexed for timing, without identifying the nature of the work (i.e., pretechnology research, applied research, or development) or who is undertaking the investment (the public sector, the private sector, or foreigners). For some studies it will be appropriate to make a formal distinction in the model between types of investment and between types of investors — e.g., domestic versus foreign as done by Zachariah, Fox and Brinkman (1989) or private versus public as done by Pray and Neumeyer (1990) and Huffman and Evenson (1992) or basic versus applied as done by Mansfield (1980) and Griliches (1986a) — as well as identifying the timing of investment flows. In addition, the generation of knowledge involves several stages of production in which outputs (research results) from one are used as inputs into the next. These stages are interdependent. The knowledge that is directly useful in agricultural production is the final stage of a scientific process that extends from basic or pretechnology research in the general sciences to production and adoption of applicable agricultural technology.

Research in the Agricultural Production Function

Usually, since the stock of knowledge cannot be observed directly, the research (knowledge) production function is more a part of the conceptual apparatus than an empirical tool. An empirically useful variant of the research (knowledge) production function is the function that relates production to lagged values of research investments.[8] Such a function is really a reduced-form hybrid of the research production function (with knowledge as its product) and the agricultural production function (with knowledge as an argument).

Loosely combining equations 2.1 through 2.5, we can suggest a reduced-form relationship between investments in research and output (or productivity) in which current output (or productivity) depends upon current flows of conventional inputs and uncontrolled factors, as well as current and past investments in agricultural research and extension.

conceptualization eventually leads to the same empirical model of the impact of extension on output.

8. Some applications have used data on patents, publications, or other direct measures of research output as the dependent variable for estimating the knowledge production function itself. For example, Griliches (1984, 1990) and the chapters and references therein used data on nonagricultural patents. Pardey (1989) used data on citation-adjusted publications in U.S. public-sector agricultural research. See also Evenson and Kislev (1975) and Adams (1990).

$$Q_t = q(X_t, W_t, H_t, P_t, Z_t, R_{t-r}, E_{t-e}) \text{ for } r, e = 0 \text{ to } \infty \tag{2.6}$$

The first two variables, conventional inputs, X, and weather, W, are conventional in production functions. Human capital variables, H, might be regarded as being conventional, too, but here they relate specifically to the effects of human capital on the utilization of knowledge rather than, perhaps, allocative efficiency or management. Prices, P, are not commonly included in production functions, but there is a recent precedent for doing so in relation to the induced-innovation hypothesis (e.g., Fulginiti and Perrin 1992). The vector of variables Z includes both infrastructural inputs (often publicly provided) that directly influence current output and the infrastructural or institutional aspects of the research system that indirectly influence output through their effects on the generation and transfer of new knowledge. In this specification of the production function *indefinitely* long lags of past research expenditures and current and lagged extension investments substitute for the accumulation of knowledge used by agricultural producers.

2.1.2 Economic Consequences of Agricultural Research

Equation 2.6 captures the essence of most of the approaches used to measure the economic consequences of agricultural research. Two broad alternatives have been used. *Econometric approaches* have estimated equations of the form of 2.6 directly. Then, using the estimated equation, economic benefits from research have been calculated as the value of the additional output attributable to the lagged research expenditures (holding other inputs constant) or the value of the savings in inputs due to the lagged research expenditures (holding output constant).

An alternative approach is to go beyond the *production function* to look at research impact on the firm and industry *supply functions*. An *economic surplus approach* can be used to evaluate the benefits from a shift in supply due to a change in productivity (as could be measured, for instance, by equation 2.6). When it changes the relationship between inputs and outputs, a technical change also affects relationships between production costs and output and thus between supply and price. In this way the consequences of research and changes in technology can be assessed by looking at the relationship between research investments and a commodity's industry-level supply function. Indeed, this has been the most popular and fruitful approach used to assess the consequences of investments in agricultural research.[9]

9. In some senses the econometric approach in practice is a variant of the economic surplus approach under some extreme elasticity assumptions. In any event, the economic surplus approach provides the theoretical support for the econometrically obtained measures of research benefits.

The Basic Supply-and-Demand Framework

Figure 2.1 is a conventional, comparative-static, partial-equilibrium model of supply and demand in a commodity market.[10] The supply curve under the original technology is denoted by S_0, and the demand curve by D. The original price is P_0 and the quantity supplied and demanded is Q_0. Adoption of new technology shifts the supply curve to S_1, resulting in a new equilibrium price and quantity of P_1 and Q_1. This model can be used to show the effects of research on a number of other variables in addition to the quantity produced, the price paid by consumers, and the price received by producers. For instance using economic surplus measures, the model can be used to identify the effects on industry revenue and to measure total increases in economic efficiency (total social benefits) as well as the distribution of

Figure 2.1:   *Gross annual research benefits*

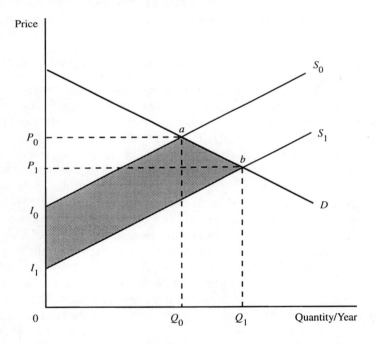

10. This is called a partial-equilibrium model (as opposed to a general-equilibrium model) because it focuses on part of the economy (e.g., agriculture or the maize industry) and treats most other economic variables as being constant (exogenous) in the analysis. The exogenous variables that are being held constant in the analysis are sometimes referred to as *ceteris paribus* conditions. It is a comparative-static model in that two (static) equilibrium situations — before and after a change or with and without a policy — are compared. Little attention is paid to the more difficult issue of the process or the path of the transition.

benefits between producers and consumers. This model can be used to consider security objectives, too, so long as those objectives can be expressed in terms of market variables, and it can be modified to incorporate trade effects, demand shifts, and pricing policies, among other things. Here, it is used mainly to illustrate the economic surplus effects of research-induced technical changes. Gross annual research benefits are measured (using economic surplus measures) as the shaded area between the two supply curves and beneath the demand curve, area I_0abI_1 in figure 2.1. This is the annual flow of economic benefits due to the supply shift from S_0 to S_1.

Lags in Research and Adoption

The comparative-static model in figure 2.1 is the cornerstone of most of what follows. It is static, however, and abstracts from some important dynamic issues. In particular, there are long, variable, and uncertain lags in the interval between commencing a research activity and generating useful knowledge, as well as between generating new technology and seeing it adopted. Further, once research leads to an increment in the stock of knowledge or an improvement in technology, that increment to knowledge or improvement in technology yields a stream of future benefits that continues until the knowledge or new technology becomes obsolete. The flow of gross annual benefits in figure 2.1 is a snapshot of only one year's worth of benefits. A successful research investment generally yields a sustained stream of such flows. The complete evaluation of a particular research investment must therefore take account of the dynamic relationships between investments in research that lead — after some, possibly long, lags — to a sustained change in the stock of productive capital and thus to a stream of future benefits. These ideas are illustrated in figures 2.2 and 2.3.

Figure 2.2 shows the hypothetical relationship between the adoption of new technology and the time after the initial investment in research. It includes a research lag (shown as five years) between the initiation of the research and the generation of pretechnology knowledge, followed by a development lag (shown as a further four years). During this time the results from pretechnology research are incorporated into useful agricultural technology, followed by an adoption lag (say a further six years) between the release of the agricultural technology and maximum adoption by producers. These assumptions about lag length are illustrative. Some projects may begin with the results from previous pretechnology research or they may begin even later in the overall process (say, by transferring in results from overseas), leading to much shorter lags between investment and adoption. On the other hand, some projects involve extremely long lags. More applied agricultural research work, typical in developing

Figure 2.2: *Research, development, and adoption lags*

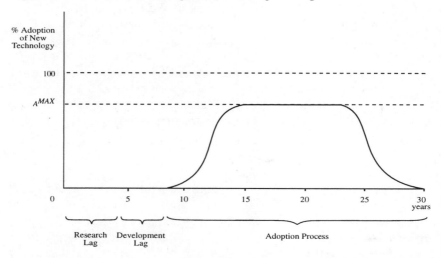

countries, is likely to involve shorter lags than the more fundamental research that is typically carried out elsewhere.

Some further features of the diagram are notable. First, adoption is drawn as an *S*-shaped curve, which is common practice following Griliches (1958) who used a logistic curve. In empirical work, simpler linear functions (e.g., Edwards and Freebairn 1981), polynomial lags (e.g., Cline 1975 and Davis 1979), or trapezoidal lags (e.g., Huffman and Evenson 1992) have often been

Figure 2.3: *Net research benefits over time*

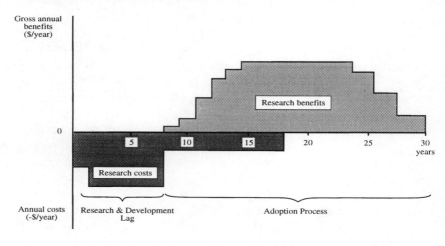

used. Second, the maximum adoption rate, A^{MAX}, is shown as less than 100 percent of the total potential adoption. Third, eventually the curve turns down when the technology depreciates or becomes obsolete and is progressively abandoned by the industry.

In practice, a discrete time approximation to a continuous adoption curve is used to develop a stream of annual flows of benefits. Figure 2.3 shows the annual flows of costs and benefits corresponding to the research investment represented in figure 2.2. It combines the information from figure 2.1, on flows of benefits for a given research-induced supply shift (the shaded area), and the information from figure 2.2, on the time path of adoption (and hence the size of the industry-level supply shift), with other information on R&D costs. In the early years there are no benefits. Once people in the industry begin to adopt the technology, there will be a supply shift of the type depicted in figure 2.1 and a corresponding flow of benefits. As the extent of adoption increases, the size of the supply shift and the corresponding flow of annual benefits also increases. Thus, the flow of benefits over time follows the shape of the adoption curve in figure 2.2. In the early years there are costs of research, development, and adoption. Even after the research results have been fully adopted, the stream of costs and benefits reflects the costs of further research undertaken to maintain the value of the technology.

Depreciation and Maintenance Research

As with most forms of capital, the economic contribution of a particular component of the stock of knowledge (i.e., a specific piece of technology or information generated by agricultural research) erodes over time because of depreciation and obsolescence. Research-based information depreciates when circumstances change in a way that makes the information less productive; it becomes obsolete when it is replaced with better information for the same conditions. Maintenance research may be needed to compensate for the inherent depreciation of information, technology, and materials. Clear examples arise with pesticides or resistant varieties that are made obsolete by the development of new chemicals or new resistant varieties and which depreciate as pests evolve to resist the chemicals or overcome natural resistance. The timing and extent of depreciation and obsolescence varies greatly among different types of research, production environments, and types of knowledge. The results of basic research are likely to depreciate more slowly than the results of very applied research because the value of basic research is usually less sensitive to changing circumstances.

The comparative-static approach compares situations with and without research, but time-subscripted data are often used for that comparison — i.e., "before and after" rather than "with and without." The hazard in such work is that the comparison will be inappropriate unless the analyst has controlled properly for variation other than that due to research. This is clearly important in the context of maintenance research. To evaluate maintenance research that succeeds in preventing yields from falling, the appropriate comparison is not between current and previous yields but rather between current yields and what yields otherwise would have been. Recent work shows that a significant fraction of agricultural research in the U.S. has been maintenance research.[11] As a consequence studies may have underestimated the initial effect of particular research investments but overstated the longevity of the contributions. This is an example of the more general point that it is important to maintain the integrity of the *ceteris paribus* assumption when conducting comparative-static analysis. This point arises in many ways in the analysis of research benefits.

Summary Measures of Economic Effects

There are several options for evaluating a stream of benefits and costs associated with a particular research program, such as the one illustrated in figure 2.3. These options are drawn from the literature on capital budgeting and benefit-cost analysis. Mostly, they entail calculating summary statistics such as the internal rate of return (IRR), the net present value (NPV), or the benefit-cost ratio, which can be used to rank programs or projects and set priorities. The NPV of a program of research undertaken in time t is calculated as the sum of the stream of future benefits, B_{t+k}, minus the costs, C_{t+k}, associated with the program, discounted at an appropriate rate, r (here, for simplicity, assumed to be a constant), as follows:

$$NPV_t = \sum_{k=0}^{\infty} \frac{B_{t+k} - C_{t+k}}{(1 + r)^k} \tag{2.7}$$

The IRR is calculated as the discount rate at which the NPV is exactly zero.

$$0 = \sum_{k=0}^{\infty} \frac{B_{t+k} - C_{t+k}}{(1 + IRR)^k} \tag{2.8}$$

Further details on these alternative methods and their advantages and disadvantages can be obtained from a number of sources (e.g., Mishan 1981).

For most purposes, the NPV method is preferred. In this approach, any program with a positive net present value is profitable. The disadvantage of

---

11. Evidence for the United States suggests that maintenance research represents about one-third of production-related agricultural research. See Adusei (1988) and Adusei and Norton (1990).

this method is that it does not provide a convenient ranking of alternatives because, although the scale of benefits is measured, the scale of the investment is not revealed. Concern over scale of investment is not an issue when funds are unlimited: all programs with a positive NPV are profitable. When funds are limited, an alternative is to express the net present value per unit of constrained input (e.g., per unit of research investment or per scientist) and rank programs accordingly. The IRR method does rank programs clearly in terms of their profitability, but it does not reveal either the scale of the investment or the value of the programs. According to this criterion, programs are profitable if the IRR is greater than the opportunity cost of funds. One criticism of IRR is that it assumes that the stream of benefits can be reinvested at the computed rate of return, which is implausible in many cases of agricultural research where very high rates of return are obtained. Often, a combination of IRR and NPV calculations can be used as complementary approaches to summarize the relevant information on the total returns to research. Typically IRRs have been used in ex post evaluation studies, while NPVs (per scientist or per unit of investment) have been used in ex ante evaluation and priority-setting studies.

Two important, related questions transcend the choice of method: What is the appropriate rate of discount (a required rate of return either for use in NPV calculations or for comparison to calculated IRRs)? How should uncertainty surrounding the estimated stream of benefits and costs be handled? Some people try to deal with both questions by requiring conservatively large rates of return. In our view (with the support of the mainstream of the literature on project appraisal), it is not appropriate to deal with uncertainty by adjusting the rate at which the streams of benefits and costs are discounted. In addition, some have argued, especially recently, that we should be using *low* discount rates so as to encourage research into technology that conserves natural resources (Cline 1992).[12] Underlying this is an implicit belief that we should attach greater weight to the welfare of future generations and that biasing the pattern of agricultural research is an appropriate way to achieve an intergenerational redistribution of welfare (Birdsall and Steer 1993). Ad hoc reduction of the discount rate is, however, unlikely to be a good way to account for externalities or to incorporate (intergenerational) distributive weights into research evaluation.[13] In most situations,

12. Ruttan (1994) points out that the impact of lowering the discount (or interest) rate on the rate of exploitation of natural resources is not entirely clear and the relationships are not simple. Lipton (1991) discusses the effects of low and high interest rates on sustainability. See also Pearce, Barbier and Markandya (1990).

13. Mikesell (1991) suggests taking explicit account of resource depletion in project analysis, instead.

there are likely to be less costly means of achieving environmental objectives (or intergenerational transfers) than biasing the pattern of agricultural research specifically towards environmentally friendly projects.

As a final note on this topic, sometimes it is helpful and important to distinguish between marginal and average effects of research and rates of return to research. It is often suggested that the research production function is characterized by diminishing returns. Indeed, if this were not the case, it might well be better to specialize much more in a smaller number of research programs or projects within programs. With diminishing returns, the marginal return to increasing the budget for a particular program will be smaller than the average return to the total investment in the program. When the relevant decision is whether to continue a program or close it down, the average return is the appropriate measure. When the relevant decision is how to allocate an increase in the total research budget among programs (or, more realistically in the current environment, how to distribute a budget cut among programs), the appropriate measure may be the marginal rate of return. Sometimes programs will be ranked differently according to marginal returns than according to average returns. Often both marginal and average rates of return are useful for providing a more complete picture of the opportunity costs of program alternatives.

2.1.3   Other Issues — Uncertainty and Adjustment Costs

Uncertainty

Agricultural research is an intrinsically risky activity, with probabilities of success akin to those in mining for diamonds or looking for oil. The uncertainty that is inherent in virtually all aspects of the research process and its effects on production and markets creates difficulties both for research administrators and scientists making decisions about their work and for the economist attempting to measure research benefits and costs.

Representing uncertainty appropriately in agricultural research evaluation and priority setting is not straightforward. Clearly, any estimation of the benefits from research inevitably involves some estimations of, or assumptions about, all of the relevant uncertain variables. In some cases, the results may be insensitive to these assumptions or estimates; in some cases the results will be highly sensitive. Most studies of research benefits do not deal with this question very well.[14] As Anderson (1991, p. 103) puts it:

14.   A few studies have looked at taking formal account of risk in research benefit calculations (e.g., Fishel 1970; Dyer, Scobie and Davis 1984; Anderson 1991; Scobie and Jacobsen 1992).

Most of the formal literature on agricultural research per se, whether of a managerial or evaluative orientation, implicitly treats research and its setting as being deterministic. In fact, of course, the process is intrinsically uncertain. Most agricultural sectors are highly variable and the observed variability is extremely unpredictable so that it is, technically speaking, risky. The conjunction of an uncertain research process with an uncertain physical and economic environment is the reality of agriculture that makes it all an extremely risky business.

There is thus a considerable mismatch between nearly all the literature on research resource allocation and that on decisions about investing in research in the risky environment in which this takes place.

The analyst's uncertainty: Uncertainty surrounds most of the variables and parameters involved in the calculation of the returns to research. It is almost tautological to note that there are uncertainties in the research process itself. The time taken to complete research is not precisely known, the scientific outcome of a particular line of research is uncertain, and the impact of the resulting new knowledge on yields, costs, and so on are also unknown at the time the research begins. It is not known in advance whether a project will lead to a commercially successful result, and the time lags and the adoption path are uncertain as well.

In ex ante studies it is important to take the possibility of the failure of research into account through the use of some measures of probabilities of success, which vary by scientist, commodity, and type of research. The results of research aimed at varietal improvement in wheat, for instance, may be fairly predictable because of the constraints imposed by the laws of quantitative genetics. On the other hand, the results of research looking at the possibility of nitrogen fixation in wheat are surely much less predictable.

Even when the scientific outcome of research is known (as happens in ex post evaluation studies), the measures of benefits are uncertain because the measures of annual flows of benefits involve market parameters that are uncertain. These include elasticities and functional forms of supply and demand and the values of those functions, as well as government policies, among other things. Also, the costs of research are uncertain. In addition, future market outcomes (either with or without successful research) are characterized by uncertainty, some of which is due to uncertainty about government policies.

It is clear that investing in a particular agricultural research project is a risky business. But the approaches being developed here are intended to be applied more at the level of the research program, involving a portfolio of individual projects, than at the level of individual projects. The riskiness of large programs may be very different from the riskiness of individual projects (formally, this depends on the covariance of returns among the individual projects within the program). It is likely that risk will be less serious at the program level.

However, even when risk or uncertainty is not a concern, it may be important to account for its effects on the mean project performance in an investment analysis (Anderson 1991, p. 126); uncertainty may affect the *expected value* of the stream of research benefits and costs. In some analyses, it might be sufficient to consider uncertainty only in so far as it affects the expected benefits, but the measures of expected benefits have a distribution around them generated by the distributions surrounding the underlying variables. In some contexts, the variance and skewness of the distribution of research benefits also may be of interest, along with the expected values.[15]

Mean-variance trade-offs in the research portfolio: The fact that markets are characterized by uncertainty, and that research investments are risky, means that research investments can be evaluated in terms of their relative riskiness as well as their expected benefits. An issue to be addressed is whether the riskiness of alternative programs ought to be considered in the evaluation and, if so, how these considerations should be introduced.

Whether the intrinsic uncertainties of doing research have a bearing on attempts to appraise the social worth of the enterprise depends on the acceptance or rejection of the controversial (but generally accepted) arguments of Arrow and Lind (1970, 1972) as to the relevant criteria for appraisal of public investments.[16] The idea here is that government can effectively "pool risk into unimportance" through its large and diversified investment opportunities (Anderson and Dillon 1992). Presuming that the risks of individual investments (be they projects, programs, or whatever) were statistically independent, Arrow and Lind (1970, 1972) showed that when such risks are publicly borne, the total cost of risk bearing is insignificant, and accordingly, for most practical purposes governments should ignore these sources of uncertainty in appraising public investments. In other words, risky research projects or programs should not be discriminated against (Parton, Anderson and Makeham 1984).

An exception to this general approach is when the research is on a commodity that accounts for a large fraction of the national (or local) earnings so that national (or local) income is correlated with research benefits. In cases such as this, or when the decision makers perceive the riskiness of research investments to be relevant, the research investment decision

15. These higher moments may be estimated crudely using sensitivity analysis for key parameters. In doing this it is important to be aware that the individual stochastic elements are unlikely to be independent, in which case covariances among variables and parameters might be important.

16. See Parton, Anderson and Makeham (1984) for a more complete discussion of this issue in this context.

might involve trading off risk against expected benefits when choosing between investments anticipated to give a higher expected payoff (and higher risk) and those anticipated to give a lower expected payoff (and lower risk).[17] In such cases, diversification strategies to reduce the riskiness of research investments are relevant. Diversification can have many dimensions in a research context. These include approaches taken, commodities chosen, sites selected, problems addressed, disciplinary perspectives used, and different investigators' perceptions about what will best contribute to knowledge (Anderson and Hardaker 1992).

If one accepts the Arrow-Lind notion that government should generally be risk neutral in its attitude towards risky research projects or programs, then policymakers and administrators of publicly sponsored research should seek to maximize the expected (i.e., mean or average) social value of research. But this in no way implies that knowledge of the range of possible outcomes of a particular line of research, as opposed to knowledge of just the "most likely" outcome, is irrelevant for decision making. If the distribution of outcomes is not symmetric, then the most likely (or modal) outcome will be a biased estimate of the expected (or mean) outcome.

In addition to these statistical quirks, there is the issue of presenting cogent information to decision makers that reflects the real-world uncertainties of the research enterprise and our imprecise perceptions of these uncertainties. In ex ante assessments of the effects of research, precision statistics (even if purely subjective) can be a useful adjunct to estimates of the expected or most likely outcome of research (Anderson 1992). This is particularly true when the expected net present values of research generated by a number of proposed activities are more or less equal. Knowledge about the confidence that can be placed on those prior expectations — as captured by the likely dispersion around the respective mean outcomes — can aid decision making.

Production risk and food security: A separate issue is the impact of research on the riskiness of agricultural production itself. Agricultural production in marginal areas, especially where rainfall is scarce and erratic, makes farmers particularly vulnerable to the vagaries of the weather. This is especially true for the semiarid areas of Africa, the Middle East, and Australia. But even in the humid tropics, where rainfall is relatively abundant and less sporadic, climate-induced fluctuations in agricultural outputs and prices (e.g., as a result of pest and disease outbreaks in intensive production systems such as irrigated rice) are also a policy concern.

Statements of national goals and objectives often refer to desires to improve security and make incomes more stable. Alternative agricultural

17. This may be so even in a "small commodity" case; for instance in a privately sponsored research unit or a quasi-public research agency that is supported in part by producer funds.

research portfolios may have different implications for the variability of agricultural production and hence for food security or income variability. Research priority-setting exercises may need to consider the effectiveness of research as a risk-reducing strategy and may need to do so with due regard to the effectiveness of other public interventions designed to stabilize output, prices, and incomes.

The Arrow-Lind argument for focusing decision-making attention on the expected (or average) outcome should not be misinterpreted to mean that the production- and market-related risks perceived by producers and consumers are not a legitimate social concern. Successful R&D might lead to technical changes that alter the riskiness of production, and such effects might be of value to producers and consumers in ways that are not reflected in conventional (deterministic) measures of benefits. To place a social value on the effects of research often requires that explicit attention be paid to the inherent variability of agricultural production and markets, the consequent uncertainties in the agricultural sector, and the degree to which research may modify these types of risks. This variability is due primarily to the variability of the natural environment over time and space, the nature of the economic environment for agricultural commodities, and political uncertainties. Anderson and Hazell (1989, p. 340 f.), summarizing the results of Weber and Sievers (1985) and others, note that the baseline levels of production variability are high in many countries, especially in semiarid areas. In addition, production variability tends to be smaller in larger countries because of the greater risk-pooling effects across crops, and regions.

Prices can vary markedly from year to year and in unexpected ways within a year. Production changes at home and abroad as a result of changes in weather can cause relatively large variations in prices for many agricultural commodities. These price swings are often especially large for commodities that are produced and marketed locally but which are difficult to transport to national or international markets. The swings can also be quite large for internationally traded goods produced in a relatively small number of locations worldwide or for goods for which one or two countries are dominant producers. Another cause of uncertainty is potential changes in the political environment. Price policies can change dramatically from year to year, and severe disruptions in an economy can occur as a result of macroeconomic adjustments, wars, coups, and other political changes.

When decision makers perceive any of these types of risk to be socially relevant, the problem of decision making becomes one of trading off perceptions of risk reductions from research against expected (or mean) benefits foregone as a consequence of this sensitivity to risk. In this instance, the weight placed on the nonefficiency objective (i.e., risk reduction) ought to reflect the decision makers' notion of the social value of such risk reductions. In determining the priority to be given to risk-reducing research, decision makers need to be aware of the efficiency of research relative to other forms of public investments (e.g., improved irrigation services) or other interventions (e.g., price stabilization schemes or buffer stocks) to achieve a certain degree of risk reduction.[18]

Adjustment Costs

The results of priority-setting exercises for research may suggest modified research programs. There are costs (related to human and physical capital) associated with changing a research program, particularly if the changes are made relatively rapidly. It generally takes some time and expense to train or retrain personnel, while newly installed buildings and equipment usually require a shakedown period before reaching their productive potential. If the cost of "organizational capital" required for growth or change is an increasing function of the speed of adjustment (as assumed, for example, by Lucas 1967 and Prescott and Visscher 1980), then rapidly growing or changing systems will have higher average cost structures than slower-growing ones.

These costs have to be considered when short-term research priorities are selected, although they become less important in the medium to long term. The implication is that the agricultural knowledge supply curve differs between the short and long run because of asset fixity. Investments in human capital (e.g., training) and physical capital are costs that must be considered when developing short- and long-run research priorities. A related cost to consider is the possible value foregone when research projects already initiated are not completed. Even when a particular commodity or type of research appears to be of lower priority than other commodities or types of research, it may pay to invest additional resources in the short run to complete work that is already underway so as to obtain the benefits of the previous research investment. Most studies have treated the question of adjustment costs informally, if at all. In a notable exception, Scobie and Jacobsen (1992) use an explicit adjustment cost function.

---

18. See section 2.5 for a discussion concerning trade-offs between efficiency and nonefficiency objectives.

2.2   Measuring Benefits and Costs Using Economic Surplus Concepts

The most common approach for analyzing the welfare effects of agricultural research in a partial-equilibrium framework has used the concept of economic surplus. Griliches (1958), Peterson (1967), and Schmitz and Seckler (1970) provide early examples of applying the economic surplus concept to ex post evaluation of agricultural research, while Davis, Oram and Ryan (1987) and Norton, Ganoza and Pomareda (1987) provide more recent examples of applying the concept in an ex ante setting.

Underlying these analyses is a body of theory and set of assumptions that are not always explicitly stated. Harberger (1971, p. 785) defended the general approach and defined three postulates that he suggested should be accepted as providing a conventional framework for applied welfare economics. These three postulates are (a) that the competitive demand price for a given unit measures the value of that unit to the demander, (b) that the competitive supply price for a given unit measures the value of that unit to the supplier, and (c) that when evaluating the net benefits or costs of a given action (project, program, or policy), the costs and benefits accruing to each member of the relevant group (e.g., a nation) should be added without regard to the individual(s) to whom they accrue. When these assumptions are valid, consumer benefits from consumption may be measured as the area beneath the ordinary demand curve, net changes in consumer welfare may be measured using Marshallian consumer surplus, and the area beneath the supply curve is a measure of total costs, so changes in the net welfare of producers may be measured using producer surplus.

In spite of the intuitive appeal of these assumptions, the approach has not been without its critics. In this section, we will illustrate the basic approach in the context of a simple closed-economy[19] case of a research-induced supply shift, review the criticisms of the economic surplus approach, and consider alternatives to the partial-equilibrium economic surplus model. Our conclusion is that, for most purposes, the partial-equilibrium economic surplus model is the best available method to evaluate returns to research.

---

19.   The term "closed economy" refers to a situation where the commodity of interest is not traded internationally and its price is determined inside the country (or region) of interest. The most important feature of this case is that consumer welfare is affected (in the typical case of a small country with an open economy, the price is exogenous). It is important to distinguish between the closed-economy case that arises as a consequence of natural protection (e.g., transportation costs) and a case where there is no trade because the border has been closed by government intervention. In the latter case the simple closed-economy model is inappropriate; a more appropriate model accounts for the effects of government intervention, as described in chapter 4.

2.2.1 *Basics of Economic Surplus Measures*

In figure 2.4 the supply curve for a commodity under the original technology is denoted by S_0, and the demand curve by D. The original price is P_0 and the quantity supplied and demanded is Q_0. Using Harberger's postulates, the total consumer surplus from consumption of the commodity is equal to the triangular area FaP_0 (the area beneath the demand curve less the cost of consumption). Similarly, the total producer surplus is equal to the triangular area P_0aI_0 (total revenue less total costs of production as measured by the area under the supply function). Total surplus is equal to the sum of producer and consumer surplus, as shown by the triangular area FaI_0 which is equal to the total value of consumption (the area under the demand curve) minus the total cost of production (the area under the supply curve). Changes in producer, consumer, and total economic surplus are measured as changes in these areas.

Cost-reducing or yield-enhancing research and adoption of the resulting new technologies shift the supply curve to S_1, resulting in a new equilibrium price and quantity of P_1 and Q_1. The *change* in consumer welfare (surplus) from the supply shift is represented by the area P_0abP_1 and the *change* in producer welfare (surplus) is represented by the area $P_1bI_1 - P_0aI_0$. Consumers necessar-

Figure 2.4: *Producer and consumer surplus measures*

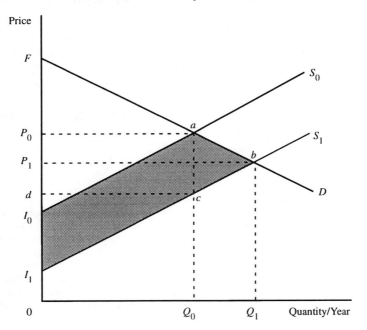

ily gain because they consume more goods at a lower price. In general, the net welfare effect on producers may be positive or negative depending on the supply and demand elasticities and the nature of the research-induced supply shift. This is so because there are two effects working in opposite directions. The producers sell more goods, but they must sell at a lower price. Both costs and revenues are affected. Producer benefits are assured if costs fall and revenues rise. But under plausible conditions, in some cases (i.e., an inelastic demand) revenue falls when supply increases. In addition, when supply shifts in a pivotal fashion against an inelastic demand, revenue falls faster than costs, and producer losses are assured. The nature of the supply shift can clearly have important implications for the distribution of benefits. In the case drawn in figure 2.4, with a linear supply curve shifting in parallel, producers necessarily benefit (by an amount equal to area $P_1bcd = P_1bI_1 - P_0aI_0$). The total (or net) welfare effect is equal to the sum of the changes in producer and consumer surplus, I_0abI_1 (which, in this case of a parallel supply shift, is also equal to area P_0abcd).

The sum of producer and consumer surplus changes measures the net welfare change in the sense that the gainers from technological change could, in principle, compensate losers and still be better off by the amount I_0abI_1. In the model in figure 2.4, compensation could mean reducing consumer benefits, perhaps through taxes, in order to provide subsidies to producers. The compensation principle assumes that such transfers could be made in a lump-sum fashion without any tax-induced distortions in consumption or production.[20] When all losers are fully compensated and there are still some net gains, the new technology constitutes a welfare improvement according to the *Pareto criterion*. Usually no compensation is paid following the adoption of new technologies produced through research. The *Kaldor-Hicks criterion* (KHC) for a net welfare improvement is that the gainers could afford to compensate the losers and still be better off, but the compensation need not take place. The KHC is a weaker, and more debatable, criterion than the Pareto criterion but it is also more practicable and underlies applied welfare economics.[21] However, several other questions have been raised about the

20. A true lump-sum transfer is therefore not possible, because some resources necessarily are consumed in making the transfer. New technology is making these costs smaller. But, even nowadays, at a minimum the cost would still be that of the labor and capital used to make an electronic transfer of funds. More usually there are substantial deadweight costs in collecting funds to finance transfers and in making transfers.

21. Bieri, de Janvry and Schmitz (1972) point out that, if compensation is not paid, the total welfare gains from research equal I_0abI_1 only if equal welfare weights are attached to producers and consumers. Attaching equal weights is clearly a value judgment. Some might argue that higher welfare weights should be attached to those who lose from technological change if compensation is not paid and if those who lose are already at the lower end of the distribution of income, and lower

use of consumer and producer surplus as welfare measures, and these are addressed below.

2.2.2 Criticisms of Economic Surplus as a Welfare Measure

The use of consumer and producer surplus has been criticized from several perspectives. Some criticisms have centered around the accuracy of what is being measured, others around the value judgments that are implied, and others around the perceived lack of policy relevance. For ease of exposition, we have grouped the complaints into six types of criticisms of surplus analysis, which we evaluate in turn.

Normativeness

The long-standing debate about the merits of positive (what is) versus normative (what should be) economics has spilled over into discussions about the merits of consumer-producer surplus analysis. As such, the criticism is broader than an attack on economic surplus; rather, it is an attack on the implicit value judgments associated with welfare economics. Mishan (1982, p. 23) points out that, at times, this criticism leaves one with the feeling that "value judgments involve nothing less than an indecent surrender of one's methodological chastity." While normative economics must draw on methods of positive economic analysis, were economists to restrict themselves to positive economics, they would be ignoring many of the vital issues of concern to society. Perhaps more fundamentally, positive economics (indeed all science) is far from value free. As Boulding (1970, pp. 121-2) puts it, "as science develops, it no longer merely investigates the world, it creates the world which it is investigating . . . [and] as science moves from pure science toward control, that is, toward creating what it knows, what it creates becomes a problem of ethical choice." In other words, value judgments are inevitable in any scientific endeavor (including economics). The important thing when conducting consumer and producer surplus analysis is to make those judgments as explicit as possible (Chipman and Moore 1978).

The issue of making value judgments explicit is important because, as noted earlier, the validity of using changes in consumer and producer surplus to measure welfare changes rests in part on the compensation principle.[22]

---

weights should be attached to those who gain. Weights could be patterned after the relationship between the marginal utility of income and the income levels. Gardner (1988) shows a Cobb-Douglas policy-preference function with the characteristic that losers are given more weight than gainers as we move from an initial position with equal weights. Harberger's (1971) third postulate explicitly assumes equal welfare weights within relevant groups.

22. When unequal weights are attached by society to gainers and losers (e.g., Harberger 1978),

Because of the difficulty in making nondistorting lump-sum transfers, distribution issues are indeed relevant.[23] Usually, compensating transfers are not made, and the welfare analysis requires an implicit or explicit value judgment.

Measurement Error

Most of the literature that discusses the validity of consumer and producer surplus analysis has focused on the conditions that must hold if consumer and producer surplus measures are to provide an accurate indicator of changes in social welfare. This vast literature will not be reviewed here. Instead, we present the key conclusions that emerge from this debate, as we see them.[24]

There are several alternative measures that have been proposed as *money metrics* for the consumer welfare change due to price changes. Whereas *consumer surplus*, CS, as defined by Marshall (1890) is the excess of the price the consumer would be willing to pay over the actual cost of the good, *equivalent variation*, EV, is the amount of additional money (income) that would leave the consumer in the *new* welfare position if it were possible to buy any quantity of the commodity at the *old* price. And *compensating variation*, CV, is the amount of additional money (income) that would leave the consumer in the *initial* welfare position if it were possible to buy any quantity of the commodity at the *new* price.

McKenzie and Pearce (1982) argue that the best cardinal representation of the ordinal utility function for the individual is a money metric related to the equivalent variation concept defined by Hicks (1946). This measure is an exact representation of an individual's utility function and can be derived from a Taylor's series expansion and written as a "fixed weight combination

compensation schemes that assume equal weights will not ensure net welfare gains from technological change. Furthermore, even if compensation is paid, the distribution of income can become increasingly skewed through time if losers are only compensated to the extent that they are no better or worse off than before the technological change. This latter result occurs if gainers are better off than before the technological change, even after they pay compensation, and if losers are in a lower income bracket. The issue of defining unequal welfare weights has received little empirical attention in the literature.

23. These transfers are difficult because government does not have sufficient information to make them. Furthermore, tax-subsidy schemes are themselves costly.

24. Some useful and relatively recent references that provide more detail on this topic are those by Currie, Murphy and Schmitz (1971), Willig (1976), Chipman and Moore (1978, 1980), Just and Hueth (1979), Hausman (1981), Mishan (1981), Just, Hueth and Schmitz (1982), McKenzie and Pearce (1982), and McKenzie (1983). Alston and Larson (1992, 1993) reviewed some more recent literature on the choice between Marshallian and Hicksian measures and discussed the issue of precision, as well as bias, in welfare measures.

of product prices, the fixed weights being constructed from first and higher order elasticities of demand and individual income changes, with elasticities evaluated at a base point" (McKenzie and Pearce 1982, p. 681). It is preferred to consumer surplus (as measured off the ordinary or Marshallian demand curve, which holds money income constant) because it accurately captures the income effect associated with a price change. For example, as price declines with a shift out in the supply curve against a downward sloping demand curve, the real income of the consumer increases, which, in effect, shifts consumer demand for the good, thereby increasing welfare.

Why then does consumer surplus continue to be used? Undoubtedly, familiarity plays a part, but more important reasons are likely to be that (a) contrary to McKenzie and Pearce (1982), consumer surplus calculations are often made with less information than would be required for calculating their exact money metric and (b) for reasons discussed below, a correct answer is *not* always preferred to an incorrect one, regardless of how difficult it may be to compute. Consumer surplus studies often do not begin by estimating demand functions. For example, evaluations of the benefits from agricultural research often begin with estimates of ordinary demand elasticities gathered from diverse sources, but comparable information may not be available for calculating the income effects of price changes.

There is little question that the McKenzie and Pearce (1982) money metric is the most accurate measure of *individual* utility under competitive equilibrium conditions.[25] No doubt, if the functional form of the Marshallian demand curve(s) is known exactly (or at least if its derivatives are known), one can deduce exact measures of the underlying preferences. But this is theoretical sophistry. As a practical matter, in most cases, the econometrics can provide little more than a local approximation to demand at a point. We must recognize that we cannot know the functional forms of supply and demand. The issue then is whether consumer surplus provides an adequate approximation of the *market-level* analogue to individual welfare changes, *given real-world limitations on available information.*

An intermediate option is to use a linear (first-order) approximation of the area behind the Hicksian demand curve (corresponding to consumer surplus behind the Marshallian demand curve), which measures the *compensating variation* or *equivalent variation* for the research-induced price change. This requires a little more information than the consumer-surplus method, but it is explicitly an approximation and does not require knowledge of the functional form for demand.

---

25. It is not clear that this superiority over consumer surplus applies also to aggregate (market level) measures as well. The issue of aggregation over consumers might swamp the issue of income effects in aggregate welfare measures.

Figure 2.5 duplicates the curves in figure 2.4 and includes, as well, two Hicksian demand curves along which money income adjusts to hold utility constant. One of these curves, H_0, holds utility at the preresearch value, u_0, corresponding to P_0 and Q_0; the other, H_1, holds utility at the post-research value, u_1, corresponding to P_1 and Q_1. The Hicksian demands are shown as less elastic (i.e., less price-responsive) than the Marshallian demand, as applies for a normal good with a positive income elasticity of demand. The Marshallian consumer surplus measure is area P_0abP_1. The corresponding area behind the first Hicksian demand (area P_0acP_1 behind H_0) is the *compensating variation* for the price change from P_0 to P_1, and the corresponding area behind the second Hicksian demand (area P_0ebP_1 behind H_1) is the *equivalent variation* for that price change. Thus, the consumer surplus overstates compensating variation and understates equivalent variation in the case of a price decrease for a normal good.

When information is available on the income elasticity of demand, η_{iY}, and the share of the good in total expenditures, s_i, as well as on the Marshallian demand elasticity, η_i, for a good i, the quantity change along the initial Hicksian curve $(Q_1 - Q_0)$ can be calculated (using the Slutsky equation) and used in the consumer-surplus formula instead of the quantity change along

Figure 2.5: *Accuracy of consumer surplus*

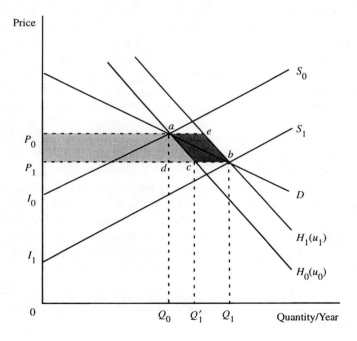

the Marshallian demand. This use of the Hicksian quantity change provides a measure of the compensating variation for the price change. The error from using Marshallian rather than Hicksian demand to measure compensating variation is equal to triangle *abc*, which corresponds to the error of using the Marshallian demand elasticity, η_i, rather than the Hicksian demand elasticity $(\eta_i^* = \eta_i + s_i\eta_{iY})$. The income effect associated with a price decrease $(- s_i\eta_{iY} \times \%\Delta P)$ is positive for normal goods (reinforcing the substitution effect) and negative for inferior goods, so consumer surplus overstates the compensating variation measure of the welfare change due to a research-induced price decrease for normal goods and understates it for inferior goods. Because triangle *abc* is only a small fraction of total benefits (and a very small fraction for small price changes), errors in approximating it are unlikely to loom large in estimates of research benefits. In other contexts, where measurement of the triangle is the main question, these errors of approximation may become relatively important, as argued by Hausman (1981).

Hausman (1981) showed how to obtain "exact" Hicksian measures of welfare change, given a Marshallian demand function, for the commonly used functional forms and argued that there was no reason not to make the correction for income effects to go from consumer surplus to either compensating variation or equivalent variation. Why use a biased measure when it is easy to correct the bias? One response may be drawn from some of the recent literature, mostly in the field of environmental economics, that has drawn attention to the *precision* of welfare measures.[26] Because the parameters of demand equations are random variables, transformations of them used to measure welfare are also random variables. If demand is estimated imprecisely, the bias in the consumer welfare effect or the deadweight loss might not be statistically significant (e.g., Kling 1992). Alston and Larson (1993) point out that, when correcting for the income effect, an additional source of imprecision in the welfare measure, variance of the income elasticity of demand, is added in order to reduce bias. There may be a trade-off of variance against bias. Using a mean-squared error criterion, they showed that the Marshallian (biased) welfare measure might be preferable to the Hicksian (unbiased) measure. The issue of precision of welfare measurement, which arises from recognizing that welfare measures are random variables, is relatively new and its implications remain as yet mostly unresolved. However, the work that has been done illustrates that considering precision may well weaken the arguments in favor of correcting for income effects to obtain Hicksian welfare measures.

26. This literature — including work by Bockstael and Strand (1987), Hayes and Porter-Hudak (1987), Kling (1988, 1991, 1992), and Smith (1990) — has been reviewed and extended by Alston and Larson (1992, 1993).

When the income effect associated with price changes is small, consumer surplus is not a bad approximation. Willig (1976) provided empirical evidence that the bias introduced by ignoring the income effect is relatively small for most goods (less than five percent), at least in a relatively developed country. The income effect is likely to be small when the income elasticity of demand for the good is small, or when a small proportion of the consumer budget is spent on the good.[27] The significance of "small" can be assessed in the context of other biases introduced from other sources during an analysis. Substantial income effects can be associated with price changes for certain foods in developing countries, but for most, the income-effect bias is likely to be swamped by errors in measuring positions of curves or shifts in them. That is to say, there are a number of sources of potential errors in the analysis and attention ought to focus on the more important ones, which in this case are not due to using consumer surplus instead of either the exact money metric or an approximate measure of compensating or equivalent variation.

The above discussion centers on consumer surplus. What about producer surplus? Producer surplus is the excess of the return to the factor owner above that necessary to induce him or her to provide the factor, and it is analogous to the concept of consumer surplus (Mishan 1981). It is meant to measure the change in producer welfare associated with a change in economic profit. However, the income effect associated with a change in a factor (or product) price is often substantial, making producer surplus a much less reliable measure of the corresponding equivalent variation or compensating variation. A change in an individual's return to labor or the value of an individual's land can have a major income or welfare effect.

There are also problems with the accuracy of producer surplus as a measure of economic profit. Producer surplus measures the return to fixed or quasi-fixed factors and thus may be thought of as corresponding closely to the concept of economic profit: income over and above the opportunity cost associated with variable factors. *Avoidable fixed costs* — costs that do not vary with output, once a decision is made to produce, but which can be avoided by choosing not to produce at all — add complications. An example may be the opportunity costs of specialized equipment. These avoidable fixed costs do affect profit but they may not be reflected in the producer surplus measure that accounts only for variable costs. However, *changes in producer surplus* are likely to provide a more accurate reflection of changes in profit, especially when the effects of relatively small changes in prices are

27. Alston and Larson (1992, 1993) reinforced Willig's (1976) result and provided some theoretical and simulation results for the case of a research-induced supply shift. The biases in measures of aggregate research benefits were indeed negligible.

measured, so that the impact on avoidable fixed costs (i.e., the impact on decisions whether to produce at all or to shut down) is minor.

An additional criticism of both consumer and producer surplus is associated with errors introduced when individual demand or supply curves are aggregated into market demand or supply curves. The underlying assumption usually is that tastes, money income, and the prices of other goods are constant across individuals in the economy (Mishan 1981).[28] However, these assumptions underlie alternative measures of welfare as well and, even if they do not hold exactly, are not likely to introduce more serious errors than other simplifying assumptions.

Finally, when estimating the benefits from agricultural research, errors are inevitably introduced by assumptions about (a) functional forms for supply and demand, (b) elasticities of supply and demand, (c) other market parameters, (d) the nature of the research-induced technical change and the corresponding shift of supply or demand, (e) the size of the research-induced productivity improvement, and (f) the timing of the flows of benefits and costs. As a practical matter, from our experience, the potential for errors from these sources is greater by orders of magnitude than that associated with the income effects of price changes or any other imperfections in the economic surplus measures of welfare changes. The results are sensitive to these aspects of the analysis and it is not possible to obtain definitive support for particular choices.

Accurate measurement of even ordinary demand-and-supply curves, particularly along their entire length, is very difficult. And it is very hard to predict the nature of shifts in these curves (Scobie 1976; Lindner and Jarrett 1978; Rose 1980). Supply-and-demand curves may be nonlinear, but they are often assumed to be linear to simplify consumer and producer surplus calculations. Errors associated with this simplification may not be too severe, but errors associated with unavoidable assumptions about the nature of the research-induced supply shift (i.e., parallel, pivotal, or some other shift) can be major (e.g., see Voon and Edwards 1991c). A parallel shift almost doubles the benefit compared with a pivotal shift. Of course, these errors only arise in consumer-producer surplus applications in which curves are shifting, such as when new technologies are being adopted.

What does economic theory tell us about the nature of these shifts? Unfortunately, not very much. To be confident about this aspect of the problem would require either (a) precise econometric evidence or (b) detailed information on the effects on individual agents, details of industry

---

28. Homothetic preferences would be sufficient to permit aggregation across consumers without introducing such errors. Otherwise, the much more restrictive assumption of equal money incomes across individuals is necessary.

structure including details on exit and entry of firms, and a complete theory of aggregation. This information is not available; assumptions are unavoidable. The consequences of assumptions for potential error in using producer and consumer surplus for predicting research impact in priority-setting exercises should be kept in mind. In most cases, the effect on producer surplus will be greater than the effect on consumer surplus.

Partial Welfare Analysis

The validity of a partial welfare analysis, which ignores the complex interrelationships with other product and factor markets in the economy, has been called into question by Little (1960) and others. Broadly speaking, there are two important considerations that influence the legitimacy of employing partial-equilibrium welfare analysis. The first is whether optimality conditions are fulfilled elsewhere in the economy. "If prices equal marginal costs in the rest of the economy, then, assuming no external economies or diseconomies, the prices of factors used in the industry under consideration will reflect their value to society elsewhere. If, however, prices exceed marginal costs elsewhere, the private costs of expanding the output of this industry will understate the real costs to society" (Currie, Murphy and Schmitz 1971, p.788). For example, if other industries are monopolistic, it may not be best for price to equal marginal cost in the sector being studied. Second, even if price equals marginal cost elsewhere, the uncounted welfare effects in factor and product markets elsewhere can be substantial if large adjustments in those sectors occur as a result of changes in the sector being studied.

The "second-best" issues arising from market distortions elsewhere, and other multi-market impacts, are not really deficiencies of economic surplus analysis, which can (at least in principle) be modified to reflect their effects. Rather, they are problems that may invalidate an economic surplus analysis if *empirically* inappropriate assumptions are made in the face of data limitations or other constraints on an analysis. Two criticisms of economic surplus (existence of externalities and transaction costs) are closely related to this general point in that they are criticisms of the conventional practice rather than criticisms of the measures in principle. In later chapters we suggest explicit adjustments to accommodate externalities and other market distortions and show more general approaches to welfare measurement, still in the economic surplus mold, that are less vulnerable to such criticisms.

Externalities and Free Riders

External economies or diseconomies (externalities) can arise which cause the marginal social value to differ from the private value or market price.

This type of market failure can occur when the welfare of one person is influenced positively or negatively by the consumption or production activities of another and when compensation is not made for these external effects.[29] If all transaction costs were equal to zero, and all property rights were assigned, then externalities should be corrected by the market. The existence of substantial, particularly negative, externalities in the world is an indication that transaction costs are important (Mishan 1981). Unless the welfare implications of externalities are explicitly accounted for in the analysis, the usual calculation of consumer and producer surplus does not include them.

A concept closely related to externalities is that of a "collective good" or "public good." We mentioned earlier that research can represent such a good because the benefits produced by certain types of research cannot be appropriated entirely by those producing or financing the work. Therefore, "free riders" become a problem because firms can receive some research benefits without incurring the full research costs. They may incur some costs in screening, adaptive research, or replication, but when these costs are much less than the initial costs of development or discovery free riding is a significant problem. When this happens, incentives to conduct research are reduced and firms produce less research than is socially optimal. This provides a justification for government intervention, such as public research, and implies that decisions to invest in public research should consider the degree of "collectiveness" of each type of research. It is also the primary justification for patents.

Transaction Costs and Incomplete Risk Markets

Consumer and producer surplus, and neoclassical welfare economics in general, has been criticized for ignoring transaction costs that arise because of asset fixity (sunk costs), imperfect information (bounded rationality), and the willingness of people to profit at the expense of others (opportunism).[30] The presence of fixed or sunk costs associated with capital items and people means that reallocating resources will involve adjustment costs that make it uneconomic to transfer capital and people immediately to their otherwise preferred uses when conditions change. Imperfect information arises because the future is uncertain. It can lead to incomplete risk markets, in which

29. Externalities do not refer to price effects associated with production or consumption, but are rather the consequences of unintended activities, such as pollution, that result from some other legitimate form of activity (Mishan 1981). Taxes or subsidies are often suggested as possible means of bringing the marginal social cost equal to the market price.

30. For instance, see Williamson (1985), Baumol (1986), and North (1984, 1987).

case competitive equilibrium is no longer *Pareto optimal* (Hart 1975; Stiglitz 1982, 1985; Runge and Myers 1985). Imperfect information and incomplete risk markets make it difficult to assess accurately the true impacts of changes in consumer and producer surplus on economic efficiency and distribution (Stiglitz 1985; Runge and Myers 1985). Because there are bounds on people's ability to calculate, it is impossible to set up complex contracts that foresee every contingency (Baumol 1986, p. 280). If it were known that participants would not try to exploit opportunities to profit at the expense of others, then contracts could be drawn up loosely and specified in more detail as circumstances became clear, but this is not the case in modern society.[31]

A conventional welfare analysis that ignores transaction costs will provide results that overstate the benefits of activities with high transaction costs both absolutely and relative to activities with relatively low transaction costs. New technologies produced through research can involve significant transaction costs because of sunk costs, imperfect information, and risk. Schmitz and Seckler (1970) and Hertford and Schmitz (1977) have pointed out that the effects of resource displacement need to be accounted for if those resources fail to find employment immediately. When a farmer's labor, for example, is displaced, there can be significant adjustment costs associated with moving the labor to a new occupation, even if it is fully employed once it arrives there. If there are adjustment costs, they have to be subtracted from the benefits. Measuring these costs is difficult. If the resource were labor, one might measure the cost to society of supporting unemployed people until they find new employment. However, it is difficult to measure the true cost to society of such adjustments.

Criticisms related to transaction costs and incomplete risk markets (which are part of a broader range of criticisms of economic surplus measures that center on "market failures" or "second-best" problems) pertain more to the assumptions conventionally used in economic surplus measurement rather than the neoclassical paradigm, which can, of course, accommodate imperfect information, transaction costs, and so on. The real issues in deciding just how to modify the empirical analysis to accommodate such problems are empirical ones.

Policy Irrelevance

Several critics of consumer and producer surplus analysis argue that the concepts are irrelevant for policy analysis. Cochrane (1980), for example,

---

31. North (1987) points out that in primitive economies, social pressures reduce opportunism because everyone knows everyone else. Thus, transaction costs are reduced. As economies grow, transaction costs rise with the impersonal nature of exchange.

argues that producers, consumers, and policymakers understand the implications of price changes but not changes in economic surplus. The "policy irrelevance" criticism tends to be based on two factors: the first is an implicit or explicit recognition of the five criticisms described above; the second stems from the way the results of consumer and producer surplus calculations are presented. They are often reported as if they came from a black box, the important assumptions and variables that drive the results are not explained, and distributional value judgments are not made explicit.

The measures of changes in consumer and producer surplus arising from agricultural research may be more useful when they are interpreted in terms of cost-reducing or yield-enhancing effects, effects on production and consumption, price effects, and other factors relevant to the type of economic surplus analysis being conducted. If a value judgment is made that income received by different people (consumers, producers, low- versus high-income people, people from different regions, and so on) has equal worth to the nation, regardless of who receives it, this should be stated. Unless care is exercised to relate the consumer and producer surplus calculations to the goals and objectives of the decision makers, those calculations are likely to be treated as irrelevant.

Summary

Six major criticisms have been leveled against consumer and producer surplus as welfare measures. Some criticisms (ignoring transaction costs, externalities, general equilibrium effects, and certain measurement errors) can be addressed, at least partially, by refinements in the measures of benefits or costs. Value judgments cannot be avoided but can be made more explicit. Policy relevance can be improved by clearer explanation of the implications of the results (or the factors driving them) and explicit consideration of distributional and other objectives.

Most procedures for assisting priority setting in agricultural research described in part III of this book use consumer and producer surplus or attempt to approximate the results of consumer and producer surplus. All of these procedures are only approximations to the "true" money metric, corrected for transaction costs, externalities, and general equilibrium effects and weighted by society's values in a policy-relevant fashion. It is impossible to obtain the truly correct welfare measure but "even those of us who sin should recognize where virtue lies."[32]

32. Comment by Martin Bailey in a different context during a conference on improved procedures for agricultural productivity measurement at the Economic Research Service, U.S. Department of Agriculture, Washington, D.C., March 31, 1988.

2.2.3   "Alternatives" to Economic Surplus Analysis

Cost-Benefit Analysis

Cost-benefit analysis is sometimes represented as an alternative to economic surplus analysis for assessing research benefits in a partial-equilibrium framework. In fact, cost-benefit analysis uses the concept of economic surplus and changes in such surplus measures, either explicitly or implicitly. For example, in a formal cost-benefit analysis, when research benefits are explicitly measured as changes in consumer and producer surplus, as represented in figure 2.4, these economic surplus changes are subsequently distributed and discounted over time. Internal rates of return, net present values, or benefit-cost ratios are calculated both to capture the time value of money and to incorporate research costs so that net benefits and not just gross benefits are calculated.[33]

Economic surplus changes may not be explicitly measured, but economic surplus calculations are still implicitly being made when internal rates of return, net present values, or benefit-cost ratios are calculated to place a value on the extra output or the inputs saved (cost reductions) because of research.[34] Moreover, one of the following two simplifying assumptions is being used.[35] The extra production is valued at a single market price that assumes that the supply curve is vertical and shifts against a horizontal demand curve (figure 2.6a). Alternatively, the value of inputs saved (cost reduction) at the current level of production is calculated, which implies that a horizontal supply curve is shifting down against a vertical demand curve (figure 2.6b). The change in economic surplus is equal to abQ_1Q_0 in the first case and abP_1P_0 in the second.[36]

The potential advantage of employing this type of implicit consumer surplus analysis is that polar demand or supply elasticities are simply imposed on the analysis by assumption, eliminating the need to obtain elasticity estimates. The disadvantages are that the implicit economic surplus calculations ignore all regional and international price effects that are due to the

---

33. See Davis, Oram and Ryan (1987) or Norton, Ganoza and Pomareda (1987) for examples.

34. See, for example, the discussion of benefit-cost analysis in Bottomley and Contant (1988). While Bottomley and Contant do not mention economic surplus analysis, they in fact are presenting an example of simplified economic surplus analysis.

35. This type of approach was introduced as an economic surplus measure of returns to research by Schultz (1953a, pp. 114-22) and Griliches (1958).

36. A parallel shift down of a linear supply function, as shown in figure 2.1, yields a gross benefit equal to a rectangle (area I_0acI_1) and a triangle (area abc). The approximation used in cost-benefit analysis in the latter case (horizontal supply shifting down against vertical demand) corresponds to the rectangle, and therefore represents a lower-bound value of benefits.

Figure 2.6:   *Implicit assumptions in cost-benefit analysis*

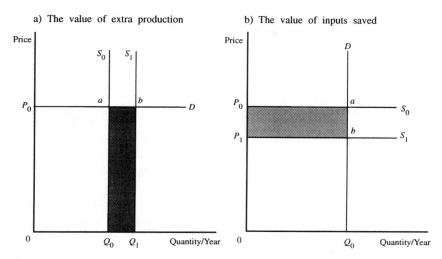

a) The value of extra production

b) The value of inputs saved

research, as well as any distributional effects. In other words, the implicit economic surplus analysis is subject to the criticisms mentioned earlier, and it adds two more. This is not to argue for or against this type of simplified economic surplus analysis, but only to point out its implications.

Econometric Models

Earlier we mentioned that some studies use econometric methods to estimate directly the relationship between past investments in agricultural research and extension and agricultural production or productivity in equations similar to equation 2.6 (see chapter 3 for more detail). The results may be used to indicate the value of the reduction in inputs for a given quantity of output or the value of additional output from a given quantity of inputs attributable to research spending. As in the case of benefit-cost approaches, this step of valuing additional output or savings in inputs is an implicit economic surplus analysis that makes extreme assumptions about market conditions (effectively assuming either perfectly inelastic or perfectly elastic supply). In this sense, the econometric approach is a variant of the economic surplus approach rather than an alternative to it. More generally, the econometric methods (or the results thereof) can be combined in a complementary fashion with a less restrictive economic surplus model to estimate the economic consequences of agricultural research investments.

Domestic Resource Cost (DRC) Models

An alternative method that has been suggested for guiding resource allocations to research while incorporating the welfare-distorting effects of government policies is a procedure called *domestic resource cost* (DRC) analysis.[37] DRC analysis involves calculating the ratio $A/(B - C)$, where A is the social value of nontraded inputs (e.g., fixed capital, labor, and land) used to produce a unit of the commodity, B is the social value of gross output, and C is the social value of traded inputs used to produce the commodity. Outputs and traded inputs are valued at their world prices. Therefore $B - C$ is the foreign-exchange value of the output minus the foreign-exchange value of traded inputs used to produce it.

A DRC ratio can be used as a cost-benefit ratio. If the DRC ratio is less than one, then it is socially profitable to produce the commodity. If the DRC ratio is greater than one, it is not socially profitable. The concept of a DRC ratio bears a close relationship to measures of comparative advantage because it provides a measure of the opportunity cost (in terms of domestic resources) of providing a net marginal unit of foreign exchange.[38] The real appeal of a DRC ratio for policy analysis is that it provides a relatively simple measure of the social value of inputs used to generate a unit of net output valued at its true social value. Unfortunately, as currently applied, DRC analysis is seriously flawed as a single or primary procedure for setting agricultural research priorities. Its fatal flaw is that it ignores one of the major determinants of the social value of conducting research on a particular commodity: the number of units (hectares, animals) to which the research benefits will apply.[39]

Because research costs are relatively independent of the number of hectares that will eventually be affected by the research results, the benefits will be substantially greater if the research affects 10,000 hectares rather than 10. The DRC does not take this into account. One could argue that if a country has a lower DRC for one commodity than for another, it should expand the number of units as well as lower the per unit costs through research. But as soon as production of the commodity expands very much, the opportunity

37. Recent applications of domestic resource cost analysis in developing countries are found in Monke and Pearson (1989) and, with reference to prioritizing research, in Byerlee (1985). For a discussion of the conceptual basis and limitations of domestic resource cost analysis see Bruno (1972), Srinivasan and Bhagwati (1978), and Tower (1984).

38. DRC is not a true measure of comparative advantage because no attempt is made to remove policy distortions on the same commodity or on other commodities in other countries that in turn are affecting world prices.

39. It also ignores the probability of research success on a particular commodity and the adoption rate of research results, but these items could be factored into a DRC analysis. For example, the denominator of DRC could be multiplied by the probability of success.

costs of the domestic resources used in production would change, input substitution would take place, and the initial DRC ratio would change. Thus a DRC is an accurate cost-benefit ratio only for marginal changes in production. In addition, if the country is a large exporter or importer, world prices could also be affected by production changes in the country. These price changes cannot be calculated without elasticities. But if elasticities are available, one might as well conduct an economic surplus analysis and include the policy distortions directly.

The Congruence Rule

The congruence rule has been used widely as a crude procedure for allocating resources to research. In this approach, funds are allocated so as to equate research intensities — research investment in relation to the value of output in gross or value-added terms — across areas. That is, research is funded in proportion to the value of production, an approach that requires minimal information.

Congruence will result in maximum economic surplus from the portfolio of research investments when all projects or programs are subject to the same per unit research (knowledge) production function (Evenson 1991).[40] The conditions under which this would occur are unlikely to be met, but in some cases there might be insufficient information available (on the flows of benefits and costs from alternative projects and programs) to justify a more complete analysis. In such cases, an application of the congruence rule might be consistent with an ultrasimplified economic surplus approach in that at least some account is taken of the scale of the industry.

2.3   Determinants of the Size and Distribution of Benefits and Costs

In section 2.1 of this chapter, we discussed the nature of agricultural research as a process that augments the stock of knowledge, which provides a flow of services as inputs to agricultural production. In that context, agricultural research is a component of a dynamic agricultural production system whose effects are spread over long periods. Using the familiar framework for supply and demand, we showed how these dynamic relations can be represented as a series of comparative-static, market equilibrium displacements. In section 2.2, we introduced the economic surplus approach

---

40. Evenson (1991) demonstrates this with a research production function (or "discovery function") of the semi-logarithmic form: $D = \alpha + \beta \ln(R)$, where D is the increment to knowledge due to research, R.

to measuring the annual economic welfare effects of a research-induced supply shift. Following a critical appraisal of that approach, we concluded that, although they are imperfect, economic surplus methods are the best available means for measuring the flows of benefits and costs of agricultural research. The purpose of this section is to extend the discussion by elaborating on (a) the key elements of the economic surplus approach and the critical choices that influence the estimates, (b) the extension of the approach to incorporate alternative market characteristics, and (c) an examination of the distributional implications of agricultural research.

2.3.1   Critical Assumptions in the Model

In figure 2.4 we schematically showed measures of producer, consumer, and total economic surplus changes associated with a research-induced supply shift. In order to measure those welfare areas explicitly, it is necessary to define explicit mathematical functions to represent supply-and-demand equations and the supply shift. In most instances it is not possible to measure these relationships econometrically with high levels of precision (if at all) and it is necessary to make assumptions rather than rely on data alone. But some aspects of the measures are sensitive to assumptions about (a) supply-and-demand elasticities, (b) functional forms of supply and demand, (c) the nature of the research-induced supply shift, and (d) the nature of the technical change. That assumptions must be made is inevitable. That they are important may be regrettable but need not be fatal to the analysis. The purpose of this section is to illustrate the nature of the sensitivity of results to assumptions in order to assist analysts in making informed choices about assumptions and in focusing their sensitivity analyses in appropriate directions.

Elasticities of Supply and Demand

To recapitulate, in figure 2.4, supply and demand are represented by linear functions. Adoption of new technology resulting from research causes supply to shift in parallel from S_0 to S_1. The resulting welfare changes are (a) ΔPS (change in producer surplus) = area $I_0abI_1 - P_0abP_1 = P_1bcd$, (b) ΔCS (change in consumer surplus) = area P_0abP_1, and (c) ΔTS (change in total surplus) = $\Delta CS + \Delta PS$ = area $I_0abI_1 = P_0abcd$. Mathematical formulas to measure these areas in terms of the size and nature of the supply shift and market parameters are provided in chapter 4. For the present purpose it is sufficient to look at these areas informally.

What are the effects of assumptions about supply-and-demand elasticities on the welfare measures? First, it is helpful to notice that in this instance, each of the surplus areas (ΔPS, ΔCS, and ΔTS) can be represented as the sum of a rectangle and a triangle. In each case the width of the rectangle is the original (preresearch) quantity, Q_0, and the width of the triangle is equal to the change in quantity produced ($\Delta Q = Q_1 - Q_0$). The heights of the rectangles and triangles depend on the absolute size of the vertical shift in supply, the per unit cost saving due to research (for ΔTS), the change in price (for ΔCS), and the difference between the change in cost and the change in price (for ΔPS). In the case of total benefits, elasticity assumptions do not affect the rectangle, P_0acd, but they do affect the triangle, *abc*: the more elastic supply or demand is, the larger the triangle and the larger the total welfare gain. As a practical matter, however, in the context of estimating research benefits, the triangles are typically very small relative to the rectangles and total benefits are relatively insensitive to elasticities of supply and demand.[41]

Elasticity assumptions (or estimates) are much more important in relation to the distribution of benefits. In particular, the more elastic supply is relative to demand, the greater the consumer share of total research benefits (and the smaller the producer share) and vice versa. In the extreme case of perfectly elastic supply with downward-sloping demand (as might occur in a competitive industry in a closed economy or in a large-country case), all of the research benefits go to consumers because the research-induced change in price is equal to the research-induced cost-saving and there is no producer surplus either before or after the supply shift (figure 2.7a). When demand is perfectly elastic (as in the case of a small, open economy which cannot affect the world price for the commodity, probably the predominant case for agricultural goods), all of the benefits go to producers because there is no research-induced reduction in price (figure 2.7b). When the elasticities are of equal magnitudes (albeit opposite signs), the benefits from research are shared equally between producers and consumers (figure 2.7c).

These conclusions about the role of elasticities, obtained using linear supply-and-demand functions with a parallel shift, apply fairly generally but there are some important additional considerations when different types of supply shifts are used. In particular, when we have a pivotal supply shift, whether producers benefit at all from research depends on the elasticity of demand — when demand is inelastic, producers lose!

41. For a $100K$ percent shift down of a linear supply function, the rectangle is equal to KP_0Q_0 and the triangle is $1/2\ K^2P_0Q_0\varepsilon\eta/(\varepsilon+\eta)$, where ε is the supply elasticity and η is the absolute value of the elasticity of demand. The triangle is equal to $50K\varepsilon\eta/(\varepsilon+\eta)$ percent of the rectangle. When the supply and demand elasticities are equal to one (or smaller), the triangle is equal to $25K$ percent (or less) of the rectangle. For commonly used research-induced supply shifts of less than 10 percent of the initial price (i.e., $K = 0.1$), the triangle would be less than 2.5 percent of the rectangle. Even when demand is perfectly elastic ($\eta = +\infty$) the triangle is only $50K$ percent of the rectangle; i.e., 5 percent when $K = 0.1$.

Figure 2.7: *Effects of elasticities on distribution of benefits*

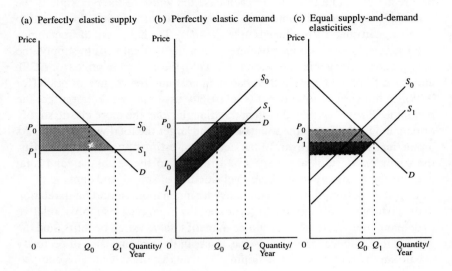

(a) Perfectly elastic supply   (b) Perfectly elastic demand   (c) Equal supply-and-demand elasticities

Functional Forms of Supply and Demand

Figure 2.4 uses linear supply-and-demand curves that make it easy to calculate the geometric areas of surplus changes using simple algebra. Linear supply-and-demand curves have been used for that reason in the majority of studies of research benefits. With such curves, the elasticities change as quantity changes along the curve, and one must be explicit about where the assumed elasticities apply — before or after the research-induced market displacement. One hazard with linear supply functions is that, when the function is *inelastic* at the supply-and-demand equilibrium, extrapolating back to the origin implies a negative intercept on the price axis (implying that positive quantities would be supplied at negative prices). Various authors have criticized the use of linear supply curves with point elasticities of less than one for that reason.[42] A linear curve does imply a negative intercept, but this can be averted by kinking the supply curve (Rose 1980). The economic surplus calculated after kinking the supply curve at the original quantity is the same as the economic surplus calculated without the kink.[43] The real problem is the poor estimate of the proportionate cost reduction due to research. With an inelastic supply curve, the proportionate cost reduction

---

42. See Kim, et al. (1987), Godyn, Brennan and Johnston (1987), and Voon and Edwards (1991c).

43. This is true whether the supply shift is pivotal or parallel.

implied by a proportional rightwards shift of supply can be unreasonable, giving rise to overestimated returns.[44]

The introduction of arbitrary kinks of supply (as by Rose 1980 and Hertford and Schmitz 1977) is effectively an abandonment of the linearity assumption. Alston and Wohlgenant (1990) suggest that when a parallel shift is used, the functional form is largely irrelevant, and that a linear model provides a good approximation regardless of the true functional form of supply. Based on that, it is safe to proceed using the algebra from the linear model, ignoring the question of any implied negative intercepts on the price axis so long as the supply shift is parallel.

The main alternative assumption that has been used is one of supply-and-demand curves of constant elasticity (e.g., Ayer and Schuh 1972; Scobie and Posada 1978). The constant-elasticity model has the supply function, regardless of its elasticity, passing through the origin. Thus, as with the linear model (in the case of inelastic supply), the constant-elasticity model has some implausible implications when we extrapolate far from the initial equilibrium. Typically the constant-elasticity assumption is combined with an assumption of a proportional (or pivotal) supply shift — because it is difficult to use a nonproportional shift with a constant-elasticity model — and, as we shall see below, that is the most important consequence of the functional form choice. A constant-elasticity supply function with a proportional supply shift is shown in figure 2.8. The surplus areas are ΔTS = area $0ab$, ΔCS = area P_0abP_1, and $\Delta PS = \Delta TS - \Delta CS$ = area $0ab$ – area P_0abP_1.

What are the implications of choosing linear versus constant-elasticity forms? The nature of the consequences will depend in part on the approximating formula being used. For example, compared with using a constant-elasticity model, the formula for a kinked supply curve provided by Rose (1980) will increase the economic surplus measure for an elasticity of supply greater than one while the formula provided by Hertford and Schmitz (1977) (for a pivotal shift) will reduce the measured economic surplus. The opposite effects would occur for a supply elasticity of less than one. The results of Rose (1980) and Hertford and Schmitz (1977) differ because Rose kinks the supply curve at the original quantity while Hertford and Schmitz kink it at the new price. Some authors have used linear approximations to calculate

---

44. Actually, if one uses an elastic supply curve, the benefits can be underestimated as well, even though the curve intersects the vertical axis at a positive price. One way that these overestimates or underestimates arise is when the proportionate vertical supply shift is calculated from the proportionate horizontal supply shift using the expression $K = J/\varepsilon$, where K = the vertical supply shift, J = the horizontal supply shift, and ε = the elasticity of supply. This relationship only holds in a small neighborhood around the original price and quantity and can give very unrealistic results for linear supply curves that are either very elastic or very inelastic. The relationships between these alternative measures of research-induced supply shifts are dealt with in detail in chapter 5.

Figure 2.8: *A proportional supply shift in a constant-elasticity model*

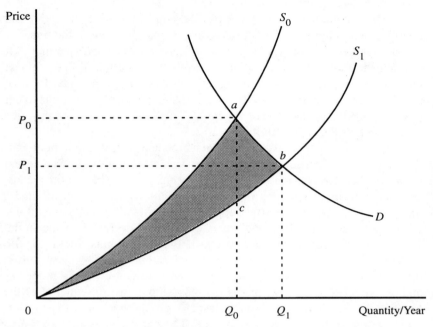

economic surplus under an assumption of a constant supply elasticity. For example, the formula used by Akino and Hayami (1975) as a linear approximation to a constant-elasticity function overestimates the economic surplus for elasticities of supply less than one and underestimates the economic surplus for elasticities of supply greater than one.

A third alternative has been suggested by Lynam and Jones (1984) and used by Pachico, Lynam and Jones (1987). This is a constant-elasticity form based on a positive intercept with the price axis, so, in fact, it is not a constant-elasticity function. This model has the virtue of greater realism than either the linear or constant-elasticity models — in that it allows a positive price intercept independent of elasticity assumptions — and it is flexible in relation to the nature of the research-induced supply shift. For instance, in figure 2.9 we have a vertically parallel shift of a constant-elasticity form of supply function. In practice the advantages of this flexibility may be illusory because of difficulties in identifying the nature of the research-induced supply shift. In addition, since this approach requires a nonlinear algorithm for its solution, the extra effort involved in solving for price and quantity changes may not be warranted (Alston and Wohlgenant 1990).

Of course, none of these is likely to be the *true* and generally unknown

Figure 2.9:   *A parallel shift down of a "constant-elasticity" supply function*

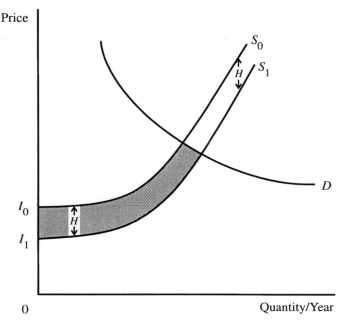

functional form. The pertinent question is whether the functional form used is an adequate approximation for the purpose. It turns out, empirically, that measures of total research benefits and their distribution between producers and consumers are quite insensitive to choices of functional form. They are much more sensitive to the related but separate choices concerning the nature of the research-induced supply shift and elasticities.[45]

The Nature of the Research-Induced Supply Shift

There has been a great deal of discussion in the literature about the effects of different types of research-induced supply shifts on the size and distribution of research benefits, and rightly so.[46] This choice in the analysis is crucially important, and by comparison, the choices about functional forms and elasticities pale into insignificance. For example, given a linear supply

45.   See Lindner and Jarrett (1978), Norton and Davis (1981), Alston and Wohlgenant (1990), and Voon and Edwards (1991c) for details and evidence.
46.   The point was comprehensively addressed by Lindner and Jarrett (1978), leading to some debate, with comments from Rose (1980) and Wise and Fell (1980) and a reply by Lindner and Jarrett (1980). The matter has never been resolved satisfactorily. Norton and Davis (1981) provide a summary discussion of the history of the question and the main points.

function, total benefits from a parallel shift are almost twice the size of total benefits from a pivotal shift (of equal size at the preresearch equilibrium). When supply shifts in parallel, producers *always* benefit from research unless supply is perfectly elastic or demand is perfectly inelastic, and even in these extreme cases, producers are no worse off as a result of research. On the other hand, as noted above, with a pivotal shift, producers benefit only when demand is elastic; when demand is inelastic, producers necessarily lose from a pivotal supply shift (e.g., Lindner and Jarrett 1978).

Unfortunately, economic theory is not informative about either the functional form of supply and demand or the functional form (parallel, pivotal, proportional, or otherwise) of the research-induced supply shift. The industry curve is based on the aggregation of supply curves for individual firms. Shifts in the industry curve depend on the effects of new technologies on the marginal costs of existing firms and on entry and exit of firms. One would need to examine the characteristics of individual firms that affect marginal costs and technology adoption in order to predict which types of firms would benefit from a particular new technology. In addition, with current techniques and typically available data, it is not possible to settle these questions econometrically. We might hope to obtain plausible estimates of elasticities at the data means, but definitive results concerning functional forms are unlikely and it is impossible to get statistical results that can be extrapolated to the price or quantity axes (i.e., the full length of the function) with any confidence. Thus, assumptions about the nature of the research-induced supply shift are unavoidable. Our conclusion is that it is important to be aware of the consequences of different assumptions.[47]

Our preference — in the absence of the information required to choose a particular type of shift — is to follow Rose's (1980) suggestion and employ a parallel shift. Rose (1980, p. 837) argued that "For most innovations, the best information available may be a cost-reduction estimate for a single point on the supply curve . . . . [It] is unlikely that any knowledge of the shape of the supply curve, or the position at which the single estimate applies, will be available. The only realistic strategy is to assume that the supply shift is parallel." We find the arguments of Rose persuasive, and therefore we are inclined to assume vertically parallel research-induced supply shifts. Under this assumption, the functional forms of supply and demand are unimportant and it is convenient to use a local linear approximation, as suggested by Alston and Wohlgenant (1990).[48]

---

47. One could always use a pivotal shift rather than a parallel shift in order to generate conservative estimates of total economic benefits.

48. A parallel shift implies the change in average cost equals the change in marginal cost at every point along the curve. Vince Smith (pers. comm.) has pointed out that often we have a reasonable

An additional advantage is that this assumption simplifies some calculations and permits consistency in the evaluation among projects and programs across a range of commodities. For priority-setting purposes, this consistency is important. Errors in assumptions are less important in relation to ranking priorities than they are in absolute terms.

A side issue is whether the shift is expressed as vertical (in the price direction) or horizontal (in the quantity direction). Of course any supply shift may be expressed, with care, equivalently in either way. The issue has arisen in going from experimental or industry yield increases to supply shifts (see chapter 5). Expressing a K percent yield increase (or cost saving) as either a K percent vertical shift or a K percent horizontal shift has different implications unless the supply elasticity is unitary.[49]

2.3.2 Extensions to the Basic Model

The basic economic surplus model may be modified in various ways (a) to disaggregate effects across multiple markets horizontally (across geopolitical regions, socioeconomic groups, or commodities) and vertically (across stages of production or among factors of production), (b) to allow interregional spillovers of research-induced price changes and research results, (c) to incorporate general-equilbrium feedback and economywide adjustments, (d) to accommodate market distortions and the effects of research on the creation (or amelioration) of market distortions caused by government intervention or production externalities, and (e) to account for the costs of taxes to finance government spending.

International and Interregional Trade

When goods are traded internationally, the basic economic surplus model measures total research benefits from a global perspective. With free trade, the total supply-and-demand functions are the horizontal summations of the underlying supply-and-demand functions of individual nations or other sub-aggregates, respectively. In this setting it is a relatively simple matter to

estimate of the change in average cost at the current equilibrium, and this is what counts for estimating the rectangle that dominates gross annual research benefits (GARB). A similar point was made by Cooke and Sundquist (1993). Thus, we do not need to know what has happened to marginal or average cost at any other point along the curve. An error in estimating the change in marginal cost, given an estimate of the change in average cost, will not cause important errors in GARB (it only affects the comparatively small triangle) although it may have important implications for distribution.

49. The equivalent horizontal supply shift, J, for a K percent vertical supply shift is given by using the definition that $dQ/Q = \varepsilon dP/P$ and, therefore, $J = \varepsilon K$, where ε is the elasticity of supply.

disaggregate the consequences of research among regions or countries. The total consumer surplus measured behind the total demand curve is the sum of the component consumer surpluses measured behind the component demand curves. Similarly, total producer surplus may be decomposed into subcomponents.

The situation may be analyzed in a disaggregated fashion either by modeling all nations in a multicountry model that explicitly involves the supply-and-demand curves of each nation (i.e., *n* markets for *n* countries), by modeling supply and demand in a country of interest and in an aggregate "rest-of-the-world" (ROW) (i.e., two markets), or by using excess supply and demand from the home country and the ROW (i.e., one market). In addition, the same approaches could be applied instead to analyze trade patterns and the distribution of research benefits among regions of a country, with regions playing the role of nations in the multinational modeling approach. All of these approaches are conceptually identical and, if implemented consistently, in a particular application give identical results for total research benefits in both the ROW and the home country. However, the different approaches yield different disaggregated details.

In deciding how to analyze research benefits for a traded good, the main question is how much detail is warranted. While it is conceptually straightforward to disaggregate to any level, in practice the information problems — of obtaining suitable measures of quantities, prices, and elasticities of supply and demand — become greater relatively quickly as one proceeds to finer disaggregations. Thus, from this perspective, it is sensible to disaggregate to the point where the requirements of the analysis are served, but no further than that. From another perspective, it may be sensible to disaggregate somewhat further in order to get a more accurate picture of the research-induced supply shift. When a technology is applicable in multiple regions that differ in their responses to the new technology, it may be necessary to disaggregate some aspects of the study to avoid aggregation biases, even if all regions are not of specific interest from a research-policy or priority-setting perspective.

From a global perspective, the total benefits from research and their distribution between "consumers" and "producers" are as defined in the basic model and are sensitive to assumptions about elasticities, functional forms, and so on, as in the basic model. When the interest is in returns from a narrower (say national or subnational) perspective, the story is altered somewhat. In addition to the factors identified in the basic model, the key determinants of national research benefits in the home country are (a) the extent to which the research results can be adopted by the ROW and (b) market power in trade (i.e., the elasticities of supply and demand that determine the distribution of benefits among nations).[50] These effects may be considered in terms of technology spillovers and price spillovers.

Technology and Price Spillovers across Geographical Areas

The results of agricultural research can have two major types of spatial spillovers. First, new knowledge or technologies produced in or targeted for one country or region can spill over into other countries or regions. Second, new technologies can affect prices, not only in the region and country adopting the technology, but in other regions or countries where the product is produced or consumed. These spillovers influence both the size and distribution of research benefits and should be considered when research priorities are set.

The ease of technology transfer across geographic boundaries depends on a variety of factors, as described by Ruttan and Hayami (1973) and by Evenson and Binswanger (1978). The relative costs of direct technology transfer and of adaptive versus comprehensive research programs, the complementarity between screening of existing technologies and carrying out applied research, the environmental sensitivity of the technology, and differences across locales in their factor scarcities are particularly important (Evenson and Binswanger 1978). Technologies themselves, as well as the capacity to create and adapt technologies, are potentially transferable. Basic research is often less environmentally specific and thus more likely to be transferred than applied research.

The fact that certain research results can be transferred from one country to another or from one region to another means that the calculations of total benefits of research to the world as a whole should consider these spillovers. Individual countries, however, have little incentive to consider the effects of their own research on other countries, except in so far as the transfer of new technology to other countries may reduce their own competitive positions in the market. Countries also have an incentive to borrow technologies when they can obtain results for less than the full cost. Smaller countries in particular may transfer in a high proportion of their new technologies because they usually cannot afford extensive research programs. There is thus an incentive to underinvest in research in the world as a whole, particularly for basic kinds of research, which suggests a need for international agricultural research centers that can generate technologies applicable to

---

50. Trade also affects distribution of benefits between producers and consumers in the home country by changing the effective elasticities and thus modifying the consequences of technical change for prices and quantities. These issues are described and analyzed, for example, by Edwards and Freebairn (1982, 1984) and Davis, Oram and Ryan (1987).

several countries. This is one rationale for the current system of centers supported by the Consultative Group on International Agricultural Research.

The existence of technological spillovers has important implications for resource allocations to research within individual countries. First, individual countries may be wise to consider new technologies being produced in international centers and in research systems in countries with similar human, natural, and physical resource bases so that research programs can be structured to complement the research conducted abroad rather than duplicating it excessively. Second, local research capacity may be needed just to enable the country to transfer in and adopt technologies developed elsewhere. Third, the differential effects of research on agricultural productivity across regions in a country may need to be considered.

International and interregional adoption of technologies implies that research in one location induces supply curves to shift out in other countries and regions, as discussed by Edwards and Freebairn (1984) and by Davis, Oram and Ryan (1987). This results not only in changes in agricultural productivity, but it also effects output prices across countries and regions. For example, if new technologies are adopted in one region (country) but not in another, producers in nonadopting regions (countries) can experience price reductions without a corresponding reduction in costs. Consumers can also benefit from the technology even though they live in regions (countries) not adopting new technologies.[51] These factors may need to be considered in an *ex ante* assessment of research priorities. They also imply a need to consider the consistency between regional and national priorities within a country.

Large countries may find it difficult to achieve a consensus on research priorities because of a divergence between regional and national priorities. Even for research that is regionally specific in its application and impact, a country must decide on its relative allocation across regions. For research with both technical and price spillovers, reconciling regional and national priorities is even more difficult. A desire to help landless laborers in one region may conflict with a second objective of increasing agricultural productivity in another region in order to provide low-cost food for urban consumers. The procedure developed for research priority setting may need to consider, and preferably to quantify, the tradeoffs associated with alternative regional allocations of research resources.

51. See Davis, Oram and Ryan (1987) and chapter 4 for a graphical and mathematical description of these effects.

Processing and Marketing Research

Two conceptual issues arise with respect to processing and marketing-sector research. First, it is frequently argued that because most of the final value of agricultural products is added beyond the farm gate, much of public agricultural research should focus on the postharvest sectors. Second, some have argued that, under reasonable assumptions, producers, processors, and consumers receive the same share of total industry benefits from research, irrespective of whether the research generates new technologies at the production, processing, or marketing stage. Considering these two, related, ideas has led some to infer that agricultural research has neglected opportunities beyond the farm gate. What determines if research affecting the processing and marketing sectors should receive priority and whether it makes a difference if research affects agricultural commodities pre- or postharvest?

Figure 2.10 is a schematic representation of production and price determination in a multistage production system for a traded good. The two stages of production include farming (that uses inputs supplied by farmers as well as purchased inputs) and processing and distribution (that uses the farm product from the first stage plus marketing and other inputs). The stages are integrated in that production and the prices of inputs and outputs at all stages of production are mutually dependent. Potential beneficiaries from research include final consumers (including foreign consumers) and suppliers of all factors used in production (farmers, farm input suppliers, and marketing input suppliers). Research may affect the supply of any of these inputs and may also affect the technology in the two stages of production. This is very similar to the multistage models analyzed by Freebairn, Davis and Edwards (1982) and Alston and Scobie (1983).

As discussed in chapter 1, the rationale for public-sector involvement in particular types of research rests on the assumption that the private sector has insufficient incentives to conduct the socially optimal quantity of those types of research. If private research incentives are insufficient, the priority placed on research in marketing and processing would then depend on the ability of researchers to generate greater net benefits in marketing and processing (by contributing to efficiency, distributional, and security goals) than in research directed at primary production. Advocates of a greater emphasis on processing and marketing research usually imply that efficiency gains would be greater if research efforts focused more on postharvest activities. This is an empirical question. However, the issue of private incentives is often ignored. Private-sector incentives may be greater in marketing and processing sectors than in primary production because of a greater ability to patent and license

Figure 2.10: *Schematics of multimarket effects of R&D*

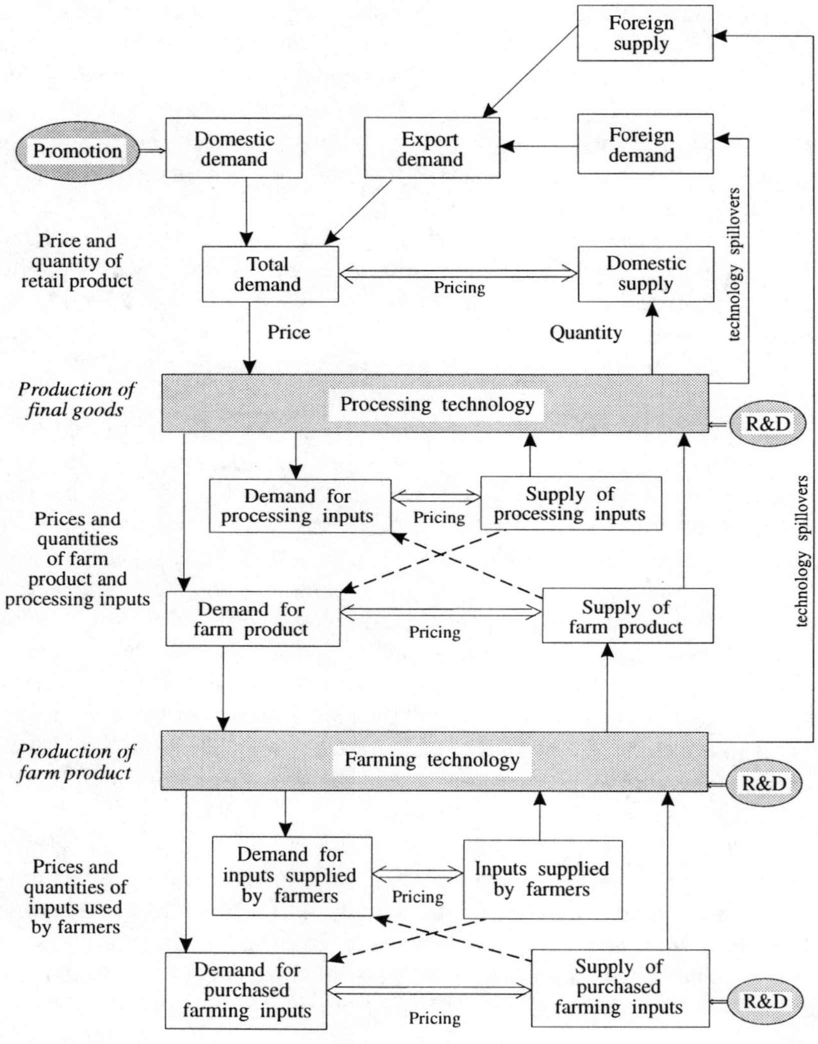

research results and thereby to appropriate the returns to research. Much processing and marketing research is related to mechanical items and new products, both of which may be easier to patent than biological innovations.

In relation to the question of who receives the gains from research at different stages in the production, processing, and marketing chain, the degree of substitutability among inputs in processing and marketing becomes quite important. Freebairn, Davis and Edwards (1982) argued that, in a processing industry using a farm and a nonfarm input, producers, processors, and consumers receive the same share of total benefits regardless of whether the research shifts the farm or processing supply curves. Alston and Scobie (1983) pointed out that this result only holds when substitution between inputs in processing is not possible. They developed a framework, allowing input substitution in processing, that can be used to assess the benefits from research at different stages in the marketing chain, and their analysis showed that a small degree of input substitution can have a large effect on the distribution of research gains among primary producers and processors. As the elasticity of substitution increases, producers generally receive larger benefits if new technologies are directed at their sector.[52]

For most agricultural products, the degree of substitution possible between a raw product and processing inputs is small. However, some substitution is possible. An important source of input substitution in the beef subsector, for example, has been the use of new technologies such as boxed beef to reduce shrinkage and spoilage. Mullen, Wohlgenant and Farris (1988) found an elasticity of substitution of 0.1 between beef and processing inputs in the U.S. beef sector that, although seemingly small, was enough to make a significant difference. Their empirical results reinforced the analytical findings of Alston and Scobie (1983).

Other assumptions can be relaxed as well. Freebairn, Davis and Edwards (1983) consider the case in which nonfarm inputs and marketing services are not available in completely elastic supply. They also consider the case of a monopolist in the marketing or input supply sector. Furthermore, calculation of benefits to research at the sector that supplies inputs to farmers (e.g., fertilizers or pesticides) involves additional complications because these inputs are used to produce several commodities and some of the commodities are produced jointly (e.g., meat and milk).[53] It is unlikely that practition-

52. This analysis of the "functional distribution" of research benefits has been extended in a number of recent studies, including Freebairn, Davis and Edwards (1983), Mullen, Wohlgenant and Farris (1988), Mullen, Alston and Wohlgenant (1989), and Holloway (1989). These studies have shown that the total research benefit and the functional distribution of research benefits among factors employed at different stages of production (or among nations when semi-processed products are traded) depend on several things in addition to those represented in the basic model unless the factors are used in fixed proportions. These additional aspects include (a) the stage of the production process to which the research applies, (b) the nature of the research-induced technical change, and (c) more detailed technological and market parameters. These results have implications for the allocation of private or public research resources within a country between programs applying at different stages in multistage production processes.

53. See Duncan (1972) for an example of a study that evaluates research on an input (pasture) which is used by another farm commodity (grazing livestock).

ers conducting priority-setting exercises will have the time and resources to consider all these potential effects for every commodity and type of research. Nevertheless, there are cases, particularly for certain types of postharvest research, where these refinements are necessary.

In less-developed countries, these issues may be thought to be of reduced importance (compared, say, with the United States or Australia) because research investments are primarily directed at production agriculture, per se, and the functional distribution of returns from research directed at further processing may be largely irrelevant for policy. However, anyone conducting an exercise in research evaluation or priority setting ought to be conscious of the implications of different types of research directed at different stages of production for the size and distribution of benefits, even when there is a strong presumption that all research efforts will be directed at farming. There are four reasons for this: (a) opportunities beyond the farm gate ought not to be neglected for the wrong reasons, (b) most places do engage in some research into postharvest handling and storage technology, (c) it is becoming increasingly fashionable to redirect research resources away from traditional agricultural technology to issues beyond the farm gate (often in pursuit of "value-adding" objectives), and (d) components of a new technology that results in direct cost savings off-farm may be embodied in outputs that are generated on-farm (e.g., new varieties that have both improved yields and improved storage or processing characteristics).

In addition, international trade in agricultural products means that the international distribution of benefits from research among nations is connected to the global distribution of benefits from research between producers and consumers. When goods are traded in raw or semiprocessed form, the international distribution of benefits also depends on where the research is applied in the chain of production (e.g., Alston and Mullen 1992). Thus, even when the interest is only in national research benefits, in the context of traded goods, the functional distribution of research benefits among stages of production or among factors of production becomes relevant.

Effects on Factor Returns

The distribution of income among factors of production is influenced by technical change because of the incentives that technical change provides for reallocating inputs among production alternatives. These incentives arise within agriculture and between agriculture and the nonagricultural sector. Several forces influence the impact of agricultural research on factor markets. The most important ones are the elasticity of demand for the commodity in question, the input bias of the technical change, the elasticity of supply of factors, the elasticities of substitution between factors of production in each sector and the input mixes for the various commodities.[54]

When the demand curve has a constant unitary price elasticity, the value of the commodity and therefore the value of the inputs to produce it are constant, no matter how the supply curve shifts. Therefore, total resources are neither entering nor leaving the sector and, with a neutral technical change, the composition of those resources is unaffected. However, when the demand is elastic, resources are drawn into the sector as supply shifts out, and when demand is inelastic, resources are forced out.[55] When new technologies are biased toward or against a factor, even if total resources are not displaced, the factor being biased against will lose relative to the other factor(s) and will probably lose absolutely (unless the product demand is very elastic). The elasticity of substitution between factors influences the impact of a technical change. The greater the elasticity of substitution between two factors, the more equal will be the effect of the technical change on both factors, regardless of their relative elasticities of supply. Finally, the relative factor intensities of the sector affect the size and distribution of research benefits. However, this effect in turn depends on the elasticity of demand for the product and the factor bias of the technical change. These qualitative effects are demonstrated formally in chapter 4 using a simple two-factor model.

Cross-Commodity Effects

Benefits and costs of research-induced technological changes might not be confined to the producers and consumers of the commodity whose production is affected directly by the new technology. Research that affects one commodity can also affect other commodities through cross-price effects, particularly on the demand side, and through technology spillovers. The cross-price effects on commodities that are substitutes or complements in demand will be most important if the commodity at which the research is directed has a relatively inelastic demand (i.e., a commodity for which the price will fall the most following the adoption of a new technology). The cross-price effects on supplies of commodities that are substitutes in produc-

---

54. Note that we have not mentioned the initial labor intensity or the number of people employed in producing the commodity. Research administrators often voice the desire to conduct more research on those commodities that employ a higher proportion of the agricultural work force than others as a means of increasing employment. The fact is, however, that in many cases, research on commodities that currently have a high labor content will reduce labor's share of income and employment unless conditions favorable to employment also hold.

55. The product demand curve is more likely to be elastic for commodities that are predominantly exported or imported than for those that are primarily produced and consumed internally.

tion may tend to be small because the lower per unit costs of production due to new technologies are partly offset by lower prices for the commodity affected.

Most studies on research priority setting are not likely to incorporate many cross-commodity effects. Cross-price elasticities are often unavailable and cross-commodity spillovers of technologies may be difficult to judge. Often it is reasonable (as well as convenient) to assume that the producer and consumer surplus measures in the market of direct interest represent the total effects, which can be true if the supply and demand curves are defined sufficiently generally (as shown by Just, Hueth and Schmitz 1982). Alternatively, conceptually at least, a more explicit accounting for these cross-commodity effects involves relatively straightforward extensions of the models presented in this and later chapters and may be developed for a limited set of commodities in some countries — depending primarily on the availability of data (e.g., see Chang et al. 1992).

Quality Change

Some types of agricultural research are intended to improve the quality of a commodity. An approach suggested by Unnevehr (1986, 1990) for evaluating the effects of research on quality is to estimate implicit prices for individual quality characteristics. Quality-enhancing research supposedly shifts the product demand curve upward to reflect the notion that consumers will demand more of a product at each price if it contains a higher proportion of a relatively higher-priced characteristic (see also Voon 1991; and Voon and Edwards 1991a). What really happens, however, is that the supply of the characteristics changes; the demand-shift representation is useful only under a limited set of circumstances.

An alternative way to conceptualize the issue is to view the market supply-and-demand curves for the commodity as an aggregation of a set of supply-and-demand curves for different types (or qualities) of the product. Each type has its own homogenous set of characteristics. Research that affects quality lowers the cost of supplying the type of the commodity with the improved characteristics. The aggregate market supply curve for the commodity also shifts to the right, and more is demanded because the aggregate price has fallen (just as the price of the higher-quality type of the commodity has fallen). At the same time, substitution effects would lead to a reduction in demand for the lower-quality types. Because of these cross-price distributional effects, in many cases the aggregate net change in economic surplus may be relatively small compared with the distributional effects on producers versus nonproducers of the higher-quality type of the commodity.

Market Distortions

It can be argued that countries should focus research resources on those commodities in which they have a comparative advantage. Unfortunately, comparative advantage can be difficult to assess because it can be obscured by misaligned exchange rates, tariffs, subsidies, and other policies, and it changes over time in response to a number of factors, including research-induced technical change. Therefore, assessments of comparative advantage must be made either with subjective judgments or with detailed analyses of the various macroeconomic and sector-specific policies affecting the countries under comparison. The latter is preferable because the existence of these policies implies some social losses that modify research benefits when supply curves shift out due to new technologies. International prices themselves are influenced by the policies of all countries. However, unless those policies are expected to be changed in a particular direction, an individual country usually is forced to take those international policies as given, particularly when assuming that the country is a relatively small producer in the world market for the commodities.

Harberger's first two postulates for the use of economic surplus analysis are that supply-and-demand functions represent both private and social benefits and costs. When markets are distorted, either by government policies or by externalities in production or consumption, these postulates are be violated and an extra effort is needed to obtain measures of social and private costs and benefits of production and consumption. Building on some initial work by Edwards and Freebairn (1981), Alston, Edwards and Freebairn (1988) presented a conceptual overview of the effects of a range of commodity programs on the size and distribution of research benefits. Subsequent work has provided some further theoretical results and empirical evidence (e.g., Oehmke 1988b, 1991; Zachariah, Fox and Brinkman 1989; de Gorter and Norton 1990; Voon and Edwards 1991b; Murphy, Furtan and Schmitz 1993; Alston and Martin 1992). This literature has identified the potential importance of market distortions for affecting both the size of research benefits (properly measured) and the potential size of errors introduced when the distortions are ignored. The results suggest that it may be unwise to ignore market distortions when conducting an assessment of research benefits, especially when the distribution of benefits and costs is being measured.

Some more recent, related literature has argued that it is logically inconsistent and perhaps unrealistic to treat market distorting policies and research policy as independent. Gardner (1988), Oehmke (1988b), Oehmke and Yao (1990), Roe and Pardey (1991), Alston and Pardey (1991, 1993) and de Gorter, Nielson and Rausser (1992) have argued for the use of political economy models in which research policies and commodity market policies are chosen jointly to maximize a welfare function in which producer welfare is weighted more or less heavily than that of consumers. This line of argument is more relevant for explaining policies than for evaluating economic welfare consequences of past or future investments in research.

The results from the work on the implications of commodity market distortions for calculating research benefits would carry over fairly directly to the situation where markets are distorted as a consequence of distortions in the exchange rate. However, there is one important difference. Exchange rate distortions result in distortions of prices of *all* traded goods, and the consequences for distortions of supply and demand in a particular commodity market are potentially quite complicated and difficult to assess (e.g., Krueger, Schiff and Valdés 1988). This topic has been neglected in the literature on research benefits. Given the pervasive nature of exchange rate distortions, especially in less-developed countries, some preliminary analysis is provided in chapter 4.

Environmental Sustainability

A further type of market distortion involves externalities in production and consumption. This topic is becoming increasingly important in the context of agricultural production and includes all of the "green" issues such as environmental pollution, the greenhouse effect, sustainability, animal welfare, and organic farming. Concern over environmental degradation has increased in several developing countries in recent years. Deforestation, soil erosion and degradation, desertification, silting of rivers and flooding, and pesticide pollution have become serious problems around the world, and research programs related to natural resource management and conservation are receiving increased emphasis. In a number of countries, environmental deterioration has become so severe that what used to appear to be potential long-run problems have become short-run problems as well. In some countries, higher incomes have meant that the demand for natural resource preservation has increased. Furthermore, research is increasingly exposing the magnitude and consequences of the problem (e.g., Pingali and Roger 1995).

Throughout the world, these issues are becoming increasingly topical, and government intervention in response to concerns about them is becoming more pervasive. Procedures for setting research priorities must be capable of considering the effects of alternative research programs on the sustainability of the agricultural resource base. The analyst now faces the problem of accounting both for the externalities and for the government intervention to correct for them. This is far from straightforward conceptually and as an empirical matter it is very difficult. To a great extent the literature has neglected this topic. Lichtenberg, Parker and Zilberman (1988) have provided a conceptual analysis of the link between commodity programs and the costs of externalities and environmental regulation in U.S. agriculture, but the issue of measuring research benefits in the presence of externalities has been neglected.[56] In addition, and perhaps worse for the economic analyst, some research may be directed specifically at reducing such problems. In such cases, it is imperative to pay specific attention to the consequences of research-induced technical changes for the amelioration of externalities.

The Full Cost of Government Funds

Most of the discussion above has related primarily to the benefits side of the equation. Typically economists assume that the marginal opportunity cost of government spending is the amount spent. Papers by Browning (1976, 1986, 1987), Ballard, Shoven and Whalley (1985), Findlay and Jones (1982) and others have shown that it is appropriate to adjust the amount spent to include the deadweight cost of taxation in order to measure the full social costs of government spending. Fox (1985) introduced this argument into the evaluation of agricultural research investments. More recently, Dalrymple (1990) presented a synopsis of the relevant literature.

The social opportunity cost of government revenue has significant implications for the calculation of net research benefits. Typically the results from the empirical studies have suggested that the social cost of government spending is in the range of 1.2 to 1.5 times the amount spent (e.g., Browning 1987). Fullerton (1991) reviewed this literature and his reconciliation of the different results leads to a suggestion that a much lower marginal welfare cost of taxation may be appropriate — implying a marginal social cost of government spending of, say, 1.07 to 1.24 times the amount spent for the United States. He shows how the answer depends on what is assumed about the disposition of the tax revenue and the income effects resulting from that disposition. Those estimates are for more-developed countries where the marginal deadweight costs of government spending may be relatively small because of relatively efficient taxation mechanisms. As a further complication, the deadweight costs of government spending apply to other forms of spending in addition to agricultural research. Alston and Hurd (1990) illustrate the issues in the context of commodity programs. Thus the complete analysis of research benefits and costs in a commodity market that involves market distortions must take account of the full opportunity costs of govern-

56. See, also, Capalbo and Antle (1988), Just and Antle (1990), and Beach and Alston (1993).

ment revenues, from the point of view of measuring both direct research costs and the effects of research on the costs of market-distorting policies that involve government revenues.[57]

2.4 Economy-Wide (General-Equilibrium) Implications of Research[58]

Research-induced technological change in agriculture can have important economy-wide implications for employment and returns to factors of production, as well as production and consumption of nonagricultural products. Through output market adjustments, technical changes in agriculture affect the relative prices of agricultural and nonagricultural products not directly affected by the new technology. These indirectly induced changes in product markets can lead to further changes in factor markets. Thus, agricultural productivity changes can affect foreign exchange earnings, food prices, domestic capital generation, labor use in nonagricultural production, rural markets for nonagricultural goods, and relative factor prices. The impacts on nonagricultural production of these research-induced factor market responses are difficult to predict in general and vary depending upon the nature of the technical change, among other things. Usually, however, one would expect impacts on nonagricultural production to yield additional benefits to augment the direct impacts measured from a partial-equilibrium model of agricultural-sector benefits.

2.4.1 *Distinguishing between Partial- and General-Equilibrium Models*

In practice, and even in theory, the distinction between *partial equilibrium* and *general equilibrium* is not always clear. We suggest that it may be thought of in terms of (a) *ceteris paribus* assumptions and (b) the variables of interest that are endogenous.[59] At one extreme is the typical model of a

57. Care is needed, however, when comparing summary statistics, like internal rates of return to research, that take account of this cost with rates of return to alternative investments that do not.

58. Several authors have drawn attention to the general-equilibrium effects of agricultural research, including Schmitz and Seckler (1970), Ayer and Schuh (1972, 1974), Musalem (1974), and Binswanger (1980).

59. Will Martin (pers. comm.) has suggested to us that there is an important distinction between (a) models in which the budget of the households in the economy is exogenous and (b) models in which household budgets are endogenous and are affected by product market equilibrium and factor payments. The latter, he suggests, is a true general-equilibrium model: the defining characteristic of a general-equilibrium model being the endogenous household budget constraint.

commodity market that takes the price and quantity of that commodity as endogenous, treating prices of all other goods as constant and exogenous to the analysis. Usually though, even in this extreme case, it is not assumed that all factor prices are entirely exogenous. At the other extreme are the detailed economy-wide models in which all prices and quantities are endogenous to, and measured in, the analysis so that extreme *mutatis mutandis* (everything allowed to change) replaces extreme *ceteris paribus* (everything else held constant). In practice, most "general-equilibrium" models impose some restrictions, so that not all economic variables are endogenous. Most economic analyses fall somewhere between these two extremes. Often when analyzing a particular commodity market, it is inappropriate to take the prices of all other goods as being exogenous, but at the same time, it is inappropriate to explicitly measure all of the endogenous adjustments. This is a quasi-general equilibrium analysis in which some prices or quantities are taken as given exogenously. The most important issue here is not what the analysis is called but rather to be clear and consistent about the *ceteris paribus* assumptions.

An alternative way to distinguish between partial- and general-equilibirum analysis is in terms of the techniques of analysis. For instance, when Marshallian supply-and-demand models are used, the analysis is typically regarded as being a partial-equilbrium analysis, whereas when a social accounting matrix (SAM) is involved, it is regarded as a general-equilibrium analysis.[60] In chapter 4, we consider research benefits in a multimarket setting that considers effects in related factor and product markets as well as in the product market of primary interest. This is an approach to incorporating general-equilibrium effects in a partial-equilibrium framework.

2.4.2 Practical Approaches for Research Evaluation

Unfortunately, economists have not developed general-equilibrium models both practical and detailed enough to provide much guidance for allocating research resources. Some models that have been developed to examine linkages among sectors (such as input-output models) are not very helpful because they fail to capture relative price changes and resource adjustments caused by technological change. The reason for the lack of practical general-equilibrium models is that any relatively complete general-equilibrium model for the allocation of research resources would require vast quantities of

---

60. A SAM uses a matrix of current inputs and outputs across activities to extrapolate the impacts of an exogenous change. This approach is general equilibrium in that it considers an entire economy, but it is limited in that it does not allow for any price responses in consumption or production.

information, beyond what it would generally be economic to collect.[61]

Some recent agricultural-sector models provide a potential compromise. For example, Chang et al. (1992) have developed a programming model of the entire U.S. agricultural sector that they have used to simulate the size and distribution of the effects of various research-induced changes in technology. This is a general-equilibrium model of the agricultural sector, but only a partial-equilibrium model in the broader sense in that the rest of the economy is exogenous. Martin and Alston (1992, 1994) have shown how to use a *balance of trade function* approach, in a modern, dual framework, to obtain Hicksian measures of the size and distribution of benefits from research in a full general-equilibrium setting, allowing for any number of market distortions. This approach, they argue, can be applied in a very aggregative way (say, for only a two-good model) as well as for detailed, disaggregated models. An alternative would be to take advantage of an existing general-equilibrium model.[62]

2.5   Reconciling Multiple Objectives of Research

Improved efficiency and equity are the primary objectives in most if not all countries, but reduced income risk and national food security or self-sufficiency are often expressed as important objectives as well, especially in less-developed countries. The concern over income risk is evident in several small countries heavily dependent on one (or a few) export crops. The desire for food self-sufficiency may reflect a feeling that there is a market failure in the world economy, or a perceived military security need. In this section we review these various social objectives and consider whether they can be achieved through public-sector agricultural research or can be better pursued using alternative policies.

---

61.   Computable general equilibrium (CGE) models have been developed, but to keep the analysis manageable, these models often employ highly simplified assumptions with respect to individual sectors (see Robinson 1986 or de Melo and Robinson 1981), and typically, the agricultural sectors in such models are aggregated to a much higher degree than would be desired for an agricultural research priority-setting study. This is a natural consequence when models are developed for other purposes, and it would be uneconomic in most cases to pay the full cost of developing a CGE model of an entire economy only for agricultural research evaluation and priority setting.

62.   Such models include the ORANI model of the Australian economy for which the agricultural sector has been developed in relatively detailed form (e.g., see Dixon et al. 1982 and Higgs 1986), Tyers and Anderson's (1992) model of global agricultural trade, Hertel's (1991) model of the global economy, the World Bank-OECD Rural Urban North South (RUNS) model (see Burniaux and van der Mensbrugghe 1991). To date we have seen very little use of these, or other, CGE models for agricultural research evaluation or priority-setting work. Martin and Alston (1993) have used the RUNS model to simulate a variety of technical changes.

2.5.1   Economic Efficiency

In chapter 1 we introduced the conventional economic arguments for public-sector involvement in agricultural research. It is widely accepted among economists that there is a market failure in the provision of agricultural research by the private sector and that, without action by the government, there would be an underinvestment in research. Specifically, a convolution of factors (incomplete markets, inappropriability of returns to invention, economies of scale, and perhaps, risk in research) can cause private returns from research investments to be lower than returns to society as a whole. Thus the private sector will be expected to neglect research opportunities that would be profitable from the point of view of the nation as a whole. These ideas are reinforced by the evidence of typically high, estimated, net social returns from public-sector research investments (e.g., Echeverría 1990). This argument gets most of its force from the application of the welfare economics perspectives (producer and consumer surplus and the compensation principle) described in this chapter. With this argument as a basis for the intervention of government, the use of those techniques to guide the intervention seems particularly appropriate.

For many economists, the application of the same set of principles and arguments leads to the conclusion that the only defensible justification for government intervention in agricultural research, and the only legitimate and achievable objective of research, is the pursuit of economic efficiency. This is not to say that other objectives (such as personal and functional income distribution and food security) are illegitimate, irrelevant, or unimportant but that there are likely to be alternative, less costly ways to achieve these other objectives than by biasing the agricultural research portfolio away from programs that will maximize total national net income. These arguments are compelling. As a further consideration, maximizing with respect to a single objective is a much simpler problem than trying to maximize a trade-off among a variety of objectives — especially when the terms of that trade-off are unclear and subjective.

At the same time we must recognize political realities. Alternative agricultural research programs have different — and occasionally profound — implications for the distribution of income, patterns of trade, regional employment, food security, and so on. These effects may be of significant concern and, if other policy instruments are not in place to pursue those objectives and correct for any negative impact of research, it may not be appropriate to ignore them in setting research priorities. The best solution, always, is to have policy instruments that aim closely at the objective, and agricultural research is a very blunt instrument for the pursuit of objectives other than economic efficiency (e.g., see Corden 1974, for a discussion of this general question). On the other hand, when the appropriate instruments are not being used, or they are being misused, a blunt instrument may be better than none.[63] In such circumstances, it is appropriate and important for the economist assessing research priorities to point out the opportunity cost of efficiency foregone when using agricultural research as an instrument of general economic, institutional, or other policy.

2.5.2 Equity (Income Distribution) and Security Objectives

A number of objectives other than efficiency are often raised in the context of agricultural research evaluation and priority setting. These fall into two broad categories: (a) equity or income distribution objectives (i.e., among different producer groups or consumer groups; nutritional status of the poor) and (b) security objectives (e.g., income risk and food self-sufficiency).

We have seen that different types of agricultural research programs can have different implications for the functional distribution of income both geographically and between different groups. Agricultural research also generates a wide range of distributional effects related to farm size, income, location, and so on.[64] In some cases it is possible to measure the distribution of costs and benefits from agricultural research between producers, consumers (and various categories of producers and consumers), and other participants in the food production, distribution, and marketing chain. This may be useful as a guide to appropriate ways of financing agricultural research as well as informing choices about alternative programs of research that have different implications for functional income distribution (distribution among factors of production).

To go beyond the effects on functional income distribution to personal income distribution requires combining information about factor ownership and consumption with information on functional income distribution effects. If research policy is used to pursue some objective of income distribution, the objective should be made clear so that the contribution of research to it can be measured explicitly. While it is tempting to make gross simplifications — such as equating the interests of the poor with a low price for staple food crops and presuming that the poor have little interest in export revenues from a capital-intensive cash crop — such gross simplifications are likely to

63. See Krueger (1990) for a discussion of "government failure" that is relevant in this context.

64. David and Otsuka (1994) provide a comprehensive study of the distributional consequences of modern rice varieties in Asia.

involve gross errors. In any event, in many cases there are more effective and less costly ways to pursue a cheap-food policy (when that is the aim) than a distorted research policy.

Different Producer Groups, Farm Size, and Tenure

The impact of technological change on the distribution of income among producer groups can be assessed in many dimensions (corresponding to several of the distributional objectives described in chapter 1). Producers with different incomes, with different farm sizes, in different locations, and with diverse tenure situations can gain or lose depending on the suitability of the new technology to their particular situations. The supply curve can be disaggregated to allow these distributional consequences to be measured within the economic surplus framework (Binswanger 1977; Hayami and Herdt 1977).

It is difficult to generalize about the effects of different types of technologies or the effects of research on particular crops on the incomes of tenants versus landlords. One might expect that biological technologies would augment land and thus help tenants. But the distribution of income gains depends on contractual arrangements for sharing costs and returns, and new technologies can induce changes in those arrangements that may offset the direct effects on tenants.

A true picture of producer benefits would need to consider the incidence of taxes paid to support public research. Scobie and Posada (1977, 1978) made such estimates (for both producers and consumers) for rice in Colombia. They divided producers into those producing upland and irrigated rice and then distributed producer benefits across farm sizes, according to estimates of production based on census data. Research costs were also distributed by farm size. In their study, small upland producers lost the most, but their losses were more than offset by gains among low-income consumers.

The issue of whether improved agricultural technologies benefit large farms more than small farms has received a great deal of attention in the literature (e.g., Ruttan 1977; Lipton with Longhurst 1989; Hazell and Ramasamy 1991). The more recent evidence suggests that neither farm size nor tenure has been a major impediment to adoption of new biological technologies, the major focus of agricultural research in less-developed countries (Scobie 1979a,b). Large farms, however, do tend to adopt new technologies first. This probably results from their economies of size in obtaining information about those technologies, their additional experience and education, and a greater ability to absorb risk. Small farms in the same region as the large farms do eventually adopt the technologies, but because the large farms adopt technologies first, they receive greater gains than small farms. And, even if all producers in a given region were to adopt a new scale-neutral technology at the same time, absolute income differences would widen (Scobie 1979b, p. 23). This reflects the effects of the unequal distribution of productive assets.

The implications for a research manager attempting to allocate research resources is that it will be more difficult to help small farms than large farms in a particular region unless the small farms are growing crops that are different from those grown on large farms or the technologies are biased toward small farms. Many technologies, for reasons beyond the nature of the technology per se, are scale-neutral or biased toward large farms, so it may be difficult to generate technologies that have a disproportionately large impact on small farms. This implies that research may not be an effective policy tool for achieving a distributional objective based on farm size. Another implication is that a desire to help small farms through research might be addressed better by focusing research on commodities grown on small farms in regions where small farms predominate instead of focusing on commodities grown on both small and large farms in regions where large farms predominate.

Different Consuming Groups

Consumers are major beneficiaries of agricultural research. There are direct benefits to *all* consumers when agricultural research results in a larger quantity being available at a lower price, as occurs when supply shifts out against a downward sloping demand curve. But because consumption patterns and demand response to price changes both vary with income, there will be a differential impact among income classes and potentially an impact on the distribution of income. Most food products are *normal goods* (i.e., they have positive income elasticities of demand — richer people consume a greater absolute quantity than poorer people) and richer individuals benefit absolutely more from lower food prices than do poorer individuals. The opposite of this may be true for some staple commodities that are *inferior goods* (i.e., having negative income elasticities) for which the poor consume absolutely more than the rich. Individually, low-income consumers tend to benefit *relatively* more from research on staple food commodities than research on other items because low-income consumers spend a high proportion of their budget on food. The reverse is likely to hold for richer consumers who spend a relatively small proportion of their incomes on food.

Nutritional Implications of Research

Some advocate using agricultural research to improve the nutritional status of the poor. Agricultural research can influence human nutrition through several mechanisms. Perhaps the four most important ones are (a) by affecting household income, (b) by altering prices paid by consumers for food commodities, (c) by influencing downside risk associated with fluctuations in food production, prices, and incomes, and (d) by increasing the production of foods consumed by the households that produce them.[65]

The effect of research on improving the purchasing power of the poor — both by raising their incomes and by lowering the prices of staple food products — is probably the major source of nutritional gains associated with agricultural research. Only the poor go hungry. Because a relatively high proportion of any income gains made by the poor is spent on food, the income effects of research-induced supply shifts can have major nutritional implications, particularly if those shifts result from technologies aimed at the poorest producers.[66]

Effects on incomes in agriculture arise in a number of ways. A shift out in the supply curve for agricultural products generates additional income streams to producers. It may also affect the demand for labor, and thereby labor income in agriculture, in either direction, depending in particular on the type of technical change.

The primary effects of agricultural research on the non-farm poor are through lower food prices. As supply shifts out against a downward sloping demand curve, consumers benefit from lower food prices. The nutritional effects due to price changes will be influenced by the price elasticity of demand for the commodities, by the inherent nutritional value of the commodities, and by the importance of particular commodities in the diets of the poor. The more elastic the demand curve is, the lower the price effect for consumers but the greater the income effect for producers.

Research can influence fluctuations in production, prices, and income and thereby alter nutrition. In years when rural incomes are low, because of lower than normal production or prices, severe malnutrition can occur in rural areas. Research can influence commodity diversification as well as the susceptibility of commodities to drought, insects, and diseases, and research

---

65. Pinstrup-Andersen (1984) lists 10 possible influences of research on human nutrition including these four. See also Pinstrup-Andersen, Ruiz de Londoño and Hoover (1976) and Perrin and Scobie (1981).

66. However, the econometric evidence to date indicates that the income and price elasticities of demand for *nutrition* are small, even in countries with comparatively low per capita incomes (such as China), and correspondingly relatively high price and income elasticities of demand for *food*. Nutrient content does not always correspond closely to food quality as perceived by consumers.

can thereby affect the variability of production, incomes, and nutrition. Improved technologies for subsistence goods can augment the nutrients available for consumption (particularly food energy).

While research can do all of these things, it is difficult to draw general conclusions about the nutritional implications of particular research portfolios because the different factors affecting the nutritional impact of research often counteract one another. Because domestic prices are strongly influenced by world market prices for most goods, nutrition is most likely to be improved by research that generates the largest income (efficiency) gains in general, particularly if those gains are realized directly by low-income producers. Therefore, research administrators should resist the temptation to emphasize research on particular commodities just because they have high nutritional content or are important in the diets of the poor.

Income Risk

Security objectives might also be rooted in a concern about the distribution of the impact of variablity among different groups of people. Economies heavily dependent on one or a few export crops such as sugarcane, bananas, or coffee often experience extreme income variability due to variability in both production and price. These countries may place a value on programs or policies that help diversify their income sources. While policy tools other than research may be more effective at reducing risk, agricultural research programs can be structured to complement diversification policies or programs. Research evaluation and priority-setting models may need to recognize this objective in certain countries.

This discussion relates to income risk from a national aggregate perspective. Income risk may also be of concern at a less aggregated level, such as a particular region, right down to the level of individual producers or consumers. For example, research aimed at producing a more drought-tolerant crop variety might contribute to reduced year-to-year or season-to-season income variability in regions (or on farms) highly specialized in its production. Alternatively, research could develop other crops to be used in those regions (or farms) in order to reduce income variability through diversification. This latter strategy might also alleviate the price variability that can be a problem for highly specialized producers.

At the level of aggregation of national, regional, and individual producers, research can contribute to a goal of reduced production or income variability. However, research alone cannot contribute much to this objective — e.g., the drought-tolerant variety or alternative crop must be adopted to have any effect. In most cases research contributes little to reduced income variability.

There are likely to be much more effective, and less costly, ways to reduce income variability than by distorting the pattern of research investments.

Self-Sufficiency and Foreign Exchange

An expressed desire for self-sufficiency can be considered a security objective, and it often reflects a concern for national pride or military security. Some recently expressed desires for import substitution may represent a hope of saving foreign exchange to meet foreign debt obligations. Research administrators ought to consider whether these obligations could better be met by exploiting comparative advantage.

Foreign exchange earned from agricultural exports (or saved on imports) can be used to ameliorate foreign debt problems. It is debatable, however, whether a country should place any importance on a separate criterion of generating foreign exchange when setting research priorities. The implicit assumptions are that foreign exchange earnings are worth more than other income gains to the economy, so focusing research on activities that generate the largest efficiency gains will not maximize the country's ability to repay debts. This is a strong assumption. In any event, it would seem to be more appropriate to make adjustments in the shadow prices to be used in a more conventional efficiency analysis than to assign extra weight to foreign exchange earnings *per se*. Calculation of the "net" foreign exchange effects of research is complicated by the fact that foreign exchange is also saved or spent on additional inputs used in the production of the commodities being researched. These effects are very difficult to calculate.[67] Davis and Bantilan (1990) present some arguments and analytical results on these effects in the context of Philippine agriculture.

2.5.3   Trading off Multiple Objectives

It is relatively easy to choose a research portfolio that maximizes economic efficiency, once the economic consequences of the alternatives have been assessed. It is much more difficult to set priorities when two or more objectives are involved, since to do so requires (a) a measure or the contribution of each of the alternative investment programs to each of the objec-

---

67.   Finally, it appears that the desire to focus research on commodities that generate foreign exchange through exports results in part from an implicit distributional objective to help large farmers. Farmers reap a higher proportion of the benefits from commodities with high rather than low own-price elasticities of demand, and these tend to be export commodities. These commodities are often grown by large farmers with political influence. Therefore, research administrators and politicians may be reacting to pressures to assist a certain group of farmers when they express a desire to increase foreign exchange earnings through research.

tives and (b) information on the relative values to be attached to the alternative objectives. The first part is difficult, sometimes impossible. The second part is extremely difficult because it involves the subjective value judgments of individuals and decisions about whose judgment is relevant. Both of these aspects are addressed in detail in later chapters.

The idea of a trade-off between multiple social objectives has been referred to by some as a social welfare function (SWF). The idea of a SWF has been criticized (e.g., Arrow 1963) but analogous ideas continue to be used widely in economic analysis. An example is the analysis of agricultural price policies using a surplus or benefit transformation curve (BTC), and a political trade-off between the welfare of producers and consumers (e.g., Gardner 1988; Alston and Hurd 1990).[68] The same type of model can be used to illustrate the trade-off between economic efficiency — maximizing the total economic benefit from research measured by the change in total economic surplus due to research — and other objectives of research, such as equity or security.

The simplest case of multiple objectives involves two objectives. To illustrate the ideas, in figure 2.11 the horizontal axis represents economic efficiency, E, and the vertical axis measures equity, V (e.g., E could represent total income or economic surplus in society and V could represent income or

68. Gardner (1988) has suggested extending the same idea to analyzing the joint optimization of agricultural research and price policies (see also de Gorter, Nielson and Rausser 1992 and Alston and Pardey 1993, 1994). It is a short step from the conceptual notion of a BTC and a political trade-off (perhaps called a SWF) to begin measuring the nature of the trade-offs involved in policy choices. In this type of analysis, the concepts of revealed preference are invoked to argue that policy choices indicate policymakers' marginal valuation of the achievement of one objective relative to another (welfare of consumers versus producers; equity versus efficiency). Efficiency in policy choices as described by Gardner (1983) requires that the benefits and costs of alternative programs be equated at the margin (i.e., there is a tangency between the SWF and the BTC), and the slopes of the curves at the equilibrium are sometimes called welfare weights (e.g., Harberger 1978). Political economy models measure and attempt to explain those welfare weights in terms of the political influence of various interest groups. Similarly, the social willingness to exchange efficiency for equity or some other objective could be measured. Until the 1970s, price policies for agricultural commodities were customarily analyzed as being designed to correct market failures, primarily directed towards efficiency but also in consideration of other objectives in a multiobjective context (i.e., in much the same way as we have described the approach to research policy in this section). More recently, agricultural economists have to an increasing extent abandoned that approach and have sought political economy explanations of farm programs instead. Similar work has barely begun on the political economy of agricultural research and much of the profession continues to treat agricultural research policy in the way we used to treat agricultural commodity price policy. Political economy models of agricultural research policy could mimic those used to study farm programs: agricultural research policy could be explained in terms of the consequences of self-serving behavior of politically powerful interest groups. Such an approach might have more empirical predictive content than the idea of trading-off efficiency versus equity and, if it did, the virtue of building such trade-offs into priority-setting exercises may be further weakened.

Figure 2.11: *A trade-off of equity and efficiency using research policy alone*

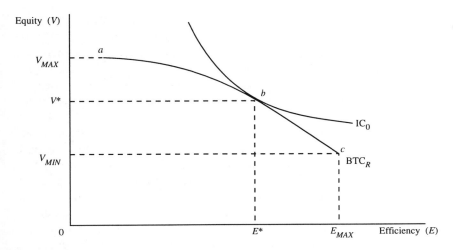

economic surplus of low-income families).[69] The curve BTC_R represents the range of *maximum* possible combinations of economic efficiency and equity that can be achieved by varying the mix of research programs in the portfolio. It is drawn as a trade-off, so in order to obtain more of one objective, some of the other must be sacrificed, as must be so in the relevant range.[70] Each point represents the maximum economic efficiency that can be achieved for a given equity outcome and vice versa. Points below the curve are attainable but clearly inferior to points on the curve; points above the curve are unattainable. Point c represents the result if the research portfolio were chosen simply to maximize economic efficiency at E_{MAX}. Moving back along the curve we can see how much economic surplus must be foregone in order to increase equity by shifting the research portfolio away from the one that maximizes economic efficiency. The other curve on the diagram is an indifference curve, IC_0, that represents the policymaker's willingness to

69. The same diagram could also be used with V representing performance against some other objective, such as security, which could be measured by income variability, for instance.

70. Clearly some technological changes increase the total income and the income going to disadvantaged groups and also reduce the variance of income. Others involve a trade-off: they increase total income at the expense of greater variability (or vice versa) or increase total income at the expense of disadvantaged groups (or vice versa) and so on. However if it is possible to increase benefits in *all* dimensions from a given R&D expenditure by changing the mix of projects, the portfolio does not lie on the efficient frontier. In such a case there can be substantial gains from inframarginal reallocations of research resources. Once the efficient frontier is reached, by definition, trade-offs are involved in any change.

substitute efficiency for equity. This particular indifference curve is tangent to the BTC and thus represents the highest level of benefits (given those preferences) that can be achieved by varying the combination of economic efficiency and equity through a change in the research portfolio. Thus, the optimal research portfolio is the one that corresponds to point b (E^*, V^*). To increase equity from V_{MIN} to V^* involves an opportunity cost of economic surplus foregone of ($E_{MAX} - E^*$), but given these preferences, this sacrifice is deemed worthwhile. This analysis could readily be extended to a case with three or more objectives as arguments of the policymaker's preference function.

Three related comments are in order here. First, deciding whose preferences are to be used to define the indifference curve is not straightforward. It might depend, for example, on whether the research evaluation or priority-setting work is being undertaken on behalf of a national government, a provincial government, or a particular research agency. Even at the national level, the preferences expressed by the ministry of finance might differ, for example, from those expressed by the ministry of agriculture. Second, there has been some success in eliciting weights for this type of trade-off among research decision makers, but it is not clear that such decision makers have been fully informed about the costs of making the trade-off through the research policy rather than other mechanisms (Norton, Pardey and Alston 1992). In any event, the work that has been done suggests that research administrators are unwilling to sacrifice very much economic efficiency for other objectives. This implies that the indifference curves are twisted away from point a toward point c. Third, the analysis has usually been conducted as if there were no other policy instruments available. A more complete analysis would allow the use of the best possible policy instrument for substituting economic efficiency for equity.

In the extreme example of a lump-sum transfer, for example, there would be no sacrifice of economic efficiency to achieve an increase in equity — the BTC for a lump-sum transfer would be a vertical line through E_{MAX}. The hypothetical lump-sum transfer involves transferring income without any effects on the economic actions of either the people taxed to provide the funds or the people who receive the transfer. True lump-sum transfers are not possible in practice, and to achieve an increase in equity necessarily involves some sacrifice of economic efficiency, which arises because people do respond to being taxed and to receiving transfers.

Thus, any policy to improve equity necessarily involves some loss of efficiency; the best policy is the one that involves the smallest sacrifice of economic efficiency in order to achieve the desired equity outcome. The relevant BTC for policy is the one that involves the use of the best possible (least-cost) policy instruments. Figure 2.12 duplicates the curves in figure 2.11 but includes two additional curves. BTC* is the optimal benefit trans-formation curve that represents the combinations of economic efficiency and equity that are possible from changing the combinations of the research portfolio and another policy instrument (say tax and income transfer). This BTC is always above the one that holds when only research policy is involved. IC_1 is the highest indifference curve that can be attained as a tangent to that BTC. In figure 2.12, the optimal outcome (point *d*) involves higher levels of both equity, V^{**}, and efficiency, E^{**}, than the optimum from research policy alone (point *b*) because the alternative approach of combining the research and nonresearch instruments is a more efficient means of pursuing the equity objective than research alone. An extreme outcome — but not an unlikely one — is where the research portfolio is chosen to maximize efficiency without regard for the equity objective, which is pursued most effectively with other policy instruments.

We can relate the ideas in figure 2.12 loosely to "Harberger triangles" of efficiency loss associated with market distortions. In the case where research policy is distorted to pursue equity, point *b* involves a deadweight loss equal to $(E_{MAX} - E^*)$. The deadweight loss when using the optimal mix of research and nonresearch instruments is smaller, $(E_{MAX} - E^{**})$. This comparison is biased because point *d* involves a higher level of equity as well. The deadweight loss from using the combined policy to achieve V^* will be

Figure 2.12: *A trade-off of equity and efficiency using the least-cost policy combination*

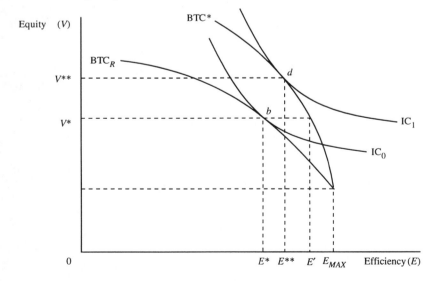

smaller still at $(E_{MAX} - E')$. The economic surplus analysis alone can be used to identify the opportunity costs involved in using research policy as an instrument of social policy. What it cannot do is indicate the *least-cost* way of achieving non-efficiency objectives. Such considerations strengthen the case for viewing research policy formulation in a holistic fashion, with regard to the availability of other instruments of social policy. From this view, it may be argued that research policy should focus, perhaps exclusively, on efficiency objectives while other policy instruments are used to pursue equity objectives.

2.6   Conclusions and Discussion

A variety of conceptual issues must be considered when designing and implementing a research priority-setting procedure. Some of these relate to the perception of the way agricultural research affects agricultural knowledge, production, and markets; some relate more to the way we translate those effects into measures of the benefits and costs of research; some are related to how we would use that information to evaluate research programs and set priorities. Each of these conceptual issues comes part and parcel with empirical challenges.

Economic surplus concepts are intimately involved in any method of estimating research benefits and, in fact, underlie the conventional economic rationale for government intervention in the provision of public-sector agricultural research. These concepts are subject to some criticisms. In implementing them in the context of agricultural research, the more important aspects are the assumptions about the nature of the research-induced supply shift and the measure of its magnitude. There are additional difficulties when markets are distorted by government policies or externalities and when international or interregional spillovers in prices or technology are involved. Methods are available to adjust for all of these factors and to consider the incidence among factors of production in a multistage system, internationally or among rich and poor people. The information and data requirements for the analysis are the binding constraints rather than the methods of economics.

While the research program may be designed primarily to increase the size of the national economic pie, inevitably the shape of the pie and the way it is sliced among groups will be affected to some extent by the choice of research priorities. There is a broad consensus among economists that agricultural research is a poor way to achieve national objectives other than economic efficiency. Still, unless other policies are in place that can correct fully for any unintended side effects of agricultural research on other objectives, it may be necessary to trade off the efficiency gains from research against other objectives such as equity or security.

The partial nature of measures chosen for the analysis, incorporation of distributional and security concerns, and the nature of the research production function each present unique challenges and suggest caution on the part of both the analyst and the people who use the results from the analysis. In the next two chapters we review alternative methods that have been used or suggested for evaluating research and setting research priorities. We discuss the extent to which these procedures can handle the important conceptual issues described in this chapter.

Part II

Measuring the Effects of
Agricultural Research

3

Econometric Measurement of the
Effects of Research

Econometric and nonparametric approaches have been used to relate measures of output, profit, or costs directly to past investments in research (and extension). Using these methods, the nature and extent of changes in technology resulting from investments in research can be computed along with the measures of research-induced savings in costs or gains in output or profit. Estimates of these effects provide summary indicators of the impact of past research investments. This chapter reviews these methods for assessing supply responses to agricultural R&D, emphasizing the evaluation of the effects of past investments in agricultural research rather than the assessment of the potential impact of current or possible future research investments. However, to the extent that the past is a useful guide to the future, such measures may also be useful as an indicator of the likely payoff to further investments in agricultural research and in designing future research strategies and priorities.

Parametric approaches involve specifying an explicit functional form that links inputs to outputs; either primal or dual methods or supply equations can be used. *Primal* approaches involve estimating either *production functions* (in which output is the relevant dependent variable), *response functions* (in which output is expressed per unit of a single input, usually land), or *productivity functions* (in which output is expressed per unit of aggregate input). In each of these alternative primal representations of the agricultural production technology, research and extension may be included directly as explanatory variables in the statistical model of production. *Dual* procedures are also feasible and, in some circumstances, preferable. The empirical

97

approaches in these instances call for research and expenditure variables to be included in either a profit function or a cost function and in the associated systems of factor demands and/or output supply equations.

Nonparametric procedures can also be used to assess the effects of past agricultural research investments. This type of approach avoids the use of functional forms altogether (hence the term "nonparametric") (Varian 1984). Instead, the data are checked for consistency with axioms of rational producer behavior, such as the *weak axiom of cost minimization* (WACM) or the *weak axiom of profit maximization* (WAPM), without the imposition of additional restrictions, such as functional forms, as joint hypotheses. In the event that the data are inconsistent with cost minimization (or profit maximization), pro-gramming algorithms have been developed that can be applied to deduce the minimum set of adjustments to the data (in the form of measures of quantity changes attributable to factor-biased and -neutral technical changes) necessary to restore consistency. This is analogous to the use of a technology index, such as time, to estimate the impact of technical change in the *parametric* approach. Alternatively, by incorporating measures of expenditures on research (and extension) in the analysis (e.g., Chavas and Cox 1992) the changes in outputs or inputs that are not attributable to changes in input or output prices or scale of production may be used to measure the effects of research (and extension) on output and productivity. This is analogous to incorporating research (and extension) as explanatory variables in a parametric model.

Index-number procedures can be used as simple accounting (i.e., aggre-gating) devices, or they can be used either directly or in conjunction with econometric approaches to assess sources of growth in agricultural output or agricultural productivity. In this way, the share of the growth of output or "total" factor productivity (TFP)[1] attributable to agricultural research invest-ments can be identified, distinguished from other sources of growth, and quantified. Index-number approaches represent an additional, and intuitively appealing, means of documenting the effects of agricultural research.

Many decisions must be made to make these econometric approaches operational. For example, when a parametric approach is chosen, a decision must be made about which particular primal or dual method to use. Decisions must also be made about functional form, the degree of spatial, commodity, and temporal disaggregation, the variables to be included in the model, and how to specify a stock-of-knowledge (or research-and-extension) variable in the model. All of these choices are governed by the nature of the question at

---

1. The term *total* is used here in deference to its common usage in the literature. Measured TFPs are more appropriately described as *multifactor* productivity indexes in recognition of the fact that measured inputs do not capture the totality of all factors of production. For more discussion on this point, see Schultz (1956) and Alston, Anderson and Pardey (1994).

hand and the availability of data and resources for the analysis. These modeling decisions can have a substantial impact on the insights to be gleaned from the data concerning technical change and the contribution of R&D to such change.

This chapter begins with a review of the relevant theory and practice in production economics as it relates to assessing research-induced technical changes. Problems with data measurement, model specification, and statistical estimation are considered. Then we discuss how to use the results from applying these econometric methods to quantify various aspects of the economic effects of research. We describe how growth-accounting techniques can be used to identify the sources of output growth, the contributions of research and extension, in particular. Then we review the procedures for translating the parameters obtained from production, productivity, and cost functions into measures of the economic benefits of research.

3.1 Conceptual Models of Production, Productivity, and Technical Change

Evaluating the effects of agricultural research and extension can be viewed as a particular application of the more generally applicable methods of production economics. But some special problems arise in applying the methods of production economics to evaluating agricultural R&D — notably the long lags in the relationship between an investment in R&D and the effects of that investment on production. And the evaluation goes beyond estimating the relationships between inputs and outputs.

When evaluating past research investments, we are usually more interested in the relationship between production (or productivity) and investments in research and extension than in the relationship between conventional inputs and outputs. However, in order to isolate the effects of R&D, it is usually necessary to measure the effects of R&D and the effects of other variables at the same time in a complete model of production. If R&D effects are important, models of production that do not account for these effects will be misspecified and the resulting estimates are likely to be biased. If R&D affects output directly or if it affects the relationship between conventional inputs and output, variables representing R&D belong in the model for econometric reasons, regardless of whether the primary purpose of the analysis is to estimate the effects of R&D or to estimate, say, the output response to fertilizer.

The methods for evaluating agricultural R&D have developed along with more general developments in production economics. Until the early 1970s, production economics used almost entirely primal approaches in which the quantity of output was modeled as a function of input quantities. Some of these models included time trends for technological change; some adjusted inputs for quality change and incorporated other variables that might be thought of as representing sources of technological changes, distinguishing between conventional and unconventional inputs; and some used explicit measures of research and extension as inputs.[2]

Simultaneity between inputs and outputs is a general problem with these primal approaches. Typically, the models have used annual data. But usually some input decisions (e.g., pest-control inputs or harvesting inputs) are made during the year after some information has become available on weather and other factors that are usually treated as exogenous, random, and part of the residual or error term of the model. This means that the error term and some included inputs move together, so that some inputs are not independent of the random part of the model. As Marshak and Andrews (1944) first pointed out, routine regression procedures are inappropriate in such circumstances. A second statistical problem with primal approaches has been multicollinearity. When all of the explanatory variables tend to move together — a common feature of highly trending time-series data — it is difficult to isolate statistically the effects of any particular variables (e.g., R&D variables) on output, independent of changes in other variables. Various devices have been developed to handle these problems, but they may introduce problems of their own.

The 1970s saw the beginning of a "new wave" in production economics, driven by two related innovations in the technology of economics: *flexible functional forms* and *duality* models of production.[3] This new wave was sustained in part by the continuing process of innovation in data processing technology and attendant developments in econometric methods. The new methods allowed researchers to tackle the estimation problems posed by the new models and to take advantage of expanded computing capacity. Dual specifications, most often based on *locally flexible* functional forms (such as the translog), have come to dominate the theoretical and empirical literature in production economics over the past twenty years and, perhaps to a lesser extent, the literature on estimating returns to research *ex post*. An offshoot from the literature on flexible functional forms has been the development of *globally flexible* models, such as the *Fourier flexible form* (Gallant 1982; Chalfant 1983), which are sometimes termed "semi-nonparametric" because the link

---

2.   See, for example, Griliches (1964), Evenson (1967, 1968), Bredahl and Peterson (1976), and Davis (1979).

3.   Theoretical papers in these areas began with, for example, Diewert (1971, 1973, 1974),Christensen, Jorgenson and Lau (1971, 1973), and Lau (1976). Applications to agriculture began almost immediately afterwards, including Binswanger (1974a and b, 1975), and Lau and Yotopoulos (1971). Chambers (1988) documents the literature.

between any single parameter and an economic concept of interest (e.g., an elasticity of substitution) is broken.[4] More recently, nonparametric models of production have been developed and applied to measure the impact of research and extension on agricultural production (e.g., Chavas and Cox 1992). These methods are relatively new, and they have considerable appeal because they avoid imposing restrictions that are not derived from economic theory as joint hypotheses when the properties of the data are evaluated (and when hypotheses about the data-generating process are tested).

Much of the literature on agricultural production economics has acknowledged the importance of incorporating technological change in the specification. Indeed, how to incorporate technological change and how to distinguish factor-biased technical changes from price-induced substitution effects or factor-neutral technical change from economies of scale have been the focus of a significant fraction of the literature.[5] Most studies have used a time index as a proxy for technological change. Only a small fraction have explicitly incorporated measures of R&D: typically, these have been studies where the focus has been on estimating the impact of research.[6]

In principle, there may be only one appropriate specification of a particular production relationship, reflecting the true data-generating process, and this specification should govern the econometric estimation regardless of the purpose of the analysis. In practice, the true data-generating process cannot be known, and empirical specifications are usually dictated by the purpose of the analysis or the available data. The choices of procedure to use, variables to include (including the representation of technical change), and functional form are intimately related and are typically made jointly in light of the objective of the analysis and in consideration of data constraints. When the primary aim is to measure a factor-substitution relationship, it may be appropriate to spend relatively more degrees of freedom attempting to increase precision in that aspect of the relationship, sacrificing accuracy

---

4. The notions of local and global flexibility, as they pertain to the choice of functional form, are discussed further below.

5. Once a functional form has been chosen (whether for a production function, cost function, profit function, or supply function), a technology index — typically a function of research and extension expenditures or time — could be incorporated either (a) as an argument of the function (an explanatory variable), (b) as a modifier of the variables already in the model of the function (e.g., defining actual and effective prices and quantities of inputs and outputs to represent input- or output-augmenting technical change), or (c) as a modifier of the parameters of the function.

6. Most studies have used time-series data, in which case a time-trend variable can be used as a proxy for changes in technology, but in studies using cross-sectional data, there is no natural ordering of the observations in terms of a "path of technology evolution," so some other index must be used. When panel data (i.e., time series of cross-sections) are used, it may be appropriate to index technology both over time (perhaps using a time trend) and cross-sectionally.

(precision and, perhaps, unbiasedness) elsewhere in the model. For instance, a functional form may be chosen that is relatively flexible in its representation of substitution responses but parsimonious in its representation of technical change. Alternatively, when the relationship between R&D and production is the focus, it may be efficient to choose a specification that sacrifices some accuracy in estimates of scale and substitution effects in order to concentrate on the response to R&D. For instance, a relatively parsimonious (and restrictive) production function may be chosen (e.g., a Cobb-Douglas) but with flexibility added by allowing its parameters to be functions of research (e.g., Fulginiti and Perrin 1992).

We now briefly review the conceptual underpinnings of these various approaches to problems in production economics and to the *ex post* evaluation of returns to R&D. Later sections address (a) the econometric issues and problems that arise with the various approaches and methods to mitigate their effects and (b) the more common measurement problems that arise, along with practicable methods to cope with them. Some of these problems are of the type that accompany any empirical econometric analysis. The discussion emphasizes the aspects that are peculiar to measuring research benefits, referring to the more general literature for information on the more general problems.

3.1.1   Parametric Approaches

Most econometric studies of returns to research have used either parametric models or index-number approaches to estimate the productivity growth attributable to R&D. In this section we consider the conceptual underpinnings and the strengths and weaknesses of the various parametric approaches. Since we are interested primarily in the effects of research on supply functions, the literature on the analysis of supply response is examined. In recent years, several review articles on the state of the art of empirical supply analysis have been written: Colman (1983), Wall and Fisher (1988), and Just (1991, 1993). However, these review articles paid relatively little attention to the incorporation of research and extension variables, so we focus on the treatment of research and extension within the frameworks suggested by the previous literature and leave out much of the more general detail because it can be found in those studies.

Colman (1983) classified econometric approaches to estimating supply functions into three broad categories in order to "facilitate examination of the role of economic theory in the different approaches, and to help assess their empirical properties and problems" (p. 202). We consider three corresponding categories of approaches to estimate supply response to, and benefits from, research and extension: (a) primal (two-stage) models, (b) dual (two-stage) models, and (c) direct single-equation supply models. As can be seen in figure 3.1 (adapted from Colman 1983, p. 205), these three approaches are intimately connected in terms of the (static) theory of the firm. The first estimates a production function and then imposes upon that function some behavioral assumptions in order to deduce the implied supply response (route 1 in figure 3.1). The second estimates a cost function and its corresponding input-demand functions, in which behavioral assumptions are embedded, and then uses derivative properties to deduce supply response (route 2 in figure 3.1), or it estimates a profit function jointly with its input-demand and corresponding output-supply functions (route 3 in figure 3.1). The third estimates the supply response directly so that behavioral assumptions are minimized, but as a result, there is no assurance that the estimates are consistent with any particular set of behavioral assumptions.

Figure 3.1:   *Economic relationships between supply functions and other functions in the theory of the competitive firm*

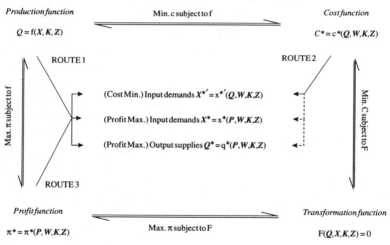

The key contrast is between the third category (i.e., directly estimated supply functions) and the other approaches. As will be seen below, both of the first two categories (using the production, profit, or cost function) draw comparatively heavily on the theory of the firm in order to impose restrictions on parameters and (presuming the restrictions to be correct) to improve the efficiency and internal consistency of the estimates. But they also involve comparatively strong restrictions on behavior, such as assumptions of static cost minimization or profit maximization and perfect knowledge. Thus, such models allow relatively little flexibility in behavioral assumptions and a rudimentary role for dynamic responses, uncertainty, and expectations. For these reasons, the ability of these models to describe and predict has been called into question, and their performance has often been disappointing in that regard. Models in the third category — the so-called *ad hoc* single-equation supply-response models that in fact predominate in the econometric supply-response literature — use relatively little of the static theory of the competitive firm under perfect knowledge and, instead, draw more heavily on the theory that has been developed for modeling dynamic response, expectation formation, and decision making under uncertainty. In comparing these approaches, Colman (1983, p. 224) concludes that

> It is clear . . . that there exist major problems with the time-series regression approach to single-commodity supply response analysis. However, this is also true of its major competitors, and it remains the case that aggregate time-series analysis is the most often used and preferred of the methods. The most significant factors in its favor are that it operates directly on the aggregate supply data which are the object of interest for projection purposes, and it handles dynamic adjustments to supply in ways in which the other procedures do not. It is the simplest of the procedures in terms of estimational methods and data requirements. . . . Finally, it is a technique which has shown itself capable of generating acceptable and useful results.

Studies of returns to research, on the other hand, have been dominated by what Colman (1983) referred to as two-stage procedures, where either a primal (production function) model or its dual equivalent (a cost function or profit function) is estimated in the first stage, sometimes jointly with the implied system of input-demand and, perhaps, output-supply equations, and the implications for research benefits are deduced from those estimates in a further step. A comparatively small number of studies have used the third approach (the "directly estimated single-equation" approach) in cases where the purpose of the study was to evaluate research on a particular commodity (e.g., Otto 1981; Zentner 1985; Haque, Fox and Brinkman 1989).

Primal Approaches

The primal approach to ex post evaluation of agricultural research involves specifying a production function f(.), in which agricultural output in time t (i.e., Q_t) depends on the quantities of conventional inputs, X_t, various "quasi-fixed" factors such as public investment in infrastructure (such as roads, communications, irrigation, and education), Z_t, the flow of services from the stock of knowledge, K_t (which we can represent by a technology index, τ_t), and uncontrolled factors such as weather and pests, U_t:

$$Q_t = f(X_t, Z_t, \tau_t, U_t) \tag{3.1}$$

Research investments can lead to a change in productivity (output per unit of conventional inputs, Q/X) by changing the quality or price of conventional inputs and outputs (i.e., through a change in the technology used to produce those inputs and outputs) or by increasing the stock of knowledge or the use of the existing stock of knowledge. Thus, the state of technology, τ_t, is endogenous, in part because the extent of *utilization* of available knowledge depends upon relative factor prices, W_t, the stock of farmers' human capital, H_t, and the extent and quality of extension services, E_t. The same infrastructural variables, Z_t, that directly affect output may also indirectly influence Q_t through their effects on τ_t. Initially we model this relationship as follows:

$$\tau_t = \tau (K_t , W_t , H_t , E_t , Z_t) \tag{3.2}$$

The current stock of useful knowledge, K_t, depreciates by an amount D_t as it is replaced by better information or when circumstances change to make it less useful, and it increases by an amount I_t because of the incorporation of results from past investments in research. Thus,

$$K_t = K_{t-1} + I_t - D_t \tag{3.3}$$

With this specification, it can be seen (by repeated substitution for K_{t-1}) that the stock of current knowledge is defined by the entire history of increments and depreciation of knowledge — an infinite lag structure.

The dynamics of the relationship between past investments in research, R_{t-r}, and extension, E_{t-e}, and current increments to useful knowledge, I_t, are complicated and uncertain. A general form of the relationship is

$$I_t = i (R_t , \dots , R_{t-L_R} , E_t , \dots , E_{t-L_E} , K_{t-1}, \tilde{Z}_t) \tag{3.4}$$

where $\tilde{Z}_t$ represents a set of quasi-fixed factors that can affect the performance of a research system, such as the orientation (e.g., commodity, technology, or problem focus) of the research and the institutional and management environment within which these research resources are deployed.

The relationship between research investments and changes in the stock of useful knowledge is sometimes termed a *research production function* or a *knowledge production function*. It is a central component in relating agricultural output to research (and extension) inputs.[7] Usually, the stock of knowl-

---

7. This model includes general research investment variables, R_t, and extension variables, E_t, indexed for timing, without identifying the nature of the work undertaken (i.e., pretechnology research, applied research, development), or who is undertaking the investment (the public sector, the private sector, or foreigners). In addition, the generation of knowledge involves several interdependent stages of production in which outputs (research results) from one stage are used as inputs into the next. Conceptually, however, the research variable in the model above can include expenditures on any type of research as part of a program or project that leads to new agricultural technology.

edge cannot be observed directly, so the research (knowledge) production function is more a part of the conceptual apparatus than an empirical tool. The empirically useful variant of the research (knowledge) production function is the function that relates output (or productivity) to lagged values of research investments.[8]

By loosely combining equations 3.1 through 3.4, a relationship between investments in research and output (or productivity) can be defined as

$$
\begin{aligned}
Q_t &= f\left(\,X_t\,,\,U_t\,,\,\tau_t\,[(R_t\,,\,\ldots\,,\,R_{t-L_R})\,,\right.\\
&\quad \left.(\,E_t\,,\,\ldots\,,\,E_{t-L_E}\,)\,,\,K_{t-1}\,,\,W_t\,,\,H_t\,,\,Z_t\,]\right) \qquad (3.5)\\
&= f(X_t\,,\,R_{t-r}\,,\,E_{t-e}\,,\,W_t\,,\,H_t\,,\,Z_t\,,\,U_t)\ \text{ for }\ r\,,\,e = 0\ \text{ to }\ \infty
\end{aligned}
$$

in which current output depends on current flows of conventional inputs, X_t, *indefinitely* long lags of past investments in agricultural research, R_{t-r}, and extension, E_{t-e}, current values of factor prices, W_t, and the stock of human capital, H_t.[9] The Z vector is commonly taken to include publicly provided "infrastructural" variables that affect the relationship between measured inputs and outputs, like public investments in such things as transportation, communication, education, and health care.[10] In equation 3.5, the vector Z subsumes the $\tilde{Z}$ variables from 3.4 that more directly affect the performance of a research and extension system; it may also include variables that reflect otherwise unmeasured changes in the quality of conventional inputs.[11] None of the variables included in Z are fixed in a literal sense; they certainly vary over a sample. But they are properly treated as fixed if they are beyond the direct control of the farmers whose production decisions are being modeled. So, they are the variables that are most unequivocally exogenous.[12]

Notice that in the transition to the second line of equation 3.5, the lagged value of the knowledge stock K_{t-1} has been dropped and, as a consequence,

8.   Some studies have attempted to estimate the research production function itself (e.g., Pakes and Griliches 1980; Pardey 1989).

9.   Conventional inputs are always included in production functions. Nowadays, human capital variables might be regarded as being conventional too, but here they relate more particularly to the effects of human capital on utilization of knowledge (rather than, perhaps, allocative efficiency or management). Prices are not commonly included in production functions, but there is recent precedent for doing so in relation to the induced-innovation hypothesis (e.g., see Fulginiti and Perrin 1992). The other variables are measures of past research expenditures and current and lagged extension investments such as those that have been incorporated in production functions in several studies (e.g., Huffman and Evenson 1992).

10.   See, for example, Antle (1983), Binswanger et al. (1987), Lau and Yotopoulos (1989), and Craig, Pardey and Roseboom (1994).

11.   Where changes in input quality are fully reflected in measured inputs, it would obviously be double counting to make a further adjustment to account for input quality.

12.   In other words, while measured output is a function of Z, the residual part of output unexplained by the X variable is uncorrelated with Z.

the infinite lags of research and extension have replaced their finite counter-parts. The role of knowledge depreciation may be implicitly reflected in the research lag structure, or some explicit treatment for depreciation may be introduced.

Previous studies have not been clear on these points and some errors may have resulted. Many studies have estimated the equivalent of the first two lines of equation 3.5 (i.e., finite lags of research and extension) but excluded the stock of knowledge, K_{t-1} (e.g., Huffman and Evenson 1989, 1992). This amounts to a problem of an omitted variable — an omission of the knowl-edge-stock variable that can be interpreted, equivalently, as having truncated the research lag. It is appropriate to omit the lagged knowledge stock only if the knowledge stock depreciates completely each year, so that only current increments to knowledge matter. In contrast, Fulginiti and Perrin (1992) effectively included an infinite lag with zero depreciation (i.e., in their model, the *useful* knowledge stock grew each year, in both gross and net terms, according to a trapezoidal lag of past research investments). In short, Huffman and Evenson (1989, 1992) effectively assumed 100% depreciation; Fulginiti and Perrin (1992) effectively assumed 0% depreciation. A more general model would allow some research-induced changes in knowledge to have effects that persist indefinitely, while some depreciate away relatively quickly. In practice, in an aggregative model, a relatively flexible specifica-tion of lags and dynamic relationships may be required. The main im-plications of omitting the knowledge-stock variable in a reduced-form model are (a) the use of a finite lag is inappropriate, a specification error that will lead to biased coefficients, and (b) the interpretation of the reduced-form coefficients on lagged research and extension variables is unclear.

A yield equation variant of this model expresses output per unit of an input (say, land), but the commonly used specifications involve some assumptions that may not be warranted.[13] Implementation of this conceptual model requires decisions about which of the variables to include (a choice that is dictated in large part by the availability of data or suitable proxies), which functional form to use, and how to specify the random part of the model that will be treated as an unexplained residual.

In order to measure returns to R&D, it is necessary to have, at a minimum, some data on research investments and conventional inputs. These minimal

13.   For example, cross-section production-function estimates in the literature are usually based on an aggregate production function such as 3.5, while the empirical model involves some scaling of the output and input variables (e.g., by hectare for a yield-response function or by number of farms). Craig, Pardey and Roseboom (1994) point out that failure to include the scaling variable then as an explanatory variable amounts to an assumption either that there are constant returns to scale among all scaled inputs or that the "aggregate" production function is appropriately defined in the scaled units. See Dillon and Anderson (1990) for an extensive treatment of the analysis of agricultural response functions.

requirements for an econometric evaluation study may be augmented with explicit measures of extension investments, human capital variables, and weather variables. But often such variables are not included in the model and their effects are left as part of the unexplained residual. The implications of this (in particular, the implications of the problem of omitted variables for bias and inconsistency in the parameter estimates) are discussed below in the section on implementation.

Decisions about functional form are intimately related to decisions on how to measure and treat the explanatory variables — especially the research and extension variables — and related decisions on estimation procedures.[14] Most of the econometric models of returns to research have used a Cobb-Douglas functional form to estimate an explicit form of an equation such as 3.5. The Cobb-Douglas model is extremely restrictive; elasticities of factor substitution are restricted to unity, output elasticities are constant and equal to factor shares under constant returns to scale, and the price elasticities of the implied compensated derived demands are invariant to the amount of output. But it has the advantage of being parsimonious with respect to parameters (one per input) and relatively easy to implement econometrically (although it may be difficult to estimate for statistical reasons). In most cases parsimony is judged to be important because a large number of lagged values for research (and extension) expenditures are included and a relatively large number of parameters are used to estimate their effects (i.e., so as not to impose too much structure on the form of the lags). Often, however, even in such otherwise relatively inflexible specifications, a great deal of structure is also imposed on the dynamics associated with research in order to conserve degrees of freedom and minimize problems of multicollinearity. The constant elasticity of substitution (CES) production function is somewhat less restrictive than the Cobb-Douglas in that the elasticities of factor substitution may differ from one, but they are still restricted to being positive numbers and constant across the data.

Over the past twenty years, a number of locally flexible functional forms have been developed that allow elasticities of substitution to vary over the

---

14. Some studies have used a two-step estimation procedure to estimate the effects of research on production or cost (e.g., Mullen, Cox and Foster 1992). In the first step, a production-function relationship is estimated in terms of conventional inputs and some other factors, including time-trend variables but excluding the determinants of the technology index. Thus, the value of the technology index is, itself, estimated as a parameter given by the changes in productivity attributable to the time-trend variables. Second, the measured technology index (or productivity) is regressed against lagged research variables. This type of two-step estimation procedure may be used to handle some of the multicollinearity that may occur when estimating a model with a large number of variables characterized by strong trends. But the factors included in the first stage could well be positively correlated with the omitted research variable. The estimated coefficients for these factors will embody part of the effects of research and, as a consequence, be biased upward. We do not recommend this approach for that reason.

sample. These locally flexible models are typically quadratic forms in some transformation of inputs and outputs. For example, the quadratic production function expresses output as a quadratic function of the quantities of inputs. The translog production function has the logarithm of output as a quadratic function of the logarithms of inputs. The generalized Leontief uses square roots of variables. These models require many more parameters than their inflexible counterparts, especially when the number of input categories is large, and this may account for their relative lack of popularity in research evaluation studies.[15] The number of parameters to be estimated may be reduced by imposing restrictions derived from theory. If these restrictions are to be tested in the analysis, as they often are, to "test down" to a more parsimonious specification, the gain in degrees of freedom is forsaken — although the illusion may remain. Globally flexible models, such as Gallant's (1982) use of a Fourier flexible form in a cost function based on a translog model, do not necessarily use many more parameters. However, unless large data sets become available, many studies will continue to use a Cobb-Douglas type of production function, with a relatively small number of input categories to both conserve degrees of freedom and avoid multicollinearity. As a result, the studies will always be vulnerable to the possibility that the estimates of R&D effects are biased because of the use of an inappropriate model specification. This issue will be addressed further in the section on empirical implementation.[16]

Once an estimate of the impact of research on production has been obtained, the remaining step is to translate that estimate into a measure of research benefits. This step involves, whether implicitly or explicitly, an economic surplus approach. It works as follows. The estimated production function can be used to partition the total output into one part that is explained by conventional inputs (and other nonresearch factors), another part that is explained by research expenditures, and an unexplained residual. One way to proceed is to calculate the value of the additional output due to research for each year in the time series being studied, by multiplying the estimate of the quantity that is attributable to research by the corresponding output price (in the case of aggregated output, a corresponding aggregate price would be used). This procedure is analogous to an economic surplus calculation in which supply is

15. For instance, with *n* input categories and assuming constant returns to scale, the Cobb-Douglas requires *n*−1 parameters, while a translog would require *n*(*n*−1)/2 parameters; in the case of five inputs, the former requires four parameters and the latter requires 10. It is common practice to preaggregate more-detailed input categories into broader classes of inputs to save on degrees of freedom, with the consequence that a number of restrictions are implicitly imposed through this aggregation procedure.

16. In general, whether in the context of primal or dual models, the flexible functional forms have been used much more often in studies undertaken for reasons other than research evaluation, where most often technological change has been incorporated by the expedient of including time as a technology index (usually either as a linear or quadratic trend).

assumed to be perfectly inelastic and demand is assumed to be perfectly elastic, so that the effect of a research-induced increase in quantity is to shift a vertical supply function to the right, in parallel, against a horizontal demand function (see figure 2.6a and the attendant discussion).[17] Once a stream of annual benefits has been estimated in this fashion, all that remains is to compare that stream to the corresponding stream of research expenditures, using conventional capital budgeting methods to compute a net present value, cost-benefit ratio, or internal rate of return.

A second approach is to compute the value of inputs that would have been required to produce the actual outputs that were produced if there had not been any research expenditure. This computation involves taking the quantity of outputs attributable to research, deducing the quantities of additional inputs that would have been needed to produce those additional outputs in the absence of the research (e.g., under constant returns to scale, all inputs would need to be increased by a proportion equal to the computed, proportional, research-induced increase in outputs), and then evaluating the stream of cost savings using the quantities of inputs saved in each year, multiplied by their corresponding input prices. This approach is analogous to a surplus analysis that involves shifting a perfectly elastic supply function up, in parallel, against a totally inelastic demand function, as a measure of the benefits foregone if the research had not been undertaken (see figure 2.6b and the attendant discussion). Again, translating the stream of benefits into a summary statistic is reasonably straightforward.

Whether the research-induced technological change is regarded as output enhancing or (input) cost saving, the primal approach is attractive in that the model directly links the research variable and the production technology. The production function itself is essentially a physical relationship, not a behavioral one (at least in principle), and important explicit behavioral assumptions are not imposed.[18] The device of multiplying the additional outputs by the output price, or the inputs saved by the input prices, does not involve any behavioral restrictions either.

17. The functional form of the production function and the way in which technical change enters it may imply a particular parallel or nonparallel supply shift due to changing technology (Davis 1981). However, the econometric estimation will typically not permit strong inferences to be drawn about the nature of the technical change or the nature of the induced supply shift (except, perhaps, locally, say, at the mean of the sample data). Thus, there is usually little basis for holding strong views about the nature of the technical change, nor for insisting on consistency between the form of technical change in the econometric model (as a local approximation) and that assumed in the welfare evaluation (as applying globally).

18. Of course observed production-function relations do incorporate some very complex behavioral assumptions concerning the choice of technology (i.e., technology adoption and use), but there are no consequences for the aspects being considered here. There are also behavioral assumptions embedded in the preaggregation of inputs and outputs that are required to estimate *any* production function.

Dual approaches embed strong behavioral assumptions as restrictions in the analysis. These behavioral assumptions save degrees of freedom by allowing the imposition of parametric restrictions in estimation. The counterpoint to this advantage is that, if the strong behavioral restrictions are inappropriate, we have merely exchanged one potential source of bias for another. The primal approach generally imposes restrictive assumptions about the technology but does not impose any especially strong restrictions on behavior; the dual approach allows a relatively flexible specification of the technology, but the price of this flexibility is the imposition of behavioral assumptions that are of questionable applicability in an agricultural setting characterized by uncertainty and dynamics.

Dual Approaches

The dual approach involves estimating a cost function (or a profit function) instead of a production function. As described above, at least for a competitive firm, for every primal representation of production, there is a corresponding dual representation.[19] The dual approach has several potential advantages. First, the use of factor prices, rather than their quantities, as explanatory variables may avoid the problems of simultaneity that arise when input choices are jointly endogenous with output; factor (and product) prices are more likely to be behaviorally, and hence statistically, exogenous to a firm and even to an industry.[20]

Second, the dual representations, combined with their derivative properties, permit the estimation of a system of equations comprising the cost function and the system of output-constrained factor-demand functions. Or in the case of the profit function, the dual approach leads to the estimation of Marshallian factor-demand equations and output-supply functions.

In a dual analogue to the model in equation 3.1 above, we can write a cost function as

$$C_t = c(\,Q_t\,,\,W_t\,,\,Z_t\,,\,\tau_t\,,\ U_t\,) \tag{3.6}$$

where c(.) is the cost function in which C_t is the minimum cost of producing

19. Young et al. (1987) provide an excellent pedagogical treatise on duality theory and applied production economics. More advanced and more comprehensive treatments of the topics can be found in Chambers (1988) and Cornes (1992).

20. However, most profit-and-cost function models use aggregate, industry-level data — with specialized factors of production for nontraded goods. And for a few traded commodities for which the country can influence world prices (e.g., corn and soybeans in the United States, jute in Bangladesh, wool in Australia), measured prices may not be statistically exogenous. In any case, one can always test for exogeneity (e.g., a Hausman test), and if variables on the right-hand side are not statistically exogenous, alternative estimation procedures (e.g., 3SLS, instrumental variables) can be employed.

output Q, given values of a vector of prices of conventional variable inputs, W_t, various quasi-fixed factors (such as publicly provided transportation, irrigation, and education facilities and services), Z_t, the state of technology, τ_t, and uncontrolled factors that are assumed to be uncorrelated with the other variables, U_t.[21] If equation 3.6 is considered a multi-output cost function, then the argument Q_t would be replaced with the vector Q_t.

As in the case of the primal model, a reduced-form expression for the cost function can be obtained by augmenting the model with other variables, including research and extension variables, as follows. Loosely combining equations 3.6 and 3.2 through 3.4, we can suggest a reduced-form relationship between investments in research and output (or productivity) in which current cost depends upon current prices of conventional inputs, W_t, *indefinitely* long lags of past investments in agricultural research, R_{t-r}, and extension, E_{t-e}, the stock of human capital, H_t, other factors such as fixed inputs, infrastructure, and (when they are not properly accounted for by adjustments in input prices) changes in input quality, Z_t, and uncontrolled factors, U_t, so that

$$
\begin{aligned}
C_t &= c\,(Q_t\,,W_t\,,U_t\,,\tau_t\,[(R_t\,,\ldots\,,R_{t-L_R})\,, \\
&\quad (E_t\,,\ldots\,,E_{t-L_E})\,,H_t\,,Z_t]) \\
&= c\,(Q_t\,,W_t\,,R_{t-r}\,,E_{t-e}\,,H_t\,,Z_t\,,U_t) \text{ for } r, e = 0 \text{ to } \infty
\end{aligned}
\tag{3.7}
$$

Here, all explanatory variables other than W_t are quantity variables. A unit- or average-cost variant of this model expresses cost per unit of output.

In order to implement this type of model, a functional form must be chosen. As with the primal approach, both relatively inflexible and parametrically parsimonious forms, such as the Cobb-Douglas, and relatively flexible alternatives, such as the translog, are available. The main issues are comparable to those raised above in relation to the primal model. The trade-off is between flexibility and parsimony, given the constraints of data and the objectives of the analysis. One important consideration is that it is desirable to incorporate the variables that are additional to those normally included in a cost function (i.e., output and the prices of conventional inputs) in ways that yield an augmented model[22] that continues to satisfy the requirements for a well-be-

21. If this model is interpreted as a long-run cost function, then all inputs are, by definition, variable. However, in the shorter run, some factors may be fixed. These can be either included explicitly at the stage of equation 3.6 or left implicit, as, in fact, they are in equation 3.6. Another issue that arises here, that does not arise in the primal approach, is the role of expectations and dynamics. In equation 3.6, the factor prices are treated as if they are known with certainty at the time decisions are made and take effect, whereas decisions about agricultural inputs are often made in an environment of uncertainty about technology, random uncontrollable factors (such as weather and pests), and prices.

22. A cost function must be continuous with respect to input prices, linearly homogeneous in input prices, nondecreasing in input prices, and concave in input prices. See Young et al. (1987) or Varian (1978).

haved cost function. Obtaining this augmented model is not always easy, and the choice of functional form for the cost function may have strong implications for the nature of the measured impact of research on output-supply and input-demand functions.

The derivation of the corresponding output-supply and input-demand equations is straightforward (see section 3.3.2). Output-supply equations are obtained by setting the derivative of the cost function with respect to output (i.e., marginal cost) equal to price and then inverting to solve for output. The input-demand equations are obtained by the application of Shephard's lemma: $X_{i,t}(.) = \partial c(.)/\partial W_{i,t}$. These output-supply and input-demand equations contain the same parameters as the cost function itself, and this fact may be imposed as a restriction in the estimation of a joint system comprising the cost function and its derivatives with respect to factor prices (or quantities). The benefit from doing this joint estimation is that, so long as the model is correctly specified, the imposition of these behavioral assumptions, with respect to factor demands and through cross-equation restrictions on parameters, means that the parameters are estimated with greater precision than if only the cost function were estimated.

Once the model has been estimated, total costs of production for each year may be partitioned into those attributable to conventional inputs (and other nonresearch factors) and those attributable to research (a negative number if research has successfully led to lower costs). Then, the contribution of research, as a cost saving, may be computed and the stream of cost savings may be evaluated.[23]

Direct Estimation of Supply

The third alternative approach is direct estimation of supply. The literature on single-equation, supply-response models for commodities is large, and the range of issues and approaches is far too great to be dealt with in any detail here. The key issues in supply-response analysis were identified sixty years ago in an article by Cassells (1933) as being how to deal with expectations and dynamics; these issues continue to be difficult. The virtue of single-equation models is that they allow considerable flexibility in the treatment of these topics. For estimating the returns to research on a particular commodity (or commodity aggregate), the direct estimation of a supply-response model may well be a better alternative than estimating a production function, precisely

---

23.   One virtue of this approach, relative to the primal approach, is that from a cost function of this type, it is possible to obtain explicit evidence on the distributional impact of research among fixed factors. One of the disadvantages, however, is that the choice of functional form may implicitly dictate the nature of the factor biases if care is not taken to allow the effects of technological variables to be treated as flexibly as the effects of prices.

because it permits the dynamics of supply response to price to be modeled in some detail along with the dynamics of supply response to research.

In general form, a supply-response model for output may be written as

$$Q_t = q(P_t, W_t, \tau_t, U_t) \qquad (3.8)$$

where q(.) is the supply function in which Q_t is the output produced given values of a vector of *expected* prices of output, P_t, and of conventional inputs W_t, a state of technology, τ_t, and other uncontrolled variables, U_t, as defined above. Loosely combining equations 3.8 and 3.2 through 3.4, we can suggest a reduced-form relationship between investments in research and output (or productivity) in which current output depends upon current expected values for prices of output, P_t, and of conventional inputs, W_t, *indefinitely* long lags of past investments in agricultural research, R_{t-r}, and extension, E_{t-e}, the stock of human capital, H_t, other factors (such as fixed inputs, infrastructure, and changes in input quality), Z_t, that are not captured by the measured input prices, and uncontrolled factors, U_t, so that

$$
\begin{aligned}
Q_t &= q\,(P_t, W_t, U_t, \tau_t\,[(R_t, \ldots, R_{t-L_R}), \\
&\quad (E_t, \ldots, E_{t-L_E}), H_t, Z_t]) \\
&= q(P_t, W_t, R_{t-r}, E_{t-e}, H_t, Z_t, U_t) \text{ for } r, e = 0 \text{ to } \infty
\end{aligned}
\qquad (3.9)
$$

Few studies have taken this type of approach in applications to research benefits, even though it dominates the more general supply-response literature (e.g., Zentner 1982; Fox, Brinkman and Brown-Andison 1987). Once the supply model has been estimated, it can be combined with a model of demand to translate the measured supply shifts into measures of the size of research benefits and their distribution between producers and consumers, using the methods sketched in section 3.3 and described in detail in chapters 4 and 5.

Modeling Technical Change

As discussed in chapters 2 and 4, the particular form of technical change may have important implications for the size and distribution of benefits (e.g., Duncan and Tisdell 1971; Scobie 1976; Jarrett and Lindner 1977; Lindner and Jarrett 1978; Rose 1980; Norton and Davis 1981). Three alternative approaches to specifying technical change are (a) directly incorporating technical-change variables in the function (e.g., Binswanger 1974; Bouchet, Orden and Norton 1989; Kohli 1991), (b) distinguishing between observed and effective quantities and prices, and output- or input-augmenting technical change (e.g., Dixon et al. 1982), and (c) using a varying-parameter specification in which the coefficients of a static model are themselves functions of technical change (e.g., Fulginiti and Perrin 1992).

In a profit function, for example, these three specifications may be represented as

$$\pi = g(P, W, Z, \tau \mid \alpha) \qquad\qquad\qquad (3.10a)$$

$$\pi = g[P(\tau), W, Z \mid \alpha] \qquad\qquad\qquad (3.10b)$$

$$\pi = g[P, W, Z \mid \alpha(\tau)] \qquad\qquad\qquad (3.10c)$$

where π is variable economic profit (i.e., the return to fixed factors), P is a vector of output prices, W is a vector of prices of variable factors, Z is a vector of quantities of fixed factors, τ is a vector of technology indexes, and α is a vector of parameters. Martin and Alston (1992) illustrate the effects of these three kinds of technical change using a second-order Taylor-series expansion around a quadratic profit function.

The first specification of technical change is well known from the empirical literature on the estimation of flexible functional forms. Technical-change variable(s) enter the function in the same way that a quasi-fixed factor would, except that they receive a zero factor return at the level of the firm. The second specification distinguishes between observed and effective quantities and prices. In this widely used approach, technical change increases the *effective* quantity of a good associated with a given physical quantity. An important feature of this specification is that there is a corresponding change in the effective price of the good; an increase in the effective quantity of an output provided by each physical unit will lower the effective price relative to that of the physical units. Using this approach, the relationship between physical and effective quantities of a particular good (i.e., input or output), Q_i, can be represented by $Q_i = Q_i^* \cdot \tau_i^e$, where Q_i is the observed quantity of the good, Q_i^* is the effective quantity of the good, and τ_i^e is the level of output-augmenting or input-augmenting technical change for good i.

The corresponding relationship between observed and effective prices is $P_i = P_i^*/\tau_i^e$, where P_i^* is the effective price of the good, P_i is the observed price, and τ_i^e is the augmentation factor. When Q_i is an input, input-saving technical advance is represented by a decline in τ_i^e, which reduces the physical quantity of the input required for one effective unit and also lowers the effective price relative to the actual price. When Q_i is an output, an increase in τ_i^e represents output-augmenting technical change; an increase raises the physical quantity associated with a given effective quantity and raises the effective price for a given actual price.[24] Producers are represented

24.   For example, consider a farm manager for whom effective outputs are measured in hectares of particular crops. A technical advance that raises yield per acre of one crop without changing its input mix increases the actual output (tonnes) attained per unit of effective output (hectares). While its actual price (in $/tonne) has not changed, its effective price (in $/hectare) has increased. Maximizing over effective

as optimizing over effective quantities and prices rather than observed quantities and prices. The profit function is then defined by replacing the variables with their corresponding effective values.

The third way of incorporating technical change is to allow the parameters of the model to be expressed as functions of a *scalar* technology index. In this approach, it is important for the functions that define the parameters to be chosen so that the desired parametric restrictions hold over the region of interest. This specification makes transparent the need to ensure that any shift remains consistent with theoretical restrictions. It has been the most popular treatment of technical change in both primal and dual approaches. Typically, technology indexes, whether they are time trends or R&D variables themselves, are included additively — basically as modifiers of only the intercepts of equations that are linear in variables or their logarithms.

3.1.2   Nonparametric Approaches

With both the primal and dual approaches, there are a number of concerns about the selection of functional form, the specification of technical change and how research expenditure variables enter the model, and the lag structure. The attraction of the *nonparametric* approach to the analysis of production and the evaluation of research is that it avoids the use of functional forms altogether (hence the term "nonparametric"). The foundations for this type of approach are papers by Hanoch and Rothschild (1972) and Varian (1984), and a good exposition can be found in the text by Varian (1992).[25] Chavas and Cox (1988) extended the models from Hanoch and Rothschild (1972) and Varian (1984) to include technical change.[26] Subsequently, Cox and Chavas (1990) applied that approach to a productivity analysis of U.S. agriculture and Chavas and Cox (1992) analyzed the effects of research on productivity.

Conventional approaches to modeling production involve estimating a parametric model and evaluating the properties of the estimated model. A disadvantage of this approach is that the results may be influenced by the functional form chosen for the model. Some such effects are trivially obvious (e.g., the use of a Cobb-Douglas model imposes the restriction that elasticities of substitution are one); some others are more subtle (e.g., even among

quantities and prices, it will be optimal to increase the effective output of this crop by withdrawing resources from other crops. Thus, actual output of this crop will go up both directly through higher output per hectare and indirectly because the higher effective price draws resources from other activities.

25.   Recent developments with applications to agriculture and agricultural productivity are reported in papers by Chavas and Cox (1988, 1992), Cox and Chavas (1990), Mullen, Cox and Foster (1992), and Lim and Shumway (1992). Examples outside agriculture include Chalfant and Wallace (1992) and Flacco and Larson (1992).

26.   See also Fawson and Shumway (1988).

locally flexible functional forms, there can be substantially different findings about technical change or scale or substitution effects estimated using a particular data set). The problem is that the true functional form cannot be known but a functional form must be imposed as a joint hypothesis with any other hypothesis test. The nonparametric approach to production analysis avoids the imposition of functional form as a joint hypothesis. Instead, in this approach, the data are checked for consistency with axioms of behavior. The two primary axioms of interest are the *Weak Axiom of Cost Minimization* (WACM) and the *Weak Axiom of Profit Maximization* (WAPM) as defined by Varian (1984) and as described by Chavas and Cox (1988).

Consider a competitive firm that maximizes profit and faces the decision problem:

$$\pi (P, \tau, h) = \underset{X}{\text{Max}}\ P'X \text{ subject to } g(X, \tau) \geq h \qquad (3.11)$$

where X is a "netput" decision vector (with positive elements corresponding to outputs and negative elements corresponding to inputs), and P is the vector of corresponding prices. The function $g(X, \tau)$ represents technology, $\tau > 0$ is a technology index, h is a scalar, and $\pi(.)$ represents the indirect objective function. It is assumed that $g(.)$ is strictly decreasing and concave in X.

The firm is observed choosing X T times, $X_1, \ldots, X_T$, and each observation is associated with a situation t characterized by market prices P_t and technology (h_t, τ_t), $t = 1, \ldots, T$. The nonparametric approach to production analysis tests the consistency of the actual decisions $X = \{X_1, \ldots, X_T\}$ with the optimization problem given by 3.11 (i.e., whether X_t could be equal to $X^*(P_t, \tau_t, h_t)$, the solution of the maximization problem above), without ad hoc specification of the functional form for $g(X, \tau)$, $\pi(X, \tau, h)$, or $X^*(X, \tau, h)$. The parametric tests involve checking a set of inequalities to see whether a production function could exist that would "rationalize" the data in the context of the maximization hypothesis. One such set of inequalities tests for consistency with profit maximization, another for consistency with cost minimization.[27]

Profit Maximization — WAPM

When h is equal to zero, technology $g(X, \tau)$ represents the implicit production frontier. In the absence of technical change, $\tau_t = 1$, for $t = 1, \ldots, T$, and $g(X_t, 1) = 0$. Profit maximization implies $P_t'(X_t - X_s) \geq 0$ for all s and t. This

---

27. Nonparametric methods can also be used to investigate many of the characteristics of production technology, such as the nature of returns to scale or various separability restrictions, or production efficiency. Here we are concerned, instead, with the use of these techniques to measure the size and factor bias of technical change in a data set and to evaluate the contribution of research to those changes.

inequality is WAPM (Varian 1984, p. 584). The interpretation is that if profits are maximized at time *t*, then it should not be possible to choose any other bundle X_s and obtain greater profit with time *t* prices. The question compares the time *t* bundle with the bundles chosen at other times in the data set.

Cost Minimization — WACM

Cost minimization is obtained from equation 3.11 when h_t denotes output (of a single product) so that $g(X, \tau)$ represents the explicit production function and X_t is the input vector (redefined here to be positive) with input prices equal to W_t. As shown by Varian (1984, p. 581), in the absence of technical change, if $h_t \leq h_s$ then cost minimization implies that $W_t'(X_t - X_s) \leq 0$ for all *s* and *t*. This inequality is WACM. The interpretation is that the inputs chosen in time *t* must cost less at time *t* prices than any other bundle that could produce greater output than h_t. If costs were minimized at time *t*, then it should not be possible to choose any other bundle X_s and obtain greater output without incurring greater cost. The question is examined by comparing the time *t* bundle with the bundles chosen at other times in the data set.

Technical change is precluded by assumption in these procedures; one would expect a substantial technical change to lead to a violation of WAPM or WACM. Chavas and Cox (1988) extended these procedures to incorporate Hicks-neutral technical change, using τ_t.[28] Subsequently Cox and Chavas (1990) allowed for both biased and neutral technical change. When technical change is allowed, the linear programming problem becomes one of solving for the minimum set of technical changes necessary to "rationalize" the data. As described by Mullen, Cox and Foster (1992), Cox and Chavas (1990) showed that the existence of a solution to the following $T(T-1)$ inequalities is necessary and sufficient for the data to be consistent with profit maximization under the input- and output-additive augmentation (translating) hypothesis

$$P_t' [Y_t - A_t - Y_s + A_s] - R_t' [X_t + B_t - X_s - B_s] \geq 0 \qquad (3.12)$$

where Y_t denotes a scalar single output with associated price P_t, X_t denotes a vector of inputs with associated prices R_t, A_t denotes output augments (higher values denote higher productivity), and B_t denotes input augments (where $B > 0$ implies factor-saving input bias and $B < 0$, factor-using input bias). Furthermore, if such a solution exists, then $Y(A_s, X_t)/Y(A_t, X_t) = 1 + (A_s - A_t)/Y_t$ is an index of total factor productivity that measures the shift in the production function between time *t* and time *s*.[29]

28.   In the notation used by Cox and Chavas (1990) A_t is equivalent to the τ_t we use in this chapter.

29.   More recently, Mullen, Cox and Foster (1992) have shown how to obtain nonparametric measures of total factor productivity, including input-based measures and output-based measures, with an applica-

Chavas and Cox (1992) proposed using their nonparametric approach to analyse the effects of research on productivity. They enumerated five virtues of the approach relative to parametric approaches (p. 584). First, it requires no a priori restrictions on substitution possibilities among inputs (e.g., via parametric restrictions). Second, the method allows joint estimation of the production technology, technical change, and the effects of research on technical progress using very disaggregate inputs. Third, the approach allows considerable flexibility in the investigation of the length and shape of the lag distribution between research and productivity. Fourth, the method permits an investigation of the separate effects of private research and public research on technical progress. Finally, the method is empirically tractable, in that it requires only a standard linear programming algorithm. They illustrate these points with an application to U.S. agriculture.

While the nonparametric approach is very attractive in principle, for the reasons outlined by Chavas and Cox (1992), there remain some questions that must be answered in practice before we can countenance a wholesale abandonment of parametric approaches. In the context of applications of nonparametric approaches to consumer demand, there has been concern about the properties of the nonparametric tests. The limited Monte Carlo work that has been done suggests that under commonly observed conditions, it can be difficult to obtain definitive results that can be taken with any confidence.[30] Presumably, there is potential for similar questions to arise in the applications to production, so we remain to some extent agnostic on the question of how generally the nonparametric approaches are applicable until further results have been obtained that establish the properties of the measures.

In addition, some recent work by Chalfant and Zhang (1994) has shown that the Chavas and Cox methodology (as developed and employed by Chavas and Cox 1988, 1992, and by Cox and Chavas 1990) is seriously flawed: the measures of technical-change bias are not invariant to the scaling (i.e., the choices of units) for prices and quantities.[31] Chalfant and Zhang (1994, p. 13)

tion to Australian broadacre agriculture.

30. Alston and Chalfant (1992) have reviewed the literature and provide a useful heuristic discussion of the application of tests for consistency of consumption data sets with revealed preference axioms. They show how to apply the equivalent of Chavas and Cox's (1988, 1992) approach to consumption data, following Sakong and Hayes (1993) to solve for the set of minimum "taste changes" necessary to rationalize the data. An important aspect of this work was the issue, raised by various writers, of the "power" of nonparametric tests and the alternative approaches that might be used to impose nonsample information (such as restrictions on elasticities or changes in elasticities from observation to observation) as restrictions on the analysis in order to increase power. While this work was conducted in relation to consumer data, the arguments are perfectly symmetrical and apply with equal force to the production side.

31. Chalfant and Zhang also point out that the same criticism applies to application of analogous procedures to measuring the size of shifts in consumer demands (e.g., by Alston and Chalfant 1992

propose that "Nonparametric methods that use the Chavas and Cox method of minimizing a (weighted) sum of taste change or technical change parameters require weights attached to these adjustments to the data whose scale varies inversely with the units of quantities . . . . Otherwise, the estimated adjustments are not invariant to scaling." In other words, in measuring technical-change biases, a price vector must be used to weight the adjustments to the input-quantity data required to restore consistency with WAPM or WACM in order for the results to be invariant with units. A disappointing aspect is that a particular price vector (e.g., corresponding to a particular observation in the sample, say, for a particular year's data) must be chosen for the analysis to weight the quantity adjustments for every observation of quantities. The results may depend on the choice of the set of relative prices to be used, and the choice is essentially arbitrary. Further work must be done to establish ways to achieve invariance that are less arbitrary. However, there can be no doubt that potentially, the nonparametric methods have much to offer, as a complement to a parametric analysis at a minimum, and there are grounds for being optimistic about further developments in this relatively new set of techniques.[32]

3.1.3   Index-Number Approaches

A working knowledge of index-number theory and practice is indispensible for econometric attempts to measure production technologies and the effects of research on those technical structures. Modern index-number procedures enable consistent and economically meaningful measures of input and output aggregates to be formed. These aggregate price and quantity measures can then be used to summarize and describe production-related data, as well as estimating aggregate production, cost, and profit functions.

Index-number procedures also enable partial and total factor-productivity measures that provide summary indications of the nature of growth in agricultural output or agricultural productivity to be constructed. These productivity measures can then be used in conjunction with econometric approaches to determine (and subsequently value) the output-enhancing effects of research, extension, and other "unconventional" inputs.

Indexes

Index numbers are involved in virtually all quantitative economics. In the index-number approach to productivity measurement, this involvement is

following Sakong and Hayes 1993).

32.   For a recent application of nonparametric techniques to an assessment of international developments in productivity and technical change, see Färe et al. (1994).

explicitly obvious, whereas in other approaches to measure the effects of technical change, the importance of the role of index numbers and index-number theory is not so apparent. Almost always, however, we must use measures of prices and quantities of inputs or outputs that have been aggregated over people, places, or time and across different qualities. The aggregated quantities (and prices) are indexes that may or may not suffer from *index-number problems* — in which quantity changes due to relative price changes are properly distinguished from other types of quantity changes. Often the only data that are available are preaggregated, and we might not know whether the aggregation was done in a way that is consistent with economic theory or, instead, in a way that leads to an over- or understatement of the actual changes in quantity (or prices) over time. Thus, an index-number problem may be inherent in the data. An index-number problem could also be generated by the analyst in making choices about how to aggregate data. In this section, we lay out the theory of index numbers that is relevant for constructing the aggregated measures of inputs or outputs that are typically used in empirical work. This theory also provides the foundation for the methods for measuring total factor productivity, discussed below.

Aggregating inputs and outputs: An economic approach to constructing index numbers is to choose a method for weighting the quantities that make up the aggregate being indexed — one that is consistent with economic theory and accommodates the optimizing responses of economic agents.[33] Inappropriate treatment of the optimizing responses leads to inappropriate weightings and over- or understatement of the aggregate quantity change. To illustrate this possibility, consider panel a in figure 3.2 where Q represents a particular quantity of output with a given state of technology, $\tau = 0$. When the price of X_2 *relative* to the price of X_1 is given by W_0, cost-minimizing producers will use the combination of inputs X_{10} and X_{20} at a point a to produce output Q. If the price of X_2 falls relative to X_1 (i.e., from W_0 to W_1), producers will substitute X_2 for X_1 to minimize the costs of producing the same output, Q, at point b (using input amounts X_{11} and X_{21}). Now assume that an input aggregate $X = g(X_1, X_2)$ is formed using a simple linear aggregation of the two inputs weighted by the respective factor prices. If the

---

33. By contrast, there is an *axiomatic* approach to index numbers (and implicitly, TFP measurement) that stems from the work of Fisher (1922) and more recently Eichorn (1976) and Eichorn and Voeller (1976), and reviewed by Diewert (1988a and b). The idea is to "test" the suitability of an index against a number of properties or conditions (e.g., characteristicity, determination, positivity, and various homogeneity and monotonicity properties) that are considered desirable for an index number. These (often statistical or empirical) properties need not bear any relationship to an economic theory of measurement or aggregation. And because no one index number satisfies all known properties, the choice of indexing procedure is based largely on the discretion of the analyst.

Figure 3.2:   *Technical change and input substitution effects*

(a) Relative input price change; no technical change

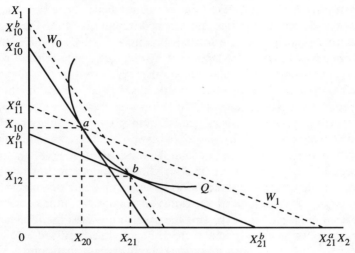

(b) Relative input price change; with technical change

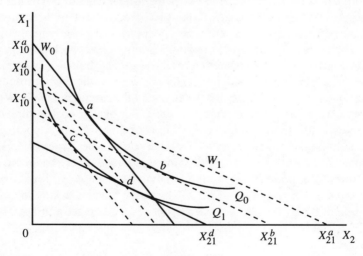

relative factor prices indicated by the slope of W_0 are used as weights, the input aggregate at point a would be valued lower (i.e., would cost less) than the point b aggregate (notice $X_{10}^a < X_{10}^b$). Consequently, an index of productivity that expresses output per unit of aggregate input would be greater if measured at point a than at b.

In a similar way, a linear aggregator that used relative input prices given by the slope of W_1 would result in the input aggregate measured at a being valued higher (i.e., more expensive) than if measured at b (notice $X_{11}^a > X_{11}^b$ and, equivalently, $X_{21}^a > X_{21}^b$). Thus, the resulting productivity index measured at a would be greater than that measured at b. In these instances, *measured* productivity has changed in the move from point a to point b, even though there has been no change in the state of technology as reflected in the shape and position of the isoquant Q.

If there is a simultaneous shift in relative prices from W_0 to W_1 and a (neutral) productivity improvement so that the same amount of output could be produced with fewer measured inputs, there is an even more subtle problem wherein the effects of technical change and factor substitution can get confounded. In panel b of figure 3.2, the shift of the isoquant from Q_0 to Q_1 (representing the same quantity of output being produced with two states of technology, i.e., $\tau = 0$ and 1, respectively) and the relative price change would lead to a change in input combination from a to d. Alternative measures of cost savings could be made with either price vector if we ever observed producers responding to the new technology at old factor prices (shifting from a to c) or using the old technology with new factor prices (shifting from b to d). The technological change measured at the original prices would be a reduction in cost from X_{10}^a to X_{10}^c. Since c is not an observed input cost, measuring the change when the input combination shifts from a to d using original prices implies smaller cost savings (a reduction from X_{10}^a to X_{10}^d). The cost savings are *understated* because the substitution effect is not factored out.

The change in technology measured using new prices (shifting from b to d) would be a cost saving given by the reduction from X_{21}^b to X_{21}^d. Since b is not observed, measuring the change from a to d using new prices indicates a reduction in costs in moving from X_{21}^a to X_{21}^d that *overstates* the cost saving. The longer the time period over which a single set of fixed price weights is used to calculate aggregates, the more likely we are to observe the effects of changes in relative prices that are confounded with changes in technology. We can understate or overstate a drop in inputs (with a corresponding upward or downward bias in a productivity index) depending on the time period over which prices are held fixed in the calculations.

Aggregation problems arise with respect to outputs that in many practical situations, are analogous to input-aggregation problem. In numerous cases, Q represents an output aggregate such as "grain crops," "livestock products," or quite commonly, "total agricultural output." The measure is formed over a set of outputs, so a *real* output aggregate is required. Again, an index that does not confuse movements along an unchanging production possibilities frontier (PPF) due to shifts in relative output prices with shifts in the PPF is desirable.

Panel a in figure 3.3 illustrates the problem of aggregating across multiple outputs. If an output aggregate $Q = h(Q_1, Q_2)$ were formed using a linear aggregation of the two outputs weighted by their relative prices given by the slope of P_0, the output aggregate at point a (producing output amounts Q_{10} and Q_{20}) would be greater than the point b aggregate (notice $Q_{10}^a > Q_{10}^b$). Conversely, using the relative output prices P_1 would result in a lower-valued

Figure 3.3:   *Technical change and output substitution effects*

(a) Relative output price change; no technical change

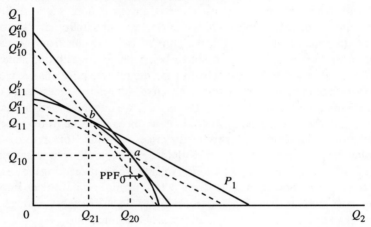

(b) Relative output price change; with technical change

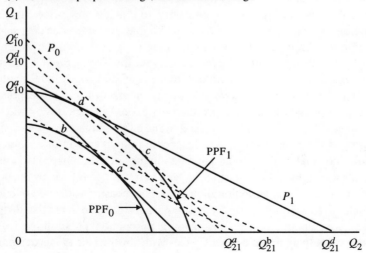

output aggregate at point a compared with point b (notice $Q_{11}^a < Q_{11}^b$). Using only one set of prices over a long period of time (whether they are P_0 or P_1) is once again likely to indicate a shift in the PPF when in fact there has been none.

When improved technology shifts the frontier (from PPF_0 to PPF_1, in panel b of figure 3.3), allowing increased quantities of either output to be produced with the same bundle of inputs, linear output aggregates will confound the effects of substitution and technical change if relative prices also change. If the economy moves from a to d because of technological change and a simultaneous increase in the relative price of good 1, movements from a to c or b to d (if observed) could be evaluated with either set of prices and give information on technical change alone. But since neither b nor c would be observed, we must rely on observed output bundles a and d. If evaluated at original prices, P_0, the technological change is *understated* ($Q_{10}^d - Q_{10}^a < Q_{10}^c - Q_{10}^a$). If the change in output is evaluated using new prices, P_1, the technological change is *overstated* ($Q_{21}^d - Q_{21}^a > Q_{21}^d - Q_{21}^b$).

Divisia indexing procedures: The method commonly used to minimize the impact of relative price changes when forming aggregate quantity indexes is to use a *Divisia* indexing procedure. As Richter (1966) and Hulten (1973) show, the Divisia index is desirable because of its invariance property; if nothing real has changed (e.g., the only input quantity changes involve movements around an unchanged isoquant) the index itself is unchanged.[34] The formula for an index of aggregate inputs is

$$XI_t^D = XI_b^D \exp \int_b^t \frac{W_s' \Delta X_s}{W_s' X_s} \, ds \qquad (3.13)$$

where XI_b^D is the index value of the base period, b, XI_t^D is the index value in period t, X_s is a vector of input quantities, W_s is a vector of input prices, and ΔX denotes changes in inputs.

If the economy of interest — measured at either the sector, industry, or even, farm level — is moving along an unchanged transformation or production surface, the sum of changes in inputs, ΔX, weighted by current factor prices, W, will be approximately zero; the index will be unchanged. If the economy's transformation surface is shifting, current price-weighted changes will be different from zero, leading to changes in the index value. This invariance property is dependent upon a maintained assumption of optimizing agents.

34. The discussion here deals with constructing indexes of quantity aggregates. An exactly analogous situation pertains to the construction of indexes of price aggregates in which quantities are used as weights. If appropriate aggregation procedures are used, the resulting price index measures the *nominal* growth of aggregate prices over time. But like its quantity counterpart, the index can also be considered "real" in the sense that it abstracts from changes in the mix of quantities in the price aggregate being measured.

Unfortunately, the calculation of a chained index such as the Divisia index requires continuous measurement of input prices and quantities. To facilitate calculations in a way that minimizes measurement error, a discrete approximation can be used to link quantities and prices across adjacent years. In any discrete approximation, some information is lost. The advantage of using a chained index involves the notion that recent quantity changes are weighted by the most recently observed prices. Intuitively, these indexes are attempting to evaluate current behavior at current prices. In proceeding from the base period to some distant period t, the small steps are chained together to minimize the measurement error that is possible when only base-period prices and period t prices are used to evaluate real changes in input quantity.

Many discrete approximations to the Divisia index are possible. Richter (1966) proposes what others have called a *Laspeyres* approximation:

$$XI_t^{DL} = XI_{t-1}^{DL} \left[1 + \frac{W'_{t-1}(X_t - X_{t-1})}{W'_{t-1} X_{t-1}} \right] = XI_{t-1}^{DL} \frac{W'_{t-1} X_t}{W'_{t-1} X_{t-1}} \tag{3.14}$$

In a similar way, we could define a *Paasche* approximation:

$$XI_t^{DP} = XI_{t-1}^{DP} \left[1 + \frac{W'_t(X_t - X_{t-1})}{W'_t X_{t-1}} \right] = XI_{t-1}^{DP} \frac{W'_t X_t}{W'_t X_{t-1}} \tag{3.15}$$

or a *Fisher ideal* approximation:

$$XI_t^{DF} = XI_{t-1}^{DF} \left(\frac{W'_{t-1} X_t}{W'_{t-1} X_{t-1}} \right)^{\frac{1}{2}} \left(\frac{W'_t X_t}{W'_t X_{t-1}} \right)^{\frac{1}{2}} \tag{3.16}$$

The *Törnqvist* (1936) or *Törnqvist-Theil* discrete approximation of the continuous version of the index given by 3.13 uses both current and lagged cost shares in weighting changes in input quantity, yielding

$$XI_t^{DT} = XI_{t-1}^{DT} \prod_{i=1}^{m} \left(\frac{X_{i,t}}{X_{i,t-1}} \right)^{\bar{S}_{i,t}} \text{ where } \bar{S}_{i,t} = \tfrac{1}{2}(S_{i,t} + S_{i,t-1}) \tag{3.17a}$$

and the input cost share for factor i in period t is given by

$$S_{i,t} = X_{i,t} W_{i,t} / \left(\sum_{i=1}^{m} X_{i,t} W_{i,t} \right) \tag{3.17b}$$

Growth rates in the input aggregate using the same formulation are calculated using cost-weighted sums of changes in input quantities:

$$\ln(XI_t^{DT}/XI_{t-1}^{DT}) = \sum_{i=1}^{m} \tfrac{1}{2}(S_{i,t} + S_{i,t-1}) \ln(X_{i,t}/X_{i,t-1}) \tag{3.18}$$

where $\ln(XI_t^{DT}/XI_{t-1}^{DT})$ is the rate of change in the input Divisia index from period $t-1$ to t.[35] In practice, a series is formed by setting $XI_b^{DT} = 1.0$ for any arbitrarily chosen base year b and accumulating the measure forward and, if necessary, backward in time according to equation 3.17.[36] Alternatively, the index can be constructed by compounding the growth rates calculated using 3.18 (forward and backward) from the base period.

As with input indexes, a Divisia aggregation procedure is used to minimize the impact of relative changes in output prices when real output aggregates are formed. The Törnqvist-Theil output index, QI_t^{DT}, is

$$QI_t^{DT} = QI_{t-1}^{DT} \prod_{j=1}^{n} \left(\frac{Q_{j,t}}{Q_{j,t-1}} \right)^{\bar{s}_{j,t}} \quad \text{where } \bar{s}_{j,t} = \tfrac{1}{2}(s_{j,t} + s_{j,t-1}) \tag{3.19a}$$

where the weight for commodity j in period t is its output revenue share:

$$s_{j,t} = Q_{j,t} P_{j,t} / \left(\sum_{j=1}^{n} Q_{j,t} P_{j,t} \right) \tag{3.19b}$$

Growth rates in the index are the sum of moving-average-share-weighted relative changes in the individual output quantitites:

$$\ln(QI_t^{DT}/QI_{t-1}^{DT}) = \sum_{j=1}^{n} \tfrac{1}{2}(s_{j,t} + s_{j,t-1}) \ln(Q_{j,t}/Q_{j,t-1}) \tag{3.20}$$

These are the output-index counterparts to the aggregate input indexes defined by equations 3.17 and 3.18. Forming the index follows the equivalent procedure described in the input aggregation discussion.

The advantage offered by any of these approximate Divisia indexes is that any substantial drift in relative prices over time is accommodated by rolling weights. In addition, theoretical work on superlative index numbers by Diewert (1976) and Lau (1979) has established that the approximate Divisia indexes are exact for specific aggregator functions. If vectors of inputs are appropriately aggregated with linear functions, the Laspeyres and Paasche

35. This rate-of-change form is the most common representation of the index. To recover the index in level form (i.e., equation 3.17), simply take the antilog of 3.18 and multiply both sides by XI_{t-1}.

36. Instead of using equation 3.18, some analysts (e.g., Romano 1987) have used

$$\ln(XI_{t+j}/XI_b) = \sum_{i=1}^{m} \tfrac{1}{2}(S_{i,t+j} + S_{i,b}) \ln(X_{i,t+j}/X_{i,b}) \text{ for all } j = 1, \ldots, T$$

Rather than using quantities and factor shares from *adjacent years*, in this (incorrect) formulation, base period quantities and cost shares are used throughout.

approximations of the Divisia offer exact measures of real quantity changes. The Fisher approximation is exact for quadratic aggregator functions. The Törnqvist Divisia index is exact for the more general class of translog aggregator functions.

If disaggregated data are difficult to obtain, we may be forced to use fixed-weight indexes, such as a Laspeyres or a Paasche index, and accept any resulting biases. However, the same amount of information is required to construct the alternative chained indexes, so what basis is there for deciding which of the Divisia approximations to use? The aggregator functions for which the various indexes are exact provide some guidance. For instance, if the translog function is deemed to be the appropriate aggregator, it implicitly takes every input type to be in some sense essential to the aggregate since the translog function is undefined when any one of the possible inputs is zero. In aggregating national accounts, the categories are typically so broadly defined that the requirement for positive quantities is not a problem. If, however, the aggregate is being formed over finely disaggregated inputs, corner solutions in which some inputs or outputs are not used or produced over part of the sample are quite likely. A linear or quadratic aggregator function, which implicitly allows for partial or complete specialization, is defined as long as at least one input is used and thus may be more appropriate than the translog in applications where some quantities of inputs (or outputs, when an output aggregate is being formed) take values of zero for some observations.

Another practical consideration is the degree to which the approximation method provides some smoothing of price weights. When commodities whose prices vary widely from period to period but whose quantity responses may lag one or more periods are aggregated, there may be less economic sense to employing weighting schemes that make use of only one period's prices. The property of *characteristicity* (Drechsler 1973) would imply using the price weights most specific to the economic activity being measured. In this respect, the Törnqvist approximation may be more appropriate than the Laspeyres for aggregating quantities when there is reason to think that producers are reacting to local prices but cannot do so instantaneously. The Törnqvist approximation implicitly smooths prices by averaging current and previous value shares when each value share is calculated using contemporaneous prices and quantities.

Direct versus implicit indexes: The discussion so far describes how to calculate direct quantity and price indexes, which are equally feasible if suitably disaggregated data are available. But, in practice, data constraints sometimes require the calculation of implicit indexes instead. Implicit indexes are consistent if the direct index satisfies Fisher's weak-factor-reversal property, wherein

$$XI_t \cdot WI_t = \frac{W_t'X_t}{W_{t-1}'X_{t-1}}$$

(3.21a)

where XI_t and WI_t are, for example, indexes of the input quantity and input price in period t, and the right-hand side of equation 3.21a represents the ratio of the current to previous period's total cost of production. Given these expenditure ratios and, say, a quantity index, the corresponding price index can be derived, implicitly, by rearranging 3.21a so that

$$WI_t = \frac{W_t'X_t}{W_{t-1}'X_{t-1}} \cdot \frac{1}{XI_t}$$

(3.21b)

Unfortunately, an implicit Törnqvist-Theil index does not conform exactly to the corresponding direct index because the translog aggregator function, for which a Törnqvist-Theil index is exact in the sense of Diewert (1976), is not self-dual. But, provided the period-to-period variation in relative prices is not "too great," the differences between a direct index and its implicit counterpart are "relatively small," i.e., equation 3.21b only holds approximately in the case of a Törnqvist-Theil index, but the approximation may be reasonably close (Allen and Diewert 1981).

Productivity Measurement

Productivity indexes are commonly constructed measures of the relationship between inputs and outputs. The most widely used productivity measure expresses output per unit of a particular input such as land or labor. These *partial factor productivities* (PFPs) are generally defined as

$$PFP_i = \frac{Q}{X_i} \qquad i = 1, \ldots, m$$

(3.22)

where Q represents output and X_i represents input i. A more careful representation is

$$PFP_i = \frac{Q^*}{X_i^*} \equiv \frac{QI}{XI_i} \qquad i = 1, \ldots, m$$

(3.23)

where Q^* represents *aggregate* output, X_i^* represents an *aggregate* of input X_i, and QI and XI_i are the corresponding indexes of aggregate output and input X_i, respectively. Equation 3.23 reflects the fact that PFP indexes are usually formed using an output aggregate such as total agricultural output (which includes different crop, livestock, and even, forestry, and fisheries output), or wheat output (which includes different grades or qualities of wheat).

More subtly, but perhaps just as significantly, the denominator in a PFP index often groups together different classes or qualities of the input X_i. Within such a factor grouping, there are aggregation problems arising from heterogeneity that are analogous to the problems of aggregating dissimilar factors such as land, labor, and capital. For example, land inputs may include a mix of different land types such as pastureland and irrigated and rainfed cropland, while the labor input may reflect hours in agriculture that are a combination of hired labor and heterogeneous operator labor of varying ages, accumulated skills, and education. In assessing measured changes in PFP, it would be useful to know whether the total effective labor input in agriculture is increasing over time because more hours of the same type of labor are being employed or because the composition of the workforce has changed to include relatively more highly skilled labor. The finer the classification scheme is for outputs and inputs, the less likely it is to confuse changes in quantity with changes in quality and, consequently, misinterpret measured changes in PFP indexes.

Even if properly constructed, PFPs pose particular problems for distinguishing (research-induced) technical changes from (price-induced) substitution effects. PFPs are affected not only by advances in the state of technology (as indexed, for example, by τ in equation 3.10) but also by changes in the effective quantities of other inputs used in production. Additional fertilizer will generally raise yields and, consequently, land productivity, while additional physical capital — be it in the form of an improved hand-held sickle or a bigger combine harvester — can raise labor productivity. A more general concept of productivity is required to distinguish between changes in output due to technical changes and those arising from changes in the mix of inputs due to shifts in their factor prices.

A measure of *total factor productivity* (TFP) can be defined as

$$TFP = \frac{Q}{X} \tag{3.24}$$

where *TFP* measures (aggregate) output Q, produced per unit of an *input aggregate*, X. From equation 3.24 it follows directly that the observed proportionate rate of growth of total factor productivity, tfp_t, is simply equal to the rate of growth of measured output, q_t, minus the rate of growth of measured inputs, x_t:

$$tfp_t = q_t - x_t \tag{3.25}$$

where

$$tfp_t = \frac{\mathrm{d}TFP_t}{\mathrm{d}t}\frac{1}{TFP_t}, \; q_t = \frac{\mathrm{d}Q_t}{\mathrm{d}t}\frac{1}{Q_t}, \text{ and } x_t = \frac{\mathrm{d}X_t}{\mathrm{d}t}\frac{1}{X_t}$$

In principle, output and input aggregates could be formed using the Divisia indexing procedure defined by equation 3.13, and from equation 3.25, it would be possible to calculate *tfp* without explicitly identifying the functional form of the underlying production relationship. The only assumptions interposing between the data and the *tfp* measures are those that concern optimizing behavior, whereby technically efficient producers substitute around isoquants and production-possibility frontiers in response to changes in relative prices of inputs and outputs. If the underlying technology is input-output separable, to the extent that the output and input aggregates, Q_t and X_t, can be formed separately, then the TFP measure follows directly.

For relatively small changes in a variable Z_t, $\mathrm{d}Z_t/Z_t = \mathrm{d}\ln Z_t \approx \ln Z_t - \ln Z_{t-1}$ (i.e., proportionate rates of change, $\mathrm{d}Z_t/Z_t$, are approximately equal to logarithmic differences, $\ln Z_t - \ln Z_{t-1}$), so a discrete approximation for equation 3.25 is

$$tfp_t \approx \ln\left(TFP_t/TFP_{t-1}\right) = \ln\left(QI_t^{DT}/QI_{t-1}^{DT}\right) - \ln\left(XI_t^{DT}/XI_{t-1}^{DT}\right) \qquad (3.26)$$

Thus, the rate of change in TFP is obtained simply by taking the difference between the growth rate of the Törnqvist-Theil indexes of aggregate output and input quantities. Work by Diewert (1976), extended for the discrete-variable case by Denny and Fuss (1983), showed that the use of the discrete Törnqvist-Theil approximation to the continuous Divisia index carries with it an implicit assumption that the underlying technology can be represented by a translog model. To the extent that the translog represents a second-order, local approximation to an arbitrary functional form, the Törnqvist-Theil index may be regarded as imposing fewer restrictions between the data and the *tfp* measure than would the Laspeyres, Paasche, or Fisher ideal index.[37]

But as Craig, Pardey and Deininger (1993) point out, agreement on the proper index formula does not resolve all measurement issues. Rather than proceeding mechanically in applying the index, important choices must be made about how many distinct inputs and outputs will be used in its construction. A fundamental insight from the literature on productivity measurement is that, regardless of the index formula used, a high level of disaggregation is required to avoid aggregation bias. Star (1974) showed that one is safe in using preaggregated inputs (e.g., taking all labor to be a single class of input) only if all inputs in the class are growing at the same rate or are perfect substitutes for

---

37. The approximation potential of the translog and other locally flexible forms has been called into question in a number of studies. For example, see Chalfant (1983, 1984) and Thompson (1988) (and the references therein for more general evidence) for a discussion of the relevant issues and an application to U.S. agriculture.

one another. If rates of change in higher-priced inputs exceed rates of change in lower-priced inputs, the rate of growth of the group will be biased downward in any index that fails to treat the inputs as separate components.

Disaggregation by itself makes it more likely that inputs and outputs will be measured in units whose quality is constant over adjacent time periods. The finer the distinction among inputs, the more confidence we have that the Xs employed in the index equations 3.23 and 3.24 are truly comparable from year to year. The same holds true for the commodity quantities, i.e., the Qs, used to form a productivity index.

Sources of Measured Productivity Growth[38]

Measuring TFP growth and identifying the sources of this growth are two distinct but directly related activities. What are the potential sources of measured productivity growth? One possible source is changes in quality of inputs or outputs that have not been accounted for properly in the analysis. Another source is mismeasurement of input or output quantities due to index-number or data problems, for reasons other than unmeasured quality change.[39] A third is improved technology as a result of either private- or public-sector R&D (and extension) or technology spill-ins.

Input quality: Improvements in input quality could include improved machinery (a "tractor" today is not the same as a "tractor" 30 years ago), improvements in quality of labor with a more educated work force, and improvements in land quality (perhaps through addition of capital or increased water rights), for example. Some of these improvements in input quality result from private-sector agricultural research on agricultural machinery, chemicals, and for many crops, seeds.

Output quality: Similar problems could arise in measuring the quantity of output, which is an aggregate of different types of outputs (as the input index is an aggregate of the different types of inputs). If the quality of, say, horticultural products had risen over time, and the measure of the quantity of horticultural products had not been adjusted accordingly, we would be *understating* the real growth in horticultural output, some of which was in

38. Reflecting on the sources of productivity growth, Schultz (1956, p. 758) wrote that "The analytical task, as I see it, is to re-establish a strong and satisfactory linkage between input and output over time. In our efforts to do this, we would do well to place before us and keep in mind the characteristics of an *ideal input-output formula* for this purpose. It would be one where *outputs over inputs* . . . stayed at or close to one. The closer we come to a one-to-one relationship in our formulation, the more complete would be our (economic) explanation." These and related issues were further discussed by Griliches (1963b).

39. Of course to the extent that research-induced quality changes are embodied in outputs and conventional inputs and that these quality changes are measured properly, they should already be captured in the productivity index.

the form of quality improvement. If we measured output without adjusting for quality change, productivity growth would be understated if quality had improved; it would be overstated if quality had declined.

Other measurement problems: Even when Divisia indexes are used in conjunction with finely disaggregated input and output data, so that index number problems are minimized, there might be some remaining problems of measurement. Perhaps the most likely one is that there is typically no explicit allowance for the reduction in the stock of environmental and natural resources associated with agricultural production in terms of land degradation, depletion of soil fertility, chemical pollution of air and groundwater, build-up of resistant pests and diseases with loss of natural predator populations, and so on. Environmental resources can be thought of as an unmeasured input into agricultural production, and part of the additional output may be attributable to consumption of the stock of natural resources.[40]

Most studies of the benefits and costs of agricultural research do not take this into account. One approach would be to include some natural resource accounting in the analysis, treating the resource base as one of the inputs in agriculture, but suitable data are not usually available for that.[41] A second approach that could be useful in the context being considered here would be to adjust the measures of research benefits to reflect a disparity between the private and social costs of production. The latter approach is more feasible, although no one has done it yet. To be done meaningfully, it would require information similar to that used in the direct approach, although data for only for a few recent years may be sufficient.

New technology: Putting aside measurement problems, the growth in measured total factor productivity that is attributable to changes in technology is taken to represent changes in output for given inputs. In turn, therefore, this productivity growth can be attributed to past expenditures on research and extension by public-sector agencies, private research, and the spill-in of technology from elsewhere.

Rates of Technical Change

Production-function approaches: The most straightforward approach to formally linking notions of technical change with measured rates of productivity growth is to assume that an index of the state of technology, τ, can be

---

40.   A *flow* of services from the stock of natural resources is always used in production but the concern here is with changes in the stock itself that will imply a reduction in future service flows.

41.   For attempts to incorporate the natural-resource-degradation and environmental-externality effects of agricultural production directly into productivity indexes, see Archibald (1988), Oskam (1991), Ehui and Spencer (1993), Antle and McGuckin (1993), and Alston, Anderson and Pardey (1994).

incorporated directly in a production function such that[42]

$$Q_t = f(X_t, \tau_t) \tag{3.27}$$

Hence, technological progress (i.e., where $d\tau/dt > 0$) is perceived as an upward shift of the production function, $f(.)$, or, equivalently, as a downward shift of the isoquant map, as depicted in the shift of an isoquant for given output from Q_0 to Q_1 in figure 3.2b. Rates of change in output over time can be partitioned into components due to changes in measured input use and to those due to changes in the state of technology. By differentiating Q_t with respect to time and dividing throughout by Q_t (or, equivalently, taking logarithms and differentiating $\ln Q_t$ with respect to time), we get

$$\frac{d\ln Q_t}{dt} = \frac{\partial \ln Q_t}{\partial \ln \tau_t} \frac{d\ln \tau_t}{dt} + \sum_{i=1}^{m} \varepsilon_{Q,i} \frac{d\ln X_{i,t}}{dt} \tag{3.28}$$

where $\varepsilon_{Q,i} = d\ln Q_t/d\ln X_{i,t}$ is the elasticity of output with respect to the quantity of the ith input. If competitive equilibrium is assumed, so that output price equals marginal cost and factors are paid the values of their marginal products, then equation 3.28 may be rewritten, equivalently, as[43]

$$\frac{d\ln Q_t}{dt} = \frac{\partial \ln Q_t}{\partial \ln \tau_t} \frac{d\ln \tau_t}{dt} + \varepsilon_{Q,C} \sum_{i=1}^{m} S_{i,t} \frac{d\ln X_{i,t}}{dt} \tag{3.29}$$

where $S_{i,t} = X_{i,t} W_{i,t}/\sum_i X_{i,t} W_{i,t}$ is the ith factor's share of total cost in time t and $\varepsilon_{Q,C} = (d\ln C_t/d\ln Q_t)^{-1}$ is the inverse of the elasticity of cost with respect to output, which can be used to define returns to scale. Notice that under constant returns to scale, where $\varepsilon_{Q,C} = 1.0$, equivalence between equations 3.28 and 3.29 requires the ith factor share to be equal to the ith factor's output elasticity, i.e., $\varepsilon_{Q,i} = S_{i,t}$. Using more compact notation, we can transform equation 3.29 to obtain a measure, g_t, of the *primal rate of technological change*, i.e.,

$$g_t = q_t - \varepsilon_{Q,C} x_t \tag{3.30a}$$

where

---

42.   Solow (1957, p. 312) used t rather than τ_t in his specification of 3.27, noting that "the variable t for time appears . . . to allow for technical change. It will be seen that I am using the phrase 'technical change' as a shorthand expression for *any kind of shift* in the production function. Thus, slowdowns, speedups, improvements in the education of the labor force, and all sorts of things will appear as 'technical change.'"

43.   To obtain this, we use the results where, under competition, each factor is paid the value of its marginal product (so that $\partial f(X)/\partial X_i = W_i/P$) and price equals marginal cost ($P = \partial C/\partial Q$). Combining these results, and manipulating the expression yields $\partial f(X)/\partial X_i = W_i/P = W_i/(\partial C/\partial Q) = W_i(\partial Q/\partial C) = W_i(Q/C)(d\ln Q/d\ln C) = W_i(Q/C)\varepsilon_{Q,C}$. We can also define $d\ln f(X) = \sum_i f(.)^{-1} [\partial f(X)/\partial X_i] dX_i$. Substituting the first result into this expression, simplifying, and consolidating terms yields $d\ln f(X) = \sum_i (W_i X_i/C)\varepsilon_{Q,C} d\ln(X_i)$.

$$g_t = \left(\frac{\partial \ln Q_t}{\partial \ln \tau_t} \frac{d \ln \tau_t}{dt} \right), \quad q_t = \frac{d \ln Q_t}{dt} \approx \Sigma_j s_{j,t} \frac{d \ln Q_{j,t}}{dt}$$

and   (3.30b)

$$x_t = \frac{d \ln X_t}{dt} \approx \Sigma_i S_{i,t} \frac{d \ln X_{i,t}}{dt}$$

and q_t and x_t are the Divisia indexes of growth in output and input, respectively.[44] In words, equation 3.30a expresses the primal rate of technological change as the rate of change of output, minus a scale-adjusted index of the rate of change in input. Hence, under the assumption of constant returns to scale, input-output separability, efficient and optimizing producers, and disembodied technical change of the extended Hicks-neutral type, the rate of change in TFP given by equation 3.25 also measures the rate of technological change or shift of the production function.

Cost-function approaches: It is also possible to use the cost or profit function to derive a *dual rate of technological change* that is a counterpart to the primal rate. Assuming that technically efficient producers act to minimize production costs at any given level of output, a minimum cost function can be written as

$$C_t = c(Q_t, \ W_t, \ \tau_t)$$ (3.31)

where c(.) is the cost function that defines C_t as the minimum cost of producing any output of Q_t, given a vector of input prices $W_t = (W_{1,t}, \ldots, W_{m,t})$ and the state of technology indexed by τ_t. Differentiating equation 3.31 with respect to time and dividing throughout by C_t (or, equivalently, differentiating $\ln C_t$ with respect to time) yields

$$\frac{d \ln C_t}{dt} = \frac{\partial \ln C_t}{\partial \ln Q_t} \frac{d \ln Q_t}{dt} + \sum_{i=1}^{m} \frac{\partial \ln C_t}{\partial \ln W_{i,t}} \frac{d \ln W_{i,t}}{dt} + \frac{\partial \ln C_t}{\partial \ln \tau_t} \frac{d \ln \tau_t}{dt}$$ (3.32)

By Shephard's lemma, the optimal (cost-minimizing) factor-demand equations are given by the derivatives of the cost function with respect to the factor prices: $X_{i,t} = \partial C_t / \partial W_{i,t} = \partial c(Q_t, W_t, \tau_t) / \partial W_{i,t}$. An equivalent representation is that factor cost-share equations are given by $S_{i,t} = \partial \ln C_t / \partial \ln W_{i,t} = (W_{i,t}/C_t)\partial c(Q_t, W_t, \tau_t)/\partial W_{i,t}$. Thus, equation 3.32 may be rewritten as

$$- \frac{\partial \ln C_t}{\partial \ln \tau_t} \frac{d \ln \tau_t}{dt} = \frac{\partial \ln C_t}{\partial \ln Q_t} \frac{d \ln Q_t}{dt} + \sum_{i=1}^{m} S_{i,t} \frac{d \ln W_{i,t}}{dt} - \frac{d \ln C_t}{dt}$$ (3.33)

Using more compact notation, we can transform equation 3.33 to obtain

44. Most analysts use time, t, as the technology index, implicitly assuming that $d \ln \tau_t / dt = 1.0$.

$$h_t = \varepsilon_{C,Q} \, q_t + w_t - c_t \qquad (3.34a)$$

where

$$h_t = \left(-\frac{\partial \ln C_t}{\partial \ln \tau_t} \frac{d \ln \tau_t}{dt} \right), \; q_t = \frac{d \ln Q_t}{dt}, \; c_t = \frac{d \ln C_t}{dt}$$

and $\qquad (3.34b)$

$$w_t = \frac{d \ln W_t}{dt} \approx \Sigma_i \, S_{i,t} \frac{d \ln W_{i,t}}{dt}$$

Thus, the dual rate of technological change, h_t, may be computed as a scale effect (actually the rate of growth of output over time, q_t, weighted by the elasticity of cost with respect to output, $\varepsilon_{C,Q} = \partial \ln C_t / \partial \ln Q_t$) plus a Divisia index of the rate of growth of factor prices, w_t, minus the rate of growth of total costs, c_t.

To establish the relationship between the dual and primal rates of technological change, the first step is to logarithmically differentiate total cost ($C_t = W_t' X_t$) with respect to time so that

$$\frac{d \ln C_t}{dt} = \overset{m}{\underset{i=1}{\Sigma}} S_{i,t} \frac{d \ln W_{i,t}}{dt} + \overset{m}{\underset{i=1}{\Sigma}} S_{i,t} \frac{d \ln X_{i,t}}{dt} \qquad (3.35)$$

Combining equations 3.30 and 3.34 allows us to respecify 3.35 as

$$h_t = -\frac{\partial \ln c(.)}{\partial \ln \tau_t} \frac{d \ln \tau}{dt} = \frac{\partial \ln C_t}{\partial \ln Q_t} \left(\frac{\partial \ln Q_t}{\partial \ln \tau_t} \frac{d \ln \tau_t}{dt} \right) = \varepsilon_{C,Q} \, g_t \qquad (3.36)$$

Primal and dual rates of technical change are equal (but opposite in sign) if and only if the elasticity of cost with respect to output equals one (i.e., $\varepsilon_{C,Q}$ = 1.0), or in other words, if the technology exhibits constant returns to scale. But constant returns to scale was required to ensure that the primal rate of technological change, g_t, equalled the rate of change of total factor productivity, *tfp*. Under this assumption, the dual rate of technological change, h_t, is also equal to *tfp*.[45]

Because of scale effects, direct estimates of the primal versus dual rates of technical progress from 3.30 and 3.34, respectively, generally differ. As Antle and McGuckin (1993, p. 182) observe, "this happens because the primal rate is computed with input levels that are held constant, whereas the dual rate is computed with input levels adjusting optimally to technological change."

45. According to Berndt and Khaled (1979) it was Ohta (1994) who first demonstrated that the primal rate of technological change is equal to the dual rate of technological change times the dual rate of returns to scale.

Factor Bias and Scale Effects

The focus of the discussion so far has been on measuring both the levels and rates of growth of total factor productivity and the link between changes in productivity and shifts in production and cost functions over time, commonly called technological change. But technological change (whether induced by research or other factors) can have *differential* effects on the productivity and, hence, utilization of specific inputs in a multiple-input production process. And these effects may be interesting and of relevance to policy-making. Indeed, one of the main reasons for constructing PFP measures is to assess the impact of technical change on the productivity of specific factors of production. An increase in labor productivity, for instance, gives some (upper-bound) indication of the increased returns to labor. Unfortunately, the extent to which (research-induced) technical change contributes to measured gains in PFP is not readily apparent because, as we have discussed, changes in the PFP of a particular input can occur simply in response to the increased use of other inputs, even in the absence of the substitution consequences of technical change. This is so even when care is taken to form the quantity aggregates used to calculate a PFP in a way that abstracts from the substitution consequences of relative price changes.[46]

Homothetic technology: To address these limitations, various measures of *technological bias* have been proposed that utilize some notion of *factor-neutral* or *factor-biased* technical change.[47] This aspect of technical change was initially discussed by Hicks (1948), who defined bias in terms of the impact of technical change on the ratio of the marginal products of the factors of production or, equivalently, the marginal rate of technical substitution (MRTS) between two factors of production.[48] From this primal perspective, neutral technical change involves a shift in the production function that leaves the MRTS unchanged (at, say, a particular point in input space — which is equivalent to holding total costs of production constant); factor-biased technical change causes the MRTS to change.[49]

---

46. In practice, there is also usually an aggregation problem to confront with the X_i variable, which is often an aggregate across different classes of X_i. For instance, when X_i represents total labor input in agriculture, this entails aggregating across hired workers, unpaid family workers, and farm operators, all of whom embody different degrees of human capital.

47. Technological change can affect the optimal quantity and mix of outputs as well as inputs, but the related concepts of *output*-neutral and *output*-biased technical change are not dealt with here. For a discussion of this topic, see Hulten (1978) and Antle and Capalbo (1988).

48. For a more complete development of the factor-bias aspects of technical change, see Binswanger (1974b, 1975, 1977) Blackorby, Lovell and Thursby (1976), Stevenson (1980), Antle (1984), and Antle and Capalbo (1988).

49. Technical change causes isoquants to shift toward the origin in a parallel (i.e., factor-neutral) way or to "twist" or, equivalently, to shift toward the origin in a nonparallel (i.e., factor-biased) fashion.

Figure 3.4 illustrates the impact of technical change on a *homothetic* technology (e.g., a Cobb-Douglas technology) where the expansion paths, *e*, are linear and the optimal factor proportions (and thus optimal factor cost shares, given fixed prices) are invariant to the scale of production. If the quantity of output were held constant at Q_0, the technical change from τ_0 to τ_1 would cause cost-minimizing producers facing constant factor prices to adjust their input mix and produce at point *b* instead of point *a* on the invariant expansion path *e* (figure 3.4). This is a Hicks-neutral change in technology because the MRTS between X_1 and X_2 remains constant for optimizing producers. This is so irrespective of whether output is held constant at Q_0 (so that technical change enables the same quantity of output to be produced for lower total cost, i.e., $C_1 < C_0$) or if more output is produced with the same total cost, in which case the quantities of inputs are held constant at point *a* and the isoquant $Q_0(\tau_0)$ is relabelled as $Q^*(\tau_1)$, where $Q_0(\tau_0) < Q^*(\tau_1)$.[50]

In contrast, the technical change from τ_0 to τ_2 causes the MRTS (i.e., the slope of the isoquant $Q_0[\tau_0]$) at point *a* to change and so is biased in the Hicksian sense. Optimizing producers facing constant factor prices would produce the same output quantity, Q_0, at point *c* instead of *a* and would thereby lower their

Figure 3.4:   *Biased technical change, homothetic technologies*

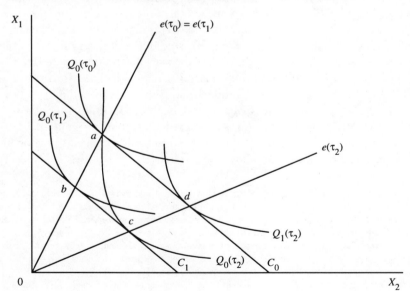

costs of production from C_0 to C_1. Similarly, if the total costs of production were held constant at C_0, optimizing producers would alter their factor mix and produce $Q_1(\tau_2)$ at point d instead of $Q_0(\tau_0)$ at point a.

Technical change from τ_0 to τ_2 induces a shift in the input ratio X_1/X_2 (or, equivalently, relative factor shares, P_1X_1/P_2X_2) that entails less of input X_1 to be used *relative* to X_2; in this sense, the technical change is factor-X_2 using and factor-X_1 saving. For homothetic technologies such as this, the direction and magnitude of the bias, as indicated by the change in the input ratio or the change in relative factor shares, is the same whether it is evaluated holding total costs constant (i.e., the shift from point a to point d) or the quantity of output constant (i.e., the shift from point a to point c) because the input ratio is independent of the scale of output.

Nonhomothetic technologies:[51] The Hicksian notion of bias, measured in terms of changes in the MRTS, does not readily carry over to the case of nonhomothetic technologies, which have nonlinear expansion paths along which the MRTS changes with the scale of production. Hence, the factor bias measured in terms of observed changes in input ratios will be sensitive to the pre- and post-technical change scale of production, and it matters whether the factor bias is measured holding total costs or the quantity of output or something else constant.

Figure 3.5 illustrates the difficulties. In panel a of figure 3.5, a change in technology from τ_0 to τ_1 enables optimizing producers to economize on inputs X_1 and X_2 and to produce the same quantity of output, Q_0, at lower cost (i.e., total costs are reduced in going from τ_0 to τ_1) at point b rather than point a. Because the MRTS between X_1 and X_2 is unaffected, the technological change is Hicks-neutral (or, by Blackorby, Lovell and Thursby's (1976) interpretation of Hicks neutrality, the technical change is expansion-path preserving) even though the input ratios and corresponding factor shares have changed. In this case, the overall bias effect of the technical change, wherein X_1/X_2 has decreased so that the technical change is factor-X_2 using and factor-X_1 saving, is entirely due to a scale effect. In panel b, the move from a to c also results in the same quantity of output being produced at a lower cost (i.e., $C_1 < C_0$) and with a different factor intensity (i.e., X_1/X_2 has again decreased). But in contrast to the case in panel a, the overall effect of factor bias can be decomposed into a Hicksian effect (i.e., a move from point a to point b, holding the total cost of production constant) and a scale effect (i.e., a move from b to c). Alternatively, the overall effect can be partitioned into a scale effect involving a move from a to d and a Hicksian effect

---

51. The discussion in this section and the next draws heavily on Antle and Capalbo (1988) and Karagiannis and Furtan (1993).

Figure 3.5: *Biased technical change, nonhomothetic technologies*

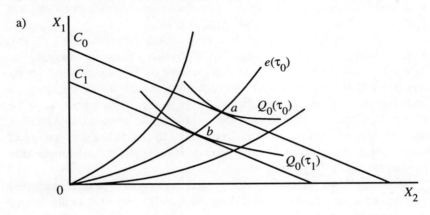

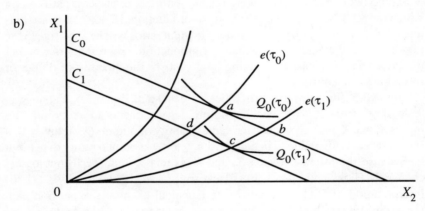

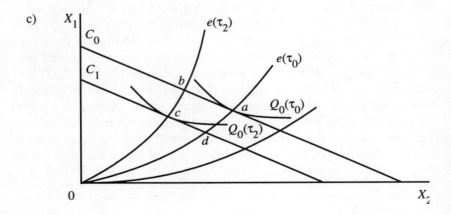

represented by a move from d to c, wherein the quantity of output is held constant at Q_0. In this case, the scale and Hicksian bias effects of the technical change are in the same direction; they are both factor-X_2 using and factor-X_1 saving.

The technical change in panel c of figure 3.5 involves an overall move from a to c that can be decomposed into a Hicksian effect, represented by a move from a to b (or, alternatively, from d to c) and a scale effect, involving a move from b to c (or, alternatively, from a to d). In this case, the scale effect is factor-X_2 using but is dominated by the Hicksian effect, which moves in the opposite direction and is factor-X_1 using, causing the overall bias effect to be factor-X_1 using.

Measuring bias: Both *pairwise* and *overall* measures of input bias are possible and commonly calculated. Following Stevenson (1980), Antle and Capalbo (1988), and Karagiannis and Furtan (1993), it is useful to categorize the factor-bias effects of technical change in terms of its effects on factor shares.[52] The overall bias relates to technology-induced changes in the cost share of a particular factor relative to the shares of all the other factors of production; pairwise bias concerns the change in the cost share of a particular factor relative to the cost share of another particular factor.

From this factor-cost perspective, pairwise bias for any pair of inputs can be formally defined as

$$B_{ij}(Q, W, \tau) = \frac{\partial \ln S_i(Q, W, \tau)}{\partial \tau} - \frac{\partial \ln S_j(Q, W, \tau)}{\partial \tau}, \; i \neq j \qquad (3.37)$$

where $S_i = \partial \ln C / \partial \ln W_i$ is the cost share of factor i. Pairwise comparisons of all inputs can be made in this fashion, with the technology being classified as factor-i using *relative to factor j* if $B_{ij} > 0$ and vice versa. But there is obviously a difficulty of interpretation when technical change uses input i relative to input j but saves input i relative to some other input, k; it is unclear whether the technical change is saving or using factor i overall. To assess this aspect of technical change, it is useful, following Binswanger (1974a, 1974b), to define the overall bias effect as

$$B_i(Q, W, \tau) = \sum_{j \neq i}^{m} S_j(Q, W, \tau) B_{ij}(Q, W, \tau) = \frac{\partial \ln S_i(Q, W, \tau)}{\partial \tau} \qquad (3.38a)$$

where S_i is the cost share and B_{ij} is the pairwise measure of bias given by

---

52. To complement this dual perspective on bias, it is also possible to calculate primal measures of factor bias in terms of the effects of technical change on the MRTS or, equivalently, relative marginal physical products. For a good discussion of these primal measures of factor bias, see Antle and Capalbo (1988) and Antle and McGuckin (1993).

3.37.[53] If $B_i > 0$, then the technical change is factor-i using overall, and vice versa; $B_i = 0$ for all i is necessary (but not sufficient) for Hicks neutrality.

To assess the degree of overall Hicks biasedness requires decomposing B_i into its Hicks (i.e., $H_i[Q, W, \tau]$) and scale (i.e., $A_i[Q, W, \tau]$) components. Antle and Capalbo (1988) show that

$$B_i (Q, W, \tau) = H_i (Q, W, \tau) + A_i (Q, W, \tau) \qquad (3.38b)$$

where the Hicksian bias in technical change is measured as a shift in the expansion path, holding the total cost of production constant so that

$$H_i (Q, W, \tau) = \frac{\partial \ln S_i (Q, W, \tau)}{\partial \tau} \bigg|_{dC = 0} \qquad (3.39)$$

and the scale effect of biased technical change due to the movement along the expansion path is given by

$$A_i (Q, W, \tau) = \frac{\partial \ln C}{\partial \tau} \left(\frac{\partial \ln C}{\partial \ln Q} \right)^{-1} \frac{\partial \ln S_i}{\partial \ln Q} = \frac{\partial \ln C}{\partial \tau} \left(\frac{1}{S_i \, \varepsilon_{C,Q}} \right) \frac{\partial S_i}{\partial \ln Q} \qquad (3.40)$$

where $\varepsilon_{C,Q} = \partial \ln C / \partial \ln Q$ is the elasticity of cost with respect to output.

Notice that if the technology is homothetic, $\partial \ln S_i / \partial \ln Q = 0$ so that the scale effect is zero (i.e., $A_i = 0$) and the overall bias effect equals the Hicksian bias effect. It is also useful to recall that the Hicksian bias effect and the scale effect do not necessarily run in the same direction so that both the overall direction of bias and the magnitude of bias depend on both the directions and relative magnitudes of the two effects.

3.2 Specification and Measurement Issues

Apart from the choice of general approach (i.e., primal versus dual or supply-function), a number of other specification and measurement issues arise in any econometric study of research benefits. Issues of the choice of variables to include, proxy measures for those variables, the representation of technical change, and the functional form for the empirical model are all intimately related and are best resolved jointly.

---

53. Time, t, is commonly used as the index of technology, τ, so that the measure of bias in technical change is also a measure of the factor share's technology-induced growth rate over time, ceteris paribus. Otherwise, to achieve the same result, it might be necessary to scale the measures of bias by the rate of change of the technology index, $d\tau/dt$.

3.2.1   Primal Models

Choices about functional form are dictated to a great extent by the availability of data and the purpose of the analysis. It is desirable to choose a specific functional form consistent with maintained hypotheses (such as positive marginal products that decline over the relevant range), which does not impose a priori the degree of economies or diseconomies of scale and which allows for both complementary and substitute relationships among inputs. These considerations favor the use of flexible functional forms.[54] Simplicity for its own sake and computational ease may also be relevant considerations. Complicated functions may contain implausible implications that are hard to detect, and they may make it difficult to compute economic effects or relationships such as the elasticity of substitution. By far the dominant criterion, however, has been data availability. This means that relatively simple and parametrically parsimonious models, which are technically and empirically undemanding, have been chosen most often.

The Cobb-Douglas Production Function

The Cobb-Douglas production function has been the basis for most econometric studies of agricultural research benefits. This function is written in standard, geometric form as

$$Q_t = \tilde{\alpha}_0 \prod_{i=1}^{m} X_{i,t}^{\alpha_i} \prod_{g=1}^{k} K_{g,t}^{\beta_g} \prod_{h=1}^{z} Z_{h,t}^{\psi_h} e^{\mu_t} \tag{3.41}$$

and for econometric estimation, it is transformed to a function that is linear in the logarithms of the variables:

$$\ln Q_t = \alpha_0 + \sum_{i=1}^{m} \alpha_i \ln X_{i,t} + \sum_{g=1}^{k} \beta_g \ln K_{g,t} + \sum_{h=1}^{z} \psi_h \ln Z_{h,t} + \mu_t \tag{3.42}$$

where Q_t is the quantity of output in period t. The X_is are quantities of conventional inputs such as land, labor, capital, and purchased inputs used in production. The K_gs are variables that determine the stock of knowledge in use, such as local and nonlocal agricultural research and extension done by the public and, perhaps, private sectors, and the Z_hs represent various institutional, infrastructural, and possibly, policy-related factors that are all treated as "fixed," i.e., beyond the direct control of the decision makers

---

54. Fuss, McFadden and Mundlak (1978), make many of the points discussed in this section with respect to choice of functional form. Other references that discuss the implications of functional forms include Heady and Dillon (1961), Chalfant (1984), Beattie and Taylor (1985), Lopez (1985b), and Just (1993).

whose production decisions are being modeled. The parameters capturing the technical structure of this model are represented by the αs, βs, and ψs, while the error term, μ, reflects other unmeasured and uncontrolled determinants of output.

Aside from being easy to estimate, this function owes some of its popularity to the straightforward and transparent way in which the estimated parameters can be used to quantify the economic effects of interest. The αs, βs, and ψs are estimates of the elasticities of output with respect to changes in the respective variables, and these elasticities are constants. The sum of the α_is is a direct estimate of the economies of scale with respect to conventional inputs, and multiplying the estimated coefficient of input X_i by the corresponding average product gives the marginal physical product of the input. But this tractability comes at some cost. The Cobb-Douglas function imposes a constant, unitary elasticity of substitution between all input pairs in addition to the constant output elasticities just noted. If such restrictions are not warranted, or are themselves the subject of investigation, then a less parsimonious specification of the structure of technology is required.

Flexible Functional Forms

The characteristic of *flexibility* — the ability to approximate an unknown functional form — has been used to classify several functional forms. A common interpretation of flexibility is based on the idea that an unknown algebraic form may be approximated over the relevant range by a Taylor's series expansion. For example, a second-order flexible functional form has been interpreted as a Taylor's series expansion, which provides a second-order approximation to the true functional form in a small neighborhood around a point.[55] The economic effects of interest, such as output quantity, returns to scale, factor shares, production elasticities, and elasticities of substitution, can generally be quantified at the point of approximation, from the estimates of the production function and its first and second derivatives, without the imposition of arbitrary restrictions. Fuss, McFadden and Mundlak (1978) showed that $(n+1)(n+2)/2$ distinct economic effects characterize the comparative-static properties of an n-input production function at a point. A second-order, locally flexible functional form can reproduce these effects without imposing any a priori restrictions across them. In particular, the

55. The fact that the approximation is good only around the point of approximation, rather than for the complete range of possibilities, leads to the term *local* flexibility rather than *global*. That is, the approximation is good only locally and becomes worse as the distance from the point of approximation increases. The Taylor's series interpretation of the approximation has been called into question (e.g., see White 1980; Gallant 1982; Chalfant 1983).

values of the matrix of second derivatives (e.g., the Slutsky matrix for a cost function) are not constrained prior to estimation.

Substitution elasticities may thus take any values at the point of approximation, but once the parameters have been estimated, there may be strong and, in some cases, implausible implications for how elasticities vary with changes in the explanatory variables. Even though the functions may approximate the relationships in the data closely at the point of approximation, it is still perilous to extrapolate far from the point of approximation. In short, locally flexible models are not a panacea for the econometric problem of selecting functional form. These problems may be particularly troublesome in the context of research evaluation, where it has been shown that the form of the research-induced supply shift is crucial.

A commonly used, locally flexible functional form is the transcendental-logarithmic (translog)[56] that can be represented for a production function with one output, m conventional inputs, and k knowledge-related inputs (but, for simplicity, suppressing the $Z_{h,t}$ variables) as

$$\ln Q_t = \alpha_0 + \sum_{i=1}^{m} \alpha_i \ln X_{i,t} + \sum_{g=1}^{k} \beta_g \ln K_{g,t}$$

$$+ \frac{1}{2} \sum_{i=1}^{m} \sum_{h=1}^{m} \alpha_{ih} \ln X_{i,t} \ln X_{h,t} + \frac{1}{2} \sum_{g=1}^{k} \sum_{h=1}^{k} \beta_{gh} \ln K_{g,t} \ln K_{h,t} \qquad (3.43)$$

$$+ \frac{1}{2} \sum_{i=1}^{m} \sum_{g=1}^{k} \gamma_{ig} \ln X_{i,t} \ln K_{g,t} + \mu_t$$

This form, initially derived by Christensen, Jorgenson and Lau (1971, 1973), has become popular because it allows the analyst to estimate the nature of factor substitution. Like the Cobb-Douglas, this function allows for calculation of returns to scale, it is easy to compute and interpret, and it permits but does not require positive and declining marginal products. In fact the Cobb-Douglas is just a special case of equation 3.43 for which parameters on all squared and interaction terms are assumed to be zero. The disadvantage of

56. Boisvert (1982) discusses the interpretation of the translog model. Because the translog model involves nonlinear transformations of the variables, rescaling the data can affect the values of economically meaningful measures such as elasticities or marginal products. It is important to ensure that the data used to compute these measures are mutually consistent and consistent with the model. For example, the arithmetic mean of the actual or predicted share of land (or some other input) is not the same as the share that would be predicted at the arithmetic mean of the exogenous variables. And combining the arithmetic means of independent and dependent variables with parameters in an elasticity formula will produce nonsensical estimates. Better alternatives for computing "average" elasticities include (a) computing elasticites at all data points and taking the average or (b) using chosen values of exogenous variables (e.g., their arithmetic or geometric means) with the corresponding *predicted* shares.

the translog is that it can require a large number of degrees of freedom, and multicollinearity often becomes a serious problem.

In order to conserve degrees of freedom and, perhaps, to mitigate multi-collinearity problems, one option is to estimate a translog function in which several but not all of the interaction and squared terms are restricted to zero. One could hypothesize a priori which coefficients are likely to be zero or close to zero, thereby reducing the demands on the data while still allowing some interactions. The cost of doing this is the potential bias arising from omitting relevant explanatory variables.

Many other flexible and less-flexible functional forms for production functions are available. Rather than discuss the advantages and disadvantages of each of these, we refer the reader to the references in footnote 54. A modified translog function as discussed above is reasonable for many production function studies designed to evaluate research, but it is certainly not the only reasonable possibility.

3.2.2   Dual Models

The dual approach is based on the correspondence that exists between a firm's production function and its profit, cost, factor demand, and supply functions under assumptions of perfect competition, cost minimization or profit maximization, and certain regularity conditions.[57] Profit function and cost function models have been used in several studies to investigate the structure of agricultural technology.[58] Most of these models have represented technical change, including the effects of research, with a time-trend variable. Recently several studies have included agricultural research, extension, and education variables in a multiproduct, profit- or cost-function approach to explore the productivity and factor-bias effects of research.[59]

The cost (or profit) function relates minimum cost (maximized profits) to input and output prices and to fixed (exogenous) or quasi-fixed factors. Once estimated, the parameters of such a model contain all the relevant information about the underlying production function. For research priority setting,

---

57.   The literature on production duality is vast. The earlier theoretical work was by Hotelling (1932), Hicks (1946), Samuelson (1953/54), Shephard (1953), McFadden (1962), and Uzawa (1964). More than 100 papers have followed with empirical applications or exploring the implications of a variety of flexible functional forms. An early example is Nerlove (1963). Other examples include Diewert (1973), Weaver (1983), Shumway (1983), Sidhu and Banante (1981), Lopez (1984), and Shumway (1988). Particularly good papers for describing the duality approach in relatively complete yet straightforward terms are Binswanger (1975), Pope (1982), and Young et al. (1987).

58.   See Binswanger (1974a), Lopez (1980, 1984), McKay, Lawrence and Vlastuin (1982, 1983), Weaver (1983), Shumway (1983), Carew, Chen and Stevens (1992), and Pardey et al. (1992).

59.   See, for example, Huffman and Evenson (1989, 1993).

a dual multicommodity approach may have appeal because it enables several supply and input demand functions to be jointly estimated without having to apportion inputs among commodities. It also facilitates calculation of research bias effects on the demands for particular inputs while still providing the coefficients on the research variables that can be used to calculate rates of return to research.

Cost Functions

The cost function can be regarded as a special case of the profit function in which output is given or predetermined rather than being variable. The cost-function approach may be preferred to the profit function for two reasons. First, it involves a much less rigorous behavioral assumption since cost minimization is required for profit maximization but may be consistent with a broad range of objectives. Second, a cost function assumes that input prices (or quantities) and output quantities are exogenous, while a profit function assumes that input prices (or quantities) and output prices, rather than output quantities, are exogenous. In many practical applications, especially those with relatively aggregated data, the assumptions that profits are maximized in relation to *realized* quantities and prices, and that output prices are exogenous, may be unreasonable. The assumptions underlying a cost-function specification may be more reasonable (although, in fact, profit functions have been used more often in studies of research benefits to date). For these reasons, the cost-function approach may be more suitable than the profit-function approach for studying the impact of technology in many cases, and we treat it explicity here.

The general form of a cost function, augmented with technology-related variables, τ, and other fixed factors, Z (that are treated as being beyond the control of farmers, but influencing their costs of production), is

$$C = c\,(Q\,,W\,,\tau, Z) \qquad (3.44)$$

where C is total variable cost so that cost is minimized with respect to a vector of fixed factors and subject to given levels of output(s), Q, and factor prices, W. The single-output, m-variable–input, Cobb-Douglas variant of a cost function takes the form[60]

$$\ln C_t = \alpha_0 + \gamma_Q \ln Q_t + \sum_{i=1}^{m}\alpha_i \ln W_{i,t} + \sum_{g=1}^{k}\beta_g \ln K_{g,t} + \sum_{h=1}^{z}\psi_h \ln Z_{h,t} \qquad (3.45)$$

60. The Cobb-Douglas is "self-dual" in that the cost function has the same functional form in input prices as the production function, 3.42, has in input quantities.

where C_t is the variable cost of producing output Q_t in period t, W_i represents prices of conventional inputs such as labor, capital services, and purchased inputs used in production, K_g represents the variables, such as research and extension, that affect the stock of knowledge in use, and Z_h represents a set of fixed factors.

A single-output, m-variable–input, translog variant of a cost function, augmented with knowledge-related variables (but for simplicity suppressing the $Z_{h,t}$ variables), is

$$
\ln C_t = \alpha_0 + \sum_{i=1}^{m} \alpha_i \ln W_{i,t} + \sum_{g=1}^{k} \beta_g \ln K_{g,t} + \gamma_Q \ln Q_t
$$

$$
+ \frac{1}{2} \sum_{i=1}^{m} \sum_{h=1}^{m} \alpha_{ih} \ln W_{i,t} \ln W_{h,t} + \frac{1}{2} \sum_{g=1}^{k} \sum_{h=1}^{k} \beta_{gh} \ln K_{g,t} \ln K_{h,t}
$$

$$
+ \frac{1}{2} \beta_{QQ} (\ln Q_t)^2 + \sum_{i=1}^{m} \phi_{iQ} \ln W_{i,t} \ln Q_t + \sum_{g=1}^{k} \beta_{gQ} \ln K_{g,t} \ln Q_t \qquad (3.46)
$$

$$
+ \sum_{i=1}^{m} \sum_{g=1}^{k} \gamma_{ig} \ln W_{i,t} \ln K_{g,t}
$$

where C_t is the cost of producing output Q_t in period t; all other variables are defined as before. This function can be regarded as a quadratic approximation to the unknown, "true" cost function when $\alpha_{ih} = \alpha_{hi}$ for all i and h.[61]

A well-behaved cost function is homogeneous of degree one in prices. That is, for a given quantity of output (and also fixed K_gs and Z_hs), total cost must double when all prices are doubled. This implies the following testable relationships among the parameters of the translog cost function:

$$
(a) \ \sum_{i=1}^{m} \alpha_i = 1; \ (b) \ \sum_{i=1}^{m} \alpha_{ih} = \sum_{h=1}^{m} \alpha_{hi} = 0 \ \text{ for all } i, h;
$$

$$ (3.47) $$

$$
(c) \ \sum_{j=1}^{n} \phi_{iQ} = 0 \text{ for all } i \ ; \ (d) \ \sum_{g=1}^{k} \gamma_{ig} = 0 \text{ for all } i
$$

This cost function does not constrain the structure of production to be homothetic, nor does it impose restrictions on the elasticities of substitution or economies of scale.

A system of m, output-constant demand functions for the factors of produc-

---

61.   Shumway, Saez and Gottret (1988) and Ball (1988) estimated multioutput versions of this type of model for U.S. agriculture, while Zhang et al. (1993) did likewise for Indonesian rice and soybean production.

tion can be derived from the factor-share equations. These *input* (cost) share equations are defined using the logarithmic form of Shephard's lemma:

$$S_{i,t} = \frac{X_{i,t}W_{i,t}}{C_t} = \frac{\partial \ln C_t}{\partial \ln W_{i,t}}$$

(3.48)

$$= \alpha_i + \phi_{iQ}\ln Q_t + \sum_{h=1}^{m}\alpha_{ih}\ln W_{h,t} + \sum_{g=1}^{k}\gamma_{ig}\ln K_{g,t}$$

where $S_{i,t}$ is the cost share of the ith input in period t.

Conventionally for estimation, it is assumed that the error terms in the cost function (3.46) and the associated cost-share equations (3.48) have intertemporally independent distributions with zero mean and nonzero contemporaneous covariance. In this framework, it is not sufficient to estimate the m-share equations (3.48) since the parameters needed to derive the impact of knowledge-related variables such as research (i.e., the α_0, β_g, β_{gQ}, and β_{gh} parameters) appear only in the cost function. The cost function and the corresponding share equations can be estimated jointly as a system of equations using maximum-likelihood methods, with cross-equation restrictions imposed on the parameters that appear in more than one equation. The benefit from using this systems approach is that as long as the model is correctly specified, the imposition of these behavioral assumptions through cross-equation restrictions on the parameters means that the parameters are estimated with greater precision than if only the cost function were used.[62]

Because cost shares must all sum to one, an input-share equation is dropped from estimation to avoid singularity of the covariance matrix in the actual estimation. Barten (1969) showed that estimation is invariant with respect to the equation dropped if maximum-likelihood estimation methods are used.[63] The parameters of the deleted cost-share equation are easily recovered using the maintained hypotheses of symmetry and linear homoge-

---

62. Typically, in practice, it would appear that little serious thought is given to where the error terms come from or how they ought to be specified. It seems they are simply tacked on to a static model to expedite statistical estimation. As Berndt (1991, p. 471) notes, the usual rationale for including additive error terms in the individual factor-demand (or -share) equations is that "firms make random errors in choosing cost-minimizing bundles." He also cites McElroy (1987), who proposes an alternative view in which the "errors" are in the eyes of the econometrician (i.e., specification or measurement errors rather than optimization errors). Given the direct relationship between the share equations and the cost function, it seems inappropriate to simply add random terms to the share equations without paying specific attention to the corresponding modifications in the cost function, itself, when the full system is being estimated. The appropriate modification to the cost function may depend on the rationale being offered.

63. In practice an iterative version of Zellner's seemingly unrelated regression procedure is often used to estimate the set of cost- and input-share equations. While the estimates obtained using Zellner's procedure are sensitive to the equation dropped, Kmenta and Gilbert (1986) used Monte Carlo methods

neity (3.47) in input prices.

Allen partial elasticities of input substitution can be computed from the cost function using

$$\sigma_{iht} = \frac{C_t\, C_{i,h,t}}{C_{i,t}\, C_{h,t}} \tag{3.49}$$

where C_i and C_h represent partial derivatives of cost with respect to inputs i and h, respectively, and σ_{iht} is calculated using the available data (i.e., the predicted values of the factor shares) and parameter estimates as (Uzawa 1964; Binswanger 1974a)

$$\sigma_{iht} = 1 + \frac{\alpha_{ih}}{S_{i,t}\, S_{h,t}} \text{ for all } i \neq h, \text{ and } \sigma_{iit} = \frac{\alpha_{ii} + S_{i,t}^2 - S_{i,t}}{S_{i,t}^2} \tag{3.50}$$

The (output-constrained) own- and cross-price elasticities of factor demand can be obtained by multiplying the Allen elasticities by the respective (predicted) factor shares so that

$$\eta_{iht} = \sigma_{iht}\, S_{i,t} \text{ for all } i \text{ and } h \tag{3.51}$$

Notice that these elasticities of factor substitution and factor demand can change over time as factor shares change, but they are often calculated at the sample means of the data.[64]

3.2.3   *Single-Equation Supply Models*

Supply functions have been estimated for research evaluation in several recent studies. Otto (1981) estimated supply functions for corn, wheat, soybeans, and sorghum in the United States including a variable for public agricultural research in each equation. The estimated coefficients were used to calculate internal rates of return to research. Zentner (1982, 1985) estimated supply equations for Canadian wheat and rapeseed including a public-research variable. He then used the shifts in the supply equations, implied by the estimated research coefficients, to calculate the change in economic

and Ruble (1968) used formal proof to show that an iteration of this procedure will converge to results of maximum likelihood and thereby the invariance property of Barten holds in this case.

64.   Mundlak (1968) and Blackorby and Russell (1989) discuss the alternative elasticity-of-substitution measures, such as that developed by Morishima wherein $\sigma_{iht}^m = S_{h,t}(\sigma_{iht} - \sigma_{hht}) = \eta_{iht} - \eta_{hht}$. Allen's elasticity of substitution corresponds to measuring how one input adjusts to a factor price change, assuming constant output, and the Morishima measure corresponds to measuring the responsiveness of two factors to a change in one price, assuming constant costs. Two factors classified as substitutes according to Allen are also substitutes according to Morishima, but not the converse. Moreover the Morishima measure is not symmetric whereas the Allen measure is.

surplus due to research. Finally, he used the surplus changes to calculate rates of return to research. A similar approach was used by Fox, Brinkman and Brown-Andison (1987) to calculate the rates of return to swine, beef, egg, dairy, broiler, and sheep research in Canada. They also included government policy variables in the econometric model and sought to account for the effects of trade and government policy on the rates of return to research.[65]

The supply function used to estimate the effects of agricultural research can be represented in general form by

$$Q = q\,(P\,,W\,,\tau, Z) \tag{3.52}$$

where Q is quantity of the commodity produced, P is expected output price, W is a vector of expected input prices, τ represents technology-related variables such as research and extension expenditures, and Z is a vector of other supply-shift variables. A number of conceptual and practical problems may be encountered in making the transition from this general form to a specific, empirical supply function.

Several of the conceptual issues associated with specifying the supply function in equation (3.52) for use in research priority setting are similar to those discussed for estimating a production function. The choice of a functional form often imposes a particular type of supply-function shift when a research variable is included (e.g., parallel or pivotal). As discussed in chapter 2 and below in chapter 4, the nature of the supply shift from agricultural research is difficult to know a priori and yet the type allowed has an important effect on the calculated research benefits.

Fox, Brinkman and Brown-Andison (1987) used a Box-Cox transformation together with an assessment of the signs and significance of individual coefficients to choose the functional form for the supply equation and, at the same time, to choose the form of the research-induced supply shift. For some commodities, they chose a partial logarithmic function and in others, a linear function. The partial logarithmic form imposed a pivotal proportional shift while the linear form imposed a parallel shift. Several cautions are in order with respect to tests for choosing a functional form and the implications of those tests for the nature of the research-induced supply shift. First, unless sufficient data are available, including data near the price axis, the results of the tests should be viewed as providing at best only an indication of the true functional form. The relationships that seem to hold at the point of approximation may not hold at all when one extrapolates away to the price axis, as is necessary in research evaluation. Further, the tests that were applied are adequate only for comparing alternatives within the Box-Cox class but not for a more general set

65. Details on using the economic surplus approach for evaluating agricultural research, with or without market-distorting policies, are provided in chapters 4 and 5.

of alternatives. Finally, and for similar reasons, it would be incorrect to assume that these tests have also provided a convincing test of the nature of the supply shift, even though a particular type of shift was selected.[66]

In addition to the specification issues that arise in applying the primal and dual methods discussed above, there are others that are specific to the supply-function approach. They arise from the flexibility of the ad hoc single-equation–modeling approach that is both its greatest strength and greatest drawback. In the primal and dual approaches discussed above, no attention was paid to the dynamics of responses over time, expectations, or uncertainty, which we know are important in agricultural decisions. Those aspects are less relevant in the primal approaches, but they are often ignored in the duality-based models simply for convenience. As discussed by Cassels (1933), Colman (1983), and Just (1991, 1993) in the context of supply models, these aspects of specification choices (along with risk and government policy variables) are important and difficult and have occupied much of the literature.

Expected prices rather than actual prices are typically used for the output price variables and sometimes for input prices. Adaptive expectations, rational expectations, or futures prices are often used to represent expected output prices. Because of its simplicity, the adaptive-expectations model has been widely used; the lagged values of the dependent variable and the output price are included in the group of right-hand–side variables.[67] Prices of substitutes and inputs, as well as other shift factors, are included to enable the estimation to identify a supply function rather than a demand function or a combination of the two. Research, extension, and education variables can be defined just as they were for the production function described earlier. Weather variables, relevant infrastructural variables, and government policy variables may also be included as shift-type variables in the model.

Another conceptual problem with specifying and estimating commodity supply functions concerns the nature of supply dynamics. One example arises in the use of time series of annual observations for commodities for which biological cycles are not annual. For example, poultry supply response may be modeled more accurately with quarterly observations (e.g., Chavas and Johnson 1982). Alternatively, some livestock industries and perennial crops involve production "cycles" of much longer than one year, and different explicit treatments to handle the dynamics of supply response to prices

66. The evidence of goodness of fit provided by the functional-form tests is based on more than the research shifter and, indeed, may be based on very few data points near the axis. The latter is a concern because a functional form that provides a good local approximation may not globally satisfy regularity conditions.

67. Nerlove (1956) discusses the adaptive-expectations model. Fisher (1982) discusses rational expectation formulations. Gardner (1976) discusses futures prices as expectation variables.

are indicated.[68] These issues of dynamics are also present, albeit slightly less obviously, in the supply-response functions of annual crops such as wheat because the dynamics relate to the use of durable specialized capital (e.g., see Burt and Worthington 1988).

3.2.4 Output and Input Data

Translating available statistics into meaningful measures of the input and output data required to study production processes, and the impact of R&D on those production processes, is often a challenging task and one that requires considerable care.[69] Aside from fundamental constraints on the statistics themselves in terms of their quantity and quality, analysts must make numerous decisions when processing and transforming the data, and these decisions can have significant implications for the eventual results. This section and the one to follow discuss these data issues, paying particular attention to the problems that arise when the available statistics are sparse and fall short of what is required to produce precise measures of the variables they are meant to represent.

Output Quantities and Prices

Quantities: Output quantity measures are required to estimate production yield, supply, and cost functions. For analyses involving only a single, homogeneous commodity, an output variable measured in quantity terms is relatively straightforward to construct. For any work using aggregate output, some index or quantity aggregate must be formed.

Agricultural data are usually reported on a seasonal or annual basis. When secondary data sources compiled by local statistical agencies or by international agencies such as the FAO or the World Bank are used, care must be taken to ensure that the reported output measure represents actual quantities *produced* in a given year or season and not quantities *available*. This is of particular concern when the output variable is derived from farm sales or marketing data that incorporate stock carryovers from one period to the next. A more serious concern in developing countries characterized by subsistence agriculture is that sales or marketing data exclude quantities consumed in the household where they are produced. For some commodities and countries,

68. For livestock, see Jarvis (1974); for perennial crops see French and Matthews (1974), Alston, Freebairn and Quilkey (1980), and Dorfman and Heien (1989).

69. This point has been stressed repeatedly by Griliches (1960, 1986b, 1994) and Gardner (1992), among others. For additional discussions of the measurement issues dealt with in this section, see Timmer (1970), Kennedy and Thirlwall (1972), Yotopoulos and Nugent (1976), AAEA (1980), Ball (1985), Shumway (1988), and Craig, Pardey and Roseboom (1994).

these quantities can represent more than half the production. Statistical agencies in many countries attempt to estimate the amount of consumption of products produced by farm households, although these estimates are frequently fairly crude. It may be necessary for analysts to derive their own estimates of home consumption in order to generate plausible output measures.

As described in section 3.1.3, additional aggregation problems arise when dealing with output aggregates such as "grain crops," "livestock products," or "total agricultural output." In these cases, some notion of a real quantity index of aggregate output is required. Unweighted and perhaps undesirable pre-aggregation may be implicit in the data-collection process even for single-commodity measures of output like tons of wheat, barley, or rice. A simple addition of high-protein (baking-quality) wheat and feed-grade wheat or malting- and feed-grade barley or an unweighted sum across various qualities of rice can result in distorted real output measures when the mix of commodities comprising the aggregrate varies over time. The potential for bias is particularly serious if the relative prices of the various commodity classes vary much across observations.[70] To form a *real* output aggregate in such cases requires data on the quantities and corresponding prices for each component of the aggregate and the construction of a Divisia output-quantity index. This aggregate is real in the sense that it abstracts from changes in measured output that are due solely to substitution effects as producers respond to changes in the *relative* prices of the components of the aggregate. In other words, a real output aggregate attempts to distinguish between changes in the size of the real commodity basket and changes in the composition of the basket.

When constructing an output index, analysts need to ensure that the form and units of the quantity data match the corresponding price data and that these aspects of the data are held constant over time. Sometimes a quantity series, say for rice, will be reported in units of "dry-stalk paddy before milling," while the corresponding output price series is reported in "milled-rice" terms. Appropriate conversion factors are generally available from local statistical agencies.

Unfortunately, often only preaggregated data on the value of production are available. If a corresponding Divisia price index were also available, then an *implicit* Divisia quantity index could be recovered from the value aggregate. In practice, Divisia price indexes are usually unavailable and some fixed-weight (Laspeyres) price index must be used to deflate the value aggregate. The longer

---

70. A related problem is when an output measure such as tons of sorghum fails to include by-products such as crop residues that are used for feeding, housing, and so on. Overlooking by-products could be an especially telling omission in the present context if the principal objective of a crop breeding program were to increase the quantity and quality of crop residues rather than just increase grain yields per se. Similarly, it may be important to incorporate manure in, say, a sheep output aggregate that also includes meat and wool.

the time horizon of the study, the more likely are fixed-weight indexes of output prices to understate the rate of change in output prices by failing to account for substitution effects. Consequently, using them to deflate output values will overstate the real changes in output. In choosing a price deflator, one should use the price index that most nearly reflects the composition of the aggregate value to be deflated.[71] To the extent that the basket of goods represented by general price indexes differs from the aggregate of interest, their use will introduce additional sources of bias into the analysis.

Prices: In addition to their use in forming real output-quantity aggregates, output prices also enter into supply, cost, and profit functions either directly or in the form of expectations. The issues of measurement and aggregation discussed above for output quantity variables carry over to the construction of output price variables. The only substantive difference is that appropriate quantity measures are used as weights in forming direct (Divisia) price aggregates. If fixed-weight quantity indexes must be used to deflate nominal value aggregates to derive implicit fixed-weight price indexes, the likely bias is to overstate price increases. This method should only be used if data limitations make that the only feasible option.

When expected prices are used instead of actual prices, the analyst must choose how to model expectations. That choice will have unpredictable implications for any subsequent use of the estimated model in evaluating the welfare impact of technological change. For the most part, however, the choice of expectation model can appropriately be based solely on econometric considerations with the aim of obtaining consistent parameter estimates, leaving the issue of interpretation to subsequent stages. One complication that ought to be anticipated is that expectation structures, such as adaptive expectations, that involve the use of lagged dependent variables involve dynamic supply responses over future time periods to a price change in the current period. These dynamics will complicate the estimation of research benefits in a model with downward sloping demand and, therefore, endogenous prices. In such a model, a one-shot research-induced supply shift might involve dynamic adjustments in quantities and prices over an indefinitely long future. An even more complicated picture emerges when the dynamic *exogenous* impact of research (through research lags, the adoption curve, and so on) generate *endogenous* dynamic responses.[72]

---

71. See Pardey, Roseboom and Craig (1992) for more discussion on this matter.

72. Care is required in the construction of such models. Indeed, some such models (such as the adaptive-expectations model) can involve dynamics applying symmetrically across the explanatory variables in the model so that the dynamics of output response to research (and other explanatory variables) would be constrained to be of the same form as the response to price changes.

Input Quantities and Prices

Labor: Although labor is one of the key inputs into agricultural production, it is notoriously difficult to obtain accurate measures of the labor actually used and the price paid for that labor. A large proportion of agricultural labor consists of operator and family labor for which observable market transactions are sparse. It is often difficult to establish the extent to which farmers and their families work full or part time at farming. Typically, the development process is characterized by a substantial but not necessarily uniform increase in the rate of part-time farming in addition to an eventual decline in the number of farms. Even in the case of hired labor, complicated sharecropping arrangements and remuneration contracts, particularly in less-developed countries, often make it difficult to price the hired-labor component.

In addition to data issues, there are the familiar conceptual and measurement problems associated with accounting for variations in quality (in this case, quality of the human agent) over space and time. A difference from other inputs and outputs is that, with labor, some of the input is provided by the individuals whose decisions and actions are being analyzed, and this may add some special problems of measurement and interpretation of prices and quantities. Further issues arise in interpreting information about labor markets, given the dynamics of education and human capital formation and their interplay with agricultural R&D (e.g., Welch 1970; Schultz 1975). Of course, if complete data were available on the prices and quantities of different categories of labor over time, the ideal index-number procedures described in this chapter could be applied in a routine fashion to obtain quantity and price indexes for the aggregate labor input. But such data never exist. The issues, then, concern appropriate approximation procedures to be used in dealing with incomplete data.

Typically, appropriate measures of wages, or the opportunity cost of time, are not readily available for any type of labor used in agriculture, especially unpaid operator and family labor, which in developing countries, constitutes most of the labor input, indeed of all inputs. When market prices are not available, they can sometimes be imputed using information from parallel labor markets. For instance, Craig and Pardey (1990) used data on the earnings of rural workers, differentiated by classes of age and education, as a measure of the opportunity cost of time for farm operators in the same classes. Then, using information on the characteristics of farm operators, they were able to construct state-level indexes of the aggregate quantity and price of labor used in U.S. agriculture. An alternative approach is to use a hedonic approach wherein a wage function is estimated by regressing wages against human-capital variables (e.g., age, education, and experience), other demographic variables (e.g., gender and ethnicity), and employment characteristics (e.g., full-versus part-time employment, operators versus hired or unpaid family), and then using the estimated model to predict the wages of farm operators in various demographic classes and by region prior to aggregation.

Capital: Capital stocks and their service flows pose a number of critical and difficult measurement problems in studies of production and productivity.[73] As development proceeds, durable inputs typically account for an increasingly large share of total inputs.[74] They also embody substantial (often privately funded) R&D output, and for these reasons, their accurate measurement and treatment are of particular importance when the productivity effects of publicly funded R&D are being assessed. The durable factors of production that are often treated as capital goods include physical inputs such as tractors, trucks, automobiles, combines, forage harvesting equipment, farm buildings, the farm plant, and other equipment, as well as biological inputs that are used for periods exceeding the frequency of the output measures. When annual data are used, this biological capital would certainly include breeding stock for cattle, sheep, pigs, goats, and chickens; milking stock such as dairy cattle and goats; and animals used for traction such as horses, buffaloes, and mules.[75]

The data commonly available are stocks of capital that are (a) either unweighted sums or value-weighted sums across different classes and/or (b) heterogeneous types of capital such as tractors of different horsepower ratings, combines of different widths or capacities, and trucks of different sizes. The service flow from capital needed for production studies or the rental rate needed for cost studies can only be inferred from information on capital stocks and their values. So measurement of service flows typically involves assumptions about the time path of the marginal physical product of capital, the relationship between the physical product and its market value, and the age and quality composition of the existing capital stock.

In competitive capital markets, the value of a unit of capital is equal to its expected, discounted real service flow. To aggregate distinct types of capital or infer actual service flows from the value of capital stocks, several character-

---

73. See Griliches (1960, 1963c), Yotopoulos (1967), and Jorgenson (1974). Craig, Pardey and Deininger (1993) give a much more detailed treatment of the issues dealt with briefly here, including coping with data limitations, forming informed guesses about key parameters, and handling quality change. For a discussion of emodical technical change cum quality-of-capital issues, see also Jorgenson (1966) and Hulten (1992).

74. For example, in 1985 capital services accounted for around 14.4% of the total production costs of U.S. agriculture (Craig, Pardey and Deininger 1993). Although comparable data are difficult to obtain, in many LDCs, the capital share is substantially lower.

75. Those biological factors of production with service lives of less than one year do not need to be treated as capital inputs. They are more appropriately viewed as *outside* inputs, as defined by Star (1974), to the extent that they are produced outside the current production period and carried over to the following (but not any future) production period. An appropriate way to deal with these factors is to define the corresponding output measure in net terms and also to exclude them from the measured inputs.

istics of the stock and flow relationship must be understood: (a) the expected lifespan of a machine (in order to incorporate likely exhaustion of a particular type of capital), (b) the pattern of physical deterioration (to incorporate economically meaningful measures of deterioration), and (c) the impact of quality differences or obsolesence on the market value of preexisting capital stock.

The assumption of competitive capital markets implies that the purchase price of a *unit* of capital at time t, P_t, is equal to the expected, discounted flow of current and future real rents, ρ_t, from that same unit of capital over its service life of length L, i.e.,

$$P_t = E\left(\rho_t + \frac{\rho_{t+1}}{D_t} + \frac{\rho_{t+2}}{D_t D_{t+1}} + \ldots + \frac{\rho_{t+L}}{\prod\limits_{k=0}^{L-1} D_{t+k}} \right) \qquad (3.53a)$$

where the discount factor is $D_t = (1 + r_t)$, and r_t is the rate of discount in period t. The discount rate represents the opportunity cost of funds, and it is typically assumed to be constant over time — i.e., $r_{t+k} = r_t = r$ for all k.[76] Then the formula reduces to

$$P_t = \sum_{k=0}^{L} \frac{\rho_{t+k}}{(1+r)^k} \qquad (3.53b)$$

To make use of this relationship, we must make further assumptions about its parameters. The real rent in period t corresponds to the real service flow from capital in period t. The relationship between values and service flows is based on expectations about the nature of current and future service flows, so purchasers must take expected usage into account. In practice, planned usage is unknown, so analysts typically assume that market data reflect the relationship between values and service flows under planned *normal* use and maintenance.

Two common assumptions about the likely profile of service flows from capital are the *lightbulb* (or *one-hoss-shay*) assumption and the *declining-balance* assumption. Under the lightbulb assumption, with normal use, the real service flow from capital is expected to remain constant throughout the capital's service life. When its service life is over, the flow stops. With a declining-balance assumption, normal use results in a linear or geometric decay

76.   In practice a long-run, real interest rate for a portfolio of government and private bonds outside the agricultural sector is an appropriate discount rate. For the United States, this rate has historically averaged around 4%. Using national account data to calculate a residual return on capital measure for the economy as a whole (e.g., Jorgenson and Griliches 1967) or the agricultural sector (e.g., Ball 1985) may be inappropriate because it includes the returns to a number of factors that are being estimated here — in particular, research.

in real service flow over time at a constant rate, δ. Service life is assumed to end when current real service flow drops below a critical threshold.

Each assumption about the service-flow profile implies a distinctive pattern of changing market valuation over the service life of the unit of capital. Craig, Pardey and Deininger (1993) show that the value of a machine or animal in year $k = 1, \ldots, L$ of its service life is given by

$$P_k = \frac{\rho_k}{\lambda(L,k,r,\delta)} \tag{3.54}$$

Under the lightbulb assumption, $\rho_k = \rho$ (so by construction, the rate of deterioration, δ, equals zero) for all years $k = 1, \ldots, L$ of a machine's working life, and

$$P_k = \left(\rho + \frac{\rho}{D} + \frac{\rho}{D^2} + \ldots + \frac{\rho}{D^{L-1-k}} \right) = \frac{\rho}{\lambda(L,k,r)} \tag{3.55a}$$

where

$$\lambda(L,k,r) = \frac{r}{1+r} \left[1 - D^{-(L-k)} \right]^{-1} \text{ for } r > 0$$

and $\tag{3.55b}$

$$\lambda(L,k,r) = (L-k)^{-1} \text{ for } r = 0$$

This service-profile assumption implies that the time path of the real value of a unit of capital is concave to the origin for positive interest rates and declines linearly when there is no discounting of future service flows.

Under a declining-balance assumption with a geometric rate of depreciation, δ,

$$P_k = \left[\rho_k + \frac{(1-\delta)\rho_k}{D} + \ldots + \frac{(1-\delta)^{L-k}\rho_k}{D^{L-k}} \right] = \rho_k \sum_{s=0}^{L-k} \left(\frac{1-\delta}{D} \right)^s \tag{3.56a}$$

$$= \frac{\rho_k}{\lambda(L,k,r,\delta)}$$

where

$$\lambda(L,k,r,\delta) = \frac{r+\delta}{1+r} \left[1 - \left(\frac{1-\delta}{1+r} \right)^{L-k+1} \right]^{-1} \tag{3.56b}$$

which collapses to $P_k = \rho_k/\lambda(r,\delta)$ where $\lambda(r,\delta) = (r+\delta)/(1+r)$ for a unit of capital with an infinite life span so that the market value of the capital declines over time at exactly the same rate as the service flow. For those units of capital with a finite service life, the time path of the real value of capital with a decaying service flow will be convex to the origin even when there is no discounting of future service flows.

Inferring real service flows from the market value of a *single* unit of capital is straightforward once the service-flow profile is parameterized. The current real service flow from a unit of capital that is k years old is a particular fraction, $\lambda(L, k, r, \delta)$, of its current market value. This *factor of proportionality* is described in equations 3.55b and 3.56b, above.

It is more complicated to infer service flows from stocks that contain different *classes* of capital, more than one machine *type* within a capital class, or more than one *vintage* of machines of a given type. For the purposes of this discussion, a capital class consists of machines that have identical service-flow profiles, i.e., identical depreciation rates and life spans, δ and L. Nevertheless, the real service flows will vary with age and type of machine, so it is crucial to know something about the age and quality distribution of types within a class. Capital types within a class, e.g., 50-, 100-, and 200-horsepower tractors, are not equally effective, but it may be tolerable to assume that the shapes of their service-flow profiles are identical.

With complete information on the numbers, ages, and productive qualities of different types of capital, figures on the aggregate value for each class could be constructed and then simply multiplied by the appropriate factor of proportionality to infer *aggregate* service flows for that class. However, to do so requires the solution of two distinct aggregation problems. First, capital must be aggregated over dissimilar types of machines within a class of capital, assuming identical service-flow profiles. This is fairly easy to do since the relative prices of machines of the *same* age will accurately reflect relative productive qualities, even if the machines embody different technologies.

A more difficult problem arises in aggregating over different vintages of capital whose productive qualities differ because of decay, exhaustion, and obsolescence. In this case there are problems in inferring service flows using relative prices because the relative prices of *used* and *new* machines are not accurate reflections of the current relative service flow from these machines, even if they have the same service profile. This arises because the decline in market valuation with age captures more than just the decay in the real service flow from capital; it also reflects the time to exhaustion of the capital stock so that $\lambda(L,1,r,\delta) < \lambda(L,k,r,\delta)$ for all $k > 1$. The appropriate measure of service flow would apply a *different* factor of proportionality to the value of each different age group.

Unfortunately, the data commonly available concerning capital are either estimates of the aggregate *market value* of the stock of capital of a particular class (e.g., the value of tractors on farms) or unadjusted *counts* of capital within a class (e.g., the number of tractors on farms). As an approximation, aggregate *service flows*, *SF*, can be inferred from aggregate market-value data, *MV*, by applying the factor of proportionality, $\lambda(L,a,r,\delta)$, appropriate for the "typical" machine. Taking the typical machine to be one whose age is the class average, *a*, yields

$$SF = \sum_{i=1}^{N} \sum_{k=1}^{L} \rho_{k,i}\, X_{k,i} \approx \lambda(L,a,r,\delta) \sum_{i=1}^{N} \sum_{k=1}^{L} P_{k,i}\, X_{k,i} = \lambda(L,a,r,\delta)\, MV \quad (3.57)$$

where *i* is an index running over the *N* types of capital in the class, *k* indexes the *L* possible vintages in the class, and $X_{k,i}$ and $P_{k,i}$ are the number and market value of vintage-*k*, type-*i* machines, respectively.

If the available figure for total capital stock for a class of capital is simply an unweighted sum of the units of all types and vintages, we must somehow account for the *likely* composition of the total in order to calculate service flows. In the absence of other information, the total stock figure may be considered to be an accurate count of the "typical" unit within each class. Here, *typical* is defined by the unit within the class of the most likely type, *x*, and age, *a*. Taking the reported total, *CC*, to be counts of typical machines, the total capital stock figure can be adjusted by the assumed rate of deterioration under normal use to reflect total effective new machines of type *x*, using

$$X_{1,x}^{*} = \sum_{i=1}^{N} \sum_{k=1}^{L} (1-\delta)^{k-1}\, \frac{\rho_{1,i}\, X_{k,i}}{\rho_{1,x}} \approx (1-\delta)^{a-1} \sum_{i=1}^{N} \sum_{k=1}^{L} X_{k,i}$$

$$(3.58)$$

$$= (1-\delta)^{a-1}\, CC$$

Aggregate service flows, *SF*, can then be inferred from this undifferentiated stock by taking the approximate machine counts, $X_{1,x}^{*}$, expressed in units of new machines of type *x*, and employing the market value of these new machines and their corresponding factor of proportionality.

$$SF = \sum_{i=1}^{N} \sum_{k=1}^{L} \rho_{k,i}\, X_{k,i} \approx \lambda(L,1,r,\delta)\, P_{1,x}\, X_{1,x}^{*} \quad (3.59)$$

When a quantity measure of the *physical stock* is desired and the only available data are the undifferentiated counts, *CC*, then the approximation in equation 3.58 can be used to express this stock in terms of new machines of type *x*. If the market value of capital in place is available, informed guesses about the age distribution must be made to derive a quantity measure. Dividing the total market rental by the rental of a new machine of type *x* would give exact counts of type-*x* machines, but we can only approximate the rental value of this undifferentiated group by taking each unit within it to be of age a. Using only the factor of proportionality for new machines of type x and its market price, $P_{1,x}$, the market value for the capital class, MV, can be converted to approximate counts of new machines of x, using

$$
X_{1,x}^* = \sum_{i=1}^{N}\sum_{k=1}^{L}\frac{\rho_{k,i}\,X_{k,i}}{P_{1,x}} = \frac{\displaystyle\sum_{i=1}^{N}\sum_{k=1}^{L}\lambda(L,k,r,\delta)\,P_{k,i}\,X_{k,i}}{\lambda(L,1,r,\delta)P_{1,x}}
$$

(3.60)

$$
\approx \frac{\lambda(L,a,r,\delta)\displaystyle\sum_{i=1}^{N}\sum_{k=1}^{L}P_{k,i}\,X_{k,i}}{\lambda(L,1,r,\delta)\,P_{1,x}} = \frac{\lambda(L,a,r,\delta)\,MV}{\lambda(L,1,r,\delta)\,P_{1,x}}
$$

An index of the real service flows from capital over time can be constructed by using the measures of service flow and physical stock described above to aggregate over M different classes of capital. For instance, to estimate the aggregate real service flow summed across multiple classes of capital such as tractors, combines, and trucks requires the actual or approximate quantities expressed in units of the numeraire of each capital class along with its corresponding service flow. Letting $\lambda_{1,c} = \lambda(L_c,1,r,\delta_c)$ represent the factor of proportionality for new machines of class c and letting SF_c represent the corresponding service flow, the formula for the Törnqvist-Theil Divisia index of the aggregate quantity of capital services is a special case of equation 3.17, namely,

$$
XI^{DT}(t) = XI^{DT}(t-1)\prod_{c=1}^{M}\left[\frac{X_{1,c}(t)}{X_{1,c}(t-1)}\right]^{w_c(t)}
$$

where

$$
w_c(t) = \frac{1}{2}\left[\frac{\lambda_{1,c}\,P_{1,c}(t)\,X_{1,c}(t)}{\displaystyle\sum_{s=1}^{M}\lambda_{1,s}\,P_{1,s}(t)\,X_{1,s}(t)} + \frac{\lambda_{1,c}\,P_{1,c}(t-1)\,X_{1,c}(t-1)}{\displaystyle\sum_{s=1}^{M}\lambda_{1,s}\,P_{1,s}(t-1)\,X_{1,s}(t-1)}\right]
$$

(3.61)

$$
= \frac{1}{2}\left[\frac{SF_c(t)}{\displaystyle\sum_{s=1}^{M}SF_s(t)} + \frac{SF_c(t-1)}{\displaystyle\sum_{s=1}^{M}SF_s(t-1)}\right]
$$

As with any other Törnqvist-Theil quantity indexes, the changes in real quantities of each capital class are weighted by its share in total capital costs. The class share, in this instance, is the two-period average of its share of total capital *rental* costs. It might be tempting to use market-value shares for weights in this index, but they differ from rental-cost shares if, as assumed here, service-life profiles differ across capital classes.

Land: The problems with measuring quantities and prices of land fall into two types. First, as with other capital, the relevant measure for many purposes is an annual flow of services from the asset rather than the market price of the asset, as described above. In many cases, data on market transactions are not available for annual land rental, so rental rates must be inferred from information on asset prices. Such imputation requires information on variables such as the discount rate, tax rates, and the expected rates of growth in rents and capital gains (e.g., Alston 1986). One virtue of land compared with other capital is that it is often reasonable to assume zero depreciation so that the problems of imputing types and rates of depreciation from sparse data may be nonexistent. However, the other variables (especially expected rates of capital appreciation over an indefinite horizon) are typically difficult to estimate, even when reliable data are available on past price movements. Second, and unlike most other capital items, the data on asset prices of land are often questionable: they are usually based on either limited numbers of observations of transactions in very thin markets or surveys of expert opinions.

Additional conceptual and measurement questions arise when land is used in rotation or in other systems that persist for several years (e.g., as in perennial crops such as coffee, cocoa, or rubber) or in production systems that allow for multiple crops within a year (e.g., irrigated rice and wheat systems in Asia where two or more crops are grown in sequence or intercropping systems where two or more crops are grown simultaneously). One conceptual problem is to match quantities with correponding prices (e.g., hectare plantings per year, rather than simply hectares, to deal with multicropping).

Like other capital, land is heterogeneous, and this heterogeneity leads to potential problems in constructing meaningful aggregates. The recommended general approach to dealing with land quality, as with other capital, is to disaggregate as much as practicable when developing indexes of land aggregates. Relevant quality attributes for land, which affect its productive potential and value, include natural characteristics (e.g., climate, topography, arability, and soil type) and human modifications of natural characteristics (e.g., fertility, disease resistance, and pest populations affected by past production practices; erosion gullies; groundwater and salinity; capital "improvements" such as terracing, roads, irrigation equipment, and infrastructure).[77]

Ideally, the value of land itself should be distinguished from the value of

77. Peterson (1986) used an international land-quality index to scale total hectares of land. It was an interesting attempt to get at the problem of heterogeneity, but the index has some problems: it was built on

fixed improvements to land (such as buildings, water storage, irrigation infrastructure, fences and roads, and in the case of perennials, the standing stock of trees and plants). Once the nonland component has been separated, it can be treated as part of the capital stock, as described more generally above. When such separation is not possible because data are incomplete, it may be necessary to attempt to treat capital improvements as an element of land quality. For instance, different classes of land (e.g., pasture versus crop, rainfed versus irrigated) can be distinguished and aggregated according to their different rental rates (e.g., Craig and Pardey 1990).

An additional set of problems can be encountered when property rights are not clear or where common-property or open-access rules apply. In such settings, it can be difficult to impute a value for the quantity of land being used in the particular crop and livestock enterprises being studied. Judging the appropriate imputation procedures is likely to require detailed information on actual production practices.

Other conventional inputs: Remaining conventional inputs include such things as irrigation inputs, fertilizers, herbicides, pesticides, seed, electricity, fuel, oil, and veterinary services. In principle, the measurement of many of these inputs is relatively straightforward, since they are typically purchased (at least to a great extent) in markets, making it possible to obtain reasonably good information on prices according to qualities. Also, they are typically nondurable, so that all of the problems associated with dynamics and imputing flows of services (which were discussed under land, labor, and capital) are unimportant, although many of these inputs are storable, and distinguishing between time of purchase and time of use may be important. In practice, however, the statistics that are available on these "other" inputs are often aggregates that have not properly accounted for quality differentials, and the measures of quantities and prices are biased (i.e., the index-number problem).

Agricultural chemicals may be measured in physical quantities (e.g., tons) rather than more relevant effective units (e.g., pounds of active ingredient for herbicides or pesticides). This is particularly a problem for pesticides where, within preaggregated categories, the mix and concentration of active ingredients has changed significantly over time. Similarly, organic and inorganic fertilizers must be distinguished, and within each of these classes, there are analogous problems arising from a varying mix and concentration of active ingredients. In inorganic fertilizer premixes, not only does the mix and concentration of, say, nitrogen, phosphorous, and potassium (N-P-K) matter, the chemical forms of the N-P-K also matter. Once again, the simple rule is to disaggregate. Additional problems arise with organic fertilizers such as

an hedonic approach using only U.S. land values that may not be representative of, nor extrapolate meaningfully to, relative prices in other parts of the world.

livestock manure, green manures, human waste, and crop residues. Clearly there are quality issues similar to those for inorganic fertilizers. In addition, since organic fertilizers are often not traded at all, but rather are an intermediate good, both produced and consumed on the same farm or group of farms (i.e., an "inside" input), data are typically woefully inadequate. The "inside" nature of these inputs means that there may be problems in imputing costs to particular production processes, although for broad output aggregates, such problems may not arise. Care must also be taken to ensure that double-counting problems do not arise (e.g., livestock feed consumed on the farms where it is produced embodies the land, labor, and other inputs used to produce it).

Weather indexes: Many production studies ignore weather as an input. As a result, typical indexes of output quantity and productivity fluctuate from year to year as a consequence of unmeasured weather influences, so the interpretation of the indexes is obscured by weather-related measurement error. In econometric production studies, the effects of weather are typically relegated to the error term. This practice will not lead to bias or problems of interpreting econometric estimates of production relationships if the omitted weather variables are uncorrelated with the included explanatory variables. In many situations, it is implausible to assume that farmers do not respond to weather within the production period (for instance, harvesting and pest-control inputs are surely affected by weather), and when that is so, some effort to explicitly account for weather effects may be worthwhile.

Serious difficulties arise in identifying meaningful measures of weather that are relevant for explaining the production of individual crops, even those for which the agronomic relationships are well understood. The problem is magnified considerably when crop aggregates are being dealt with. For instance, dryland wheat yields depend on both the timing and quantity of rainfall (evapotranspiration), both immediately prior to planting and at harvest. And other cereal crops depend on similar rainfall variables. The main problem is that different crops depend on different weather variables (rainfall, temperature, humidity) at different times within the year (e.g., Geigel and Sundquist 1984).

Among the U.S. studies attempting to account for weather effects, widespread use has been made of a procedure suggested by Stallings (1960). To construct a "weather index," Stallings regressed *experimental* yields of seven crops from various locations against a linear time trend; the amounts of nonweather inputs were presumed constant over time and space. The index for each location and for each crop was defined as the ratio of actual yield to the yield predicted from the regression. Aggregate indexes across regions were formed by weighting the indexes for the individual locations according to corresponding regional production. These, in turn, were aggregated across crops to obtain an overall index.

Proxies, policy variables, and other problems: In practical econometric work, it is customary to replace the economic constructs in a theoretical model with more readily available variables that are intended to proxy for the "true" variable. For instance, *all* of the indexes discussed in this chapter are, necessarily, approximations to the true quantities and prices that are included in theoretical models (because they use discrete data and so on, as discussed above). But some proxies are much cruder, involving much greater leaps of faith than that involved in using a discrete approximation to a Divisia index. For instance, wholesale prices may be used as proxies for their farm-level counterparts, or the price of a particular fertilizer may be used as a proxy for all fertilizers or all agricultural chemicals (or, at least, as a proxy to compute a rate of change for the broader price aggregate).

The main statistical problem with using proxies is that they are invariably imperfectly correlated with the "true" variable, and the resulting "errors-in-the-variables" problem means that the estimates are biased and inefficient. The statistical problems extend to parameters on variables that are measured precisely, not just the one being proxied. In addition, problems of interpretation may arise when the units of proxies for prices or quantities differ from those of the corresponding "true" variables. This problem is so pervasive (and inescapable) in practical econometric work that it is almost never mentioned. Most practitioners seem reconciled to accepting whatever biases are involved and hoping that they are not too important.

Policy proxies are particularly problematic. Here, the question is not so much whether a proxy is a close enough approximation to the true variable but, rather, whether it belongs in the model at all. In many cases, the effects of policies are already (or ought to be) reflected in the measures of prices and quantities of inputs and outputs. The additional inclusion of explicit policy proxies is a form of double counting if the other variables are measured properly. Meaningful inferences based on the results from such models are unlikely.

On the other hand, certain policies, whose effects are not reflected in appropriate measures of quantities and prices (e.g., the provision of infrastructure in the form of public goods such as rural roads, education, police, and hospitals), might well warrant the inclusion of an appropriate proxy (Antle 1983; Binswanger et al. 1987; Lau and Yotopoulos 1989; Hu and Antle 1993). Drawing the distinction between which variables should be included in principle and interpreting the estimated coefficients on proxies for those variables in practice is bound to be difficult. Craig, Pardey and Roseboom (1994) suggest that such variables may be providing indirect information on the roles played by conventional inputs — particularly physical and human capital that have been mismeasured — as well as the direct effects they would be supposed to capture.

A final set of measurement issues that arises, particularly in less-developed countries, concerns the differentiation between the productive and consumptive uses of inputs and, relatedly, the household use versus marketed quantity of output. Home consumption of farm output remains significant, even in more-developed countries, and is a major aspect of peasant farming systems. Typically, it is difficult to distinguish the consumptive use of land and buildings from their uses as productive assets. The same is partly true of vehicles and fuel. Attribution of inputs, especially operator and family labor, among activities is particularly troublesome in the context of part-time farming, which is becoming a prevalent form of farming in more-developed countries, moreso where farming is regarded in part as a hobby or leisure pursuit.

3.2.5   Research and Extension Variables

Most of the difficulties associated with including variables representing research, R, and extension, E, in primal or dual models of production arise because research affects agricultural production neither directly nor instantaneously. There are considerable time lags between investment in research and the generation of usable technologies, and there are lengthy lags in the uptake of technologies. As new technologies depreciate or become obsolete, their output-enhancing or cost-saving effects may eventually wane. Specification of the length and shape of the lag relationship and, relatedly, the depreciation of the existing stock of research-induced knowledge, has been largely ad hoc. Past attempts to estimate rather than impose these parameters on the analysis have been inconclusive. Indeed, recent, and essentially exploratory, studies by Pardey and Craig (1989) and Chavas and Cox (1992) raise more fundamental questions about the common parameterizations used to estimate the productivity effects of research, and they suggest there may be much to gain from more work in this area.

In addition to current and past local research, research by other states, regions, and countries on similar production problems, commodities, or factors of production would be expected to have a positive effect on local production technologies. However, environmental factors, among other things, place natural constraints on the degree to which increments to the agricultural knowledge stock made in (or for) one locale can be transferred to others.[78] Attempts to identify the magnitude and significance of these research-spillover

---

78.   This new knowledge may be embodied in new plant varieties, agricultural chemicals, or agricultural machinery, or it may consist of pretechnology material, such as new breeding lines for crops and

effects have produced mixed results and have usually been derived under particularly strong and, in many respects, unrealistic hypotheses. Because the modeling decisions made with regard to these research-lag and spillover issues have a crucial and direct bearing on the measured effects of research, they are discussed here in some detail.

Measuring Research[79]

Constructing the time-series data on research expenditures required for the ex post methods described in this chapter, as well as the ex ante approaches described elsewhere in this book, can be difficult and time consuming. Often there are no consolidated research budgets or expense reports that present data in sufficient detail over a long enough period to enable a lengthy series of aggregate research expenditures to be readily assembled. These data difficulties are compounded if research expenditures are required for a single commodity or clearly defined group of commodities, such as food crops, cereals, or small ruminants. There are problems in apportioning aggregate expenditures among specific commodities, particularly for institutes that share research facilities and equipment across a number of commodities or lines of research. It is also common to find a multiplicity of executing, funding, and reporting agencies that provide incompatible, incomplete, and even conflicting data.

When data are being compiled, it is helpful to first develop a clear understanding of the institutional history of the local research system, paying special attention to details of institutional mergers and divisions, as well as mandate changes, so that a consistent time series is developed. Reporting standards and disbursement practices differ, so it is often useful to compile data on the research funds available or, more appropriately, on research expenditures according to their source and type. On this basis, three broad expenditure classes can be identified.

Core funding: The first category includes funds from state, provincial, and national governments in support of routine or core expenditures. These core expenditures typically cover basic and on-going operational costs such as salaries, utilities, maintenance, consumables, administration, and essential travel and communications. If these data are not available from "performer-based" records (i.e., by summing across the funds received or spent by all the agencies actually performing the research), it will be necessary to compile them from "source-based" reports. Public funds for research may

livestock, as well as the new research know-how, techniques, and so on that are reported in journals, books, or symposia.

79. For some additional guidelines on compiling data of this type see OECD (1981), UNESCO (1984), Pardey and Roseboom (1989), and Pardey et al. (1992, appendix 2).

come from a disparate set of government agencies, such as the ministries of agriculture, science and technology, and education, so care is needed to ensure that all relevant funding sources are included. For state and provincial research systems, a significant portion of their funds may also come from the national government, as in the case of the U.S. state agricultural experiment stations, where about 26% of the funds come directly from federal government sources (Huffman and Evenson 1993, p. 223).

Data obtained from performer-based records could well understate the resources used for research to the extent that administrative overhead and even the salaries of research-related staff appear in ministerial budgets separately from the reported allocations to agricultural research. Conversely, source-based records may overstate the resources actually used in support of research by including all the administrative and salary costs associated with managing agricultural development and support programs (or teaching activities), where research represents but one, and possibly a minor, component.[80] An additional concern when research expenditure data are being assembled from either source- or performer-based records is the need to capture actual expenditures and not amounts budgeted; the differences can often be substantial.

Other government funds: The second expenditure category is publicly provided funds from domestic governments used for development or project-related purposes. These include the costs of executing specific research activities such as additional support for construction, equipment, experimentation and related travel, research data collection, analysis and reporting, project administration, and dissemination of research results. While these expenditures are generally more volatile than core expenditures, they can usually be allocated to particular research programs more readily than is the case with core expenditures. Not all research programs relate to a specific commodity or narrowly defined group of commodities. Research on factors of production (e.g., soils and water) or research of a more basic nature (e.g., development of modern biotechnology techniques, cytology, or fundamental studies of growth hormones) can have productivity-enhancing effects across a range of commodities. This makes it difficult to apportion these types of expenditures to a particular commodity in any meaningful way.

But to the extent that these aspects of a research program do or should ultimately have a commodity impact, albeit often a multicommodity impact, it is reasonable to consider them as a component of the relevant commodity

---

80.   If government bureaucracies are bloated because of public-sector job-creation practices, it might be difficult to justify charging the extraordinarily large "administrative overheads" of the central government bureaucracies that come with this overstaffing against the research agency being evaluated. In fact, it has been argued that overly bureaucratic systems stifle research ingenuity and actually reduce the stream of benefits coming from research.

program(s) and apportion them accordingly.[81] One practical option for doing so is to assume that the share of project-related expenses that can be readily identified with a specific commodity program is representative of the overall commodity orientation of the research so that

$$R_{j,t} = r_{j,t} + \left(r_{j,t} / \sum_{j=1}^{n} r_{j,t} \right) \times \left(R_t - \sum_{j=1}^{n} r_{j,t} \right) = R_t \left(r_{j,t} / \sum_{j=1}^{n} r_{j,t} \right) \qquad (3.62)$$

where $R_{j,t}$ is the estimated total expenditure on commodity j in year t, R_t is total research expenditure in year t, $r_{j,t}$ is project-related expenses in year t that are readily allocated to commodity j, and $\sum_j r_{j,t}$ is the sum of project-related expenses in year t that can readily be allocated to one of n commodities.

Allocating preaggregated core expenditures to specific commodities is problematic. Given that a substantial fraction (often 60% to 70%) of core budgets is used for salaries, a plausible approach is to compile data on the time researchers spend working on particular commodities (preferably measured in full-time equivalents of actual time spent doing research) and use this information to partition total core expenditures. An alternative approach is to use the share of project-related or development costs going to each commodity as the basis for apportioning the core budget. The human capital component that typically dominates core budgets gives rise to higher degrees of "fixities" relative to project-related budgets (e.g., it may be difficult to convert a rice breeder rapidly into a corn breeder). Thus, it may be useful to smooth the fluctuations in development expenditures when using them to prorate preaggregated core expenditures by adopting some variant of the following equation:

$$R_{j,t}^* = R_t^* \times \frac{1}{n} \sum_{k=0}^{n-1} \left(r_{j,t-k} / R_{t-k} \right) \qquad (3.63)$$

where $R_{j,t}^*$ = the imputed core budget expenditures on commodity j in year t, R_t^* = total (or unallocated portion of) core budget in year t, $r_{j,t-k}$ = development or project-related expenditures on commodity j in year $t-k$, and R_{t-k} = total project-related expenses in year $t-k$.

Donor funds and grants: The third class of expenditures includes funds received from other sources, such as loans or grants from donor governments, public agencies, and private-sector organizations; funds recouped from fee-for-service activities; sales of farm produce; funds from the sale of new technologies; user fees, such as patent royalties or licence charges; and

---

81. Presumably, research on improved soil management practices, for example, is targeted toward a particular, and usually representative, site and/or production system, for which the likely commodity mix is readily apparent.

so on. Each of these raises its own particular set of measurement difficulties.

In measuring the flow of donor-sourced funds going to research, particular care is needed to distinguish between actual expenditures and funds allocated or made available. Nontrivial and unpredictable lags between the commitment and the actual disbursement of donor funds mean that in many cases, a sizable portion of the funds allocated to a multi-year project is never actually spent. The mismatch between funds available and expenditures is compounded by the fact that donor support is often biased toward lumpy capital items such as new buildings, plant, and equipment. Unfortunately, in many instances, the available data are restricted to information on budget totals and project starting and ending dates. In this case, the practical option is to assume that the appropriated or, preferably, the expended budget total was disbursed in equal annual amounts for the duration of the project. It is common for donor-funded projects to cover a number of commodities (e.g., a research project on food crops, on upland agriculture, or on farming systems) and to include nonresearch activities (e.g., development of irrigation infrastructure or joint research-extension activities). These budget data are often reported along functional rather than programmatic lines. In the absence of a detailed accounting of the use of the funds, the judgment of knowledgeable research scientists and administrators can be used to estimate the portions of project funds going to research on particular commodities.

There can also be difficulties in identifying the research component of farm operations that may be undertaken in support of agricultural research. To the extent that such farm operations are necessary to execute a program of research, it is appropriate for them to be included as part of the cost of doing research. But some systems engage in farming operations well beyond what is required to support research. In some cases, the surplus earnings from farm sales are used not only to support research but also to support a whole host of nonresearch activities. In these instances, including all of the resources devoted to farm operations can substantially overstate the costs of doing research.

Research expenditures are a more accurate measure of the funds used to do research than simple budget or funds-available figures where, for example, the year-to-year carryover of unspent funds can lead to a significant mismatch between the temporal pattern of funds allocated versus funds actually spent on research. The capital budgeting exercises described in section 5.4.2 make it clear that the pattern of research expenditures (as well as the patterns of research benefits flowing from these expenditures) can significantly alter the estimates of discounted research costs and benefits, or rates of return to research, coming from such an exercise.

Research expenditures versus service flows: A research expenditure series might not be a particularly accurate measure of the *real* resources actually used to do research. The major problem in this regard arises when a large share of total expenditures is invested in physical capital inputs such as new or refurbished buildings and research facilities, equipment and autos, or the upgrading of human capital.[82] This is especially common in newly established or rapidly growing systems. Such an expenditure aggregate overstates the flow of services coming from these research inputs in years of high capital expenditures and correspondingly understates them in subsequent years. This is because the resources spent in constructing new buildings and training scientists can produce a stream of research services for many years after the investment has been made — assuming adequate maintenance, repair, and in the case of scientists, continued training and opportunities for professional development. It is the service stream, not the corresponding expenditure series, that is the best measure of the resources actually used to do research. To express a research input aggregate in terms of service flow, it would be necessary to identify expenditures on durable inputs, such as buildings and equipment, autos, and training of personnel, apply the procedures described in section 3.2.5 to derive service-flow estimates for these capital inputs, then combine these estimates with recurrent costs such as salaries and consumables to give a measure of aggregate service flows (Pardey, Craig and Hallaway 1989).

A basic distinction must be drawn between research *expenditures* (a measure of the costs of research) and an index of the *quantity* of research inputs. The *expenditure* series simply adds up expenditures across cost categories, giving them equal weights. In contrast, a quantity index aggregates across different categories — flows from research capital stocks, such as buildings, land, and equipment (as measured by aggregate service flows), as well as from current consumption of nondurables and labor — as described above, using different weights for the different categories.

These two ways of measuring research are used for different, but related, purposes. Consider an analysis of a time series of annual investments in research. An economic evaluation of the stream of research must use the expenditure series, while the economic explanation of the consequences of research, in an econometric model, is best served by using the quantity index for each year. This is because the *evaluation* involves comparing the stream of actual costs to measured benefits, whereas the *explanation* attempts to aggregate across different categories of expenditure, accounting for changes in the composition of that expenditure, since different types of expenditure

---

82.   During its formative years, the state agricultural experiment station system in the United States spent upwards of 29% of its total expenditures on capital inputs. For some states in some years the share was around 60% (Pardey, Craig and Hallaway 1989).

have a different impact on the production of new knowledge, and a constant relationship is posited between the production of new knowledge and the quantity of research.

In a practical evaluation study, the quantity index may be used in the first stage to estimate the parameters of the research production function. Then, in a subsequent step, alternatives are simulated. In order to evaluate the alternatives, it is necessary to translate the series of simulated counterfactual quantity indexes into a research-expenditure counterpart. This step is usually left implicit, and we suspect the issue has been largely overlooked. To our knowledge, all previous studies have used research expenditures directly in the econometrics, ignoring the index-number problems. That omission has involved an implicit assumption that the composition of total research expenditure is constant or, at least, that changes in the composition of expenditures are econometrically unimportant. Such an assumption is convenient in that data to enable a better index to be constructed are often unavailable.[83] Also, work remains to be done on how best to design counterfactual simulations of the streams of component expenditures.

Measuring Extension

Throughout this book, we have regarded and treated extension as a component of a continuum of types of R&D activities that interact and together determine the impact of R&D expenditures. On this view, extension is the same, conceptually, as any other R&D input: the measurement issues are no different and the approaches are the same as for agricultural research, as discussed above. And the typical distinction between research and extension is somewhat arbitrary; similar distinctions might also be drawn, with equal or greater justification, among other categories within the R&D aggregate (e.g., between pretechnology, applied, and development research; or public, private, and foreign research, as discussed in chapter 2).

Like different types of research, different types of extension have different types of effects. Some research conducted in U.S. agricultural experiment stations, for instance, bears no perceptible relationship to production agriculture, including some applied work on nonagricultural topics as well as basic research. Similarly, some extension work is directed toward urban issues. In some cases where there might be a connection to production agriculture, its nature may be vague (e.g., 4-H extension activities, home economics, etc.). Some previous studies (e.g., Huffman 1978) have attempted to distinguish

83. See Pardey, Craig and Hallaway (1989) for an example of decomposing research costs into various categories. See also Mansfield (1987) and Bengsten (1989a and b) for a related discussion of R&D price indexes.

between extension work that affects *productive* efficiency and that which affects *allocative* efficiency. Such distinctions are difficult to draw conceptually, let alone in the data that are typically available.

Typically, for both research and extension, we must aggregate across types of expenditures (as well as over time), and more often than not, extension is aggregated with research in a single R&D variable (e.g., Griliches 1964; Evenson 1968; Cline 1975; Mullen, Cox and Foster 1992). Such aggregation is undesirable to the extent that research and extension have different kinds of effects on knowledge or output. It is also undesirable where there is some interest in differential effects or where the mix of research and extension has been changing over time so that aggregation bias is likely to result from aggregating research and extension.[84] In any of these cases, it would be preferable to include separate research and extension variables (perhaps allowing for interaction effects), but in practice, multicollinearity is likely to be a problem. The use of preaggregated research and extension variables, as by Huffman and Evenson (1992), might be necessary to circumvent the statistical problems that can arise when both research and extension variables are included in an econometric model.

Like research, while much of the extension effort is carried out in the public sector, a significant and increasing amount is being done privately by agribusiness, either as part of their marketing effort or on a fee-for-service basis. And farmers themselves invest heavily in search and screen activities among private and public information sources, which are increasingly accessible through electronic and print media. Data on either agribusiness or farmer investments in extension-related activities are typically not available in a form suitable for econometric analysis, if at all, so the main implication of this is that one must be aware of the potential biases from excluded variables when interpreting estimates from an incomplete model. A similar caveat applies with equal or greater force to the very common (almost universal) practice of estimating models including public- but not private-sector research.

---

84. In particular, it is commonly suggested that extension lags are shorter than research lags, and spillover effects may be important for research (for which the model might need to include research spill-in variables as well as local research) but not for extension (for which it might be sufficient to include only local expenditures).

Aggregating Research and Extension — Temporal Aggregation

The capital-theory approach to modeling the generation and use of knowledge in agriculture defines a stock-of-knowledge variable, K_t, in terms of the (depreciated) stock of existing knowledge, K_{t-1}, and net increments to that stock, I_t, as in section 3.1.1. Assuming that a geometric, declining-balance, depreciation process applies to the knowledge stock, such that $D_t = (1 - \delta_K)K_t$, equation 3.3 becomes

$$K_t = I_{t-1} + (1-\delta_K)K_{t-1} \tag{3.64}$$

where δ_K is the rate at which existing knowledge becomes obsolete because it is replaced by better information or circumstances change to make it less useful. Crop management practices developed and used in the 1950s may be of limited use today given the availability of genetically superior crop varieties, improved agricultural chemicals, improved farm machinery, and so on. Such obsolescence is reinforced by biological deterioration through, for example, the evolution of resistant diseases and pests that lower yield potential and may increase the yield variability of existing crop varieties over time.[85] Changing economic circumstances can shift relative prices in a particular locale and lead to changes in local output and factor mixes that lower the productive value of existing agricultural knowledge targeted for that locale.

The notion of a stable relationship between research expenditures and increments to the stock of knowledge follows naturally from the perception that in general, science progresses by a sequence of marginal improvements rather than through a series of discrete, essentially sporadic, breakthroughs.[86] The systematic aspects of this input-output relationship in research are directly related to the degree of aggregation being employed. For instance, the annual publication count or knowledge output of individual scientists may vary quite capriciously, but this random variation is less important at higher levels of aggregation (e.g., at the project, program, or system level).[87] A general form for the knowledge or research production function was defined in section 3.1.1 (equation 3.4) as

$$I_t = i\,(R_t, \ldots, R_{t-L_R}, K_{t-1}, \tilde{Z}_t) \tag{3.65}$$

where current increments to knowledge, I_t, are determined by the historical pattern of research expenditures, the existing stock of knowledge (here

85. See Anderson and Hazell (1989) and the references therein.

86. See, for example, Minasian (1969), Rosenberg (1976), Griliches (1979), Pakes and Griliches (1980), Kamien and Schwartz (1982), and Pardey (1986).

87. For this reason, among others, it does not make much sense to use these procedures to evaluate the effects of a narrowly defined field of research.

broadly defined to include fundamental and pretechnology types of knowledge) and a set of institutional variables, $\tilde{Z}_t$, related to the management and deployment of research staff and the resources with which they work. The mix of research may matter. When budget cuts curtail the fundamental sciences, the marginal gains from continued investments in the more applied agricultural sciences may fall.[88] Similarly, the efficacy of agricultural research is likely to vary with the commodity, site, and problem focus of the research. Some production problems for some commodities (e.g., rust in wheat or black sigatoka in bananas) are simply harder and, consequently, more costly and time-consuming to solve than others.

Taking equations 3.64 and 3.65 together, it is convenient to view *maintenance research* — which seeks to replace or replenish the (research-induced) productivity gains from past research investments — as leading to new knowledge that substitutes for declines in the stock of usable knowledge. Ruttan (1982, p. 60) speculated that the rate of knowledge decay, δ_K, is likely to increase as agricultural production systems become more knowledge intensive so that a larger share of research resources is needed simply to maintain the exisiting knowledge stock. This decay rate is an additional source of "instability" in the relationship between research and knowledge stocks. If a particular crop in a specific locale is analyzed, then the relevant δ_K may well be quite volatile over time and not constant as depicted here. For instance, in the early 1970s, outbreaks of brown planthopper in Indonesia inflicted a great deal of damage on improved but nonresistant varieties of rice, implying a significant and sudden increase in δ_K for genotypic-based rice technologies used in parts of Indonesia. As the commodity and locational focus of the analysis broadens, one would expect a lower and more stable rate of knowledge decay.[89]

The extent of utilization of the existing stock of knowledge (i.e., the service flows, F, arising from the existing knowledge stock) depends upon the relative prices of products, P_t, and factors, W_t, the stock of farmers' human capital, H_t, and the extent and quality of extension services, E_t, among other things, so that

$$F_t = \mathrm{f}\,(K_t, P_t, W_t, H_t, E_t) \tag{3.66}$$

Combining equations 3.64, 3.65, and 3.66, it is possible to accommodate these conceptual ideas in an empirically tractable way by defining the stock of knowledge *in use* as

88. Evenson and Kislev (1975, ch. 8) develop this idea in more detail. Recent examples of this phenomenon are modern technologies of gene manipulation and control, which had their origins during the early 1970s in the health sciences (Persley 1990) and have given rise to the "biotechnology revoution" that offers the promise of significant technology advances within the agricultural sciences.

89. Although in a shift to more intensive, monocropping systems, a consequent narrowing of the genetic base in use may offset this tendency.

$$K_t = k\,(R_t^*, E_t^*) \tag{3.67a}$$

where the effects of prices and human capital variables are suppressed, for simplicity. Assuming a constant-elasticity functional form for the lag relationship, the stock of knowledge in use may be defined as[90]

$$K_t = \prod_{r=1}^{\infty} R_{t-r}^{\lambda_r} \prod_{e=1}^{\infty} E_{t-e}^{\phi_e} \tag{3.67b}$$

where, in this instance, λ_r and ϕ_e are the lag coefficients that specify the shape of the lag profile linking local research expenditures in period $t-r$, R_{t-r}, and extension expenditures in period $t-e$, E_{t-e}, to the stock of knowledge being *used* in period t.

The process by which investments in research and extension lead to changes in technology is complex.[91] Quantifying the process usually entails aggregating across a portfolio of research activities (e.g., across different technology types, commodities, or institutions) that vary in many respects, not least in their lag profiles. The lag between the inception and completion of a line of research (i.e., the research gestation lag) can be around two to three years for some crop-management types of research (e.g., developing improved fertilizer recommendations). The lag may be even shorter if the research is highly adaptive or of a search-and-screen nature that builds directly on earlier work. In contrast, conventional breeding programs for cereals usually take six to ten years to develop a new variety, while similar work on perennial crops such as coconuts or bananas can take up to fifteen years.

All of these lags are influenced by the specific research problems being addressed and by the experience and talent of the researchers doing the work. For example, a barley breeding program may seek to increase yield potentials, improve nutritional or malting qualities, incorporate some degree of pest or disease resistance, or involve some combination of all of these traits. Lags are also affected by the institutional environment in which the work is carried out. For example, persistent problems of insufficient or untimely disbursement of

90. It is important to note that the choice of functional form for the construction of the index of the stock of knowledge in use is not dictated by theory and may have implications that are undesirable. Here, for instance, the choice of a geometric (linear-in-logarithms) form means that every past value of research or extension is *necessary* in the sense that if the value of any one of them is zero, the value of the stock will fall to zero. The linear-in-logarithms form is econometrically convenient when combined with a Cobb-Douglas model and has been popular for that reason. A linear-in-levels form would not have the problem of all past values being necessary but it could imply increasing returns to scale in some specifications. This is another example of the general problem that analytical convenience and tractability, which often dominate specification choices, may not always fit well with the other requirements of the analysis.

91. Nelson and Winter (1982), for example, develop an evolutionary model of technical change that tries to incorporate some of these complexities.

operational funds may result in missed growing seasons and considerably longer research cycles. Research programs with limited experience or expertise in a particular line of research may incur substantial start-up costs or delays that do not apply to on-going, "mature" research programs.

Once new technologies are available, there are further, and often substantial, lags in their adoption. While many of the green-revolution technologies have been developed and extended in package form (e.g., new plant varieties plus recommended fertilizer, pesticide, and herbicide use, along with water control measures) many of the components of these technological packages are taken up in a piecemeal, often stepwise, fashion (Herdt and Capule 1983; Byerlee and de Polanco 1986). Eventually, new technologies are given up as they are replaced by superior or substitute technologies. Natural, economic, and political forces all have a direct bearing on adoption and disadoption processes.[92] The role of public and private extension services — broadly defined to include the technology-transfer activities of the input-supply sector and the search-and-screen activities of farmers themselves — are particularly pertinent in this regard. At the same time, some countries have unduly cumbersome or inefficient seed certification and distribution systems that cause additional delays in getting new technologies into farmers' fields. Such complications make it difficult, both conceptually and empirically, to isolate the effects of research from those of extension. The specification provided in equation 3.67 implies that it is possible to estimate separate effects of research and extension on agricultural output or productivity growth. To the extent that the effects of research are not independent of expenditures on extension, it might be appropriate to incorporate a research-extension interaction term (or terms) into this specification (Evenson 1988; Huffman and Evenson 1993).

In practice, the *temporal weights* λ_r and ϕ_e in equation 3.67 are reduced-form lag coefficients linking current and past research and extension expenditures to agricultural output, variable costs, profit, or productivity measures; they represent a complex convolution of a whole array of activities involving knowledge-cum-technology generation and transfer. The nature of these lag profiles is sensitive to the mixes of activities included in the research and extension aggregates. Changing the commodity orientation of research or its technology, disciplinary, or problem focus is likely to induce changes in the lag structures.

Typical, finite lag structures: Some rather loose priors concerning the likely shape and length of the R&D gestation, adoption, and obsolescence phases of a specific technology (e.g., a new crop variety or an improved pest-control practice) have been used to impose well-defined and deterministic structures on lag coefficients. This is usually done to reduce the number of

---

92. See Lindner (1981) and Feder and Umali (1993) for a review of the pertinent adoption literature.

coefficients being estimated in order to skirt degrees-of-freedom constraints or avoid multicollinearity problems. But in the absence of complete information on the mix of research included in the knowledge *aggregate* being modeled and measured, it is not clear whether such priors are appropriate. In particular, it is questionable whether a *finite* lag process can properly represent the effects of past research and the entire knowledge stock on current output, productivity, costs, or profits even when a finite lag process might well characterize increments to the knowledge stock. An infinite lag requires a different approach to empirical specification and estimation. Even if a finite lag is appropriate, imposing a form for its structure a priori involves obvious dangers.

This set of reservations notwithstanding, figure 3.6 depicts the finite lag structures commonly used to form a preaggregated research expenditure variable, R_t^*, for inclusion as a regressor in a production, cost, profit, supply, or productivity function.[93] The lag coefficients, λ_r, for an inverted-V (or *DeLeeuw*) lag profile are given by

$$\lambda_r = r\lambda \qquad \text{for } 0 \leq r < \frac{L_R}{2}$$

$$\qquad (3.68a)$$

$$= (L_R - r)\lambda \quad \text{for } \frac{L_R}{2} \leq r \leq L_R$$

where here, by construction, $\lambda_0 = \lambda_{L_R} = 0$ and r takes values from 0 to L_R.[94] Thus,

$$R_t^* = \prod_{r=0}^{L_R/2} R_{t-r}^r \prod_{r=(L_R/2)+1}^{L_R} R_{t-r}^{(L_R - r)} \qquad (3.68b)$$

or, in corresponding logarithmic form,[95]

$$\ln R_t^* = \sum_{r=0}^{L_R/2} r \ln R_{t-r} + \sum_{r=(L_R/2)+1}^{L_R} (L_R - r) \ln R_{t-r} \qquad (3.68c)$$

It is the preaggregated research variable, $\ln R_t^*$, that is included as an explan-

---

93. If we were using the form given by equation 3.67b, then $R_t^* = \prod_{r=0}^{L_R} R_{t-r}^{\lambda_r}$.

94. See Maddala (1977) for additional discussion of this and other lag structures.

95. This is the form most commonly used to preaggregate current and lagged research (and extension) expenditures for inclusion as an argument in Cobb-Douglas or translog-type functions expressed in logarithmic form. There is, in fact, no intrinsic reason why a linearly preaggregated research variable, wherein $R_t^* = \sum_r \lambda_r R_{t-r}$, could not be used in these instances. Use of the geometric aggregation procedure anticipates the need to recover the coefficients on individual R_{t-r}'s when calculating the temporal effect of research (see section 3.3.2).

Figure 3.6:   *Finite research lag structures*

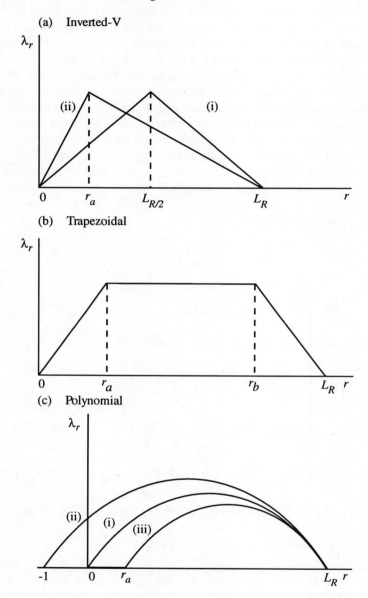

(a)   Inverted-V

(b)   Trapezoidal

(c)   Polynomial

atory variable in the production functions (3.42 or 3.43) or the cost functions (3.45 or 3.46). The coefficient on $\ln R_t^*$ is an estimate of λ. If R_t^* were taken to represent a knowledge stock, then λ measures the effect of marginal changes in the knowledge stock on output, profit, or variable costs. However, many other components of the knowledge stock have been left out.[96] Substituting the estimate of λ in 3.68a gives estimates of the λ,s, $r = 1, \ldots, L_R$. These λ,s can be interpreted as measures of the partial impact of research in time $t-r$ on output in time t or, equivalently, the partial impact of research in time t on output in time $t+r$.

A nonsymmetric variant of an inverted-V specification is obtained by respecifying equation 3.68a so that

$$
\begin{aligned}
\lambda_r &= r\lambda && \text{for } 0 \le r < r_a \\
&= (L_R - r)\lambda && \text{for } r_a \le r \le L_R
\end{aligned}
\tag{3.69}
$$

where $0 \le r_a \le L_R$ and $\ln R_t^*$ from equation 3.68c is suitably respecified. The trapezoidal structure can be viewed simply as an extension of the inverted-V specification whereby

$$
\begin{aligned}
\lambda_r &= r\lambda && \text{for } 0 \le r < r_a \\
&= r_a\lambda && \text{for } r_a \le r < r_a \\
&= (L_R - r_a - r)\lambda && \text{for } r_b \le r \le L_R
\end{aligned}
\tag{3.70a}
$$

and, by construction, $\lambda_0 = \lambda_{L_R} = 0$ so that

$$
\ln R_t^* = \sum_{r=0}^{r_a} r \ln R_{t-r} + r_a \sum_{r=r_a+1}^{r_b} \ln R_{t-r} + \sum_{r=r_b+1}^{L_R} (L_R - r_a - r) \ln R_{t-r}
\tag{3.70b}
$$

Once again the coefficient on $\ln R_t^*$ is as an estimate of λ, which can be substituted into 3.70a to give an estimate of the λ,s.

Imposing a polynomial or *Almon* lag structure on the λ,s has been the most popular means of forming an aggregate of research expenditures. Based on the rather informal prior reasoning that the impact of the new knowledge arising from research first rises and then falls, a quadratic polynomial is usually specified such that

$$
\lambda_r = \alpha_0 + \alpha_1 r + \alpha_2 r^2 \quad \text{where } r = 0, \ldots, L_R
\tag{3.71a}
$$

so that

96. For instance, the components of the knowledge stock created by private-sector agricultural research, private- or public-sector agricultural research conducted elsewhere, and basic science or nonagricultural research are all typically excluded.

$$\ln R_t^* = \sum_{r=0}^{L_R} (\alpha_0 + \alpha_1 r + \alpha_2 r^2) \ln R_{t-r}$$

$$= \alpha_0 \ln R_{0,t}^* + \alpha_1 \ln R_{1,t}^* + \alpha_2 \ln R_{2,t}^* \qquad (3.71b)$$

where

$$\ln R_{0,t}^* = \sum_{r=0}^{L_R} \ln R_{t-r} \, ; \, \ln R_{1,t}^* = \sum_{r=0}^{L_R} r \ln R_{t-r}$$

and   (3.71c)

$$\ln R_{2,t}^* = \sum_{r=0}^{L_R} r^2 \ln R_{t-r}$$

In this instance the preaggregated research variables $\ln R_{0,t}^*$, $\ln R_{1,t}^*$, and $\ln R_{2,t}^*$ are used as regressors in production or cost functions to yield direct estimates of the αs, which can then be used in conjunction with 3.71a to obtain estimates of the λ_rs. Unfortunately, the three parameters obtained using the computationally simple Almon lag approach can generate implausible, negative lag coefficients (i.e., λ_rs) for individual years at the beginning or end of the lag structure (Ravenscraft and Scherer 1982). To avoid this possibility, "endpoint constraints," such that $\lambda_{-1} = \lambda_{L_R+1} = 0$, are commonly imposed so that

$$\alpha_0 = -\alpha_2 (L_R + 1) \quad \text{and} \quad \alpha_1 = -\alpha_2 L_R \qquad (3.71d)$$

and hence 3.71b reduces to[97]

$$\ln R_t^* = \sum_{r=0}^{L_R} (r^2 - L_R r - L_R - 1) \ln R_{t-1} \qquad (3.71e)$$

where the coefficient on the research aggregate, $\ln R_t^*$, from 3.71e is simply α_2 from equation 3.71a. The estimate α_2 can be used in conjunction with equations 3.71d and 3.71a to obtain estimates of the lag coefficients, λ_r, for $r = 0, \ldots, L_R$. Imposing the two endpoint constraints reduces the number of research coefficients to be estimated from three (in equation 3.71c) to one (in equation 3.71e), thereby avoiding the multicollinearity problems that often arise in practice from including $\ln R_{0,t}^*$, $\ln R_{1,t}^*$, and $\ln R_{2,t}^*$, in the estimating equation.

More flexible lag structures: Preaggregating lagged research expenditures using the DeLeeuw, trapezoidal, or polynomial lag structures described

---

97. Substituting $r = -1$ and $r = (L_R+1)$ into $\lambda_r = \alpha_0 + \alpha_1 r + \alpha_2 r^2$ gives $0 = \alpha_0 - \alpha_1 + \alpha_2$ and $0 = \alpha_0 + \alpha_1 (L_R+1) + \alpha_2 (L_R+1)^2$, respectively, which in turn simplify to 3.71e.

above makes it possible to reduce the variances of the estimated short-run effects of research, i.e., the variance on the individual $\lambda_i s$, but only at the cost of introducing an unknown degree of bias in the resulting estimates. In many (if not all) cases the priors imposed through these lag structures are ad hoc (Griliches 1967). It is common for analysts to argue that it is "plausible" for the weights on the R&D lag structure to have a particular shape and to use these "priors" to impose a definite shape on the individual year coefficients.

If the analysis is focused on a particular commodity, it may be possible to use extraneous information on the average lag between the inception of research and the availability of new technology for various lines of research on that commodity, as well as information on the subsequent pattern of adoption of a "representative" technology (e.g., a new crop variety), to impose some meaningful structure on the analysis. Even if some smoothness priors are imposed on these lag weights and the general shape of the lag structure can be presumed, many aspects of these structures (such as lag length, mean lag, and skewness) are unknown but are implicit in any parameterization of a particular lag structure. One way of addressing this problem is to use the sample data to pretest the lag length along with various other parameters of a specific lag form. This is usually done by searching over a range of alternative parameterizations and choosing the set of restrictions that minimize the sum-of-squared residuals. Studies by Smith, Norton and Havlicek (1983) and Swallow, et al. (1985), for example, presumed a second-order polynomial lag structure (with or without end-point constraints) and tested for lag length, while Evenson (1980) performed grid searches over the three parameters (i.e., r_a, r_b, and L_R in equation 3.70b) that define a specific trapezoidal structure. The problem with this approach is that these specification searches are performed with a particular, inflexible lag form (e.g., inverted-V, trapezoidal, or polynomial) as a maintained hypothesis.

A number of other practical options for imposing smoothness priors on these lag weights entail less severe prior restrictions than the above approaches and more reasonably reflect our still rudimentary prior knowledge. One is to presume an "equivalence" between the more flexible probability-generating functions described by Solow (1960), Griliches (1967), and others and the lag operators that give the weights used in forming an R&D expenditure aggregate.

Probability-generating functions such as the *binomial* distribution (see Ravenscraft and Scherer 1982) or the *Pascal* distribution (see Solow 1960) have quite flexible shapes, subject to the constraint that the individual lag effects are positive and smooth. Using the binomial function, the lag weights are given by

$$\lambda_r = \left(\frac{L_R!}{(L_R-r)!r!} \right) \theta^r (1-\theta)^{L_R-r} \quad r = 0, 1, \ldots, L_R \qquad (3.72)$$

where θ is the binomial parameter. For the Pascal distribution, the weights are defined as

$$\lambda_r = \left(\frac{\phi + r - 1}{r} \right) \gamma^r (1 - \gamma^\phi) \quad r = 0, 1, \ldots, L_R \qquad (3.73)$$

where ϕ and γ are the two Pascal parameters. Estimates can be made by searching over values of θ or ϕ and γ for a specification that minimizes the sum-of-squares residuals after imposing L_R.

If $\theta = 0.5$, the binomial lag structure approximates a symmetric, *normal* distribution; with small values of θ the distribution is skewed right (i.e., with the peak near zero so that the mode is always less than the mean); for very small values a *geometric* (e.g., *Koyck*) distribution is approximated; for $\theta > 0.5$ the distribution is skewed left. A Pascal distribution is skewed to the right if γ is large, with smaller ϕ leading to greater skewness. If $\gamma = 1$, the Pascal is simply a *geometric* distribution; it approaches a *Poisson* (of mean m) as $\gamma \to 0$ and $\gamma\phi \to m$, and if m is large, the limiting form is a *Gaussian* distribution.

Form-free lag structures: While these types of distributions are quite flexible, the choice of any one distributional form, a priori, still imposes a definite (and not necessarily appropriate) shape on the individual lag coefficients. An altogether different approach is to use the form-free distributed lag technique developed by Hatanaka and Wallace (1980) and apparently first used by Silver and Wallace (1980). In the Hatanaka and Wallace approach, it is not the lag structure per se but the moments (i.e., the total lag effect or sum of coefficients, μ_0, the mean of the distribution, μ_1, the variance of the distribution, μ_2, and higher-order moments)[98] of an arbitrary lag distribution that are estimated directly.

Applying the Hatanaka and Wallace (1980) form-free approach to estimating R&D lag structures would mean including current and lagged research expenditures as separate regressors in the function being estimated. While the λ_r coefficients on the individual research expenditure variables (measuring the short-run effects of research on output, variable cost, or profit) are generally estimated with low precision, linear combinations of these coefficients are likely to have lower variances than the individual coefficients. This is because positively autocorrelated variables, such as most time series of research (and extension) expenditures, give rise to estimated regression coefficients that by

---

98. With this notation, the i subscript on μ_i indicates the order of the moment, so that $i = 0$ is a zero-order moment, $i = 1$ is a first-order moment, and so on.

and large have negative covariances. Therefore, the sum of the λ_r, coefficients has a variance smaller than the sum of their variances. Moreover, Hatanaka and Wallace (1980) argue that in their method, the lower-order moments (i.e., the total effect, $\mu_0 = \sum_r \lambda_r$, the mean $\mu_1 = \sum_r r \lambda_r$, and the variance $\mu_2 = \sum_r r^2 \lambda_r$), which are of greater practical interest, are generally estimated with greater precision. Moreover, there is a hierarchy of precision: $V(\mu_0) < V(\mu_1) < V(\mu_2)$.

Directly estimating the moments of a lag distribution using a procedure that imposes no priors on the shape — but which does require the fairly plausible notion of smoothness and non-negativity concerning the lag weights and also presumes a given lag length — affords the analyst various options.[99] One option is to employ the method-of-moments technique to estimate the relevant parameters of a flexible probability density function using the moments obtained from a first pass through the data, and then to impose shape restrictions that are not at variance with the data when research expenditures are preaggregated for a second round. This approach is described by Silver and Wallace (1980), for example.

Spatial Aggregation

The new knowledge generated from research by other states, regions, or countries on similar outputs, inputs, or production problems can have a positive effect on the performance and payoff to local research. The importance of *spillover effects* has been studied for a number of different industries (Jaffe 1986; Bernstein and Nadiri 1988, 1989) in addition to agriculture (Evenson and Kislev 1975; Evenson 1989) and was recently reviewed by Griliches (1992). Empirical estimates for spillover-intensive industries in the United States attribute up to two-thirds of the research-induced productivity gains to spillovers (Bernstein and Nadiri 1989).

A form-free approach to assessing the spillover effects of nonlocal research, which is analogous to the form-free approach described above with respect to temporally aggregated research expenditures, would be to include temporally preaggregated research expenditure variables in the analysis for each of the nonlocal research sites deemed relevant in terms of their potential to generate research spill-ins to the site of interest. For example, if the units of analysis were states or provinces within a country, then separate research expenditure variables would be included for all other states, regions or countries doing research that is potentially relevant to the "home state." This approach is usually not feasible because of problems with multicollinearity

---

99. Truncating the fitted structure so that it is short relative to the "true" (but unknown) lag structure will cause estimates to be biased; including lagged terms whose coefficients are zero does not bias the estimates but does increase the variances.

or degrees of freedom.

In a manner analogous to the temporal aggregation procedures discussed above, the most tractable approach is to define a plausible set of *spatial weights,* γ_{hk}, which enable research conducted in a number of other locations, $R^*_{h,p}$ to be combined into a research spillover aggregate, $S^*_{k,t}$, that reflects the pool of nonlocal research that may spill in to the home region, k, such that

$$S^*_{k,t} = \prod_{\substack{h \neq k}}^{H} (R^*_{h,t})^{\gamma_{hk}} \tag{3.74}$$

Then an augmented version of 3.67a can be formed so that

$$K_{k,t} = k\left(R^*_{k,t}, \; S^*_{k,t}, \; E^*_{k,t} \right) \tag{3.75}$$

where $K_{k,t}$ represents the current (period t) stock of knowledge in use in the kth locale, and $R^*_{k,p}$ $S^*_{k,p}$ and $E^*_{k,t}$ respectively represent the preaggregated local research, nonlocal research, and local extension variables that pertain to the kth locale.

In constructing $S^*_{k,p}$ one option is simply to sum all the nonlocal research (i.e., $\gamma_{hk} = 1.0$ for all h and k). This is not a particularly fruitful approach. It does not address the question of how to decide what constitutes *relevant* research, and in so doing, it inappropriately treats all nonlocal research as being *equally* relevant from the perspective of its spill-in potential to a particular locale. In practice, most country studies exclude all research done abroad (i.e, the γ_{hk}s are implicitly set to zero when h indexes research carried out by other countries), even though there is clear evidence, for at least some commodities, that substantial international technology transfers are possible.[100] And for those studies where the unit of analysis has been states or regions within a country, there has been little uniformity in the way out-of-state research has been treated.

For several reasons, distance from the source of information plays a significant role in shaping research spillover potentials, particularly in agriculture, (e.g., Lindner, Pardey and Jarrett 1982), but spatial closeness is an incomplete indicator of spillover potential. Evenson (1980, 1989), Otto (1981), and others have used the concept of an *agroecological zone* and the relationship between geopolitically defined *regions* (e.g., states within the United States) and these *zones* when defining the γ_{hk}s. The idea is that the potential for agricultural research to spill over is higher between locations that are in some sense agroecologically similar than between locations that are not. While this is intuitively appealing, it is often difficult to implement. First, there are problems in defining the technical criteria (e.g., aspects of

---

100. See, for example, Brennan (1986) in the case of wheat and Pardey et al. (1992) for rice.

soil, climate, and topography) by which to construct relevant agroecological zones (Wood and Pardey 1993). Second, depending on the scale at which they are defined, the agroecological zones may not correspond closely to the geopolitical regions by which research expenditures and other economic variables are usually reported. Deciding which zone (or part thereof) and hence which γ_{hk} is pertinent for any two regions h and k is problematic.

Studies that aggregate across a number of commodities or technologies that vary in their site-specificity face further problems. Some subsectors (e.g., intensive livestock operations or glasshouse horticulture) may be less sensitive to variations in the natural environment, so the potential for spillovers to occur over greater physical distances is higher. In addition, economic, institutional, and other factors exacerbate or ameliorate the ecological constraints to technology transfers.

Given the conceptual and practical difficulties of formally using agro-ecological zones to measure region-to-region spillover potentials (i.e., the γ_{hk}s), some less-demanding "reduced-form" procedures may be in order. It is reasonable to expect that the economic, ecological, and social characteristics of a region are reflected in the commodity orientation and input use within the region. On the presumption that local research is congruent with local commodity (and input) mixes, a measure of *technological proximity*, γ_{hk}^p, can be used as a proxy for spillover potential. Given an n-dimensional vector of outputs and an m-dimensional vector of inputs, the "position" of region s in input-output space can be characterized by a vector $F_s = (f^1, \ldots, f^n, f^{n+1}, \ldots, f^{m+n})$ where each of the elements of F_s denotes the region's or state's quantity of outputs, $j = 1, \ldots, n$, or quantity of inputs $i = 1, \ldots, m$, respectively. Following Jaffe (1986, 1989), a measure of the *technological proximity*, γ_{hk}^p, between any two regions h and k in input-output space can be defined as

$$\gamma_{hk}^p = \frac{F_h F_k'}{\sqrt{(F_h F_h')(F_k F_k')}} \tag{3.76}$$

Clearly, γ_{hk}^p equals one if both input and output quantities — up to a factor of proportionality — are identical and will approach zero the more dissimilar the input and output mix is between any two regions. If the output bundles of two regions are dominated by corn, for example, then the research portfolios of both regions will be similarly biased toward corn. In this case, the spillover potential would be higher than if the comparison were between a predominantly corn-producing region and, say, a coconut-producing region. Differences in the factor mix across regions — for instance region 1 produces corn using "low-input" rainfed technologies while region 2 uses "high-input" irrigation technologies — means that the spillover potential of corn-related research is lower than if patterns of factor use *and* technology structures were similar across the regions.

3.2.6   Statistical and Econometric Issues

In addition to the conceptual and measurement issues discussed above, several econometric problems can arise in models used for research evaluation. The most severe problems typically include (a) specification error, (b) multicollinearity, and (c) simultaneity problems.

Specification Error

If relevant variables are omitted from a model, then the included variables must explain the effects of other omitted variables as well as their own effects. As Griliches (1957) and others have shown, in a linear model, $E(b_1) = \beta_1 + \beta_2 P_1$ where β_1 is the "true" coefficient, b_1 is the OLS estimate of that coefficient when another relevant variable has been omitted (and $E(b_1)$ is the expected value of the OLS estimate of β_1), β_2 is the coefficient that would have been found on the omitted variable, and P_1 is the regression coefficient that would be found if the omitted variable were regressed on the included variable.

If the omitted variable is not correlated with the included variable (i.e., $P_1 = 0$), the estimated coefficients on the included variables will be unbiased. If $P_1 \neq 0$, the bias depends on the signs and magnitudes of β_2 and P_1. In the examples discussed earlier, if extension, education, and private research are omitted, and these variables are expected to positively influence production and are positively correlated with research, then the research coefficient will be biased upward.

When a variable is included but mismeasured, the coefficients of included variables may be biased as a result. For example, if the quality of an input has changed over time but a quality adjustment has not been made, the coefficient on the research variable will be biased if research is correlated with the quality of the input. There has been a debate in the literature over whether inputs should be left unadjusted for quality changes that result from research so that a more complete assessment of the impact of research can be obtained from the research variable.[101]

Multicollinearity

Multicollinearity can be a serious problem, particularly with time-series data, when production functions are used to evaluate agricultural research. Many variables move together over time, and research, extension, and

---

101.   See Denison (1961, 1969) and Jorgenson and Griliches (1967).

education are often highly correlated, particularly if the formulation of the lag structures calls for the inclusion of more than one variable for each factor. When multicollinearity is serious, the large variances on regression coefficients for the collinear variables mean that limited confidence can be placed in the parameter estimates.[102] The model becomes highly sensitive to specification and to sample coverage. Parameters exhibiting large standard errors — instability and lack of conformity to prior expectations — may indicate multicollinearity. Sometimes, however, problems arising from specification error are attributed to multicollinearity.[103]

There are no easy solutions. More data, more prior information, or some other means of making fewer demands on the data are the only options. Sometimes prior beliefs can be imposed as restrictions on the coefficients on nonresearch variables (e.g., making use of mixed estimations in which coefficients on conventional inputs in a Cobb-Douglas production function are constrained to be equal to their factor shares). This procedure assumes profit-maximizing behavior and equilibrium.[104] Biased estimation procedures such as ridge regression and principal-components regression are also feasible. These procedures trade off variance for bias, but selection of a final regression must be based on highly subjective tests.[105] Ridge regression can be expected to perform best in situations where the data are highly collinear and all coefficients are expected to be of the same sign and roughly the same size, as may arise in production functions estimated with time-series data.[106]

Multicollinearity among nonresearch, extension, or education variables is likely to be less of a problem with cost, profit, or supply functions than with production functions because most real input and output prices are less highly correlated than production inputs. On the other hand, serial correlation may be more serious.

Simultaneity and Causality

Simultaneity is often a problem when a production function is estimated to evaluate agricultural research.[107] The problem arises for two major reasons.

102. For example, see Belsley, Kuh and Welsch (1980).

103. Diagnostic tests based on variance inflation factors, condition indexes, and variance proportions, which are available with many regression packages, can be used to detect some such problems.

104. The use of productivity functions may be thought of as a further example of this type of approach, where the structure of the technology is effectively imposed as a prior restriction in order to focus the estimation on the response to research.

105. For examples of ridge regression applied in an evaluation of agricultural research, see Norton, Coffey and Frye (1984) and Leiby and Adams (1991).

106. See Brown and Beattie (1975).

107. See Marschak and Andrews (1944).

First, conventional inputs may not be behaviorally and, hence, statistically exogenous variables. Uncontrollable factors *during* a production period (e.g., weather or pests) commonly affect *both* inputs and outputs (affecting the input-output relationship), so the measured effects of inputs become biased because the input quantities are correlated with the error terms in the model. Second, future output and its profitability may depend on past research, but research expenditures in turn may depend on both past output and expectations about its future.[108] These two sources of simultaneity are related but arise in somewhat different ways.

Simultaneity between the quantity, price, or value of production of a commodity and the value of research spending can arise from funding arrangements that use output levies or taxes, for example. In these cases, a rise in output (say, in response to an increase in demand) will lead to an automatic increase in the total funds available for research. Similar forces might also be at work in situations without explicit tax arrangements if, for instance, research resources are allocated according to a congruence rule — in proportion to the value of output. Also, while farmers do not directly choose a level of research in the same way as they choose conventional inputs, changes in output levels can lead producers to pressure governments to adjust support for research in general or for particular commodities.

These forces are not likely to result in serious statistical problems of simultaneity because of timing: current research does not affect current output but current (or recent) output can affect current research. The relationship is more likely to be recursive than simultaneous. Using a set of causality tests, Pardey and Craig (1989) provide evidence that while research expenditures do cause output changes, output indexes also carry information that helps predict future research expenditures. Their results suggest that part of what is measured as an effect of research on output may in fact reflect the effect of output changes on research. The empirical significance of simultaneity problems is difficult to assess and there is no truly satisfactory solution to the problem in the production-function framework. While an instrumental-variables approach may be tried, in a study that involves estimating a large number of commodity production functions, it might be preferable simply to acknowledge the possible bias.

It is often argued that simultaneity is less of a problem with profit- or cost-function models because many of the independent variables are prices. In a competitive market, prices are determined by the market and not by individual farmers. Hence, price variables and error terms should be uncorrelated (Varian 1978). However, while such reasoning may be valid for models estimated with farm-level data, it may be less valid when aggregate national,

---

108.   See Griliches (1979), Pardey and Craig (1989), and Schimmelpfennig and Thirtle (1994).

regional, or state-level data are used. For example, if national time-series data are used, observed output prices may be influenced to some extent by aggregate output levels. Furthermore, just as with the production function, research expenditures may be influenced by aggregate output levels. With either of these situations, the independent variables might be correlated with the error term.

Simultaneity between output and price may be reduced by use of lagged or futures prices, but it probably will not be completely eliminated, particularly with futures prices. There is little that can be done to reduce the problem associated with output causing research expenditures, although the problem is mitigated somewhat by the fact that research expenditures are included in a lagged fashion. An instrumental-variables approach could be used in which the instrument for the research variables would be fitted values from regression of research expenditures on their lagged values, lagged expected output prices, and other variables hypothesized to influence research expenditures. Simultaneity may also be a problem with single-equation supply models.[109]

3.3   Calculating the Effects of Research

Econometrically estimated production, productivity, cost, and, profit functions can provide useful summary measures of the structure of production technologies and their change over time. Aspects of these production technologies are represented by the size and sign of the marginal product of inputs and their associated output (cost or profit) elasticities, economies of scale and economies of scope, elasticities of input substitution, and so on. Our primary interest is in estimating the effects of agricultural R&D on output, cost, profit, and input use, with a particular emphasis on developing measures of the benefit streams flowing from past investments in research. To the extent that changes in the more familiar production parameters for quantifying the effects of R&D matter, they will be given due attention, but mostly we refer readers to texts on production economics for a review of the specific details on measurement and interpretation concerning these production parameters.[110]

3.3.1   Growth Accounting

The rates of growth in aggregate agricultural output and its components differ markedly over time and across regions and countries. While the

109. See Huffman and Miranowski (1981) for an example of combining a demand function with a supply function that includes a research variable.

110. See, for example, Ferguson (1975), Fuss, McFadden and Mundlak (1978), Beattie and Taylor (1985), and Chambers (1988).

increased use of conventional inputs such as land, labor, and capital, as well as purchased inputs such as fertilizers, pesticides, and energy, often accounts for a sizable share of the measured growth in output, it is by no means the only important source of growth. Changes in the quality of conventional inputs — such as improvements in the human capital aspects of labor and new and improved agricultural machinery, fertilizers, and pesticides — can also be significant sources of growth. For our purposes, it is desirable to distinguish the growth consequences of the new technologies and know-how attributable to investments in public agricultural research and extension from other growth-promoting influences that stem more directly from private R&D investments and public spending on education, health, and rural infrastructural services. Accounting for these various sources of growth in order to get quantitative indications of their importance and to identify whether their relative contribution has changed over time is a useful way of summarizing the agricultural sector's historical pattern of development and the contribution of research to that development process.

A simple yet informative first step in this direction is to quantify the relative importance of yield versus area effects on the measured growth in agricultural output. Because

$$Q_t \equiv A_t\,(Q_t/A_t) \tag{3.77a}$$

where Q_t is output in period t, and yield, $Y_t = Q_t/A_t$ is output divided by area, it follows directly from taking the logarithmic differential of equation 3.77a that

$$q_t = a_t + y_t \tag{3.77b}$$

where

$$q_t = \frac{dQ_t}{dt}\,\frac{1}{Q_t}\,, \quad a_t = \frac{dA_t}{dt}\,\frac{1}{A_t}\,, \quad \text{and} \quad y_t = \frac{dY_t}{dt}\,\frac{1}{Y_t}$$

Dividing through equation 3.77b by q_t enables the rate of change in output to be partitioned into that *proportion* due to changes in area and that due to changes in yield.[111]

Using the econometric procedures described in this chapter, a more complete accounting of the sources of growth is possible. Taking the deriva-

---

111. Notice that if area is measured in terms of stock (e.g., hectares in rice) rather than in terms of flow (e.g., hectare plantings or area sown to rice), then multiple-cropping effects will be captured as part of the measured increase in yield rather than an increase in area. To the extent that these multiple-cropping effects are the result of research, this is an appropriate modeling approach if the rate of change in yield is to be taken as an (upper-bound) indication of the effects of research.

tive with respect to time of the Cobb-Douglas production function expressed in logarithmic form (3.42), it follows directly that

$$q_t = \sum_{i=1}^{m} \alpha_i \, x_{i,t} + \sum_{g=1}^{k} \beta_g \, k_{g,t} + \sum_{h=1}^{z} \psi_h \, z_{h,t} + \dot{\mu}_t \tag{3.78}$$

where q_t, x_i, k_g, and z_h are the rates of growth of the respective variables, and $\dot{\mu}_t$ is the rate of growth in output unaccounted for by the included variables. The estimated coefficients of equation 3.78 (i.e., the αs, βs, and ψs) can be multiplied by the rates of growth in the corresponding input variables and divided by the growth rate of output, q_t, to provide measures of the shares of output growth attributable to the individual inputs. In most empirical applications, the marginal rates of change in outputs and inputs are replaced by their discrete counterparts, while the residual rate of growth, $\dot{\mu}_t$, is constructed as an accounting residual to ensure that equation 3.78 holds as an identity, irrespective of the actual rates of growth in outputs and inputs used in the calculation.

If a translog production function is used, the growth-accounting principles just described are still valid, but putting them into practice becomes a little more demanding. In this case, the growth-accounting equation is obtained by differentiating equation 3.43 with respect to time and rearranging terms to give

$$\begin{aligned} q_t = \; & \sum_{i=1}^{m} (\alpha_i + \sum_{h=1}^{m} \alpha_{ih} \ln X_{h,t} + \sum_{g=1}^{k} \gamma_{ig} \ln K_{g,t}) \, x_{i,t} \\[2mm] & + \sum_{g=1}^{k} (\beta_g + \sum_{h=1}^{k} \beta_{gh} \ln K_{h,t} + \sum_{i=1}^{m} \gamma_{ig} \ln X_{i,t}) \, k_{g,t} + \dot{\mu}_t \end{aligned} \tag{3.79}$$

where, again, q_t, x_i, and k_g are the rates of growth of the respective variables, and $\dot{\mu}_t$ is the rate of growth of the accounting residual. Terms in brackets represent the elasticities of output to changes in the corresponding X_i and K_g variables. For a Cobb-Douglas production function, these elasticities are constant over time, but in the translog, they vary in response to changes in input levels. In most practical situations, translog growth rates are calculated at the means of the data, although some studies use values for the sample's median year and others use an average of beginning- and end-of-year observations.

3.3.2   Research-Benefit Streams

This chapter has focused on the specification, measurement, and statistical aspects of estimating production, cost, productivity, or supply functions that are designed to capture the effects of research and extension. Along with conventional input and output price and quantity variables, the models include research and extension variables (or time-trend variables) and, where appropriate, other fixed factors that are considered beyond the direct control of the economic agents being modeled. We now turn to conceptual and practical issues that arise in using the parameter estimates, along with the data used to generate them, to construct measures of the economic benefits from research.

In section 3.1.1 we identified procedures for estimating the impact of research on production, costs, and profit. Research (and extension) variables can be included as explanatory variables in the respective production, productivity, cost, and profit functions — and, where appropriate, their derived factor-demand and output-supply functions. The coefficients on these variables give various and not necessarily equivalent measures of the effects of research.

In the case of the production function, these coefficients indicate the output-enhancing effects of marginal changes in the research variable, holding the quantities of inputs and various fixed factors constant. The corresponding cost-function coefficients indicate the cost-saving effects of research at a particular level of output, holding values for prices of variable inputs and quantities of fixed factors constant and assuming cost-minimizing behavior. Finally, the profit function estimates measure the profit-enhancing effects of research, holding input and output prices constant, as well as any other fixed factors that might be included in the model, and assuming profit-maximizing behavior. While the appropriate approach for a particular problem depends largely on the characteristics of the problem outside the control of the analyst — the suitability of particular behavioral assumptions in conjunction with alternative estimation procedures, the ultimate purpose for the estimates, and data availability — the choice may have consequences for the estimates of research benefits. In principle, from the duality relationships among production, profit, cost, and supply functions, all of the alternatives are capable of reflecting the same technological relationships and the same changes in technology induced by research. In practice, the results may differ among the alternative approaches for a host of reasons.[112]

Production Functions

Cobb-Douglas production functions: For simplicity, we begin with the Cobb-Douglas production function given by equation 3.42 in which the

---

112. One of the alternatives might be chosen with a view to dealing with specific characteristics of the problem — for instance, a single-equation model might be used where it is believed that dynamics and expectations are important and cross-commodity effects are not; a production-function approach might be ruled out by multicollinearity problems; a profit function might be ruled out in a case where output prices are thought to be unreliable. Availability of suitable data might also be a pertinent criterion.

current stock of knowledge or research-stock variable, K_t, is determined entirely by a finite distributed lag of current and past local research expenditures, where R_{t-r} represents research expenditures in year $t-r$ $(r = 0, \ldots, L_R)$ (ignoring, for the time being, nonlocal or spill-in research expenditures and extension expenditures) so that

$$\ln Q_t = \alpha_0 + \sum_{i=1}^{m} \alpha_i \ln X_{i,t} + \beta_K \ln K_t + \mu_t \tag{3.80}$$

For a Cobb-Douglas production function, the elasticity of output with respect to the *research stock* is simply the respective regression coefficient because

$$\xi_{Q_t,K_t}^{CD} = \frac{\partial Q_t}{\partial K_t} \frac{K_t}{Q_t} = \frac{\partial \ln Q_t}{\partial \ln K_t} = \beta_K \tag{3.81}$$

It then follows that the marginal product of the research stock, in terms of changes in current output with respect to changes in the research stock, is

$$MP_{Q_t,K_t}^{CD}(t) = \frac{\partial Q_t}{\partial K_t} = \xi_{Q_t,K_t}^{CD} \frac{Q_t}{K_t} = \beta_K \frac{Q_t}{K_t} \tag{3.82}$$

Although the stock-of-research elasticity derived under the assumption of a Cobb-Douglas technology (i.e., equation 3.81) is invariant over the sample data, the marginal product of this stock varies over time with changes in output, Q, or the research stock, K.

Degrees-of-freedom constraints or multicollinearity problems often dictate that a preaggregated, research-stock variable such as K_t be included in the production function being estimated. But for the purposes of comparing a stream of research benefits with its corresponding costs, it is more relevant to identify the effect of (time-dated) *research expenditures*, not simply the effect of the stock of research, on output. The elasticity of output in year t with respect to research expenditures in year $t-r$ is given as[113]

$$\xi_{Q_t,R_{t-r}}^{CD} = \frac{\partial Q_t}{\partial R_{t-r}} \frac{R_{t-r}}{Q_t} = \frac{\partial Q_t}{\partial K_t} \frac{\partial K_t}{\partial R_{t-r}} \frac{R_{t-r}}{K_t} \frac{K_t}{Q_t}$$

$$\tag{3.83}$$

$$= \xi_{Q_t,K_t}^{CD} \frac{\partial K_t}{\partial R_{t-r}} \frac{R_{t-r}}{K_t} = \beta_K \lambda_r$$

113. Recall that

$$K_t = \prod_{r=0}^{L_R} R_{t-r}^{\lambda_r} \quad \text{or, alternatively,} \quad \ln K_t = \sum_{r=0}^{L_R} \lambda_r \ln R_{t-r} \quad \text{so that} \quad \partial \ln K_t / \partial \ln R_{t-r} = \lambda_r$$

So for Cobb-Douglas technologies, the percentage increase in output in year t from a one percent increase in research expenditures in year $t-r$ is equal to the product of the estimated coefficient on the corresponding stock-of-research variable, β_K, and the temporal weight on research expenditures in year $t-r$ used to form the research stock (i.e., the λ_r). To derive the marginal product of R_{t-r} on output in year t, the elasticity estimate from 3.83 is simply scaled by the appropriate average product of research because

$$MP^{CD}_{Q_tR_{t-r}}(t) = \frac{\partial Q_t}{\partial R_{t-r}} = \xi^{CD}_{Q_tR_{t-r}} \frac{Q_t}{R_{t-r}} = \beta_K \lambda_r \frac{Q_t}{R_{t-r}} \tag{3.84}$$

Effects of a permanent increase in research: To find the total effect of a permanent unit increase in annual research spending (i.e., a one-dollar increase in all past years and the present year) on current output in the Cobb-Douglas model, we can define the "total" marginal product of research as

$$TMP^{CD}_{Q_tR_{t-r}}(t) = \sum_{r=0}^{L_R} MP^{CD}_{Q_tR_{t-r}}(t) = \sum_{r=0}^{L_R} \beta_K \lambda_r \frac{Q_t}{R_{t-r}} \tag{3.85a}$$

Equation 3.85a gives the effect on current output of a sustained unit increase in research expenditures over the past L_R years (or longer — earlier increases in research have no current impact). Alternatively, the total effect on output in a future year, $t + T$, of a permanent unit increase in research beginning in the current year, t, can be obtained as the sum of the marginal impacts over the next T years (noting that only L_R lags of research affect output in any year), as follows

$$TMP^{CD}_{Q_{t+T}R_t}(t) = \sum_{r=0}^{T \le L_R} MP^{CD}_{Q_{t+r}R_t}(t) = \sum_{r=0}^{T \le L_R} \beta_K \lambda_r \frac{Q_{t+r}}{R_t} \tag{3.85b}$$

The total marginal product of research in period t derived from 3.85a is identical to that derived from 3.85b as the benefit in a future year $t + T$ ($T \le L_R$) only if $Q_t/R_{t-r} = Q_{t+r}/R_t$ for all $r = 0, \ldots, L_R$. This is different from assuming that the ratio of *current* output to *current* research expenditures (i.e., Q_{t-r}/R_{t-r}, the inverse of the commonly calculated research-intensity ratio) was constant for all t and $r = 0, \ldots, L_R$. In fact, it is unlikely that the total marginal products of research derived from equations 3.85a and 3.85b would be equal. Such outcomes are attributable to the use of the Cobb-Douglas functional form, which involves constant elasticities rather than constant marginal products.

The distinction between the total marginal products of research obtained from 3.85a versus 3.85b is rarely made in practice. A common approach is to use an averaging or approximating procedure to calculate the total marginal product of research, wherein sample average values of output and research expenditures are used to form $\overline{Q}/\overline{R}$, or even the sample average of the output-to-research expenditure ratio $(\overline{Q/R})$, which is then used in place of Q_t/R_{t-r} or Q_{t+r}/R_t to calculate

$$\overline{TMP^{CD}_{Q_tR_{t-r}}} = \overline{TMP^{CD}_{Q_{t+r}R_t}} = \sum_{r=0}^{L_R} \beta_K \lambda_r \frac{\overline{Q}}{\overline{R}} = \beta_K \frac{\overline{Q}}{\overline{R}} \sum_{r=0}^{L_R} \lambda_r = \beta_K \frac{\overline{Q}}{\overline{R}} \qquad (3.87)$$

if the temporal weights λ_r are normalized so that $\Sigma_r \lambda_r = 1$.[114] The research "benefit" associated with these shortcut procedures is obtained by valuing the approximate total marginal product of research at the sample average output price $\overline{P}$ so that

$$\widetilde{VMP^{CD}_{Q_tR_{t-r}}} = \widetilde{VMP^{CD}_{Q_{t+r}R_t}} = \beta_K \frac{\overline{Q}}{\overline{R}} \overline{P} \qquad (3.88)$$

Because this aggregation does not take explicit account of the time-dated nature of the benefit stream, the economic interpretation of such total marginal products, or how they may be used in a benefit-cost analysis, remain unclear.

The commonly employed procedure of using the sample average price of output, $\overline{P}$, to value the marginal product of research means that this assumption is embedded in the estimated benefits from research.[115] Of course a variable output price could easily be incorporated into a research-benefit calculation using a production-function approach if P_t were used instead of $\overline{P}$ when valuing the marginal product of research.

Effects of a one-shot increase in research: Alternatively, the model can be used to consider, or evaluate, the impact over time of an increase in research spending *in a particular year*. Equation 3.84 expresses the impact on current output of a unit change in past research, expressed as marginal products. The equivalent representation for the impact of current research on future output is given by

$$MP^{CD}_{Q_{t+r}R_t}(t) = \beta_K \lambda_r \frac{Q_{t+r}}{R_t} \qquad (3.89)$$

The total benefit through time involves aggregating these marginal benefits. They can be expressed in value terms by multiplying each marginal physical

114. Using sample values of average output and research expenditures may be appropriate given that the estimated regression coefficient used in these calculations to measure the elasticity of output with respect to the stock of research is itself "averaged" over the sample data.

115. Recall that no explicit assumptions are made about output price when a production function approach is used to estimate the marginal product of research.

product by the corresponding price, and these benefit streams can, in turn, be used in the capital budgeting procedures described in section 5.4.2 to provide summary measures of the effects of research, such as the net present value of research or the internal rate of return to research, for the case of a "one-shot" unit change in research spending.

For instance, looking forward from the current year to evaluate a one-shot increase by one dollar in the flow of research spending for the current year t, the formula for the net present value of that change is

$$
NPV_{R_t}^{CD}(t) \quad = \quad \sum_{r=0}^{L_R} \left[\frac{VMP_{Q_{t+r}R_t}^{CD}(t)}{(1+\rho)^r} \right] - 1
$$

$$
= \quad \frac{\beta_K}{R_t} \sum_{r=0}^{L_R} \left[\frac{\lambda_r \, P_{t+r} \, Q_{t+r}}{(1+\rho)^r} \right] - 1
$$

(3.90)

where ρ is the interest rate. This formula can be simplified considerably if we can presume, as above, that the price, quantity, and research variables will be projected as unchanging over the relevant future period using either historical averages or current values. Then (projecting current values, for example) the net present value is simply equal to the present value of the future lag weights, $\Sigma \lambda_r / (1+\rho)^r$, multiplied by the constant term $\beta_K P_t Q_t / R_t$.

Simulating alternative scenarios: Algebraic manipulations of the sort shown above yield useful results only when simplifying assumptions, such as constant prices and output and constant research spending (or constant changes in it), are imposed. More generally, when one desires to evaluate the benefits of particular research alternatives, the easiest method is to use the estimated model to project forward or backwards under alternative assumptions and then to evaluate the difference in output under the alternative assumptions. For instance, to evaluate a permanent increase of research spending by one unit in every future year, production could be simulated over the indefinite future under two scenarios: first, assuming a base level of spending (e.g., the most recent value) and, second, assuming the base value plus one dollar. The additional output could be valued at the current price or some other projection of price, and the present value of the additional output could be compared with the present value of one dollar per year in perpetuity. Scobie and Eveleens (1987) provide an example of this approach. Two virtues of this method are that (a) it permits projection under a consistent set of ceteris paribus conditions that may vary over time (e.g., prices or fixed factors may vary or the impact of changing the ceteris paribus conditions on measured benefits may be examined) and (b) any set of alternatives that is of interest (e.g., a one-shot increase or decrease by any amount or letting research be reduced to zero to deduce an average value of research benefits) can be simulated.

A translog production function: If a translog production function (such as 3.43) is used to assess the output-enhancing effects of research, then the elasticity of output with respect to the stock of research is simply

$$\xi_{Q_t K_t}^{TL} = \frac{\partial \ln Q_t}{\partial \ln K_t} = \beta_K + \beta_{KK} \ln K_t + \sum_{i=1}^{m} \frac{1}{2}(\gamma_{iK} + \gamma_{Ki}) \ln X_{i,t} \tag{3.91}$$

It follows that the marginal product of R_{t-r} on output in year t when the technology takes a translog form is

$$\begin{aligned}
MP_{Q_t R_{t-r}}^{TL} &= \xi_{Q_t K_t}^{TL} \frac{Q_t}{R_{t-r}} \\
&= \left[\beta_K + \beta_{KK} \ln K_t + \sum_{i=1}^{m} \frac{1}{2}(\gamma_{iK} + \gamma_{Ki}) \ln X_{i,t} \right] \lambda_r \frac{Q_t}{R_{t-r}}
\end{aligned} \tag{3.92}$$

Summing over the lag distribution (i.e., $r = 0, \ldots, L_R$) yields the total marginal product of research. Multiplying the marginal product by the current price gives the current-value marginal product of research, which may be aggregated similarly using the lag weights.

Productivity Functions

In many studies, a productivity function is estimated instead of a production function. This is usually done for statistical reasons such as a shortage of data or in response to multicollinearity problems in an initial attempt to estimate a production function directly. The principle in adopting the productivity-function approach is to impose restrictions on the estimation (and by implication on the parameters and the nature of the technology being estimated) in order to obtain better estimates of the research-related coefficients.

General approach: Consider the agricultural production function from equation (3.5):

$$Q_t = f(X_t, R_{t-r}, E_{t-e}, U_t), \text{ for } r, e, = 0 \text{ to } \infty \tag{3.93}$$

where, in year t, Q_t is output, X_t is a vector of conventional inputs, U_t is a measure of uncontrolled, random factors (such as weather), and R_{t-r} and E_{t-e} represent infinite streams of past investments in research and extension (other influences, such as prices and human capital, are left implicit for now). It may be ambitious to attempt to estimate all of the parameters of a relationship such as equation 3.93 jointly with a single time-series data set, especially in light of the long lags between research and its effects on output. When the main interest is in the relationship between research and extension and output (or when the focus is on productivity per se), degrees of freedom can be saved, and the odds of a successful estimation may be improved by imposing structure on the relationship between conventional inputs and outputs. One option is to assume, say, a Cobb-Douglas relationship between inputs and outputs and use factor shares to deduce the component of output attributable to conventional inputs (as done by Griliches 1963b). A similar principle, but a less restrictive set of implicit assumptions, is involved when an index-number approach is used to approximate an unknown technology.

Assuming weak separability, equation 3.93 may be represented as

$$Q_t = g(X_t).h(R_{t-r}, E_{t-e}, U_t), \text{ for } r,e, = 0 \text{ to } \infty \tag{3.94}$$

Then, it is a small step to transform this to a model of total factor productivity (TFP)

$$\frac{Q_t}{g(X_t)} = TFP_t = h(R_{t-r}, E_{t-e}, U_t), \text{ for } r,e, = 0 \text{ to } \infty \tag{3.95}$$

Since a desirable (and typical) feature of an input-quantity index is that it is homogeneous of degree one in its component inputs, using a conventional TFP index in an equation such as 3.95 involves an implicit assumption that the technology being approximated is characterized by constant returns to scale, as well as separability, in the conventional inputs, X.

Deducing research impact: Thus, a TFP index could be constructed, as described earlier in this chapter, and it could be regressed against a distributed lag of past investments in research and extension. Then, the resulting estimates could be used to deduce the effects of changes in research investments (marginal or total and one-shot or permanent) on the time pattern of productivity. This could be done algebraically (as described above in the context of production functions) or by numerical simulation. The results could then be evaluated using the capital budgeting methods outlined above.

Alston, Pardey and Carter (1994) — hereafter referred to as "APC" — provide an example of applying the numerical simulation version of this approach to estimate the rate of return to public-sector agricultural research in California. Their econometric approach for estimating rates of return to research involves three steps. First, total factor productivity is regressed against measures of research and extension. Next, the estimated parameters are used to simulate the stream of total factor productivity (and, hence, output) that would be associated with (a) the actual past stream of research expenditures and (b) different (hypothetical) past streams of research expenditures. These streams may be used to derive marginal effects (for small decreases in research), or total effects (when simulating output streams with research fixed at zero). In the final step, the simulated differences in the value of output and corresponding changes in the cost of research are used to deduce rates of return.

To simplify the estimation problem, APC constructed a preaggregated research variable using the finite trapezoidal lag structure of Huffman and Evenson (1992). In this specification, the research stock variable, K_t, in year t, is a weighted sum of research expenditures, R_t, over the past 35 years. That is,

$$K_t = \alpha_1 R_{t-1} + \alpha_2 R_{t-2} + \ldots + \alpha_{35} R_{t-35} \tag{3.96}$$

The lag weights are zero for the first three years, they increase linearly up to year nine, then they are constant until year 15, after which they decline linearly to year 35. The weights are normalized so that they sum to one. APC estimated various regression models, with total factor productivity (TFP_t in year t) as the dependent variable, and in the preferred model, TFP was a quadratic function of the research stock variable.

$$TFP_t = \alpha_0 + \alpha_K K_t + \alpha_{KK} K_t^2 \tag{3.97}$$

To analyze the effects of research on productivity, they compared actual production in California with predictions from the model if the research variable had been equal to zero beginning in 1914 (the earliest year of research that affects output in 1949, given a 35-year lag). The value of the *additional* output attributable to research-induced productivity growth was computed for each year from 1949-1985 using the parameters from the statistical model as

$$GARB_t = GVP_t \frac{\Delta TFP_t}{TFP_t} = GVP_t \frac{(\hat{\alpha}_K K_t + \hat{\alpha}_{KK} K_t^2)}{TFP_t} \tag{3.98}$$

That is, the gross annual research benefit in year t, $GARB_t$, is equal to the proportional change in total factor productivity in year t attributable to research, multiplied by the actual value of output (i.e., gross value of production, GVP) in year t.

To compute a rate of return to research, the stream of benefits, $GARB$, from 1949 to 1985 is compared with the stream of research expenditures, R, from 1914 to 1985. Since these streams of benefits and costs are in nominal (undeflated) terms, the corresponding internal rate of return is comparable to nominal (i.e., observed) interest rates without requiring any adjustment for inflation. The comparison of $GARB$ and R is biased in that research after 1914 had some effects on output between 1914 and 1949 that is not being valued;

also, research up to 1985 has effects that persist for up to 35 years into the future, and benefits beyond 1985 are left out as well. In this sense, the estimated annual internal rate of return — 21.4 percent — is conservatively low. On the other hand, although APC left out benefits for certain years, they also left out costs of extension and private research that might be responsible for some of the measured benefits. A second internal rate of return was computed by adding the costs of extension, E, in every year since 1914 to the costs of research and computing an internal rate of return comparing those total costs $(R+E)$ to the stream of $GARB$ from 1949 to 1985. Adding extension costs reduced the rate of return to 19.1 percent. This still excludes private research costs and spill-in effects. As a crude adjustment, APC also computed rates of return to research and to research and extension by repeating these calculations but using half the values for measured benefits (i.e., using $GARB/2$). The estimated annual internal rates of return were reduced to 19.5 percent (including research costs alone) and 17.1 percent (when the sum of research and extension costs were used). Thus, the rate of return to research was quite insensitive (varying from 17.1 to 21.4 percent) to whether the stream of estimated benefits was cut in half or extension costs were included along with research costs. The explanation for this insensitivity is that timing is all-important. The annual research cost is small relative to the maximum annual benefits, but it is spent over many more years.

APC pointed out that a number of additional caveats should be kept in mind when these estimates are interpreted and used, and similar caveats would apply to other studies using similar approaches. First, the analysis involved a large extrapolation (to zero research) from the historical experience reflected in the data used in the statistical model. Such extrapolations are hazardous in that the statistical confidence we can attach to them may be low. The "average" rate of return computed in this fashion is valuable for some comparisons, but it is likely to differ from the "marginal" rate of return that should be used for considering marginal changes in research budgets (as opposed to the effects of elimination of public-sector research for which the average return is pertinent). A marginal analysis was made difficult (if not precluded) by APC's use of a preaggregated research-stock variable with presumed lag weights and a presumed lag length. This introduces a second major caveat. The assumptions about the lag structure were based on work by Huffman and Evenson (1992) that might not be applicable to California.[116]

116. On the other hand, the work by Pardey and Craig (1989) supported the use of long lag lengths — greater than 30 years — as subsequently assumed by Huffman and Evenson (1992).

Cost Functions

The measured effects of research on the cost of production can also be used to value the stream of benefits coming from past investments in research. In this case, the research-benefit stream reflects the marginal, cost-reducing effects of research given a fixed level of output(s), fixed quantities of "fixed" factors, and fixed prices of "variable" factors. This contrasts with the production-function approach to estimating the benefits from research, where the marginal, output-enhancing effect of research was obtained holding the quantities (not necessarily the prices) of all inputs constant.

For the Cobb-Douglas cost function (3.45), the elasticity of cost with respect to the research stock is

$$\xi_{C_t K_t}^{CD} = \frac{\partial C_t}{\partial K_t} \frac{K_t}{C_t} = \frac{\partial \ln C_t}{\partial \ln K_t} = \beta_K \tag{3.99}$$

where K_t, the stock-of-research variable, represents the full set of knowledge-related variables in equation 3.67. Taking the marginal, cost-saving benefits from changes in the stock of research to be the cost-function counterpart to the research-benefit measure obtained using primal procedures (i.e., using equation 3.82), then for Cobb-Douglas cost functions, it follows that

$$MB_{C_t K_t}^{CD}(t) = -\frac{\partial C_t^{CD}}{\partial K_t} = -\frac{\partial \ln C_t^{CD}}{\partial \ln K_t} \frac{C_t}{K_t} = -\xi_{C_t K_t}^{CD} \frac{C_t}{K_t} = -\beta_K \frac{C_t}{K_t} \tag{3.100}$$

If the translog cost function (3.46) were used, the cost saving from changes in the research stock would be

$$MB_{C_t K_t}^{TL}(t) = -\frac{\partial C_t^{TL}}{\partial K_t} = -\frac{\partial \ln C_t^{TL}}{\partial \ln K_t} \frac{C_t}{K_t} = -\xi_{C_t K_t}^{TL} \frac{C_t}{K_t}$$

$$\tag{3.101}$$

$$= -\left(\beta_K + \beta_{K K} \ln K_t + \sum_{i=1}^{m} \gamma_{i K} \ln W_{i,t} + \beta_{KQ} \ln Q_t \right) \frac{C_t}{K_t}$$

where symmetry has been imposed on the cross-partial derivatives of the cost function with respect to the knowledge-stock variable, K, and for simplicity, nonresearch contributors to the knowledge stock have been suppressed.

Dual analogues to the primal procedures can be used to derive estimates of the stream of marginal benefits arising from changes in research expenditures, rather than from changes in the corresponding stock of research. To do this, we substitute

$$\prod_{r=0}^{L_R} R \, \tfrac{\lambda}{t-r} \text{ for } K_t$$

in the respective cost function and develop corresponding measures of the marginal benefits (cost savings) from research investments. For a Cobb-Douglas cost function, this stream of research benefits is given by

$$MB^{CD}_{C_t R_{t-k}}(t) = -\frac{\partial C^{CD}_t}{\partial R_{t-k}} = -\frac{\partial \ln C^{CD}_t}{\partial \ln K_t} \frac{\partial \ln K_t}{\partial \ln R_{t-r}} \frac{C_t}{R_{t-r}}$$

(3.102)

$$= -\xi^{CD}_{C_t R_{t-r}} \frac{C_t}{R_{t-r}} = -\beta_K \, \lambda_r \frac{C_t}{R_{t-r}}$$

If the translog cost function (3.46) were used, the cost saving from changes in research would be

$$MB^{TL}_{C_t R_t}(t) = -\left(\beta_K + \beta_{KK} \ln K_t + + \sum_{i=1}^{m} \gamma_{iK} \ln W_{i,t} \right.$$

(3.103)

$$\left. + \beta_{KQ} \ln Q_t \right) \lambda_r \frac{C_t}{R_{t-r}}$$

The cost-saving, research-benefit streams given by 3.102 or 3.103 can then be incorporated into the capital budgeting exercises described in section 5.4.2. The calculations may be simplified by the use of sample average values of production costs, $\overline{C}$, and research expenditures, $\overline{R}$, to derive approximate measures of the stream of cost-saving benefits from research. As with the production-function approaches, however, only a limited range of questions can be addressed in that fashion. Greater flexibility is available when the estimated model is used to simulate streams of costs of production under alternative research investment scenarios and then the streams of costs and benefits are evaluated in a second step.

Supply Functions

The last approach we consider for estimating research impact and evaluating benefits is directly estimated supply functions. The general form of such equations is as set out in equation (3.8):

$$Q_t = q(P_t, W_t, R_{t-r}, E_{t-e}, Z_t, U_t), \text{ for } r,e, = 0 \text{ to } \infty \qquad (3.104)$$

where, in year t, Q_t is output of a commodity of interest, P_t is a vector of (expected) output prices (of the commodity of interest and related commodities), W_t is a vector of (expected) prices of conventional inputs, R_{t-r} and E_{t-e} represent indefinite streams of past investments in research and extension, Z_t represents fixed factors (including human capital for now), and U_t represents uncontrolled factors.

In the literature on estimating commodity supply functions, attention has focused to a great extent (following Cassels 1933) on the problems of specifying dynamics and expectations variables. Choices about these aspects of model specification have implications for the use of the estimated supply function for evaluating research benefits. For example, in a model with endogenous prices due to downward-sloping demand, the use of a Nerlovian distributed lag (to represent either dynamics of supply in a partial adjustment framework or adaptive expectations) implies that a research-induced supply shift today will have an impact on production and prices (and research benefits) over the indefinite future. In contrast, in a static model with expected prices equal to actual prices, the same supply shift would have an effect only in the current period.

One virtue of the approach of using directly estimated supply functions to measure research benefits, on the other hand, is that it makes the closest possible connection between the statistical model and our conceptual supply-and-demand model of research benefits. As a consequence, the output from this type of model can be used relatively directly in an economic-surplus model of research benefits.

Two alternative approaches suggest themselves. One approach is to use the econometrically estimated supply function to deduce a measure of K for each year to be simulated (to be used in an all-or-nothing evaluation of past research, perhaps); the other is to use the estimated supply function to simulate prices and quantities under alternative scenarios (e.g., under the actual pattern of research investments and under counterfactual alternatives — marginal or total, one-shot or permanent changes from the actual values). Then, the values of the streams of producer (and consumer and, perhaps, taxpayer) surpluses under the actual past stream of investments and the counterfactual alternatives may be evaluated and compared. Finally, as discussed above in relation to production functions, the simulated change in the stream of benefits (the difference between the actual and counterfactual surplus measures) can be compared with the change in the stream of research costs used to define the counterfactual experiment in a benefit-cost analysis.

Consider the stylized case of a linear supply function with only the own-price, P_t, and the research stock, $K_t = \rho_1 R_{t-1} + \ldots + \rho_{L_R} R_{t-L_R}$, as its arguments, with exogenous prices and no market distortions (notice that this model assumes that actual prices coincide with expected prices). The estimated supply function is given by

$$\hat{Q}_t = \beta_0 + \beta_1 P_t + \hat{\rho}_1 R_{t-1} + \hat{\rho}_2 R_{t-2} + \ldots + \hat{\rho}_{L_R} R_{t-L_R} \tag{3.105}$$

Assuming that supply is inelastic (recall that the formulas for producer research benefits with a linear supply function depend on whether supply is elastic or inelastic), the producer (and, in this case, total) gain from research in year t is equal to the research-induced change in quantity, ΔQ_t, multiplied by the price, P_t. That is, $\Delta PS_t = P_t \Delta Q_t$. Thus, all that is necessary for this analysis is to simulate the quantities under the actual research expenditures, R, and some counterfactual alternative of interest (e.g., no research in a particular year or in all years, or a marginal change in a particular year or in all years), R^*, and then the stream of *changes in producer surplus* can be compared and evaluated against the stream of *changes in research expenditure* ($\Delta R = R^* - R$) associated with it. One advantage of the linear model, in this simplest of cases, is that this stream is easy to compute, as shown below, without the intermediate step of simulating quantities having to be gone through:

$$\Delta PS_t = P_t \Delta \hat{Q}_t = P_t (\hat{rho}_1 \Delta R_{t-1} + \hat{\rho}_2 \Delta R_{t-2} + \ldots + \hat{\rho}_{L_R} \Delta R_{t-L_R}) \tag{3.106}$$

Then, the net present value of the change in research spending could be computed using

$$NPV = \sum_{n=-L_R}^{L_R} \Delta PS_{t-n} (1 + r)^n - \sum_{n=1}^{L_R} \Delta R_{t-n} (1 + r)^n \tag{3.107}$$

It would be a trivial extension to this analysis to accommodate endogenous output prices or other supply shifters, although endogenous prices would require computing changes in quantities explicitly, as well as a different calculation for producer benefits. And there would be no problem to calculate research benefits in the case of elastic supply, using the formulas presented in appendix A5.2.

More serious challenges arise when one goes from the static model to a model with dynamics and expectations. In such a case, it would seem sensible, as a matter of course, to use the estimated model to simulate prices and quantities with and without research, to simulate costs of production as the integral beneath the estimated supply function, and to compute producer surplus for each period as the simulated revenue minus simulated costs of production. While all of this would seem straightforward in principle, it may well be that the effort involved in putting such approaches into practice (compared, say, with a productivity function) can account for the limited use that has been made to date of directly estimated supply functions, with dynamics and expectations embedded in them, for evaluating research benefits.

4

Economic Surplus Methods

The concept of economic surplus underlies most of the methods used by economists to estimate the benefits and costs of agricultural research or to assess agricultural research priorities. In this chapter, the introductory material presented in chapter 2 is extended to demonstrate how variations on the basic economic surplus approach can be used to model and measure the economic effects of research-induced technical changes in the market settings that commonly confront practitioners. We consider the size and distribution of research benefits in the context of multiple factors, multiple product markets, and market distortions.

This chapter begins with the basic economic surplus model that considers a single market in a closed economy. Then the model is extended to consider various multimarket settings, mainly to disaggregate the measures of benefits that are obtained from the basic model (to allocate the "producer surplus" among individual productive factors as quasi-rents and to allocate consumer surplus among different groups of consumers).[1] First, a horizontal disaggre-

---

1. If some of the fixed factors are only fixed in the short or intermediate term, the rents accruing to them are usually called *quasi-rents*, following a tradition begun by Alfred Marshall. If they are fixed in the long run they are called *rents*, following a tradition begun by David Ricardo. The term *producer surplus* is an unfortunate one because producer surplus represents either quasi-rents or rents to owners of fixed factors and usually are not returns to producers per se except as those producers are owners of the fixed or quasi-fixed factors. The supply curve used for economic surplus analysis in aggregate agriculture is often said to be the long-run supply curve, which slopes upward because of variable inputs being applied to a fixed supply of land. In fact, the curve often used is estimated from annual observations on prices and quantities. Therefore, the curve is really an intermediate-run curve and the measured producer surplus is quasi-rent (returns to quasi-fixed factors such as producers' and input suppliers' own labor and fixed capital) as well as rent (returns to land). More important, the supply curves used in research evaluation and priority setting are for individual commodities. Therefore, land is also a quasi-fixed rather than a fixed factor.

gation (across different markets for a product or for different producing and consuming groups and across different products) is presented. Next, vertical disaggregation of research benefits (among factors of production or across stages of a multistage production system) is discussed. Then, the effects of market distortions on the size and distribution of research benefits are considered. These distortions include a range of commodity policies and programs (such as trade-distorting policies or domestic programs affecting factors and products), exchange-rate distortions, and finally, externalities.

We present this analytical framework as a set of principles that can be applied to a range of situations beyond those specifically considered here. How to collect and use the data and information required to make these models operational is discussed in chapter 5 with specific reference to developing summary measures of the effects of research.

Some important simplifying assumptions are retained throughout. First, supply-and-demand curves are assumed to be linear and to shift in parallel as a result of research-induced technical changes.[2] Second, a static (single-period) model is used and dynamic issues are put aside. Third, competitive market clearing is imposed. Fourth, as discussed in chapter 2, Harberger's (1971) "three postulates" are invoked so that standard surplus measures may be used as measures of welfare change. Under these assumptions, for a range of situations, comparative static models of the effects of a research-induced supply shift, are presented. The qualitative effects are shown using supply-and-demand diagrams, and formulas to compute the effects are presented. The formulas express research-induced surplus changes as functions of technical, market, and policy parameters.

4.1 The Basic Model

4.1.1 Surplus Distribution in the Basic Model

The basic model of research benefits in a closed economy is shown in figure 4.1. In this model D represents the demand for a homogeneous

---

2. Much has been written about the implications of functional forms of supply and demand, elasticities of supply and demand, and the nature of research-induced supply shifts for the size and distribution of research benefits (e.g., Lindner and Jarrett 1978; Norton and Davis 1981). These arguments are summarized in chapter 2. In relation to total benefits, functional forms and elasticities are relatively unimportant compared with the nature of the supply shift. In relation to the distribution of benefits, functional forms are relatively unimportant compared with the sizes of elasticities and the nature of the supply shift. The assumption of a parallel shift is very important. Alston and Wohlgenant (1990) have shown that with parallel shifts, the choice of functional form has little effect on either the size or distribution of benefits. See also Voon and Edwards (1991b).

Figure 4.1: *Surplus distribution in the basic model of research benefits*

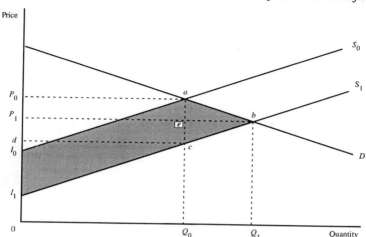

product, and S_0 and S_1 represent, respectively, the supply of the product before and after a research-induced technical change. All curves are defined as flows per unit time, typically annually, as are the economic surplus measures. The initial equilibrium price and quantity are P_0 and Q_0; after the supply shift they are P_1 and Q_1.

The total (annual) benefit from the research-induced supply shift is equal to the area beneath the demand curve and between the two supply curves (ΔTS = area I_0abI_1). This area can be viewed as the sum of two parts: (a) the cost saving on the original quantity (the area between the two supply curves to the left of Q_0 — area I_0acI_1) and (b) the economic surplus due to the increment to production and consumption (the triangular area abc, the total value of the increment to consumption — area Q_0abQ_1 — less the total cost of the increment to production — area Q_0cbQ_1). Alternatively, we can partition the total benefit into benefits to consumers in the form of the change in consumer surplus (ΔCS = area P_0abP_1) and benefits to producers in the form of the change in producer surplus (ΔPS = area P_1bI_1 minus area P_0aI_0). Under the special assumption of a parallel supply shift (where the vertical difference between the two curves is constant), area dcI_1 = area P_0aI_0 and the change in producer surplus is equal to the net benefit on current production (area P_1ecd) plus the gain on the increment to production from Q_0 to Q_1 (area bce) for a total producer surplus gain of area P_1bcd. As shown in box 4.1, these effects can be expressed algebraically as follows:[3]

3. The text equations are for the case of a parallel supply shift. For a pivotal shift in the basic closed-economy case, the formulas for change in total surplus, ΔTS, change in consumer surplus, ΔCS, and

$$\Delta CS = P_0 \, Q_0 \, Z \, (1 + 0.5 Z \eta) \qquad (4.1a)$$

$$\Delta PS = P_0 \, Q_0 \, (K - Z)(1 + 0.5 Z \eta) \qquad (4.1b)$$

$$\Delta TS = \Delta CS + \Delta PS = P_0 \, Q_0 \, K \, (1 + 0.5 Z \eta) \qquad (4.1c)$$

where K is the vertical shift of the supply function expressed as a proportion of the initial price, η is the absolute value of the elasticity of demand, ε is the elasticity of supply, and $Z = K\varepsilon/(\varepsilon+\eta)$ is the reduction in price, relative to its initial (i.e., preresearch) value, due to the supply shift.

4.1.2 Disaggregating Benefits and Costs

The model in figure 4.1 may be used to measure research benefits in terms of supply and demand defined at the farm, retail, or some intermediate stage of the marketing system. The measurement of total benefits is not affected by the choice of where to measure benefits in the marketing chain — the total producer and consumer surplus (or total change in surplus) is the same at all market levels. What is affected by this choice is whose benefits are included in producer surplus and whose are included in consumer surplus.[4]

When research benefits are measured at the retail level, producer surplus includes quasi-rents to all factors employed in producing the retail product (including marketing, distribution, and processing that takes place beyond the farm level) as well as quasi-rents to farming inputs; consumer surplus measures the surplus of consumers who buy at retail. When research benefits are measured at the farm level, producer surplus includes only the quasi-rents accruing to inputs used in farming; quasi-rents accruing to off-farm processing and marketing inputs are included along with final consumer surplus in "consumer surplus" measured at the farm level. Thus, choosing the market level for the analysis implies a choice about the aggregation of owners of productive factors and final consumers in the welfare analysis — i.e., the vertical aggregation.

Implicit choices about horizontal aggregation of surpluses are also made in the basic model. At a given market level we have aggregated all suppliers together and all demanders together.[5] For some purposes, it may be desirable

change in producer surplus, ΔPS, are

$$\Delta TS = 0.5 K P_0 Q_0 (1 + Z \eta)$$
$$\Delta CS = Z P_0 Q_0 (1 + 0.5 Z \eta)$$
$$\Delta PS = \Delta TS - \Delta CS$$

where K is the proportionate vertical shift down in the supply curve due to a cost reduction.

  4. See Just and Hueth (1979), Just, Hueth and Schmitz (1982), and chapter 2.

  5. In addition to these choices, some more subtle questions of aggregation arise from choices about whether to use general-equilibrium or partial-equilibrium definitions of the supply-and-demand curves. When a general-equilibrium definition (allowing for the feedback effects when other product prices adjust)

BOX 4.1: *Algebra for Research-Benefit Calculation for the Closed-Economy Case in Figure 4.1*

The model: The relative reduction in price is defined as $Z = K\varepsilon/(\varepsilon+\eta) = -(P_1 - P_0)/P_0$, where P_0 and Q_0 are equilibrium price and quantity before the supply shift, ε is the supply elasticity, and η is the absolute value of the price elasticity of demand. The equation for Z is obtained by solving linear supply-and-demand equations for price as a function of slope and intercept parameters, treating a research-induced supply shift as an intercept change, and converting to elasticities:

Supply: $\qquad Q_S = \alpha + \beta (P + k) = (\alpha + \beta k) + \beta P$

Demand: $\qquad Q_D = \gamma - \delta P$

where k is the shift *down* of supply due to a cost saving induced by research. In figure 4.1, $k = (P_0 - d)$, and the supply shift relative to the initial equilibrium price is $K = k/P_0 = (P_0 - d)/P_0$.

Equilibrium price change: Setting $Q_S = Q_D = Q$ yields the equilibrium price $P = (\gamma - \alpha - \beta k)/(\beta+\delta)$. When $k = 0$, $P_0 = (\gamma - \alpha)/(\beta + \delta)$; when $k = KP_0$, $P_1 = (\gamma - \alpha - \beta KP_0)/(\beta + \delta)$. The research-induced change in price is $(P_1 - P_0) = -\beta KP_0/(\beta + \delta)$ and the absolute value of the relative change in price is given by $-(P_1 - P_0)/P_0 = \beta K/(\beta + \delta)$. Converting the slopes to elasticities (multiplying through the numerator and denominator by P_0/Q_0) yields $Z = K\varepsilon/(\varepsilon+\eta) = -(P_1 - P_0)/P_0$.

Consumer surplus: In figure 4.1, the consumer surplus change is given by $\Delta CS = P_0abP_1 = $ rectangle $P_0aeP_1 + $ triangle $abe = (P_0 - P_1)Q_0 + 0.5(P_0 - P_1)(Q_1 - Q_0)$ or $\Delta CS = (P_0 - P_1)Q_0[1 + 0.5(Q_1 - Q_0)/Q_0]$. Using the definition above that $Z = -(P_1 - P_0)/P_0$ so that $(Q_1 - Q_0)/Q_0 = Z\eta$ yields $\Delta CS = P_0Q_0Z(1 + 0.5Z\eta)$

Producer surplus: The producer surplus change is $\Delta PS = P_1bI_1 - P_0aI_0 = P_1bcd + dcI_1 - P_0aI_0 = P_1bcd$ given that $dcI_1 = P_0aI_0$ under the assumptions of a parallel supply shift and linear supply and demand. $\Delta PS = P_1bcd = $ rectangle $P_1ecd + $ triangle $bce = (P_1 - d)Q_0 + 0.5(P_1 - d)(Q_1 - Q_0)$. Thus, $\Delta PS = (P_1 - d)Q_0[1 + 0.5(Q_1 - Q_0)/Q_0]$. We may define $(P_1 - d) = (P_0 - d) - (P_0 - P_1) = KP_0 - ZP_0$ and $(Q_1 - Q_0)/Q_0 = Z\eta$. Thus, $\Delta PS = (K - Z)P_0Q_0(1 + 0.5Z\eta)$.

Total surplus: Note also that $\Delta TS = \Delta PS + \Delta CS = P_0abcP_1 (= P_0acd + abc)$, which in this instance equals $I_0abI_1 (= I_0acI_1 + abc)$ given that $P_0acd = I_0acI_1$ under the "laws of parallelograms."

---

to disaggregate suppliers or demanders into subcategories according to geopolitical boundaries (e.g., domestic or foreign), according to income classes, or according to their business characteristics (e.g., small or large farms, adopters or nonadopters of the new technology). A further complication is that the total research benefit and its distribution may be affected by

is used, the surplus measures reflect welfare effects in other commodity markets as well as the one being studied. When a partial-equilibrium definition (assuming that other commodity prices are constant) is used, some further analysis may be needed to compute the effects of any induced price changes in related markets that feed back into the market of interest.

price-distorting policies and externalities. When government revenues are involved in commodity policy, it can be important to distinguish the effects of new technology on government revenues (or taxpayers) from the effects on consumers, producers, or factor owners.

4.2   Horizontal Market Relationships

The basic model refers strictly to the case of a homogeneous product being sold in a single market. Now we consider multiple markets for a single product, multiple products, and possible shifts in demand arising from research-induced quality changes. In section 4.3 we consider "vertical" market relationships — in particular the distribution of benefits among factors of production (or across stages in a multistage production process).

4.2.1   Multiple Markets for a Single Product

One type of horizontal market relationship that is often important is the case of an internationally traded good. While some commodities, particularly root crops and several of the main fruits and vegetables, are produced and consumed almost exclusively domestically, most commodities are also either exported or imported. When a country is a large enough producer or consumer of a commodity in the world market that its production or consumption affects world prices, part of the gains or losses from a shift in its supply curve will be realized in other countries. In addition, when research conducted by one country is transferable to other countries, technology spillovers can cause further reductions in the world price, which in turn affect the initial country conducting the research.

Even when there is no international trade, there may be significant inter-regional trade within a country, and therefore, price or technology spillovers among regions within a country may matter. The approaches given below for considering the national implications of research on an internationally traded good are applicable to the regional implications of research on an in-tranationally traded good or to the intranational implications of research on an internationally traded good.

Several studies have developed models for evaluating agricultural research in the context of trade. Some of these studies have assumed that the country conducting the research is a small exporter or importer of the commodity in the world market and thus does not influence world price.[6]

---

6. Examples of studies in which the small-country case with international trade has been considered include Akino and Hayami (1975), Nguyen (1977), de Castro and Schuh (1977), Hertford and Schmitz

Some studies have allowed for price spillovers. Some have allowed for technology spillovers in which research results from one country or region are adopted in another. Others have allowed for both output price effects and spillovers of research results to other countries.[7]

There are two primary means of modeling technology and price spillovers. The first is to develop a commodity model with equations to represent the home country (country A) and equations to represent the rest of the world (ROW) or region B as a group (e.g., Edwards and Freebairn 1981, 1982, 1984). The second is to develop a commodity model with equations for country A and for each of the other major countries in the world — a less aggregative treatment of the ROW (e.g., Davis, Oram and Ryan 1987). Yet another approach is to treat the ROW as an aggregate but to disaggregate the domestic economy into two or more regions.

The rationale for the first approach is that an individual country is often concerned with spillovers only to the extent that they affect the total domestic research benefit and, perhaps, its distribution between consumers and producers, but not the spatial distribution of domestic benefits. It may be easier to obtain an accurate estimate of the aggregate excess-demand curve (elasticity) facing the country than it is to obtain accurate estimates of *all* the individual supply-and-demand curves in other countries, which are influenced by their domestic and international trade policies and other factors. However, Davis, Oram and Ryan (1987) used secondary and synthetic estimates of demand-and-supply elasticities for most countries of the world and attempted to measure the extent of technology spillovers by commodity by country. This approach is justified when there is a specific interest in the disaggregated cross-country effects. We begin here with the two-market case and then extend the analysis to the *n*-market case. The general representation can be interpreted in terms of any geopolitical aggregation — of regions within countries or among countries — or aggregation according to other criteria.

Two Markets with No Technology Spillovers

Price spillovers occur when a technical change in one country or region has an effect in other countries or regions through effects on the prices of goods traded between the countries or regions. Such price spillovers arise only when the innovating country is a *large country* in trade (i.e., able to influence international prices for the commodity). To analyze research-induced price spillovers in an excess-supply, excess-demand framework, we

(1977), Flores-Moya, Evenson and Hayami (1978), and Norton, Ganoza and Pomareda (1987).

7. Examples include, Martin and Havlicek (1977), Edwards and Freebairn (1982, 1984), Davis, Oram and Ryan (1987), Mullen, Alston and Wohlgenant (1989), and Mullen and Alston (1990).

model the worldwide market in terms of trade between the home country (country A) and all other countries (ROW) so that market clearing is enforced by equating excess supply (the difference between domestic demand and supply) and excess demand (the difference between ROW demand and supply). This is represented in figure 4.2 in which panel a represents supply and demand in the home country (country A) and panel c represents aggregated supply and demand in the ROW (i.e., region B). In the case shown here, the home country is a "large-country" exporter and the ROW is a "large-country" importer. All of the supply-and-demand curves are assumed to be linear.

The excess (export) supply in country A is shown as $ES_{A,0}$ in panel b — given by the horizontal difference between domestic supply (initially $S_{A,0}$) and demand (initially $D_{A,0}$). The initial excess (or import) demand from the ROW is shown as $ED_{B,0}$ in panel b — given by the horizontal difference between ROW demand (initially $D_{B,0}$) and supply (initially $S_{B,0}$). International market equilibrium is established by the intersection of excess supply and demand at a price P_0. The corresponding domestic quantities are shown as consumption, $C_{A,0}$, production, $Q_{A,0}$, and exports, QT_0; the ROW quantities are shown as consumption, $C_{B,0}$, production, $Q_{B,0}$, and imports, QT_0. Research in the home country causes a parallel shift of domestic supply from $S_{A,0}$ to $S_{A,1}$, and in consequence, the excess supply shifts from $ES_{A,0}$ to $ES_{A,1}$. The new equilibrium price is P_1. The corresponding domestic quantities are shown as consumption, $C_{A,1}$, production, $Q_{A,1}$, and exports, QT_1; the ROW quantities are shown as consumption, $C_{B,1}$, production, $Q_{B,1}$, and imports, QT_1.

The research-induced supply shift in country A causes the world price to fall. Consumers in both countries and producers in country A gain, while ROW producers lose. From the domestic standpoint (in panel a), consumer benefits (as measured by the change in consumer surplus) are given by area P_0aeP_1 behind the demand curve and the benefits to producers are given by the area P_1bcd behind the supply curve. This area corresponds exactly to the same area (also P_1bcd) in figure 4.1 for producer benefits in the case of a nontraded good. From the standpoint of domestic producers, the relevant measure of surplus is unaffected by whether the consumers are domestic or overseas. The determinants of producer benefits in both cases are the size of the research-induced supply shift, the resulting decline in price and the initial output. Indeed, the formula for domestic producer surplus continues to be equation 4.1b with the interpretation that the relevant demand elasticity is that for total demand (i.e., domestic plus ROW) rather than simply domestic demand. From the ROW perspective (in panel c), consumer benefits are given by the area behind the demand curve, P_0fgP_1, and producer *losses* are represented by the area behind the supply curve, P_0hiP_1. Box 4.2 shows the algebra for these areas.

Figure 4.2: *Size and distribution of research benefits for a traded good (exporter innovates, no technology spillovers, large country)*

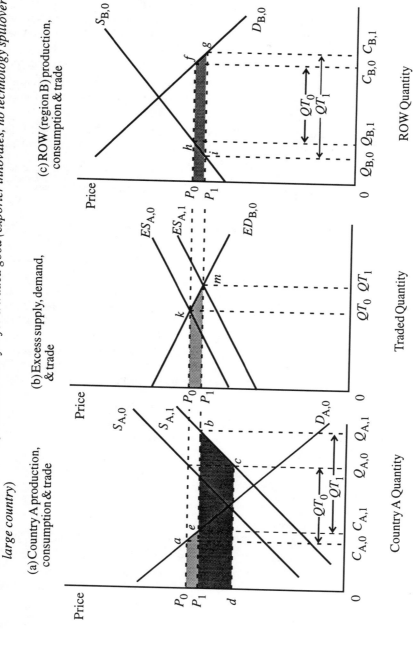

(a) Country A production, consumption & trade

(b) Excess supply, demand, & trade

(c) ROW (region B) production, consumption & trade

Since both consumers and producers benefit, in the home country national research benefits are unambiguously positive. In the ROW, there are two effects in opposite directions — producers lose but consumers gain. However, we can see that the consumer gain must be greater than the producer loss. The change in "consumer surplus" measured off the ROW excess demand (area P_0kmP_1 in panel b) measures the net ROW benefit (i.e., consumer benefit less producer loss) and is equal to the area *fgih* in panel c. This diagram, therefore, shows that both countries must benefit from a research-induced technical change in the exporting country.

If the innovating country, country A, is an importer (as shown in figure 4.3), consumers worldwide benefit from the research-induced price decrease

---

BOX 4.2: *Algebra for Research-Benefit Calculation for the Open-Economy Case in Figure 4.2*

The model: The percentage reduction in price in the case of an open economy is defined as

$$Z = \varepsilon_A K/[\varepsilon_A + s_A \eta_A + (1-s_A) \eta_B^E] = -(P_1 - P_0)/P_0$$

where s_A is the fraction of production consumed domestically (i.e., in country A), ε_A is the domestic supply elasticity, η_A is the absolute value of the elasticity of domestic demand, and η_B^E is the absolute value of the elasticity of export demand (i.e., the ROW, or region B, excess demand), all defined at the initial equilibrium, and other variables are as previously defined.

This price reduction is obtained by solving linear supply-and-demand equations for price as a function of slope and intercept parameters, treating a domestic research-induced supply shift as an intercept shift, and converting the following to elasticities:

Domestic supply: $Q_A = \alpha_A + \beta_A (P+k) = (\alpha_A + \beta_A k) + \beta_A P$
Domestic demand: $C_A = \gamma_A - \delta_A P$
ROW supply: $Q_B = \alpha_B + \beta_B P$
ROW demand: $C_B = \gamma_B - \delta_B P$

where k is the shift *down* of supply due to a cost-saving technological change.

Equilibrium prices: We can solve for the equilibrium price by setting $Q_A + Q_B = C_A + C_B$ to obtain

$$P = (\gamma_A + \gamma_B - \alpha_A - \alpha_B - \beta_A k)/(\beta_A + \gamma_A + \beta_B + \delta_B)$$

When $k = 0$, $P = P_0 = (\gamma_A + \gamma_B - \alpha_A - \alpha_B)/(\beta_A + \delta_A + \beta_B + \delta_B)$.
When $k = KP_0$, $P = P_1 = (\gamma_A + \gamma_B - \alpha_A - \alpha_B - \beta_A KP_0)/(\beta_A + \delta_A + \beta_B + \delta_B)$.
Thus, the change in price is $P_1 - P_0 = -\beta_A KP_0/(\beta_A + \delta_A + \beta_B + \delta_B)$, and the absolute value of the *relative* change in price is $Z = -(P_1 - P_0)/P_0 = \beta_A K/(\beta_A + \delta_A + \beta_B + \delta_B)$.

(continued on next page)

Box 4.2: *(continued)*

Multiplying through the numerator and denominator by $P_0/Q_{A,0}$ and converting to elasticities yields

$$Z = -\ (P_1 - P_0)/P_0 = (\beta_A K)\ (P_0/Q_{A,0})/[(\beta_A + \delta_A + \beta_B + \delta_B)\ (P_0/Q_{A,0})]$$

$$= \varepsilon_A K/[\beta_A\ (P_0/Q_{A,0}) + \delta_A\ (P_0/C_{A,0})\ (C_{A,0}/Q_{A,0})$$

$$+ (\beta_B + \delta_B)\cdot[P_0/(C_{B,0} - Q_{B,0})]\cdot[(Q_{A,0} - C_{A,0}/Q_{A,0}]$$

$$= \varepsilon_A K/[\ \varepsilon_A + s_A\ \eta_A + (1\ -\ s_A)\eta_B^E\ ]$$

where we have defined the elasticity of the ROW's excess-demand curve as $\eta_B^E = (\beta_B + \delta_B)\ P_0/(C_{B,0} - Q_{B,0})$ and used the fact that the traded quantity,

$$QT_0 = C_{B,0} - Q_{B,0} = Q_{A,0} - C_{A,0}.$$

Welfare effects: In figure 4.2, the domestic consumer surplus change is given by $\Delta CS_A = P_0 a e P_1$ in panel a. By analogy with the closed-economy case in figure 4.1, the domestic consumer surplus change is $\Delta CS_A = P_0 C_{A,0} Z(1 + 0.5Z\eta_A)$. Similarly, also by analogy with the closed-economy case, the domestic producer surplus change is $\Delta PS_A = P_1 bcd = P_0 Q_{A,0}(K - Z)(1 + 0.5Z\varepsilon_A)$. The ROW surplus change is equal to area $P_0 km P_1$ in panel b, and this area is equal to $P_0 QT_0 Z(1 + 0.5Z\eta_B)$ by analogy with the closed-economy case.

The same answer for welfare effects could have been obtained by substituting the relative price change, Z, into equations 4.4a and 4.5b after substituting for $E(P_{d,i}) = E(P_{s,i}) = Z$ for $i =$ A or B and defining $E(Q_{d,i}) = \eta_i Z$ and $E(Q_{s,A}) = \varepsilon_A(K - Z)$ and $E(Q_{s,B}) = \varepsilon_B Z$. The disaggregated ROW welfare effects would be $\Delta CS_B = P_0 C_{B,0} Z (1 + 0.5Z\eta_B) =$ area $P_0 fg P_1$ in panel c of figure 4.2 and $\Delta PS_B = P_0 Q_{B,0} Z (1 + 0.5Z\varepsilon_B) = -$ area $P_0 hi P_1$. The sum of these two effects (i.e., the difference between the two areas) is

$$\Delta TS_B = \Delta CS_B + \Delta PS_B$$

$$= P_0(C_{B,0} - Q_{B,0})\ Z\{1 + 0.5\ Z\ (\eta_B\ C_{B,0}/[C_{B,0} - Q_{B,0}] - \varepsilon_B Q_{B,0}/[C_{B,0} - Q_{B,0}])\}$$

$$= P_0\ QT_0\ Z\ (1 + 0.5\ Z\ \eta_B^E\ )$$

and therefore this area is equal to area $P_0 km P_1$ in panel b of figure 4.2.

(domestic consumers gain $P_0 ij P_1$ in panel a and ROW consumers gain $P_0 kl P_1$ in panel c), producers in country A gain (area $P_1 bcd$ in panel a) and ROW producers lose (area $P_0 fh P_1$ in panel c). Once again, the innovating country unambiguously gains. In contrast with the previous case, the ROW loses because the loss to ROW producers (area $P_0 fh P_1$ in panel c) exceeds the benefit to ROW consumers (area $P_0 kl P_1$ in panel c). The net ROW loss is shown as the area $P_0 eg P_1$ in panel b (which equals area $P_0 fh P_1$ minus area $P_0 kl P_1 =$ area $kfhl$ in panel c) of figure 4.3.

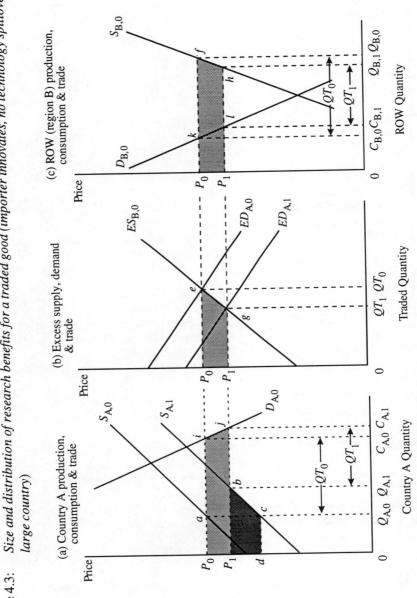

Figure 4.3: Size and distribution of research benefits for a traded good (importer innovates, no technology spillovers, large country)

(a) Country A production, consumption & trade

(b) Excess supply, demand & trade

(c) ROW (region B) production, consumption & trade

218

Technology Spillovers

Technology spillovers arise when some parts of the ROW are able to adopt the results from country A's research. Thus the research-induced supply shift in country A is accompanied by a supply shift in the ROW. The ROW supply shift is likely to be smaller than country A's because a given country's research results are likely to be less applicable elsewhere, especially results from relatively applied research. Figure 4.4 duplicates figure 4.2 (the case where country A is a "large country" exporter) with adjustments to reflect spillovers of technology from country A to the ROW.

In figure 4.4, all of the curves from figure 4.2 are as previously defined, but there are two extra curves ($S_{B,1}$ and $ED_{B,1}$). In panel c, $S_{B,1}$ represents ROW (i.e., region B) supply after a research–spillover-induced supply shift. Correspondingly, in panel b, there is a reduction in excess demand facing country A from $ED_{B,0}$ to $ED_{B,1}$. Thus, the international spillover of technology augments the initial effect, further depressing the world price from P_1 to P_2, and in consequence, consumer benefits in both countries are greater. In addition, producer benefits in country A are smaller and ROW producer losses are reduced and perhaps even turned into a gain.

The ROW unambiguously benefits from both the initial supply shift in country A and the spillover supply shift in the ROW. The benefits to country A are reduced by the spillover. One way to see this is to view the initial supply shift in country A and the ROW supply shift as independent events. The initial (own) supply shift in the exporting country yields a net domestic benefit (see figure 4.2). The subsequent supply shift in the (foreign) importing country imposes a cost in the exporting country because it leads to a reduction in demand for exports from which the loss to producers is greater than the benefit to consumers in the exporting country. Nonetheless, country A still benefits overall from the research-induced supply shift. Indeed, country A producers unambiguously benefit so long as the overall price reduction (from P_0 to P_2) is smaller than the initial vertical supply shift in country A, and that will be so even in the extreme case when the ROW supply function shifts by the same amount (i.e., when the technology is fully transferable). As the diagram in figure 4.4 is drawn, ROW producers are net losers, even with some adoption of country A's research results (i.e., area P_2ij is less than area P_0hk in panel c), but in general they could gain or lose. The benefits to producers in country A are shown as the area P_2bcd in panel a; the benefits to consumers in country A and the ROW are shown as area P_0aeP_2 in panel a and area P_0fgP_2 in panel c, respectively.

The case of research spillovers when country A is an importer can be illustrated by including a research-induced supply shift in the ROW in figure

Figure 4.4: Size and distribution of research benefits for a traded good (exporter innovates, with technology spillovers, large country)

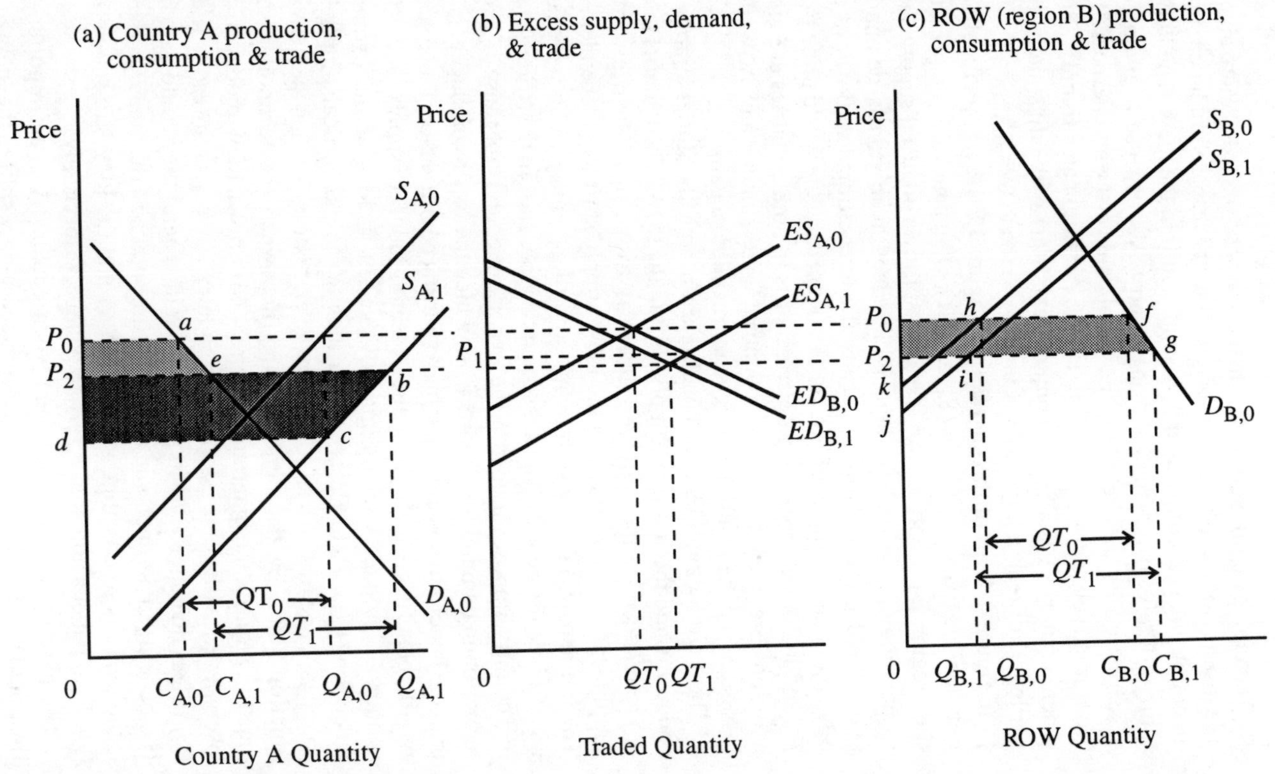

(a) Country A production, consumption & trade

(b) Excess supply, demand, & trade

(c) ROW (region B) production, consumption & trade

4.3. As an importer, country A benefits from transfers of its research results to the ROW, although research benefits to domestic producers are reduced as a result of the price-depressing effect of overseas adoption of those results. A general method of deriving the formulas for calculating economic surplus changes in the case of technology spillovers is presented in the next section.

The Case of n Countries or Regions

The above analysis has dealt with two regions with research-induced technical change, allowing the possibility of interregional technology spillovers. More generally, an arbitrary number of groups of suppliers and consumers can be considered with market-clearing conditions imposed on quantities and prices. This corresponds to the approach of Davis, Oram and Ryan (1987). In the context of multiple regions of a nation, technology may be better regarded as being specific to agroecological zones rather than to geopolitical regions. With this in mind, the formulation of technology spillovers can be recast to reflect multiple zones adopting new technologies to a greater or lesser extent, depending on their natural endowments of resources and climate, where the potential impact (i.e., the local supply shift or K effect) of the new technologies also varies spatially. Thus, supply-shift variables among regions may be related, either because technology spills over from one region to another or because technology becomes available to all regions but is not equally applicable, and also not as readily adopted, in all regions.

The following model assumes that total quantity demanded and total quantity supplied are equal and prices are set competitively with zero transport costs among markets.[8]

Supply: $$Q_{s,i} = f_i (P_{s,i}, B_i) \qquad (4.2a)$$

Demand: $$Q_{d,j} = g_j (P_{d,j}, A_j) \qquad (4.2b)$$

Market clearing: $$\sum_{i=1}^{n} Q_{s,i} = \sum_{j=1}^{n} Q_{d,j} \qquad (4.2c)$$

$$P_{s,i} = P_{d,i} = P_{s,j} = P_{d,j} = P \text{ for all } i \text{ and } j \qquad (4.2d)$$

where $Q_{s,i}$ is the quantity supplied, $P_{s,i}$ is the supply price, and B_i is a supply-shift variable for the ith group of suppliers or producers; $Q_{d,j}$ is the quantity demanded, $P_{d,j}$ is the demand price, and A_j is a demand-shift variable for the jth group of demanders or consumers. Equation 4.2d is the market-

---

8. Market-distorting policies are easily incorporated in this model as ad valorem taxes or subsidies. For example, see Alston (1991) and chapter 5.

clearing price condition that could be adjusted to reflect price wedges due to policies or transportation costs.

This model can be solved either by using specific functional forms for the supply-and-demand equations or by taking a logarithmic differential approximation.[9] When a change in technology causes a small shift from an initial equilibrium, changes in prices and quantities may be approximated linearly by totally differentiating equations 4.2a through 4.2d and converting them to elasticity form. Differentiating throughout and adding exogenous shocks yields the following system of equations — expressed in terms of relative changes and elasticities:[10]

Supply:

$$E(Q_{s,i}) = \varepsilon_i [E(P_{s,i}) + \beta_i] \qquad (4.2a')$$

Demand:

$$E(Q_{d,j}) = -\eta_j [E(P_{d,j}) - \alpha_j] \qquad (4.2b')$$

Market change:

$$\sum_{i=1}^{n} ss_i E(Q_{s,i}) = \sum_{j=1}^{n} ds_j E(Q_{d,j}) \qquad (4.2c')$$

$$E(P_{d,j}) = E(P_{d,i}) = E(P_{s,i}) = E(P_{s,j}) = E(P) \qquad (4.2d')$$
for all i and j

where E denotes relative changes (i.e., $E(Z) = dZ/Z = d\ln Z$), η_j is the absolute value of the elasticity of demand, and α_j is a vertical shift *upwards* in the jth demand function (an increase in demand relative to the initial equilibrium price); ε_i is the elasticity of supply and β_i is a vertical shift *down* in the ith supply function (reflecting an increase in supply, measured relative to the initial equilibrium supply price).[11] In equation 4.2c' the share-weighted sum of relative changes in quantities supplied equals the share-weighted sum of relative changes in quantities demanded, where the ith supply share is $ss_i = Q_{s,i}/(\sum_i Q_{s,i})$ and the jth demand share is $ds_j = Q_{d,j}/(\sum_j Q_{d,j})$.

The exogenous shift parameters (α_j, β_i) express equilibrium displacements relative to an initial equilibrium. Thus, for instance, setting $\alpha_j = 0.1$ would imply a 10 percent increase in the jth group of consumers' willingness to pay for the initial quantity of the product. While the shift of demand is expressed as a fraction of the initial price, it cannot be presumed that there

9. Edwards and Freebairn (1981, 1982, 1984) and Davis, Oram and Ryan (1987) assumed linear supply and demand, for example. Alston and Wohlgenant (1990) have shown that the logarithmic differential (linear elasticity) approximation is good for small changes with constant elasticity supply and demand and is exactly correct with linear supply and demand.

10. Perrin and Scobie (1981) use this type of *horizontal* multimarket model to analyze Colombian food policy. They present general algebraic solutions as well as numerical results.

11. Thus β_i corresponds to K_i, the proportional research-induced shift in the price direction of the ith supply function.

has been a proportional shift of demand. Rather, α_j measures the vertical shift in the jth demand, g_j, at a point, locally, for any type of demand shift (e.g., proportional, parallel, or pivotal). Similarly, β_i measures the shift down of the ith supply, f_i, with the magnitude of the reduction in marginal cost (at the point of approximation, the initial equilibrium) being expressed relative to the initial price of the good.

In this specification nothing is presumed about the magnitude of the supply (or demand) shift at other points along the supply (or demand) curve. The nature of the shift (e.g., proportional, parallel, or pivotal) is treated as a separate question from the amount of the shift relative to the initial equilibrium. For the most part, parallel shifts of supply and demand are assumed but those shifts are expressed relative to initial prices and quantities. Further, for the most part it is assumed that all supply-and-demand curves are linear — at least in the relevant range of the equilibrium displacement. But these assumptions are not necessarily implied by the specification of the equations of the equilibrium-displacement model. At the same time, they are wholly consistent with the equations of the model when we make it clear that we are using the model to approximate the consequences of parallel displacements of linear supply-and-demand equations.

The assumptions of (approximately) linear supply-and-demand functions with parallel shifts *are* required for the economic surplus measures that are used below. In cases where different assumptions are made about the functional forms or nature of the supply-and-demand shifts, it may still be convenient to use the linear-elasticity equilibrium-displacement model to estimate changes in prices and quantities — and for small shifts, it is likely to be a good approximation. However, the surplus formulas below are correct only for parallel shifts of linear supply and demand; nonparallel shifts require different equations (albeit only slightly different in many cases) to compute changes in economic surpluses.

The system of equations 4.2a′ through 4.2d′ can be solved for the endogenous relative changes in prices and quantities as functions of the elasticities of supply and demand, shares, and exogenous shift variables (see chapter 5). The solution for the relative change in price is[12]

$$E(P) = \frac{\Sigma_i \, (ds_i \, \alpha_i \, \eta_i - ss_i \, \beta_i \, \varepsilon_i)}{\Sigma_i \, (ds_i \, \eta_i + ss_i \, \varepsilon_i)} \tag{4.3}$$

This price equation shows how a research-induced increase in supply in one region ($\beta_i > 0$ for region i) depresses the price in all regions. The extent of

12. In some situations it might be helpful to note that $\Sigma_i ss_i \varepsilon_i = \varepsilon_W$ and $\Sigma_i ds_i \eta_i = \eta_W$, where ε_W and η_W are the aggregate (world) elasticities of supply and demand.

the effect depends on the size of the shift, the relative importance of that region, ss_i, in world production of the commodity, and the elasticities of supply and demand. Alternatively, a research-induced increase in demand (perhaps as a reflection of improvements in processing technology) in region i ($\alpha_i > 0$) will increase price in all regions. Again, the price increase depends on the size of the shift and the share of that region in total consumption (i.e., ds_i). Thus we have a relatively general representation of price spillovers in a model that allows for simultaneous, independent supply-and-demand shifts in any of the n regions.

This is one type of spillover: the pecuniary effect when innovation by one group of producers affects prices received by another group of producers. The other type of spillover occurs when technology developed by one country (or group of producers) is adopted elsewhere. In the context of the model given above this "leakage" of research results can be analyzed by treating the supply shifters, the β_is, as mutually dependent so that there is a supply shift in one region as a consequence of a supply shift in another region. Specifically, when an innovation in region i partially leaks out to other regions, we might define the shift parameters in the other regions as $\beta_j = \theta_{ji}\beta_i$ where θ_{ji} is the supply shift in region j as a fraction of the shift in region i.[13] Similarly, a technical change that causes a supply shift and also involves a concomitant demand shift (say, due to a quality change) can be modeled by relating a demand shift to the research-induced supply shift.

Once the situation of interest has been parameterized (by defining the nature of supply and/or demand shifts and the elasticities and market shares), equation 4.3 can be used to calculate the relative change in the product price. Effects on quantities may then be obtained by substituting this result into the country-specific supply-and-demand equations (in 4.2a′ and 4.2b′). While all regions in this model experience identical changes in equilibrium prices, changes in quantities supplied may vary regionally because of differences in local supply-and-demand characteristics (as reflected in local elasticities of

---

13. For instance, suppose a technology developed by country 1 that reduces costs by one percent is adopted at the same time by country 2 but is not adopted by country 3. This could be analyzed by setting the shift parameters as $\beta_1 = \beta_2 = 0.01$ and $\beta_3 = 0$. The qualitative results are that "leakage" of results will increase global total benefits, increase global producer benefits in total, increase global consumer benefits in total, and reduce benefits to producers in country 1 and country 3, relative to the case where only country 1's costs are reduced. Country 2 clearly benefits from leakage. International leakage of research results from country 1 to country 2 may involve a net benefit or a net cost in countries 1 and 3. This is an empirical question, the answer to which will depend on the characteristics of the markets and trade in the affected commodity. More generally, for n countries, one can think of an $n \times n$ spillover matrix containing coefficients, θ_{ij}, that are used as multipliers to indicate the extent of spillovers of supply shifts from country i to country j. The diagonal elements, θ_{ii}, represent the own-country effects, and the off-diagonal elements, $i \neq j$, represent international spillovers. This matrix need not be symmetric.

supply and demand) and the size of localized shifts in supply and/or demand. These changes in quantities and price, along with the original information on the supply-and-demand shifts, are sufficient to calculate the full welfare consequences of the equilibrium displacements. For large numbers of distinct groups of suppliers and demanders, particularly with price wedges in the model, it might not be sensible to try to obtain analytic solutions to the system of equations 4.2′, but numerical solutions are possible.[14] Gross annual research benefits accruing to the various groups of producers and consumers may be computed using

$$\Delta CS_i = -P_{d,i}\, Q_{d,i} \left[\, \mathrm{E}\,(P_{d,i}) - \alpha_i\,\right]\left[1 + 0.5\mathrm{E}\,(Q_{d,i})\,\right] \qquad (4.4a)$$

$$\Delta PS_j = P_{s,j}\, Q_{s,j} \left[\, \mathrm{E}\,(P_{s,j}) + \beta_j\,\right]\left[\,1 + 0.5\mathrm{E}\,(Q_{s,j})\,\right] \qquad (4.4b)$$

$$\Delta TS = \Sigma_i\, \Delta CS_i + \Sigma_j\, \Delta PS_j \qquad (4.4c)$$

where subscript d denotes demand prices and quantities and s denotes supply prices and quantities, subscript i denotes the different groups of consumers, and j the different groups of producers. Equation 4.4c measures global benefits.[15] Benefits to any subaggregate of consumers and producers can be computed using the relevant components from equations 4.4a and 4.4b. For instance, benefits to "country" i could be computed as $\Delta TS_i = \Delta PS_i + \Delta CS_i$.

Suppose the subscripts "i" denote different countries. In the above model, a supply (or demand) shift in any one country will affect the price, quantity, and economic surpluses in every other country. Thus research-induced technical changes in one country have effects that are not confined to the country where the innovation takes place. In this model it is easy to show the intuitively reasonable result that when a subset of producers adopt an improved technology, all consumers benefit, while those producers who do not adopt the innovation lose (e.g., see Edwards and Freebairn 1982, 1984).

The multiple market (or trade) model described here is essentially the same as those of Edwards and Freebairn (1981, 1982, 1984) and Davis, Oram and Ryan (1987) — i.e., it deals with a single commodity, research shifts a linear supply function down in parallel, and there may be spillover effects in other supply functions. There is one important difference, however: it is possible to combine this multimarket model with the multifactor model described in the next section so that we can consider multiple markets (i.e., international trade) and multiple factors (i.e., multistage production)

14.   The algebra and its solutions can become quite messy and complicated and the results may not be clear, in which case the value in obtaining analytic solutions is not clear.

15.   If there were any tax wedges we would need to augment the measures with changes in government revenues as well.

jointly and in a theoretically consistent manner. This was done, for example, by Mullen, Alston and Wohlgenant (1989) in their study of the international incidence of the benefits and costs of Australian investments in research applicable to various stages of the world wool industry, allowing for both technology and price spillovers.

Special Cases

The above model provides general results for the case of interregional trade among any number of regions under conditions of competitive market clearing and zero transport costs (and no other price wedges). Using that model, we can measure the size and distribution of economic welfare effects (along with price, quantity, and trade effects), allowing for spillovers of prices and technology. It would be relatively simple to introduce price wedges into the model. Most studies do not use a model as general as the one shown above for n regions (even with the restriction of costless arbitrage so that prices are equal among regions). Typical alternatives can be represented as special cases of this model, however, and the welfare effects of research-induced supply shifts may be measured using the surplus formulas 4.4a, 4.4b, and 4.4c.

In a common example, the innovating country, A, is a *small country in trade*. This can be defined by taking the limit of equation 4.3: as the supply share, ss_i, of the innovating country i approaches zero so does $E(P)$. The "small country" model takes as an extreme approximation that $E(P) = 0$. Then, setting all of the other demand-and-supply shift variables at zero (i.e., assuming an absence of locally generated or spill-in technical change elsewhere and no change in demand structures), the welfare consequences of innovation in country A are given by substituting β_A into equations 4.4a through 4.4c. In this case, all of the research benefits accrue to country A's producers regardless of whether the country is an exporter or an importer.

The small-country assumption is often appropriate — most agricultural products are tradable and most regions or countries do not influence international prices significantly. The impact of research on a small-country importer or exporter of a commodity is illustrated in figure 4.5 (panel a represents the case of a small exporter and panel b represents a small importer). The initial equilibrium is defined by consumption, C_0, and production, Q_0, at the world market price, P_W, with a traded quantity, QT_0 (representing exports or imports), equal to the magnitude of the difference between consumption and production. Research causes supply to shift from S_0 to S_1 and production to increase to Q_1. As a result, exports increase (or imports decrease) to QT_1. Because the country does not affect the world price, the economic surplus change (equal to area I_0abI_1) is all producer surplus. One advantage of the

Figure 4.5: *Research benefits in a small open economy*

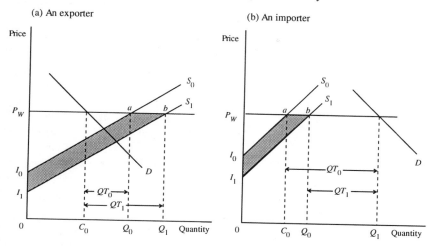

small-country assumption is that, even when the government intervenes in the commodity market (see section 4.4 below), all the research benefits continue to accrue domestically and there is no need to consider the ROW (unless there is leakage of research results and consequent price spillovers feeding back from the ROW). The world price, P_W, is a constant in the analysis and defines the opportunity cost of resources used in production and consumption.

In this case of a small open economy, the formula for research benefits from a K percent (where $K = \beta_A$) parallel shift down of supply is simply

$$\Delta PS = \Delta TS = P_W Q_0 K (1 + 0.5K \varepsilon) \tag{4.5a}$$

This equation can be obtained by taking the limit of equation 4.1b or 4.4b (where equation 4.2a′ has been substituted for $E[Q_{s,j}]$) as the demand elasticity approaches infinity (and $E[P_{s,j}]$ goes to zero). It applies for both an exporter and an importer. When we allow for trade in the product, we may also have to consider the possibility of technology spillovers, as discussed above in a more general context. Technology spillovers are relatively simple to incorporate as

$$\Delta PS = \Delta TS = P_W Q_0 (K - Z_B) [1 + 0.5 (K - Z_B)\varepsilon] \tag{4.5b}$$

where Z_B is the proportional change in the world price due to the technology spillover, which may be calculated as $Z_B = K_B \varepsilon_B /(\varepsilon_B + \eta_B)$. The subscript B denotes ROW (i.e., region B) coefficients corresponding to the domestic coefficients defined in equations 4.1a through 4.1c, and K_B denotes the ROW supply shift due to the leakage of the technology that caused the K proportional home-country supply shift.

We can also see the price change in a *closed economy* (the basic model) as a special case of equation 4.3. In this case there is only one region, and we can drop the subscripts and use supply-and-demand shares (ss_i and ds_i) equal to one. Making these simplifications in equation 4.3, a research-induced supply shift of β_A causes a price change of $E(P) = \beta_A \varepsilon/(\varepsilon+\eta)$. This price change is exactly that defined above in relation to the basic model (using K instead of β_A). Furthermore, substitution of this measure of the price change into equations 4.4a, 4.4b, and 4.4c will yield precisely 4.1a, 4.1b, and 4.1c. Finally, the two-sector case (country A and the ROW) analysed in detail above is easily dealt with as a special case of the n-sector framework. Thus, the equations of the model can be used to measure the areas of surplus changes shown on figures 4.2, 4.3, and 4.4.

4.2.2   *Disaggregating Consumer and Producer Surplus*

So far we have shown how to disaggregate welfare among a range of producer and consumer groups. In the discussion above, in the context of traded goods, the interpretation was that the groups differed according to where they lived. More generally, the multigroup model — as defined above in equations 4.2a′ to 4.2d′ — could be interpreted with groups defined according to any criterion. For example, the groups of consumers could be various categories of domestic consumers (e.g., according to income class) in a closed-economy model. Elasticities of demand that vary across income classes could be incorporated, and thus the differential impacts of technical change on the various groups could be identified. Similarly, producer categories of various types could be included (e.g., large versus small farms, adopters and nonadopters). The main limitation on such analyses is likely to be the availability of meaningful estimates of parameters and data to describe the groups of interest. Here, we introduce some special examples of disaggregating consumer and producer surplus according to characteristics other than regional location.

Household Consumption

In many countries, a significant proportion of food production is consumed in the farm household where it is produced, with the proportion varying by commodity, location, and farm size. When producers of a good consume significant quantities of the good they produce, producer surplus alone will be an incomplete measure of the welfare consequences of price changes for producers. A more complete measure would augment their producer surplus with their consumer surplus from consuming their own product. In the context of the model above, this could be done by having one group of producers and two groups of consumers (i.e., producers and non-producers) with producer welfare being measured by their consumer and producer surplus combined. The remaining consumer surplus would accrue to consumers who are not also producers.

In a developing-country context, household consumption of home-produced goods tends not to be very responsive to price and, therefore, has been represented in several studies with a perfectly inelastic demand (e.g., Hayami and Herdt 1977; Nagy 1984; Norton, Ganoza and Pomareda 1987). Thus the consumer surplus benefit to producers is equal simply to the research-induced price change multiplied by the quantity consumed by producers. The change in total economic surplus is the same as before but part of the consumer benefits remains with producers. This highly simplified approximation of the benefits to home consumption could be refined by assessing more accurately the price elasticity of demand for home consumption.

Benefits Among Producer Groups

The impact of technological change on the distribution of income among producer groups can be assessed in many dimensions (corresponding to several of the distributional objectives described earlier). Producers at different income levels, with different farm sizes, in different locations, and with diverse tenure situations can gain or lose depending on the suitability of the new technology to their particular situations. The supply curve can be disaggregated to allow measurement of these distributional consequences within the economic surplus framework (e.g., Hayami and Herdt 1977; Binswanger 1980). The *n*-sector model above could be reinterpreted to represent groups of producers according to some characteristic other than geographic location (i.e., adopters or nonadopters, small or large farms) and the surplus formulas could be applied without any modification.

A related type of analysis can be used to show the distributional effects of technological change on the relative incomes of landlords and tenants. If the tenant pays a fixed amount to the landlord, the tenant's producer surplus is always reduced by the amount of rent paid to the landlord (which may represent all the producer surplus on marketed production). After the technical change, the tenant can earn rents (producer surplus) on the land being farmed until the landlord raises the rent charged for the use of the land. If the tenant pays the landlord a fixed share of the output, the division of any producer surplus depends on the relative sharing of production costs as well. If all output and costs were shared equally, they would each earn the same producer surplus but the amount would be one-half that earned by an owner-operator. Of course these are ad hoc approaches and it would be better to analyze the *functional* distribution of income between landlords and tenants using the methods described in section 4.3 for analyzing surplus distribution among factors of production in vertically related markets.

Benefits among Consumer Groups

The relative benefits by consumer income groups can be calculated by disaggregating the market demand curve into demand curves by income groups, as illustrated by Pinstrup-Andersen, Ruiz de Londoño and Hoover (1976), Pinstrup-Andersen (1977), and Perrin and Scobie (1981).[16] Separate price elasticities of demand could be obtained for each consumer group and then applied to calculate benefits by group. A rougher but quicker method for apportioning total consumer benefits is to distribute them across consumer groups in proportion to the quantity consumed initially by each group.[17] Similarly, consumer benefits can be disaggregated by region and combined with the regional benefits to producers to arrive at an estimate of total research benefits by region. As an approximation, benefits may be distributed across consumer groups in proportion to the quantity consumed initially by each group. This is equivalent to assuming equal demand elasticities among the groups. This approach was used by Hayami and Herdt (1977) and Scobie and Posada (1977, 1978) and was criticized by Pinstrup-Andersen (1977, p. 27).

4.2.3   Multiple Products: Some General Issues

Types of Multiproduct Situations

A few studies have dealt formally with the incidence of research benefits and costs among industries (e.g., Coble et al. 1992). Changes in technology in one industry (affecting one commodity) will affect industries producing different commodities that are related either in consumption or production to the one where the innovation occurs. For example, an improvement in technology in the chicken meat industry will result in a shift in the supply of

16. Scobie (1980) pointed out and corrected an error by Pinstrup-Andersen (1977).

17. Scobie and Posada (1978, pp. 88-89) followed a similar procedure in apportioning consumer benefits from rice research in proportion to the consumption by various income groups. Pinstrup-Andersen, Ruiz de Londoño and Hoover (1976) conduct a more detailed analysis in which they estimate separate price characteristics for five consumer income strata.

chicken and a reduction in its price. A second-round effect of this change will be a reduction in demand for beef (a substitute in consumption) and, at the same time, a reduction in the supply of beef due to increased feed-grain costs (assuming the change in the technology was not feed saving) because beef and chicken compete for feed grains. Alternatively, as a second example, improvements in the technology of feed-grain production will lower costs for both chicken and beef, but the effects may differ in size and the net effects on either may be unfavorable because of substitution in consumption.

A third alternative multiproduct situation is where the two goods are directly related in production (rather than through a shared factor), such as in the Australian sheep wool and meat industries or in the dairy-processing industry that uses milk to produce a range of products. In these two examples the various products will be related in three ways: (a) substitution in consumption (say, between butter and cheese), (b) complementarity in production (say, between butter and skim-milk powder), and (c) competition (or substitution) between products in the use of specialized factors (say, between using milk to produce butter and skim-milk powder and using milk to produce cheese). A change in technology may be of the kind that affects joint product relationships or the kind that affects factor use (neutral or factor-biased technical changes), as considered below.

Particular situations might involve one or more of these types of interactions among products. In the humid tropics, for example, multiple cropping is common. Technical change that affects one crop directly may affect another through its effects on resource requirements and growing season, through effects on soil structure and fertility and pests and diseases, and through substitution in consumption.

General-Equilibrium Feedback and Double Counting

Welfare measures taken in the context of a single-market model may reflect the welfare changes in related markets. Consider the first example, an improvement in the technology of chicken production. A conventional partial-equilibrium analysis of welfare changes in the chicken market will reflect induced shifts in demand for beef but will still be correct so long as the beef price is exogenous. It will be incorrect, however, if the beef price is affected, and it will be complicated further when there is feedback from the beef market into supply or demand in the chicken market. A natural impulse would be to add up the areas of welfare changes in the beef and chicken markets, but adding up effects across markets could involve double counting.

Alternatively, a general-equilibrium definition of the supply-and-demand equations for chicken could be used. The normal (*ceteris paribus*) Marshallian demand curve shows how consumption of a good responds to changes in its own price, holding all other prices and money income constant. A general-equilibrium (*mutatis mutandis*) demand function shows how consumption of a good responds to changes in its own price, allowing prices of related goods to adjust in response to the own-price changes and allowing the *ceteris paribus* demand for the good to shift in response to these induced changes in prices of related goods. The elasticity of this type of general-equilibrium demand curve corresponds to the "total elasticity" concept introduced by Buse (1958).[18] The supply-side counterpart allows for induced changes in the prices of related products to feed back into the supply curve of interest.

The welfare measures taken off those supply-and-demand equations will reflect welfare changes in the beef market (and any other related markets) as well as the welfare of the participants in the chicken market; the single-market model *can* measure the full effects. Just, Hueth and Schmitz (1982, p. 192) put it succinctly: "net social welfare effects over the economy as a whole of intervention in any single market can be measured completely in that market using equilibrium supply and demand curves of sufficient generality."

There are two correct ways to measure welfare effects when there are multiple price changes and cross-price effects induced by a supply shift in one market. The first is to add up effects across markets using the welfare areas measured off *ceteris paribus* supply-and-demand curves in all of the affected markets, all of which may shift as a consequence of an exogenous supply (or demand) shift; it will be correct (and path-independent) only if integrability conditions are met. The second is to use the *mutatis mutandis* supply-and-demand curves for the commodity of interest, in which case there are no *endogenous* shifts of any of the curves, and there is no need to add up across related markets. When a "general equilibrium" model is used to measure the quantity and price changes caused by a supply shift in one market, those measured responses will reflect feedback from related markets. If those responses were used to compute welfare changes, it would be double counting to add them up across markets. The main point is that it is important to be aware of the dangers of double counting (and partial counting) and to ensure that the welfare measures are calculated in a fashion that is consistent with the structure of the model.

---

18. The "total" elasticity is equal to the Marshallian elasticity obtained holding the price of other goods constant, $\partial \ln Q_i / \partial \ln P_i$, plus a term reflecting the effect of induced cross-price changes and their effects on the demand for the good in question:

$$\frac{d \ln Q_i}{d \ln P_i} = \frac{\partial \ln Q_i}{\partial \ln P_i} + \frac{d \ln P_j}{d \ln P_i} \frac{\partial \ln Q_i}{\partial \ln P_j}$$

Correct Measures of Welfare Change

Two difficult questions remain. First, how can the effects among the related commodity markets be disentangled and, from there, apportioned among factor suppliers and consumers? Second, what can be done when two or more exogenous displacements occur simultaneously?

Some recent work provides a partial answer to the first question: Thurman (1991a, 1991b) explores the welfare significance (and nonsignificance) of general-equilibrium supply-and-demand curves. He considers two goods that may be related through substitution in consumption, substitution in production, or both. He verifies the results of Just, Hueth and Schmitz (1982, p. 192) that, if care is taken, the total welfare effects in both markets can be measured in the context of a single market. In addition, he points out that the areas behind the general-equilibrium supply-and-demand curves for a commodity may have no welfare significance taken separately (in that they may not measure the welfare of an identifiable group) although they do have welfare significance when taken together (as a measure of the total change in welfare). This is because the conventional welfare areas reflect welfare changes in related markets (for example, the area that conventionally represents changes in *consumer* surplus for beef may now contain some components due to changes in *producer* surplus for chicken). Thurman's most useful result — for the present purpose — is to show that when there is only one source of feedback (i.e., when the goods are related through either consumption or production but not both), the conventional measures of welfare change taken off the general-equilibrium supply-and-demand curves *do* have welfare significance (i.e., they do measure changes in the welfare of identifiable groups).

These results mean that, with only one source of general-equilibrium feedback, it is possible to measure the total welfare change — and its incidence — due to a displacement in one market, taking account of general-equilibrium adjustments. In applications to research-induced market displacements, we have a remaining problem of defining the impact of technical change as a displacement of a general-equilibrium supply or demand function. What is the percentage shift of a *general-equilibrium* supply curve for chicken in response to a K percent reduction in the cost of chicken production?[19] The implications of Thurman's (1991b) results are clearest for either (a) a supply shift when there is feedback to demand through substitution in consumption or (b) a demand shift when there is feedback to supply through substitution in production. In these cases we can use the conventional (partial-equilibrium) measures of research-induced displacements.

19. See chapter 5 for more discussion on estimating K.

With regard to the second question, welfare measurement with only one displacement is difficult enough in a general-equilibrium setting with only one source of feedback. To allow two or more changes to occur simultaneously would be very difficult, even with limited options for feedback. It is not difficult to model price, quantity, and revenue changes in multiple factor and product markets with general-equilibrium feedback and multiple displacements occurring simultaneously (e.g., see Mullen, Alston and Wohlgenant 1989). The difficulty is to measure the welfare consequences. Thus, where general-equilibrium issues are thought to be important, with multiple sources of general-equilibrium feedback, an entirely different approach is necessary. A full general-equilibrium treatment would allow measurement of the full welfare consequences (e.g., Ballard, Shoven and Whalley 1985). This requires a model of the entire economy, an exercise that is likely to be beyond the scope of most research evaluation and priority-setting studies.

An Explicit General-Equilibrium Model Using the Balance of Trade Function

Martin and Alston (1992, 1994) have described and illustrated an "exact" approach for measuring the benefits from new technology using a modification of the widely utilized *distorted trade expenditure function* or *balance of trade function* (e.g., Lloyd and Schweinberger 1988; Vousden 1990; Anderson and Neary 1992).[20] The balance of trade function may be defined for a single-household economy as

$$H^i = e\,(\,p,\,w,\,u^i\,) - g\,(\,p,\,w,\,v,\,\tau\,) - (\,p - p^w\,)'\,\mathbf{m}\,(\,p,\,w,\,v\,) - f \qquad (4.6)$$

and the money-metric measure of total welfare in the economy, H^i, given an intitial utility of u^i, is based on four components: (a) the minimum expenditure necessary to obtain a given level of utility from consumption, e(.), (b) income to owners of factors of production, g(.), (c) government revenues from trade taxes, $(p - p^w)'\mathbf{m}(.)$, and (d) net transfers from abroad, f.

These four components are obtained as follows. The function e(.) is the net expenditure function of a composite household for a given vector of domestic product prices, p, a vector of domestic factor prices, w, and a level of utility that is exogenously specified at level u^i since this measure is based upon the Hicksian money-metric measures of welfare change. The function g(.) defines the maximized profit generated from production in the economy

20. In this approach, advantage is taken of the modern, duality methods for modeling general equilibrium trade and welfare. While a complete model is required of the economy of interest, interest may be confined to a subset of the entire economy and, through judicious use of separability assumptions and aggregation, the model can be kept quite small.

for given domestic prices of outputs, prices of endogenously supplied factors, w, a vector of fixed factors, v, and a vector of technology variables, τ, representing the state of the available technology. For a vector of world prices, p^w, the second-last term in equation 4.6 is the government revenue generated by tariffs (or spent on export subsidies). It is calculated as the inner product of the vector of trade taxes on each commodity $(p - p^w)$ and the vector of *actual* import levels, $\mathbf{m}$, which are determined by product and factor prices and the resource endowment.[21] The tariff revenues are assumed to be redistributed without cost to the composite consuming household. Finally, f, is the financial inflow from abroad in the form of net transfers, net factor income flows, or foreign borrowings utilized by the economy.

The use of the expenditure function approach, as in equation 4.6, means that money measures of the compensation required to maintain a particular level of utility are derived in a consistent manner, avoiding the discrepancies that can arise when compensation is considered one market at a time (see Thurman 1991a; Hueth and Just 1991). The modified trade-expenditure function presented in equation 4.6 can be generalized in several ways. First, it can be extended from a single household to any number of households simply by identifying the expenditure and revenue functions associated with each household or household group. Similarly, vertical market linkages through intermediate inputs can be incorporated by identifying separate net revenue functions for the input-supplying and input-using sectors. Domestic taxation on production, consumption, or factor returns can be incorporated in the same manner by distinguishing between the prices paid by demanders and received by suppliers and by accounting for the resulting government revenues in the same way as for tariff revenues.

An exact money-metric measure of the welfare change resulting from technical change can be obtained from equation 4.6 simply by comparing the net expenditures required to achieve a given level of utility, u^i, under the initial technology, τ_0, and under the new technology, τ_1. The *compensating variation* version of the measure, with the utility level in the expenditure function held constant at u^0, is

$$H_1^0 - H_0^0 = H\,(\,p_1, p_1^w, w_1, v_1, \tau_1, u^0\,) - H\,(\,p_0, p_0^w, w_0, v_0, \tau_0, u^0\,) \qquad (4.7)$$

The equation for *equivalent variation* is the same except that utility is held at u^1 rather than u^0. Since the components of changes in H shown in 4.6 are

---

21. Tariff revenues are calculated using the actual level of imports rather than the quantity of imports that would result if compensation had been made to hold utility at u^i, following the approach of Martin and Alston (1992) (based on the suggestion of Mayshar 1990). If preferred, the actual import demands — $\mathbf{m}$ (p, w, v) — in equation 4.6 can be replaced with the compensated demands to provide a welfare measure based on actual, rather than hypothetical, compensation.

expressed purely in money terms, they can simply be added across different types of households or firms as long as different distributional weights are not being imposed. Different distributional weights can be incorporated if desired.

The welfare evaluation in equation 4.7 is based on changes in product and factor prices from the intial period (subscript 0) to the final period (subscript 1) as a result of the change in technology from τ_0 to τ_1. These price changes are established by the simulation of market equilibrium using Marshallian supply-and-demand curves, a simulation that is logically prior to and separate from the welfare evaluation. For consistency, these Marshallian supply-and-demand curves must be derived from, and share parameters with, the relevant components of the modified trade-expenditure function, equation 4.6. The basic surplus model in section 4.1 may be regarded as a special case of the more general model defined by equation 4.7, which applies when all product prices but one are exogenous and there are no distortions. In such a case, the only remaining differences are that (a) the basic model uses the Marshallian measure of consumer welfare change rather than the Hicksian measure and (b) the producer surplus measured in the basic model may differ from the change in producer profit in equation 4.7.

The balance of trade function approach greatly expands the problems for which accurate welfare evaluation can be undertaken without requiring any data or parameters beyond those needed for the traditional approach. A behavioral model, constructed as described above, may be used to solve for a baseline and a perturbed solution for the price, quantity, expenditure, and revenue variables in the model. Because of the structure of the formulation, the behavioral model must be a general-equilibrium model. However, when the commodity (or commodities) of interest and all other goods can be assumed to be separable, the model need not be any more complicated (and requires little if any additional information to parameterize) than the more traditional partial-equilibrium approach.

Once a general-equilibrium model has been used to compute the prices and quantities under the old and new technologies, the total welfare change and each of its components can be computed. If the supply-and-demand curves used to generate the prices and quantities are derived directly from the underlying preferences and technology, then the welfare measures will be exact. In sharp contrast with the traditional approach, multiple sources of general-equilibrium feedback present no problems for the calculation and interpretation of exact measures of the welfare effect and its distribution at any level of aggregation. The procedures identified above can be implemented without modification in the presence of multiple sources of price change and endogenously determined prices.

The use of the balance of trade function approach in conjunction with a general-equilibrium model seems to hold the potential to resolve in a satisfactory way many of the problems that have arisen when attempts have been made to expand the range of settings in which research benefits are evaluated. The conventional graphical approach becomes increasingly difficult as the problem becomes more complicated. In principle one should get the same answer from the system of supply-and-demand equations, by integrating back, as one gets by starting with the expenditure function and modeling equilibrium in terms of the supply-and-demand equations derived from it (i.e., the duality should work in both directions). In practice, however, supply-and-demand equations may not be integrable and the results obtained by starting from supply and demand may not be the same as those obtained by specifying the full integrable model at the outset.

At least in situations where the market situation to be studied is complicated by distortions and multiple sources of general-equilibrium feedback, it will usually be better to use Martin and Alston's (1992, 1994) approach rather than to attempt to build welfare measures from a single-market analysis. It is also likely to be appropriate to apply that type of approach more generally. Whether that is so in a particular study will depend on the additional costs of using the theoretically more defensible approach relative to the benefits in terms of greater precision and consistency of results. Further work is necessary with these relatively new methods to establish the dimensions of that trade-off.[22] When markets are less complicated, the graphical single-market approach is adequate, and it is preferable in terms of its transparency and minimal requirements for data and modeling expertise. Such situations are likely to be the norm in typical research evaluation and priority-setting studies. Thus, the remainder of this chapter emphasizes relatively simple partial-equilibrium models that, for the most part, do not involve important problems of a general-equilibrium nature.

4.2.4   Multiple Products Related in Consumption

The simplest case of multiple products has two (or more) products that are substitutes in consumption but entirely unrelated in production (i.e., the

22. As illustrated by Martin and Alston (1994), in the context of an evaluation analysis, the additional work may not be too onerous. They showed that a three-good model (i.e., two goods of interest, and a numeraire representing all other goods) could easily be set up and run on a spreadsheet to evaluate benefits from research-induced changes in technology for one or more goods with market distortions. Martin and Alston (1993) report results from a full global general-equilibrium model, the OECD-World Bank RUNS model. What remains to be established by further empirical work is the magnitude of the gains in precision to be obtained by doing the extra work, to the extent that extra work is involved, in going from ad hoc partial-equilibrium approaches to a consistent general-equilibrium approach.

technologies of production are independent and there are no specialized factors in common — any factors that are used in both products are perfectly elastically supplied to both industries). A supply-and-demand model for this case with n products could be written as

Supply:
$$Q_i = f_i(P_i, B_i) \tag{4.8a}$$

Demand:
$$Q_i = g_i(P_1, \ldots, P_n, A_i) \tag{4.8b}$$

for $i = 1, \ldots, n$. The supply of each product i depends only upon its own price and exogenous supply shifters, B_i, but demand for each product depends on the prices of all the products and exogenous demand shifters, A_i. In logarithmic differential form, for two products, the system of supply-and-demand equations may be written as

Supply:
$$E(Q_i) = \varepsilon_i \left[E(P_i) + \beta_i \right] \tag{4.8a'}$$

Demand:
$$E(Q_i) = \eta_{i1} E(P_1) + \eta_{i2} E(P_2) - \eta_{ij} \alpha_i \tag{4.8b'}$$

for $i = 1$ or 2. In these equations the parameter definitions are slightly different from those used in the single-product model. The elasticity of supply of product i (ε_i) is as before, but the own-price elasticities and cross-price elasticities of demand, η_{ij}, are the natural values rather than absolute values so that own-price elasticities are negative ($\eta_{ii} < 0$ for $i = 1$, 2). The solutions for relative changes in prices are

$$E(P_1) = -[(\eta_{11}\alpha_1 + \varepsilon_1\beta_1)(\varepsilon_2 - \eta_{22}) + \eta_{12}(\alpha_2 - \beta_2)]/D' \tag{4.9a}$$

$$E(P_2) = -[(\eta_{22}\alpha_2 + \varepsilon_2\beta_2)(\varepsilon_1 - \eta_{11}) + \eta_{21}(\alpha_1 - \beta_1)]/D' \tag{4.9b}$$

where

$$D' = (\varepsilon_1 - \eta_{11})(\varepsilon_2 - \eta_{22}) - \eta_{12}\eta_{21}$$

The equations for gross annual economic welfare changes have the same form as equations 4.4a and 4.4b, but the interpretation is that the subscripts denote different *commodities* rather than the same commodity in different countries or regions:

$$\Delta CS_i = -P_i Q_i [E(P_i) - \alpha_i][1 + 0.5 E(Q_i)] \tag{4.10a}$$

$$\Delta PS_i = P_i Q_i [E(P_i) - \beta_i][1 + 0.5 E(Q_i)] \tag{4.10b}$$

In addition, and in contrast to the single-product case, it is not appropriate to simply add these measures up across is (now commodities rather than countries) to get a measure of total welfare change. As suggested by the quote above from Just, Hueth and Schmitz (1982), the *total* welfare changes due to a supply (or demand) shift in the *i*th market are reflected in the general-equilibrium measures of consumer and producer surplus changes *in that market alone*. The welfare measures in equations 4.10a and 4.10b are based on general-equilibrium changes in quantities and prices; so they are general-equilibrium welfare measures. Adding up these measures of the welfare effects of a particular supply (or demand) shift across markets would lead to double counting. In general, to measure the incidence of a change, we have to look across markets in a disaggregated fashion.

For example, consider an increase in supply of good 1 ($\beta_1 > 0$) with no other exogenous shifts ($\alpha_1 = \alpha_2 = \beta_2 = 0$). The correct measures of welfare change taken in the market for good 1 (assuming a parallel shift) are

$$\Delta CS^* = -P_1 Q_1 E(P_1)[1 + 0.5E(Q_1)] \tag{4.10c}$$

$$\Delta PS_1 = P_1 Q_1 [E(P_1) - \beta_1][1 + 0.5E(Q_1)] \tag{4.10d}$$

$$\Delta TS = \Delta CS^* + \Delta PS_1 \tag{4.10e}$$

where ΔCS^* is the change in consumer surplus measured off the general-equilibrium demand curve for good 1, and it comprises consumer surplus from both goods plus producer surplus on good 2 ($\Delta CS^* = \Delta CS_1 + \Delta CS_2 + \Delta PS_2$). To disaggregate these measures further,

$$\Delta PS_2 = P_2 Q_2 E(P_2)[1 + 0.5E(Q_2)] \tag{4.10f}$$

$$\Delta CS = \Delta CS^* - \Delta PS_2 \tag{4.10g}$$

To clarify these points, consider figure 4.6: panel *a* represents the market for one good (say, chicken meat) and panel *b* represents the market for a substitute (say, beef). The initial demand curves ($D_{C,0}$ and $D_{B,0}$) are defined in the usual way as conditioned on the price of the other good being constant at its initial value ($P_{C,0}$ or $P_{B,0}$). When the supply curve for chicken meat shifts (from $S_{C,0}$ to $S_{C,1}$), a series of general-equilibrium-type adjustments take place in both markets: a fall in the price of chicken causes a fall in demand for beef (because they are substitutes); the subsequent fall in beef price causes a fall in demand for chicken and so on. Ultimately, a new equilibrium is achieved at prices $P_{B,1}$ and $P_{C,1}$ with corresponding demand curves $D_{C,1}$ and $D_{B,1}$.

The curve D_C^* is the *"general" equilibrium* demand curve for chicken that traces out the demand response to exogenous price changes in the chicken market *holding constant the supply curve for beef*. The usual treatment — holding constant the price of beef — is a special case that applies when the supply curve for beef is perfectly elastic. The solutions from the equilibrium-displacement model for relative changes in prices and quantities reflect these

Figure 4.6: *Welfare effects with feedback in consumption*

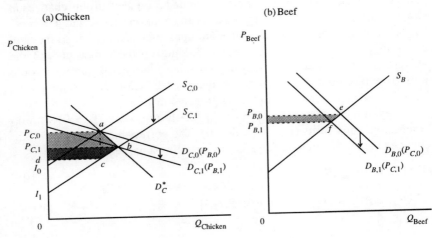

general–equilibrium-type responses, a fact that must be borne in mind when the solutions are being used to compute welfare changes.

In figure 4.6, the full welfare consequences of the shift in the supply of chicken can be measured as the area beneath the demand curve D_C^* between the two supply curves ($S_{C,0}$ and $S_{C,1}$). This area ($I_0 ab I_1$) comprises the "consumer surplus" of area $P_{C,0} ab P_{C,1}$ and (with parallel supply shifts) "producer surplus" equal to area $P_{C,1} bcd$. In this case, the change in "consumer surplus" comprises changes in consumer surplus from consumption of both beef and chicken and changes in beef producer surplus. These components could be disentangled with a little effort; note that the fall in beef producer surplus is given by area $P_{B,0} ef P_{B,1}$.

4.2.5 *Multiple Products Related in Production*

So far we have considered interactions among products only through substitution in consumption. Now we consider cases where multiple products are related either through their production technology or through factor use. Clearly in some cases production processes are interdependent among products. An alternative way for product markets to interact is when they share the use of a specialized factor of production.[23]

23. Clear examples are (a) when livestock industries (e.g., hogs and chicken) affect feed-grain prices, the supply functions of livestock products will be related, and (b) the use of milk in production of various dairy products (e.g., see Perrin 1980). In these examples the products are also related in consumption and, perhaps, through production technology.

Mullen, Wohlgenant and Farris (1988, pp. 247-49) presented a two-product, two-input model that they applied to the U.S. beef processing sector. In this model two products are produced using two specialized factors. The products are related in production and through factor markets, but not in consumption. The key assumptions are that the production function is (a) characterized by constant returns to scale and (b) separable between inputs and outputs. Their model is outlined below.

The *production function* has the form

$$Q = q(Q_1, Q_2) = f(X_1, X_2) = F \tag{4.11a}$$

Because q is linearly homogeneous in X_1 and X_2, the *cost function* is separable in prices and quantity:

$$C = h(W_1, W_2)Q \tag{4.11b}$$

Corresponding *output-constrained input-demand functions* are (by Shephard's lemma)

$$X_1 = h_1(W_1, W_2)Q \tag{4.11c}$$

$$X_2 = h_2(W_1, W_2)Q \tag{4.11d}$$

The second part of the problem is to maximize revenue subject to a constrained level of inputs, *F*. Homogeneity conditions result in a separable *revenue function*:

$$R = r(P_1, P_2)F \tag{4.11e}$$

Corresponding *input-constrained output-supply functions* are (by Hotelling's lemma)

$$Q_1 = r_1(P_1, P_2)F \tag{4.11f}$$

$$Q_2 = r_2(P_1, P_2)F \tag{4.11g}$$

The system of logarithmic differential equations describing equilibrium becomes

Final demand: $E(Q_1) = -\eta_1[E(P_1) - \alpha_1]$ (4.11a′)

$E(Q_2) = -\eta_2[E(P_2) - \alpha_2]$ (4.11b′)

Constrained output supply (transformation) and factor demand (substitution):

$$E(Q_1) - E(Q_2) = \tau[E(P_1) - E(P_2)] \tag{4.11c′}$$

$$E(X_1) - E(X_2) = \sigma \, [E(W_1) - E(W_2)] \qquad (4.11d')$$

Market
equilibrium:
$$m_1 E(P_1) + m_2 E(P_1) = s_1 E(W_1) + s_2 E(W_2) \qquad (4.11e')$$

$$m_1 E(Y_1) + m_1 E(Y_2) = s_1 E(X_1) + s_2 E(X_2) \qquad (4.11f')$$

Factor supply:
$$E(X_1) = \varepsilon_1 [E(W_1) + \beta_1] \qquad (4.11g')$$

$$E(X_2) = \varepsilon_2 [E(W_2) + \beta_2] \qquad (4.11h')$$

In these equations (with some slight changes from the notation used by Mullen, Wohlgenant and Farris 1988), the parameters and variables are defined as follows: the quantity of product i is Q_i and its price is P_i, the price of factor i is W_i and its quantity is X_i, the fraction of revenue accounted for by product i is m_i, the fraction of cost accounted for by factor i is s_i, the absolute value of the demand elasticity for product i is η_i, the supply elasticity for factor i is ε_i, the elasticity of product transformation is τ, and the elasticity of factor substitution is σ. This model includes only two types of equilibrium displacements — those due to shifts of final demand and those due to shifts of factor supply (the shift of demand for product i is α_i, and the shift of supply for factor i is β_i) — and it does not allow for the products to interact in consumption. Mullen, Wohlgenant and Farris (1988) show how to obtain numerical solutions to this model using matrix algebra. The solution is a vector of values for the relative changes in prices and quantities of the factors and products. Measures of welfare changes can then be computed by substituting the relative price and quantity changes into the following formulas:

$$\Delta CS_i = -P_i Q_i [E(P_i) - \alpha_i][1 + 0.5 E(Q_i)] \qquad (4.12a)$$

$$\Delta PS_i = W_i X_i [E(W_i) + \beta_i][1 + 0.5 E(X_i)] \qquad (4.12b)$$

$$\Delta CS = \Sigma_i \, \Delta CS_i \qquad (4.12c)$$

$$\Delta PS = \Sigma_i \Delta PS_i \qquad (4.12d)$$

$$\Delta TS = \Delta PS + \Delta CS \qquad (4.12e)$$

where equation 4.12a measures the change in consumer surplus in consumption of good i, equation 4.12b measures the change in producer surplus in supplying factor i, equation 4.12c measures the change in consumer surplus across both products, equation 4.12d measures the change in producer surplus on all factors, and equation 4.12e measures the total welfare change. The aggregated results for producer surplus in equation 4.12d are the same whether they are summed using components from 4.10b to represent the sum of producer surplus changes across commodity markets, or whether they are summed using components from 4.12b to represent the sum of changes in surpluses accruing to factor suppliers, under competitive equilibrium assumptions. The consumer surplus formulas, 4.10a and 4.12a, are identical.

4.2.6   Demand Shifts

Quality Change

A recurring problem in analyzing the effects of new technology is the question of whether changes in technology involve changes in product quality characteristics as well as changes in factor use for a product. In rice, for example, broken grains, shape, chalkiness, amylase content, glutination temperature, gel consistency, and fragrance are varietal quality characteristics that may be subject to research (Unnevehr 1986, 1990). A further example is the mechanical tomato harvester that *required* tomatoes to be sufficiently robust to withstand the process. Higher-yielding wheat varieties may have lower protein content, while barley varieties differ by malting characteristics (Brennan 1984; Ulrich, Furtan and Schmitz 1986, 1987; Macagno 1990; Voon and Edwards 1992). Lemieux and Wohlgenant (1989) considered the effects of consumer preferences for lean meat when analyzing the impact of porcine somatotropin, the primary impact of which is yield improvement or cost saving (see also Voon and Edwards 1991a).

Differentiated products, which vary according to some quality characteristics, face differential demands so that higher-quality goods command a premium. Farm products may be perceived as being of higher quality either because they have attributes that lead to higher quality from the retail viewpoint or because they have attributes that are advantageous from the viewpoint of intermediaries. For instance, Macagno (1990) used a multistage model to represent the malting quality of barley as an embodied technology, the initial benefits of which accrue to malsters and brewers. In this case there is no tangible change in the quality of the final product. Similar approaches may be appropriate for a wide range of other products (such as cotton, where milling costs are affected by uniformity of fiber quality, and higher-protein grains that yield flour with better baking quality but not necessarily an appreciable change in the characteristics of the final product).

In most cases it seems likely that technological changes will involve some changes in product characteristics, and sometimes these changes will be very important. For the most part agricultural economists have sidestepped the question of jointly modeling technical changes and associated changes in product quality.[24] One approach is to use a multiproduct model of the type described in the previous section(s) and either to treat product characteristics as products (so that "quality" is continuously variable) or to treat different qualities of products as different products (discrete variation in "quality"). The latter approach may be more restrictive but it is probably more practicable. The most common approach is to introduce an *ad hoc* shift in demand for the product induced by changes in quality. Technical change that leads to a change in product quality is a change in supply conditions *not* demand conditions, and it would be better to model it as such.[25]

The implication is that different qualities should be modeled using a multiproduct modeling approach. The difficulty with this approach is that the substitution effects between the different qualities of a particular product that are the most important (that determine the own- and cross-price elasticities of demand) are very difficult to measure — especially for ex ante studies where the different qualities might not exist when the analysis is being undertaken. In addition, substitution effects in production (say, between two varieties of wheat) are likely to be too important to dismiss when various qualities of a particular product are dealt with and when these too are difficult to quantify. Thus, to model quality changes formally may require using a model with multiple sources of general-equilibrium-type feedback. We have seen above that measuring welfare changes may be difficult in such a setting. However, in some cases, where product quality change is important, a formal attempt to analyze its effects in a logically consistent fashion may be worthwhile.

The previous approaches in the literature (treating quality change as a demand shift) have avoided the difficulties by treating different qualities as perfect substitutes in consumption (up to a constant premium for quality) and treating the supply choice as exogenous, implying no substitution in production in response to price changes (either a total switch from one quality to another or a partial switch determined exogenously, independent of prices).[26]

---

24. Some exceptions are Unnevehr (1986, 1990), Lemieux and Wohlgenant (1989), Voon (1991), and Voon and Edwards (1991a, 1992). The studies by Ulrich, Furtan and Schmitz (1987) and Macagno (1990) are pertinent as well.

25. For instance, the development of technology for filtered cigarettes may have had gross effects similar to those from an increase in demand for the aggregate good, "cigarettes" (i.e., greater sales at a higher price), but it might at the same time have led to a reduction in demand for tobacco per cigarette with an ambiguous net effect on demand for tobacco. Modeling this change simply as an increase in demand for cigarettes would lead to an erroneous conclusion that demand for all inputs used in cigarettes had increased.

26. Mullen and Alston (1994) treated different qualities of lamb as perfect substitutes in consumption (i.e., linear indifference curves) but with different production and marketing costs and consumer willingness to pay. Then they modeled quality change in the context of a model of consumption and production aggregated over different qualities. A change in the product mix was modeled as leading to a shift in

Under these restrictive assumptions, it is possible to analyze quality change as a demand shift (the addition of a premium for improved quality) and to obtain meaningful measures of the size and distribution of benefits. However, when less restrictive assumptions are applied, it may not be safe to treat quality change as an equivalent shift of demand.

Income, Population, and Other Demand Shifters

The production effects of agricultural research are generally realized over several years. As a result, demand can change a lot over time, particularly because of changes in population and per capita income.[27] The effect of adding an exogenous demand shift is illustrated in figure 4.7. The original price and quantity are P_0 and Q_0. If research were to shift the supply curve down with no exogenous shift in demand, the new price and quantity would be P_1 and Q_1. However, if demand were to shift out exogenously, the new (post-research) price and quantity would be P_1' and Q_1' and the research-induced changes in total economic surplus, consumer surplus, and producer surplus would be I_0abI_1, $P_0'abP_1'$, and $I_0abI_1 - P_0'abP_1' = P_1'bcd$, respectively. In addition, this diagram can be used to illustrate the case where the demand shift is endogenous. For instance, putting aside our reservations about this approach, when new technology involves both an improvement in quality and cost savings, we could model it that way (e.g., Lemieux and Wohlgenant 1989). Alternatively, when improved agricultural technology leads to capital accumulation and growth outside agriculture, with concomitant effects on per capita incomes, and those effects are not already represented in the demand curves, an adjustment to demand due to technical change will be appropriate.

Equations 4.1a, 4.1b, and 4.1c can be used to calculate changes in total, consumer, and producer surplus but with P_0' substituted for P_0, Q_0' substituted for Q_0, and with the elasticities of supply and demand and the percentage shift in supply defined at the initial equilibrium being adjusted to reflect the new pre-research equilibrium (i.e., the move from point d to point a in figure 4.7). Those adjusted numbers are not directly observable, but estimates of rates of population and income growth can be used to inflate the initial quantities and prices from their base values (as described in chapter 5) before the research-induced supply shift is introduced.

---

farm-level supply for total lamb, a change in the overall marketing margin, and an increase in aggregate demand for lamb of all qualities.

27. These changes occur both domestically and internationally. One of the few studies to explicitly incorporate domestic demand shifts over time is Norton, Ganoza and Pomareda (1987).

Figure 4.7:   *Effects of exogenous demand shifts on the size and distribution of research benefits*

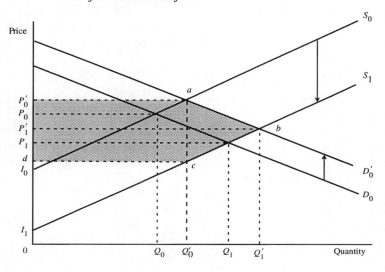

4.3   Vertical Market Relationships

To study vertical market relationships in multistage production systems, we abstract from the temporal ordering of the stages of production and treat the different stages as if they occur at one time. The participants in different stages of the production system are represented as input suppliers and their welfare is reflected in the distribution of economic surplus among inputs. The multistage nature of input decisions can be reflected in constraints on substitutability among inputs through separability assumptions. The case of a single product (in partial equilibrium) produced with two factors in fixed proportions is discussed first and then we proceed to variable proportions, and then multiple factors.

4.3.1   Two Factors with Fixed Factor Proportions

The simplest case we can consider is when two factors of production are used in fixed proportions to produce a homogeneous product. The case of derived factor demand and output supply with two factors and fixed factor proportions is illustrated by Friedman (1976) with the example of knives, blades and handles. That model can be used to show market equilibrium and surplus distribution between, for example, two farming inputs (say land and other inputs) used to produce a farm product. Alternatively, we may use the same approach to analyze a multistage production system — say when a farm product and marketing inputs (such as transportation, processing, and distribution inputs) are used to produce a retail product.

Equilibrium in Factor and Product Markets

Figure 4.8 represents the markets for a farm product and a composite marketing input that are used in fixed proportions to produce a retail food product. The market situation is defined by (a) the technology of production (i.e., the fixed amounts of the two factors used to produce a unit of the retail product), (b) the supply conditions for the factors of production (the farm product supply is SF_0 and the supply of marketing inputs is SM_0 with the units of factor quantities *defined per unit of the retail product*), and (c) the demand function for the retail product, DR_0. Because the factors are used in fixed proportions, it is straightforward to derive the retail supply and factor demand equations. The retail supply function, SR_0 is given as the vertical sum of the underlying factor supply functions (SF_0 and SM_0) so that the marginal cost of a quantity of the retail product is equal to the sum of the marginal costs of the corresponding factor quantities. The derived demand function for the farm product, DF_0, is given by the vertical difference between the retail demand and the supply of marketing inputs. Similarly, the derived demand for marketing inputs, DM_0, is given by subtracting the supply function for the farm product (vertically) from the retail demand function.

The initial equilibrium in the product market is defined by the intersection of retail supply and demand at price PR_0 and quantity QR_0. Equivalently, equilibrium may be defined in terms of one of the factor markets: equilibrium of supply and demand of the farm product is at price PF_0 and quantity QF_0; supply and demand for marketing inputs are in equilibrium at price PM_0 and quantity QM_0.

Increase in Supply of Marketing Inputs

Now, suppose the supply function for marketing inputs shifts down (say, in response to technical change) in parallel from SM_0 to SM_1. This shift affects the equilibrium in all three markets. The supply of the retail product shifts down (by the same absolute amount per unit) from SR_0 to SR_1. The demand for the farm product shifts up in parallel (also by the same absolute amount per unit) from DF_0 to DF_1. All quantities increase in proportion (to QR_1, QM_1, and QF_1). The prices of the marketing input and the retail product fall (to PM_1 and PR_1), and the price of the farm product rises (to PF_1).

Figure 4.8: *Research benefits with two factors in fixed proportions*

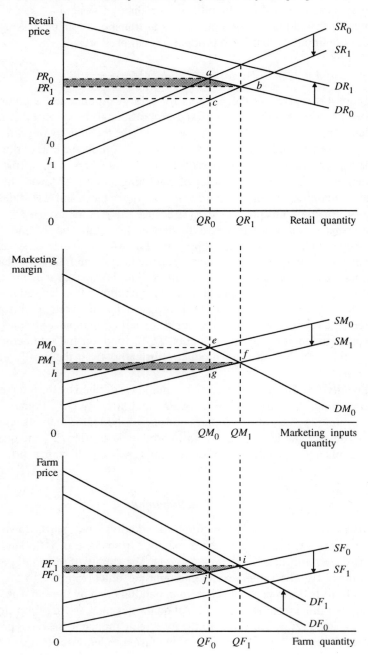

As a consequence of these changes, there is a total welfare gain of I_0abI_1, comprising a change in consumer surplus, $\Delta CS = PR_0abPR_1$, and a change in producer surplus, $\Delta PS = PR_1bcd$. The change in producer surplus comprises a change in surplus to suppliers of marketing inputs ($\Delta MS = PM_1fgh$) and a change in surplus to suppliers of the farm product ($\Delta FS = PF_1ijPF_0$). We can express these effects algebraically in the same form as we did for the basic model as follows:

$$\Delta CS = PR_0QR_0Z(1 + 0.5Z\eta) \qquad (4.13a)$$

$$\Delta PS = PR_0QR_0(K - Z)(1 + 0.5Z\eta) \qquad (4.13b)$$

$$\Delta TS = \Delta CS + \Delta PS = PR_0QR_0K(1 + 0.5Z\eta) \qquad (4.13c)$$

where K is now the vertical shift of the supply function for marketing inputs expressed as a percentage of initial *retail* price, PR_0, η is the absolute value of the elasticity of demand at retail, ε is the elasticity of supply to retail and $Z = K\varepsilon/(\varepsilon+\eta)$ is the percentage reduction in retail price due to the supply shift.

The components of the change in producer surplus are

$$\Delta FS = PF_0QF_0(K - Z)(\varepsilon/\varepsilon_f)(1 + 0.5Z\eta) \qquad (4.13d)$$

$$\Delta MS = PM_0QM_0(K - Z)(\varepsilon/\varepsilon_m)(1 + 0.5Z\eta) \quad \text{and} \qquad (4.13e)$$

$$\Delta PS = \Delta MS + \Delta FS \qquad (4.13f)$$

where ε_f is the elasticity of supply of the farm product and ε_m is the elasticity of supply of marketing inputs.

Equivalently, we could measure the total benefits in the market for marketing inputs as the area beneath the demand curve, DM_0, between the two supply curves (SM_0 and SM_1). This area comprises "producer surplus" (i.e., $\Delta MS = PM_1fgh$) and "consumer surplus" in the market for marketing inputs (PM_0efPM_1 — which includes ΔCS to final consumers and ΔFS to suppliers of the farm product). Alternatively, we could measure the total benefits and their distribution in the market for the farm product; the total benefits in this case are equal to the area between the two demand curves and above the supply curve. The increase in "producer surplus" in the market for the farm product reflects benefits to producers of the farm product, ΔFS, and the increase in "consumer surplus" reflects benefits to final consumers and suppliers of marketing inputs (i.e., $\Delta CS + \Delta MS$).

This set of results may be extended to any arbitrary number of factors of production. Considering individual factors, in any factor market the "producer surplus" refers to surplus of suppliers of that factor while the "consumer surplus" refers to surplus of both final consumers and suppliers of all other factors. Alternatively, we can consider surplus in markets for intermediate products. At any market level, the "producer surplus" is the sum of quasi-rents accruing to all factors used in the production of the intermediate good (i.e., factors used up to that market level). The "consumer surplus" is the sum of final consumer surplus and the quasi-rents accruing to all factors used in conjunction with the intermediate good (i.e., beyond that market level).

Another feature of the results warrants emphasis: the *distribution* of benefits is entirely independent of which of the curves shifts. That is, the total benefit and distribution of benefits would be the same from a shift down of the farm product supply function by the same amount per unit — i.e., to SF_1 (or, for that matter, from a shift up of the final demand function by the same amount per unit — i.e., to DR_1), so long as the shifts are parallel. Thus, in this setting, farmers could afford to be indifferent both about where new technology applies in the production and marketing system and about where a levy to fund research is collected; maximizing total benefits will maximize farmer benefits.

Change in Processing Technology

So far we have treated technical change in terms of either a shift of the supply of the marketing inputs or a shift of the supply of the farm product. An alternative type of technical change would be a change in the production function that combines the raw materials (the farm product and marketing inputs). The change could be neutral (reducing the amount of both inputs required to produce a unit of the product but maintaining factor proportions), biased (reducing the amount of only one of the inputs required per unit of the product), or some combination of biased and neutral changes (changing the proportions and amounts of both inputs required per unit of the product). Figure 4.9 shows the effects of a biased technical change (saving marketing inputs) in the context of the market model described in figure 4.8. The technical change reduces — in proportion — the amount of marketing inputs used per unit of the farm product and per unit of the retail product. This amounts to a proportional shift down of the supply of marketing inputs (where the input quantities are expressed per unit of the final product) from SM_0 to SM_1 from the point of view of the producers of the retail product (equivalently, a percentage reduction in the cost of supplying "efficiency units" of the marketing input).

The welfare effects are slightly more complicated in this case. For the retail product, consumer surplus is increased by $\Delta CS = PR_0abPR_1$ and total surplus is greater by $\Delta TS = I_0abI_1$. For suppliers of the farm product, producer surplus increases by $\Delta FS = PF_1 cdPF_0$. For the marketing input, the number of "efficiency units" (QM_1^*) is greater, but the actual use of marketing inputs (QM_1) is smaller. The effect of the technical change on surplus accruing to marketing inputs is equal to the difference $\Delta MS = PM_1 fh - PM_0 eg$. This difference may be positive or negative, depending, primarily, upon the elasticity of final demand; a sufficient condition is that it will be negative when final demand is inelastic. Thus, farmers and consumers necessarily benefit from a biased (marketing-input-saving) technical change; marketing input suppliers may gain or lose.

Technical change biased against the farm product could be modeled in the same way by switching the roles of the farm product and marketing inputs in figure 4.9. By analogy, then, farmers may gain or lose from a farm-product-saving technical change in the food industry. Notice that biased technical change has effects that are similar to those of a proportional downward shift of the factor supply function.[28]

With a neutral technical change, it is relatively easy to show that when both factor supply functions slope up, both inputs will benefit when demand for the product is elastic (in which case total expenditure on both inputs rises with an increase in output), and conversely, both will lose when demand for the product is inelastic. These issues are more easily addressed as a special case in the context of the model of technical change with variable factor proportions that will be developed next.

4.3.2 Two Factors with Variable Factor Proportions

The assumption of fixed factor proportions is an extreme one. Clearly, the extent of input substitution possibilities is an empirical matter, and there is some empirical support for using a less restrictive assumption that allows the possibility of substitution between farm inputs or substitution between farm products and marketing inputs (e.g., Wohlgenant 1989). We saw above that the analysis of research benefits and their distribution for any number of inputs (or stages of production) is quite straightforward under the assumption of fixed factor proportions. With variable proportions it is difficult to get useful algebraic results for more than three factors of production.[29]

28. As shown by Mullen, Wohlgenant and Farris (1988), a biased technical change that is X_1-saving may be modeled as an "equivalent" shift in the supply of X_1. It will not be equivalent in all senses, however, and care must be exercised in assuming equivalence.

29. For two factors the results are fairly transparent (e.g., see Alston and Scobie 1983) but for three factors the analytics are quite cumbersome and the transparency is reduced (see Holloway 1989). Numerical rather than algebraic solutions are likely to be necessary for studies involving three or more factors. Wohlgenant (1982) provided a general solution for the case of one output and n factors.

Figure 4.9: *Biased technical change with fixed proportions*

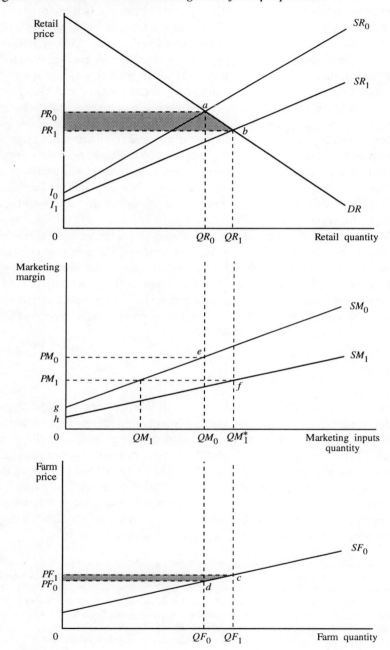

Freebairn, Davis and Edwards (1982) analyzed the distribution of research benefits in a three-stage model with fixed proportions between purchased farming inputs, a farm product, and marketing inputs. They illustrated their results with an application to the U.S. hog industry. Their key points were that with parallel shifts of linear supply functions, (a) innovation at any stage of a multistage production process confers positive benefits on consumers and producers in all stages (i.e., factors) of production and (b) the distribution of benefits is independent of where the innovation applies in the system. In a comment on Freebairn, Davis and Edwards (1982), Alston and Scobie (1983) demonstrated that the distribution of research benefits among factors (or stages) of production depends crucially upon the elasticity of substitution. Their approach to modeling benefits from technical change has subsequently been adopted, adapted, and extended in several studies.[30] The approach owes its origin to Muth (1964), who presented an elegant, simple model of equilibrium displacement in a two-factor model of supply and factor demand in a competitive industry.[31] First, a slightly modified version of Muth's (1964) model of market equilibrium displacements is presented below. Then the welfare economic effects of research-induced technical changes are considered.

The Muth Model

Following Muth (1964), we can model the market equilibrium of a competitive industry producing a homogeneous product using two factors of production in terms of the following six general equations:

Consumer demand: $Q = f(P)$ (4.14a)

Production: $Q = q(X_1, X_2)$ (4.14b)

Factor demand: $W_1 = Pq_1$ (4.14c)

$W_2 = Pq_2$ (4.14d)

Factor supply: $X_1 = g(W_1)$ (4.14e)

$X_2 = h(W_2)$ (4.14f)

The endogenous variables in the model are industry output, Q, the amounts

30. Examples include studies by Mullen, Wohlgenant and Farris (1988), Mullen, Alston and Wohlgenant (1989), Lemieux and Wohlgenant (1989), Holloway (1989), Mullen and Alston (1990), and Wohlgenant (1993).

31. Gardner (1975) used a very similar model to analyse marketing margins. Miedema (1976) clarified the connection between the Muth (1964) and Gardner (1975) models. More recently, Gardner (1987) applied the same type of modeling approach to a range of agricultural policy issues.

of the two factors used by the industry (X_1 and X_2), the price per unit of the final product, P, and the factor prices (W_1 and W_2). Table 4.1 summarizes the notation used in the Muth model. Equation 4.14a is the demand for the industry's output, equation 4.14b is the production function, equations 4.14c and 4.14d are factor-demand equations with each factor being paid the value of its marginal product ($q_i = dq[.]/dX_i$ for factor i), and equations 4.14e and 4.14f are the factor-supply equations. Constant returns to scale is assumed at the industry level.[32]

Totally differentiating equations 4.14a through 4.14f, converting them to elasticity form, and adding exogenous shocks yields the following system of logarithmic differential equations — expressed in terms of relative changes and elasticities:[33]

$$E(Q) = -\eta[E(P) - \alpha] \tag{4.14a'}$$

$$E(Q) = s_1 E(X_1) + s_2 E(X_2) + \delta \tag{4.14b'}$$

$$E(W_1) = E(P) - (s_2/\sigma)E(X_1) + (s_2/\sigma)E(X_2) + \delta + \gamma \tag{4.14c'}$$

$$E(W_2) = E(P) + (s_1/\sigma)E(X_1) - (s_1/\sigma)E(X_2) + \delta - (s_1/s_2)\gamma \tag{4.14d'}$$

$$E(X_1) = \varepsilon_1[E(W_1) + \beta_1] \tag{4.14e'}$$

$$E(X_2) = \varepsilon_2[E(W_2) + \beta_2] \tag{4.14f'}$$

where E denotes relative changes (i.e., $E(Z) = dZ/Z = d\ln Z$), η is the absolute value of the elasticity of demand, α is a vertical shift in the demand function reflecting an *increase* in demand, s_i is the cost share of factor i ($s_i = W_i X_i / PQ$) and, under an assumption of constant returns to scale, $s_1 + s_2 = 1$, δ is a (neutral) upward shift in the production function, γ is a biased (X_2-saving) technical change, σ is the elasticity of substitution between X_1 and X_2, ε_i is the elasticity of supply of factor i, and β_i is a vertical shift down in the supply of factor i reflecting an increase in its supply.[34]

The exogenous shift parameters (α, β_1, β_2, δ, and γ) express equilibrium displacements relative to an initial equilibrium. For instance, setting $\alpha = 0.1$

---

32. See Diewert (1981) for a discussion of this assumption.

33. Muth (1964) shows how to do this for the case being considered here. Mullen, Alston and Wohlgenant (1989, pp. 44-5) show the steps involved in this transition for the three-factor case, approaching the problem from the dual side (i.e., using a cost function rather than a production function).

34. Freebairn, Davis and Edwards (1983) objected to the Muth (1964) specification of biased technical change and suggested an alternative treatment in which only one factor-demand equation is affected. This objection is primarily terminological. Muth claimed correctly that any technical change could be modeled as a combination of his biased component (twisting the isoquant — γ) and a neutral component (relabelling isoquants or relabelling the axes — δ). Neither treatment allows the possibility of a technical change that would alter the elasticity of substitution (i.e., the curvature of the isoquants).

Table 4.1: *Notation Used in the Muth Model*

Variable or parameter	Definition
Endogenous variables	
Q	Quantity of product
P	Price of product
X_i	Quantity of factor i (for $i = 1,2$)
W_i	Price of factor i (for $i = 1,2$)
Q_i	Marginal product of factor i (for $i = 1,2$)
Market parameters	
η	Absolute value of the elasticity of final demand
ε_i	Elasticity of supply of factor i (for $i = 1,2$)
s_i	Cost share of factor i (for $i = 1,2$)
σ	Elasticity of factor substitution
Exogenous shift variables	
α	Relative increase in demand (vertical shift *up* in the price direction)
β_i	Relative increase in supply of factor i (vertical shift *down* in the price direction)
γ	Relative increase in marginal product of factor X_1 due to an X_2-saving biased technical change, holding output constant
δ	Relative increase in output and marginal products of both factors due to a neutral technical change

would imply a 10% increase in consumers' willingness to pay for the initial quantity of the product. As in the case of the multiproduct model, while the demand shift is expressed as a percentage of the initial price, a proportional shift of demand cannot be presumed. Rather, α measures the vertical shift in demand at a point, locally, for any type of demand shift (e.g., proportional, parallel, or pivotal). Similarly, β_i measures the shift down of the supply of factor X_i with the magnitude of the reduction in marginal cost (at the point of approximation, the initial equilibrium) being expressed relative to the initial price of the factor. These shifts are shown in figure 4.10 which is a diagrammatic representation of the model in equations 4.14a′ through 4.14f′.

Solutions to the Muth Model

As we can see in the equations of the model (i.e., equations 4.14a′ through 4.14f′) or in figure 4.10, mutually consistent changes in prices and quantities of factors and products may arise from shifts of the final demand, a, either factor supply function, b1 or b2, a neutral technical change, d, or a biased technical change, g. Algebraic solutions may be obtained by a sequence of substitutions (as by Muth 1964, see also box 4.3a) or by matrix algebra methods (as shown in box 4.3b). The parameters and variables in the Muth model are defined in table 4.1, and the reduced-form solutions are shown in table 4.2 as equations 4.15a through 4.15f. These equations are derived from Muth (1964, p. 233) but with slightly different notation (the parameters are all defined as positive and the shift variables are defined so that when they have positive values, the relevant quantity increases), and we have corrected the error in Muth's equation 24 noted by Freebairn, Davis and Edwards (1983).

4.3.3   Research Benefits with Input Substitution

To measure the surplus changes associated with the equilibrium displacements described by the two-factor model above, it is necessary to define the functional forms of the factor-supply and-demand functions and the nature of the shifts induced by the various changes. As Lindner and Jarrett (1978) and others have shown in the context of the "basic model," the functional form and nature of the supply shift have important implications for measures of benefits — the nature of the shift is especially important.

Surplus Measures

The model in equations 4.14a′ through 4.14f′ does not involve any explicit or implicit assumptions about the functional forms of supply and demand. It is a local approximation to unknown functions; the approximation is linear in logarithmic differentials (i.e., relative changes) and elasticities; it is not assumed that the elasticities are constant.[35] In the work that follows, it is assumed that supply-and-demand functions are approximately linear in the region of interest and that the curves shift in parallel as a result of exogenous factors (α, β_i, γ, and δ). Under these assumptions, the benefits accruing to consumers (ΔCS) and factors of production (ΔPS_i for $i = 1,2$) may be measured in terms of the changes in factor and product prices and quantities from equations 4.15a through 4.15f, using

$$\Delta CS = -P_0 Q_0 [E(P) - \alpha][1 + 0.5E(Q)] \tag{4.16a}$$

$$\Delta PS_i = W_i X_i [E(W_i) + \beta_i][1 + 0.5E(X_i)] \tag{4.16b}$$

---

35. For instance, it is perfectly valid to use this type of model to analyze the effects of parallel shifts in the case of linear supply and demand functions. Alston and Wohlgenant (1990) have shown that this type of linear elasticity model is exactly correct for linear supply and demand and only approximately correct for constant elasticity functions when using $E(X) = dX/X$. The opposite is true when using $E(X) = d\ln X$.

Figure 4.10:   *The Muth equilibrium-displacement model*

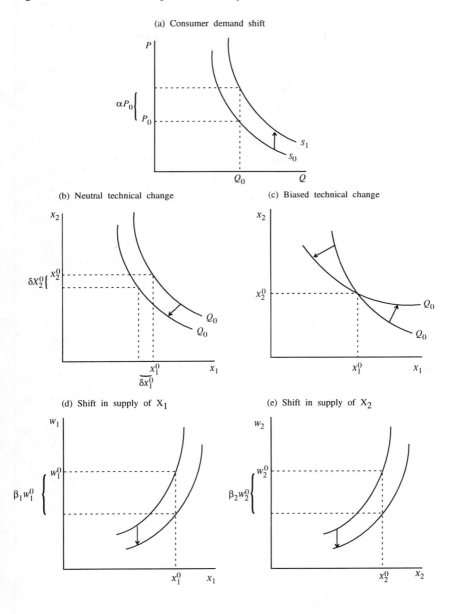

BOX 4.3a: *Solving the Muth Model by Substitution*

The equations of the model may be written as

$$E(Q) = -\eta E(P) + \eta\alpha \tag{4.3.1}$$

$$E(Q) = s_1 E(X_1) + s_2 E(X_2) + \delta \tag{4.3.2}$$

$$E(W_1) = E(P) - (s_2/\sigma)[\, E(X_1) - E(X_2)\,] + \delta + \gamma \tag{4.3.3}$$

$$E(W_2) = E(P) + (s_1/\sigma)[\, E(X_1) - E(X_2)\,] + \delta - (s_1/s_2)\gamma \tag{4.3.4}$$

$$E(W_1) = (1/\varepsilon_1)E(X_1) - \beta_1 \tag{4.3.5}$$

$$E(W_2) = (1/\varepsilon_2)E(X_2) - \beta_2 \tag{4.3.6}$$

Substituting 4.3.5 into 4.3.3 and 4.3.6 into 4.3.4 yields

$$(1/\varepsilon_1)E(X_1) - \beta_1 = E(P) - (s_2/\sigma)[\, E(X_1) - E(X_2)\,] + \delta + \gamma \tag{4.3.7}$$

$$(1/\varepsilon_2)E(X_2) - \beta_2 = E(P) + (s_1/\sigma)[\, E(X_1) - E(X_2)\,] + \delta - (s_1/s_2)\gamma \tag{4.3.8}$$

Setting 4.3.1 equal to 4.3.2 and solving for $E(P)$ yields

$$E(P) = \alpha - (s_1/\eta)E(X_1) - (s_2/\eta)E(X_2) - \delta/\eta \tag{4.3.9}$$

Substituting 4.3.9 into 4.3.7 and 4.3.8 eliminates $E(P)$ and yields

$$\begin{aligned}(1/\varepsilon_1)E(X_1) - \beta_1 = \alpha - (s_1/\eta)E(X_1) - (s_2/\eta)E(X_2) - \delta/\eta \\ - (s_2/\sigma)\,[E(X_1) - E(X_2)] + \delta + \gamma\end{aligned} \tag{4.3.10}$$

$$\begin{aligned}(1/\varepsilon_2)E(X_2) - \beta_2 = \alpha - (s_1/\eta)E(X_1) - (s_2/\eta)E(X_2) - \delta/\eta \\ + (s_1/\sigma)\,[E(X_1) - E(X_2)] + \delta - (s_1/s_2)\gamma\end{aligned} \tag{4.3.11}$$

Collecting terms involving X_1 and X_2 yields

$$\begin{aligned}[(1/\varepsilon_1) + (s_1/\eta) + (s_2/\sigma)]E(X_1) + [(s_2/\eta) - (s_2/\sigma)]E(X_2) \\ = \beta_1 + \alpha + \delta(1 - 1/\eta) + \gamma\end{aligned} \tag{4.3.12}$$

$$\begin{aligned}[(1/\varepsilon_2) + (s_2/\eta) + (s_1/\sigma)]E(X_2) + [(s_1/\eta) - (s_1/\sigma)]E(X_1) \\ = \beta_2 + \alpha + \delta(1 - 1/\eta) - (s_1/s_2)\gamma\end{aligned} \tag{4.3.13}$$

or, more succinctly,

$$A_1 E(X_1) + A_2 E(X_2) = A_3 \tag{4.3.12'}$$

$$B_1 E(X_1) + B_2 E(X_2) = B_3 \tag{4.3.13'}$$

where

$$A_1 = (1/\varepsilon_1) + (s_1/\eta) + (s_2/\sigma) = (\sigma\eta + \sigma\varepsilon_1 s_1 + \eta\varepsilon_1 s_2)/\sigma\,\eta\varepsilon_1 \tag{4.3.14a}$$

$$A_2 = (s_2/\eta) - (s_2/\sigma) = s_2(\sigma - \eta)/\sigma\,\eta \tag{4.3.14b}$$

$$A_3 = \beta_1 + \alpha + \delta(1 - 1/\eta) + \gamma \tag{4.3.14c}$$

$$B_1 = (s_1/\eta) - (s_1/\sigma) = s_1(\sigma - \eta)/\sigma\,\eta \tag{4.3.14d}$$

(continued on next page)

Box 4.3a: (*continued*)

$$B_2 = (1/\varepsilon_2) + (s_2/\eta) + (s_1/\sigma) = (\sigma\eta + \sigma\varepsilon_2 s_2 + \eta\varepsilon_2 s_1)/\sigma\,\eta\varepsilon_2 \qquad (4.3.14e)$$

$$B_3 = B_2 + \alpha + \delta(1 - 1/\eta) - (s_1/s_2)\gamma \qquad (4.3.14f)$$

Solving 4.3.12′ and 4.3.13′ for $E(X_1)$ and $E(X_2)$ gives

$$E(X_1) = (A_2 B_3 - A_3 B_2)/D \qquad (4.3.15a)$$

$$E(X_2) = (A_3 B_1 - A_1 B_3)/D \qquad (4.3.15b)$$

where $D = A_2 B_1 - A_1 B_2$

Substituting the terms above into the expression for D and simplifying it yields

$$D = -[\sigma\,\eta + \sigma\,(s_1\varepsilon_1 + s_2\varepsilon_2) + \eta(s_1\varepsilon_2 + s_2\varepsilon_1) + \varepsilon_1\varepsilon_2]/\sigma\,\eta\varepsilon_1\varepsilon_2$$

Multiplying the numerator of equation 4.3.15a by $-\sigma\,\eta\varepsilon_1\varepsilon_2$ yields

$$E(X_1) = [(A_3 B_2\sigma\,\eta\varepsilon_1\varepsilon_2) - (A_2 B_3\sigma\,\eta\varepsilon_1\varepsilon_2)]/D' \qquad (4.3.16)$$

where $D' = \sigma\,\eta + \sigma\,(s_1\varepsilon_1 + s_2\varepsilon_2) + \eta(s_1\varepsilon_2 + s_2\varepsilon_1) + \varepsilon_1\varepsilon_2$

Substituting from equations 4.3.14 and simplifying we get

$$A_3 B_2\sigma\,\eta\varepsilon_1\varepsilon_2 = A_3\,(\sigma\,\eta + s_2\sigma\varepsilon_2 + s_1\eta\varepsilon_2)\,\varepsilon_1 \text{ and } B_3 A_2\,\eta\varepsilon_1\varepsilon_2 = B_3 s_2(\sigma - \eta)\varepsilon_1\varepsilon_2$$

After substituting for A_3 and B_3 we have the solution for $E(X_1)$. Since the solution is linear in the shift terms, its elements can be derived for each shift parameter in turn. Thus, the term involving the demand shift, α, is equal to

$$E(X_1|\alpha) = \{\,[(\sigma\,\eta + s_2\sigma\varepsilon_2 + s_1\eta\varepsilon_2)\varepsilon_1] - [s_2(\sigma - \eta)\varepsilon_1\varepsilon_2]\,\}\,\alpha/D'$$
$$= \eta\varepsilon_1(\sigma + \varepsilon_2)\,\alpha/D'$$

The terms involving the factor-supply shifts are given by

$$E(X_1|\beta_1) = (\sigma\,\eta + s_2\sigma\varepsilon_2 + s_1\eta\varepsilon_2)\varepsilon_1\,\beta_1/D'$$

$$E(X_1|\beta_2) = -s_2(\sigma - \eta)\varepsilon_1\varepsilon_2\,\beta_2/D'$$

The terms involving the technical changes are given by

$$E(X_1|\delta) = \{\,[(\sigma\,\eta + s_2\sigma\varepsilon_2 + s_1\eta\varepsilon_2)\varepsilon_1] - [s_2(\sigma - \eta)\varepsilon_1\varepsilon_2]\,\}\,(1 - 1/\eta)\delta/D'$$
$$= -(1 - \eta)\varepsilon_1(\sigma + \varepsilon_2)\,\delta/D'$$

$$E(X_1|\gamma) = \{\,[(\sigma\eta + s_2\sigma\varepsilon_2 + s_1\eta\varepsilon_2)\varepsilon_1] + (s_1/s_2)[s_2(\sigma - \eta)\varepsilon_1\varepsilon_2]\,\}\,\gamma/D'$$
$$= \sigma\varepsilon_1(\eta + \varepsilon_2)\,\gamma/D'$$

The equation for $E(X_1)$ is given by the sum of these five terms. The equation for $E(X_2)$ can be derived using the same approach but eliminating $E(X_1)$, instead of $E(X_2)$, from equations 4.3.15. Equations for the other four endogenous variables (the output quantity and the three prices) are readily derived using the solutions for the input quantities and the equations of the model (4.3.1, 4.3.2, 4.3.5, and 4.3.6).

BOX 4.3b: *Solving the Muth Model Using Matrix Algebra*

The matrix algebra approach is more tractable than the substitution approach, especially for problems involving larger numbers of equations (when there are more inputs or outputs, as shown later in this chapter). The first step is to transform the model so that the exogenous shocks are on the right-hand side. In the two-factor, one-product case, the model (i.e., equations 4.14) thus may be represented as follows:

$$E(Q) + \eta\, E(P) = \eta\, \alpha$$

$$E(Q) - s\, E(X_1) - s_2\, E(X_2) = \delta$$

$$E(W_1) - E(P) + (s_2/\sigma)E(X_1) - (s_2/\sigma)E(X_2) = \delta + \gamma$$

$$E(W_2) - E(P) - (s_1/\sigma)\, E(X_1) + (s_1/\sigma)\, E(X_2) = \delta - (s_1/s_2)\gamma$$

$$E(X_1) - \varepsilon_1 E(W) = \varepsilon_1\beta_1$$

$$E(X_2) - \varepsilon_2 E(W_2) = \varepsilon_2\beta_2$$

In matrix form this can be written as

$$M\,Y = X$$

where Y is a vector of endogenous prices and quantities of interest (of length $n = 6$ in this case), X is a vector of exogenous shocks of length n, and M is an $n \times n$ matrix of parameters. That is

$$
\begin{bmatrix}
1 & \eta & 0 & 0 & 0 & 0 \\
1 & 0 & -s_1 & -s_2 & 0 & 0 \\
0 & -1 & (s_2/\sigma) & -(s_2/\sigma) & 1 & 0 \\
0 & -1 & -(s_1/\sigma) & (s_1/\sigma) & 0 & 1 \\
0 & 0 & 1 & 0 & -\varepsilon_1 & 0 \\
0 & 0 & 0 & 1 & 0 & -\varepsilon_2
\end{bmatrix}
\begin{bmatrix}
E(Q) \\
E(P) \\
E(X_1) \\
E(X_2) \\
E(W_1) \\
E(W_2)
\end{bmatrix}
=
\begin{bmatrix}
\eta\alpha \\
\delta \\
\delta + \gamma \\
\delta - (s_1/s_2)\gamma \\
\varepsilon_1\beta_1 \\
\varepsilon_2\beta_2
\end{bmatrix}
$$

The solution vector is

$$Y = M^{-1} X$$

It remains to solve for the inverse of the parameter matrix, M. For some problems, a numerical solution will be sufficient; for others, an analytic solution may be wanted. An analytic inverse can be derived either by hand, using standard methods or using a computer program such as *Mathematica©* or *Derive©*. The solutions shown as equations 4.15 in table 4.2 are then obtained by collecting together the terms in the solution to $M^{-1}X$ involving each of the different individual elements of the exogenous shock terms (i.e., α, β_1, β_2, δ, and γ).

Table 4.2: *Solutions to the Muth Model*

$$E(Q) = [\eta \{ \varepsilon_1\varepsilon_2 + \sigma(s_1\varepsilon_1 + s_2\varepsilon_2) \}\, \alpha + s_1\varepsilon_1\eta(\sigma+\varepsilon_2)\beta_1 + s_2\varepsilon_2\eta(\sigma+\varepsilon_1)\beta_2 + \eta \{ \sigma(1 + s_1\varepsilon_1 + s_2\varepsilon_2) + \varepsilon_1\varepsilon_2 + s_1\varepsilon_2 + s_2\varepsilon_1 \}\, \delta$$
$$+\, s_1\sigma\eta(\varepsilon_1 - \varepsilon_2)\gamma]/D \tag{4.15a}$$

$$E(P) = [\eta(\sigma + s_2\varepsilon_1 + s_1\varepsilon_2)\alpha - s_1\varepsilon_1(\sigma+\varepsilon_2)\beta_1 - s_2\varepsilon_2(\sigma+\varepsilon_1)\beta_2 - \{ \sigma(1 + s_1\varepsilon + s_2\varepsilon_2) + \varepsilon_1\varepsilon_2 + s_1\varepsilon_2 + s_2\varepsilon_1 \}\, \delta - s_1\sigma(\varepsilon_1 - \varepsilon_2)\gamma]/D \tag{4.15b}$$

$$E(X_1) = [\eta\varepsilon_1(\sigma + \varepsilon_2)\alpha + \{ \eta\sigma + (s_2\sigma + s_1\eta)\varepsilon_2 \}\, \varepsilon_1\beta_1 - s_2(\sigma - \eta)\varepsilon_2\varepsilon_1\beta_2 - (\sigma+\varepsilon_2)\,(1 - \eta)\varepsilon_1\delta + \varepsilon_1\sigma(\varepsilon_2 + \eta)\gamma]/D \tag{4.15c}$$

$$E(X_2) = [\eta\varepsilon_2(\sigma + \varepsilon_1)\alpha - s_1(\sigma - \eta)\varepsilon_1\varepsilon_2\beta_1 + \{ \eta\sigma + (s_1\sigma + s_2\eta)\varepsilon_1 \}\, \varepsilon_2\beta_2 - (\sigma+\varepsilon_1)(1 - \eta)\varepsilon_2\delta - (s_1/s_2)\varepsilon_2\sigma(\varepsilon_1 + \eta)\gamma]/D \tag{4.15d}$$

$$E(W_1) = [\eta(\sigma + \varepsilon_2)\alpha - (s_1\sigma + s_2\eta + \varepsilon_2)\varepsilon_1\beta_1 - s_2(\sigma - \eta)\varepsilon_2\beta_2 - (\sigma+\varepsilon_2)(1 - \eta)\delta + \sigma(\varepsilon_2 + \eta)\gamma]/D \tag{4.15e}$$

$$E(W_2) = [\eta(\sigma + \varepsilon_1)\alpha - s_1(\sigma - \eta)\varepsilon_1\beta_1 - (s_2\sigma + s_1\eta + \varepsilon_1)\varepsilon_2\beta_2 - (\sigma+\varepsilon_1)(1 - \eta)\delta - (s_1/s_2)\sigma(\varepsilon_1 + \eta)\gamma]/D \tag{4.15f}$$

Note: $D = \sigma(\eta + s_1\varepsilon_1 + s_2\varepsilon_2) + \eta(s_2\varepsilon_1 + s_1\varepsilon_2) + \varepsilon_1\varepsilon_2$, and $D > 0$ for $\eta > 0$, $\sigma > 0$, and ε_1 and $\varepsilon_2 > 0$.

$$\Delta TS = \Delta CS + \sum_{i=1}^{n} \Delta PS_i \qquad (4.16c)$$

Mullen, Alston and Wohlgenant (1989) present equivalent formulas for the case of three factors. Equations 4.16a through 4.16c may be used for an arbitrary number of factors (or stages of production) to estimate total benefits and the distribution of those benefits from equilibrium displacements under the assumptions being used here. They can also be used to examine the effects of a combination of displacements (which add linearly) or individual changes. Freebairn, Davis and Edwards (1983) present formulas for surplus changes that correspond to these equations after substituting terms from equations 4.15a to 4.15f.

Qualitative Results

The qualitative results considering individual exogenous shifts in isolation are shown in table 4.3. With the exception of the biased technical change, consumers always gain from the displacements associated with positive values for any of the exogenous shift variables; they either shift demand up, α, or shift final market supply down (β_i, δ). In the case of a biased (X_2-saving) technical change, consumers will benefit only when the elasticity of supply of X_1 is greater than that of X_2 (i.e., $\varepsilon_1 > \varepsilon_2$). Freebairn, Davis and Edwards (1983) suggested an alternative specification of biased technical change that they found more plausible and which avoided this ambiguity. Factor suppliers gain from a parallel shift down of their own supply function (i.e., surplus to producers of X_1 increases with positive values of β_1 and surplus to producers of X_2 increases with positive values of β_2). However, the cross-effects of factor-supply shifts may be positive or negative, depending upon whether the two factors are gross substitutes or gross complements.

When the elasticity of substitution is *less* than the absolute value of the demand elasticity ($\sigma < \eta$), the two factors are gross complements (i.e., the cross-price elasticity of factor demand is negative so that a fall in price of either factor will increase the demand for the other factor). In this case, both factors benefit when either factor-supply function shifts down. In the extreme case of fixed proportions ($\sigma = 0$), the distribution of benefits is independent of which factor-supply function shifts and the results are as derived in section 4.3.1 above. When the elasticity of substitution is *greater* than the absolute value of the demand elasticity ($\sigma > \eta$), the two factors are gross substitutes (i.e., the cross-price elasticity of factor demand is positive so that a fall in price of either factor will reduce the demand for the other factor). In this case, suppliers of X_1 lose when the supply function for X_2 shifts

Table 4.3: *Incidence of Benefits from Technical Change in the Muth Model*

Type of change in technology	Interest groups		
	Suppliers of X_1	Suppliers of X_2	Consumers
Demand increase ($\alpha > 0$)	+	+	+
Increase in supply of X_1 ($\beta_1 > 0$)	+	$\sigma < \eta$	+
Increase in supply of X_2 ($\beta_2 > 0$)	$\sigma < \eta$	+	+
X_2-saving ($\gamma > 0$)	+	−	$\varepsilon_1 > \varepsilon_2$
Neutral ($\delta > 0$)	$\eta > 1$	$\eta > 1$	+

Note: Entries denote conditions under which interest groups benefit.
+ indicates that benefits are positive under all conditions.
− indicates that there are no conditions under which benefits are positive.
All entries are subject to the assumptions that η, σ, ε_1, and $\varepsilon_2 \geq 0$.
Entries in the row for X_2-saving technical change assume σ is strictly positive. When $\sigma = 0$, there are no effects from biased technical change as defined by Muth (1964); all the entries in that row become zeros.

down ($\beta_2 > 0$) and suppliers of X_2 lose when the supply function for X_1 shifts down ($\beta_1 > 0$). Both factors gain from a neutral technical change ($\delta > 0$) when demand is elastic ($\eta > 1$); both factors lose when demand is inelastic. Factor X_1 benefits from a biased (X_2-saving) technical change and factor X_2 loses unless we have fixed proportions ($\sigma = 0$), in which case there is no effect on quantity or price of output and no effect on quantity or price of either factor.

Alston and Scobie (1983) and also Freebairn, Davis and Edwards (1983) considered the distribution of benefits of these various types of technical change in the two-factor case (between a farm product and marketing inputs). They concluded that in contrast to the case of fixed-factor proportions, when there is input substitution, the distribution of benefits depends on the nature of the research-induced technical change. They also suggested that the model can be used to measure the incidence of costs of a levy to fund research. When there is input substitution, the incidence of a research levy on the farm product will be different from the incidence of benefits from research, other than research directed at shifting the farm-product supply function. These issues have been explored further in empirical models.[36]

36. Empirical studies that have considered the implications of input substitution for the distribution of benefits from different types of technical change include, for example, Mullen, Wohlgenant, and Farris

One issue that has not been resolved in this literature is how best to model biased technical change. Muth (1964) suggested one approach: shifting both factor-demand curves — in effect, twisting the isoquant to change the ratio of marginal products but holding output constant. Freebairn, Davis and Edwards (1983) criticized that approach and offered an alternative: incorporating a shift variable in only one factor-demand equation. Mullen, Wohlgenant and Farris (1988) suggested that a biased (X_2-saving) technical change (of the type defined by Muth) could be modeled as an "equivalent" shift of factor-supply functions (i.e., there is some combination of values for β_1 and β_2 that has effects equivalent to those from a particular value of γ). It is not completely clear in what sense(s) the shifts will be "equivalent," however.

4.3.4 Models with More Than Two Factors of Production

Three-Factor Models

Several studies have provided numerical estimates of the size and distribution of research benefits across three (or more) factors of production (e.g., Mullen, Alston and Wohlgenant 1989). However, the only published algebraic solutions are those of Holloway (1989). Those results serve, among other things, to illustrate how quickly the analysis becomes intractable for analytical results (although numerical simulation is always possible) when the number of stages of production increases. Holloway (1989) extended the two-factor case studied by Alston and Scobie (1983) to a three-factor case (a farm product with two marketing stages, processing and distribution). Holloway's (1989) key results are summarized in box 4.4.

n-Factor Models

Muth (1964), Gardner (1975), Perrin (1980, 1981), and Holloway (1989) all tackled the problem from the primal side (specifying production functions). Wohlgenant (1982) suggested using a dual approach (specifying a cost function instead), and he used it to illustrate solutions for the case of n factors. Several studies have followed that suggestion (e.g., Mullen, Wohlgenant and Farris 1988; Mullen and Alston 1990; Mullen, Alston and Wohlgenant 1989). In this approach, the equations of the model in the case when n factors are used to produce a single product are specified in logarithmic differential form as

Final demand: $E(Q) = -\eta[E(P) - \alpha]$ (4.17a)

(1988), and Mullen, Alston and Wohlgenant (1989). Alston and Mullen (1992) looked at the differential incidence of different ways of funding R&D and different types of technical change in Australian wool.

BOX 4.4: *Research Benefits in an Industry with Two Marketing Stages*

Holloway (1989, p. 341) showed that farmers always gain from increases in final demand or from biased technical change that is farm-product using (i.e., technical change that saves distribution or processing services). Conditions for farmers to gain from other types of research are

1. Increase in the supply of
   (a) "distribution services": $\eta > \sigma_d$
   (b) "processing services": $(\sigma_d - \sigma_p)(\varepsilon_d + \eta) > s_i(\sigma_d - \eta)(\varepsilon_d + \sigma_p)$

2. Neutral technical change in
   (a) "distribution": $\eta > 1$
   (b) "processing": $(\sigma_d - 1)(\varepsilon_d + \eta) > s_i(\sigma_d - \eta)(\varepsilon_d + 1)$

3. Primary-input-saving technical change in
   (a) "distribution": $\eta > \sigma_d$
   (b) "processing": $(\sigma_d - \sigma_p)(\varepsilon_d + \eta) > s_i(\sigma_d - \eta)(\varepsilon_d + \sigma_p)$

   where σ_d = the elasticity of input substitution in the distribution industry, σ_p = the elasticity of input substitution in the processing industry, ε_d = the elasticity of supply of distribution services, η = the absolute value of the elasticity of final demand, and s_i = the cost share of the intermediate input.

Market clearing: $$E(P) = \sum_{j=1}^{n} s_j\, E(W_j) \qquad\qquad (4.17b)$$

Factor supply: $$E(X_i) = \varepsilon_i\, [E(W_i) + \beta_i] \qquad\qquad (4.17c)$$

Factor demand: $$E(X_i) = \sum_{j=1}^{n} \eta_{ij}^*\, E(W_j) + E(Q) + \delta_i \qquad\qquad (4.17d)$$

This system consists of $2n+2$ simultaneous equations in which the variables are as previously defined (i.e., W_i is the price of factor i, P is the final product price, X_i is the quantity of factor i, and Q is the quantity of the product). The parameters are the absolute value of the elasticity of final demand, $\eta > 0$, elasticities of factor supply, ε_i (where $i = 1, \ldots, n$), output-constant own- and cross-price elasticities of factor-demand, η_{ij}^*, and factor cost shares, s_i. The exogenous-shift variables are a final demand shift, α, shifts of factor supply functions, β_i, and shifts of factor demand functions, δ_i. This specification has used the assumption of constant returns to scale of the industry production function. The elasticities of factor demand may be expressed in terms of cost shares and Allen partial elasticities of factor substitution (i.e., $\eta_{ij}^* = s_j\sigma_{ij}$ for $i \neq j$). Restrictions on the parameters can be derived from assumptions of symmetry of the cost function ($\sigma_{ij} = \sigma_{ji}$) and homogeneity of the cost function in the factor prices $\Sigma_{j=1}^{n} \eta_{ij}^{*} = 0$. Using these restrictions, the full set of n^2 (output-constant) factor-demand elasticities can be represented by $n - 1$ factor shares and $n(n - 1)/2$ elasticities of substitution.

Equations 4.17a through 4.17d can be used to solve numerically for the price and quantity effects of a range of types of technical changes in the case where a single product is produced using a variety of factors of production (as described in box 4.5, for example). Then the size and distribution of the total benefits from research may be computed by substituting the results into equations 4.16a through 4.16c.

4.4   Market-Distorting Policies and Research Benefits

The benefits from agricultural research can be influenced by government policies that distort output and input prices. These distortions can reduce short-run allocative efficiency, can significantly alter the distribution of research benefits, and may influence the size and direction of research investments and technical change in the long run.[37] Several recent studies have examined the benefits from agricultural research under a variety of output pricing and other government policies.[38] In one of the first of these studies, Alston, Edwards and Freebairn (1988) analyzed the qualitative implications of a range of commodity price policies for the size and distribution of research benefits under a range of market conditions (e.g., closed economy, small or large country, importer or exporter).[39] Their main findings (pp. 285-7) may be summarized as (a) all of the forms of intervention studied modify the pattern of research benefits relative to free trade, (b) world research benefits may be increased, reduced, or left unchanged, depending on the market circumstances and the form of intervention, (c) a government intervention reduces (increases) total welfare gains from a research-induced

37.   For example, see Schultz (1977, 1978) and Ruttan (1982, pp. 88-90). Mellor and Johnston (1984, p. 558) suggest that "the indirect long term effects of price distortions on the orientation of research and the bias of technical change may well be more important than their adverse effects on short-run, allocative efficiency." Alston, Edwards and Freebairn (1988) explored the effects of price policy on research investments informally. More recently, Gardner (1988) presented a formal political economy model in which research policy and price policies are jointly endogenous. See also de Gorter, Nielson and Rausser (1992), Roe and Pardey (1991), and Alston and Pardey (1991).

38.   See Akino and Hayami (1975), Nguyen (1977), Edwards and Freebairn (1981), Alston, Edwards and Freebairn (1986, 1988), Norton, Ganoza and Pomareda (1987), Oehmke (1988a, b), Haque, Fox and Brinkman (1989), Zachariah, Fox and Brinkman (1989), de Gorter and Norton (1990), Anania and McCalla (1991), Martin and Alson (1992, 1993, 1994), Alston and Martin (1992, 1995), Murphy, Furtan and Schmitz (1993), and Chambers and Lopez (1993).

39.   In their earlier paper, Alston, Edwards and Freebairn (1986) provided some quantitative illustrations in an application of their analysis to the Australian wool industry.

BOX 4.5: *A Numerical Solution for the n-Factor, One-Product Problem*

Computer programs are available for solving linear systems of simultaneous equations. Alternatively, the model can be solved using matrix algebra methods in a generalization of the solution to the 2-factor, one-product problem (the Muth model) as shown in box 4.3. The first step is to transform the model so that the exogenous shocks are on the right-hand side. In the n-factor, one-product case, the model (i.e., equations 4.17) may be represented as follows

$$E(Q) + \eta E(P) = \eta \alpha$$
$$s_1 E(W_1) + s_2 E(W_2) + \ldots + s_n E(W)_n - E(P) = 0$$
$$E(X_1) - \eta^*_{11} E(W_1) - \eta^*_{12} E(W_2) - \ldots - \eta^*_{1n}(E(W_n) - E(Q) = \delta_1$$
$$E(X_2) - \eta^*_{21} E(W_1) - \eta^*_{22} E(W_2) - \ldots - \eta^*_{2n} E(W_n) - E(Q) = \delta_2$$
$$\cdot \qquad \cdot \qquad \qquad \cdot \qquad \cdot \qquad \cdot$$
$$\cdot \qquad \cdot \qquad \qquad \cdot \qquad \cdot \qquad \cdot$$
$$E(X_n) - \eta^*_{n1} E(W_1) - \eta^*_{n2} E(W_2) - \ldots - \eta^*_{nn} E(W_n) - E(Q) = \delta_n$$
$$E(X_1) - \varepsilon_1 E(W_1) = \varepsilon_1 \beta_1$$
$$E(X_2) - \varepsilon_2 E(W_2) = \varepsilon_2 \beta_2$$
$$\cdot \qquad \cdot \qquad \cdot$$
$$E(X_n) - \varepsilon_n E(W_n) = \varepsilon_n \beta_n$$

In matrix form this can be written as

$$M Y = X$$

where Y is a vector of the endogenous prices and quantities of interest, of length $2(n+1)$, X is a vector of exogenous shocks of length $2n+2$, and M is a $(2n+2) \times (2n+2)$ matrix of parameters. That is

$$
\begin{bmatrix}
0 & - & 0 & 0 & - & 0 & 1 & \eta \\
0 & - & 0 & s_1 & - & s_n & 0 & -1 \\
1 & - & 0 & -\eta^*_{11} & - & -\eta^*_{1n} & -1 & 0 \\
| & \backslash & | & | & \backslash & | & | & | \\
0 & - & 1 & -\eta^*_{n1} & - & -\eta^*_{nn} & -1 & 0 \\
1 & - & 0 & -\varepsilon_1 & - & 0 & 0 & 0 \\
| & \backslash & | & | & \backslash & | & | & | \\
0 & - & 1 & 0 & - & -\varepsilon_n & 0 & 0
\end{bmatrix}
\begin{bmatrix}
E(X_1) \\
| \\
E(X_n) \\
E(W_1) \\
| \\
E(W_n) \\
E(Q) \\
E(P)
\end{bmatrix}
=
\begin{bmatrix}
\eta \alpha \\
0 \\
\delta_1 \\
| \\
\delta_n \\
\varepsilon_1 \beta_1 \\
| \\
\varepsilon_n \beta_n
\end{bmatrix}
$$

The solution vector is, as in the two factor case

$$Y = M^{-1} X.$$

A numerical solution can be obtained after substituting values for the elements into the parameter matrix M and choosing values for the exogenous shocks in the X vector and simulating solutions using any computer program with capability to invert matrices.

supply shift by an amount equal to the increase (reduction) in social costs of the market intervention resulting from that same supply shift.[40] Unfortunately, there are no more general rules about the implications of commodity market distortions for the size and distribution of research benefits. Thus, each type of intervention in each market situation must be considered in a case-by-case fashion.

More recent studies have extended the range of policies analyzed to include input market distortions (e.g., de Gorter and Norton 1990), to measure the quantitative importance of the issue (e.g., Oehmke 1988b, 1991) and to adjust measures of research benefits to allow for the effects of price-distorting policies (e.g., Haque, Fox and Brinkman 1989).

Some further studies in this area have taken a different tack. Gardner (1988), Roe and Pardey (1991), and de Gorter, Nielson and Rausser (1992), for example, have argued that price policies and public-sector research investments are jointly determined in a political-economy process.[41] According to their arguments, the instruments of policy are chosen to maximize a weighted sum (rather than a simple sum) of benefits to producers and consumers (who are also taxpayers).

From the standpoint of those papers it does not make sense to examine the implications of price policies for incentives to fund research because the price policies themselves are determined jointly with the research policies. This argument is plausible, and integrates research policy into the public-choice models of agricultural policy that to date have focused on price policy. It does call into question Alston, Edwards and Freebairn's (1988) inferences that, since price policies affect the size and distribution of research benefits and, therefore, the incentives of different groups to fund research, price policies might account for underinvestment in research. It suggests, alternatively, that another factor, differential political power of different groups, accounts for *both* price-distorting policies and research policies. This line of argument might not work so well in relation to some price distortions (e.g., exchange-rate distortions) that are unlikely to be endogenous to agriculture in the same way as commodity market distortions. In any event, Alston, Edwards and Freebairn's (1988) results would lead to the same predictions if combined with welfare weights. In the present context, we are not concerned with deducing the optimal combination of research and commodity price policies to maximize a weighted welfare

40. Alston and Martin (1992) prove this proposition formally.

41. Alston and Pardey (1991) reviewed this literature and argued that, given the nature of the timing of the impacts of decisions on research policy and price policy, and given the typical separation of the decision-making bodies for the two types of policies, it is too great a simplification to treat the two policies as being simultaneously determined by a single decision maker. See also Alston, Chalfant and Pardey (1993).

function. Rather, we are concerned with the problem facing research administrators: evaluating research and setting research priorities treating any price policies as determined elsewhere. For this problem, the issues raised by Gardner (1988), Roe and Pardey (1991), and de Gorter, Nielson and Rausser (1992) are not relevant and the approach suggested by Alston, Edwards and Freebairn (1988) is applicable.

Since there are no simple general rules, in this section we provide details on the size and distribution of research benefits in a range of commonly occurring market and policy situations. We use supply-and-demand diagrams to illustrate the economic surplus measures of research benefits accruing to domestic consumers, ΔCS, domestic producers, ΔPS, domestic taxpayers, ΔGS, and the ROW (foreigners), ΔFS. In addition, total domestic benefits, ΔTS, and world research benefits, ΔWS, are measured as aggregates of the other measures. Throughout, we assume a parallel research-induced supply shift in the home country. We show these surplus measures for each market and policy situation, both as areas on diagrams and by formulas to compute those areas in terms of market, policy, and technological parameters.

The analysis includes a fairly comprehensive range of typical policies, including (a) price-fixing schemes, such as minimum (target) prices, maximum (ceiling) prices, or variable import levies, (b) subsidies or taxes on production, inputs, or trade, (c) quantitative restrictions (on inputs, outputs, or trade), and (d) exchange-rate distortions. We begin with a closed-economy case, then we extend the analysis to the case of a small, open economy. Most countries (or regions within a country) are in one of these two categories in relation to most agricultural commodities they produce. This is especially so in relation to the relatively long-run horizon in which research benefits accrue. We show a limited number of examples for the more unusual situation in which a country has market power in international agricultural commodity trade.

A number of issues, which warrant some consideration in many situations, are put aside in this analysis. First, in the calculations of surplus areas, changes in government revenues are used to represent changes in taxpayer surplus. This ignores the deadweight cost of taxation to raise government revenues (as discussed, for example, by Fox 1985; Dalrymple 1990; Alston and Mullen 1992). Second, the analysis is conducted at a single market level — although this raises no special problems as long as care is taken in the interpretation of the calculated surpluses. Third, the analysis retains Harberger's postulates for the surplus measurement after adjustment for the particular distorting policies of interest. That is, we assume no other relevant distortions.

Once we allow for one distorting policy (e.g., a target-price policy) it is tempting to worry about another as well (e.g., the deadweight costs of government spending). Indeed, in some cases the policies must be analyzed as consisting of the joint action of several instruments, as pointed out by de Gorter and Norton (1990) in relation to U.S. farm commodity programs in which supply controls offset the output subsidies. It is tempting, in particular, to include production externalities along with market-distorting policies. But this can go too far. We end up quickly in a second-best world in which we can say little unequivocally about economic welfare effects. This situation arises, in particular, in the context of analyzing the implications of exchange-rate distortions that are addressed later in this section. The questions of production externalities and sustainability, however, are deliberately kept separate from the question of commodity market policies and are dealt with separately in section 4.5, below.

The appendix to chapter 5 includes formulas for computing the price, quantity, and welfare effects of research-induced supply-and-demand shifts in the presence of the types of policy distortions discussed below.

4.4.1 Closed-Economy Examples

Price Supports (Minimum Target Prices with Deficiency Payments)

The benefits from research in the presence of a simple price-support scheme are illustrated in figure 4.11.[42] The output price to producers is supported at P_{MIN} (by government deficiency payments) above the competitive equilibrium price, P_0. As a result, the quantity supplied increases from Q_0 to Q_0', and P_0' is the price at which the commodity is sold on the domestic market in order to clear that quantity. The government incurs a cost of area $P_{MIN}abP_0'$, while the net social cost of this policy is the triangle abc. As a consequence of research, the supply curve shifts from S_0 to S_1, producers gain area I_0adI_1, consumers gain $P_0'bfP_1$, the government incurs additional costs due to its price-support policy of $adfP_1P_0'b$, and the social cost of the price policy is given by triangle dfg. Research benefits are estimated as the change in producer surplus plus the change in consumer surplus minus the change in government cost. Although research-induced changes in total producer and consumer surpluses are larger, the net social benefits to research under this regime, compared with a situation without a price support, are lower by

42. This case has been discussed by Alston, Edwards and Freebairn (1988), Oehmke (1988b), and de Gorter and Norton (1990).

an amount equal to the difference between *dfg* and *abc*.

Suppose, instead, a government wants to support producer prices but only up to a certain amount of production (which is assumed to be less than or equal to the free trade quantity, Q_0).[43] The quantity produced in excess of that amount receives only the market price. Such a policy is also illustrated in figure 4.11, where Q_R represents the quantity on which producer price supports are paid. In this situation, the price policy acts like a decoupled income transfer to producers. The income from price supports is independent of production beyond the supported quantity. Marginal decisions relate to market prices, so producers continue to produce the competitive quantities and research benefits are unaffected by the subsidy transfer.

Price Ceilings (Maximum Prices)

The price-support policy illustrated above includes subsidies to producers while consumers gain because of lower prices. An alternative "cheap-food" policy, at least in the short run, is to set a price ceiling, say at P_{MAX}, which is below the competitive equilibrium price, P_0, as illustrated in figure 4.12. The

Figure 4.11: *Research benefits in a closed economy with a target price and deficiency payments*

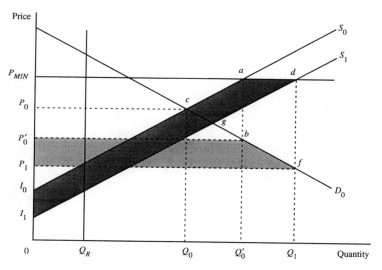

43. There are two alternative situations where Q_R is greater than the competitive quantity. When it is greater than the quantity supplied at the minimum price, Q_0', the quantity limitation is irrelevant. When it is between Q_0 and Q_0', it is binding on producers and consumers.

result is a reduction in production to Q_0' and an increase in quantity demanded to C_0'. The implications of this response for consumption and welfare depends on how the government acts to clear the market (e.g., see Alston and Smith 1983). Unless the excess demand $(C_0' - Q_0')$ is satisfied somehow (e.g., by imports that are purchased by the government), shortages will occur in the market and some other mechanism (e.g., queueing or black markets) will be necessary to clear it. A variety of policies have been used by governments when (maximum) price ceilings have been imposed to ration demand. For purposes of illustration, we assume the government buys imports (at a price P_M above the regulated maximum price) and makes them available at P_{MAX}. Thus, in the initial (distorted) equilibrium situation, the government incurs a net consumption subsidy cost equal to the price difference $(P_M - P_{MAX})$ per unit times the quantity of imports $(M_0 = C_0' - Q_0')$.

When research causes supply to shift from S_0 to S_1, the quantity supplied increases from Q_0' to Q_1, consumption is not affected, and imports fall by this amount to M_1. The benefits from research are equal to a gain in producer surplus of area I_0cdI_1 and a gain to the government of $(P_M - P_{MAX})(Q_1 - Q_0')$ of reduced subsidy expenditure.[44] In the absence of the price ceiling, total research benefits would be equal to area I_0abI_1 and would be shared between producers and consumers depending on the elasticities of supply and de-

Figure 4.12: *Research benefits in a closed economy with a maximum price ceiling*

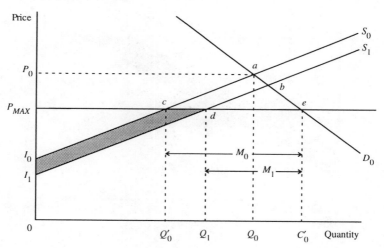

44. If the supply curve shifts out beyond point *e* in figure 4.12, the policy becomes irrelevant and the calculation of research benefits is slightly more complicated.

mand. Clearly, consumer research benefits are reduced (i.e., eliminated) by this price policy. On the other hand, the government becomes a beneficiary of research under a price ceiling. The effects of the price policy on research benefits to producers and the nation are ambiguous, depending upon the size of the price distortions between the regulated price, P_{MAX}, the unregulated price, P_0, the cost of imports, P_M, and the relative sizes of the elasticities of supply and demand. Producer research benefits *could* be greater under this price policy than under a competitive closed-economy arrangement.

Subsidies on Inputs or Output

The effects of an output subsidy on the size and distribution of research benefits in a closed economy are illustrated in figure 4.13. This case is described in detail by Alston, Edwards and Freebairn (1988). Here we consider a research-induced shift down of supply by k per unit, with and without an output subsidy. An output subsidy or negative tax $(-\tau^Q$ per unit) shifts the commodity supply curve down from S_0 to S_0'. Research shifts the supply curve from S_0 to S_1 without the subsidy and from S_0' to S_1' with the subsidy.

In summary, the effects of the subsidy policy on research benefits are to change the distribution but not the size of total benefits. Producer and consumer benefits from research are greater but this is exactly offset by the increase in government costs as a result of research. By the same token, research does not change the social costs of the subsidy policy — initially the social cost is triangle *ace*; after the research-induced supply shift, it is triangle *bdf* (which is equal to *ace*). The effects of output taxes are symmetric but opposite. The producer research benefits under this policy are shown as area $P_1'dhg$ and consumer research benefits are equal to area $P_0'cdP_1'$. Total research benefits are equal to the sum of these areas less the increase in government subsidy costs due to research, the subsidy per unit multiplied by the research-induced change in output $|\tau^Q| (Q_1' - Q_0')$, where $\tau^Q < 0$. In figure 4.13 the total research benefit — with and without the subsidy — is also given by area I_0abI_1.

Developing countries often subsidize inputs such as fertilizer and pesticides. In some instances an input subsidy is exactly equivalent to an output subsidy. Assuming that all producers use the same (fixed) amount of the input, X, per unit of production, Q, before and after the technical change (i.e., it is a neutral change with fixed factor proportions), an input subsidy or negative input tax of $-\tau^X$ per unit of input (where $\tau^X < 0$) is identically equivalent to an output subsidy of $-\tau^Q = -\tau^X (X/Q)$ per unit of output.[45] The

---

45. Of course this is a very restrictive special case. When input subsidies change relative factor prices,

Figure 4.13: *Research benefits in a closed economy with a per unit subsidy*

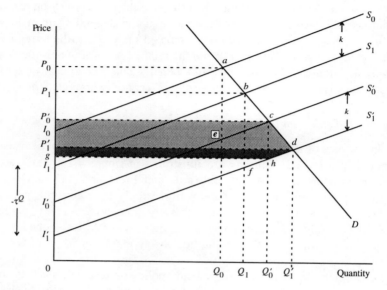

shift down in the product supply curve would be equal to the shift down in the factor supply curve multiplied by the number of units of the factor used per unit of the product (i.e., X/Q). Equivalently, the percentage (parallel) shift of output supply could be determined by multiplying the percentage cost reduction in the input supply curve by the share which that input represents in the cost of producing the commodity. Under different assumptions (i.e., biased technical change or variable factor proportions), the effects of input price policies may be quite different from output price policies, requiring additional work to evaluate the effects.

Output Controls

The policies discussed so far all involve the use of government revenues. Supply controls are sometimes used as a way of supporting producer incomes at the expense of consumers, avoiding any budget costs. The idea is to restrict supply to the market and thereby raise prices. In many cases the

and when there are opportunities for factor substitution, the input mix will change in response to an input subsidy and there will be a greater output supply shift than in the case of fixed factor proportions. On the other hand, the benefits from greater precision in allowing for this substitution effect in the context of measuring research benefits are unknown and in most cases it would not be feasible or worthwhile to go beyond treating input subsidies as equivalent output subsidies.

controls are applied to inputs (e.g., land used to grow a crop or the number of livestock on hand) rather than outputs as such; the usual explanation is ease of enforcement. Input controls are identical to output controls when there is no opportunity to substitute inputs in order to increase yields and reduce the constraint of the policy. In most cases there are some opportunities for substitution, and "slippage" becomes a problem. As with input subsidies, substitution among inputs complicates the economic welfare implications of input controls. Where it is thought to be important to do so, the effects of input subsidies or input controls with input substitution could be explored formally using models of the types developed in section 4.3. Here we consider only explicit output controls (or equivalent input controls with fixed proportions). The case of an output quota in a closed economy is illustrated in figure 4.14.

When a quota restricts output from Q_0 to Q_0', the price paid by consumers rises from P_0 to P_0' and quota owners receive a quota rent equal to area $P_0'abc$. Often, but not always, quota owners are producers. When research causes supply to shift from S_0 to S_1, there is no effect on quantity supplied or on price. All the research benefits in this case accrue to quota owners in the form of increased quota rents (which increase to area $P_0'ab'c'$); there are no research benefits either to consumers or to producers *per se*. The total research benefit (the increase in quota rents) is equal to the research-induced cost saving per unit multiplied by the quota quantity. In the absence of the quota, research benefits would be equal to area I_0deI_1. Total research benefits are lower under the quota, compared with the unregulated situation, by an amount equal to area $bdeb'$.

4.4.2   The Small-Country Trader Case

The models of effects of price-distorting policies discussed thus far have assumed a closed economy. The more typical example is one where trade occurs or would occur in the absence of trade-distorting policies. In addition, in most cases, the small-country assumption is appropriate. The impact of research on a small-country importer or exporter of a commodity in the absence of market-distorting policies was described earlier (see figure 4.5). In the closed-economy case, we considered policies of (a) price fixing, (b) input and output subsidies (and taxes), and (c) output controls. In the context of traded goods, we can consider all of these policies, and in addition, there are border policies including (a) trade taxes (or subsidies) and (b) quantitative restrictions on trade. Often a country will use a mix of policies for a traded good — in particular, to be effective, domestic policies often require the assistance of an embargo (or some other restriction) on imports.

Figure 4.14: *Research benefits in a closed economy with an output quota*

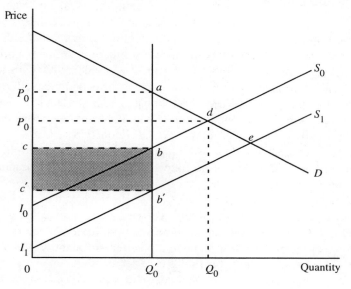

Price Supports (Minimum Prices) or Output Subsidies

The benefits from research in the presence of output price supports (i.e., target prices with deficiency payments or the equivalent per unit output subsidy) in a small country (exporter or importer) are illustrated in figure 4.15.[46] Before the research, with prices supported at P_{MIN}, producers supply Q_0'. Domestic consumers continue to face the world price, P_W, and consume C_0, as if there were no policy. The government incurs a subsidy cost of deficiency payments equal to $(P_{MIN} - P_W)Q_0'$. After the research, production increases from Q_0' to Q_1 and exports increase (or imports decrease) by the same amount. As a result of research, producer surplus rises by area $I_0 cdI_1$. Government subsidy costs rise by an amount equal to the per unit subsidy times the increase in quantity supplied $(P_{MIN} - P_W)(Q_1 - Q_0')$, which in this instance, is equal to area $acdb$. National research benefits are unaffected but the distribution is changed by the policy. Specifically, the increase in producer surplus is greater by the amount of the increase in government subsidy costs, which is used as a measure of the reduction in taxpayer surplus, ΔGS.

$$\Delta GS = -(P_{MIN} - P_W)Q_0'K'\varepsilon' \tag{4.18a}$$

46. The size and distribution of benefits in the case of free trade are illustrated in figure 4.5 and described in the accompanying text.

277

Figure 4.15: *Research benefits in a small open economy with price supports (or output subsidies)*

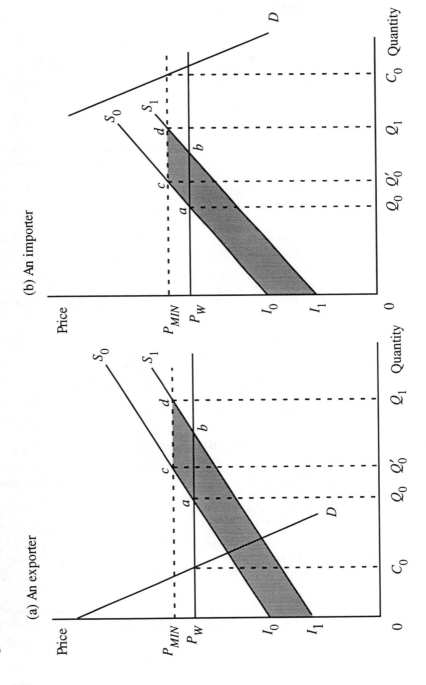

(a) An exporter

(b) An importer

$$\Delta PS = P_{MIN}\, Q_0'\, K'\, (1 + 0.5K'\varepsilon') \tag{4.18b}$$

$$\Delta TS = \Delta PS + \Delta GS \tag{4.18c}$$

where ε' is the elasticity of supply and K' is the proportionate supply shift effect both defined at the (generally observed) preresearch, distorted equilibrium price and quantity (i.e., P_{MIN}, Q_0').

The results are identical when an output subsidy of $(P_{MIN} - P_W)$ per unit is used instead of the price support and deficiency payments. As in the case of the closed economy, under some circumstances input subsidies are equivalent to output subsidies, and this model could also be used to represent the research benefits in the presence of input subsidies.

Output Price Ceilings (Import Subsidies or Export Taxes)

When a small country imposes a price ceiling below the world price to protect domestic consumers, it usually must also introduce a trade barrier or tax in order to prevent the policy from being undermined by trade. Assuming that producers and consumers face the same (maximum) price, there will be increased consumption, lower production, and lower exports (increased imports) due to the ceiling. The example of research combined with a price ceiling is illustrated in figure 4.16. In this analysis it is assumed that the government effectively taxes exports (subsidizes imports) to ensure domestic market clearing at the regulated maximum price, P_{MAX}.

Although this policy does not change the total net domestic research benefits, it does affect the distribution. In the context of given world prices, consumers do not benefit from research — whether there is a maximum price or not. Producer benefits are lower but government revenue is greater because a research-induced supply shift leads to reduced subsidy costs (in the case of imports) or increased tax revenue (in the case of exports). Of course, if there were different approaches taken by the government to clear the market, entirely different results could obtain.

Before the research, with prices fixed at P_{MAX}, producers supply Q_0' and consumers consume C_0'. In the case of an exportable good (panel a), the government imposes an export tax and generates tax revenue of $(P_W - P_{MAX})(Q_0' - C_0')$; in the case of an importable good (panel b), the government incurs a subsidy cost of $(P_W - P_{MAX})(C_0' - Q_0')$. After the research, production increases from Q_0' to Q_1 and exports increase (or imports decrease) by the same amount. As a result of research, producer surplus rises by area I_0abI_1. Government revenues rise (or subsidy costs fall) by an amount equal to the per unit tax (or subsidy) times the increase in quantity supplied domestically $(P_W - P_{MAX})(Q_1 - Q_0')$, which is equal to area $acdb$.

Figure 4.16: *Research benefits in a small open economy with maximum domestic prices*

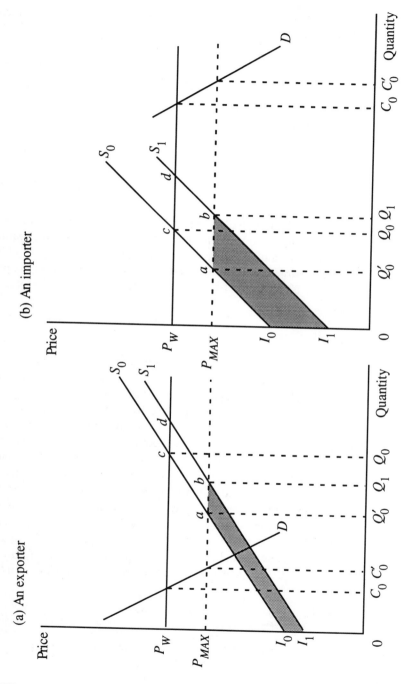

(a) An exporter

(b) An importer

279

National research benefits are unaffected but the distribution is changed by the policy. Specifically, the increase in producer surplus is *smaller* by the amount of the increase in government revenue in the case of an exporter (or by the amount of the decrease in subsidy costs in the case of an importer), the taxpayer benefit, ΔGS. The formulas are

$$\Delta GS = (P_W - P_{MAX})\, Q_0' K' \varepsilon' \tag{4.19a}$$

$$\Delta PS = P_{MAX}\, Q_0' K'\, (1 + 0.5 K' \varepsilon') \tag{4.19b}$$

$$\Delta TS = \Delta PS + \Delta GS \tag{4.19c}$$

where ε' is the elasticity of supply and K' is the proportionate supply shift effect defined at P_{MAX}, Q_0'.

These results are identical to those that would hold if an export tax (for an exportable) or an import subsidy (for an importable) of $(P_W - P_{MAX})$ per unit were used as such without setting a ceiling price. As in the case of the closed economy, when different policies are used in conjunction with a ceiling price to clear the market, they could have entirely different effects from what has been shown here.

Import Tariffs and Import Quotas

Import tariffs are widely applied in agricultural markets, in developed and developing countries alike. The range of tariff policies employed includes *ad valorem* (percentage) and *specific* (per unit) tariffs and they may be either fixed or variable (i.e., most tariff rates are fixed but some countries use variable tariff rates, such as the European Community variable levies). For present purposes, the differences among types of tariffs are relatively unimportant, especially in the small-country case.[47] We will consider an *ad valorem* tariff, only. In some contexts an import quota has effects identical to those of an import tariff but, as we shall see below, not in the context of measuring the size and distribution of research benefits.

Figure 4.17 shows the effects of a tariff ($100T$ percent) on imports by a small country. The tariff raises the domestic price from P_W to $(1+T)P_W$ and generates tariff revenue for the government, equal to $TP_W(C_0' - Q_0')$ in the absence of research. Producer benefits from research, with the tariff, are

47. Differences between per unit and ad valorem tariffs arise when the world price changes (i.e., the two are equivalent only for a particular value of the world price). Similarly, there is a particular import quota that corresponds to a particular tariff (of either sort), given particular positions of the functions and competition. However, this equivalence breaks down when there is imperfect competition or when the curves shift (due to growth, for instance). In a comparative-static, competitive model the three policies are equivalent in the small-country case because the world price is constant.

Figure 4.17: *Research benefits in a small importing country with a tariff*

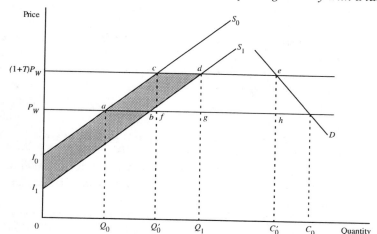

equal to area I_0cdI_1. The research-induced supply shift reduces imports from $(C_0' - Q_0')$ to $(C_0' - Q_1)$ and reduces tariff revenue by area $cdgf =$ area $acdb = TP_W(Q_1 - Q_0')$.[48] The total benefit from research (area I_0abI_1) is unaffected by the tariff but the producer benefit is greater, offsetting reduced government revenues from tariffs. The formulas for research benefits in this case are identical to those for a support-price or output-subsidy scheme — equations 4.18a through 4.18c — after we replace the support price, P_{MIN}, with the tariff-ridden price, $(1+T)P_W$:

$$\Delta GS = -TP_W Q_0'K'\varepsilon' \qquad (4.20a)$$

$$\Delta PS = (1 + T)P_W Q_0'K'(1 + 0.5K'\varepsilon') \qquad (4.20b)$$

$$\Delta TS = \Delta PS + \Delta GS \qquad (4.20c)$$

This equivalence of formulas arises from the equivalence of the policies in their effects on the size and distribution of research benefits. In the former case, research increased output-subsidy costs; in the latter, it reduced government revenues from tariffs. In both cases, the increased private benefits for producers exactly matched the reduction in government revenues.

Now we consider the effects of an import quota that is sometimes used as a substitute for a tariff. In most analyses, the main difference between a tariff

48. Note that the change in quantity due to the tariff is $Q_0' - Q_0 = T\varepsilon Q_0$ where ε is the supply elasticity defined at the preresearch, undistorted equilibrium. Alternatively the change in quantity $Q_0' - Q_0 = T\varepsilon' Q_0'/(1+T)$ where ε' is the elasticity of supply defined at the preresearch, distorted equilibrium price and quantity (i.e., $(1+T) P_W, Q_0'$). See appendix A 5.2 for more details.

and an import quota is that the tariff generates tariff revenue for the government whereas the import quota generates quota rents, which are often private benefits. Thus, a tariff and a quota are in some senses equivalent, and often are regarded as such. An import quota is illustrated in figure 4.18. Initially, the quota is set at M_0 (corresponding to $[C_0' - Q_0']$ in figure 4.17 if the quota were set to be equivalent to the tariff rate, T). What happens when research causes supply to shift from S_0 to S_1? In the case of the tariff, increased domestic production was accommodated with reduced imports. In the case of the import quota, imports will continue at the quota level, M_0, as long as there are quota rents to be earned, and any research-induced increase in production must be sold on the domestic market. Thus, unlike the case of the tariff, in this case research causes a decline in domestic price (from P_0' to P_1). As a result, there are now some consumer benefits, area $P_0'abP_1$, but producer benefits (shown by area P_1cde) are lower. Quota rents to owners of the import quota are reduced by the amount of the decline in the domestic price multiplied by the import quantity, $(P_0' - P_W)M_0$. The research has led to a reduction in the price distortion (the distortion in both production and consumption) due to the import quota. Initially, the net social cost was triangle *fgh* plus triangle *amk*; after the research-induced supply shift, it is triangle *cji* plus triangle *bml*. Compared with free trade, research benefits are greater by the amount of the research-induced reduction in the triangles of deadweight loss associated with the import quota policy.[49] In the absence of

Figure 4.18: *Research benefits in a small country with an import quota*

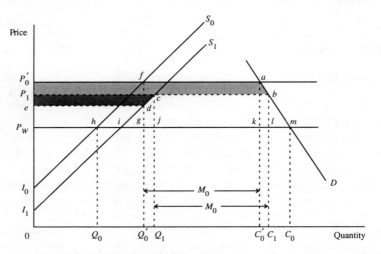

49. This result was asserted by Alston, Edwards and Freebairn (1988), who illustrated a number of cases, and proved by Alston and Martin (1992) as a general second-best proposition.

the quota the total research benefits (also equal to the national research benefits in this case) would be area I_0hiI_1; with the policy, total research benefits are equal to area I_0hiI_1 plus $(fgh - cji)$ plus $(amk - bml)$.

Output Controls

In the case of a small-country trader, output controls would seem to serve little purpose — they involve a net social cost and there are no clear beneficiaries. Output controls reduce the domestic quantity produced and the balance of trade, and research benefits continue to be concentrated in the hands of producers (quota owners). How do we explain the pervasive use of measures to control supply in countries that seem to have no market power in trade? The most likely explanation is that the output control is only one component of a package of policies (e.g., as a complement to a subsidy scheme to limit government obligations, as discussed above). There are relatively few examples of a pure supply control program in a small-country setting. Hence, it is important to model the actual policies accurately. When a quota scheme is applied in the context of a small trading country, it will usually be in conjunction with a prohibitive trade barrier (e.g., an embargo against imports, as is common for fresh milk or eggs) and the correct form of analysis will be as described above for the case of a closed economy with additional steps to account for research-induced changes in the social costs of the embargo.

Revenue-Pooling Price-Discrimination Schemes

As a final example, many countries have schemes that price-discriminate against the domestic market and pay producers a weighted average of the (high) home price and the (low) export price.[50] In figure 4.19, the domestic price to consumers is fixed at P_d, above the world price P_w. Producers are paid a weighted average of these two prices so we can represent average revenue — the effective demand facing producers — with the pooled price line, aP_p, which asymptotically approaches the export price line from above. Equilibrium is now defined by the intersection of supply with the pooled price line at P_0' and Q_0' before a research-induced supply shift from S_0 to S_1 and P_1 and Q_1 afterwards. Whether the policy is applied or not, all of the research benefits accrue to producers because research does not affect the price paid by consumers in either case. Thus, in either case, all of the research-induced increment to production is sold on the export market.

50. Alston and Freebairn (1988) provide a comprehensive discussion of this type of scheme. Alston, Edwards and Freebairn (1988) show the results described here. See also Freebairn's (1992) study of the Australian dairy industry.

Figure 4.19: *Research benefits in a small country with a revenue-pooling price-discrimination scheme*

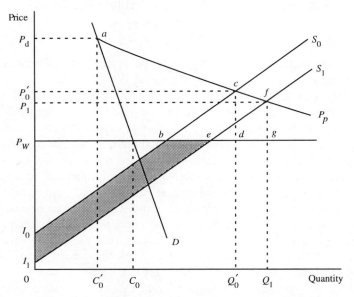

In the absence of the policy, the total producer (and national) research benefit is equal to area I_0beI_1. Under the policy there is a deadweight cost of resource distortions in production, shown as triangle *bcd* before research and the smaller triangle *efg* afterwards. In this case, as with an import quota, an added benefit is that research reduces the social cost of the policy. Using Alston and Martin's (1992) results, total producer (and national) benefit from research is equal to the benefit in the absence of distortions, area I_0beI_1, plus the change in cost of distortions induced by the supply shift, *bcd – efg*.

4.4.3   Large-Country Trader Models

We have examined the effects of a range of policies in the context of a closed economy or a small open economy. These cover the vast majority of situations likely to be encountered in the context of work on research priority setting and evaluation. In a few cases, an individual country will produce enough of a commodity that it can affect international prices, but such cases are rare, especially over the relatively long run, which is the appropriate context for research evaluation and priority setting. Often, when a country is treated as having market power in a commodity market, the context is the short to medium term. Even when countries have some market power in the short to medium term, they usually do not have significant market power in the relevant long run. In most cases, therefore, even when it seems that a country might have some market power in international trade, a small-country model is better for evaluating research and setting priorities.[51] In this section we illustrate the effects of selected policies in the case when domestic policies and output can affect international prices.

A key point to be made here is that, when a country can affect its international terms of trade in a commodity market, free trade in that commodity *may not* maximize domestic welfare — even when we maintain all of the standard assumptions. When a country has some monopoly or monopsony power in international markets, it can gain by exercising that power. When the private sector is competitive, and therefore cannot take advantage of that market power, the government can intervene to achieve an equivalent result (from the point of view of a nation as a whole) through the application of *optimal export taxes* or *optimal tariffs*. The story becomes more complicated when we consider the potential for strategic interaction among governments and retaliatory policies, especially when the industry is not purely competitive.[52] The distinction between market power of firms and market power of nations becomes especially important in this context. We retain the assumptions of competitive behavior of firms and assume no retaliation. Then, a nation with market power in trade may benefit by applying an import tariff, an export tax, or an equivalent policy.

Alston, Edwards and Freebairn (1988) showed that generally benefits from a research-induced supply shift are greater or smaller under a price policy than under free trade, to the extent that research reduces or increases the magnitude of the social costs of divergence from the policy that maximizes domestic welfare. For a closed economy or a small-country trader, the optimal policy is free trade; for a large country, it is the optimal trade tax. We illustrate these ideas with four examples: (a) output price supports for an exporter, (b) export taxes, (c) import tariffs, and (d) supply controls.

Output Price Supports

The benefits from research in the presence of output price supports in a large exporting country are shown in figure 4.20. This is virtually identical to figure 4.10, which represents the closed-economy case. Here we identify the domestic component of total demand as D_d, and the curve D_0 represents

51. This line of argument implies that an explicitly dynamic treatment of the response of supply and export demand to price changes (i.e., dynamic price elasticities) is required for optimal exploitation of market power in trade in general as well as in relation to understanding the interaction of research-induced supply shifts with trade policy.

52. For example, see Vanzetti (1989) and McNally (1993).

total demand — the sum of domestic and export demand (in the case of a nontraded good in figure 4.10, the corresponding total demand was entirely domestic demand). The output price to producers is supported at P_{MIN} (by government deficiency payments) above the competitive equilibrium price, P_0. As a result, quantity supplied increases from Q_0 to Q_0' and P_0' is the price at which the commodity is sold on the domestic and export markets in order to clear that quantity. The government incurs a cost of area $P_{MIN} abP_0'$.

As a consequence of research, the supply curve shifts from S_0 to S_1, producers gain area $I_0 adI_1$, domestic consumers gain $P_0'ceP_1$, and the government incurs additional costs because of its price-support policy of $adfP_1P_0'b$. Research benefits are estimated as the change in producer surplus plus the change in consumer surplus minus the change in government cost. Although research-induced changes in total producer and consumer surpluses are larger, the net social benefits from research under this regime, compared with a situation without a price support, are lower. Here, research widens the disparity between the actual policy and the optimal policy in two ways. It widens the divergence between domestic costs and prices while, at the same time, it increases the effective subsidy on exports when the optimal policy is to tax exports. Thus the exporter's research benefits are lower than they are with free trade — indeed, research benefits could be negative (e.g., Oehmke 1988b, 1991).[53] However, ROW research benefits are greater in the presence of an export subsidy in the innovating country.

Export Taxes

Less-developed countries often impose export taxes either to raise government revenue or as part of a "cheap food" policy. The implications of agricultural research in the context of an export tax in a large country are illustrated in figure 4.21. The initial quantities produced, consumed, and exported by country A are Q_0, C_0, and QT_0. First we introduce an export tax of τ^E per unit. Then we introduce a research-induced supply shift. The export tax is represented as a shift down in the ROW excess-demand curve from $ED_{B,0}$ to $ED_{B,1}$ such that the preresearch net of tax export (and domestic) price falls from P_0 to P_0'. As a consequnce of research, the supply curve shifts from S_0 to S_1. At the same time, the excess-supply curve shifts from $ES_{A,0}$ to $ES_{A,1}$

---

53. The idea of negative returns to research is not new. The literature on immiserizing technological change includes articles by Bhagwati (1958, 1968), Gruen (1961), and Johnson (1958, 1967) that illustrate the possibility of immiserizing effects due to terms-of-trade effects or to government intervention in markets. Some recent articles have shown examples from agriculture (e.g., Oehmke 1988b, 1991; Chambers and Lopez 1993; Murphy, Furtan and Schmitz 1993) where a negative return may be attributable to distortions in commodity markets. Alston and Martin (1992) synthesize the recent literature and the older, immiserizing growth literature.

Figure 4.20: *Research benefits in a large country with a target price and deficiency payments*

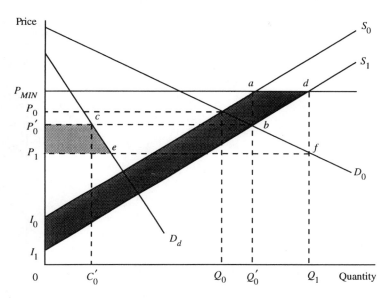

and the final price is P_1. Relative to the tax-distorted equilibrium, research has caused an increase in domestic consumption (from C_0' to C_1), an increase in production (from Q_0' to Q_1), and an increase in exports (from QT_0' to QT_1). Associated with these changes is a gain in producer surplus equal to area P_1cde in panel a and a gain in consumer surplus equal to area $P_0'abP_1$ in panel a. If we were to ignore the tax, the sum of these two areas would be a measure of total domestic research benefits. However, the research-induced supply shift also leads to an increase in tax revenue equal to area *fghi* in panel b (because exports increase), which is an additional component of domestic benefits. Exactly offsetting this, from the world standpoint, is a reduction in research benefits to the ROW.

Import Tariffs

The implications of agricultural research in the context of a tariff imposed by a large importing country are illustrated in figure 4.22. The initial quantities produced, consumed, and imported by country A are Q_0, C_0, and QT_0. First, we introduce an import tariff of τ^M per unit. Then we introduce a research-induced supply shift. The tariff is analyzed as a shift up in the ROW excess supply curve from $ES_{B,0}$ to $ES_{B,1}$ such that the preresearch, duty-paid

288

Figure 4.21: *Research benefits for a large-country exporter with an export tax*

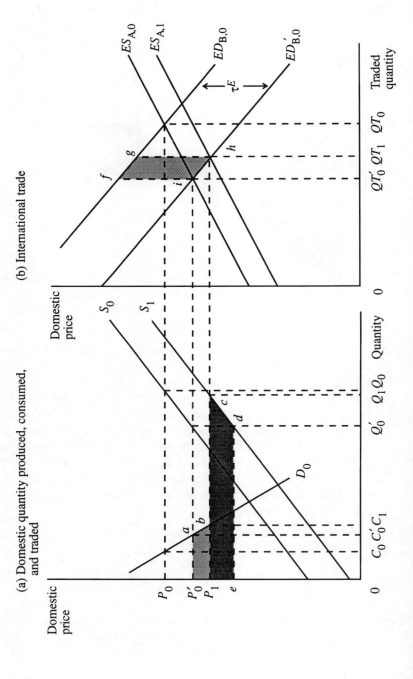

(a) Domestic quantity produced, consumed, and traded

(b) International trade

import (and domestic) price rises from P_0 to P_0'.[54] As a consequence of research, the supply curve shifts from S_0 to S_1. At the same time, the excess-demand curve shifts from $ED_{A,0}$ to $ED_{A,1}$ and the final price is P_1. Relative to the tax-distorted equilibrium, research has caused an increase in domestic consumption (from C_0' to C_1), an increase in production (from Q_0' to Q_1) and a decrease in imports (from QT_0' to QT_1). Associated with these changes is a gain in producer surplus equal to area P_1cde in panel a, and a gain in consumer surplus equal to area $P_0'abP_1$ in panel a. If we were to ignore the tariff, the sum of these two areas would be a measure of the total domestic research benefits. However, the research-induced supply shift also leads to a reduction in tariff revenue (because imports decrease) equal to area $fghi$ in panel b, which offsets some private domestic benefits.

Supply Controls

For a large-country exporter, supply controls have some of the virtues of export taxes (for example, see Sumner and Alston 1986; Johnson 1965): they do allow the monopolistic exploitation of foreign markets but they involve some distortions in domestic consumption that the export tax avoids. Output quotas greatly simplify the problem of measuring research benefits. The same result holds regardless of whether the country is an importer or exporter, large or small. So long as the quota is binding on production — with and without the research — the total research benefit is equal to the cost saving per unit multiplied by the total quota quantity. This total benefit accrues entirely to quota owners who may also be producers. Thus, the model described in detail for the closed-economy case is equally valid for the small- or large-country trader, although as discussed above, pure supply controls are unlikely to be used in isolation from other policies by a small-country trader.

A More General Approach

The four cases discussed in this section illustrate a general point. When measuring research benefits (with or without policy-induced price distortions), there is one set of formulas to measure the welfare consequences that can be applied in every case. The implications of price distortions are that (a) different market participants may face different prices, (b) the policies may affect the research-induced price changes, and (c) government revenues may

---

54. This policy could be analyzed, alternatively, by treating the tariff as an equivalent shift of the importer's excess demand for imports. As always for competitive industry, the ultimate incidence of a tax does not depend on its initial incidence. The choice is arbitrary but the shifting of exporter's excess supply yields a clearer picture.

Figure 4.22:   *Research benefits for a large-country importer with an import tariff*

(a) Domestic quantities produced, consumed,
and traded

(b) Excess supply, demand, and trade

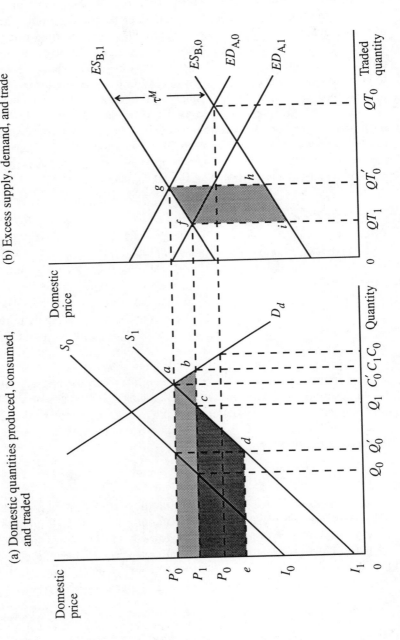

change as a result of the policies and effects on government revenues must be accommodated. Some relatively general formulas for components of the domestic welfare change due to research in the presence of policies are

$$\Delta PS = P_P Q_P [E(Q_P)/\epsilon][1 + 0.5E(Q_P)] \tag{4.21a}$$

$$\Delta CS = P_C Q_C [E(Q_C)/\eta][1 + 0.5E(Q_C)] \tag{4.21b}$$

$$\Delta GS = \tau_C\, Q_C\, E(Q_C) + \tau_P\, Q_P\, E(Q_P) + \tau_T\, Q_T\, E(Q_T) \tag{4.21c}$$

$$\Delta TS = \Delta PS + \Delta CS + \Delta GS \tag{4.21d}$$

where P_P and Q_P denote the producer price and quantity before research, P_C and Q_C denote the consumer price and quantity before research, Q_T is the quantity traded, ϵ and η are the absolute values of elasticities of supply and demand, and τ_C, τ_Q, and τ_T are per unit taxes on consumption, production, and trade (for subsidies they can be negative numbers). What is needed to complete the analysis is a model of the market that can be used to calculate the relative changes in quantities produced, consumed, and traded, given by $E(Q_P)$, $E(Q_C)$, and $E(Q_T)$, respectively. Specific reduced-form formulas for research benefits under particular policies and market structures can be derived (as done above, for example, in equations 4.18, 4.19, and 4.20) by substituting analytic solutions for the relative changes in quantities into equations 4.21a through 4.21d or their equivalent. However, it may be more useful and appropriate not to do that. Instead, in many cases, it will be better to keep the model of research-induced price and quantity effects separate from the calculation of the welfare effects associated with those market adjustments, as is shown in the appendix to chapter 5.

4.4.4   Overvalued or Undervalued Exchange Rates

Exchange rate distortions are pervasive, especially in agricultural markets in less-developed countries. The most common scenario is one where the exchange rate is overvalued (i.e., fixed above the rate that would be reached if the currency were freely floating). In such cases it is effectively a tax on all exports (and a subsidy on all imports) although it does not generate any tax revenue as such. An undervalued exchange rate has the opposite effect. Sometimes a country will use different official exchange rates for different commodities or sectors and these exchange-rate distortions — in relation to the market exchange rate — amount to discriminatory taxes. To fully analyze exchange rate distortions requires a general-equilibrium model with the macro-economy explicitly treated. For the present, we will use a partial-equilibrium approach and, where appropriate, introduce general-equilibrium connotations.

First, consider the case where an official exchange rate (overvalued relative to the market rate that applies to goods in general) is applied only to one commodity that is exported by a small-country trader. What are the implications for research benefits? The answer depends on the mechanism used to enforce the policy. Suppose the government insists on changing all the foreign currency earned from exporting the good in question into local currency at the official rate. This is a typical policy when a specific official rate is applied to a particular commodity; it is tantamount to an ad valorem export tax on the commodity at a rate given by the ratio of the official and market exchange rates. This case can be seen by reinterpreting panel a of figure 4.16 so that P_W denotes the world price in domestic currency at market exchange rates and P_{MAX} denotes the corresponding price using an overvalued official exchange rate.

Differences between a policy of an overvalued exchange and an export tax may arise in the greater potential for tax avoidance through falsifying invoices or through barter trade under the former. When an overvalued exchange rate is enforced costlessly in a way that enables the home-country government to keep the difference between export revenues and payments to producers, the appropriate measures of research benefits are those that would apply for an explicit export tax. Changes in government revenues (area *acdb* in figure 4.16a) must be incorporated explicitly in total benefits if private benefits are measured using the distorted prices (area I_0abI_1); an equivalent measure of total benefits is obtained by using the undistorted prices (and the corresponding quantities) to measure what benefits would have been without the distortion (area I_0cdI_1).

An extreme alternative situation is one where all of the "export tax" revenue is wasted from the home-country viewpoint, either because the policy is operated in such a way that it creates rents for foreign importers or because all of the rents are dissipated in "tax" avoidance, black markets, and so on. In such a scenario, the only research benefits that exist are the private benefits measured by the supply shift relative to the distorted "net of tax" price received by producers (i.e., area I_0abI_1 in figure 4.16a), and the potential "tax revenue" benefit (area *acdb*) is wasted. When enforcement of exchange rate rules is costly, something that lies between these two alternative measures may be appropriate.

Now consider the case where the exchange rate distortion is not discriminatory but applies to all traded goods. This creates two additional problems for the analysis of research benefits for a particular good. First, there will be general-equilibrium feedback of the effects in all commodity and factor markets, displacing both supply and demand for the good in question in ways that may be difficult to quantify. Second, it becomes less clear what happens to the potential rents or implicit tax revenues created by the policy. As before, in the partial equilibrium context, if the "rents" are not collected by the government, they may be lost from the country altogether, either through waste or to foreigners. Given these problems, and additional problems that are encountered when an attempt is made to define and deduce a measure of the "market exchange rate" that would apply if official rates were absent,[55] it may be best simply to ignore the existence of *general* exchange rate distortions when research benefits are calculated using partial-equilibrium commodity models.

Moreover, even when a country does not have an explicit policy of exchange rate management, other trade-distorting policies (such as general tariffs against imports) have similar effects through their effects on the balance of trade and exchange rates. For example, from the point of view of exporting industries, a general tariff on imports leads to an appreciation of the exporter's currency and is tantamount to an export tax applied to all exports. Sometimes an explicit exchange rate policy serves to counter other trade-distorting policies. It may be more misleading to account for only part of the policy set rather than ignore it altogether. Thus, accounting for economywide policies such as those affecting exchange rates and general trade policies may be too difficult to be worth attempting. This is an example of the more general second-best problem.

4.5   Sustainability Issues and Other Externalities

A further potential source of distortions in incentives is externalities in production. While there has been some work on the general economic implications of environmental externalities in agriculture, we are unaware of any studies of the implications for returns to research.[56] Externalities from agricultural production — and broader, related, environmental or "green" issues such as sustainability, global warming, preservation of wilderness areas, animal welfare, food safety, and species preservation — have received increasing attention in discussions of agricultural policy in recent years. That trend can be expected to accelerate. All of these issues, conceptually at least, can be considered in the framework of a conventional supply and demand model, allowing for a divergence between private and social costs or benefits from production.[57] This is similar to incorporating price-distorting policies

55. For example, see Krueger, Schiff and Valdés (1988, 1991).
56. See Pingali and Roger (1995) for an example of the environmental implications of agricultural research.
57. As Summers (1992, p.71) recently observed, "Certainly, the idea of sustainable development has

but different in that the distortions are not the creations of governments. We begin with an illustrative example of an environmental externality and then discuss some issues that relate to agricultural research in this context.

4.5.1 Research Benefits in the Presence of Environmental Externalities

There are many types of external effects in agriculture, and we have already considered two types of spillovers — price spillovers and technology spillovers. An *externality* arises when there is a spillover effect of one person's actions on another person's economic opportunities and where that effect is not fully compensated through a market transaction. Price spillovers are not externalities, but technology spillovers usually are. Here we are concerned with externalities of a different type. One example would be where the use of agricultural chemicals on a crop suppresses the population of beneficial natural predators and increases the costs of pest control (in that industry or in some other industry), but individual producers disregard that external effect when making their pest-management decisions. Another example is where agricultural production causes pollution of groundwater with agricultural chemicals or salt or causes pollution of surface water with eroded soil, salt, or agricultural chemicals. A third and more abstract example is when the clearing of rainforests results in species depletion, reduction of pristine wilderness, or other environmental damage that is regarded as a cost by some people but where that cost is not considered in decisions about clearing the forest. In all these cases, the social cost of agricultural production is greater than the private cost perceived by farmers. In most cases, the externality is borne within the country (or region) within which it is created, although not necessarily by consumers or producers of the commodity in question, or even within the agricultural sector. In some cases (such as global warming), the effects are also borne by foreigners. A further example is where the use of an agricultural chemical leaves residues on food that are hazardous to consumers but difficult to detect. Here the cost of the residue may be borne by the consumers of the product in the first instance, but eventually, if the practice continues, all producers might experience a loss of markets due to consumer concerns about the unreliability of the product.

Figure 4.23 illustrates supply and demand for a commodity produced by a small-country exporter in the case where there is a negative externality

drawn attention to environmental problems that were ignored for too long. But there is no intellectually legitimate case for abandoning accepted techniques of cost-benefit analysis in evaluating environmental investments . . . The answer does not lie in blanket sustainability criteria, or in applying special discount rates, but in properly incorporating environmental costs into the appraisal of projects."

associated with production (e.g., pollution created by the use of agricultural chemicals). The preresearch supply curve and demand curves are S_0 and D, and the market clears at the world price P_W with quantities produced, consumed, and traded equal to Q_0, C_0, and QT_0. However, the marginal social cost of production is given by S_0' and it does not coincide with supply. Instead, marginal social cost is greater by E per unit (which is a measure of the *external costs* experienced by *all* agents in the domestic economy). From a national viewpoint there is excess production equal to the difference between Q_0 and Q_0' and there is a net social cost due to the externality equal to the triangle $a'ca$ (the total cost of the externality is E per unit times a quantity Q_0, equal to the parallelogram $I_0'caI_0$, but some of that is offset by producer surplus equal to $I_0'a'aI_0$ on the extra production, $Q_0 - Q_0'$). A constant per unit externality, E, is assumed for convenience and means that S_0 and S_0' are parallel.

Suppose research reduces the social costs of production by k^s per unit *without affecting the externality*. Then, when research shifts supply from S_0 to S_1, it also shifts the marginal social cost from S_0' to S_1'. The net social cost of the externality is unaffected (triangle $b'c'b$ is identical to triangle $a'ca$). However, the total social cost of the externality does increase by $E(Q_1 - Q_0)$, which is equal to area $acc'b$ or area $a'cc'b'$. The producer benefit from

Figure 4.23: *Research benefits in a small country with a negative production externality*

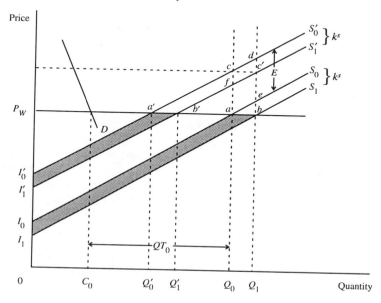

research is area I_0abI_1 ($= I_0'cc'I_1'$). Total benefits are given by deducting the amount of the increased external cost from producer benefits (there are no effects on consumer welfare). The result is that total research benefits are equal to area $I_0'a'b'I_1'$ and are unaffected by the presence of the externality. Only the distribution of benefits is affected — producer benefits are greater, but offsetting this is increased external costs.

This example is relatively stylized. A large number of alternative scenarios might be considered. For instance, suppose the research-induced supply shift was not associated with an identical shift in marginal social costs — so all of the private cost savings were merely increases in the externality without any reduction in social costs. In this case, the producer benefits would be as described above but the research would lead to a net social cost equal to area *acdb*.

Alternatively, suppose the effect of the research were to reduce the externality by k^s without any effect on private costs. In this case, there would be no producer benefits but total research benefits would be equal to $I_0'cfI_1'$. Both of these are extreme examples, but it is perhaps equally unlikely that a research-induced technical change would be neutral with respect to an externality, especially if that externality is associated with the use of a particular input.[58] As a further complication, an externality may not be constant per unit of output, and research-induced technical changes might cause nonparallel shifts of nonlinear functions that are difficult to judge. Finally, for both traded and nontraded goods, the international distribution of externalities might be an important issue from an international perspective, if not a national one. In particular, for example, this might apply in the context of global warming.

What should we do about externalities in the evaluation of agricultural research and priority setting? The general answer is the same as the one given for agricultural policies. Externalities are like taxes or exchange rate distortions. When measuring research benefits, we ought to take into account the total effects on the welfare of all affected groups when we can. To do this, we compute the effects of research-induced supply shifts on producer surplus, consumer surplus, government revenues, and now, those who bear the costs of externalities. Then the total benefit is obtained as the sum of benefits and costs to all groups. A shortcut approach would be to evaluate the effects by adjusting first for the externality and working off the marginal-social-cost curves instead of the supply curves. This is not recommended for two reasons. First, it is difficult and, if the information is available to allow it to be done, it is not necessary. Second, information on the distribution of

---

58. Indeed, a great deal of current research in many countries is directed at reducing the demand for chemicals and enhancing water-use efficiency, all with a view to reducing adverse environmental effects.

benefits and costs will be lost. In the event that good information is unavailable on the size of externalities and the effects of agricultural research on them but these effects are thought to be important, there is little that can be done except to heavily qualify the results of an analysis that does not take them into account.

4.5.2 Resource Depletion, Intergenerational Equity, and Agricultural Research

An increased rate of exploitation of the resource base is inherent in the "green revolution" technologies that involved a greater intensity of use of land and other resources. Problems that have arisen from intensified land use include soil salinization and acidification, erosion, and the like, and in some cases this has been reflected in declining yields. Greater reliance on chemical pesticides and cherbicides, especially in monoculture systems, leads to problems over time because of the development of resistance and the destruction of natural predators.

Many people are concerned that the capacity of agricultural systems (globally or locally) is being depreciated too rapidly by excessive exploitation of the natural resource base.[59] Underlying this concern is an implicit belief that agricultural decision makers are discounting the future too heavily, that they find it optimal to consume the natural resource base too quickly, compared with some standard. Two possible rationales are that (a) private discount rates are greater than social discount rates and (b) some individuals attach too little weight to the welfare of future generations. These rationales are both open to challenge, but it must be said that they are among the thornier issues in economics and there is no clear consensus. Why do we think landowners fail to value their assets properly? By whose values are future generations being underweighted? By the same token, what about the starving members of the current generation — are they being underweighted, too, according to the same argument? Graham-Tomasi (1991) and Crosson and Anderson (1993) discuss some of these questions in the context of sustainability and agricultural research.

Notwithstanding the heat generated by this debate, it is not clear that there are any useful implications for the measurement of expected economic surplus arising from improved technology. Lacking clear evidence to the contrary, the best approach remains that prices are our measure of opportunity costs and the unadjusted economic surplus measures are appropriate.

---

59. As Alston, Pardey and Carter (1994, p. 97) observed, "A *flow* of services from the stock of natural resources is always used in production but the concern here is with changes in the stock itself that will imply a reduction in future service flows."

Where there is evidence of a market failure such that social costs and benefits diverge from private costs and benefits, the analysis can be adjusted as shown above for the case of an externality.

The political nature of these issues means that there may be implications for research priority setting and evaluation even when there are none for expected economic surplus. Projects aiming to develop more environmentally sensitive technology, or likely to contribute to sustainability, seem likely to be given priority, everything else being equal. There are two roles for the economist here. The first is to clarify the issues surrounding sustainability (and other similar objectives) such that decision makers can develop informed weightings for that objective compared with other objectives. The second is to use the expected economic surplus analysis to demonstrate the opportunity cost of using research to pursue objectives such as sustainability.

It is not clear that biasing the research portfolio is the best way to counter the effects of environmental problems. However, research has the potential to address some of the problems that have been identified as arising in part from the dynamics of modern production systems, and as those problems become increasingly important, the likelihood increases that such research will be a part of the optimal portfolio.

4.6   Conclusion

A benefit-cost analysis based on the calculation of economic surplus provides a framework for agricultural research evaluation and priority setting capable of incorporating most of the conceptual elements discussed in chapter 2. Although all procedures are subjective and only provide an approximation of the "true" model, the economic surplus model provides a logically consistent approximation and is a useful evaluation tool.

A common misperception is that economic models, and their creators, relate only to pecuniary or monetary issues, so questions of income distribution, nutrition, or sustainability, for example, must be dealt with separately from the economic analysis. In this chapter we have shown that a comprehensive approach can explore these different types of economic questions at the same time. The analysis aims to quantify the physical effects of different technology scenarios, to translate them where possible into economic values, and to derive summary measures of those values that can be used to rank alternatives on a consistent basis. The great strength of this approach — over alternatives that consider multiple aspects of the problem in a piecemeal fashion — is that it is comprehensive and internally consistent.

We have illustrated the application of supply, demand, and economic surplus models to a wide range of situations. Often, a simple aggregate model of either a closed economy or a small open economy will suffice. For most cases this will provide the information necessary to evaluate alternatives against a criterion of economic efficiency. Sometimes, however, consequences other than economic efficiency will be of interest. In most instances, agricultural research is not the best way to achieve nonefficiency objectives. Usually there is a better policy available for achieving a specific nonefficiency objective (such as income distribution, nutrition), or to address sustainability or natural resource conservation concerns. Nevertheless, the economic surplus analysis can be extended to consider a range of the distributional effects of research along with the efficiency effects. A variety of horizontal disaggregations (according to agroecological zones, types of producers, income classes of consumers, countries or regions of a country, and so on) are readily incorporated in the analysis if data are avaliable. Similarly, vertical disaggregations across stages of a multistage system of production permit us to examine the distributional consequences among producers, consumers, and market intermediaries.

Some problems might warrant relatively simple models. Some may call for sophistication to allow for research-induced quality changes, general-equilibrium feedback effects, market-distorting policies, and other distortions in incentives such as externalities. We have shown how to incorporate some of these aspects into an economic surplus model, too. While we have not considered every possibility, we have dealt with the most important ones and the reader should be able to draw on these examples to deal with most of the situations likely to be encountered. In particular, we have not considered the implications of distortions arising from the exercise of market power by individual firms. There is little written on the effects of the market power of firms on the size and distribution of research benefits in agriculture. This may be because of a widespread belief that the competitive model provides a good approximation for agriculture.[60]

The next step is to consider how to obtain and use the economic surplus measures in practice. The following chapter provides details on implementing the procedures, including algebraic formulas for surplus measures for the main examples, and in an appendix examples of computer programs are provided that can be used in either a spreadsheet or in the interactive computer program, *Dream©*, that we have written for research evaluation.

---

60. One exception is Kim et al.'s (1987) reconsideration of the benefits from the tomato harvester in California, although their assumption of pure monopsony (i.e., a single processing firm) may be more misleading than an assumption of competition.

Part III

Evaluation and Priority Setting
in Practice

5

Economic Surplus Measurement and Application

This chapter describes how to implement an economic surplus analysis to evaluate agricultural research and how to use the results for setting priorities and allocating research resources. We break the implementation process down into five components and relate those components to the underlying conceptual constructs, such as the knowledge-production function and economic surplus models presented in earlier chapters.

Defining the problem: A research evaluation study is a research project itself and, like all research projects, should have clear, explicit objectives. At the outset, it is important to decide which questions the analysis hopes to answer, as well as how the results will be used and for what types of decisions. This defines the *objectives for the analysis*.[1] Only then is it possible to define the scope of the analysis in terms of the research programs for which benefits and costs are to be assessed and the kinds of decisions to be made about those research programs.[2] A statement of the *objectives of the system*, against which performance is to be measured, helps define the

---

1. The *client*, who commissions a research evaluation study, might also be asked to identify the objectives *of the research system* to which the study relates, as a basis for defining the relevant measures of benefits and costs. These two notions of objectives — the objectives of the study of the research system and the objectives of the system itself — can be related to one another (particularly in terms of who defines them) but they are very different ideas.

2. Research programs are often defined by the institutional structure in which research is carried out. Sometimes they are defined according to the commodities they affect (in an institute structured along commodity lines), the disciplinary focus (where research is organized into fields such as entomology or soil science), and spatial aggregates (where research is organized among regional institutes or where spatial incidence is an issue).

relevant measures of costs and benefits (which will often be limited to measures of total economic surplus and its distribution, the subject of this chapter). Together, these two sets of objectives, along with the definitions of measures of costs and benefits, are the terms of reference for the study. Then, given a budget for the study and in consideration of other constraints such as data availability, a modeling strategy can be developed to define the degree of detail for the analysis in terms of the degree of disaggregation of both research program alternatives and measures of performance.

Compiling the data: The next step is to define and compile the research- and market-related data — some of which may be obtained from published sources and some elicited from scientists and others. The modeling strategy and scope of the analysis define the data requirements. Essentially, data on prices and quantities produced or consumed are required for each group of producers and consumers identified by the client as being of particular interest. Corresponding elasticities of supply or demand will be required for each identified group. In addition to these *market-related* data, *research-related* data are required to identify the nature, magnitude, and timing of the research-induced shifts of supply.

Measuring K: As discussed in chapters 2 and 4, by far the most important parameter defining total benefits, and perhaps the hardest to measure, is the size of the research-induced supply shift, K. An ex ante assessment of program alternatives usually involves eliciting the values of the potential impact of successful research (often expressed as yield effects). These are combined with estimated probabilities of success and information on likely adoption paths to derive a time path for K for each program alternative. Conceptual and practical issues in estimating K are raised and resolved below.

Analyzing the data: The fourth step is to calculate research benefits and validate the results. Spreadsheets or other computer aids are helpful for this task, and the *Dream©* interactive computer package, discussed and documented in appendix A5.1.2, could be used. Depending on the purpose of the analysis and the nature of the data, in addition to estimates of total benefits, estimates of the effects on the distribution of benefits among different groups or measures of the effects of research on income variability may also be needed. For ex post studies, the set of choices is limited, but it may still be relevant to compute both total benefits from the total investment and marginal benefits (using small changes from the actual past investments). For ex ante analyses, it may be necessary to compute benefits in relation to (a) the current allocation of resources to research, (b) allocations representing changes from a baseline of the current allocation, (c) allocations of a given amount to each of a range of programs, or (d) more than one of these options.

In every case, benefits and costs have to be converted to comparable units (such as net present value per unit of research resources or internal rates of return) by capital-budgeting methods, as described in section 5.4.2.

Interpreting and using the results: The fifth component involves making the results useful for the client, either as a set of summary statistics, a set of decisions about priorities, or an institutionalized process of thinking about decisions regarding the allocation of resources to research. Once gross and net benefits have been calculated for each of the alternatives being analyzed, they can be converted into summary statistics such as rates of return or net present values (perhaps per dollar of research spending) and used as aids in decision making. Usually, it is important to validate the results in consultation with the client (the decision maker for whom they are being developed), which might involve some adjustment of results while a consensus is being built.[3] The process will usually not be linear, as laid out here, but will involve iteration in which goals for the analysis are reviewed and revised after preliminary results have been obtained and digested.

5.1   Defining the Problem

The variety of problems and situations that call for research evaluation is too great to be covered fully here. It is not our purpose to provide a manual that deals with all possible situations. Rather, we provide a set of principles and general approaches that can be tailored to specific situations. In order to illustrate those principles, we use as our central example the common case of a public agricultural research system in a developing country deciding how to allocate a fixed amount of research resources among a given set of research program areas.

5.1.1   Clients for the Analysis — Decisions to Be Served

The process by which resources are allocated to agricultural research is complex. It is shaped by the conjunction of a large number of scientific, economic, and political factors, and many decision makers have an interest in or are responsible for allocating resources to agricultural research (chapter 1). While many are interested in (and, indeed, have an economic stake in) agricultural research decisions, few have any direct say in decision making. For any particular research budget, there is a person or group of people who have the

---

3.   Both as part of the validation, and as a management strategy to effectively implement the results of the exercise, other scientists and lower-level managers typically are (and should be) involved at this stage.

authority and responsibility for allocating funds among the broad alternatives being considered in strategic analyses such as this. This person or group is the primary *client* for a research evaluation or priority-setting study.

Several individuals may be potential clients. For instance, the minister of agriculture may be responsible for allocating a total budget for national agricultural research (and might delegate that authority to the permanent secretary). The secretary of agriculture may allocate a total research budget among research institutes (although it would be more typically delegated to a systemwide director of research, council, or board). In turn, a director of a research institute may be authorized to allocate the research institute's budget among programs and projects. Usually, however, the delegation is less than complete. The minister and secretary often take an interest in the distribution of the budget among institutes and the programs within them, and the national director or board often plays an active role in determining the research programs of individual institutes.

A first step in any research evaluation project is to identify the client (or clients). Typically, the client is the senior manager (or a small group of senior managers) in the research system being evaluated. Often research evaluation is undertaken on an explicit consultancy basis, where the contractual arrangement makes clear the objectives of the work and explicitly identifies the client. But in-house reviews are common, too. In those studies, as well, it is necessary to be clear about which decision maker within the organization will play the role of the client for the work, what decisions the work will serve, and what questions it will try to answer.

5.1.2   *The Objectives of the Analysis — Terms of Reference*

Within a public agricultural research system, a variety of questions might be raised about the value of research, perhaps calling for a variety of evaluation approaches. There is often a demand for information on rates of return to justify support for research. Estimated rates of return are usually based on ex post analysis of past research (see chapter 3 for examples). Sometimes this ex post evaluation is treated as if it provided a basis for setting priorities for future research — an extrapolation that often is not justified. The other main type of evaluation work pertains to decisions about allocating resources for the future — either for ongoing research programs or for new initiatives, that is, for setting priorities. In a priority-setting context, the types of decisions being made can include

- how much to allocate to research (and extension) in total
- how to allocate that total among different programs of research
- whether to accelerate, slow down, or even discontinue existing programs

- whether to introduce new programs

In principle, we might envision a process of equating marginal social benefits and costs among all possible alternatives so as to maximize net social benefits. In a practical setting, it is necessary to define a specific finite set of alternative *decisions* about research programs so that those decisions can be evaluated and compared. For example, an estimate of the net benefits for the current program alone is of little use in decision making; it is much more useful to compare the net benefits of the current program to a relevant alternative (e.g., an across-the-board 10% cut in current programs).[4]

Here we focus on the example of research evaluation that relates to the question of how to allocate a fixed quantum of research resources among a given set of commodity research programs. This question calls for a forward-looking analysis in which *prospective* programs of research (i.e., research not yet done) are evaluated ex ante. A great many troublesome issues arise even in the context of this somewhat circumscribed example. Along the way, we elaborate on some of these issues. And occasionally we refer to differences that arise in other cases that we do not cover in detail — such as ex post analysis of research that has already been done in either individual programs or total systems, or ex ante analysis when the research budget is not fixed.

5.1.3   The Scope of the Analysis — Research Programs and Program Alternatives

Before collecting data, it is necessary to define the research programs of interest and the alternatives to be evaluated. The list of programs might be defined in terms of commodity and noncommodity programs and also might be disaggregated regionally. For an ex post research evaluation, the list may be relatively short. However, for a priority-setting analysis, the list can be long, and programs on commodities that are clearly of low priority, perhaps because of their very small current and potential value of production, are candidates for exclusion from formal analysis.

If research is to be prioritized by noncommodity research programs or by components of commodity research programs (e.g., plant breeding, plant protection, or animal nutrition), a list of perhaps three to four broad programs

---

4.   Even if the appraisal of current programs shows that the rates of return (or net present value per unit of constrained resource) are different among programs, permitting a *ranking* of programs, more information is needed to support a *decision* to change the allocation of resources: Should programs with lower rates of return be cut and programs with higher rates of return expanded? Not always. If a program with a relatively low rate of return is to be reduced, how much should it be reduced? Answers to questions such as these depend on the curvature of the research-production relationship, the extent of sunk costs in a particular research program, and the degree of fixity in research resources, among other things. If a particular set of alternatives has been evaluated, decisions can be supported by the analysis.

(representing a logical aggregation of more specific research areas) that correspond to existing or potential programs can be developed. An example of typical research areas is included in table 5.1. However, because of the difficulty of quantifying the effects of research in certain noncommodity areas, a decision may be made to formally analyze only a subset of the areas explicitly using economic surplus models. For instance, economics and other social sciences, agroforestry, and agroclimatology might be excluded because of the conceptual and empirical difficulty of applying an economic surplus analysis to them. Alternative methods (perhaps informal economic surplus approaches) must be used to evaluate these programs.

Table 5.1:   *An Illustrative List of Commodity and Noncommodity Research Programs*

Crop programs	Cross-commodity programs
Plant breeding	Agroclimatology
Plant cultural practices	Agroforestry
Plant protection	Economics and other social services
Livestock programs	Mechanization
Animal health	Postharvest technologies
Animal nutrition	Soils and fertilizers
Animal reproduction	Water management

Having defined the relevant research programs, what remains to be defined are the decisions about the programs to be evaluated — decisions such as whether to support particular programs at all or, alternatively, whether to redistribute funds in a particular way among existing programs. Even when the total budget for research is fixed, it is informative to consider varying the allocation of resources to particular programs in order to measure the benefits and costs of potentially relevant alternatives. For instance, one approach is to evaluate each research program at the current level of funding and plus or minus 10% of that amount. The results from such evaluations could be used in a decision-making model to reallocate the fixed total resources for research among the existing programs in order to try to maximize overall net benefits. When shutting down a program or introducing an altogether new program is being considered, it is appropriate to compute the benefits and costs of those "all-or-nothing" decisions rather than the benefits and costs of marginal changes.

5.1.4   Objectives for the Research System — Measures of Benefits

The scope of the analysis defines the alternatives to be assessed. The next step is to define the yardstick to be used in making that assessment: the measures of benefits corresponding to the objectives for the system being analyzed. The "clients" for the analysis — typically national and regional research directors or an agricultural research council or board — must define the objectives for agricultural research. Usually it is productive for the analyst(s) conducting the study to meet with the clients to discuss the list of potential objectives and to ensure that they are in agreement. A generic list of objectives is presented in table 5.2. The list for a particular study is usually more specific. For example, if a regional distributional objective is specified, it must indicate which regions are to receive additional emphasis.[5]

It is important during this step not to confuse *objectives* with the *means and measures* of achieving them. For example, improving nutrition, increasing production and employment, and generating foreign exchange are means or measures of achieving increased economic and physical well-being. Each objective for the research system implies the economic impact of research to be measured, if possible. For example, an objective of increasing total net benefits implies a need to estimate research-induced changes in total economic surplus. An objective related to the regional distribution of benefits implies a need to calculate changes in economic surplus by region.

Also, it may be necessary to put some effort into resolving what the *real* objectives implied by the stated objectives are. For instance, a stated objective of "sustainability" is not clearly meaningful. Through discussion with the client, the analyst may be able to identify a more explicit concern about conservation of the natural resource base. In turn, that concern can be identified more explicitly as either a concern that the opportunity cost of natural resources be measured properly (an economic *efficiency* consideration) or that resources be conserved so that they are available for the following generations (an intergenerational *distributional* objective). Failing to identify the real objectives in this fashion could lead to unnecessary complications in the analysis due to the inclusion of redundant objectives or, perhaps even worse, to double-counting of effects.

As discussed in chapters 2 and 4, consideration of objectives other than economic efficiency makes the analysis much more expensive and problem-

---

5.   The decision to undertake economic surplus analysis at a spatial level other than national might also be due to a concern that the effects of research on reducing per unit costs or increasing yields cannot be modeled accurately at the aggregate level, or because decisions need to be taken within regions. Regions can be based on agroecological or political considerations. There may be some correlation between the two but seldom do politically based regions and agroecological zones coincide exactly. Suggestions on how to define the boundaries of agroecological zones and relate them to regions are presented later in this chapter.

Table 5.2:   *An Illustrative List of Agricultural Research Objectives*

Broad societal goals	Objectives for the research system
1. Efficiency — raise the average level of well-being in the economy	1. Increase the total or average well-being of producers and consumers taken in aggregate
2. Equity — increase the well-being of particular groups	1. Improve the well-being of specified income group(s) (e.g.,, low-income groups)
	2. Improve the well-being of people living in particular locations
	3. Improve the well-being of owners of particular factors of production (e.g., providing employment for landless laborers)
	4. Improve the well-being of people with specific farm sizes (e.g.,, small farms)
	5. Improve the well-being of people in specified farm-tenure situations
	6. Improve the well-being of consumers and producers differentially
3. Security — reduce the variability of well-being over time or increase food safety	1. Reduce year-to-year income fluctuations
	2. Increase food self-sufficiency or self-reliance
	3. Improve food safety

atic. Limiting attention to economywide economic efficiency means that only the total domestic impact of economic surplus must be assessed. This is still a formidable task, given that the evaluation involves assessing the total costs and benefits for each research program (and each option being considered for each program) and given the likelihood that a regional disaggregation (either international or domestic) will be required to permit an accurate assessment of domestic benefits. Estimating the effects on different groups in the domestic economy might not involve too much extra work if the model has been parameterized in reasonable detail. Making use of the information about distributional impacts may be more problematic; as noted in the earlier chapters, research is a blunt and ineffective instrument for achieving distributional, or security, objectives.

One valuable contribution of the economic surplus analysis is that it allows an assessment of the opportunity cost of using agricultural research to pursue nonefficiency objectives, reflected as lower total benefits from the overall research program. Those opportunity costs can be estimated by considering research programs that are designed to pursue nonefficiency objectives such as income distribution or security. This requires measuring the contributions of different research program choices to the nonefficiency objectives of interest. With that in mind, although this chapter is primarily about measuring economic surplus and its distribution, some attention is given to measuring the impact on variability as an example of a nonefficiency objective.

5.1.5 Strategy for the Analysis — Degree of Detail

One primary decision is whether the analysis will lead to relatively precise, detailed, disaggregated estimates of benefits or, instead, will be relatively aggregative and approximate. Some studies require highly disaggregated and precise estimates of impact on a large number of groups of people (regional or otherwise); others are served adequately by rough estimates of aggregated (say, national) welfare impacts.

The Simplest Case — Aggregate Impacts, No Price Effects

Suppose all weight is placed on the efficiency objective so that only global total benefits are of interest (and no consideration is given to the distribution of benefits among various groups). In such a case, the gross annual research benefit from a K percent per unit cost saving (or increase in yield) can be closely approximated without regard to research-induced changes in prices and quantities (and therefore without requiring any information on elasticities and market shares) as being equal to KV_0, where V_0 is the initial value of production. Thus, the analysis simply involves estimating the time-specific values of the increased production or of the inputs saved due to research. This model, which was presented in figure 2.6 in chapter 2, is implicit in both simple benefit-cost analysis and the econometric approach to research evaluation discussed in chapter 3. Although changes in prices and quantities are not explicitly accounted for, this simple model can provide a first approximation of total research benefits because such market effects tend to influence the distribution of benefits more than the total benefits.

This *simple* model requires roughly the same effort at identifying research-related information (effects on yield or per unit costs, probabilities of research success, adoption rates, and base price and quantity data) as more sophisticated forms of economic surplus analysis (for a given set of alternatives). But it is simplified in its requirements for market-related information:

it does not require information on price elasticities of demand or supply (assumed zero or infinite) or market shares. However, it implicitly imposes some extreme assumptions about price policies, technological spillovers (they are absent), and market structure (it is irrelevant), which can be relaxed in more detailed modeling approaches. It would be a minor variation on the theme in such an analysis to adjust for some of these aspects while preserving the essential parsimony of the approach.

This type of simplified economic surplus model is used most often when a long list of alternatives must be compared but total resources for the analysis are limited, or where only rough approximations are judged to be adequate for the purpose at hand. This approach has been combined with other criteria, attempting to weight multiple objectives for research, in simple scoring models that are reviewed and critiqued in chapter 7.[6] It has also been used for project-level evaluations of improved technologies (e.g., IAC 1976).

Extensions — Some Price Effects, Some Disaggregation

The approximations and the degree of aggregation involved in the simple model mean that it is unable to deal with the distribution of benefits. It may also result in significant measurement errors. Where commodities are traded and technologies are transferable outside the region of direct interest, in such a way that benefits accrue beyond the place where the research is carried out, the simple model might not be adequate for measuring aggregate domestic effects. In addition, a measure of distribution of domestic benefits and costs may be of direct interest (e.g., it may make a difference if benefits accrue to farmers rather than consumers or to the farmers in a particular region). A more detailed economic surplus analysis allows for public policies, interregional and international trade, and regional price and technology spillovers, providing a measure of the distributional impact of research and thereby a more precise measurement of the domestic impact of interest. This type of analysis distinguishes the impact of domestic welfare from international impact; it can also distinguish between impact on domestic producers, consumers, and taxpayers. The analysis can be disaggregated horizontally to account for the spatial distribution of research benefits and costs within a country and to incorporate research spillover effects both within and between countries.

A country's research can affect world trading prices in one of two ways. First, if the country is *large in trade* in the commodity, its production response to research affects world trading prices (i.e., the price spillover effects of research). Second, if the country is *large in research*, the adoption of its research results by other countries leads to changes in world production that

6. See, for example, the study by Cessay et al. (1989) of research priorities in the Gambia.

affect world prices (i.e., the price effects of technology spillovers). Thus, price spillover effects can arise without international technology spillovers only when a country is large in trade, but the price effects of technology spillovers can originate from a country small in trade if the country is large in research.

Technology spillovers might be ignored if they had no price effects.[7] However, when the domestic price effects of price and technology spillovers are significant, it is necessary to use a multimarket model to measure their domestic consequences. Of course, if the client is interested in international impact (e.g., the CGIAR or international donors to domestic systems), there is another set of reasons for paying attention to the global multicountry impact of domestic R&D.[8]

Even when the spatial distribution of benefits within the country is not of direct concern, there may be grounds for disaggregating some aspects of the analysis to improve the accuracy of the measures of total research benefits. In particular, agroecological diversity within a country often means that disaggregated data on the local impact of research (in terms of cost effects and rates of adoption) are needed to obtain accurate measures of the aggregate research-induced supply shift, K. Similar points apply to the estimation of other parameters (e.g., demand elasticities), but the potential for aggregation bias is typically more important in estimating K.

The more detailed analysis requires the same research-related information as the simple model, but it is more detailed in its treatment of markets and, therefore, more demanding in its requirements for market-related data. In addition to the information required by the simple model, it requires estimates of commodity-specific price elasticities of supply and demand, quantities traded internationally, and agricultural policies. Also, depending on the concerns with aggregation and the potential for the price effects of technology spillovers, it might also require a spatially disaggregated treatment of the supply response to research, both domestically and internationally.

Some version of this more detailed approach is likely to be used in any serious ex ante priority-setting exercise conducted by a NARS (except perhaps in the smallest systems) because it incorporates the virtual minimum of market-related and research-related data necessary to obtain meaningful

7. This typically would be the case, for instance, when the ROW countries that adopt the research results are collectively small in trade in the commodity, in that changes in their production have a negligible effect on global exports or imports. It is also true when the combination of relative smallness of spillover effects on production combined with relative smallness of countries in trade means that the spillover effects on prices are small, or when government interventions in markets prevent the effects from being reflected in international prices.

8. For instance see Edwards and Freebairn (1981, 1982, 1984), Davis, Oram and Ryan (1987), McCalla and Ryan (1992), and Traxler and Byerlee (1994).

measures of national research benefits. Such an approach has been used extensively for research evaluation and for priority-setting analysis.[9] While more time, information, and effort are required than for the simple model, the difference should not be too great if basic data are available on elasticities, trade, and pricing policies. One purpose of this book is to facilitate the application of models with more detail (and hence more accuracy) in research evaluation and priority setting.

Further Extensions

In chapter 4, we discussed extending the simple model to disaggregate impacts vertically among the stages of a multistage production system, which requires information on the elasticities of substitution among inputs, factor shares, and factor-supply elasticities for inputs used in the marketing chain. Such models have not been applied often in research priority-setting contexts,[10] but they are likely to become more widely used as data and techniques become better and cheaper. Also, some recent studies have developed and applied more comprehensive general-equilibrium models to evaluate specific questions in relation to research benefits (e.g., Coble et al. 1992; Martin and Alston 1993). Such studies have tended to relate more to broader questions of research policy than to applied evaluation and priority-setting work. However, these relatively new approaches require further development and refinement before they can be applied to practical research evaluation and priority-setting problems. Hence, we see limited use of such models in the immediate future for most of the questions that concern us in this book, and we do not go into them further here.

5.2   Market-Related Data

A major step in implementing an economic surplus analysis is defining the specific data and other information required, deciding who should provide particular types of information, designing questionnaires (if necessary) to obtain that information, and collecting the information. The specific types of information needed for our hypothetical study on behalf of a developing-country NARS, and their likely sources, are described below.

The economic surplus measures presented in chapter 4 require, at a minimum, data on quantities produced and consumed, prices received and paid, and

---

9. See Norton, Ganoza and Pomareda (1987), Dey and Norton (1993), Palomino and Norton (1992a), and Lima and Norton (1993).

10. Exceptions include Mullen and Alston (1990) and Scobie and Jacobsen (1992).

the corresponding price elasticities of supply and demand for each identified group of producers and consumers. An ex ante analysis requires a few years of price and quantity data (perhaps the most recent three or four years) for a benchmark.[11] Data on prices and quantities of exports and imports, exchange rates, rates of population and income growth, and information on government price policies and any other relevant market interventions may be required for some commodities. A discount rate is required for the capital budgeting framework. These items are discussed individually below.

Decisions must be made about the "level" in the production-marketing-consumption system at which to apply the analysis, and these decisions are usually governed by practical considerations of the availability of data and the degree to which a commodity is recognizable as such (e.g., wheat versus bread), as well as a desire to relate the analysis closely to the objectives identified by the client. This constellation of considerations usually implies that an analysis should apply at the farm level or at the wholesale level. The latter is especially apt to be used for traded goods to ensure that domestic and traded quantities and prices are treated consistently.[12] It is unusual for a study of research benefits to use retail prices and retail goods. When farm-level prices are used, it may be necessary to consider spatial variation in prices for a given quality and price variation due to variations in quality when forming a representative price index. For traded goods, it may be appropriate to use the border price — either c.i.f. or f.o.b., depending on whether the good is importable or exportable.

As noted above, once the set of goods has been defined explicitly (including the market level), at a minimum, quantities are required on production and consumption for every distinct group of producers and consumers identified in the objectives. Producer and consumer prices will be required for every such identified quantity. Of course, if there were no policy interventions or other reasons for price differences, all consumers and producers would effectively face the same price.

---

11.   An ex post analysis typically requires detailed data on prices and quantities for a single commodity aggregate of interest on an annual basis for all past years for which benefits are to be assessed. As discussed in chapter 3, econometric studies require even more data.

12.   As discussed in detail in chapter 4, the choice of market level for the analysis involves an implicit choice about the aggregation of surpluses accruing to farmers and others on the supply side (in "producer surplus") and consumers and others on the demand side (in "consumer surplus").

5.2.1   Price and Quantity Data

Quantities Produced

Information is needed on the annual production of each commodity included on the list of research programs. Usually a three- or four-year average is taken to reduce the effects of abnormal years. For ex ante evaluation, the most recent three to four years are typically used as a benchmark.[13] If there are regional distributional objectives and a more completely disaggregated analysis is being undertaken, explicitly taking trade into account, the same information must also be gathered on a regional basis. Data are also needed on the recent world production of tradable commodities for which the country influences world market prices.[14] Data on own-country production are usually available from national statistical sources. World production for particular commodities can be obtained from a source such as the most recent FAO *Production Yearbook*.[15] But users need to be aware that such data are not always completely reliable — it is best to double-check.

Quantities Consumed and Traded

Unless the simplest model is being used, information is needed on exports and imports (for the same years as production) for those commodities for which the country can influence world prices, either through its own production or through spillovers of its research results. The most recent FAO *Trade Yearbook* and the other references listed in footnote 15 are potential sources for these data. Data on interregional trade within the innovating country are needed as well when regional distributional objectives are specified. These data may be obtained from state, provincial, or national statistical agencies.

Consumption data can be obtained from national statistical sources by adding imports to and subtracting exports from production (and by adjusting

13. For ex post analysis, there is a general problem of inferring a stream of without-research prices and quantities using time-denominated with-research data that vary partly as a result of variables not included in the model (e.g., weather, policy changes), unlike the ex ante analysis where, by assumption, other things are held equal or are explicitly modeled. Problems of double counting or inappropriate attribution can arise when studies apply a measure of K to actual past quantities and prices (i.e., time-subscripted data) rather than projecting the entire series forward or backward, based on a benchmark as for ex ante analysis. It is important to be conscious of the potential problems. One "safe" course is to carry out an ex post analysis in the same way as an ex ante analysis, projecting the entire series from a benchmark as described in appendix A5.1.2, in which case the *same* information is required for benchmarking.

14. Most countries are unable to influence the world price of *any* commodity, over the relevant length of run, through international trade; at most there may be one of these commodities in a typical country study.

15. A number of government organizations and international agencies have made useful data available on diskette for a nominal charge. These include (a) FAO's *AGROSTAT* data, (b) USDA's *World Agriculture and Trade Indicators* files, and (c) The World Bank's *World Tables* data series.

for changes in stocks if data are available). Consumption data must be converted to the same units as production and trade data.[16] For example, information may be needed to convert slaughtered weight of livestock to its equivalent live weight or to convert various processed forms of food crops (e.g., dried, shelled, milled) into a standardized equivalent form to maintain units consistent with production data. World consumption data are also needed for those commodities. World consumption of a commodity can be assumed to be roughly equal to world production.

If there is an interest in the disaggregated effects on consumers according to regions within the country, data on consumption by region may be required. These data are unavailable for many countries, but they do exist in several of the larger, more populous countries. In any event, even when not available directly, values for consumption can often be inferred using information on the regional population pattern and either (a) per capita incomes and results from studies on income-consumption relationships or (b) data on rural/urban per capita consumption patterns that can be used to apportion aggregate consumption among regions.[17] The latter is likely to be more accurate.

Prices

Data to match the production and consumption data (i.e., the same commodities at the same market levels in the same places and for the same years) are need for the prices on each commodity. It is usually necessary to determine whether these domestic prices are free-market prices or the result of a tax or subsidy policy and to measure the extent of any price interventions. When regional objectives on income distribution are included, and therefore regional income distribution effects are to be measured in the analysis, regional prices and information on regional pricing policies are needed as well.[18] If the analysis

16. Relevant conversion factors can usually be obtained from local statistical agencies.

17. The data on per capita consumption may be obtained from periodic consumption surveys (often carried out by local statistical agencies).

18. Although we have abstracted from transport costs, regional differences in prices attributable to transport costs might be significant — especially for perishables such as fresh fruit and milk — and it might not be appropriate to treat prices as being equal among regions for the welfare analysis, even when the supply-and-demand model does not include explicit spatial equilibrium considerations. Options as approximations in models where prices differ regionally include (a) treating individual regions as closed economies in trade in certain commodities (not necessarily in technology), (b) treating regional prices as being in fixed proportion to one another (equivalent to a constant percentage price difference) and solving for each regional price given a percentage change in the national price, and (c) treating the price differences as being constant and solving for each regional price given a value for the national price. Since it is the change in prices that matters for welfare analysis, it might not be worth the effort of trying to allow for regional price differences in such ways in the welfare analysis if the market equilibrium model does not explicitly account for the causes of those differences. In many cases, it will be appropriate to use *changes*

is to be disaggregated vertically in the marketing chain to deal with multiple market levels, as discussed in chapter 4, data will be needed on marketing margins. Data on marketing margins may be required for converting prices received by farmers to retail or wholesale, or vice versa, even when benefits are not to be disaggregated vertically.

Typically, an analysis will be undertaken with all monetary variables expressed in real terms (usually current purchasing power). This can be achieved by deflating nominal prices by an appropriate price index, with the initial year for the economic surplus calculation taken as the base.[19] When international data are included in the analysis, it is usually desirable to convert all money units to the same currency so that benefits can be compared and summed across countries. This can be accomplished by multiplying the local currency price by the exchange rate between that currency and, say, the U.S. dollar. In some instances it might be appropriate to adjust the published official exchange rate, based on an estimate of the percentage over- or undervaluation of the currency (e.g., Krueger, Schiff and Valdéz 1988). Alternatively, purchasing-power-parity indexes, such as those developed for the agricultural sector by Rao (1993), could be used instead of market exchange rates.

Government Policies

The specific government price policies to be included in the analysis of individual commodities can be determined by examining historical policies and by consulting with policymakers about likely future output- and input-pricing and trade policies. These policies can be incorporated into the economic surplus measures in ways described in chapter 4. It may be tempting to treat policies as ad valorem tax or subsidy equivalents and to use available data on producer subsidy equivalents. However, it is important to be aware that, as discussed in chapter 4, such approximations can invalidate the welfare analysis (the actual instruments of protection matter), especially in relation to the distributional impacts of research. Indeed, assuming that actual policies can be modeled as tax or subsidy equivalents may distort the findings more than assuming that price policies are absent (as pointed out by de Gorter and Norton 1990). More generally, if policies are to be included, it is important to take the problem of representing the actual policy and all of the relevant components seriously.

Many analysts may be inclined to ignore domestic price policies. Although it is difficult to generalize, in most cases this will lead to an overstatement of

---

in the national border price (or equivalent for nontraded goods) in conjunction with actual regional quantities that relate to region-specific prices.

19.   Chapter 3 provides information on index-number theory and construction.

the social benefits from research on protected commodities and an understatement of the social benefits from research on commodities that are taxed. The percentage over- or understatement will often be approximately equal to the percentage producer subsidy equivalent (which includes the effects of commodity policies, input subsidies, and other measures, as described below). Thus, a consideration of the differentials in rates of protection among commodities will give some guidance as to the potential importance of explicitly accounting for policies in the analysis. Where distribution of research benefits is of concern, it is especially important to take explicit account of price policies and to consider the actual policies, because the main effect of price distortions is on the distribution of benefits between producers, consumers, and government (Alston, Edwards and Freebairn 1988).

Information on the policies, and measures of them that can be included in supply-and-demand models, can be obtained from the government of the country being studied or from published studies. Methods for representing agricultural policy in models have received a great deal of attention recently, especially in connection with the Uruguay round of GATT negotiations. Producer subsidy equivalents (PSEs) and consumer subsidy equivalents (CSEs) have been proposed as summary measures of policy distortions and the FAO (1973), OECD (1987), and USDA (1988) have published PSE and CSE estimates for the major individual commodities produced by most countries. These measures are summary subsidy equivalents that might be equivalent to the actual policies for some purposes (e.g., measuring trade-distorting effects) but are surely not equivalent for deducing the size and distribution of research benefits. However, in estimating PSEs and CSEs, FAO, the USDA, and OECD have also quantitatively documented the specific instruments of protection as well.[20] Thus, the PSE-CSE data could be useful for parameterizing the types of models laid out in chapter 4. Other studies have documented other aspects of policy distortions for modeling work (e.g., Tyers and Anderson 1992).

5.2.2 Elasticities

When the simplest economic surplus model is being used, the domestic price elasticities of supply and demand are implicitly assumed to be zero or infinite. To go beyond the simplest models, domestic price elasticities of supply, as well as domestic price and income elasticities of demand, are required for all of the relevant commodities. For those commodities for which the country can influence world price, a "rest-of-world" excess-sup-

---

20. Josling and Tangerman (1988) compared the policy coverage of the PSE estimates available from these three sources.

ply curve (for an importer) or excess-demand curve (for an exporter) may be used to summarize the "rest-of-world" role in the market in conjunction with a model of domestic supply and demand. Then, a corresponding excess-supply or excess-demand elasticity is required along with the domestic supply-and-demand elasticities. This excess-supply–excess-demand approach is appropriate for estimating domestic benefits, but more detailed elasticities are needed for all countries for which benefits are to be calculated when a client (e.g., a donor to a national system or the CGIAR) wants to know the detailed, international, cross-country distribution of benefits. Additionally, if interregional or other multimarket research effects are calculated, domestic price and income elasticities may be needed by region, by consumer income group, and so on. Obtaining all these elasticities is a tall order. Fortunately, there are several ways to approximate both domestic and foreign elasticities.

Demand Elasticities

Domestic price elasticities of demand can be obtained from (a) published results of previous studies, (b) estimations of demand system equations, and (c) approximations using economic theory.[21] Option b is usually too expensive for an agricultural research priority-setting study. Option a is the least-cost approach, but usually a combination of a and c is used. Economic theory can be used to deduce an estimate of an unknown price elasticity of demand. Theoretical restrictions (homogeneity, symmetry, and adding-up rules) can be used to get some economically meaningful consistency into the set of demand elasticities and fill in any missing values.[22] For instance, the "homogeneity condition" means that, for commodity j, the own-price elasticity of demand, η_{jj}, the income elasticity of demand, η_{jI}, and the relevant cross-price elasticities, η_{ij}, sum to zero. That is,

$$\sum_{i=1}^{n} \eta_{ij} + \eta_{jI} = 0 \qquad (5.1)$$

For normal goods, the income elasticity of demand is positive, and for highly aggregated commodities with limited substitution possibilities (e.g.,

---

21. For example, see Nerlove (1956), Frisch (1959), Carter and Gardiner (1988), and Tsakok (1990, appendix D) and the references therein.

22. The restrictions on demand elasticities implied by theory are documented and discussed by, for example, Phlips (1974), Deaton and Muellbauer (1980a and b), and Johnson, Hassan and Green (1984). In addition to homogeneity, the most useful restrictions are (a) that the Slutsky matrix of second derivatives of the consumer-expenditure function is negative semidefinite and symmetric (Slutsky symmetry), which implies that compensated elasticities of demand, η_{ij}^*, satisfy the restriction that $\eta_{ij}^*/s_j = \eta_{ji}^*/s_i$ where s_j is the budget share of good j and (b) the Engel-aggregation condition in which the share-weighted average of income elasticities is one: $\sum_j s_j \eta_{jI} = 1$.

meat or cereal grains), the sum of the cross-price elasticities is usually a small positive number, so the own-price elasticity of demand is usually a negative number that is slightly larger in absolute value than the income elasticity. Even when the income elasticity of demand is unknown, it can be approximated if one knows whether the good is a staple, a normal good, or a luxury good. Staples in the diet have very small or even negative income elasticities of demand, normal goods (the majority of foods) have η_{ji} between zero and one, and luxury foods (primarily meats and other higher-priced foods) have η_{ji} greater than one.[23]

Another formula that can be used to estimate η_{jj} is $\eta_{jj} = \varepsilon_j [s_j - (1-s_j\varepsilon_j/\omega)]$, where ε_j is the expenditure elasticity of demand for commodity j, which is roughly equal to η_{ji}, s_j is the proportion of the consumer budget spent on commodity j, and ω is the "money flexibility," which equals $(du/dy)(y/u)$, where u is the marginal utility of money income and y is money income.[24] While ω can vary from zero to a large negative number, in most developing countries ω would lie between -1.0 and -5.0, decreasing in absolute value as incomes rise. A value of $\omega = -1.0$ might be typical of a middle-income developing country while $\omega = -5.0$ would be typical of a low-income country.

Supply Elasticities

Domestic supply elasticities can be obtained from previous studies in the country or region. Most published elasticities of supply for agricultural products fall between 0.1 and 1.0. These elasticities, primarily estimated with annual time-series data, are likely to have been biased downward, however, as a result of problems with the specification of the dynamics of supply response, problems with specification of price expectations, incomplete representation of alternatives, and the nature of data in which prices of alternative products tend to move together (e.g., see Cassells 1933; Colman 1983; Burt and Worthington 1988; Just 1993).[25] Part of the problem is that supply elasticities increase with

23.   Note that the classification of goods as luxuries and normal goods varies with income as, along with the patterns of consumption, income elasticities depend on per capita income. In some relatively rich countries, for instance, most meats would be normal goods, not luxuries. See Schultz (1953b) for a good discussion of this issue regarding farm and food products.

24.   In this approach it is assumed that the marginal utility derived from each good is independent of the quantity of any other good consumed. This is known as want-independence. Demands for goods are still related through the budget constraint, however, and therefore want-independence does not imply the much stronger assumption of demand-independence. Pinstrup-Andersen, Ruiz de Londoño and Hoover (1976), Pomareda (1978), and Norton, Ganoza and Pomareda (1987) used this formula to calculate own-price elasticity. See, also, Scobie (1980).

25.   For these kinds of reasons, part of what is often attributed to trend and technological change may be due to changes in relative prices that are not captured by conventionally used price indexes (Griliches 1960; Peterson 1979). See, also, Binswanger et al. (1987).

increases in the length of run (i.e., as more time is allowed for adjustments in response to a price change and as more "fixed" factors become "variable"). As pointed out by Cassells (1933), econometric studies tend to estimate intermediate rather than long-run elasticities.

The supply elasticity depends in known ways on a number of things in addition to the length of run. The supply elasticities of the factors used to produce a commodity make up an important determinant its own elasticity of supply. Arable land can be a limiting factor, but often this will be so only for very important commodities (e.g., corn in the United States, rice in Asia) or very aggregated commodities (e.g., grains). Thus, the supply of relatively important commodities (or relatively aggregated commodities) tends to be relatively inelastic because of an inelastic supply of factors that account for a large share of the total costs of production. Livestock industries and perennial crops tend to have smaller supply elasticities because a component of specific capital (existing breeding stock or trees) is fixed for a time.

Other things to consider are the ease of factor substitutability (greater substitutability among factors in the production of a commodity leads to a greater supply elasticity) and the nature of economies of size or scale in the industry (diseconomies of size or scale lead to a less elastic supply). Thus, theory suggests that an industry such as the tobacco industry — that uses only a little arable land and relatively few other specialized factors and which can be regarded as having close to constant returns to scale at the industry level — is likely to have a highly elastic supply.[26] Similar arguments indicate that in most countries, the intensive livestock industries (pork, poultry, and in some cases, dairy) are likely to have relatively elastic supplies.

Clearly, long-run elasticities for most individual agricultural products are greater than one (and for many products they may be infinite), but even short- or intermediate-run supply elasticities are probably close to one. For most priority-setting work, the relevant length of run will be intermediate, and in the absence of better information, an elasticity of 1.0 is an appropriate starting point — this is especially true in relation to translating *J*s (measuring horizontal shifts) into *K*s (vertical shifts).

Excess Supply-and-Demand Elasticities

In many studies, it is convenient to represent the "rest of the world" in summary form in the analysis, using excess-supply and excess-demand concepts. For a given country (or region or group of countries), the excess-supply/excess-demand function is given by the algebraic difference between

---

26. This theoretical idea has been borne out in empirical work by Sumner and Alston (1986), Goodwin and Sumner (1990), and Fulginiti and Perrin (1993) who all found a highly elastic supply of U.S. tobacco.

its domestic supply function and domestic demand function. Global market clearing can be represented equivalently by either (a) the intersection of the algebraic sum of all demand functions and the algebraic sum of all supply functions or (b) the intersection of the "rest-of-world" excess supply (or demand) with the "own-country" excess demand (or supply) when the home country is an importer (exporter).

In the most common case, the home country is a small country, unable to influence world prices. Then the rest-of-world excess-supply/excess-demand function can be represented by a horizontal (i.e., perfectly elastic) price line. In a few cases, a country or region will be able to influence world prices for a product, and then an estimate of the price responsiveness of excess supply/excess demand will be needed.

Own-country and the rest-of-world excess supply-and-demand elasticities can be approximated as follows. First, for a good that is exported by the home country,

$$\varepsilon_{XA} = \left(\frac{Q_{s,A}}{Q_{s,A} - Q_{d,A}}\right)\varepsilon_A + \left(\frac{Q_{d,A}}{Q_{s,A} - Q_{d,A}}\right)\eta_A$$

$$= \frac{Q_{s,A}}{Q_{x,A}}\varepsilon_A + \frac{Q_{d,A}}{Q_{x,A}}\eta_A$$

(5.2a)

where ε_{XA} is the elasticity of excess supply (i.e., supply of exports) for the commodity in the home country (country A), ε_A is the domestic supply elasticity, η_A is the absolute value of the domestic price elasticity of demand for the commodity, and $Q_{s,A}$ and $Q_{d,A}$ are domestic production and consumption of the commodity. $Q_{x,A}$ is exports of the commodity.

Second, for a good that is imported by the home country,

$$\eta_{MA} = \left(\frac{Q_{s,A}}{Q_{d,A} - Q_{s,A}}\right)\varepsilon_A + \left(\frac{Q_{d,A}}{Q_{d,A} - Q_{s,A}}\right)\eta_A$$

$$= \frac{Q_{s,A}}{Q_{m,A}}\varepsilon_A + \frac{Q_{d,A}}{Q_{m,A}}\eta_A$$

(5.2b)

where η_{MA} is the elasticity of excess demand (i.e., demand for imports) for the commodity in the home country and $Q_{m,A}$ is imports of the commodity into the country.

Third, for a good being imported by the home country,

$$\varepsilon_{XB} = \left(\frac{Q_{s,B}}{Q_{s,B} - Q_{d,B}}\right)\varepsilon_B + \left(\frac{Q_{d,B}}{Q_{s,B} - Q_{d,B}}\right)\eta_B$$

$$= \frac{Q_{s,B}}{Q_{m,A}}\varepsilon_B + \frac{Q_{d,B}}{Q_{m,A}}\eta_B$$

(5.2c)

where ε_{XB} is the excess supply elasticity of the commodity in the rest of the world (i.e., region B), ε_B and η_B are the elasticities of supply and demand (absolute value) in the rest of the world, $Q_{s,B}$ and $Q_{d,B}$ are the rest-of-world production and consumption of the commodity, and $Q_{m,A}$ is imports of the commodity into country A (equal to exports from country B).

Finally, for a good being exported by the home country,

$$\eta_{MB} = \left(\frac{Q_{s,B}}{Q_{d,B} - Q_{s,B}}\right)\varepsilon_B + \left(\frac{Q_{d,B}}{Q_{d,B} - Q_{s,B}}\right)\eta_B$$

$$= \frac{Q_{s,B}}{Q_{x,A}}\varepsilon_B + \frac{Q_{d,B}}{Q_{x,A}}\eta_B$$

(5.2d)

where η_{MB} is the excess-demand elasticity for the commodity in the rest of the world (i.e., the rest of the world's demand for imports) and the other variables are as defined above.[27]

5.2.3   Discount Rate and "Exogenous" Growth Factors

Discount Rate

Economists do not agree as to whether the appropriate social discount rate should reflect the alternative value of public resources in consumption or in investment. There is little disagreement, however, that when the analysis is conducted using benefits and costs expressed in constant value (i.e., real) terms, the rate should be a real rate of interest (adjusted for inflation), and most would argue that it should reflect any restrictions placed on alternative uses of the funds. In many situations, the real discount rate will fall in the 3% to 5% range. This rate corresponds to a long-term, risk-free rate of return (e.g., the real yield from long-term government bonds).[28] Ray (1986, pp.

27. For discussions of these equations and their simplifying assumptions, particularly with respect to the elasticity of price transmission, see Horner (1952), Tweeten (1967, 1977), Johnson (1977), Bredahl, Myers and Collins (1979), and Carter and Gardiner (1988).

28. In some places the government bond rate might include a risk premium, but it could still be appropriate to use as a measure of the opportunity cost of government funds. Some have suggested that a

92-101) discusses theoretical and conceptual issues surrounding the choice of discount rate and reviews the relevant literature.

In chapter 2 we argued that it is inappropriate to adjust the discount rate to reflect the riskiness of research or, for example, to reflect concerns with sustainability because adjusting the discount rate does not account properly for concerns about risk or intergenerational equity, and other approaches are better. Not everyone will take this advice, so it is important when comparing net present values among studies to check what discount rates were used and to make sure they are comparable.[29] Sensitivity analysis is useful for assessing the effects of the discount rate on the net present value of net research benefits. Section 5.3 discusses using the results from economic surplus and provides details on the use of discount rates in capital budgeting.

Exogenous Growth in Demand

For priority-setting work, projections of population and income growth rates for the next 15 to 20 years are needed to project exogenous demand shifts. In a future year, T years from now, the projected population, N_{t+T}, will be equal to the current population, N_t, scaled by the exponential population growth rate, $g_{N,\,t+k}$, in year $t + k$:

$$N_{t+T} = N_t \prod_{k=1}^{T} (1 + g_{N,\,t+k})$$

$$= (1 + g_N)^T N_t \quad \text{if } g_{N,t+k} \text{ is invariant over time.}$$

(5.3)

Then, for a given per capita consumption, total consumption would be projected to increase in proportion to population — i.e., scaled up by $(1 + g_N)^T$. In the absence of information to the contrary, the same approach can be applied for income growth, but it is necessary to multiply the projected growth in per capita income by the relevant income elasticity to deduce the implied growth in consumption. Thus, ignoring the effects of population growth, total consumption of commodity j in T years' time would be projected to be $C_{j,t+T} = [(1 + g_I)^T - 1] \eta_{jI} C_{j,t}$, where g_I is the exponential growth rate in per capita income. More details on these procedures are provided in appendix A5.1.2, which documents the *Dream©* computer model.

higher discount rate might be appropriate for developing countries to reflect their greater scarcity of capital. This ought to be reflected in the government bond rate, if it is relevant.

29. In particular, according to Birdsall and Steer (1993), the World Bank uses a discount rate of 8% to 10% for project evaluation in the context of a less-developed country — on the grounds that this represents the opportunity cost of capital in developing countries. They claim that the opportunity cost of capital is higher in developing countries than in industrial countries, belying the globalization of international capital markets.

Population growth rates can be included at the current rate estimated by the World Bank or other sources and then allowed to follow standard projections for the country over time. Recent historical experience and other factors can be considered in projecting income growth rates.

Exogenous Growth in Supply

The "without-research" quantity may be projected to change either as a result of changes in area (for crops) or herd size (for livestock) or as a result of changes in yield. Such changes could result from (a) responses to market forces with given technology (e.g., changes in output prices leading to greater planned output or changes in input prices leading to intensification), (b) price-induced changes in technology, or (c) the effects of research spillover. In addition, when the relevant alternative is less research rather than none, the relevant projection of output for the benchmark case is output given the lower amount of research. What is important here is to be clear about the alternatives being compared and, therefore, about what conditions are applicable for projecting future outputs.

In practice, current output may be projected forward using recent past changes in output to infer a growth rate and to obtain a first approximation of a benchmark stream of "without-research" quantities. Then appropriate revisions to that benchmark stream can be made, based on advice from scientists and others for the case of either (a) no research or (b) a baseline program of research spending. In either case, the benchmark should incorporate the effects of research spill-ins and autonomous growth in supply in response to exogenous changes in factor and product markets. Alternatively, in some cases it might be preferable to project yield and area (or herd size) in the baseline case and to combine the results to project output. In the *Dream©* model, as described in appendix A5.1.2, exponential growth rates in area and yield that are not attributable to research are added together to derive an overall exogenous growth rate of output.

5.3 Measuring the Research-Induced Supply Shift

To measure changes in economic surplus due to research-induced shifts in the supply curve, information on variables that quantify the knowledge production function described in chapter 2 is required. That function relates research costs (and how they are deployed) to actual or expected per unit cost reductions or yield increases; to lags in research, adoption, and depreciation; and to probabilities of research success.

The size of the research-induced supply shift — the *K-factor* — is a crucial determinant of the total benefits from research. The accuracy of the estimate of *K* and its path over time, reflecting adoption lags and so on, will determine the accuracy and validity of the estimates of research benefits and any research priorities that are derived, based on those estimates. In short, *K* (and its associated distribution) is critical.

The most important questions concern the size of the research-induced shift in a commodity supply function for a given expenditure on research and how that shift varies over time. In order to answer these questions for a given research program, the analyst has to combine technical, scientific, and economic information from a number of sources. For ex ante analysis, some of the information can be obtained primarily from researchers and extension workers — especially technical information about the likely impact of the research on, say, experimental yields or on commercial yields under various scenarios and on the likely time path of the adoption of various technologies. However, it is important to use appropriate sources for any such information. Scientists are often unable to give meaningful answers to questions about impact on industry-level costs or supply functions, so economists can play an important role in translating scientific information into economic information. Also, scientists might be too optimistic about their chances of success, the likely size of the eventual impact of their work if successful, the time required to complete the research, and the speed and extent to which it would be adopted. If the economic surplus analysis is ex post, the results of previous experimental trials can be used to assess changes in cost and yield. Even with ex ante analysis, such past results are indispensable for assessing information from other sources and providing a benchmark for future projections.[30]

In section 5.3.1, we lay out some of the conceptual issues that arise in relating changes in production, productivity, or cost to a measure of *K* to be used in research evaluation. Then in section 5.3.2, we consider some specific measurement issues that arise in particular alternative approaches to estimating *K*, including ex post econometric studies and ex ante approaches based on elicited information.

The ex post measures obtained from econometric models reflect the adoption response. In section 5.3.2, we emphasize how to measure the *maximum* shift corresponding to full adoption when research is successful. We turn to the modifications that must be made in ex ante evaluation in section 5.3.3 — to account for the distribution of possible research outcomes and the time path of the adoption. Sample questionnaires and some discussion of the practical

30. In appendix A5.3, we discuss the use of experiment and industry data to help assess potential supply shifts at the industry level.

aspects of eliciting the interview information needed for ex ante evaluation and for validating responses are provided in appendix A5.4. Although variables are discussed individually, they interact in shifting the supply curve over time, amplifying the importance of the manner in which questions are posed to scientists, extension workers, and those asked to validate their responses.

5.3.1 Conceptual Issues

At the level of the individual farm firm, a research-induced supply shift may be decomposed into two components: (a) one part arising from changes in productivity that would occur if input use were held constant at the optimum that applied before the technological change and (b) one part associated with changes in the input mix to optimize input combinations under the new technology. The latter augments the former.[31]

In order to measure the impact on profitability, the measured increase in productivity should reflect a change to a new optimal input mix, and correspondingly, measures of research-induced cost savings ought to reflect research-induced changes in the use of inputs *and their opportunity costs*. At the level of the individual firm, this means that estimated per unit cost savings ought to reflect the complete difference in the commodity enterprise budgets between the new and old technologies. In principle, this difference could be measured by preparing a detailed enterprise budget for production (applicable at the national or, if relevant, regional preresearch quantity), using each of the alternative technologies. The resulting differences in unit costs could be used as a measure of the research-induced reduction in marginal and average costs at the preresearch equilibrium.

But it is difficult to measure these differences in a reliable or meaningful way for technologies that are not yet developed, let alone adopted. At best, we can make an informed guess about the likely impacts on yield or on some aspects of cost, and this guess will be conditional to holding some things constant that will not be constant in practice.[32] This highlights the point that it is the result of producers optimizing their responses to the availability of new technology, not the new technology per se, that is relevant for measuring K.

---

31. This is according to the *Le Châtelier Principle* — when a constraint is removed, you can do at least as well as, and possibly better than, you could when the constraint was in force.

32. Evenson (1992) argued that unless the details of the research program are known, the effects of the research will be unpredictable. This is a reasonable view. But it is rarely true that we have *no* information to support making an informed estimate of the likely research outcome, and such an estimate may be more relevant than ex post information on past research effects, or it can be combined with information on past effects in a Bayesian-type approach. We do not agree with Evenson's (1992, p. 68) conclusion that "one may as well acknowledge that ex post evidence is all that one can bring to bear on such questions."

Results from using shortcut methods to infer this difference — such as translating a yield increase into a cost saving — must be adjusted to reflect changes in input use. For instance, as a matter of sound scientific practice, experimental yields generally hold the input mix constant across experimental alternatives in order to isolate the effects of the specific component of the technology being studied.[33] Thus, to the extent that optimal input mixes vary among alternatives, the *experimental* yield increase (or corresponding cost saving) will misstate the *economically optimal* yield increase (or cost saving). If the experimental input mix is optimal for the old technology but not for the new technology, then the cost saving from switching to the new technology will be understated (i.e., futher reductions in costs will be achieved by changing the input mix). Conversely, if the input mix is optimal for the new technology, the cost saving relative to the old technology will be overstated (i.e., the costs under the old technology will be overstated because they could be reduced by changing to an optimal input mix). Alternatively, if the input mix is varied across alternatives so that it is optimal for each of the alternatives, it will be necessary to account for changes in input use in deducing the research-induced cost saving (this also includes a charge for the opportunity cost of so-called "fixed" factors if their use changes). And in going from yield changes to cost changes, it will be necessary to account for that part of the increased yield that is attributable to changes in input use.

The same kinds of issues arise when the analysis is at the industry level rather than at the level of the firm, but they are buttressed with some additional ones. First, some inputs that are "variable" for firms (having exogenous prices) are quasi-fixed from the point of view of the industry. The endogenous prices of variable factors can complicate the evaluation of the impact of an input-saving or input-using technical change on the per unit costs of outputs, but they are unlikely to be a serious problem in most instances. Second, the prices of outputs that are exogenous to individual firms can be endogenous at the industry level, giving rise to the possibility of general-equilibrium feedback from related product markets through shifts of the industry supply function. Such changes complicate both the problem of *measuring* the research-induced supply shift and the problem of *interpreting* it in relation to a welfare analysis and evaluation (e.g., see chapter 4 for a discussion).

---

33. Thus, for example, in typical variety trials, the use of chemical fertilizers and the timing of operations will be held constant across different varieties even though different varieties might respond differently and call for different agronomic treatments. Similarly, for instance, in order to maximize profits when using bovine somatotropin to increase the milk yields of dairy cows, there must be an increase in rations and a change in the composition of the rations and the feeding schedules for the cows, compared with the optimum when the growth hormone is not being used.

These ideas are represented schematically in figure 5.1: four curves are shown representing different industry-level supply functions under different technological and market conditions. Initial output is Q_0. S_0 represents the initial supply curve, reflecting the use of the optimal input combinations under the original technology. S_1 represents the supply curve that would result if the new technology were adopted but the input mix were the same as under the original technology (S_1 is shown as lying below S_0, but with certain types of biased technological change, where achieving cost savings relies on changing the input mix, it might not lie below S_0 and could even lie above it).[34] S_2 represents the supply curve that applies when the optimal input mixes are used for the new technology, but this assumes that variable input prices are fixed and the quantities of "fixed" factors (such as land) used in

Figure 5.1: *Components of research-induced supply shifts*

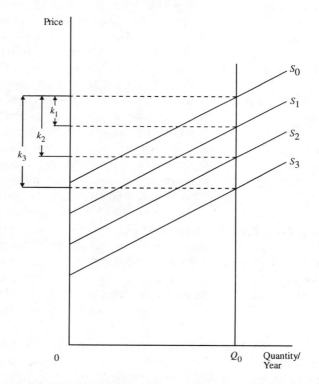

34. Of course producers would be unlikely to adopt such technologies if they did imply higher costs. A case where a new technology implies higher costs when input combinations are not optimized — but lower costs when they are optimized — provides a graphic illustration of the importance of optimally varying input mixes when technologies are compared for research evaluation.

producing the commodity are indeed fixed. The difference between the curves S_1 and S_2 is the cost saving due to optimizing the input mix for the new technology. Finally, S_3 represents the supply curve after all optimizing responses have been made, including the drawing of "fixed" factors into (or out from) the production of the commodity whose profitability has been increased by the introduction of the new technology.

Which of these supply shifts should we attempt to approximate to include as K in our assessment of research benefits: S_0 to $S_1 = k_1$, S_0 to $S_2 = k_2$, or S_0 to $S_3 = k_3$? The research-induced cost saving is understated by k_1 because it does not allow for economizing on the input mix. The unthinking use of experiment data or the results from a production-function econometric study (where the quantities of variable inputs are held constant for evaluating the output-enhancing effects of research) could lead unconsciously to a measure that corresponds to k_1 unless explicit account is taken of the input-mix change. Adjusting for the optimal input mix would lead to a measure that corresponds to k_2 (e.g., Bernhart and Perrin 1989; Lemieux and Wohlgenant 1989; Perrin 1992). This could well correspond to the measures of the research-induced supply shift derived from a cost-function study, for instance (where the prices of variable inputs and quantities of output and fixed inputs are held statistically constant), as well as the measures derived from a thoughtful ex ante study based on experiment data.

What about k_3? The estimate of the research-induced supply shift from an econometric estimation of either a directly estimated supply function or a single-commodity cost function might correspond to k_3, which represents the entire research-induced supply shift, including the component of cost reduction (or output increases) that is attributable to drawing in quasi-fixed factors (e.g., allocatable fixed factors such as land in a multi-output setting). The problem is that the measure of k here is a measure of *single-commodity* cost changes, some of which have been achieved at the expense of cost increases (decreases in producer surplus) in other commodities, from the production of which the quasi-fixed factors have been drawn. The difference between S_2 and S_3 is not a net benefit; it is a gross benefit for which there is a corresponding cost (associated with a leftward shift of the supply of competing products) and the net social benefit is zero (see Martin and Alston 1994 for a discussion and heuristic proof).[35]

Unless a full general-equilibrium analysis is being undertaken, in which case it would be desirable to explicitly measure the impact of commodity-market–factor-market interactions of the type involved in shifting from S_1 or S_2 to S_3, it

---

35. In commenting on Lindner and Jarrett (1978), Rose (1980) was concerned with this issue of allocatable fixed factors (especially land) and deriving appropriate measures of quasi-rents.

would be best to attempt to estimate k_2 rather than k_3. This implies adjusting estimates obtained from either scientists, experiment data, or production-function studies for changes in the input mix, with appropriate cost adjustments. It also implies adjusting measures obtained from econometric models for the impact, if any, of changes in quasi-fixed factors. An advantage of the sector-wide econometric models of total agriculture over their individual-commodity counterparts is that at the sector level (say provincial, state, or national agriculture as a whole), quasi-fixed factors may reasonably be regarded as fixed.[36] In individual-commodity studies, a significant component of the supply response to research might be a reflection of changes in intensity of land use, which might lead to an overstatement of research benefits unless an appropriate adjustment is made for the opportunity cost of land. In a sectorwide model, it is necessary to account for the effects of research program alternatives that involve shifting several individual-commodity supply curves simultaneously.

5.3.2   Practical Measurement

As noted above, the key piece of information for any research evaluation study is the per unit cost reduction that has resulted from research or that is anticipated if the research is successful and the resulting technologies are adopted. A number of options are available for estimating K, depending on the purpose of the analysis data available, and the overall methodological approach being applied in the study.

In ex post studies, the cost and impact of the research can be known and measured, at least conceptually; in ex ante studies, they can neither be known nor measured. In either case, we must make an estimate that will be subject to error, but in the case of the ex ante studies, we know much less about the statistical distribution of the estimation errors. Unlike ex post studies, in ex ante studies we don't know whether the research will be successful; we must estimate the odds of success. We must draw on people's subjective estimates (either as individuals or in some type of consensus approach), both of the costs of a research program and of a number of the components of the corresponding K-factor: the probability that research will be successful, the likely impact on productivity if the research is successful and the results are adopted, and the likely time path of adoption (replicated by region when a geographically disaggregated analysis is being undertaken).

---

36.   Offsetting this "advantage" is the fact that the resulting estimate of the aggregate K is a weighted average of the individual Ks across individual commodities. This will be inappropriate for any particular commodity when the individual Ks vary much among commodities.

Research Costs

Information is required on research costs, both for relating the calculated research benefits to their corresponding costs and for developing a benchmark of the size of the research program for scientists responding to questions about expected yield changes, probabilities of research success, and so on.[37] Historical data on research costs are necessary for ex post analyses and are useful for establishing a benchmark for ex ante studies. For many developing and developed countries alike, cost data are seldom broken down by commodity and research program. Hence, it can be useful to use information on numbers of scientists working in different programs (or, more appropriately, their full-time equivalents) to assist in apportioning the costs. Administrative costs must also be spread across programs (see chapter 3 and appendix A5.4 for details).

The evaluation exercise requires a statement of total research costs for each program alternative to be evaluated. At the outset, it is usually appropriate to define a benchmark of the current research effort in terms of the total resources being invested, the composition of those resources — capital (buildings and equipment), personnel (disaggregated between nonscientists and different types of scientists), and operating expenditures, as well as their deployment among current programs. This information can be obtained either (a) from "central administration" files, reports, and other documents or (b) by asking scientists or administrators for information on the current scientific staffing and costs for each research program. Discrepancies from these alternative approaches to gathering data on the current research effort are likely to be evident in the results, and it may help to combine the two. The advantage of the second approach is that the costs reported by scientists are based on their recent experiences.[38]

The benchmark value for each research program can be used as a base for the analysis when information is elicited from scientists about expected research results. The base can be varied (perhaps 10% higher or lower) to

---

37.   When an extension component is explicitly involved as part of the research program, its costs must also be measured. The inclusion of this aspect can have implications for the benchmarking of research impacts, especially as extension would be expected to affect the adoption process. In addition, it may be appropriate to scale the research program costs upwards to reflect a measure of the full social opportunity cost of government funds (e.g., as discussed by Fox 1985 and Dalrymple 1990 and done by Alston and Mullen 1992). Care should be exercised to ensure that results from different studies are consistent in their treatment of this issue.

38.   A third approach can be used in which research costs are ignored initially, a particular percentage (or set of percentages) reduction in production costs due to research is assumed, and then scientists are asked what it would cost to arrive at that percentage reduction (Davis, Oram and Ryan 1987). This has implications for the probabilities of success, research lags, and so on that are relevant. Various approaches to incorporating costs can be used, but the choice will influence subsequent steps in the analysis.

elicit information on expected results for different total research investments.[39] Another plausible alternative to evaluate might concern the redeployment of existing resources within a current program — i.e., changing the spatial orientation of the program, changing the problem orientation of the program (e.g., in relation to genetic improvement, agronomy, or pest and disease control), or changing the ratio of scientists to support staff.

One way to help scientists provide meaningful information is to ask them what would be possible if resources were "entirely unlimited." Scobie and Jacobsen (1992) asked scientists two questions: First, how much total scientific resources could be spent productively on a given research program? Second, given that amount, how would you spend it and what would be the expected outcome? As well as providing an observation of the maximum point of the research production function attainable in the short to medium run, this approach provides a fixed reference point against which to define what is possible with more realistic levels of resources — our primary concern. In this way, information is provided on the scientists' view of diminishing returns in the research production function.

Econometric Measures of Research-Induced Supply Shifts

Ex post evaluation studies using econometric approaches (as described in chapter 3) will, as a matter of course, yield parameter estimates that either directly represent the research-induced supply shift (when supply functions are estimated directly) or that can be translated into a measure of the research-induced supply shift (when a production function, cost function, or profit function is estimated with research as an argument or when index-number methods are used to derive a measure of productivity growth).

Directly estimated supply functions: A number of studies have estimated commodity supply functions directly, with past expenditures on agricultural research and extension included as arguments.[40] In these studies the lag relationships between research and adoption are estimated jointly as part of the supply response to research. Thus, it is possible to use the estimated supply function and deduce (or simulate) an entire time path of research-induced supply shifts associated either with the total research investment or with marginal changes in it. For example, suppose the supply function for commodity j was estimated as follows:

---

39. Scientists might not appreciate the possible impact of a 10% reduction in *total* budget. Often a higher percentage change in operating costs (say 30% to 50%, perhaps implying a 5% to 10% change in total costs) is used in this elicitation instead, in order to get scientists' attention and to obtain a meaningful response from them about the implied change in research productivity.

40. Examples include Otto (1981) and Zachariah, Fox and Brinkman (1989).

$$Q_{j,t} = \alpha_j + \beta_j \, P_{j,t} + \sum_{r=0}^{\infty} \delta_{jr} \, R_{t-r} \tag{5.4}$$

where in year t, $Q_{j,t}$ and $P_{j,t}$ are the quantity and price of commodity j and R_{t-r} is expenditure on research in year r-years past.[41] Then, assuming the past effects of research carry forward into the future, the future time path of proportional reductions in the marginal cost of the commodity (i.e., shifts down in supply relative to the commodity price) for a one-shot marginal change in research spending (say \$1) in the current year, t, could be projected as

$$\hat{K}_{j,t+r} = \hat{\delta}_{jr} / (\hat{\beta}_j \, \hat{P}_{j,t+r}) \quad \text{for} \quad r = 0, \dots, L_R \tag{5.5a}$$

where the "hats" denote projected values of variables and estimated values of parameters.

Alternatively, the model could be used to simulate the impact of a permanent change in funding that would involve summing across research-lag weights for the relevant years in which research had changed. For instance, to simulate the effect in the current year of research being reduced by \$1 in *all* past years, the corresponding estimate of $K_{j,t}$ would be

$$\hat{K}_{j,t} = \sum_{r=1}^{L_R} \hat{\delta}_{jr} / (\hat{\beta}_j \, P_{j,t}) \tag{5.5b}$$

Either equation 5.5a or 5.5b could be used to generate a stream of estimated values of K to be used in an economic surplus model for evaluating research. In each case, the directly estimated supply shift reflects the combined effects of adoption and of supply shifts for those who adopted. The difference between the two is in the counterfactual experiment being carried out: a temporary or a permanent change in research funding by \$1 per year.

Production functions: For estimating aggregated rates of return for agricultural research as a whole, a more common approach has been to estimate a production function, or productivity function, in which past expenditures on research (and extension) are included as arguments.[42] In these studies, the research and adoption lag relationships are estimated jointly as part of the output response to research. Thus, it is possible to use the estimated production function and deduce (or simulate) an entire time path of research-induced supply shifts (reflecting either input savings for a given output or additional

---

41. This is similar to the corresponding model developed in chapter 3, but it is different in that (a) the "other" supply-shift variables are suppressed here for simplicity (subsumed in α_j) and (b) the research variables have not been preaggregated.

42. Examples include Griliches (1963a, 1964), Bredahl and Peterson (1976), Evenson (1967), and Scobie and Eveleens (1987).

output due to research) associated with either the total research investment or marginal changes in it. For example, suppose the production function for commodity j was estimated, using a Cobb-Douglas model, as

$$\ln Q_{j,t} = \alpha_j + \beta_j \ln X_{j,t} + \sum_{r=1}^{L_R} \delta_{jr} R_{t-r} \qquad (5.6)$$

Then, in terms of percentage change, the time path of changes in output (or productivity) for a one-shot marginal change in research spending (say \$1) in the current year, t, would be projected as $J_{j,t+r} = \delta_{jr}$.[43] This could be translated into a shift down in the price direction by dividing by the supply elasticity: $K_{j,t+r} = \delta_{jr}/\varepsilon_j$.[44] It is important to be aware that, as discussed above (in relation to figure 5.1), this measure represents a supply shift only under restrictive conditions that might not be satisfied at the industry level (and assuming that the future mirrors the past).[45]

Cost and profit functions: Modern duality-based specifications of systems of equations representing output supply and factor demand permit the joint estimation of research impacts in multiple dimensions. There have been a small number of studies that have taken this type of approach to measure the size and bias of technical changes (e.g., Lopez 1980; Ray 1982; Ball and Chambers 1982; Zhang et al. 1993), but they have usually included one or more time-trend variables and have not included explicit research variables. One exception is Huffman and Evenson (1989), who estimated a multi-output profit-function system, representing aggregate U.S. production of crops and livestock products on cash-grain farms and incorporating a range of research and extension variables. As with the supply or production-function models mentioned above, the parameters from the profit (or cost) function can be translated into measures of a research-induced supply shift.

Productivity functions: A common alternative approach is to calculate a measure of productivity (or productivity growth) using index-number procedures. Econometric models can be applied to estimate the relationship between productivity and past research (and extension) investments, among other

---

43. If $\ln R$ were used instead of R in equation 5.6 (a more typical approach in the Cobb-Douglas model), then δ_{jr} would measure the percentage change in output for a *one-percent* change rather than a unit change in research expenditure.

44. An equivalent approach, in many respects, has been to calculate the productivity growth attributable to research using index-number procedures or assumptions about technology and to regress those estimates against distributed lags of research and extension expenditures. The results from those studies could be translated into supply shifts as was done here. See chapter 3 for further details.

45. The critical assumptions are (a) exogenous prices of "variable" factors (i.e., there are no variable factors at the firm level that are specialized at the industry level) and (b) exogenous quantities of "fixed" factors (i.e., there are no allocatable fixed factors).

things. The econometric estimates can be used to deduce values for K to be used to estimate streams of research benefits (chapter 3 provides details).

In a recent article, Cooke and Sundquist (1993) proposed a procedure for measuring the "K-shift" in the supply function when new technology is introduced. They illustrated their procedure in an application measuring benefits from growth in U.S. soybean productivity. Their approach involves several critical explicit or implicit assumptions. In particular, it seems that their approach may be valid only under an assumption of constant returns to scale, and it might require an additional assumption that average and marginal costs are equal, which would imply a horizontal supply curve.

The K-shift is defined by Cooke and Sundquist (1993) — drawing upon Lindner and Jarrett (1978), Rose (1980), Edwards and Freebairn (1984), and by implication, Mishan (1972) — as being equal to both (a) the proportionate reduction in average cost of production excluding rent, relative to initial average cost excluding rent, and (b) the proportionate shift down in the equilibrium supply curve (i.e., marginal cost), relative to the inital price (or marginal cost). This would seem to be equivalent to assuming that marginal and average costs are equal both before and after the supply shift. Cooke and Sundquist (1993) illustrate the problem of not being able to observe this K shift, the research-induced change in costs, directly. They propose to measure it indirectly by first measuring an index of total factor productivity growth and then deriving a cost-efficiency index from that. This second step uses theory that relates an index of total factor productivity growth to an index of cost efficiency.

Cooke and Sundquist (1993, p. 173) argue that "a Fisher cost efficiency index approximately equals the inverse of a Törnqvist total factor productivity index (Diewert, 1976, p. 124). Both indexes are 'superlative' in that they reflect second-order approximations of nonhomothetic production and unit-cost functions, respectively. Therefore, K_a or the proportionate reduction in average cost excluding rent is approximately equal to one minus the inverse of the Törnqvist index of total factor productivity." Thus the proportional reduction in average cost excluding rent (i.e., K) is measured by the proportional growth in total factor productivity. This seems to be remarkably simple and easy.

Cooke and Sundquist do not discuss any restrictions on the production technology that are needed to make this measure valid. In chapter 3 we suggested that under the assumption of constant returns to scale — in addition to the assumptions of input-output separability, efficient and optimizing producers, and disembodied technical change of the extended Hicks-neutral type — the rate of change of total factor productivity (TFP) given by equation 3.29 would be equal to both the primal rate of technological change (or the shift of the production function) and the rate of dual technological change (or the change in cost of production). Similar assumptions are likely to be required for validity in the Cooke and Sundquist approach, notwith-standing their explicit suggestion, quoted above, that their approach would apply to nonhomothetic technologies.

There are even more fundamental problems in using proportional changes in measured TFP as estimates of K-shifts that in turn are used to measure benefits attributed to R&D. As we also discussed in some detail in chapter 3, measured growth in TFP occurs for a good many reasons in addition to agricultural R&D or, more particularly, public-sector R&D. Some of the additional sources of growth in measured TFP include mismeasured or unmeasured improvements in the quality of inputs, such as land and labor, through the provision of irrigation, communication, and education services and the acquisition of these services by individuals, firms, and governments; unrecorded quality improvements in seeds, machinery, and agricultural chemicals due to private R&D; and economies of scale. Simply attributing all of this productivity growth to R&D will surely overstate the implied benefits from public-sector research and in some cases seriously so.

Experiment and Industry Data

Experiment data: Experiment data take several forms. A major distinc-tion in kinds of experiment data is between the results from long-term trials over many years (say, monitoring crop yields with old and new varieties) and the results from one-shot or short-term studies (e.g., studies of particular cultural aspects, fertilizer trials, or specific varietal comparisons). The latter often allow an investigation of crop performance at a number of locations, whereas the former allow an investigation over time.

Data from long-term trials allow response functions to be estimated for the specific alternatives included under a range of weather conditions; data from one-shot multilocational trials allow paired comparisons of response functions under a range of agroecological conditions. Thus, the different types of experiment data provide different types of information about differ-ent types of research questions. Of course neither long-term trial data nor one-shot multilocational trial data are perfect because, for research evalua-tion, we want to control for both site effects (i.e., over space) and weather (over time). Distinguishing the effects of uncontrolled factors is sometimes difficult with either type of experiment.

Ex post studies[46] might use experiment data and information on adoption rates and so on to deduce the pattern of past supply shifts attributable to a

---

46. Experimental yields have been used in ex post analysis as a proxy for industry yields or supply shifts in a number of more recent studies. Examples are provided by Echeverría, Ferreira and Dabezies (1989), Pardey et al. (1992), and Palomino and Norton (1992b).

particular set of technological changes (e.g., Griliches 1957b). In ex ante studies, too, it is necessary to integrate information about the per unit cost saving for those who adopt the technology with information on the time pattern of adoption — often, in both cases, information that involves people's subjective judgments. For ex post work, results of on-farm yield trials and other experiment data for key types of research are essential for estimating per unit cost reductions or yield changes for farmers who adopted. For ex ante analysis, this information is also useful as background information for the scientists who are being asked to project future cost or yield changes.[47]

It is not always easy to translate increases in experimental yields into industry-level cost savings — even when we put aside the questions of adoption responses. Experimental yields are typically higher than commercial yields (the so-called "yield-gap" phenomenon) and gains in experimental yields often exceed gains experienced on farms.[48] But the sizes of these differences vary among places and technologies, and it is difficult to make empirical generalizations. There is some basis for scaling down experimental yield *gains* to better reflect likely on-farm *gains* — but it would probably be an overcorrection to scale down the gains in proportion to the difference between research-station yields and on-farm yields.

In addition to differences between experimental and farm responses, and differences between individual farm and industry supply responses (discussed above), there are issues arising from the factor bias of the technical change interacting with factor cost shares, elasticities of factor substitution, and elasticities of factor supply. Appendix A5.3 examines the relationships between the industry (final product) supply shift, experimental yields, and changes in industry yields for different types of technical changes. The relative increase in experimental yield, Y, will translate into an equal, proportional, rightwards shift of industry supply in the quantity direction (i.e., $dY/Y = E(Y) = J$) under a neutral technical change with fixed factor proportions. To translate this into a measure of K (the percentage shift down of supply in the *price* direction), we divide by the elasticity of supply: i.e., $K = J/\varepsilon = E(Y)/\varepsilon$. If the technical change is not neutral (i.e., there is some factor bias, as is most likely) or if the factor proportions are not fixed (i.e., some factor substitution is possible, as is most

---

47. In many cases a detailed record of the results of an experiment is not available, and occasionally even summary statistics on experiments are not kept. In such cases there may be no more information available than average gains in experimental yields, perhaps only at one location. However, in some cases useful records have been maintained and it can be possible to develop measures of the site-specific effects of new technologies on the average outcome as well as the variability of outcomes.

48. For additional discussion, see Swanson (1957), Johnson (1957), Davidson and Martin (1965), and Davidson, Martin and Mauldon (1967). Scobie and Posada (1977, 1978) dealt appropriately with this issue when attempting to estimate returns to research on improving rice varieties in Colombia.

likely) then experimental yields will not translate so simply into industry supply shifts. The value for the industry supply-response elasticity, ε, is a critical factor in converting an experimental yield into an industry-level, per unit, cost saving. When actual or hypothetical experimental yields are being used to deduce values for K and information on supply elasticities is lacking, it is often expedient to use a supply elasticity of 1.0.[49]

Industry data: Historical data on yields over time and in different locations are often more readily available and more complete than experiment data. These may be analyzed informally or using statistical techniques. Yields may have changed over time for a host of reasons in addition to the research-induced technical changes of specific interest. These reasons can include secular productivity gains arising from other research carried out locally, including private-sector research, or as a spill-in effect. They can also include the transitory effects of weather variations and of pest and disease factors. A careless use of statistical methods could be misleading. With appropriate care in model specification and interpretation of the results, best done in consultation with relevant scientists, the historical record can be very informative for providing a benchmark for current situations and potential future changes. Such data are particularly useful when combined with, and juxtaposed against, experimental data (e.g., Pardey et al. 1992; Constantine, Alston and Smith 1995).

Eliciting K from Scientists

In some cases, a commodity enterprise budget can be developed with old and new technologies. The proportionate cost reduction can then be based on this information. More often, for priority-setting work, researchers are asked to project the percentage yield increase (or, in some cases, cost reduction) as a "best-guess" estimate.[50] If scientists provide estimates of yield changes resulting from new technologies (as opposed to per unit cost reductions), they should be asked about changes in input requirements so that changes in input costs can be netted out in translating yield changes into cost changes. The effects of research expenditures on per unit costs or yields are unlikely to be in constant proportion, independent of the scale of expenditure, and research on some commodities is more expensive than on others. Thus, scientists can be asked about the effects of research at two or three levels of funding or staffing.

49.   When using J/ε to estimate K, clearly the value of the supply elasticity is critical. For instance a supply elasticity of 0.1 would imply a value for K 10 times the value of J and 10 times the value implied by a supply elasticity of 1.0, or one-hundredth that implied by a supply elasticity of 10. Thus, a 10% yield increase could be translated into a 100% cost saving or a 1% cost saving, depending on whether the supply elasticity is assumed to be 0.1 or 10.

50.   Scientists usually find cost changes much more difficult to estimate than yield changes. Hence, their cost estimates tend to be less precise than their yield estimates.

This estimation (or elicitation) process is not simply a matter of asking scientists to provide a number to be used as a value for K for each program. Deducing a value for K (or, more appropriately, a distribution of K^{MAX}) from what scientists know involves combining various pieces of information intelligently in a structured fashion. Consider the example of a research program for a particular crop. In order to elicit a meaningful value of K (and spillover effects) for a given program of expenditure, it is necessary (a) to look in some detail at the individual impacts of components of that program of expenditure (e.g., plant breeding versus agronomy versus pest control work), (b) to consider the substitution or complementary relationships among the components of the research program, and (c) to obtain a clear picture of the relevant alternatives (e.g., what would happen to yields in the absence of the research).[51]

Research program components: The different components of a research program are likely to have different potential effects on yield, creating a possibility for aggregation bias. But apart from the potential for aggregation bias, there is another reason for considering their disaggregated effects. Some scientists may not be able to give a sensible estimate of an entire program's impact on yield, even when they have very good information about its individual components. Further, different scientists know about different components, and different program components can yield very different time profiles for cost savings. For example, research lags and the rate of uptake both differ between, say, developing a new, disease-resistant variety and developing new fertilizer recommendations. Eliciting information on the individual components jointly with information on their aggregate effects provides a check on the consistency of the estimates. Such information can also allow a structured assessment of intraprogram allocations of resources to research.

In all such work, it is necessary to be clear about what is being held constant, something that becomes potentially more serious when disaggregated components are being dealt with.[52] Even if disaggregated information

---

51. Even within relatively narrow "fields" of research there can be significant diversity and associated aggregation questions. For instance, plant breeders have many objectives in breeding new cultivars, including improving yield potential, pest and disease resistance, tolerance of adverse environmental conditions (e.g., cold and drought), and a number of different grain characteristics that interact to determine "quality." Apart from the determinants of quality, many other genotypic characteristics have their main expression through yield. Therefore yield is an extremely useful summary statistic, which reflects a diversity of objectives pursued by researchers. But yield changes may not reflect all the cost changes associated with the adoption of new technologies. Traxler and Byerlee (1993) show the economic trade-offs involved in the effects of grain yield versus straw in modern, semidwarf wheat varieties. See also Byerlee, Igbal and Fisher (1989).

52. This disaggregation could be taken beyond the point where it is useful. As the degree of disaggregation increases, the potential interactions among disaggregated components and the difficulties of obtaining meaningful estimates can quickly become overwhelming.

is not collected formally (say on the individual components of a research program or in relation to different agroecological zones) and it is decided to estimate an *aggregate* supply response directly for a given program of research, it can be very useful to talk through these points first with the scientists and to have some relevant past data at hand.

Aggregation, substitution, and complementarity: Estimates of the yield-enhancing impact of individual components of the research program can be added together so long as they can be regarded as independent. More often than not, they will not be independent. For instance, high-yielding "green-revolution" varieties were relatively responsive to new crop management and fertilizer regimes, so there was a complementarity between research on variety improvement and management. And the joint impact of the components of the technological package was greater than the simple sum. On the other hand, a new high-yielding variety will preclude the adoption in a particular selection of an alternative disease-resistant variety, and in this context the total potential effect of the research program will be less than the sum of the potential effects of its individual components. The problem of double counting mutually exclusive technologies is likely to be more pronounced with programs that involve multiple institutions or multiple research sites conducting similar lines of research designed to produce technologies that can be adopted in the same places. These positive and negative interactions may be accounted for by drawing the different scientists together and eliciting their views on the combined effects of the entire set of program components.[53] These considerations are also directly relevant to the notions of maintenance research and research spillovers discussed below.

Maintenance research and benchmarks: When scientists' projections of the yield impact of research are being elicited, it is essential to be clear about the reference point. At a minimum we want two sets of projections: one in the absence of the research program being evaluated and the other if the research program is successful and fully adopted. From this perspective, there is no meaningful distinction to be drawn between maintenance research and any other type of research.[54] All research in this context is directed toward increasing yield *relative to what it would have been otherwise*. Unless scientists are questioned carefully, they are only likely to give estimates of changes relative to current yields. But differences between current yields and future yields (without research) might reflect perceptions of a decline due to deterioration or

---

53. Of course, if detailed data were available on the yield effects of each component, and corresponding specific adoption rates, the potential for double counting innovations could be avoided in a much more explicit way.

54. Maintenance research is typically defined as the research required to maintain the status quo in terms of yields or costs of production per unit of output.

obsolescence, or a gain due to other innovations, that must be distinguished from future yield changes due to the research program of interest. One way to develop benchmark yield projections is to project historical time-series data forward statistically as a basis for discussion (see the discussion in this section on industry and experiment data). This could be done with spatially disaggregated data when there are significantly different yield trends (or differences in anticipated yield response) among agroecological zones. Where it is believed there will be significant differences in yield response to research among zones, a disaggregated treatment of zones in the elicitation process may reduce spatial aggregation biases.

Local and spillover effects in an international setting: In a multinational market model, in the context of a NARS evaluation study, the supply-and-demand functions for other countries must be projected for a baseline simulation. Again, ceteris paribus issues arise: what is being held constant when those projections are being made, and is there potential for double counting? For instance, a projection from the historical trends in wheat yields in Australia would be based on past yield growth that was driven in considerable part by technology spillovers from CIMMYT (Brennan 1986). The analyst modeling the effects of future CIMMYT wheat research might want to project Australia's wheat production in the absence of CIMMYT research, and the gross historical pattern may provide little guidance. Where spillovers are likely to be important in the future, they are likely to have been important in the past, and vice versa.

Spillover effects are difficult enough to analyze when research results that are embodied in technologies (e.g., new machinery, production practices, or crop varieties) are being examined. Further difficulties arise when research results themselves are being transferred. For example, a new crop variety could be used directly by farmers, but it might, instead, be used as an input into an ongoing breeding program to produce further new varieties. Measuring the potential spillover effects is a greater challenge in the latter case than in the former.

Some studies have attempted to explicitly forecast own-country research effects while *simultaneously* allowing for the adoption of research results from other countries. In such work asking scientists to make forecasts they might be unqualified to make, or using rules of thumb related to spillover potentials, introduces a real potential for double counting (Pardey and Wood 1994). With a number of countries involved in such a model, all generating technologies that can spill over internationally, there is a greater potential for double counting research results than in the more common approach where only one country's R&D is explicitly included, albeit perhaps with multi-country impact.

Multicountry studies might involve an analysis of the global or regional (e.g., west African or southeast Asian) consequences of research done by individual countries within the region, or they might focus on a country of interest, taking its multicountry context into account. The regional consequences of research will not be equal to the sum of the effects across countries within the region unless care is taken to define the individual country measures so that they are mutually consistent (i.e., to avoid double counting or other mismeasurement of spillover effects).

International research spillovers are important for both multicountry studies of the effects of research from a multinational perspective (a perspective that we are not taking in this chapter) and for country-specific studies (the perspective we have adopted here), where research and technology spillovers in both directions can modify the domestic effects of the research undertaken by the country of interest. In either kind of study, it is important to be clear about which of these perspectives is being adopted before deciding what types of information to collect for analysis. Also, as in any economic analysis, it is important to be clear about what is being held constant and what is being allowed to vary between any pair of alternatives that are being compared. When one country's research is being evaluated in the context of a multicountry model with international price and technology spillovers, such ceteris paribus considerations assume particular importance. Explicit decisions must be made about whether research by other countries will be held constant at a baseline (with corresponding baseline spill-ins to the country of interest), held constant at zero (with zero spill-ins), or allowed to vary *in response to* research by the country of interest. Different choices here may involve eliciting different information for the analysis. Vagueness here may mean that the elicited information does not correspond to the information required for the particular analysis that is eventually carried out.

Further questions arise concerning whether effects are additive or mutually exclusive. Consider, for example, a situation in which *all* countries directly experience an increase in productivity from locally conducted research. If spillovers among all countries are presumed to be additional to their own research effects (i.e., country i can simultaneously adopt, *to some extent*, all technologies developed everywhere else), then

$$K_i^{MAX} = \theta_{i1}\, K_{1,1}^{MAX} + \ldots + \theta_{ii}\, K_{i,i}^{MAX} + \ldots + \theta_{in}\, K_{n,n}^{MAX} \tag{5.7}$$

where $K_{j,j}^{MAX}$ represents the maximum attainable local effect of country or region j's research and the θ_{ij} coefficients are multipliers that reflect the confluence of factors determining $K_{i,j}^{MAX}$, the maximum potential impact of country j's research on supply in country i, given $K_{j,j}^{MAX}$, so that $K_{i,j}^{MAX} =$

$\theta_{ij} \, K_{j,j}^{MAX}$.[55] With this formulation, the θ_{ij} coefficients represent the cross-country or interregional "transferability" of research results to the extent that they reflect the maximum potential shift in supply when using region j technologies in region i *relative* to the local impact of region j technologies. Letting $\theta_{ii} = 1$, equation 5.7 simplifies to

$$K_i^{MAX} = K_{i,i}^{MAX} + \sum_{\substack{j \neq i}}^{n} \theta_{ij} \, K_{j,j}^{MAX} \qquad (5.8)$$

However, a more plausible specification would adjust for the likelihood that some imported and domestic technologies are mutually exclusive (e.g., it is not possible to simultaneously adopt high-yielding domestic and foreign varieties on all hectares). In other words, we must account for differences between *potential* spillovers given by 5.7, and *actual* spillovers, allowing for crowding-out effects. Avoiding the problems of double counting requires additional information about the local rate of uptake of these various new technologies. Introducing adoption parameters into equation 5.8 gives

$$K_{i,t} = A_{i,i,t} \, K_{i,i}^{MAX} + \sum_{\substack{j \neq i}}^{n} A_{i,j,t} \, \theta_{ij} \, K_{j,j}^{MAX} \qquad (5.9)$$

where $A_{i,i,t}$ is the local (i.e., region i) rate of uptake of locally produced technologies in period t, $A_{i,j,t}$ is the period t rate of adoption in region i of technologies developed in region j, and $K_{i,t}$ is the overall supply-shifting effect of local and nonlocal technologies in period t.[56]

Obtaining plausible estimates of the $n \, (2 + t)$ values for the $A_{i,j,t}$, θ_{ij}, and $K_{j,j}^{MAX}$ parameters required to estimate the $K_{i,t}$s is clearly a tall order. It is asking a lot (if not too much) of scientists and others to have meaningful views on the supply-shifting effects of both local *and* spill-in technologies that have yet to be developed, as well as the likely rate of uptake of these new technologies. It may be reasonable to seek opinions about the local effects of local research from scientists familiar with or likely to carry out the research. However, it is unreasonable to expect them to have enough knowledge of the current or planned research being done in other countries to be able to give plausible and highly disaggregated estimates of the spill-in potential of

55. Thus $\theta_{ij} = K_{i,j}^{MAX}/K_{j,j}^{MAX}$. The θ_{ij}s usually range between 0 and 1 but may be greater than one if the research results are better suited to the region into which the research spills (i.e., region i) than the region where it was done (i.e., region j). One of the difficulties with this approach is that simply by disaggregating the world further, one can obtain bigger effects (e.g., by adding up a greater number of mutually exclusive technologies). This leads to the implication that, when in doubt, there might be "gains from aggregation" in terms of reducing the rest of the world to a single aggregate.

56. As elaborated below, to avoid double counting benefits, the $A_{i,i,t}$s and $A_{i,j,t}$s must be defined appropriately so that the adoptions are mutually exclusive when that is appropriate.

technologies. At best, they may have some relevant knowledge about specific research being done in selected countries. Consequently, they may only be able to provide broad indications of the *aggregate* spill-in potential of research, based on past experience and a limited knowledge of related work being done by researchers in other locales.

In the face of these constraints, there are few options here to reduce the information required to estimate the $K_{i,t}$s. One approach is to presume, in the absence of compelling evidence to the contrary, that the rates of local uptake of all nonlocal technologies are roughly equal (i.e., $A_{i,j,t} \approx A_{i,t}^*$ for all $j \neq i$) so that

$$K_{i,t} \approx A_{i,i,t} K_{i,i}^{MAX} + A_{i,t}^* \sum_{\substack{j \neq i}}^{n} \theta_{ij} K_{j,j}^{MAX} \tag{5.10}$$

With this assumption, it is possible to preaggregate (or, more usually, form an estimate of) the local supply-shifting effects of all imported or spill-in technologies, (i.e., to estimate the overall spill-in effects, $\sum_{j \neq i} \theta_{ij} K_{j,j}^{MAX}$), scale this aggregate by $A_{i,t}^*$, and add it to the local impact of locally produced research to estimate the overall supply-shifting effects of research. A further simplification is to assume identical lag structures for all technologies, irrespective of their source, so that

$$K_{i,t} \approx A_{i,i,t} \theta_{ii} K_{i,i}^{MAX} + A_{i,i,t} \sum_{\substack{j \neq i}}^{n} \theta_{ij} K_{i,j}^{MAX}$$
$$= A_{i,i,t} \sum_{j=1}^{n} \theta_{ij} K_{i,j}^{MAX} \tag{5.11}$$

Clearly, adopting assumptions or rules of thumb along the lines used to form equations 5.10 and 5.11 is a recipe for double counting.[57] These procedures pay no regard to the types of technology being developed at each site and presume that the local impact of all these technologies are additive. In many cases this is an unrealistic assumption to make. If two countries develop new crop varieties, it is inappropriate to think of the combined supply-shifting effect of the two technologies to be a simple sum of their separate effects in a given locale. If any rule of thumb were to be applied, it might be more reasonable to

---

57. Davis, Oram and Ryan (1987) and Ryan and Davis (1990) used similar variants of these simplifying assumptions concerning the adoption aspects of local and spill-in technologies. Davis, Oram and Ryan appear to have assumed that the ceiling levels of adoption for local and all spill-in technologies were equal, while Ryan and Davis (p. 11) varied these ceilings in unspecified ways based on considerations of "rural infrastructure such as roads, fertilizer consumption, and so on." In both studies, the shapes of the local and spill-in adoption profiles were equal while the "mean adoption lag" for all spill-in technologies was taken to be 12 years, one year longer than the corresponding lag for local technologies.

assume that there are negligible spill-ins of nonlocal varieties (i.e., $A_{i,j,t} \approx 0$ for all $j \neq i$) on the presumption that locally produced varieties (for local conditions) will generally outperform varieties transferred from elsewhere. But even this presumption has been questioned recently regarding the international transferability of CIMMYT wheat varieties that are apparently widely adaptable (Maredia 1993; Traxler and Byerlee 1994).

In reality, farmers in a particular country or region within a country often use a mix of locally and nonlocally developed varieties at any point in time. This is partly because varieties do not generally perform uniformly well within the spatial aggregates commonly used for evaluation purposes, so wtihin a given area, different varieties will find different niches in which they perform best. In any event, it is simply not enough to know the local supply-shifting effects of local and spill-in technologies to form an estimate of $K_{i,t}$. Some notion of the types of technologies under development will help identify whether the technologies are potentially "complementary" (e.g., locally developed management practices and spill-in varietal technologies) or potentially "substitutable" (e.g., competing varietal technologies). If they are complementary, they may well have somewhat similar patterns of adoption, but if they are potential substitutes, for instance, they may have dissimilar, and indeed polar, patterns of adoption. So to estimate $K_{i,t}$ requires knowledge of both the relevant values of $K_{i,j}^{MAX}$ and the corresponding $A_{i,j,t}$.

In addition to the problems of translating potential effects into actual or realized effects (i.e., translating $K_{i,j}^{MAX}$ to $K_{i,t}$), there is the problem of estimating the values of $K_{i,j}^{MAX}$ themselves. Rather than directly eliciting or estimating the values of $K_{i,j}^{MAX}$ (the maximum attainable supply-shifting effect of region j technology in region i), an alternative and commonly used option is to jointly estimate the domestic impact of region j technology (i.e., $K_{j,j}^{MAX}$) with the performance of region j technology in region i *relative* to its performance in region j (i.e., θ_{ij}). A consideration of the agroecological basis for variation in the spatial performance of past or potential technologies is helpful in forming these estimates. Ongoing developments in geographical information system (GIS) (in conjunction with elicitation techniques, crop simulation models, and so forth) will yield more structured and, it is hoped, more realistic estimates of the $K_{i,j}^{MAX}$ and θ_{ij} parameters. These approaches reflect the influence of variations in agroecological conditions on the performance of many agricultural technologies. The potential yield superiority of a new crop variety is likely to vary less across areas that have similar edaphic, terrain, and climatic characteristics than across dissimilar agroecological zones (AEZs).

Using GIS procedures to overlay AEZs on geopolitical regions and existing production areas makes it possible to develop more refined estimates of the values of $K_{i,j}$ by disaggregating *region i* into a series of agroecological *zones*.

Using this approach, $J_{i,j,z}^{MAX}$ (the output- or yield-enhancing response in zone z of region i to region j's research) can be obtained and then summed across the relevant agroecological zones to form an estimate $J_{i,j}^{MAX}$ so that

$$J_{i,j}^{MAX} = \sum_z (Q_{i,z}^0/Q_i^0) \, J_{i,j,z}^{MAX} \tag{5.12}$$

where $Q_{i,z}^0$ is the preresearch output in the zth zone of the ith region and Q_i^0 is the preresearch output in region i. Because supply curves are aggregated horizontally, the aggregate supply-shift effect is formed by horizontally summing across values for $J_{i,j,z}$ (the research-induced shift in output quantities holding output price constant), rather than using output shares as weights to vertically sum the cost-saving effects of research (i.e., the corresponding values of $K_{i,j,z}$ s). This approach can improve the precision of the estimates of $K_{i,j}^{MAX}$ when there is substantial spatial variation in the effects of research because of agroecological diversity; it also provides information on the trade-offs involved when research is targeted to different zones within a region.[58]

Local and spillover effects in a domestic setting: Similar problems can arise in within-country applications when research programs involve multiple institutions or multiple sites within institutions. In order to minimize the potential for double counting, and in acknowledgement of the site-specific nature of many research results in which locally developed technologies locally dominate technologies developed elsewhere, Wood and Pardey (1993) suggest assuming no *within-country* spillovers between those locales where a national research program is simultaneously developing new technologies. Of course, when there is information to the contrary (such as where one site specializes in plant breeding and another in agronomy), the potential for spillovers should not be ruled out.

Two options are (a) to conduct a spatially disaggregated analysis within a country, which may involve an explicit treatment of within-country spillovers or (b) to preaggregate zones into the market aggregates to be used to evaluate the supply-shifting effects of research, obviating the need to measure spillovers. The latter approach runs a risk of aggregation bias but reduces the cost of information gathering in the process.[59]

58. Similar spatial aggregation techniques can be used to improve the estimates of the regional adoption parameters. In this case the basic area of analysis is defined in terms of uniformity with regard to adoption potential (in contrast to the agroecological zones used to partition regions into areas that have uniform supply-shifting potential).

59. The horizontal shift in an aggregate supply function (representing the sum of a number of competitive supply functions) is equal to the sum of the shifts of the individual curves in the quantity direction. This implies an approach to aggregation and to choosing weights for the aggregation — i.e., according to regional shares of preresearch output.

In the above model of spillovers in an international setting, the time profile of adoption of all the research results emanating from one region is commonly restricted to being equal among all regions. A more flexible approach would use separate parameters to measure the maximum spillover and the time profile of spillovers. As we discussed above, suitable information to support such disaggregation is unlikely to be available for any commodity research programs in an international setting, but it may be available for some commodities in a disaggregated domestic setting. The most sophisticated analysis would disaggregate regionally within a country and measure the own-region effects and spillover effects in each region, properly allowing for different time profiles of adoption of own-research results and spill-in research results among the regions and allowing these parameters to vary among research programs. But the information requirements for such highly disaggregated studies are great, and simplifying assumptions are inevitable. It is incumbent on the analyst to make sensible simplifications and to test the sensitivity of the results to changes in the assumptions.

Bias in subjective data: When information for calculating Ks for prospective research is elicited from scientists, it is necessary to guard against unrealistic responses that would invalidate the analysis and the use of the results for evaluating research or setting priorities. A particular risk of bias arises because scientists know the purpose of the analysis and often have (or perceive) a vested interest in a high measured rate of return to research. Three ways of dealing with this potential bias are (a) using objective data on past experimental results, historical yield trends, and perhaps, total factor productivity growth rates to calibrate the elicitations, (b) creating an environment of peer review and, perhaps, a competitive process (e.g., Delphi methods) that will reduce the potential for personal incentives to bias estimates of technical parameters, and (c) creating an institutional setting in which scientists will be held accountable for systematic biases in their estimates of research impact (e.g., by comparing actual achievements within programs over time against scientists' forecasts of what would be achieved).

5.3.3 Research Risk and Lags in Research, Development, and Adoption

The temporal nature of the knowledge production function was described in chapter 3. It takes time to complete research, adoption takes time and is incomplete, and most research knowledge eventually depreciates. Thus, as described above, there are long lags in the process of research, development, and adoption. Pardey and Craig (1989) estimated that the effects of research on aggregate U.S. agricultural productivity persist for at least 30 years after the research is begun. For research benefit calculations, the shape of the lag distribution in the earlier years is relatively important, and this shape, as well as the lag length, varies among research programs and among technological options within programs. In short, the time path of the flows of research benefits and costs is dynamic and uncertain — as discussed in section 2.1.3.

Some of this uncertainty stems from the fact that the results from investing in research are inherently unpredictable, some from the fact that the industry response to the information is uncertain (so that K is uncertain), and some from uncertainty about technological and market parameters (so that translation of a known K into measures of benefits is uncertain). A further factor complicating the translation of a "known" K into benefits is that the underlying supply-and-demand functions may involve dynamics (uncertainty and expectations) and leads and lags in relation to price responses as well as in relation to technical change. These dynamics mean that the elasticities, which we treat as constant parameters in economic surplus formulas, vary with length of run. In most studies of research benefits, these dynamics are put aside and the problem is treated as a comparative-statics exercise. The uncertainty is "managed" by conducting the analysis in terms of expected or, more pragmatically, most likely values and by carrying out some sensitivity analysis.

Dynamics continue to be involved through variations in the size of the research-induced supply shift over time. A number of approaches may be used. In the typical approach for ex ante research evaluation, the first step is to estimate the proportional cost reduction, K^{MAX}, that would apply with successful research and full adoption of the resulting technology by the entire industry. That value is multiplied by the probability of success (treating "success" as an all-or-nothing outcome, rather than allowing a continuous range of degrees of success with corresponding probabilities occurrence) and by the likely rate of adoption. Then it is adjusted for any anticipated research depreciation to yield an annual value, K_t, for inclusion in the research benefit formula for that year.

An alternative shortcut approach is to calculate the flow of benefits, B^{MAX}, corresponding to the maximum value, K^{MAX}, and then to scale that flow of benefits according to the probability of success, adoption rate, and depreciation rate. Gross annual benefits, B, are a quadratic function of the supply shift, K, but for small values of K, the quadratic term vanishes and the function is approximately linear. Thus, these two approaches are approximately equivalent for small values of K so long as the same formula (i.e., with the same parameters) is used to translate K_t into a measure of B_t for all values of t. However, in some cases, it may be desirable to use different parameters for different future time periods (reflecting, for instance, the effects of income and population growth on the underlying supply and demand or allowing different elasticities for longer run lengths). In such cases, the two approaches will not be equivalent and the approximation may not be a good one.

Hence, when dynamics are incorporated quantitatively in these models, there are three related components to estimate:

- the research lag
- the adoption or uptake phase
- the depreciation or obsolescence phase

In this section we deal with each of these components in turn. For ex ante evaluations, we also have to deal with the related question of the probability of research being successful.

Research Risk[60]

In ex post studies, we know what research was successful and what was not, at least from the point of view of meeting a scientific objective. And we can find out whether the research led to a commercially successful new idea, method, technology, or input that was adopted by farmers or others. In ex ante evaluation, it is not known in advance whether research will be successful in either the scientific or commercial sense. A measure of the odds of success will be required for each program alternative being considered. Success, however measured, will depend on the degree of aggregation within programs: highly disaggregated programs or individual projects might be highly risky; highly aggregated programs are more predictable if their outcomes are either uncorrelated or negatively correlated and if, as a result, uncertainty is reduced by pooling.

While it is typical, and often convenient, to view success in absolute terms (i.e., the achievement of a particular result), a given program of research might be judged successful across a range of outcomes. For instance, it may be useful for some purposes to think of research as being successful if it generates a $Z\%$ increase in experimental yields. However, the same research would surely be a success if it led to a yield increase *greater than $Z\%$*. Many (especially biological) research projects admit a continuous range of possible outcomes, and the outcome of research can be viewed in terms of the statistical distribution of the random variable used to indicate it (e.g., the experimental yield or gain in yield). In such cases the use of a discrete analogue to represent success or failure is an approximation for analytical convenience, and it might not be very convenient for the analysis.

Consider a plant breeding program, for example, for which the outcome of the research is measured by the increase in experimental yields relative to

---

60. See Fishel (1970) for an early discussion of research risk issues related to research evaluation, planning, and resource allocation and Anderson (1991) for a more recent discussion of these same issues.

existing varieties $(z = \Delta Y)$.[61] In figure 5.2, the distribution of experimental yield *gains*, as perceived before the research is undertaken, is represented by $f(z)$, and z^* is the minimum experimental yield gain that will lead to a commercially successful new variety. Research success is defined in the absolute sense as $z \geq z^*$. The probability of research success is defined as

Figure 5.2:   *Presumed probability distribution of experimental yield gains*

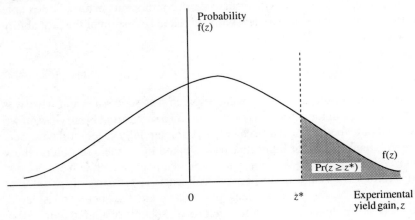

$$\text{Pr} \, (z \geq z^*) = \int\limits_{z^*}^{\infty} f(z)dz \tag{5.13}$$

The expected value of the experimental yield gain, given successful research, is

$$\xi(z \, | \, z \geq z^*) = \int\limits_{z^*}^{\infty} z \; f(z)dz \tag{5.14}$$

The expected yield gain attributable to research is often calculated by multiplying the expected yield gain, given successful research, i.e., $\xi(z \, | \, z \geq z^*)$, by the probability that the research will be successful, i.e., $\text{Pr}(z \geq z^*)$:

$$\Delta \hat{y}^* = \bar{z}^* = \text{Pr} \, (z \geq z^*) \times \xi \, (z \, | \, z \geq z^*) = \int\limits_{z^*}^{\infty} f(z)dz \int\limits_{z^*}^{\infty} z \; f(z)dz \tag{5.15a}$$

61.   The arguments could apply as well to conceptualizing a distribution of changes in industry yields due to research. When an experimental yield distribution has been defined, as discussed below, it is necessary to adjust for differences between experimental gains and commercial gains. Scientists are typically better able to judge experimental outcomes than outcomes in the field.

Alternatively, one could directly estimate the expected yield gain attributable to the research by integrating the distribution of possible research outcomes over the entire range:

$$\Delta\hat{y} = \bar{z} = \xi(z) = \int_{-\infty}^{\infty} z \ f(z) dz \tag{5.15b}$$

This is the unconditional expected value of the yield gain from research. Either of these two alternatives (equation 5.15a or 5.15b) could be involved implicitly or explicitly when scientists are being asked to quantify the uncertain outcome from research.

In many studies, the equivalent of equation 5.15a is used with estimates of the "probability of success" and the "conditional expectation of (experimental) yield gains given successful research" that have been solicited directly. One drawback in using this approach is that the statistical meanings of the terms "probability" and "conditional expectation" might not be fully appreciated by the people providing the information. The meaning of "success" has not always been clear, either.[62] As a consequence, the validity of the measures of K may be questionable.

An alternative approach is to solicit information on the distribution of experimental outcomes, instead — i.e., $f(z)$ — and a definition of successful outcome — i.e., z^* — and use that information to deduce a measure of the conditional (equation 5.15a) or unconditional (equation 5.15b) expected yield gain due to research. For instance, scientists could be asked to estimate a higher-bound (or maximum possible) experimental yield gain, z_h, a lower-bound (or minimum possible) yield gain, z_l (which could be a negative number), and a most-likely value, z_m. Then, assuming a triangular distribution, as in figure 5.3, the complete distribution of experimental outcomes is defined.[63]

Alternatively, the scientists could be asked to estimate points on the cumulative distribution function (i.e., probabilites of experimental yields greater than various values — $\Pr[z \geq z_i]$). The results of this elicitation could be used either to define the entire distribution or as a direct estimate of the critical value associated with the definition of "success": $\Pr(z \geq z^*)$.

---

62. For instance, some scientists have interpreted "success" to mean meeting the stated objectives of a program — such as successfully completing experimental trials — which might not have any economic implications. Others might have a notion of z^* in mind that is well beyond what is necessary for commercial success. Unless success is defined explicitly, and meaningfully, it is difficult to assess the validity or meaning of the information elcited from scientists and others.

63. In section 5.4.4 we show how to parameterize a triangular probability distribution and use it to calculate measures of the dispersion of the distribution to include in models accounting for research risk.

Figure 5.3:   *Triangular probability distribution of experimental yield gains*

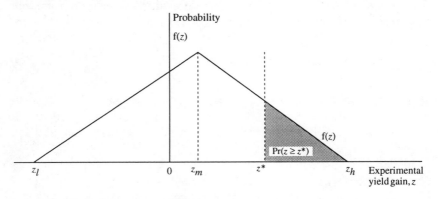

Knowledge of the experimental yield distribution could be used to generate either the summary statistics of the research outcome defined above or other summary statistics (such as a variance). Two drawbacks may be encountered when using this type of approach. First, the triangular distribution is a restrictive approximation, which, in some cases, may involve a loss of information compared with what is actually known about the potential research outcome — but the same approach may be used with more flexible distributions if necessary. Second, even using the simple triangular distribution, the information requirements are significant when only one level of research funding is being evaluated. Later we advocate varying the size of the research budget for each program in order to evaluate the shape of the research payoff relationship. It might be unrealistic, or simply too expensive, to attempt to parameterize an experimental yield distribution across a range of program budgets for each program.

In what follows, we have adopted the conventional approach of combining an estimate of the probability of research success with an estimate of the expected yield gain (or cost saving), given successful research. This encompasses approaches that elicit the estimates directly, as well as those that use the preferred approach (when resources permit) of eliciting information on the distribution of outcomes from which the probability of success and expected values can be derived.[64]

Experienced research scientists are likely to be the best source of information about the distributions of possible outcomes from alternative re-

---

64.   Eliciting explicit details on the distribution of experimental outcomes makes possible the consideration of the joint distribution of the research outcome and the adoption of research results. In sophisticated studies it might be of interest to take this into account when the expected benefits are computed. It is likely that some type of Monte Carlo approach would be necessary to do this properly.

search programs, their expected outcomes, and their probabilities of research success. These scientists can be asked to provide the required information for each research program alternative and for a given program budget and time schedule to complete the research, taking into account the fixed resources available for the research, previous research, information available in other countries, and so on.

Time Required to Complete the Research

Some types of research inherently require more time to complete (or to obtain partial results) than others. The sooner benefits are received, the more they are worth. Scientists should, therefore, be asked to estimate the length of time between incurring an expenditure on research and the release of new technologies.

This is easier to do for disaggregated projects (e.g., wheat variety development) than for an aggregative program (e.g., wheat research including a range of crop management projects and programs in addition to new variety work). The problem is that different components of an aggregated program are characterized by different research lags. What is required for ex ante evaluation of programs is a meaningful estimate for a profile of an "average" research lag for each program. Similar to eliciting K for an aggregate program, it might be best to ask scientists about the disaggregated components along with the aggregate.

Insights into the nature of the research production function (as well as the roles of diminishing returns and fixed factors in research) may be gleaned by asking scientists about the implications of changing the time taken to complete a given program of research. Often, scientists will have a clearer picture of the implications of speeding up or slowing down a particular line of work than the implications of changing the resources available for the work. For instance, they could be asked to consider the effects of finishing an ongoing project (say, with a five-year horizon) one year earlier than originally planned. Given the same annual budget, the same facilities and support staff, and the same expected result if the research is successful (i.e., K^{MAX}), what would be the effect on the probability of success of shortening the horizon? Or, holding the probability of success constant, what quantity of extra resources would be needed to complete the research one year earlier? This type of approach was used, for instance, by Scobie and Jacobsen (1992).

Extent of Adoption

The geographical spread of research results and the time path of adoption, both domestically and internationally, are important determinants of total benefits of research and its distribution. These adoption rates depend on many geoclimatic and socioeconomic factors.[65] Because these factors differ by region and their importance differs by commodity, adoption will seldom approach 100% in a country as a whole, even if it is 100% within a village or local area.

Ex post adoption studies: Ex post sudies of the adoption of research results have included (a) econometric studies where an adoption process is estimated jointly with other characteristics of the supply response of a particular commodity (or commodity aggregate) to aggregate research and extension and (b) studies using survey data on the uptake of specific new technologies (CIMMYT 1993). Lindner (1981), Feder, Just and Zilberman (1985), and Feder and Umali (1993) surveyed much of the literature in this area.

The econometric approach predominates. It is of questionable use for extrapolating to an ex ante analysis of individual commodity research programs because (a) extrapolating from the past may be suspect,[66] (b) aggregate (i.e., sectorwide) responses are not informative about disaggregated (i.e., commodity-specific) responses, and (c) key aspects of the lag structure underlying the adoption curve are typically imposed rather than estimated in the analysis. The second approach, based on a survey (either formal or informal) of the past adoption of new technologies, has a better chance of yielding results that are relevant for ex ante evaluation of research programs but only as a basis for a benchmark. In addition, published data are sometimes available on the spread of varieties of a crop. These data may be used for ex post evaluation but may also provide a benchmark for forward-looking analyses of similar innovations.

Ex ante models: For ex ante evaluation work, we have suggested treating the adoption process as a modifier that translates potential research effects, K^{MAX}, into actual effects over time, K_t. As discussed above, different components of a commodity research program will generate technologies that have different adoption paths in different locations. Potential complementarities and substitution effects among components of technologies further complicate the determination of likely adoption paths for individual components.

Extension workers and others who have observed the adoption of previous research results are primary candidates from whom to elicit information on adoption. A useful approach for eliciting a synthetic adoption path applicable

---

65. The agroecological factors include rainfall, temperature, soils, topography, and the photoperiodicity of crops; the socioeconomic ones include land tenure, farmer education, quantity and quality of extension, transportation, availability of credit, communications, market structure, religion, cultural differences in preferences, and incentives created or destroyed by output pricing and input subsidy policies.

66. It may be thought that the future will be like the past because, in the past, the future was like the past (Weinberg 1975).

to a broad program of research is to discuss the general set of questions and interdependencies and then infer adoption responses for the aggregate. This is similar to the approach for eliciting K^{MAX} and information about research lags, where we suggested considering individual components explicitly; there are complementary aspects of collecting the various types of information on these disaggregated components together. To focus the discussion, it is often useful, at least for crops, to begin with research on new varieties, recognizing that the agronomic and pest and disease research results are likely to be adopted in concert with new varieties.[67]

To define the entire adoption curve corresponding to a particular technology (or results from a particular program of research), it is necessary to choose a functional form. A linear form for adoption response is widely used as a component of a trapezoidal lag structure. Appendix A5.1.2 describes in detail how to specify a trapezoidal research lag structure, including a linear adoption phase (following an initial research lag) and a linear decline. The main alternative is an S-shaped (usually logistic) curve that involves a similar number of parameters. The logistic curve can be specified as[68]

$$A_t = \frac{A^{MAX}}{1 + e^{-(\alpha + \beta t)}} \tag{5.16}$$

where A^{MAX} is the maximum adoption rate (commonly expressed as a fraction of the total area ultimately planted to a crop), A_t is the actual adoption rate t years after the release of the new technology, and α and β are parameters that define the path of the adoption rate that asymptotically approaches the maximum. Thus, a logistic adoption curve can be defined completely by three parameters: A^{MAX}, α, and β. The entire curve can be generated, also, by defining any three points on the curve (preferably with two near-extreme values).

A variety of approaches has been used to elicit values that will define the parameters of a logistic adoption curve. A wise choice would be dictated by judgments about which points on the curve are easier to guess. It is usually reasonable to assume very low adoption in the year of release (say, $A_0 = 0.01$, or 1%) to define one point on the curve. It is also reasonable to try to elicit an estimate of the ceiling rate of adoption. One more point is needed. The scientists and extension workers could be asked either (a) to estimate the most likely adoption rate in a particular year, say seven years after release of

---

67. Some studies have considered piecemeal adoption of components of a technological package (e.g., Byerlee and de Palanco 1986), but these studies have usually concerned ex post evaluation of relatively disaggregated research programs. In ex ante evaluation of aggregate research programs, it is usually difficult to predict such details.

68. For useful discussions of the use of the logistic adoption curve in this context and its derivation, see Griliches (1957b) and Lekvall and Wahlbin (1973).

the technology or (b) to give a best estimate of the number of years required after release of the technology before adoption reaches 50% of the maximum (e.g., if it takes 11 years, $A_{11} = 0.5A^{MAX}$).

Using such information, it is easy to parameterize the curve as follows. Taking logarithms of equation 5.16 yields an equation for β as a function of α, A^{MAX}, A_t, and t:

$$\beta = \left[\ln \left(\frac{A_t}{A^{MAX} - A_t} \right) - \alpha \right] \frac{1}{t} \qquad (5.17)$$

We know A^{MAX} and two combinations of A_t and t. Substituting those values into equation 5.17, we can solve for values of α and β.[69]

Research Depreciation

Many types of research results depreciate over time for various reasons. Crop varieties become susceptible to insects and diseases and eventually begin to yield less. Particular pesticide practices may become less effective as insects and diseases develop resistance to pesticides, and so on. Economic depreciation may not be the same as physical depreciation. Even if a technology doesn't physically depreciate, it can become obsolete and be superseded as a result of changes in market conditions or other changes in technology.[70] Consequently, estimates of research depreciation should be made to adjust expected research impact downward a few years after use of the new technology begins. The effects of discounting mean that early years are weighted much more heavily than later years so that an accurate estimation of research depreciation is less important than an accurate estimation of the time needed to complete the research and of the adoption rates, but it can still be important. For ex ante analysis, scientists and extension workers can be asked to estimate how rapidly they expect the results of the proposed research to degenerate. For ex post analysis, survey results may be available on when the use of particular varieties or other technologies slowed or stopped.

69. Scobie and Jacobsen (1992) show how to do this in a particular setting. See also Pardey (1978), who describes the Pearl-Reed method of fitting logistic curves as given in Pearl (1924, pp. 576-81) and Davis (1941, pp. 216-8).

70. The relevant notion of economic depreciation of technology depends on the particular technological alternatives being considered — that is, it depends on the ceteris paribus conditions. The effects of a one-shot research investment in a particular year are defined given fixed values for the investments in all other years. When considering the effects of a program of research spending over several years, the baseline simulation will refer to a baseline of no investment in the several years in question in the particular program. An extreme example is when the program is regarded as permanent — applying over the indefinite future. The relevant notion of research depreciation will differ between these two types of investments (i.e., one-shot versus multiyear or permanent).

As for other forms of capital, the economic depreciation of the output from successful research (be it new machinery, new genetic material, or new ideas) is commonly represented in one of three ways:

- "one-hoss-shay" depreciation, in which the technology holds its value (i.e., $K_t = K^{MAX}$) until a point in time, L_R, when it becomes worthless instantly (i.e., $K_{L_R + r} = 0, r \geq 0$)
- "straight-line" depreciation, in which, after some point, the value of the technology declines linearly to zero (as described in detail in appendix A5.1.2)
- "declining-balance" depreciation, in which, at some point, the value of the technology begins to decline by a constant proportion each period — i.e., T years after release of the technology it begins to depreciate according to $K_{T+n} = (1 - \delta)^n K^{MAX}$

Variations on each of these approaches to delineating the profile of the agricultural research lag can include specifying the depreciation as applying to the gross measure of K (avoiding the problem of modeling the disadoption process explicitly) or as applying to the technology itself (with endogenous disadoption decisions). In the latter case, for example, it would be necessary to estimate both the decline in yields and the share of production affected. The former approach is more common and is illustrated in appendix A5.1.2 for the straight-line depreciation approach.

Questionnaires

For ex ante analysis, interview questionnaires can be used to obtain information from scientists, extension workers, and research directors on expected yield increases or per unit cost reductions, probabilities of research success, time to complete the research, adoption rates, and research depreciation. It is impossible to define a questionnaire or elicitation process that will be generally applicable. In appendix A5.4 we provide some illustrative examples.

Combining the Information

Box 5.1 shows how to deduce a time path for the research-induced supply shift for a program of research using elicited information on the expected yield gain, adoption rates, probability of success, additional input use, and research depreciation.

Box 5.1: *Combining Information to Calculate* k *and* K

Suppose the following information has been collected for a research program on commodity j:

(a) The research has a probability p_j of successfully leading to a new technology that when fully adopted, will result in a 100 E(Y_j)% increase in commercial yields (after allowing for the optimization of the input mix when switching from existing technology to new technology and allowing for differences between changes in commercial yields and changes in experimental yields) — e.g., E(Y_j) = 0.30 so that 100 E(Y_j) = 30%.

(b) The fraction of the total industry (area or output) adopting the new technology is defined in relation to years, t, from commencement of the research as $A_{j,t}$ (where the particular values might be derived from a logistic curve or some other model) and there is a declining-balance rate of depreciation in the new technology, δ_j. (Here we treat the depreciation rate as applying from the point at which the project commences, but in many cases, it will be preferable to defer the commencement of depreciation until later, say, T years after maximum adoption is achieved.)

(c) The supply elasticity is ε_j and the current producer price is $PP_{j,0}$ per tonne.

(d) The increase in commercial yields involves an *additional* cost of purchased inputs (e.g., fertilizer, fuel, or pesticides) of ΔC_j (or 100 E$[C_j]$%) in costs per hectare that can be translated using preresearch yields, $Y_{j,0}$, to a change in cost per tonne of output of $\Delta C_j / \{[1+E(Y_j)]Y_{j,0}\}$. This could be a positive or negative number. The percentage change in costs per tonne — obtained by dividing by average costs per tonne $(C_j/Y_{j,0})$ — is equal to E$(C_j)/[1+E(Y_j)]$.

(e) The increase in commercial yields involves a 100 E(F_j)% *increase* in the use of allocatable fixed factors (e.g., land or operator labor and managerial inputs) per tonne of output. And quasi-rents to allocatable fixed factors account for a fraction, s_j, of preresearch costs per tonne. E(F_j), too, could be a positive or negative number.

Given this elicited information on potential yield changes, adoption rates, and so on, values for the *absolute* reduction in costs per tonne, $k_{j,t}$, for all future years can be projected as follows. First, assuming the use of variable or quasi-fixed inputs does not change in order to bring forth the projected yield increase

$$k_{j,t} = [\text{E}\,(Y_j)/\varepsilon_j]\, p_j A_{j,t}\, (1-\delta_j)^t\, PP_{j,0}$$

Second, allowing for changes in input use,

$$k_{j,t} = \left[\frac{\text{E}\,(Y_j)}{\varepsilon_j} - \frac{\text{E}(C_j)}{1+\text{E}\,(Y_j)} - s_j\,\text{E}\,(F_j)\right] p_j A_{j,t}\, (1-\delta_j)^t\, PP_{j,0}$$

(*continued on following page*)

Box 5.1: (*continued*)

Notice that in both cases, we have included $PP_{j,0}$ so that $k_{j,t}$ is computed as the change in cost per tonne of output rather than the *percentage* change in cost per tonne of output. This approach has the advantage that the computed effect of the technology on per unit costs of production does not depend on exogenous growth in demand or supply that would affect the price. If the calculation were in percentage terms, the absolute effect would depend on prices. Relative shifts of supply could be derived as $K_{j,t} = k_{j,t}/PP_{j,t}$ where $PP_{j,t}$ is the projected producer price in the absence of the technical change.

It is also pertinent to note that we have not said here how to go from hypothetical changes in experimental yields to an estimate of optimized commercial yield. That topic is dealt with in the text and in appendix A5.2. Unlike δ, A, and p, the supply elasticity, ε, is not bounded between 0 and 1 and errors in its estimation could have relatively important quantitative implications. Thus, we have advocated using $\varepsilon = 1$ for this step so that $K = J$.

5.4   Application — Analyzing and Using the Data and the Results

The data analysis involves several components, including (a) calculating the economic surplus measures of streams of benefits and costs accruing to each defined interest group for each defined program alternative, (b) converting those streams of benefits and costs into summary statistics using capital budgeting methods, (c) calculating any other desired measures of research program performance (such as contributions to security objectives), and (d) using the resulting information to help choose among program alternatives.

5.4.1   Calculating the Streams of Research Benefits and Costs

Once the basic data and other information have been collected in tables and on interview summary forms, a spreadsheet template can be created for each commodity in Lotus©, Quattro©, or some similar program. Spreadsheets are useful for

- structuring the basic data for the analysis (e.g., prices, quantities, and elasticities)
- incorporating the data into formulas for measuring research effects on prices and quantities
- calculating changes in consumer and producer surplus due to agricultural research
- calculating present values or internal rates of return
- summarizing the results in tabular or graphical form

Thus, a spreadsheet can be used to calculate changes in the total economic surplus, the distribution of benefits, the net present value of research, and the internal rate of return to research (using algorithms embedded in the spreadsheet package). Appendix A5.1.1 outlines two examples of spreadsheets that can be used in this way.

A spreadsheet is just one of the possible means of implementing the economic surplus model on a computer. A number of other computer programs are available. For example, Lynam and Jones (1984) developed a program for research evaluation called MODEXC, which formed the basis for a program developed by Antony (1989). The Australian Centre for International Agricultural Research (ACIAR) developed a Fortran program called RE4 to implement the model of Davis, Oram and Ryan (1987) (the program is reported in their appendix). Also, as described in appendix A5.1.2, a flexible, menu-driven program, *Dream©*, has been developed at ISNAR to facilitate application of the economic surplus model under a variety of market situations.

As well as documenting the logical structure of *Dream©*, appendix A5.1.2 provides some practical guidance for more general implemention of economic surplus models of research benefits. The appendix shows how to parameterize linear supply-and-demand functions using information on elasticities, prices, and quantities produced and consumed. It also shows how to incorporate adjustments in those functions for autonomous growth in consumption or production and how to parameterize a trapezoidal profile of the research-adoption lag. A generic representation of market-distorting policies, as tax-subsidy equivalents, is also described.

5.4.2 Capital Budgeting

The economic surplus models can be used to derive annual flows of research benefits and costs. To compare and evaluate alternative investments, this information usually has to be compressed into a summary statistic by aggregating the flows over time. This can be done using the methods of cost-benefit analysis in which anticipated costs and benefits are calculated on an annual basis and summarized as either an anticipated net present value or an internal rate of return for each research program alternative. Typically, this will be done only for the aggregate measures of benefits (i.e., the efficiency measures), not the distributional effects on particular groups, and nonefficiency objectives will be put aside for the calculation.

Net Present Value

Net present value (NPV) is calculated using the following formula:

$$NPV = \sum_{t=0}^{\infty} \frac{B_t - C_t}{(1 + r)^t}$$ (5.18)

where r is the discount rate (as discussed earlier in this chapter), B_t is the calculated value for annual research benefits t years in the future, obtained by calculating the total economic surplus for the year based on the methods described earlier, and C_t is the annual research cost expended t years in the future.[71]

It is usually convenient to express all of the flows of future (or past) benefits and costs in terms of current (real) value, and therefore it is appropriate to use a real discount rate. For priority setting, the NPV is often used to measure the contributions of research programs to the efficiency objective.

Sometimes the present value of *gross* research benefits is computed separately from the present value of research costs. The difference between the present value of gross benefits and the present value of research costs is, plainly, the net present value. The ratio of the two is a benefit-cost ratio, as commonly stated.

Internal Rate of Return

For ex post research evaluation, the internal rate of return (IRR) to research is often calculated. It is computed as the discount rate that would result in a value of zero for the net present value

$$0 = \sum_{t=0}^{\infty} \frac{B_t - C_t}{(1 + IRR)^t}$$ (5.19)

In other words, the IRR is the rate of return that would make the present value of benefits equal to the present value of costs. It provides an annual real rate

---

71. A more general formula for net present value allows the discount rate to vary over the life of the investment:

$$NPV = (B_0 - C_0) + \sum_{t=1}^{\infty} \left[\frac{B_t - C_t}{\pi_{k=1}^{t} (1 + r_k)} \right]$$

As in equation 5.18, it is typically assumed for analytical and empirical convenience that the relevant discount rate is constant over the life of the investment. In some cases, it might be appropriate to allow the discount rate to vary, reflecting anticipated variations in future, real, risk-free interest rates. This is closely related to discounting investments that have different horizons at different rates. Likewise, the term structure of interest rates can be used to deduce values for discount rates that vary over the future horizon. Chapter 3 contains some discussion of these issues.

of return (when the benefits and costs are defined in real terms) that can be compared against alternative public investments (see chapter 2).

While projects can be ranked by either IRR or NPV, NPV is preferred for priority setting because it can be normalized in a way that considers the size of the research program. IRR and NPV can also yield different rankings of projects. One reason is that NPV reflects the scale of the investment. If NPVs of net benefits are divided by the corresponding present values of costs, a type of benefit-cost ratio is obtained that can be used to rank programs, taking account of scale. The scale-adjusted rankings of NPVs still might differ from the scale-independent IRR rankings, but the conditions under which that situation arises are not likely to be found in research program evaluations where the costs occur early and the benefits occur later in the time period being analyzed (see Mishan 1976).

In addition, while present-value measures can be used to consider distribution of benefits and costs, typically IRR cannot. This is because computing a meaningful IRR requires a stream of costs as well as corresponding benefits — if an interest group pays no costs but receives some benefits (e.g., domestic consumers or particular groups of producers who do not pay any cost of research funded by general government revenues), their IRR is infinite. Only in unusual cases (such as where research is funded in part by producer groups) will it be possible to apportion costs and benefits in ways that permit IRRs to be computed for different groups. Most agricultural research is funded from general revenues, and the incidence of funding costs among beneficiaries of research is difficult to calculate.[72]

5.4.3   Calculating Other Consequences of Research

Distributional Impacts

The economic surplus analysis can generate information on the *functional* distribution of research benefits (i.e., between domestic and foreign people, among suppliers of various factors of production and consumers, and perhaps disaggregated further according to where people live within the home country). The ultimate incidence of research costs can also be calculated in the same ways. However, these measures of functional distribution of benefits and costs might not represent all the distributional impacts that are of concern — for instance, the objectives might pertain to the effects on the

72. However, net present values of benefits or rates of return to particular interest groups, for instance, could be calculated and have been upon occasion. For example, Scobie, Mullen and Alston (1991) calculated rates of return from wool research from the point of view of Australian wool producers and from the point of view of Australia as a whole.

urban poor or particular classes of domestic producers. It is feasible in some cases to calculate some such distributional impact, but as we argued in chapter 2, it is usually difficult to measure such effects and there are almost always better instruments than agricultural research for pursuing objectives related to *personal* income distributions. Nevertheless, it might be useful to incorporate a measure of performance against such objectives if only as a basis for measuring the opportunity cost of using research to pursue them.

Variability of Incomes

Income variability in agriculture — arising from unpredictable weather, prices, and government policies — is a problem for agricultural producers and, sometimes, for the nation as a whole (i.e., when it leads to problems of poverty and malnutrition or, worse, famine).[73] Different agricultural technologies can imply different degrees of yield variability or different exposure to the risk of bankruptcy (say, where a greater amount of purchased inputs is being used), and thus the choice of a research portfolio might have implications for risk and uncertainty in agriculture. To the extent that this is so and that it can be understood and measured, research priorities might take into consideration the impact of research on variability. In most practical settings, the implications of the differential variability of research alternatives are not well understood because the relationships are complicated and the effects can be subtle — they cannot be measured with confidence (there may be little relevant information available on the implications of the variability of hypothetical technologies). It may well be better, therefore, to avoid the issue altogether in most cases.[74]

5.4.4   Variance of the Research Portfolio and Sensitivity Analysis

Variance of the Research Portfolio

An entirely different notion of variability relates to the uncertainty surrounding computed values for the NPVs of research program alternatives. We argued in section 2.1.3 that public-sector agricultural research portfolios ought not to be based on a mean-variance trade-off, but a measure of the variability surrounding the estimates can be useful for interpreting estimates for decision making. In particular, a measure of variability indicates the degree of confidence that can be placed in a point estimate of research benefits. And some research institutions will want to consider mean-variance

73.   See Anderson and Hazell (1989) and section 2.1.3.
74.   Anderson and Hazell (1989) disagree.

trade-offs. An example is the use of a portfolio approach by Scobie and Jacobsen (1992) to analyze Australian Wool Research Council research priorities.

In section 5.3.2, we considered the problem of parameterizing the uncertain impact of research on yields and suggested using a triangular distribution to represent potential research impact. A probability distribution surrounding an estimate of the technical impact of research implies a corresponding probability distribution around the measures of benefits (indeed, a particular specification of the distribution of K^{MAX} might translate into a specific distribution of benefits). Of course, other parameters (including A^{MAX}, α, β, the discount rate, and research and adoption lags) are also uncertain and can be viewed as random variables with probability distributions, so the translation of uncertain K^{MAX} into a distribution of NPVs is not simple.

Sprow (1967) suggested a method for estimating variances and covariances associated with research programs, and Scobie and Jacobsen (1992) interpreted and applied that approach in the following way.[75] The first step is to simulate the economic benefits, with each simulation based on a different set of randomly drawn parameters. These parameters can be drawn from a triangular probability density function, PDF. The triangular distribution is characterized by three parameters, namely the modal or most likely outcome, z_m, the lowest possible, z_l, and the highest possible, z_h. These values are portrayed as a triangle (panel a in figure 5.4) and can be mapped onto a cumulative distribution function, CDF, with two quadratic segments, one beginning at zero for the lowest outcome and the other begining at one for the highest possible outcome (panel b in figure 5.4). These two segments, which correspond to the linear segments of the triangular PDF, meet at the mode.

In order to parameterize this approach, three values are needed for each uncertain variable or parameter. If this approach is to be used, information should be collected in the elicitation process on the most likely, minimum, and maximum values for the variables underlying the measures of K_t, the elasticities, and so on. In eliciting the parameters of the underlying distributions of K^{MAX}, A^{MAX}, α, β, and research and adoption lags, it is important to remember that they are jointly determined and jointly distributed (in the statistical sense). Such information can be elicited in various ways, but there is some potential for eliciting meaningless numbers that are mutually incompatible, and something must be done to limit the number of alternative combinations being considered. For example, one approach is to fix the

---

75. Anderson, Dillon and Hardaker (1977), Anderson and Dillon (1992), and Scobie and Jacobsen (1992) have described the approach first used by Sprow (1967) to evaluate research expenditures using triangular distribution functions and Monte Carlo methods. See, also, Anderson (1991).

Figure 5.4:   *The triangular probability distribution*

(a) Probability distribution function (PDF)

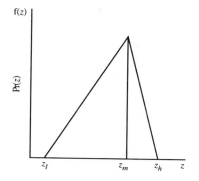

(c) PDF for a uniform
variate

(b) Cumulative distribution function (CDF)

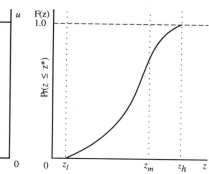

Source: Adapted from Anderson, Dillon and Hardaker (1977) and Scobie and Jacobsen (1992).

research costs and then consider the distribution of K^{MAX} conditional on the other determinants of K_t being held constant.

Letting z be a random variable (say, the experimental yield gain, as in equations 5.13 through 5.15b) for which we have elicited the highest, modal (or most likely), and lowest values, its CDF is given by two quadratic CDF segments that meet at the mode so that

$$F(z) = \frac{(z - z_l)^2}{(z_h - z_l)(z_m - z_l)} \qquad z_l \leq z < z_m \qquad (5.20a)$$

$$F(z) = 1 - \frac{(z_h - z)^2}{(z_h - z_l)(z_h - z_m)} \qquad z_m \leq z \leq z_h \qquad (5.20b)$$

where $F(z_i)$ represents the probability that $z \leq z_i$. It is analytically convenient to equate $F(z)$ with a uniform variate, u, with a probability density function $f(u)$, as shown in panel c of figure 5.4. Because u and $F(z)$ each lie between zero and one, it is possible to determine the z value for any particular u that is drawn from the uniform distribution by using the following equations:

$$z = z_l + [u(z_h - z_l)(z_m - z_l)]^{0.5} \qquad \text{if} \quad 0 \leq u < \frac{z_m - z_l}{z_h - z_l} \qquad (5.21a)$$

$$z = z_h - [(1 - u)(z_h - z_l)(z_h - z_m)]^{0.5} \qquad \text{if} \quad \frac{z_m - z_l}{z_h - z_l} \leq u \leq 1 \qquad (5.21b)$$

A uniform variate is equally likely to take any value between zero and one. Random draws of uniform variates can be obtained from most statistics textbooks, from a computer spreadsheet program, or by drawing from a hat. The procedure can be applied, say, 200 times and it can be replicated for each parameter being treated as a random variable (e.g., K^{MAX}, A^{MAX}, α, β, research and adoption lags). A Monte Carlo simulation can be used to compute corresponding draws of economic surplus measures and thereby generate a distribution of values for economic surplus from which we can compute measures of its central tendency (e.g., the mean or mode) and of dispersion (e.g., variance or coefficient of variation).[76] If information is available on the *joint* distributions of two or more parameters (e.g., K^{MAX} and A^{MAX}), it would be appropriate to draw from their joint distribution(s) for a Monte Carlo simulation, conditional on the remaining parameters.

While we have proposed considering alternative funding levels relative to the baseline, it might not be worth the trouble to run all such alternatives through a Monte Carlo simulation. If a stochastic simulation is undertaken only for the benchmark case, it might be reasonable to assume that the variance (or perhaps the coefficient of variation) of NPV is constant at different levels of funding.[77] Scobie and Jacobsen (1992) discuss why the variance might rise or fall as the level of funding rises. On the other hand, the value of the NPV obtained from taking every parameter at its most likely value will differ from the expected value derived from the simulation if the

---

76. In the Monte Carlo simulation, the random values of the parameters are combined to estimate the economic surplus change due to research — for example, by inserting the values into the appropriate economic surplus formula in *Dream©*.

77. Anderson (1991) gives examples that support the likely constancy of coefficients of variation across programs.

distributions are asymmetric and the relationships between parameters and benefits are nonlinear.

Sensitivity Analysis

Sensitivity analyses in which prices, per unit cost reductions, and other factors are allowed to vary can provide useful information on the robustness of the results. If a range of values (say highest, middle, and lowest) have been elicited for uncertain parameters, it is possible to derive a distribution of possible NPVs for each research program that reflects the joint distributions of the unknown parameters using Sprow's (1967) approach. Even if the variance is not computed formally, an informal impression of uncertainty about returns to a research program can be gleaned by computing the returns for a range of combinations of parameters and computing a measure of dispersion (e.g., variance, coefficient of variation, or minimum and maximum).

In this type of analysis, one should keep in mind the fact that the parameters are mutually dependent. For instance, the adoption rate probably depends positively on the size of the maximum yield gain. Treating the parameters as independent, which is implied by varying each parameter from high to low and considering all combinations, can give a misleading impression.

When multiple objectives are included, the weights on objectives can be varied to explore the implications for the rankings of programs (see chapters 6 and 7). In particular, by simulating a reallocation of research resources in order to satisfy nonefficiency objectives and by evaluating the effect of such reallocations on the NPV, it is possible to obtain a quantitative measure of the opportunity cost of using research to pursue nonefficiency objectives. In order to choose research programs with a view to meeting nonefficiency objectives, it is necessary to take a measure of the contribution of different research programs to different objectives.

5.4.5   Using the Results in Decision Making

Maximizing Efficiency

Ranking a given set of programs: Suppose the evaluation considers only one option for each research program — say, the current level of total support and the current mix of research components within each program. How could the results be used? In the simplest setting, we would have available a measure of the anticipated or most likely NPV for each research program and that would allow us to rank the programs according to their total NPVs or NPVs expressed per dollar of research funding (perhaps in present value terms) or per scientist or per some other constraint. A more detailed analysis might also provide information on the degree of dispersion of each NPV (say, around their most likely values) and on the benefits to particular groups.

The NPV measure is absolute — programs with positive NPVs (such that the present value of benefits exceeds the present value of costs) are economically worthwhile. Programs with negative NPVs should be shut down, according to the economic efficiency criterion — that is, those funds could be reallocated profitably to a nonresearch use (the discount rate indicates the cost of borrowing and may also represent the rate of return that could be earned by using the funds for other public goods) or to new research programs with positive NPVs.

It might be tempting to redirect research resources toward the existing programs with the highest NPVs. But for programs with positive NPVs, there is little or no information in a ranking of programs according to NPVs about what would happen if the funds were reallocated within the research portfolio. Thus, such a ranking does not lead to any decisions without additional information. Specifically, in order to make *marginal* decisions about reallocating research resources among programs, we need to have information about the *changes* in research benefits and costs associated with such marginal reallocations.

Rankings can be more meaningful when constraints on research programs mean that not all programs with positive NPVs can be supported. In such a case, research programs can be ranked from highest to lowest according to NPV per unit of constraint (e.g., scientists or research cost in present-value terms). Then the decision about which programs to support involves moving down the list of programs until the constraint is binding overall and ruling out all programs below the line. This will be an optimum, given the constrained choice between the given alternatives, but it will not necessarily maximize the overall NPV per unit of constraint (which is the constrained efficiency objective) because the programs are presented as discrete alternatives and some reallocation of resources among the programs might lead to an increase in the overall NPV.

Again, however, as with the unconstrained choice, the ranking alone does not provide any information about the benefits of marginally reallocating resources among the programs because the marginal effects have not been measured. The NPVs per unit of resources committed to research represent *average* benefits that might not be equal to the *marginal* benefits (or costs) if a unit of resources is added to (or subtracted from) the program. Only if the research program is characterized by constant returns to scale will the marginal and average rates of return (or benefits per unit of resources) be equal.

Additional information is needed on the relationship between marginal and average benefits (or on the benefits associated with explicit program alternatives given by marginal changes from the baseline) in order to establish the returns to changing the budget for research in total or to reallocating the total constrained research resource. A high average NPV per unit is likely to be associated with a high marginal NPV, so the average figures may indicate the direction in which research resources should flow (e.g., from low- to high-average-NPV programs), but explicit alternatives must be explicitly evaluated in order to decide how far the reallocation should go. The exception is the extreme (and extremely unlikely) case of constant returns to scale (average NPV equals marginal NPV) where *all* available resources should be allocated to the program with the highest average NPV (per unit of constraint).[78]

In other words, research administrators usually want to know not only *whether* resources should be redirected from program A to program B, they also want to know how much of program A's resources should go to program B — or, indeed, to program C. Optimal decisions require information about the marginal relationships — on how the marginal benefit from each program varies with the size of the program.

Beyond ranking — explicit variations in program size: It is not appropriate to redirect resources among programs with positive NPVs based on an ordinal ranking alone — even when the ranking is of NPVs per unit of constraint (e.g., research resources). Decisions regarding resource allocations require comparisons of explicit alternatives. When the question is how to maximize the social benefits from a given research budget, it is necessary to explore the implications of changes in the budget allocation. It is also necessary to consider discrete alternatives, but it is desirable to do so in a way that limits the number considered and sheds light on alternatives not explicitly considered. To do this, we have suggested looking at three options for each program: say 10% above and below a baseline of the current research funding.

With such information available, it is possible to contemplate the full set of 3^n explicit combinations (with n programs) and choose the one with the highest aggregate net present value; it is also possible to solve for the combination that will maximize the aggregate net present value for the same or different total budgets. And it is possible, thereby, to look at alternative ways of distributing increases or decreases in the total budget.

The same principles can be applied to consider any variation within the research program, be it the emphasis on different regions or zones, the

---

78. Similarly, if the research budget were unlimited, under constant returns to scale, an unlimited amount of funding could be spent profitably on any program with a positive NPV.

emphasis on different lines of research (e.g., basic versus applied research, plant breeding versus agronomy, or even one crop versus another in a crop program), or the mix of resources used (i.e., the balance between scientists and support staff or capital-labor ratios). The important point to note is that if such variation is to be optimized, its implications must be assessed.

Optimization algorithms: The number of alternative allocations to be considered can become very large as the number of things to be varied grows. This problem can be mitigated by dealing with a comparatively small number of aggregated programs and by restricting the number of alternatives to be considered within each program at the stage of resource allocation decisions.[79] To manage the information, even when there is only one objective (efficiency) and a small number of options, it may be desirable to use an optimization algorithm to search among the alternatives rather than make all possible comparisons. Optimization techniques (e.g., linear or nonlinear programming models) could be applied to information on discrete alternatives to maximize the total benefits from the portfolio, given resource constraints and given the resource demands associated with the alternatives. And in some cases, it might also be possible to extrapolate (or interpolate) beyond the discrete alternatives and infer a continuous relationship between funding and benefits that could then be used to deduce an optimum allocation. Chapter 6 discusses this in more detail in relation to mathematical programming approaches.

Maximizing with Multiple Objectives

Specifying a distributional objective, such as placing additional emphasis on the benefits to low-income groups, implicitly argues that an extra unit of income to a poor person is weighted more than an extra unit of income to the average person. Placing a distributional weight on a nonefficiency objective in a research priority-setting analysis may also imply a belief that the opportunity cost to society of meeting that objective by distorting research investments is lower than the cost of meeting it entirely with other types of policies.

Conceptualizing the trade-off: The idea of maximizing the benefits from research with multiple research objectives is analogous to the conventional textbook utility-maximization problem. The "utility" function of the research system (the revealed preferences of the "clients" for an analysis) defines the relative contributions of different types of research benefits (e.g., greater efficiency, E, or greater equity, V) to the goals of the research system. Mathematically, this can be represented by

---

79.   Recall that less aggregated treatments might still be involved at the stage of parameterization in order to optimize the accuracy of the estimates of NPVs.

$$U = U(E, V, R) \tag{5.22}$$

where U is the total "utility" or "social benefit" from research and R is the quantity of research or research expenditure. Research expenditure does not give utility directly, but it is included to reflect the opportunity cost of research. Totally differentiating this equation and setting the result equal to zero yields

$$
\begin{aligned}
dU &= \frac{\partial U}{\partial E}\, dE + \frac{\partial U}{\partial V}\, dV + \frac{\partial U}{\partial R}\, dR \\[2mm]
&= U_E\, dE + U_V\, dV + U_R\, dR \tag{5.23} \\[2mm]
&= 0
\end{aligned}
$$

In this equation, the coefficients U_E, U_V, and U_R are the marginal contributions of greater efficiency, greater equity, and research expenditure to the objective function. It is convenient to define $U_R = -1$ (i.e., the marginal cost of a dollar of research spending is \$1) and this defines the units for the other coefficients, too, in terms of what is foregone by using resources for research. These coefficients can be thought of as representing the (marginal) weights to be attached to the different research objectives (Harberger 1978). Thus,

$$0 = U_E\, dE + U_V\, dV - dR$$

Holding U and R constant ($dU = dR = 0$), the slope of an indifference curve is equal to the marginal rate of substitution between E and V:

$$\frac{U_E}{U_V} = -\frac{dV}{dE} \tag{5.24}$$

An efficient research portfolio is one in which the marginal rate of substitution (in terms of preferences) between the objectives E and V is equal to the marginal rate of transformation (in terms of production possibilities) between E and V that arises from changing the mix of research programs. This relates directly to the discussion of benefit-transformation curves, BTCs, and indifference curves, ICs, presented in chapter 2. These curves are reproduced in figure 5.5. We remind the reader that the horizontal axis represents efficiency, E, and the vertical axis represents equity, V.[80] The curve BTC_R represents the range of

---

80. These *benefit*-transformation curves may be thought of as a generalization of the *surplus*-transformation curve. In the surplus-transformation curve, the benefits are measured as economic surpluses accruing to particular groups. In the BTC, the benefits could be economic surpluses or something else. We need to be clear about the interpretation of the origin of these curves, what is being held constant, and what the units are. One option is to measure the contributions of the research portfolio to the objectives measured along the axis — so the units are *additional* benefits relative to a world with no research portfolio, and the origin represents zero benefits from research. This would mean the diagram represents incremental welfare. Alternatively, the axes could represent total benefits from all economic activities in the economy,

Figure 5.5:   *Assessing the trade-off between equity and efficiency*

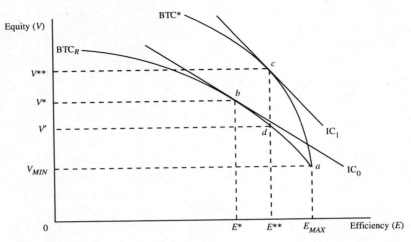

maximum possible combinations of economic efficiency and equity that can be achieved by varying the mix of research programs in the portfolio, in the absence of other policy instruments. An efficient portfolio is one that corresponds to a tangency between a BTC and an IC.

Point *a* represents the result if the research portfolio were chosen simply to maximize economic efficiency at E_{MAX}. Moving back along the curve reveals how much economic surplus must be foregone in order to increase equity by shifting the research portfolio away from the one that maximizes economic efficiency. The curve labeled IC_0 represents a policymakers' indifference curve, or the willingness to substitute equity for efficiency. This particular indifference curve is tangent to BTC_R at point *b*, which represents the best combination of economic efficiency and equity (given these preferences) that can be achieved by varying the research portfolio. To increase equity from V_{MIN} to V^* involves an opportunity cost of economic surplus foregone equal to $(E_{MAX} - E^*)$, but given the preferences, this sacrifice is worthwhile.

Nonresearch policies: Figure 5.5 includes a second benefit-transformation curve, BTC^*, which represents the most efficient combinations of economic efficiency and equity that are possible from jointly changing the portfolio of research and a second policy instrument (say a tax and income-transfer scheme). This combined BTC can never be below the one that holds

including research. Then, the origin would represent zero benefits from all economic activities. The former view is attractive for simplicity but the latter is necessary for coherence with theory. Thus, we take the latter approach here.

when only research is involved. IC_1 is the highest indifference curve that can be attained as a tangent to BTC*. The optimal outcome (point c) involves higher levels of both equity, V^{**}, and efficiency, E^{**}, than the optimum from research policy alone (point b) because combining research with other policy instruments is a more efficient (i.e., less costly) means of pursuing the equity objective than is research alone.

Transfers of direct income or assets are never costless in themselves and, in many developing countries, the cost may be high. However, as pointed out in chapter 2, research is a very blunt instrument for redistributing incomes, and research policymakers should be made aware of this fact if they attach heavy weight to the distributional objective in the research priority-setting context. The same is likely to be true of most other nonefficiency objectives as well. Some of the most severe problems facing the agricultural sector in any given country simply cannot be solved by research; many are better solved by other means.

If research policymakers treat research as the only policy instrument available for meeting social objectives, they might select a research portfolio that trades off substantial efficiency for additional equity. If they recognize the availability of other policy instruments, however, they might be less willing to trade off efficiency for equity in selecting a particular research portfolio because the equity concern can be better met through another policy. That is, other policies may be more efficient than research at contributing to equity.

Assume that a research portfolio represented by point d on BTC_R is selected. This selection might imply that research policymakers believe that their indifference curve, IC_0, is tangent to BTC_R at this point. Alternatively, it might imply that they are aware there is a tangency with a higher IC at point c, achieved by combining research and other policies on the unobservable BTC*. In this case, they select point d on the observable BTC_R because they have a reasonably good feel for the contribution that research can make to their objectives compared with the other policy instruments.

Discrete and continuous alternatives: We began this section with a consideration of ranking discrete program alternatives according to their NPVs. Discrete research program alternatives could also be ranked according to their impact on objectives other than efficiency. It may be difficult, however, to use such information for making decisions because it is very difficult to make a mutidimensional comparison among a large number of alternatives. With two objectives, the alternatives could be plotted on a graph (one axis measuring efficiency and the other measuring the contribution to the other objective). This would reveal inferior options (where the outcome would lie below the efficient frontier) and would also indicate the dimensions of the trade-off. It would not, however, correspond to BTC_R because the alternatives being considered are discrete ones that have not necessarily optimized the trade-offs between E and V. In some NARSs, current programs might lie below the frontier, especially if economic criteria have not been used. Thus, there may be opportunities to move to the frontier, increasing contributions to all objectives simultaneously.

To find the efficient portfolio of programs with multiple objectives requires considering continuous variation in the sizes of alternative research programs. This is so, even when the individual programs are characterized by constant returns to scale in relation to each objective (i.e., when marginal and average effects are equal). Where multiple objectives are involved, it could be especially important to use a formal optimization algorithm because it requires a clear definition of the objective function and the terms of the trade-off between efficiency and alternative objectives.

Measurement issues: Considering multiple objectives adds to the reasons for wanting information on the marginal returns to individual research programs. In addition, it means that the marginal and average contributions of individual research programs to nonefficiency objectives must be measured as well. Also, and perhaps of greatest concern, the weights attached to both efficiency and nonefficiency objectives must be estimated. Some of these things are hard to measure. Including nonefficiency objectives therefore adds to the cost of the analysis and also adds some potential inaccuracy. It is to be avoided if possible, given these considerations and the fact that there are doubts about using research to pursue nonefficiency objectives. But, if nonefficiency objectives affect decisions about allocating resources to research, evaluating their effects may be particularly valuable as a guide to their efficiency costs.

The biggest single problem concerns the elicitation of weights (which are not needed if only one objective is being pursued) corresponding to U_E and U_V in equation 5.20. In that equation the weights reflect marginal benefits from changes in E and V. Clearly, their values will depend on the measures of E and V (for instance, and trivially, if E is measured in millions of dollars, its weight will be 1000 times the weight that would apply if E were measured in billions).[81] When we use proxies for the true "objectives" (such as using a variance of yields to represent a concern about income variability), the units have implications for the weights that might not be obvious. In such situations the problem of *jointly* determining weights and measures can be serious, if not intractable. These problems are surely insurmountable in a

81.   Moreover, weights are most likely to vary as the size of the total research program varies so that particular (fixed) weights might be applicable only for a limited set of alternatives. In other words, the functional form of the "utility" function could matter, and constant weights are implied only by a linear form.

typical scoring analysis, as discussed in chapter 7, where large numbers of "criteria" are scored and there is no possibility of using intelligent sensitivity analysis to deduce the appropriate weights to attach to the criteria.

One practical way to proceed is first to find the research decision that maximizes the efficiency objective. Then, the implications (cost of efficiency benefits foregone) of incrementally placing little weight on the nonefficiency objectives can be observed by seeing how the decisions change and comparing their efficiency outcomes. Relating these concepts to figure 5.5, if the analyst initially places all weight on the efficiency objective, assuming a budget constraint, this results in a research portfolio that corresponds to point a on the benefit-transformation curve BTC_R. Then, as weights on equity are increased in small increments, implying changes in the slopes of the indifference curves, new research portfolios are generated as new tangencies between IC_0 and BTC_R are reached. These preliminary aggregate rankings can be discussed with decision makers, and changes can be made in the weights until there is consensus about which research ranking or portfolio to select. This revised portfolio can then be compared with the current research emphasis in the system. Weights can be changed to select other portfolios (points on BTC_R) or changes can be made in underlying assumptions (e.g., prices, quantities, and percent cost changes due to research), which would shift the BTC_R.

5.5   Conclusion

The economic surplus approach is a practical and theoretically justifiable approach to agricultural research evaluation and priority setting. While data and information needs are nontrivial, application of the approach can add valuable structure to the research priority-setting process. Use of the procedure also provides research directors with a justification for their decisions regarding resource allocations when they are confronted with pressures from policymakers to change research directions in response to short-term crises. A by-product of the analysis is a set of internal rates of return and net present values that can be used to justify research budgets relative to alternative public expenditures. Such information is particularly useful for discussions within the ministries of agriculture and finance, as well as with donors and policy-making bodies.

5.5.1   Reality Check

The budget for research evaluation and priority setting is typically small (and often nonexistent), and it is under the same pressures for justification as other uses of research funds. Some expenditure on research evaluation and priority setting is surely justified in any system — as a complement to, and often as a partial replacement for, bureaucratic structures for research management. But even in the most generously supported system, it will not be worth overly investing in formal cost-benefit analysis of program alternatives. There are a number of aspects of reality that determine what it is practical and economically desirable to do.

Too Much Information

Research evaluation and priority-setting studies generate a lot of information. Sometimes it is costly and difficult to make sense of a mass of information relating to a wide range of alternatives. While the procedures are designed to accommodate and reduce a large amount of information, more detailed analysis of a large number of alternatives can still leave many options to be compared. Thus, in an unthinking application of these methods, the analyst might lose sight of the problem they were designed to serve.

Especially in settings where the approaches are new, it may be helpful to begin the analysis by focusing on a small number of alternatives for which the data needs and analysis are relatively straightforward (e.g., commodities within a crop program). Starting small means that it is possible to illustrate the kinds of information that are required for the analysis and that can be generated from it while educating policymakers about the scope of the approach and the economic way of thinking about agricultural research.

Too Little Information

Even when the analyst is ambitious and resources are available, the available data and other information might not support a detailed study. Information about the research-induced supply shift may be hard to get for some commodity-based programs. And for noncommodity research programs and certain types of pretechnology research, measuring effects in the framework of a commodity or factor market could be problematic. But this concern is often overstated. Many pretechnology and noncommodity research programs can be translated, with some effort, into a supply-and-demand setting and evaluated accordingly. For example, the supply-and-demand framework is directly applicable to the evaluation of research on land, air, and water resources. Research on these resources has an effect on multiple commodities, which would seem to make the task impossible, but the solution is to study the market for the factor itself. Chapter 4 lays out the types of vertically disaggregated multimarket models that can be used to study research that affects the supply or demand functions for particular factors. In many cases, research directed at environmental issues can also be considered the same way, so long as information can be obtained on the external environmental costs of production and the impact of research on them.[82] There may be more serious difficulties in studying pretechnology research, the commodity- and factor-market impacts of which are less direct and harder to predict.

5.5.2 Achieving a Balance

Limitations on the scope for measuring the economic impact of some types of research programs diminish the virtue of measuring very precisely the impact of others that are easy to evaluate. The economist who takes the formal evaluation of commodity research programs to extremes, while ignoring noncommodity programs, is like the drunk who lost her keys in the car park but only looks under the lamp-post because the light is better there.[83] It would be poor practice to bias a research portfolio away from some research programs solely because their effects were difficult to assess. Still, the laws of economics apply to research on research. Everything else being equal, it is economic to spend relatively more effort on relatively easy problems. The fact that some research programs are difficult, or impossible, to evaluate formally cannot be altered — at least in the short run. Even for the hardest problems, it is worthwhile at a minimum to apply economic principles in a qualitative consideration of the determinants of the likely payoff from the research. At this level of analysis, all research programs are comparable. The incorporation of an economic way of thinking into research management is worthwhile even if the analysis goes no further.

It is important to keep in mind the objectives and purpose of the analysis. We are seeking to improve decision making and decisions — not to perfect them. An informed use of the principles and methods laid out here can lead to a better decision-making environment even if we go no further than evaluating a limited number of alternatives, informally comparing and ranking them. In some cases, however, the information will warrant a more formal priority-setting application to complement the evaluation exercise. Chapter 6 discusses the use of mathematical-programming models for setting priorities when measures of the multidimensional impacts of multiple research program alternatives are available. Chapter 7 discusses shortcut procedures, such as scoring approaches, that may be seen as crude approximations to both formal measurement of economic impact (as described in the present chapter) and formal optimization (as described in chapter 6).

---

82. For example, see Crosson and Anderson (1993).
83. This analogy was used by McCloskey (1985) in a different context in reference to the preoccupation of econometricians with sampling errors.

Appendix A5.1   Computing Research Benefits

To facilitate the implementation of the methods described in this book, in this appendix we document two ways of calculating the returns to research. The alternatives differ in degree of detail. The spreadsheet approach, presented first, is useful for relatively simple analysis; more comprehensive analysis is possible using the *Dream*© computer program, which is based on the logic described in section A5.1.2.

A5.1.1 A Spreadsheet Approach

In this section, two spreadsheet examples are laid out to illustrate the computation of research benefits in either a small, open economy or a closed economy. Any real application would probably not want to use the explicit simplifying assumptions built into these examples. In the open-economy example, exogenous growth in output is built into the spreadsheet. In both examples, a relatively simple treatment of the market is used (no horizontal or vertical disaggregation, no market distortions), and some additional simplifying assumptions about research impact (i.e., the adoption process and research risk) are embedded. A more flexible, general approach to some of these aspects is developed in section A5.1.2. It can be applied easily using the *Dream*© computer program.

Small Open-Economy Example

An example of a spreadsheet used to project national research benefits for a commodity produced in an open market with a small-country assumption is presented in table A5.1.1. The following discussion works the reader across the spreadsheet, column by column, to indicate how research benefits (i.e., change in total economic surplus) are calculated. The formula from chapter 4 for the change in total economic surplus is $\Delta TS_t = K_t P'_t Q'_t (1 + 0.5 K_t \varepsilon)$, where P'_t is the preresearch price, Q'_t is the preresearch quantity in year t (after accounting for exogenous [i.e., nonresearch] shift effects), ε is the elasticity of supply, and K_t is the proportionate shift down in the supply curve in period t due to research (see box 5.1 for a related discussion and definition of variables). The latter is calculated here as

$$K_t = \left[\frac{E(Y)}{\varepsilon} - \frac{E(C)}{1 + E(Y)} \right] pA_t (1 - \delta_t)$$

Column A: Year	Annual benefits are projected for 15 years after research commences ($t = 1, \ldots, 15$).
Column B: Supply elasticity	Single values are specified for the supply-and-

Table A5.1.1: *Sample Spreadsheet to Evaluate Research in a Small Open Economy*

A	B	C	D	E	F	G	H	I	J
Year	ε	η	Max. yield change	Gross cost change per ton	Input cost change per ha.	Input cost change per ton	Net cost change	Prob. of success	Adopt. rate
1994	0.8	0.8	0.16	0.20	0.10	0.086	0.114	0.50	0
1995	0.8	0.8	0.16	0.20	0.10	0.086	0.114	0.50	0
1996	0.8	0.8	0.16	0.20	0.10	0.086	0.114	0.50	0
1997	0.8	0.8	0.16	0.20	0.10	0.086	0.114	0.50	0
1998	0.8	0.8	0.16	0.20	0.10	0.086	0.114	0.50	0
1999	0.8	0.8	0.16	0.20	0.10	0.086	0.114	0.50	0.05
2000	0.8	0.8	0.16	0.20	0.10	0.086	0.114	0.50	0.10
2001	0.8	0.8	0.16	0.20	0.10	0.086	0.114	0.50	0.15
2002	0.8	0.8	0.16	0.20	0.10	0.086	0.114	0.50	0.20
2003	0.8	0.8	0.16	0.20	0.10	0.086	0.114	0.50	0.25
2004	0.8	0.8	0.16	0.20	0.10	0.086	0.114	0.50	0.30
2005	0.8	0.8	0.16	0.20	0.10	0.086	0.114	0.50	0.35
2006	0.8	0.8	0.16	0.20	0.10	0.086	0.114	0.50	0.35
2007	0.8	0.8	0.16	0.20	0.10	0.086	0.114	0.50	0.35
2008	0.8	0.8	0.16	0.20	0.10	0.086	0.114	0.50	0.35

demand elasticities used in the spreadsheet as an approximation, even though the correct procedure would be to adjust elasticities for changes in quantities and prices and for shifts in the linear curves. The symbol is ε.

Column C: Demand elasticity   The absolute value of the demand elasticity, η.

Column D: Proportionate yield change   Expected proportionate yield change per hectare, $E(Y)$, presuming research is successful and is fully adopted.

Column E: Gross proportionate reduction in marginal cost per ton of output   Column D/Column B converts the proportionate yield change to a proportionate gross reduction in marginal cost per ton of output, $E(Y)/\varepsilon$.

Column F: Proportionate change in input cost per hectare   Proportionate change in variable input costs per hectare, $E(C)$, if any, to achieve the expected yield change.

Table A5.1.1: *Sample Spreadsheet to Evaluate Research in a Small Open Economy (contd.)*

K	L	M	N	O	P	Q	R	S
Depre. rate	K_t	Price	Exogen. output growth rate	Quan.	ΔTS_t	Res. cost	Net benefit	NPV
1.00	0	140.0	0.01	2958.3	0	6000	-6000	9806
1.00	0	140.0	0.01	2987.9	0	6000	-6000	
1.00	0	140.0	0.01	3017.8	0	6000	-6000	
1.00	0	140.0	0.01	3047.9	0	6000	-6000	
1.00	0	140.0	0.01	3078.4	0	6000	-6000	
1.00	0.003	140.0	0.01	3109.2	1240		1240	
1.00	0.006	140.0	0.01	3140.3	2507		2507	
1.00	0.009	140.0	0.01	3171.7	3803		3803	
0.95	0.011	140.0	0.01	3203.4	4869		4869	
0.90	0.013	140.0	0.01	3235.4	5828		5828	
0.85	0.015	140.0	0.01	3267.8	6676		6676	
0.80	0.016	140.0	0.01	3300.5	7408		7408	
0.75	0.015	140.0	0.01	3333.5	7012		7012	
0.70	0.014	140.0	0.01	3366.8	6607		6607	
0.65	0.013	140.0	0.01	3400.5	6194		6194	

Column G: Proportionate input cost change per ton of output

Column F/(1 + Column D) converts proportionate input cost change per hectare to a proportionate input cost change per ton of output.

Column H: Net proportionate change in cost per ton of output

(Column E – Column G) nets out the effect of variable input cost changes associated with the yield change to give the maximum potential net change in marginal cost per ton of output.

Column I: Probability of research success

Probability, p, that research will achieve the yield change in column D.

Column J: Adoption rate

Reflects the rate of adoption, A_t, defined in relation to years, t, from the commencement of research. Assumed here that research takes five years before technologies are available. Then adoption occurs on five percent of the land devoted to that commodity in year six, ten percent in year seven, and so on.

Column K:	Depreciation factor	$1 -$ rate of annual depreciation of the technology, $(1 - \delta_t)$. Linear depreciation begins eight years after research commences.
Column L:	Proportional supply shift in year t	K_t : Column H × Column I × Column J × Column K, giving the cumulative proportionate shift down in the supply curve.
Column M:	Price	In this case, price remains constant at P_0 because although the commodity is traded, the country is not assumed to influence world price. Units are, say, constant 1994 dollars per ton. (If desired, exogenous changes could be built in so that the exogenous world price varies over time.)
Column N:	Exogenous output growth rate	The anticipated proportionate change in output not due to research in each year. The exogenous output growth rate is equal to the sum of the growth rates of area, g_A, or yield, g_Y, *not* due to research: $g_Q = g_A + g_Y$.
Column O:	Quantity	Q_t': $Q_0 \times [$ $(1+$ Column N$)$ **$($ Column A - 1993$)]$ where $Q_0 = 2929$ thousands of tons is the initial base quantity; $Q_t = Q_0 (1 + g_Q)^t$ is the initial quantity, adjusted by exogenous output growth.
Column P:	Changes in total surplus in year t	ΔTS_t : Column L × Column M × Column O × $[1 + (0.5 \times$ Column L × Column B$)]$. This column represents change in total economic surplus equal to $K_t P_t Q_t (1 + 0.5K_t \varepsilon)$. Units are thousands of base-year dollars per year.
Column Q:	Research cost	Annual research cost for the commodity corresponding to expected yield increase, and so on, described above. Units are thousands of constant (base year = 1994) dollars.
Column R:	Net benefit	Column P – Column Q.
Column S:	NPV	Net present value (using the formula embedded in the spreadsheet program). In this case, a real discount rate (e.g., 0.03) must be selected for the analysis because benefits and costs are expressed in real terms (see section 5.6.1). Units are thousands of base-year dollars.

Closed-Economy Example

The spreadsheet example in table A5.1.1 is relatively simple because of the assumed market situation. If a closed-economy market situation is assumed, the economic surplus formulas are more complicated. The formulas from chapter 4 for the change in total economic surplus, ΔTS, and in consumer surplus, ΔCS, for a closed economy with no exogenous shifts in demand or supply are as follows: $\Delta TS_t = K_t P_0 Q_0 (1 + 0.5 Z_t \eta)$ and $\Delta CS_t = Z_t P_0 Q_0 (1 + 0.5 Z_t \eta)$, where $Z_t = K_t \varepsilon/(\varepsilon+\eta)$. The columns shown in table A5.1.2 are the same as in table A5.1.1 through Column M: those columns refer to the base parameters and variables used to compute the series of research-induced supply shifts and to the base price. A description of the added columns is as follows:

Column N:	Proportionate decrease in price in year t	$Z_t = K_t \varepsilon/(\varepsilon + \eta)$ = Column L × [Column B/(Column B + Column C)].
Column O:	Quantity	The preresearch quantity is constant, equal to the base quantity.
Column P:	Change in total surplus in year t	ΔTS_t: Column L × Column M × Column O × [1 + 0.5 × (Column N × Column C)].

Table A5.1.2: *Sample Spreadsheet to Evaluate Research in a Closed Economy*

A	B	C	D	E	F	G	H	I	J
				Gross cost	Input cost	Input cost			
			Max. yield	change	change	change	Net cost	Prob. of	Adopt.
Year	ε	η	change	per ton	per ha.	per ton	change	success	rate
1994	0.8	0.8	0.16	0.20	0.10	0.086	0.114	0.50	0
1995	0.8	0.8	0.16	0.20	0.10	0.086	0.114	0.50	0
1996	0.8	0.8	0.16	0.20	0.10	0.086	0.114	0.50	0
1997	0.8	0.8	0.16	0.20	0.10	0.086	0.114	0.50	0
1998	0.8	0.8	0.16	0.20	0.10	0.086	0.114	0.50	0
1999	0.8	0.8	0.16	0.20	0.10	0.086	0.114	0.50	0.05
2000	0.8	0.8	0.16	0.20	0.10	0.086	0.114	0.50	0.10
2001	0.8	0.8	0.16	0.20	0.10	0.086	0.114	0.50	0.15
2002	0.8	0.8	0.16	0.20	0.10	0.086	0.114	0.50	0.20
2003	0.8	0.8	0.16	0.20	0.10	0.086	0.114	0.50	0.25
2004	0.8	0.8	0.16	0.20	0.10	0.086	0.114	0.50	0.30
2005	0.8	0.8	0.16	0.20	0.10	0.086	0.114	0.50	0.35
2006	0.8	0.8	0.16	0.20	0.10	0.086	0.114	0.50	0.35
2007	0.8	0.8	0.16	0.20	0.10	0.086	0.114	0.50	0.35
2008	0.8	0.8	0.16	0.20	0.10	0.086	0.114	0.50	0.35

Table A5.1.2:   *Sample Spreadsheet to Evaluate Research in a Closed Economy (contd.)*

K	L	M	N	O	P	Q	R	S	T	U
Depr. rate	K_t	Price	Z_t	Quan.	ΔTS_t	ΔCS_t	ΔPS_t	Res. cost	Net benefit	NPV
1.00	0	140	0	2929	0	0	0	6000	-6000	5782
1.00	0	140	0	2929	0	0	0	6000	-6000	
1.00	0	140	0	2929	0	0	0	6000	-6000	
1.00	0	140	0	2929	0	0	0	6000	-6000	
1.00	0	140	0	2929	0	0	0	6000	-6000	
1.00	0.003	140	0.001	2929	1167	584	584		1167	
1.00	0.006	140	0.003	2929	2336	1168	1168		2336	
1.00	0.009	140	0.004	2929	3506	1753	1753		3506	
0.95	0.011	140	0.005	2929	4442	2221	2221		4442	
0.90	0.013	140	0.006	2929	5263	2631	2631		5263	
0.85	0.015	140	0.007	2929	5967	2983	2983		5967	
0.80	0.016	140	0.008	2929	6553	3277	3277		6553	
0.75	0.015	140	0.007	2929	6143	3071	3071		6143	
0.70	0.014	140	0.007	2929	5732	2866	2866		5732	
0.65	0.013	140	0.006	2929	5322	2661	2661		5322	

Column Q: Change in consumer surplus in year t

ΔCS_t : Column M × Column N × Column O × [1 + (0.5 × Column N × Column C)].

Column R: Change in producer surplus in year t

ΔPS_t: Column P – Column Q.

Column S: Research cost

See explanation for table A5.1.1.

Column T: Net benefit

Column P – Column S.

Column U: NPV

See explanation for table A5.1.1.

Many other spreadsheet examples could be provided for other market and policy scenarios. The above examples can be modified using either the formulas or the methods provided in chapter 4 for developing new formulas. Shortcut formulas for calculating surpluses as measures of research benefits are summarized in appendix A5.2.

A5.1.2 The Dream© Approach

In order to illustrate more clearly the economic surplus method in practice, this appendix presents a model that can be used to estimate the present value of research benefits in the following cases:
- multiple regions, i
- producing a homogeneous product
- with linear supply and demand in each region
- with exponential (parallel) exogenous growth of linear supply and demand
- with a parallel research-induced supply shift in one region (or multiple regions)
- with a consequent parallel research-induced supply shift in other regions
- with a range of market-distorting policies
- with zero transport costs (at least initially)
- with a research lag followed by a linear adoption curve up to a maximum
- with an eventual linear decline

This example for one commodity could be duplicated across a range of commodities (or research programs for a single commodity or several commodities) in a priority-setting study. It considers only the benefit side of the cost-benefit equation. Additional work would be needed, measuring the present value of the costs of achieving the supply shift, to complete the analysis.

The model, developed in detail below, is the conceptual basis for the *Dream©* computer program that has been developed for research priority setting and evaluation. In addition, at the end of this appendix, we present some shortcut methods and summary formulas that can be applied in the common situation where "back-of-the-envelope" estimates of benefits are desired, without going into the full analysis of growth over time, present-value calculations, multiple markets, or nontariff distortions in markets. For the archetypal cases of a small or large country in trade with and without a distortion at the border (i.e., a tariff or an export subsidy), a closed economy (with and without a commodity tax), and a large country in trade (with no distortions), we present summary formulas for the benefits to producers, consumers, taxpayers, and the economy as a whole from a given research-induced parallel supply shift.

General Form of Supply and Demand

For region i in year t, linear supply-and-demand equations for a particular commodity (subscript suppressed) are specified as

Supply: $Q_{i,t} = \alpha_{it} + \beta_i PP_{i,t}$ (A5.1a)

Demand: $C_{i,t} = \gamma_{it} + \delta_i PC_{i,t}$ (A5.1b)

The first subscript, i, refers to a region, and the second subscript, t, refers to years from the initial starting point of the evaluation. The slopes are assumed to be constant for each region for all time periods. The intercepts may grow over time to reflect underlying growth in supply or demand due to factors other than research (i.e., growth in productivity or income). All of the variables are expressed in real terms so that any growth is real growth. One important implication of this is that the discount rate used in subsequent analysis to compare costs and benefits of research over time must be a real rate.

Initial Parameterization

The parameters of the supply-and-demand equations are defined by beginning with initial ($t = 0$) values of
- quantity consumed in each region – $C_{i,0}$
- quantity produced in each region – $Q_{i,0}$
- producer price in each region – $PP_{i,0}$
- consumer price in each region – $PC_{i,0}$
- elasticity of supply in each region – $\varepsilon_{i,0}$
- elasticity of demand in each region – $\eta_{i,0}$ (< 0)

In many cases, the initial values of elasticities would be assumed to be equal among regions (a convenient, but not necessary, assumption). These initial values are sufficient to allow us to compute the slope and intercept of supply and demand in each region for the initital year:

$$\beta_{i0} = \varepsilon_{i0} Q_{i,0} / PP_{i,0}$$ (A5.2a)

$$\alpha_{i0} = (1 - \varepsilon_{i0}) Q_{i,0}$$ (A5.2b)

$$\delta_{i0} = \eta_{i0} C_{i,0} / PC_{i,0}$$ (A5.2c)

$$\gamma_{i0} = (1 - \eta_{i0}) C_{i,0}$$ (A5.2d)

Exogenous Growth in Supply and Demand

We incorporate average exponential growth rates to reflect growth in demand (due to growth in population and income) and supply (due to growth in productivity or an increase in area cropped) that is expected to occur regardless of whether the research program of interest is undertaken.

$$\alpha_{it} = \alpha_{it-1} + \pi_i^Q Q_{i,t} \text{ for } t > 0$$ (A5.3a)

$$\gamma_{it} = \gamma_{it-1} + \pi_i^C C_{i,t} \text{ for } t > 0$$ (A5.3b)

where

$\pi_i^C =$ the growth rate of demand (e.g., population growth rate + income elasticity × income growth rate)

$\pi_i^Q =$ is the growth rate of supply (e.g., area growth rate + yield growth rate not attributable to research)

Now we have sufficient information to parameterize the supply-and-demand equations for each region in each year under the no-research scenario.

Research-Induced Supply Shifts

Local effect of research: Let region i undertake a program of research with

- probability of success p_i, which, if the research is successful and the results are fully adopted, will yield
- a cost saving per unit of output equal to c_i percent of the initial price, $PP_{i,0}$ in region i, while
- a ceiling adoption rate of A_i^{MAX} percent holds in region i

Then it is *anticipated* that the supply function in region i will shift *down* (in the price direction), eventually, by an *amount per unit* equal to

$$k_i^{MAX} = p_i \ c_i \ A_i^{MAX} \ PP_{i,0} \geq 0 \qquad\qquad (A5.4)$$

The *actual* supply shift in any particular year is some fraction of the eventual *maximum* supply shift, k_i^{MAX}, defined above. In order to define the actual supply shift, we can combine the maximum supply shift with other information about the shape of the time path of $k_{i,t}$ based on data about adoption and depreciation-cum-obsolescence factors. Assuming a trapezoidal shape for the adoption curve, in order to define the entire profile of supply shifts over time, we need to define the following parameters:

- research lag in years – λ_R
- adoption lag (years from initial adoption to maximum adoption) – λ_A
- maximum lag (years from maximum adoption to eventual decline) – λ_M
- decline lag (years from the beginning to the end of the decline) – λ_D

Then we can define the supply shifts (in the price direction) for region i in each year t as follows:

$$k_{i,t} = 0 \qquad\qquad\qquad \text{(for } 0 \leq t \leq \lambda_R)$$

$$k_{i,t} = k_i^{MAX} (t - \lambda_R)/\lambda_A \qquad\qquad \text{(for } \lambda_R < t \leq \lambda_R + \lambda_A)$$

$$k_{i,t} = k_i^{MAX} \qquad\qquad \begin{aligned} &\text{(for } \lambda_R + \lambda_A < t \leq \lambda_R \\ &\quad + \lambda_A + \lambda_M) \end{aligned}$$

$$k_{i,t} = k_i^{MAX} \frac{(\lambda_R + \lambda_A + \lambda_M + \lambda_D - t)}{\lambda_D} \qquad \text{(for } \lambda_R + \lambda_A + \lambda_M < t \le \lambda_R \\ + \lambda_A + \lambda_M + \lambda_D)$$

$$k_{i,t} = 0 \qquad \text{(for } t > \lambda_R + \lambda_A + \lambda_M + \lambda_D)$$

Figure A5.4.2 in appendix A5.4 shows the trapezoidal adoption curve and shows how the parameters above (λ_R, λ_A, λ_M, and λ_D) may be used to define the entire curve. Options for deriving S-shaped adoption curves are discussed in section 5.3.3 and appendix A5.4.

Spillover effects of research:[84] The *spillover effects* from region i to other regions, j, are parameterized in relation to the supply shifts in region i, implicitly assuming the same adoption curve applies in every region.

$$k_{j,t} = \theta_{ji} \, k_{i,t} \text{ for all } i \text{ and } j \qquad (A5.5)$$

where

θ_{ji} = supply shift in j due to research-induced supply shift in i ($\theta_{ii} = 1$)

With-Research Supply and Demand

To model the with-research case (denoted by superscript R on all relevant variables and parameters), we take the intercepts from the without-research case (but include the effects of exogenous supply growth), add the effect of the supply shift to them, and include the result in the supply equation:

$$\alpha_{j,t}^R = \alpha_{jt} + k_{jt} \, \beta_j \qquad (A5.6)$$

The models for supply and demand that reflect the local and spillover effects of research are

$$Q_{i,t}^R = \alpha_{it}^R + \beta_i \, PP_{i,t}^R \qquad (A5.7a)$$

$$C_{i,t}^R = \gamma_{it} + \delta_i \, PC_{i,t}^R \qquad (A5.7b)$$

The only substantive difference from the corresponding without-research equations (A5.1a and A5.1b) is in the supply intercept, but as noted above, the prices and quantities are labeled differently (the R superscript) to distinguish them from the without-research values:

- quantity consumed in each region – $C_{i,t}^R$
- quantity produced in each region – $Q_{i,t}^R$

---

84. The spillover coefficients, θ_{ji}, are defined as if they were constant for all types of research-induced supply shifts and, for a given technological change, constant over time, implying that the relative shifts always occur in fixed proportion. These might not be reasonable restrictions for all problems. Between agroecological zones i and j, the spillover relationships are very likely to differ among commodities, among types of technological changes for a given commodity, and over time for a given technological change and a given commodity. For some problems, it might be necessary to redefine the spillover matrix for different types of technologies and different times after release of a technology.

- producer price in each region – $PP_{i,t}^R$
- consumer price in each region – $PC_{i,t}^R$

Market-Clearing Rules

For all of the scenarios to be considered, there is an overall quantity clearing rule to the effect that the sum of quantities supplied equals the sum of quantities demanded in each year. Considering n regions,

$$Q_t = (Q_{1,t} + Q_{2,t} + \ldots + Q_{n,t}) = C_t = (C_{1,t} + C_{2,t} + \ldots + C_{n,t}) \qquad \text{(A5.8)}$$

All of the market-clearing rules express policies in terms of price wedges that permit differences between consumer and producer prices within and among regions consistent with clearing quantities produced and consumed.[85]

Free trade: The easiest case is that of free trade, where

- with-research prices: $PP_{i,t}^R = PC_{i,t}^R = PC_{j,t}^R = PP_{j,t}^R = P_t^R$
- without-research prices: $PP_{i,t} = PC_{i,t} = PC_{j,t} = PP_{j,t} = P_t$

are defined for all regions i and j and for any year t.

Making this substitution into each of the n regional supply-and-demand equations and then substituting them into equation A5.8 yields a solution for the equilibrium price for each year. To simplify, let us define the following aggregated parameters for each year, t:

- $\gamma_t = \gamma_{1t} + \gamma_{2t} + \ldots + \gamma_{nt}$
- $\alpha_t = \alpha_{1t} + \alpha_{2t} + \ldots + \alpha_{nt}$
- $\alpha_t^R = \alpha_{1t}^R + \alpha_{2t}^R + \ldots + \alpha_{nt}^R$
- $\delta_t = \delta = \delta_{10} + \delta_{20} + \ldots + \delta_{n0} < 0$
- $\beta_t = \beta = \beta_{10} + \beta_{20} + \ldots + \beta_{n0} > 0$

Then the without-research and the with-research market-clearing prices under free trade are given by

$$P_t = (\gamma_t - \alpha_t)/(\beta - \delta) \qquad \text{(A5.9a)}$$

$$P_t^R = (\gamma_t - \alpha_t^R)/(\beta - \delta) \qquad \text{(A5.9b)}$$

These are always positive numbers, with $P_t > P_t^R$, because the intercepts

---

85. Transportation costs influence trade among countries and should theoretically be incorporated into the analysis if possible. However, accurate calculation of these costs is often difficult because it requires knowing the transportation differentials for each commodity between the home country being studied and each of its major trading partners, as well as the pattern of commodity flows. If international research spillovers are included in the analysis, either (a) information should be collected on the likely destinations and transportation costs between the home country and each other country involved so that a relatively accurate assessment can be made of the price wedge to be driven between the excess-supply and excess-demand curves or (b) transportation costs should be ignored. When regional analyses within a country are being conducted, regional transportation costs also may be needed.

on the *quantity* axis satisfy $\gamma_t > \alpha_t^R > \alpha_t$, — unless we make a mistake such as letting supply grow too fast relative to demand.[86]

We can substitute the results for prices from equations A5.9a and A5.9b into the regional supply-and-demand equations to compute regional quantities produced and consumed with and without research and, as we shall see later, then calculate the regional consumer and producer welfare effects.

Generalized taxes and subsidies: We can define a general solution for a large variety of tax or subsidy regimes by setting out a general model in which a *per unit* tax is collected from consumers in every region and from producers in every region.

- T_i^C = per unit consumer tax in region i
- T_i^Q = per unit producer tax in region i

Different policies can be represented as different combinations of taxes and subsidies

- consumption tax in region i at T_i per unit: $\quad T_i^C = T_i\;; \quad T_i^Q = 0$
- production tax in region i at T_i per unit: $\quad T_i^C = 0\;; \quad T_i^Q = T_i$
- export tax in region i at T_i per unit: $\quad T_i^C = -T_i\;; \quad T_i^Q = T_i$
- import tariff in region i at T_i per unit: $\quad T_i^C = T_i\;; \quad T_i^Q = -T_i$

A subsidy is a negative tax, so it is also possible to use these to represent subsidies on output, consumption, imports, or exports. One way to think about this is to imagine a region with no taxes or subsidies in which the prices to producers and consumers are $P_t = PC_t = PP_t$ and $P_t^R = PC_t^R = PP_t^R$. Thus, P_t (expressed in common currency units, either local currency or $US) is the border price for an exporter or an importer whose internal consumer or producer prices will be equal to that price in the absence of any domestic distortions. The arbitrage rules are that the prices in all regions are equal to

- $PP_{i,t} = P_t - T_i^Q$
- $PC_{i,t} = P_t + T_i^C$
- $PP_{i,t}^R = P_t^R - T_i^Q$
- $PC_{i,t}^R = P_t^R + T_i^C$

for all regions i and j and for any year t.

Making this substitution into each of the n regional supply-and-demand equations and substituting them into equation A5.9 yields a solution for the equilibrium price for each year. As for the case of free trade, let us define the following aggregated parameters for each year:

86. For instance, we could violate this condition by setting the *autonomous* growth rate of supply so much greater than the *autonomous* growth rate of demand that in some set of future projections a point would be reached where supply and demand did not cross in the positive orthant — i.e., the *quantity* intercept of supply would become greater than the *quantity* intercept of demand in either the with- or without-research case.

- $\gamma_t = \gamma_{1t} + \gamma_{2t} + \ldots + \gamma_{nt}$
- $\alpha_t = \alpha_{1t} + \alpha_{2t} + \ldots + \alpha_{nt}$
- $\alpha_t^R = \alpha_{1t}^R + \alpha_{2t}^R + \ldots + \alpha_{nt}^R$
- $\delta_t = \delta = \delta_{10} + \delta_{20} + \ldots + \delta_{n0} < 0$
- $\beta_t = \beta = \beta_{10} + \beta_{20} + \ldots + \beta_{n0} > 0$

In addition, we can define the following aggregated demand-and-supply shifts in the quantity direction because of consumer and producer taxes:

- $T_t^C = T_{1t}^C \delta_{10} + T_{2t}^C \delta_{20} + \ldots + T_{nt}^C \delta_{n0}$
- $T_t^Q = T_{1t}^Q \beta_{10} + T_{2t}^Q \beta_{20} + \ldots + T_{nt}^Q \beta_{n0}$

$$P_t = (\gamma_t + T_t^Q + T_t^C - \alpha_t)/(\beta - \delta) \qquad \text{(A5.10a)}$$

$$P_t^R = (\gamma_t + T_t^Q + T_t^C - \alpha_t^R)/(\beta - \delta) \qquad \text{(A5.10b)}$$

To check the signs intuitively, taxes on production in all regions will raise the equilibrium world trading price P_t — which is equal to the producer price in any country or region with no producer taxes and the consumer price in any country or region with no consumer taxes. Taxes on consumption in all regions will lower it.[87] Of course this hypothetical price, P_t, might not actually apply anywhere.

To compute the actual consumer and producer prices in any region, the results of equations A5.10a and A5.10b are substituted into the arbitrage (market-clearing) rules given above (under the heading "generalized taxes and subsidies"). Then the individual prices can be used in the individual supply-and-demand equations (equations A5.1 and A5.7) to compute quantities with and without research, and from there to compute surplus effects. Notice that this set of results includes the free-trade model as a special case (i.e., when all of the taxes and subsidies are zero).

The small-country case: The small-country case can be represented in this model without modification. However, to do that requires getting information — that is not useful otherwise — on quantities produced and consumed in the rest of the world. The alternative is to define the market-clearing price for equations A5.10a and A5.10b as an exogenous parameter:

$$P_t = P_t^R = \overline{P}_t$$

It might require defining a growth rate for P_t to obtain a series of exogenous world prices based on a starting value for P_0. Then corresponding quantities

87. A positive value of T_i^Q for all i leads to a *positive* value of T_t^Q and thus a higher value of P_t. A positive value of T_i^C for all i leads to a *negative* value of T_t^C (because the demand slopes $\delta_{i,0}$ are negative numbers) and a lowering of the price, P_t.

can be obtained by substituting into the relevant supply-and-demand equations.

Other policies: Quantitative restrictions on production or trade can be treated approximately as tax/subsidy equivalents with a little care to distribute "tax revenue" as quota rents. The approximation is somewhat unreliable in a dynamic model, but it might suffice for our purposes. A target price, deficiency-payment scheme might involve more work. Conceptually, the approach is to define target price and allow it to determine output in regions where it applies. Then, with that supply as exogenous, supply equations in the other regions and demand equations in all regions would interact to determine price.

Welfare Effects

The following equations for welfare effects should be correct for most (if not all) types of policies (i.e., market-clearing rules).

$$\Delta PS_{j,t} = (k_{j,t} + PP^R_{j,t} - PP_{j,t})\, [Q_{j,t} + 0.5\, (Q^R_{j,t} - Q_{j,t})] \qquad (A5.11a)$$

$$\Delta CS_{j,t} = (\,PC_{j,t} - PC^R_{j,t}\,)\, [C_{j,t} + 0.5\, (C^R_{j,t} - C_{j,t})] \qquad (A5.11b)$$

$$\Delta GS_{j,t} = T^C_{jt}\, (C^R_{j,t} - C_{j,t}) + T^Q_{jt}\, (Q^R_{j,t} - Q_{j,t}) \qquad (A5.11c)$$

where

$\Delta PS_{j,t}$ = producer research benefit in region j in year t

$\Delta CS_{j,t}$ = consumer research benefit in region j in year t

$\Delta GS_{j,t}$ = government research benefit in region j in year t

Aggregation over Time and Interest Groups

The model so far is capable of generating an indefinitely long time series of prices, quantities, and economic surplus measures for the regions of interest for a range of tax or subsidy policies. The remaining problem is to aggregate those measures into summary measures of research benefits. For a given policy scenario, we have the measures of benefits — $\Delta PS_{i,t}$, $\Delta CS_{i,t}$, $\Delta GS_{i,t}$ — *for each region in each time period.*

The *real* discount rate must be defined for the computation of the present value of the stream of benefits. A reasonable approach is to fix a single value for all regions, interest groups, and years so that

$$r_{i,t} = r_{j,s} = r$$

We need to define a relevant planning horizon. Thirty years should be adequate for most purposes if we are using discount rates of 5 % per year or greater. The *present values* of benefits to interest groups are then defined as

$$VPS_i = \Sigma_{t=0}^{30} \Delta PS_{i,t}/(1+r)^t$$
$$= \Delta PS_{i,0} + \Delta PS_{i,1}/(1+r) \tag{A5.12a}$$
$$+ \Delta PS_{i,2}/(1+r)^2 + \ldots + \Delta PS_{i,30}/(1+r)^{30}$$

$$VCS_i = \Sigma_{t=0}^{30} \Delta CS_{i,t}/(1+r)^t$$
$$= \Delta CS_{i,0} + \Delta CS_{i,1}/(1+r) \tag{A5.12b}$$
$$+ \Delta CS_{i,2}/(1+r)^2 + \ldots + \Delta CS_{i,30}/(1+r)^{30}$$

$$VGS_i = \Sigma_{t=0}^{30} \Delta GS_{i,t}/(1+r)^t$$
$$= \Delta GS_{i,0} + \Delta GS_{i,1}/(1+r) \tag{A5.12c}$$
$$+ \Delta GS_{i,2}/(1+r)^2 + \ldots + \Delta GS_{i,30}/(1+r)^{30}$$

If a longer planning horizon is appropriate, we can either simply increase the number of years from 30 (probably the best way) or approximate the effects beyond 30 years using an infinite series (which is risky when the markets are growing and research effects are depreciating). Then we are free to add these present values up across the different producing and consuming groups in whatever fashion we find useful.

Appendix A5.2: Selected Formulas for Calculating Research Benefits

The *Dream©* model is relatively general, and for some situations that generality may be a disadvantage. Sometimes it is considered unnecessary, for instance, to go to the trouble of allowing for exogenous growth in supply and demand or to do a full capital-budgeting analysis. Some studies implicitly assume that the time structure of costs and benefits is constant across research alternatives, and therefore they compare the gross annual research benefits after full adoption. These simplifying assumptions, whether made implicitly or explicitly, are very restrictive. It is therefore questionable whether the results obtained under such assumptions would be valid generally. However, in some situations such assumptions will be made either because they are believed to be an appropriate approximation or because the analysis is necessarily a shortcut one. In order to facilitate the analysis in those cases, we provide some formulas for measures of the total gross annual research benefit (GARB) and its distribution in some typical market-structure scenarios. All of these shortcut formulas may be obtained as special cases of those in the model above; that is, they are based on an assumption of approximately linear supply and demand with a parallel research-induced supply shift in the home country (or region).

A5.2.1 Simplified, Two-Country Model

Dropping redundant time subscripts (i.e., to consider only a one-shot, comparative static analysis) and considering only two countries or regions, the variables in the model are, for regions j = A (the home or innovating country or region) or B (the rest of the world or the "other" noninnovating country or region)

- producer price in region $j - PP_j$
- consumer price in region $j - PC_j$
- production in region $j - Q_j$
- consumption in region $j - C_j$
- production tax in region $j - T_j^Q > 0$ ($T_j^Q < 0$ for production subsidy)
- consumption tax in region $j - T_j^C > 0$ ($T_j^C < 0$ for consumption subsidy)
- producer research benefit in region $j - PS_j$
- consumer research benefit in region $j - CS_j$
- government research benefit in region $j - GS_j$
- national research benefit in region $j - NS_j$

Research-Induced Supply Shifts

As a special case of equation A5.4, we assume that the supply function in the home country (region A) will shift down (in the price direction) by an amount per unit equal to

$$k = k_A = K\, PP_A \tag{A5.13}$$

where K is the percentage shift down of supply relative to the initial producer price, PP_A.

Research-Induced Changes in Prices and Quantities

In order to measure the welfare impact, what remains to be defined are the changes in prices (ΔPP_j and ΔPC_j for $j = $ A and B) and quantities (ΔQ_j and ΔC_j for $j = $ A and B) due to the research-induced supply shift in terms of the magnitude of the supply shift, k_A, the parameters of supply and demand, and the policy wedges. The policy wedges may be represented (using the per unit consumption and production taxes, T^C and T^Q, respectively, and the hypothetical price, P, as before) as

$$PP_A = P - T_A^Q\,;\, PC_A = P + T_A^C\,;\, PP_B = P - T_B^Q\,;\, PC_B = P + T_B^C \tag{A5.14}$$

Then, we may write the supply-and-demand equations, including the tax wedges and the supply-shift parameter, to reflect research-induced technical change, as

$$Q_A = \alpha_A + \beta_A\,(P - T_A^Q + k\,) \tag{A5.15a}$$

$$C_A = \gamma_A + \delta_A\,(P + T_A^C\,) \tag{A5.15b}$$

$$Q_B = \alpha_B + \beta_B\,(P - T_B^Q\,) \tag{A5.15c}$$

$$C_B = \gamma_B + \delta_B\,(P + T_B^C\,) \tag{A5.15d}$$

Market clearing in this system of four equations is enforced by setting aggregate supply equal to aggregate demand (i.e., $Q_A + Q_B = C_A + C_B$). The without-research case is obtained by setting k equal to zero in equation A5.15a. The general solution for the research-induced change in price is given by

$$\Delta P = -\,k\beta_A / (\beta_A + \beta_B - \delta_A - \delta_B\,) < 0 \tag{A5.16}$$

It is an interesting and useful feature of the linear and additive structure of this model, with fixed per unit taxes/subsidies, that the research-induced *changes* in all producer and consumer prices are equal. That is,

$$\Delta PP_A = \Delta PC_A = \Delta PP_B = \Delta PC_B = \Delta P \tag{A5.17}$$

Thus, the research-induced changes in quantities are given by

$$\Delta Q_A = \beta_A\,(k + \Delta P)\,;\, \Delta C_A = \delta_A \Delta P\,;\, \Delta Q_B = \beta_B \Delta P\,;\, \Delta C_B = \delta_B \Delta P \tag{A5.18}$$

Welfare Impact

The following equations for welfare effects are special cases of equations A5.11a through A5.11c, where the welfare effects in the *home country or region*, (i.e., country A) are given by

$$\Delta PS_A = (k + \Delta P)(Q_A + 0.5\Delta Q_A) \tag{A5.19a}$$

$$\Delta CS_A = -\Delta P(C_A + 0.5\Delta C_A) \tag{A5.19b}$$

$$\Delta GS_A = T_A^C \Delta C_A + T_A^Q \Delta Q_A \tag{A5.19c}$$

$$\Delta NS_A = \Delta PS_A + \Delta CS_A + \Delta GS_A \tag{A5.19d}$$

and the welfare effects in the *other country or region*, or the rest of the world (i.e., denoted B) are given by

$$\Delta PS_B = \Delta P(Q_B + 0.5\Delta Q_B) \tag{A5.19e}$$

$$\Delta CS_B = -\Delta P(C_B + 0.5\Delta C_B) \tag{A5.19f}$$

$$\Delta GS_B = T_B^C \Delta C_B + T_B^Q \Delta Q_B \tag{A5.19g}$$

$$\Delta NS_B = \Delta PS_B + \Delta CS_B + \Delta GS_B \tag{A5.19h}$$

In these equations, Δ denotes the difference between the with-research and without-research values of variables. Total regional (national) benefits in region j are defined as ΔNS_j, and global benefits, ΔWS, may be obtained by adding up regional (national) benefits.

Examples

Small, open economy with no distortions: The simplest case of all is that of a small country in trade for which the export (or import) price is exogenous and unaffected by the research-induced supply shift. In this case, taking the limit as $\beta_B \to \infty$, $\Delta P = 0$ so that welfare of the ROW in total, and welfare of domestic consumers, are unaffected. Also, in the absence of price-distorting policies, taxpayer welfare is unaffected. In short, only domestic producer welfare is affected, and the measure of gross annual producer (and national and global) research benefits is $\Delta PS_A = \Delta NS_A = \Delta WS$

$$\Delta PS_A = k(Q_A + 0.5\Delta Q_A) = k(Q_A + 0.5\beta_A k)$$

$$= kQ_A(1 + 0.5\beta_A k/Q_A) \tag{A5.20a}$$

If we choose to express the supply shift, k, as a fraction of the initial price, P_A, i.e., let $K = k/P_A$, then we may express the result above in terms of the percentage supply shift and the elasticity of supply, ε_A, as

$$\Delta PS_A = KP_A \, Q_A \, (1 + 0.5K\varepsilon_A) \tag{A5.20b}$$

where the values of P_A and Q_A refer to the preresearch equilibrium and the elasticity of supply has been evaluated at that point.

Small, open economy with a border distortion subsidy or tax: In the case of a small country in trade with a border tax (or subsidy), the welfare of the ROW in total and of domestic consumers is still unaffected by domestic supply shifts. However, in this case, taxpayer welfare is affected. The measure of producer research benefits is, as before,

$$\Delta PS_A = k \, (Q_A{}' + 0.5\Delta Q_A) = k \, (Q_A{}' + 0.5k\beta_A)$$

$$= K' \, P_A{}' \, Q_A{}' \, (1 + 0.5K' \, \varepsilon_A{}') \tag{A5.21a}$$

where $K' = k \, P_A{}'$ defines the supply shift as a proportion of the *distorted* preresearch price. Here, the values of $P_A{}'$ and $Q_A{}'$ refer to the distorted preresearch equilibrium and the elasticity of supply, $\varepsilon_A{}'$, has been evaluated at that point. In addition, there is the welfare impact on taxpayers to consider. An import tariff of T per unit (or an equivalent *ad valorem* tariff at a rate $\tau = T/P_A$) on an imported good is equivalent to an output subsidy of T per unit and a consumption tax at the same rate. Thus, for an imported good with a tariff, as a result of the research-induced increase in supply, taxpayers lose an amount equal to the per unit tax multiplied by the reduction in imports (i.e., the increase in output):

$$\Delta GS_A = - \, T\Delta Q_A = - \, T \, \beta_A \, k = - \, \tau P_A{}' \, Q_A{}' \, K'\varepsilon_A{}' \tag{A5.21b}$$

The same formula would apply for an export good with an export subsidy, while the sign would be reversed in the case of an import subsidy or an export tax. Net domestic benefits from the research-induced supply shift are obtained by adding effects on taxpayer welfare and producer welfare. Recall that with linear supply and demand and a fixed per unit tax or subsidy, in the small-country case, national research benefits are unaffected by the presence of the distortion. That is, producer research benefits are higher under a tariff by an amount exactly equal to the research-induced reduction in tariff revenues. This result (shown by Alston, Edwards and Freebairn 1988, and generalized by Alston and Martin 1992) can be verified using the equations above.

Small, closed economy with no distortions: In a small country, price is exogenous. The simplest case with endogenous prices is that of a closed economy with no market distortions. In that case, the change in producer and consumer price is equal to

$$\Delta P = -k\beta_A / (\beta_A - \delta_A) = -k\varepsilon_A / (\varepsilon_A + \eta_A)$$
$$= -KP_A \, \varepsilon_A / (\varepsilon_A + \eta_A) = - ZP_A \qquad \text{(A5.22a)}$$

where $Z = - K\varepsilon_A / (\varepsilon_A + \eta_A)$ is the fall in price relative to its initial value, and η_A is the absolute value of the price elasticity of demand in country A, so that the corresponding change in quantity is

$$\Delta Q_A = \Delta C_A = -k\beta_A \delta_A / (\beta_A - \delta_A) = k \, (Q_A / P_A) \, \varepsilon_A \eta_A / (\varepsilon_A + \eta_A)$$
$$\qquad \text{(A5.22b)}$$

$$= KQ_A \varepsilon_A \eta_A / (\varepsilon_A + \eta_A) = ZQ_A \eta_A$$

and the welfare effects are given by

$$\Delta PS_A = (k + \Delta P) \, (Q_A + 0.5\Delta Q_A) = (K - Z) \, P_A Q_A \, (1 + 0.5Z\eta_A) \quad \text{(A5.22c)}$$

$$\Delta CS_A = -\Delta P \, (C_A + 0.5\Delta C_A) = ZP_A Q_A \, (1 + 0.5Z\eta_A) \qquad \text{(A5.22d)}$$

$$\Delta NS_A = k \, (Q_A + 0.5\Delta Q_A) = KP_A Q_A \, (1 + 0.5Z\eta_A)$$
$$= \Delta PS_A + \Delta CS_A \qquad \text{(A5.22e)}$$

Small, closed economy with distortions: As for the small open-economy case, the introduction of market distortions (in the form of per unit taxes or subsidies) with linear supply and demand does not change the impact of research on any of the prices. The introduction of distortions does, however, change the quantities produced and consumed, to which those price changes are applied in order to evaluate the welfare impact. Hence, the formulas for changes in prices and quantities, and for the welfare of producers and consumers, are the same as for the undistorted closed economy (i.e., equations A5.22a-d). The measured welfare effects will differ, however, because the base quantities for the calculation differ between the distorted and undistorted cases. In addition, there is the impact on taxpayer welfare to consider, and the formula for taxpayer welfare is as given in equation A5.19c for any combination of consumer and producer taxes or subsidies. Since output and consumption are equal, the taxpayer welfare effect is simply $\Delta GS_A = T_A \Delta Q_A$, where T_A is the net per unit tax rate on consumption (or production). Therefore,

$$\Delta PS_A = (k + \Delta P) \, (Q_A' + 0.5\Delta Q_A)$$
$$= (K' - Z') \, P_A' Q_A' \, (1 + 0.5Z' \, \eta_A') \qquad \text{(A5.23a)}$$

$$\Delta CS_A = -\Delta P \, (C_A' + 0.5\Delta C_A) = Z' \, P_A' \, Q_A' \, (1 + 0.5Z' \, \eta_A') \qquad \text{(A5.23b)}$$

$$\Delta GS_A = T_A \Delta Q_A = T_A \, Q_A' \, Z' \, \eta_A' \qquad \text{(A5.23c)}$$

$$\Delta NS_A = k\,(Q_A' + 0.5\Delta Q_A) + T_A \Delta Q_A$$
$$= K' P_A' Q_A'\,(1 + 0.5Z'\,\eta_A') - T_A\,Q_A'\,Z'\,\eta_A' \tag{A5.23d}$$

As in the other cases shown here, the effect of the distortions is to change the incidence of the benefits from research but not to change the total benefits (Alston, Edwards and Freebairn 1988). It may be important to note that in this case, unlike the small-country cases, the preresearch price is affected by the tax so that the value of K in equations A5.23a-d (i.e., K') will be different from that in equations A5.22a-d (i.e., K) for a given value of k.

Large, open economy with no distortions: The case of a large, open economy is significantly more complicated than the closed economy or small, open economy because it includes complications arising (a) from the fact that prices are endogenous and (b) because the quantities consumed domestically differ from the quantities produced domestically. Equation A5.16 defines the research-induced price change, and that equation may be transformed into elasticity form as follows:

$$\Delta P = -\frac{k\beta_A}{\beta_A + \beta_B - \delta_A - \delta_B}$$

$$= -\frac{Ks_A\varepsilon_A P}{s_A\varepsilon_A + (1 - s_A)\varepsilon_B + d_A\eta_A + (1 - d_A)\eta_B} = -ZP \tag{A5.24a}$$

where $s_A = Q_A/(Q_A + Q_B)$ is the domestic share of global production, $d_A = C_A/(C_A + C_B)$ is the domestic share of global consumption, and Z is the decline in the domestic (and world) price, which depends on overseas as well as domestic supply-and-demand parameters. The corresponding changes in production and consumption are as defined in equation A5.18, and these may be expressed in terms of elasticities as follows:

$$\Delta Q_A = \varepsilon_A\,(K - Z)\,Q_A\;;\;\Delta C_A = \eta_A\,ZC_A$$
$$\Delta Q_B = -\,\varepsilon_B\,ZQ_B\;;\;\Delta C_B = \eta_B\,ZC_B \tag{A5.24b}$$

Then, formulas for domestic welfare effects can be obtained by making the appropriate substitutions in equations A5.19a-h. In elasticity form, these equations are

$$\Delta PS_A = (k + \Delta P)\,(Q_A + 0.5\Delta Q_A)$$
$$= (K - Z)\,P_A Q_A\,[1 + 0.5\varepsilon_A\,(K - Z)\,] \tag{A5.24c}$$

$$\Delta CS_A = -\,\Delta P\,(C_A + 0.5\Delta C_A) = Z\,P_A C_A\,(1 + 0.5\eta_A) \tag{A5.24d}$$

The net domestic benefits in this case would be equal to the sum of the

producer and consumer benefits thus obtained. It would be relatively straightforward to compute welfare effects in the other country and global effects as
well.

However, in order to deal with distortions in the large-country case, another
layer of complications is introduced, and it is significantly more complicated
to derive analytical solutions for the welfare effects on the different groups in
terms of elasticities and so on when the different groups face different prices.
That is, when different consuming and producing groups are involved that face
different prices, the formulas do not simplify as readily as when quantities
produced equal quantities consumed and buyers and sellers face the same
prices. Further problems may arise unless care is taken to be consistent in the
definition of the analysis. In particular, results may depend on whether a supply
shift is defined as a proportion of the undistorted preresearch price (i.e., K) or
as a proportion of the distorted preresearch price (i.e., K'). These issues are
illustrated next in the case of a small, open economy.

A5.2.2 Alternative Formulas for a Small, Open, Distorted Economy

In the analysis of research benefits with distorted markets, we assume linear
supply shifting in parallel by a given amount, k, in the price direction, against
a horizontal demand equation (in the small-country case, there is no price
change). Subscripts 0 and 1 denote quantities with and without the research-induced supply shift and the prime (′) is used to denote quantities produced and
consumed in the presence of policy (defined as a price wedge corresponding
to a tax equal to T per unit). In this illustration, a negative value for T could
represent the effects of an output subsidy or an import tariff or a floor price
scheme, and a positive value could represent the effects of an output tax or a
price ceiling, for example.

Policy-induced change in quantity is equal to $-\beta T = Q_1' - Q_1 = Q_0' - Q_0$,
where β is the slope of the supply function (i.e., when β and T are both
positive, a tax causes a fall in output from Q_0 to Q_0'). The research-induced
change in quantity ($\Delta Q = Q_1' - Q_0' = Q_1 - Q_0 = \beta k$) is unaffected by per unit
susbidies or taxes. This means that the effect of price policy on producer
research benefits arises only through a change in the initial quantity, upon
which the given per unit benefit, k, is received (i.e, the base of a rectangle),
from Q_0 to Q_0'. The triangle of producer benefits is unaffected by the presence of policy (because the height of the triangle, k, and the slope of supply,
β, are unaffected). In every case, then, the research benefits are given by the
following:

with policy

$$\Delta PS = kQ_0' + 0.5k\Delta Q$$
$$= k(Q_0 - \beta T) + 0.5k^2\beta \qquad (A5.25a)$$
$$= kQ_0 - k\beta T + 0.5k^2\beta$$

$$\Delta GS = T\Delta Q = k\beta T \qquad (A5.25b)$$

$$\Delta TS = \Delta PS + \Delta GS$$
$$= kQ_0 + 0.5k^2\beta \qquad (A5.25c)$$
$$= kQ_0 + 0.5k\Delta Q$$

without policy

$$\Delta PS = kQ_0 + 0.5k\Delta Q$$
$$= kQ_0 + 0.5k^2\beta \qquad (A5.26a)$$

$$\Delta TS = \Delta PS \qquad (A5.26b)$$

The difference in producer surplus, between the with- and without policy cases, is equal to $(Q_0' - Q_0)k = -T\beta k$ which is equal to the research-induced increase in subsidy cost. Thus, as can be seen above, the total (net) benefit is unaffected by the policy. In the formulas that use elasticities and percentage changes, these relationships can become obscured and they will hold in practice only when care is taken about the initial price (from which the supply shift is defined as a percentage change) and the initial quantity (to which the supply elasticity is applied to deduce the induced change in quantity — i.e., the implied value of β depends on the initial price and quantity combined with the supply elasticity).

General Formulas in Terms of Elasticities

The next step is to convert these formulas into formulas involving elasticities and price wedges (i.e., $T = \tau P_W$) and percentage research-induced supply shifts. We confine attention to the with-distortion formulas from above and show the effects of different assumptions about whether the percentage supply shift, K, applies to the undistorted or distorted supply price [i.e., $k = KP_W$ or $k = K(1 - \tau)P_W$, respectively].

Supply Shift Defined Relative to Undistorted Price ($k = KP_W$)

Producer surplus in terms of the undistorted quantity: From the formulas above,

$$\Delta PS = kQ_0 - k\beta T + 0.5k^2\beta \qquad (A5.27a)$$

Substituting for k and T gives

$$\Delta PS = (KP_W)Q_0 - (KP_W)\,\beta\,(\tau P_W) + 0.5(KP_W)^2\beta, \text{ or}$$

$$\Delta PS = KP_WQ_0[1 - \tau\,(\beta P_W/Q_0) + 0.5(\beta P_W/Q_0)]$$

(A5.27b)

Then, using the definition that $\varepsilon = \beta P_W/Q_0$ is the supply elasticity at the undistorted equilibrium, P_W, Q_0, the formula for producer benefits simplifies to

$$\Delta PS = KP_WQ_0\,(1 - \tau\varepsilon + 0.5K\varepsilon)$$

(A5.27c)

Producer surplus in terms of the distorted quantity: Alternatively, suppose we begin with the formula

$$\Delta PS = kQ_0' + 0.5k\Delta Q$$

(A5.25a)

Substituting for k gives

$$\Delta PS = (KP_W)Q_0' + 0.5(KP_W)^2\beta, \text{ or}$$

$$\Delta PS = KP_WQ_0'\,[1 + 0.5K\,(\beta P_W/Q_0')]$$

(A5.28a)

Then, using the definition that $\varepsilon' = \beta(1 - \tau)P_W/Q_0'$ is the supply elasticity at the distorted equilibrium, $(1 - \tau)P_W, Q_0'$, the formula simplifies to

$$\Delta PS = KP_WQ_0'\,[1 + 0.5K\varepsilon'/(1 - \tau)]$$

(A5.28b)

This is equivalent to the previous result but expressed now in terms of the *distorted* equilibrium quantity and the corresponding supply elasticity.

Government revenues: The effects of research on government revenues are computed according to

$$\Delta GS = T\Delta Q = k\beta T$$

(A5.25b)

Substituting for k and T gives

$$\begin{aligned}\Delta GS &= (KP_W)\,\beta\,(\tau P_W)\\ &= KP_WQ_0\tau(\beta P_W/Q_0)\\ &= KP_WQ_0\tau\varepsilon\end{aligned}$$

(A5.29a)

Alternatively, for a measure in terms of the distorted quantity,

$$\begin{aligned}\Delta GS &= (KP_W)\,\beta\,(\tau P_W)\\ &= KP_WQ_0\tau\,[\beta(1 - \tau)P_W/Q_0']/(1 - \tau)\\ &= KP_WQ_0'\tau\varepsilon'/(1 - \tau)\end{aligned}$$

(A5.29b)

Net welfare: In the small-country case, the net (or total) welfare effect is equal to the sum of the effects on producer surplus and government revenues.

Beginning with the formulas defined in terms of the undistorted quantity,

$$\Delta TS = \Delta PS + \Delta GS$$
$$= KP_wQ_0 [1 - \tau\varepsilon + 0.5K\varepsilon] + KP_wQ_0\tau\varepsilon \quad \text{(A5.30a)}$$
$$= KP_wQ_0 [1 + 0.5K\varepsilon]$$

Alternatively, using the formulas defined in terms of distorted quantities,

$$\Delta TS = \Delta PS + \Delta GS$$
$$= KP_wQ_0' [1 + 0.5K\varepsilon'/(1 - \tau)] + KP_wQ_0'\tau\varepsilon'(1 - \tau) \quad \text{(A5.30b)}$$
$$= KP_wQ_0' [1 + \tau\varepsilon' (1 - T) + 0.5K\varepsilon'/(1 - \tau)]$$

This formula is equivalent to the one above defined in terms of the undistorted quantity.

Supply Shift Defined Relative to Distorted Price $(k = K'(1 - \tau)P_w)$

Producer surplus in terms of the undistorted quantity: From the formulas above,

$$\Delta PS = kQ_0 - k\beta T + 0.5k^2\beta \quad \text{(A5.25a)}$$

Substituting for k and T gives

$$\Delta PS = [K' (1 - \tau)P_w]Q_0 - [K' (1 - \tau)P_w] \beta (\tau P_w)$$
$$+ 0.5[K(1 - \tau)P_w]^2\beta,$$

or

$$\Delta PS = K' (1 - \tau)P_wQ_0 [1 - \tau(\beta P_w/Q_0)$$
$$+ 0.5K(1 - \tau)(\beta P_w/Q_0)] \quad \text{(A5.31a)}$$

Then, using the definition that $\varepsilon = \beta P_w/Q_0$ is the supply elasticity at the undistorted equilibrium, P_w, Q_0, the formula simplifies to

$$\Delta PS = K'(1 - \tau)P_wQ_0 [1 - \tau\varepsilon + 0.5K'(1 - \tau)\varepsilon] \quad \text{(A5.31b)}$$

Producer surplus in terms of the distorted quantity: Alternatively, suppose we begin with the formula

$$\Delta PS = kQ_0' + 0.5k\Delta Q \quad \text{(A5.25a)}$$

Substituting for k gives

$$\Delta PS = [K'(1 - \tau)P_w]Q_0' + 0.5[K(1 - \tau)P_w]^2\beta, \quad \text{or} \quad \text{(A5.32a)}$$

$$\Delta PS = K'(1 - \tau)P_wQ_0' [1 + 0.5K(\beta(1 - \tau)P_w/Q_0')]$$

Then, using the definition that $\varepsilon' = \beta(1 - \tau)P_w/Q_0'$ defines the supply elasticity at the distorted equilibrium, $(1 - \tau)P_w, Q_0'$, the formula simplifies to

$$\Delta PS = K'(1 - \tau)P_wQ_0' [1 + 0.5K'\varepsilon'] \tag{A5.32b}$$

This is equivalent to the previous result but expressed now in terms of the *distorted* equilibrium quantity and the corresponding supply elasticity.

Government revenues: The effects of research on government revenues are computed according to

$$\Delta GS = T\Delta Q = k\beta T \tag{A5.25b}$$

Substituting for k and T gives

$$\begin{aligned}
\Delta GS &= [K'(1 - \tau)P_w] \beta (\tau P_w) \\
&= K'(1 - \tau)P_wQ_0\tau(\beta P_w/Q_0) \\
&= K'(1 - \tau)P_wQ_0\tau\varepsilon
\end{aligned} \tag{A5.33a}$$

Alternatively, for a measure in terms of the distorted quantity,

$$\begin{aligned}
\Delta GS &= [K'(1 - \tau)P_w] \beta (\tau P_w) \\
&= K'P_wQ_0'\tau [\beta(1 - \tau)P_w/Q_0'] \\
&= K'P_wQ_0'\tau\varepsilon'
\end{aligned} \tag{A5.33b}$$

Net welfare: Beginning with the formulas defined in terms of the undistorted quantity,

$$\begin{aligned}
\Delta TS &= \Delta PS + \Delta GS \\
&= K'(1 - \tau)P_wQ_0[1 - \tau\varepsilon + 0.5K'(1 - \tau)\varepsilon] \\
&\quad + K'(1 - \tau)P_wQ_0\tau\varepsilon \\
&= K'(1 - \tau)P_wQ_0[1 + 0.5K'(1 - \tau)\varepsilon]
\end{aligned} \tag{A5.34a}$$

Alternatively, using the formulas defined in terms of distorted quantities,

$$\begin{aligned}
\Delta TS &= \Delta PS + \Delta GS \\
&= K'(1 - \tau)P_wQ_0'(1 + 0.5K'\varepsilon') - K'P_wQ_0'\tau\varepsilon' \\
&= K'(1 - \tau)P_wQ_0'(1 - \tau\varepsilon' + 0.5K'\varepsilon')
\end{aligned} \tag{A5.34b}$$

This formula is equivalent to the one above defined in terms of the undistorted quantity.

Implications

In many studies, the most readily available information relates to the distorted equilibrium, so the natural place to begin is there. The formulas for producer surplus and government revenues using the quantity-and-supply elasticity at the observable (distorted) equilibrium are reasonably straightforward. The analyst is free to choose whether the K percent supply shift refers to current marginal cost (i.e., the distorted value) or the shadow value of output. The summary formulas for total welfare effects are somewhat more cumbersome and it might be simpler to compute the components separately and add them up. On the other hand, when the interest is only in the total (or net) effects, one can either deduce the prices and quantities at the undistorted equilibrium and apply the K shift to the standard formula (since we know that in this model the presence of distortions of these types does not affect the total benefit), or alternatively, one can use the formulas developed above. In some cases, it might be simpler, and less prone to errors, to parameterize the linear supply-and-demand curves themselves, rather than rely on using elasticities, and to use a per unit k rather than a percentage K to calculate welfare effects.

Selected Formulas

Some examples of formulas that can be used in common cases for measuring research impact on the welfare of producers, consumers, and government revenues are given in table A5.2.1.

Table A5.2.1: *Selected Formulas for Computing Changes in Economic Surpluses*

Model	Formula	Corresponding chapter 4 figure
Closed-economy models		
1. Basic closed economy	$\Delta CS = P_0 Q_0 Z (1 + 0.5 Z\eta)$ $\Delta PS = P_0 Q_0 (K - Z)(1 + 0.5 Z\eta)$ $\Delta TS = P_0 Q_0 K (1 + 0.5 Z\eta)$	Figure 4.1
2. Closed economy with exogenous demand shift	$\Delta CS = P_0' Q_0' Z (1 + 0.5 Z\eta)$ $\Delta PS = P_0' Q_0' (K' - Z)(1 + 0.5 Z\eta)$ $\Delta TS = P_0' Q_0' K' (1 + 0.5 Z\eta)$	Figure 4.7
Open-economy models		
3. Small open economy (home-country effects)	$\Delta CS = 0$ $\Delta PS = \Delta TS = P_w Q_0 K(1+0.5K\varepsilon) = P_0 Q_0 K(1 + 0.5K\varepsilon)$	Figure 4.5, panels a and b
4. Large open economy (no technology spillovers): $Z = -(P_1 - P_0)/P_0$		
4a. Home-country (i.e., country A) effects	$\Delta CS_A = P_0 C_{A,0} Z(1 + 0.5 Z\eta_A)$ $\Delta PS_A = P_0 Q_{A,0} (K - Z)(1 + 0.5 Z\varepsilon_A)$ $\Delta TS_A = \Delta CS_A + \Delta PS_A$	Figure 4.2 and 4.3 box 4.2
4b. Rest-of-world (i.e., region B) effects	$\Delta CS_B = P_0 C_{B,0} Z(1 + 0.5 Z\eta_B)$ $\Delta PS_B = - P_0 Q_{B,0} Z(1 + 0.5 Z\varepsilon_B)$ $\Delta TS_B = \Delta CS_B + \Delta PS_B$	Figures 4.2 and 4.3

Table A5.2.1: *Selected Formulas for Computing Changes in Economic Surpluses (contd.)*

Model	Formula	Corresponding chapter 4 figure
4c. Global (i.e., world) effects	$\Delta CS_W = \Delta CS_A + \Delta CS_B$ $\Delta PS_W = \Delta PS_A + \Delta PS_B$ $\Delta TS_W = \Delta TS_A + \Delta TS_B = \Delta CS_W + \Delta PS_W$	Figures 4.2 and 4.3
5. Large open economy (with technology spillovers): Note that Z here is necessarily a different value than Z with no spillovers		
5a. Home country (i.e., country A) effects	$\Delta CS_A = P_0 C_{A,0} Z(1 + 0.5Z\eta_A)$ $\Delta PS_A = P_0 Q_{A,0} (K_{A,A} - Z)(1 + 0.5Z\varepsilon_B)$ $\Delta TS_A = \Delta CS_A + \Delta PS_A$	Figure 4.4
5b. Rest-of-world (i.e., region B) effects	$\Delta CS_B = P_0 C_{B,0} Z(1 + 0.5Z\eta_B)$ $\Delta PS_B = P_0 Q_{B,0} (K_{B,A} - Z)(1 + 0.5Z\varepsilon_B)$ $\Delta TS_B = \Delta CS_B + \Delta PS_B$	Figure 4.4
5c. Global (i.e., world) effects	$\Delta CS_W = \Delta CS_A + \Delta CS_B$ $\Delta PS_W = \Delta PS_A + \Delta PS_B$ $\Delta TS_W = \Delta TS_A + \Delta TS_B = \Delta CS_W + \Delta PS_W$	Figure 4.4
6. Small open economy with output price supports (home-country effects): $P_{MIN} = (1 - \tau)P_W$ where $\tau < 0$		
6a. Proportionate supply shift defined relative to distorted market equilibrium ($k = K' P_{MIN}$)	$\Delta CS = 0$ $\Delta PS = K'(1 - \tau)P_W Q_0' (1 + 0.5K'\varepsilon')$ $\Delta GS = \tau K'(1 - \tau)P_W Q_0'\varepsilon'$ $\Delta TS = \Delta CS + \Delta PS + \Delta GS$ $= K'(1 - \tau)P_W Q_0' (1 + 0.5K'\varepsilon') + K'(1 - \tau)P_W Q_0'\tau\varepsilon'$ $= K'(1 - \tau)P_W Q_0' (1 + \tau\varepsilon' + 0.5K'\varepsilon')$	Figure 4.15

Table A5.2.1: *Selected Formulas for Computing Changes in Economic Surpluses (contd.)*

Model	Formula	Corresponding chapter 4 figure
6b. Proportionate supply shift defined relative to undistorted market equilibrium ($k = KP_W$)	$\Delta CS = 0$ $\Delta PS = KP_W Q_0 (1 - \tau\varepsilon + 0.5K\varepsilon)$ $\Delta GS = \tau P_W Q_0 K\varepsilon$ $\Delta TS = \Delta CS + \Delta PS + \Delta GS$ $\quad = P_W Q_0 K(1 + 0.5K\varepsilon)$	Figure 4.15

7. Small open economy with output price ceiling (home-country effects): $P_{MAX} = (1 - \tau)P_W$ and $\tau > 0$

Model	Formula	Corresponding chapter 4 figure
7a. Proportionate supply shift defined relative to distorted market equilibrium ($k = K'P_{MAX}$)	$\Delta CS = 0$ $\Delta PS = K'(1 - \tau)P_W Q_0' (1 + 0.5K'\varepsilon')$ $\Delta GS = \tau K'(1 - \tau)P_W Q_0'\varepsilon'$ $\Delta TS = \Delta CS + \Delta PS + \Delta GS$ $\quad = K'(1 - \tau)P_W Q_0'(1 + 0.5K'\varepsilon') + K'(1 - \tau)P_W Q_0'\tau\varepsilon'$ $\quad = K'(1 - \tau)P_W Q_0'(1 + \tau\varepsilon' + 0.5K'\varepsilon')$	Figure 4.16
7b. Proportionate supply shift defined relative to undistorted market equilibrium ($k = KP_W$)	$\Delta CS = 0$ $\Delta PS = KP_W Q_0 [1 - \tau\varepsilon + 0.5K\varepsilon]$ $\Delta GS = \tau P_W Q_0 K\varepsilon$ $\Delta TS = \Delta CS + \Delta PS + \Delta GS$ $\quad = P_W Q_0 K(1 + 0.5K\varepsilon)$	

Table A5.2.1: *Selected Formulas for Computing Changes in Economic Surpluses (contd.)*

Model	Formula	Corresponding chapter 4 figure
8 Small open economy with import tariff (home-country effects), i.e., $\tau < 0$		
8a. Proportionate supply shift defined relative to distorted market equilibrium $(k = K'(1 + TP_W))$	$\Delta CS = 0$ $\Delta PS = K'(1 - \tau)P_W\, Q_0'(1 + 0.5K'\epsilon')$ $\Delta GS = \tau K'(1 - \tau)P_W\, Q_0'\epsilon'$ $\Delta TS = \Delta CS + \Delta PS + \Delta GS$ $\quad = K'(1 - \tau)P_W\, Q_0'(1 + 0.5K'\epsilon') + K'(1 - \tau)P_W\, Q_0'\tau\epsilon'$ $\quad = K'(1 - \tau)P_W\, Q_0'(1 + \tau\epsilon' + 0.5K'\epsilon')$	Figure 4.17
8b. Proportionate supply shift defined relative to undistorted market equilibrium $(k = KP_W)$	$\Delta CS = 0$ $\Delta PS = KP_W\, Q_0(1 - \tau\epsilon + 0.5K\epsilon)$ $\Delta GS = \tau P_W\, Q_0 K\epsilon$ $\Delta TS = \Delta CS + \Delta PS + \Delta GS$ $\quad = P_W\, Q_0 K(1 + 0.5K\epsilon)$	Figure 4.17

Note : See text on pages around the figures in chapter 4 that are cited above for definitions of variables. For notational simplicity, country and regional subscripts have sometimes been suppressed. Unless otherwise indicated, all surplus changes refer to home-country effects. In all of these formulas, the demand elasticity is in terms of absolute values (i.e., $\eta > 0$), K defines the proportional shift down of supply (*not* change) (i.e., $K > 0$ for a decrease in marginal cost) and Z is the proportional reduction (*not* change) in price (i.e., $Z > 0$ for a decrease in price). Differences between the measures from models 6a and 6b (or 7a and 7b or 8a and 8b) arise in part because (a) a different proportionate supply shift is implied (i.e., $K'P_{MIN}$ versus KP_W) and (b) the elasticity of supply (ϵ' versus ϵ) in the formula applies to a different point on the supply curve (i.e., Q_0' versus Q_0, where $Q_0' = (1 - \tau\epsilon)\, Q_0$ when ϵ is defined at Q_0 and $Q_0' > Q_0$ when $\tau < 0$), so that a different supply slope and a different research-induced change in quantity is implied unless care is taken to adjust the elasticity accordingly. Note, also, that formulas for distorted markets are the same for the minimum or maximum price policy or tariff (models 6, 7, and 8) once the policy is expressed as an "equivalent" ad valorem tax, τ. The signs of the effects vary depending on whether τ is a tax ($\tau > 0$) or a subsidy ($\tau < 0$). Thus, $\tau > 0$ implies an increase in government revenue due to research and smaller research benefits for producers.

Appendix A5.3: Estimating K Using Industry and Experiment Data

Studies of returns to research using economic surplus models require an estimate of the shift in supply due to research-induced technical change. In the literature, the supply shift has been represented either as a vertical shift down, K, or a horizontal shift to the right, J. To estimate the value of J or K for a particular technical change — or for a particular research investment — a number of approaches have been used. For example, experimental yields have been used in *ex post* analysis as a proxy for industry yield or supply shifts. Echeverría, Ferreira and Dabezies (1989), Pardey et al. (1992), and Palomino and Norton (1992b) present recent examples. In *ex ante* evaluations, scientist questionnaires and other mechanisms for eliciting information about potential J or K have been employed, as discussed earlier in this chapter. The purpose of this appendix is to clarify the relationships between the industry (final product) supply shift (J or K), experimental yields, and industry yield changes for different types of technical changes. Neutral and biased technical change are considered in a two-factor linear-elasticity equilibrium-displacement model. The results illustrate the importance of the supply elasticity and the elasticities of substitution among factors of production in determining the interrelationships among changes in experimental yields, industry yields, and final product supply.

A5.3.1 A Two-Factor Equilibrium-Displacement Model

Following Alston (1991), we can model the effects of technical change on the market equilibrium of a competitive industry producing a homogeneous product using two factors of production in terms of the following six linear elasticity equations (equivalent to text equations 4.14a' to 4.14f'):

$$E(Q) = \eta E(P) \tag{A5.35a}$$

$$E(P) = s_1 E(W_1) + s_2 E(W_2) \tag{A5.35b}$$

$$E(X_1) = \eta_{11} E(W_1) + \eta_{12} E(W_2) - \delta_1 \tag{A5.35c}$$

$$E(X_2) = \eta_{21} E(W_1) + \eta_{22} E(W_2) - \delta_2 \tag{A5.35d}$$

$$E(X_1) = \varepsilon_1 E(W_1) \tag{A5.35e}$$

$$E(X_2) = \varepsilon_2 E(W_2) \tag{A5.35f}$$

where E denotes relative changes (i.e., for a variable Z, $E[Z] = dZ/Z = d[\ln Z]$), η is the elasticity of demand for the product measured in natural units (i.e., $\eta < 0$), s_i is the cost (and revenue) share of factor i (i.e., $s_i = W_iX_i/PQ$) and in this two-factor case, $s_1 + s_2 = 1$, η_{ij} is the uncompensated cross-price elasticity of demand for factor i with respect to price of factor j, δ_1 and δ_2 are factor-demand-shift variables reflecting changes in technology, and ε_i is the elasticity of supply of factor i.

The endogenous variables in the model are industry output, Q, the amounts of the two factors used by the industry, X_1 and X_2, the price per unit of the final product, P, and the factor prices, W_1 and W_2. Equation A5.35a is the demand schedule for the industry's output, equation A5.35b is a zero-profit condition reflecting a constant-returns-to-scale industry production function, equations A5.35c and A5.35d are derived factor-demand equations, and A5.35e and A5.35f are the factor-supply equations. The solutions to this model are

$$E(W_1) = -(\varepsilon_2 - \eta_{22})\delta_1/D - \eta_{12}\delta_2/D \tag{A5.36a}$$

$$E(W_2) = -\eta_{21}\delta_1/D - (\varepsilon_1 - \eta_{11})\delta_2/D \tag{A5.36b}$$

$$E(X_1) = -\varepsilon_1(\varepsilon_2 - \eta_{22})\delta_1/D - \varepsilon_1\eta_{12}\delta_2/D \tag{A5.36c}$$

$$E(X_2) = -\varepsilon_2\eta_{21}\delta_1/D - \varepsilon_2(\varepsilon_1 - \eta_{11})\delta_2/D \tag{A5.36d}$$

$$E(P) = -[s_1(\varepsilon_2 - \eta_{22}) + s_2\eta_{21}\delta_1 + s_2(\varepsilon_1 - \eta_{11}) + s_1\eta_{12}\delta_2]/D \tag{A5.36e}$$

$$E(Q) = -[s_1(\varepsilon_2 - \eta_{22}) + s_2\eta_{21}\delta_1 + s_2(\varepsilon_1 - \eta_{11}) + s_1\eta_{12}\delta_2]\eta/D \tag{A5.36f}$$

where

$$D = (\varepsilon_2 - \eta_{22})(\varepsilon_1 - \eta_{11}) - \eta_{21}\eta_{12} > 0$$

Using Slutsky symmetry and the homogeneity of the cost function, we can define the four own- and cross-price elasticities of factor demand using factor cost shares, s_i, the final demand elasticity, η, and the elasticity of substitution between X_1 and X_2 (i.e., σ)

$$\begin{aligned}
\eta_{11} &= -s_2\sigma + s_1\eta \quad ; \quad \eta_{12} = s_2\sigma + s_2\eta \\
\eta_{21} &= s_1\sigma + s_1\eta \quad ; \quad \eta_{22} = -s_1\sigma + s_2\eta
\end{aligned} \tag{A5.36g}$$

Substituting equation A5.36g into equations A5.36c, A5.36e, and A5.36f gives

$$E(X_1) = -\varepsilon_1(\varepsilon_2 + s_1\sigma - s_2\eta)\delta_1/D - \varepsilon_1s_2(\sigma + \eta)\delta_2/D \tag{A5.36c'}$$

$$E(P) = -[s_1(\varepsilon_2 + \sigma)\delta_1 + s_2(\varepsilon_1 + \sigma)\delta_2]/D > 0 \tag{A5.36e'}$$

$$E(Q) = -[s_1(\varepsilon_2 + \sigma)\delta_1 + s_2(\varepsilon_1 + \sigma)\delta_2]\eta/D > 0 \tag{A5.36f'}$$

where

$$D = \sigma \, (s_1 \, \varepsilon_1 + s_2 \, \varepsilon_2 - \eta) - \eta \, (s_1 \, \varepsilon_2 + s_2 \, \varepsilon_1) + \varepsilon_1 \, \varepsilon_2 > 0$$
$$\text{for } \eta < 0 \text{ and } s, \varepsilon_1, \varepsilon_2 > 0$$

The relative change in yield $(Y = Q/X_1)$ is

$$E(Y) = E(Q/X_1) = E(Q) - E(X_1) \tag{A5.37a}$$

Substituting equations A5.36c$'$ and A5.36e$'$ into equation (A5.37a) gives

$$E(Y) = [(s_1\sigma[\varepsilon_1-\eta] - \eta[s_1\varepsilon_2 + s_2\varepsilon_1] + \varepsilon_1\varepsilon_2)\delta_1$$
$$+ s_2\sigma(\varepsilon_2 - \eta)\delta_2 \,]/D \tag{A5.37b}$$

Experimental Yield Data

Neutral technical change: Consider a neutral technical change that we can model by setting $\delta_1 = \delta_2 = \delta$ in the equations above. The results are

$$E(X_1) = - \varepsilon_1(\sigma + \varepsilon_2)\delta/D > 0 \tag{A5.38a}$$

$$E(P) = - (s_1\varepsilon_2 + s_2\varepsilon_1 + \sigma)\delta/D < 0 \tag{A5.38b}$$

$$E(Q) = - (s_1\varepsilon_2 + s_2\varepsilon_1 + \sigma)\delta\eta/D > 0 \tag{A5.38c}$$

$$E(Y) = [\sigma(\varepsilon_1- \eta) - \eta(s_1\varepsilon_2 + s_2\varepsilon_1) + \varepsilon_1\varepsilon_2] \, \delta/D > 0 \tag{A5.38d}$$

To represent an experimental setting in which both input quantities are held constant we make the factor supply functions perfectly inelastic (i.e., $\varepsilon_1 = \varepsilon_2 = 0$). Under these conditions, the change in yield is equal to the change in output $(E(Y) = E(Q))$. A neutral technical change, δ, would increase output and experimental yields by $E(Y^*) = - \eta\sigma\delta/D = \delta$ (when $\varepsilon_1 = \varepsilon_2 = 0, D = - \eta\sigma$). This would be the observed change in experimental yields due to the change in technology. In a firm or industry setting (i.e., allowing factor-supply response), the change in yield might be quite different, depending upon the extent to which inputs are variable and substitutable for one another. The shift in the industry supply function might be proxied by the increase in experimental yields, but that might not be a good idea.

To measure the vertical shift in industry supply, K, due to the neutral technical change, we set $\eta = 0$ in equation A5.38b and get

$$K = - E(P) \; (given \; Q \,)$$
$$= \delta \, (s_1\varepsilon_2 + s_2\varepsilon_1 + \sigma \,)/[\sigma \, (s_1\varepsilon_1 + s_2\varepsilon_2) + \varepsilon_1\varepsilon_2] > 0 \tag{A5.39}$$

To measure the horizontal shift in industry supply, J, due to the neutral technical change, we set $\eta = - \infty$ in equation A5.38c to get

$$J = E(Q) \ (given \ P \ ) = \delta > 0 \tag{A5.40}$$

Notice that $J = \varepsilon_T K$, where ε_T is the elasticity of supply of the industry product, Q, and is given by

$$\varepsilon_T = [\sigma \ (s_1 \varepsilon_1 + s_2 \varepsilon_2) + \varepsilon_1 \varepsilon_2]/(\sigma + s_2 \varepsilon_1 + s_1 \varepsilon_2) \tag{A5.41}$$

Thus, for neutral technical change (as defined) the increase in experimental yields is a good measure of J, the *horizontal* supply shift at the industry level. However, it might not be a good measure of K, the corresponding *vertical* supply shift. The correct measure of the vertical supply shift is $K = \delta/\varepsilon_T$ and to get $K = \delta$ requires restrictions on elasticities of factor supply, factor substitution, or factor cost shares such that the elasticity of product supply is 1.0.

Biased (land-saving) technical change: Let us suppose that X_1 is land. To model a biased (land-saving) technical change, set $\delta_2 = 0$ in equations A5.36c′, A5.36e′, A5.36f′, and A5.37b to get

$$E(X_1) = - \varepsilon_1(\varepsilon_2 + s_1 \sigma - s_2 \eta)\delta_1/D < 0 \tag{A5.42a}$$

$$E(P) = - s_1(\varepsilon_2 + \sigma)\delta_1/D < 0 \tag{A5.42b}$$

$$E(Q) = - s_1(\varepsilon_2 + \sigma)\delta_1 \eta/D > 0 \tag{A5.42c}$$

$$E(Y) = [s_1\sigma(\varepsilon_1 - \eta) - \eta(s_1\varepsilon_2 + s_2\varepsilon) + \varepsilon_1 \varepsilon_2]\delta_1/D > 0 \tag{A5.42d}$$

where

$$D = \sigma(s_1\varepsilon_1 + s_2\varepsilon_2 - \eta) - \eta(s_1\varepsilon_2 + s_2\varepsilon_1) + \varepsilon_1\varepsilon_2 > 0 \text{ for } \eta < 0$$
$$\text{and } \sigma, e_1, \varepsilon_2 > 0.$$

The effect of this technical change on experimental yields (holding factor quantities constant by setting $\varepsilon_1 = \varepsilon_2 = 0$) is given by $E(Y^*) = E(Y)$ (*given X_1 and X_2*) $= E(Q)$ (*given X_1 and X_2*) $= s_1\delta_1$. To measure the vertical shift in industry supply due to the biased technical change, we set $\eta = 0$ in equation A5.42b to get

$$K = - E(P) \ (given \ Q \ )$$
$$= s_1 \ (\varepsilon_2 + \sigma) \ \delta_1/[\sigma (\ s_1\varepsilon_1 + s_2\varepsilon_2) + \varepsilon_1\varepsilon_2] > 0 \tag{A5.43}$$

Setting $\eta = - \infty$ in equation A5.42c, the corresponding horizontal shift in supply is

$$J = E(Q) \ (given \ P)$$
$$= s_1 \ (\varepsilon_2 + \sigma) \ \delta_1/[\sigma + s_1\varepsilon_2 + s_2\varepsilon_1] = \varepsilon_T K > 0 \tag{A5.44}$$

Thus, with biased (land-saving) technical change, the increase in experimental yields ($E(Y^*) = s_1\delta_1$) is not likely to be a good measure of either the vertical or horizontal shift in industry supply. Parametric restrictions are needed to make experimental yield increases a good measure of the vertical or horizontal supply shift (either K or J) resulting from land-saving technical change. For instance, when the factor-supply elasticities are equal ($\varepsilon_1 = \varepsilon_2$), $J = \sigma_1 \delta_1 = E(Y^*)$ and $K = s_1 \delta_1 \varepsilon_T = E(Y^*)$. This situation seems unlikely.

Biased (land-using) technical change: To model a biased (land-using or X_2-saving) technical change, set $\delta_1 = 0$ in equations A5.36c′, A5.36e′, A5.36f′, and A5.37b and get

$$E(X_1) = -\varepsilon_1 s_2(\sigma + \eta)\,\delta_2/D > 0 \tag{A5.45a}$$
$$\textit{iff } \sigma + \eta < 0 \quad \text{(i.e., inputs 1 and 2 are gross complements)}$$

$$E(P) = -s_2(\varepsilon_1 + \sigma)\delta_2/D < 0 \tag{A5.45b}$$

$$E(Q) = -s_2(\varepsilon_1 + \sigma)\eta\delta_2/D > 0 \tag{A5.45c}$$

$$E(Y) = s_2\sigma\,(\varepsilon_1 - \eta)\delta_2/D > 0 \tag{A5.45d}$$

where

$$D = \sigma(s_1\varepsilon_1 + s_2\varepsilon_2 - \eta) - \eta(s_1\varepsilon_2 + s_2\varepsilon_1) + \varepsilon_1\varepsilon_2 > 0 \text{ for } \eta < 0$$
$$\text{and } \sigma, \varepsilon_1, \varepsilon_2 > 0$$

The effect of this technical change on experiment yields (holding factor quantities constant by setting $\varepsilon_1 = \varepsilon_2 = 0$) is given by $E(Y)$ (*given* X_1 and X_2) $= E(Q)$ (*given* X_1 and X_2) $= s_2\delta_2$.

To measure the vertical shift in industry supply due to the biased (X_1-saving) technical change, we set $\eta = 0$ in equation (A5.45b) and get

$$K = -E(P) \; (\textit{given } Q)$$
$$= s_2\,(\varepsilon_1 + \sigma)\,\delta_2/[\sigma\,(s_1\varepsilon_1 + s_2\varepsilon_2) + \varepsilon_1\varepsilon_2] > 0 \tag{A5.46}$$

The corresponding horizontal shift in supply due to the biased technical change (i.e., with $\eta = -\infty$ in A5.45c) is

$$J = E(Q) \; (\textit{given } P)$$
$$= s_2\,(\varepsilon_1 + \sigma)\delta_2/[\sigma + s_1\varepsilon_2 + s_2\varepsilon_1] = \varepsilon_T \; K > 0 \tag{A5.47}$$

The experimental yield increase from a land-using technical change is analogous to that from the land-saving technical change: $E(Y^*) = s_2\delta_2$. Again (as with land-saving biased technical change), the experimental yield data are unlikely to provide an accurate measure of either the vertical or horizontal shift of the industry supply function.

Industry Yield Data

An alternative approach to measuring J and K is to look at the growth in industry yields as a consequence of the introduction of new technology. The corresponding measure is $E(Y)$ in the equations above. That too may lead to misleading results. The algebraic results for the effects of neutral and biased technical changes on experimental yields, $E(Y^*)$, vertical supply shift, K, horizontal supply shift, J, and industry yields, $E(Y)$, are summarized in table A5.3.1.

A5.3.2 Summary of Algebraic Results

In table A5.3.2 it can be seen that a *neutral technical change*, δ, will lead to an increase in experimental yields by the same percentage, and the increase in experimental yields, $E(Y^*)$, will be the same as the consequent *horizontal* shift of supply, J. However, the increase in experimental yields will be a good measure of the *vertical* supply shift, K, only when the output-supply elasticity is unitary; otherwise (and more generally) it is necessary to divide the increase in experimental yields by the supply elasticity to get the vertical supply shift. The increase in industry yields will be a good measure of the increase in supply, J, when the factor proportions are fixed (i.e., the elasticity of factor substitution is zero: $\sigma = 0$); otherwise it might not be a very good measure.

In the case of a biased (*land-saving*) technical change, δ_1, the increase in experimental yields, $\delta_1 \sigma_1$, is a good measure of the *horizontal* shift of supply, J, only when the factor-supply elasticities are equal, $\varepsilon_1 = \varepsilon_2$. Again, it is necessary to divide the horizontal supply shift, J, by the output-supply elasticity, ε_T, to estimate the vertical supply shift, K. As with the neutral technical change, the change in industry yields will be an accurate measure of the horizontal supply shift when factor proportions are fixed.

In the case of a biased (*land-using*) technical change, δ_2, the increase in experimental yields, $\delta_2 \sigma_2$, is a good measure of the *horizontal* shift of supply, J, only when the factor-supply elasticities are equal. Again, it is necessary to divide the horizontal supply shift, J, by the output-supply elasticity, ε_T, to estimate the vertical supply shift, K. The change in industry yields, $E(Y)$, will be zero in the case of fixed proportions.

Theoretical conditions under which changes in experimental yields and industry yields are accurate measures of the shift of industry supply are shown in table A5.3.2.

Table A.5.3.1: *Consequences of New Technology for Yields and Supply Shifts*

Effect	Type of technical change		
	Neutral (δ)	Land-saving (δ_1)	Land-using (δ_2)
$E(Y^*)$	δ	$\delta_1 s_1$	$\delta_2 s_2$
J	δ	$\dfrac{\delta_1 s_1(\varepsilon_2 + \sigma)}{\sigma + s_1\varepsilon_2 + s_2\varepsilon_1}$	$\dfrac{\delta_2 s_2(\varepsilon_1 + \sigma)}{\sigma + s_1\varepsilon_2 + s_2\varepsilon_1}$
K	$\dfrac{\delta(\sigma + s_1\varepsilon_2 + s_2\varepsilon_1)}{\sigma(s_1\varepsilon_1 + s_2\varepsilon_2 + \varepsilon_1\varepsilon_2)}$	$\dfrac{\delta_1 s_1(\varepsilon_2 + \sigma)}{\sigma(s_1\varepsilon_1 + s_2\varepsilon_2) + \varepsilon_1\varepsilon_2}$	$\dfrac{\delta_2 s_2(\varepsilon_1 + \sigma)}{\sigma(s_1\varepsilon_1 + s_2\varepsilon_2) + \varepsilon_1\varepsilon_2}$
$E(Y)$	$\dfrac{\delta[\sigma(\varepsilon_1 - \eta) - \eta(s_1\varepsilon_2 + s_2\varepsilon_1) + \varepsilon_1\varepsilon_2]}{D}$	$\dfrac{\delta_1[s_1\sigma(\varepsilon_1 - \eta) - \eta(s_1\varepsilon_2 + s_2\varepsilon_1) + \varepsilon_1\varepsilon_2]}{D}$	$\dfrac{\delta_2 s_2\sigma(\varepsilon_1 - \eta)}{D}$

Note: $D = \sigma(s_1\varepsilon_1 + s_2\varepsilon_2) + \varepsilon_1\varepsilon_2 - \eta(\sigma + s_1\varepsilon_2 + s_2\varepsilon_1)$.

J = the percentage horizontal (rightwards) shift of product supply

K = percentage vertical (downwards) shift of product supply

$E(Y^*)$ = the percentage change in experimental yields (Q/X_1) holding factors fixed

$E(Y)$ = the relative change in industry yields

In every case,

$K = J/\varepsilon_T$, where $\varepsilon_T = [\sigma(s_1\varepsilon_1 + s_2\varepsilon_2) + \varepsilon_1\varepsilon_2]/(\sigma + s_1\varepsilon_2 + s_2\varepsilon_1)$

Table A5.3.2: *Sufficient Conditions under Which Yield Changes Accurately Reflect Supply Shifts*

	Type of technical change		
	Neutral (δ)	Land-saving (δ_1)	Land-using (δ_2)
$E(Y^*) = J$	always	when $\varepsilon_1 = \varepsilon_2$	when $\varepsilon_1 = \varepsilon_2$
$E(Y^*) = K$	when $\varepsilon_T = 1$	when $\varepsilon_1 = \varepsilon_2$ and $\varepsilon_T = 1$	when $\varepsilon_1 = \varepsilon_2$ and $\varepsilon_T = 1$
$E(Y) = J$	when $\sigma = 0$	when $\sigma = 0$ and $s_1(1 - \varepsilon_2) = (1 - s_1)\varepsilon_1$	when $\varepsilon_1 = \varepsilon_2 = 0$
$E(Y) = K$	when $\sigma = 0$ and $\varepsilon_T = 1$	when $\sigma = 0$ and $s_1(1 - \varepsilon_2) = (1 - s_1)\varepsilon_1$ and $\varepsilon_T = 1$	when $\varepsilon_1 = \varepsilon_2 = 0$ and $\varepsilon_T = 1$

Appendix A5.4: Data for Estimating the Supply-Shifting Effects of Research

In chapter 5, the basic data required to implement a research-evaluation priority-setting study were described. Both the market- and research-related data used in these types of analyses were reviewed and some of the main conceptual and empirical issues were also discussed. This appendix builds directly on that discussion and develops in more detail a set of procedures and guidelines for eliciting information and compiling data to estimate the research-induced shift in supply.

In compiling these data, it is important to proceed in an organized and structured fashion. This facilitates estimating the economic consequences of research. And well-constructed primary data themselves are useful decision-making aids. Moreover, institutionalizing the evaluation process demands a structured and documented approach to data gathering and processing, given the relatively frequent turnover of analysts and decision makers in many agricultural research institutions, particularly those in developing countries. Accumulating primary market- and research-related data over time on a consistent basis can also confer significant economies of size and scope regarding the data acquisition and processing aspects of this work. It also builds the basis for the whole evaluation cum priority-setting exercise to take on a monitoring function as well. Systematically cross-checking scientists' best guesses about the future impact of their current work against the current impact of their past work is valuable from various vantage points, be it scientists thinking about the prospects of socially valuable impact coming from their planned research or those individuals operating at more strategic levels in the decision-making hierarchy who are reviewing the likely consequences of reallocating resources between or within different programs.

While the data requirements are much the same for ex post and ex ante analyses, the emphasis here is on compiling estimates of the economic consequences of research that is yet to be done. By explicitly linking these likely research effects to the planned deployment of research resources, it is possible to gain a structured appraisal of the implications of alternative resource allocation decisions, information that is valuable for choosing among alternatives. The topics dealt with in the elicitation forms and guidelines on data compilation described below include
- Research resources
  - research personnel (commodity focus, research program areas)
  - research costs (total resources, research program details)
- Research impact

— aggregate, local yield effects
— factor bias and additional input costs
— spatial variation in yield effects
• Research dynamics
— research and development lags
— adoption parameters (including research depreciation)
• Research risk
— sensitivity analysis
• Reconciliation

The topics are grouped and ordered in a sequence that should prove acceptable for, or that can be adapted to suit, most evaluation studies.[88] However, it is simply not feasible to design a questionnaire or elicitation process that is of direct use in all applications. Nevertheless, these prototypical forms and their accompanying notes should be relevant in many circumstances, particularly when it is the economic consequences (at the farm level) of broad programs within a national agricultural research system or agency that are being evaluated and prioritized. In any case it is a relatively straightforward job to modify these forms so that they can be used in other contexts, e.g., when dealing with research that affects the costs of production at various stages in the production-marketing chain or when applying the procedures to a multicountry, regional priority-setting exercise.

Benchmarking: Simply asking scientists and others to estimate likely yield increases or unit cost reductions, the time required to complete the research, the riskiness of the research, and adoption and research depreciation rates will not suffice. The approach adopted here is to assemble both historical and projected or elicited data, so that analysts can combine information from various sources in an intelligent fashion, drawing on the ideas and arguments discussed in chapter 5 to derive estimates of parameters. Wherever possible, historical data on past experimental and industry yield gains, prior rates of uptake of new technologies, the current cost structures of production, and so on should be explicitly incorporated into the elicitation process to condition and thereby calibrate the responses of scientists and others.

Alternative research scenarios: Research evaluation involves assessing and comparing alternatives. When eliciting research-related data and evaluating the economic consequences of the research, it is incumbent on the analyst to be clear about just what research scenarios are being assessed and compared. In particular, it is necessary to be completely clear about what is being held constant and what is being allowed to vary between any pair of alternatives that are being compared.

---

88. These illustrative elicitation forms are based on Pardey et al. (1992), Scobie and Jacobsen (1992), Dey and Norton (1993), and Bantilan and Lantican (1994).

In many ex ante studies, it is an ongoing rather than a new program of research that is being evaluated. This has direct consequences for the definition of the with- and without-research scenarios. When evaluating an ongoing research program, the with-research scenario often implies or explicitly uses a baseline that presumes an indefinite continuation of the current program of research. The corresponding without-research situation usually implies that none of the baseline research is conducted. But other interpretations are possible. Some scientists might think that without-research means without any research by anyone, rather than simply eliminating the specific program being discussed. Or, a scientist might make the common mistake of confusing information about changes over time (i.e., before and after) with the information being sought about changes attributable to changes in a particular factor, research (i.e., with and without). Having established the baseline *with* and *without* cases, the implications of deviating from this baseline (e.g., plus or minus 15% of the baseline research budget) can be established to give some indication of the marginal trade-offs involved in reallocating research resources. Generally, when doing this type of sensitivity analysis, the without-research situation continues to be a case in which none of the baseline research is undertaken.

Alternatively, the baseline could involve a smaller temporary or permanent change in the current program of research. For example, the baseline (with-research) scenario may involve a continuation of the existing pattern of research investments while the "without"-research case refers to a one-shot, permanent, decrease in funding from the baseline. Or, the "without"-research situation could involve a change in funding that persists only for a finite period, say one round or cycle of research that runs for the time it takes to develop a new crop variety. Alternatively, the baseline could be defined as a sequence of research program expenditures that differs from the current program, and the alternative could be different in any way thought to be relevant for comparison. One of the most difficult, and potentially useful parts of a research evaluation cum priority-setting project is to define meaningful, relevant alternatives to be assessed. A closer correspondence between the alternatives defined for assessment (on which explicit information is elicited) and the real options being considered enhances the possibility of a useful outcome.

Exactly which scenario is being evaluated has important implications for what data to collect or elicit and how to interpret the results of the subsequent analysis. Many studies are unclear on this point, so the elicited parameters (particularly regarding depreciation and adoption) used to estimate a research benefit stream involve a confusion of scenarios that often don't properly correspond to the cost stream used as the basis for analysis.

Joint determination of research parameters: Both in practice and in their elicited responses, scientists may well trade off smaller maximum yield gains for shorter R&D lags, or longer R&D lags for a higher probability of successfully completing the research, or various other combinations of these research-related parameters. And most adoption studies find that profitability is a critical determinant of adoption rates: the rate of uptake of a new technology is positively related to the size of the yield-increasing or cost-reducing effects of research.

These trade-offs should be dealt with explicitly in the research evaluation framework. A preferred option may be to benchmark the elicitation of all these parameters on a baseline deployment of research resources, making it clear to those from whom the information is elicited that the parameters are to be viewed as *jointly* determined. This makes it possible to consider in a structured way the effects of changes in research resources on all the parameters that are relevant for estimating the likely benefits from research. An important aspect of the elicitation-cum-parameter estimation process is reviewing and reconciling the various estimates to ensure that they are internally consistent for a given research scenario and meaningfully comparable among alternative research options.

An alternative approach, and one adopted by Davis, Oram and Ryan (1987), is to fix the (maximum potential) unit cost reduction at 5% of current production costs for each commodity being analyzed and to elicit, or estimate, the R&D lags, probabilities of research success, and adoption parameters compatible with the presumed unit cost reduction. One difficulty with this approach is that the baseline 5% unit cost reduction may lie well outside the range of previous experience or future prospects, making meaningful estimates of the remaining research-related parameters unlikely. Another, and perhaps more fundamental, difficulty is that this approach treats k^{MAX} as an exogenous parameter. Estimates of the R&D lags, probabilities of research success, and adoption parameters are elicited, conditional on a 5% k^{MAX} but without explicitly linking those estimates to the *change* in research resources thought necessary to achieve such a supply shift. It seems much more natural to think of the research resources themselves as the exogenous (or decision) variable and to analyze the likely supply-shifting effect, given various research scenarios that are of interest to decision makers. Modeling the changes in the research program that are thought necessary to generate a 5% decrease in unit costs across all commodity research programs may provide little in the way of useful information. Indeed, if an option being considered were to close down one research program and redeploy the resources among other programs, for instance, it would be much more natural and meaningful to model that reallocation.

Guidelines: The following guidelines are developed with the typical research evaluation study in mind. The usual sequence of events is to (a) compile the relevant data on research input and resource deployment to benchmark the cost side of the analysis, (b) assemble and process pertinent data, such as historical yield trends, current cost of production, past adoption practices, as well as relevant agroecological data (to both benchmark scientists' responses and help structure the elicitation of the technical parameters used to estimate the benefit side of the analysis), and (c) jointly elicit the set of research-related parameters corresponding to clearly defined research program alternatives, using the current program as a benchmark.

Naturally, not all studies proceed in such a linear fashion. In some cases a pilot evaluation exercise for a limited number of commodity research programs will be undertaken to familiarize scientists, analysts, and decision makers with all the steps in the process before proceeding with a more comprehensive priority-setting exercise. A careful evaluation exercise involves a good deal of interaction with scientists and decision makers. Elicited research-related parameters are often recalibrated and revised when new information becomes available, often as a consequence of the evaluation process itself, or as various sensitivity analyses are performed to provide decision makers with relevant information on which to assess the implications of alternative research options. A well-integrated evaluation-cum-priority-setting effort will be cycling through various versions of data elicitation, data processing, and result presentations as new questions and new opportunities for doing worthwhile analyses present themselves.

A5.4.1   Elicitation Form Cover Sheet

Table A5.4.1:   *Example of an Elicitation Form Cover Sheet*

Institute Name: Institute Address:					
	Respondent details			Elicitor details	
Commodity/ research area	Name	Position	Research specialty	Name	Date

Note: To expedite data reviews and revisions, it is helpful to keep track of who performed and who participated in the data-elicitation exercise.

A5.4.2   *Research Resources*

Personnel

Table A5.4.2:   *Research Resources: Human Resource Information by Commodity*

Year:	Scientists[a]		Technical support staff[a]	
Commodity/ research area	Number	Share	Number	Share
	(fte)	*(%)*	*(fte)*	*(%)*
Other				
Institute total	x	100%	x	100%

Note: Research personnel data that are stratified by commodity or research area for the current year or, preferably, the past several years (or, even more desirable, a lengthy time series of past years) provide a useful indication of the current and likely future focus of a research institute, organization, or system. For evaluation purposes at least, it is recommended that the resources devoted to factor-oriented research (e.g., research on soil, water, and so on) be identified as a component of a specified commodity program whenever it is possible and appropriate to do so. Much, if not most factor-oriented research is done to improve the value of a natural resource that is (or is likely to be) used to produce a known output. With this approach, only the resource management and conservation research that is difficult to allocate in this way (because, for example, it jointly affects multiple outputs) is classified in a residual, "noncommodity," or "other" research category. Explicit use of vertically disaggregated market models may be required to model and measure the effects of this type of research.

[a]It is often easier to allocate full-time equivalent (fte) researchers and associated support staff, rather than research expenditures, to specific research areas. If the program-specific fte researchers are difficult to obtain from published records or by elicitation, it may be useful to identify the fte total for the institute or system being evaluated, determine the *share* of total ftes working for specific commodity programs, and then prorate the fte total to specific programs using the corresponding share figures.

Research Program Area

Table A5.4.3: *Research Resources: Human Resource Information by Research Program Area*

Commodity:		Year:
	Scientists	
Research program areas[a]	Number	Share
	(fte)	*(%)*
Plant breeding		
Plant protection		
Soil management and fertilizer		
Crop production practices[b]		
Other		
Post-harvest[c]		
Commodity total	x	100%

Note: Having identified the commodity orientation of the research being assessed, it is useful for evaluation and resource-allocation purposes to identify the research program areas of each commodity program. This information could be compiled from existing management and accounting data, perhaps drawn from databases developed using the *INFORM* program (Gijsbers 1991). It is also useful to elicit this same information from scientists as a check against data obtained from other sources published and unpublished) or as a substitute for such data when they are not available.

[a]Corresponding categories for livestock research are animal breeding (or genetic improvement), animal health (including the veterinary sciences), livestock management, and perhaps, a separate category for feed and nutrition (which may include research on pasture management).

[b]Includes research on planting densities and timing, cropping patterns and rotations, irrigation practices, and so on.

[c]Postharvest areas of work include a wide range of research related to on- and off-farm issues that need to be explicitly identified in each case. If a significant share of the research is postharvest in nature, then vertical-market models and commensurate data will need to be assembled to preform the evaluation. See Scobie and Jacobsen (1992) for details of such an evaluation-cum-priority-setting exercise.

Research Costs

Detailed information should be gathered on the total costs and, where possible, on the form of expenditure (e.g., capital versus labor) at the level of the relevant alternatives to be assessed, and with a view to total constraints (table A5.4.4). Thus, for instance, if the analysis pertains only to a particular research institute, information would be gathered on the total expenditure by that institute over recent years, the mix of expenditures on different types of research inputs, and the mix of expenditures on different research programs carried out by the institute that are to be considered separately in the analysis. Details are usually not available on the expenditure mix by major research programs, but such information may be available in some cases and could be useful. Alternatively, a NARS might want to collect disaggregated details on research costs by institute as well as by program, depending on the alternatives to be assessed in the analysis.

Research Program Details

To benchmark the analysis around the current deployment of resources, it is helpful to get a structured view of the research orientation of the current program. To do this, it could be useful to compile a list of current (and, if relevant, proposed) projects, identifying each project or research theme (consisting of a logical grouping of projects or areas of research) by its

- commodity focus (see table A5.4.2)
- research program area (see table A5.4.3)
- spatial (agroecological) focus
- research problem focus
- linkages among projects within the program and to projects in other areas

Table A5.4.4 *Total Resources and Disposition*

| Year | | Capital costs | Maintenance costs | Operating costs | Labor[a] | | | Total research costs | Total extension costs[b] |
No	Date				fte	Cost per fte	Total labor costs		
1	1990	x	x	x	x	x	x	x	x
2	1991	x	x	x	x	x	x	x	x
3	1992	x	x	x	x	x	x	x	x
4	1993	x	x	x	x	x	x	x	x
5	1994	x	x	x	x	x	x	x	x
6	1995								
7	1996								
8	1997								
9	1998								
10	1999								
11	2000								
12	2001								
13	2002								
14	2003								
15	2004								

Note: For an ex ante evaluation, data files from management and accounting, or, in their absence, elicited data, can be used to establish the baseline deployment of research and extension funds. The baseline is usually taken to be the current spending pattern, or, preferably, the average spending pattern for the past three years. A time series of past expenditures in conjunction with elicited data from research administrators, scientists, and others is usually the best basis for projecting forward the baseline spending scenario. Pardey and Roseboom (1989) and Roseboom and Pardey (1993) discuss data compilation and processing issues while Pardey et al. (1993, appendix 2) provide substantial details on the methods used to compile commodity-specific, time-series, research spending data for Indonesia. See also Pardey, Roseboom and Craig (1992) for further details on deflation and currency conversion issues related to aggregates of agricultural research spending.

[a] It might only be possible to distinguish between capital and noncapital costs, in which case a labor cost series could be estimated by scaling up estimates of cost per fte using the number of fte researchers. Likewise, noncapital costs might be projected forward using current and projected noncapital costs per researcher, scaled by the corresponding fte researcher series.

[b] Extension agencies are generally more labor intensive than research operations. Projecting baseline labor costs forward per fte (perhaps using extension personnel data) and making suitable adjustments for anticipated noncapital costs and changes in personnel could generate an acceptable cost series for extension.

428

A5.4.3 Research Impact — Estimating k^MAX

The effects of research on shifting supply functions — assuming full adoption of the results, the k^{MAX} parameters — can be estimated using experiment or industry data for ex post analysis. In ex ante studies, it is necessary to use estimates of the effects of hypothetical research alternatives; past experiment or industry yield data can be used to ensure realism in the elicitation of those estimates.

Aggregate Industry Yield Effects

In order to estimate a value of k^{MAX} for use in computing research benefits, it is necessary to define two scenarios between which yields (or costs) can be compared. A baseline scenario is commonly defined as a basis against which one or more alternative programs are to be compared; the k^{MAX} estimate refers to the shift in supply from the baseline due to the difference in research expenditure under the alternative. For ex post evaluation of past programs, studies have treated the actual program as the baseline and the alternative is a counterfactual scenario of no expenditure on the research program of interest. This will yield a measure of average returns. For forward-looking analysis, actual expenditure is not known and the baseline is hypothetical, along with the alternatives. A reasonable approach is to project the current (or recent past) forward as the baseline and to consider variations from that baseline (say plus or minus 15%) as relevant alternatives. This latter approach will generate an estimate that is closer to a marginal than an average rate of return.

For forward-looking analysis, for both the baseline and alternative scenarios, scientists and others are usually asked to estimate yields if the research is successful and the results are fully adopted, and the estimated yields are used to deduce measures of k^{MAX}. It is likely that elicited estimates will be more accurate if past yields are used to benchmark the projections. One approach is to graph past yields and ask scientists and others to juxtapose their estimates of "lowest," "most likely," and "highest" future yields — given a particular research program alternative — against the historical record, as shown in figure A5.4.1.

In figure A5.4.1, information on a single research option is shown. Alternatively, and perhaps preferably, a table such as table A5.4.5 could be used, in conjunction with the historical yield plot in figure A5.4.1, to elicit information on the distribution of potential outcomes from each of several research alternatives. A moving average of yields over several recent years may be used to adjust for weather effects. Alternatively, the elicitation form might be constructed to simultaneously collect additional information, such as research lags, on a single research alternative.

Figure A5.4.1: *Benchmarking elicited yield effects for a single research option*

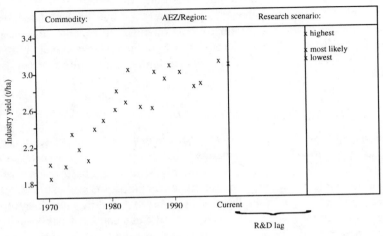

Table A5.4.5: *Sample Data Sheet for Recording the Yield Effects of Various Research Options*

Commodity:		AEZ/ Region:		
Research		**Yield**		
Scenario	I.D. No.	Lowest	Most likely	Highest
		(t/ha)	(t/ha)	(t/ha)
Baseline	1			
No research	2			
Baseline + 15%	3			
		Yield gain		
Research Alternative		Lowest	Most likely	Highest
		(%)	(%)	(%)
1 vs 2				
1 vs 3				

Estimates of industry yield effects might also be based on experimental data. In such cases, care must be taken in the elicitation to contrast experimental and industry yields and to account for differences in experimental and industry conditions, cultural practices, and input use.

Factor Bias and Additional Input Costs

As discussed in section 5.3.2 and in box 5.1, the elicited estimates of increases in industry yields identified in table A5.4.5 may involve a change in the cost of purchased inputs (such as fertilizer, fuel, and pesticides) or a change in the use of allocatable fixed factors (such as land or operator labor) per tonne of output. Such induced changes in input costs must be accounted for when elicited yield changes are translated into measures of the per unit cost reductions attributable to research (i.e., k^{MAX}). Table A5.4.6 can be used to assist in compiling the data to make the appropriate adjustments for changes in input costs when k^{MAX} is estimated. Note that in order to make these adjustments, it is necessary to use information on shares of total costs attributable to those factors whose costs are changing.

Table A5.4.6: *Sample Data Sheet for Recording Changes in Input Costs*

Commodity:						
	Preresearch cost share	Most likely cost change			
Input		Decrease	No change	Increase	Rate of change
Variable ($/ha)	(%)		(*check one*)		(%)
Hired labor					
Fertilizer					
Pesticides					
Irrigation					
Fuel					
Other					
Total variable					100 E(C)
Allocatable/fixed ($/tonne of output)					
Machinery					
Land					
Operator labor					
Total fixed					100 E(F)

Note: E(C) is the rate of change in variable-factor costs, and and E(F) is the rate of change in allocatable, fixed-factor costs (see box 5.1). These cost increases are simply equal to the cost-share-weighted sum of the increases in specific factor costs, e.g., E(C) $= \Sigma_j S_j$ E(C_j) where S_j is the share of the input j in total variable costs, and E(C_j) is the proportionate rate of cost change in input j.

Spatial Variation in Yield Effects

Direct effects: Within a country or region, there may be a good deal of spatial variation in agroecological characteristics, giving rise to a large spatial variation in yield response to new technologies. It may be worthwhile to take this zonal variation into account when constructing a measure of the aggregate supply shift in order

- to improve the estimates of the overall regional or country-level effect of new technologies, even when the regional supply shifts themselves are not of immediate interest
- to distinguish between the local and spillover effects of research, both within and between countries
- to provide information on differential spatial impacts where they are of direct interest

This spatial variation could be taken into account by directly eliciting information on yield responses to the new technology (and associated cost changes) for each of several different zones, using the tables above. Another approach is to infer regional differences using other information on relative productive performance among the zones.

Spillover effects: A practical problem when dealing with multiple sources of technology concerns the ceteris paribus assumptions used to estimate the $K_{i,j}$s and $K_{j,j}$s. The principle espoused in this book is that the shift effect should reflect the with- versus without-research situation rather than the before- versus after-research situation, thereby explicitly capturing the "maintenance effects" of research in the evaluation. But with multiple sources of technology (i.e., multiple research sites), the "without-research" situation needs careful elaboration. This amounts to no more than being clear about what is being held constant, and what is being varied, across the alternatives being evaluated.

From country i's perspective, the baseline scenario could be defined as a particular program of local research (perhaps the current program of local research), with or without nonlocal or spill-in research. In many cases, where nonlocal research programs are beyond the control of the client, it is appropriate to treat the supply of research from those programs as exogenous (and in most cases this will translate in effect to treating the yield consequences of those programs as exogenous and constant across the alternatives being compared). Hence, the usual situation (and treatment) is not "zero nonlocal research" but, rather, "zero induced change in nonlocal research."

Where there is an interest in the multiregional impact of multiregional research, the analyst might initially fix research programs in all places of interest at a baseline and establish a baseline scenario for yield patterns. The second step is then to evaluate the effects of alternatives to the baseline (allowing a full matrix of spillovers) by varying research, as appropriate, in one or more locations and reevaluating the supply-shifting effects. This more involved approach might be more appropriate for addressing the issues concerning international centers or large countries with multiple research institutes and a concern with regional impact, than for the usual NARS analysis.

A5.4.4   Research Dynamics

Information of various types is needed to parameterize the dynamics of the research process, in order to translate the measures of potential supply shift, k^{MAX}, into measures of anticipated supply shifts over time, k_t. These dynamics relate, in particular, to lags in the research process itself, in commercialization of the results, and in adoption.

Research and Development Lags

The baseline scenario implies a particular time pattern of expenditures on research and a particular corresponding time path over which results are developed and become available for adoption. These R&D lags are usually taken to represent the most likely time from when a particular line of research is initiated to when a new technology has been developed. For a plant breeding program, this is the time required to develop a new, improved variety; for crop-production practices, it may be the time taken to develop new planting recommendations; for fertilizer technologies, it could be the time required to develop a new premix or, alternatively, the time required to isolate the effects of a particular trace element, depending on the nature of the research. In eliciting R&D lags from scientists, it is important for them to understand that the question is not "how long until the next new results are available from the ongoing research?" but, rather, "how long would it take for a newly initiated project, say, within the current ongoing program, to yield results?"

Typical R&D lags vary across subcommodities within an aggregated commodity program, as well as across lines of research on the same commodity, in part varying according to the funding support that is available. For this reason, when eliciting an average or overall estimate of the R&D lag to be applied to an entire program of research, it is important to take account of the mix of research to be undertaken within the particular program alternative being discussed and to be sure that the R&D lag estimate is fully consistent with the corresponding elicited values for yield response and research costs.

Table A5.4.7 may be useful for eliciting R&D lags for research program areas within a particular commodity program, as a basis for either evaluating individual areas or for developing an estimate of the overall average R&D lag.

Table A5.4.7   *Sample Data Sheet for Eliciting R&D Lags for Research Program Areas*

Commodity:

Research program area	Most likely time (in years) to *develop* new technology (check)										
	≤1	2	3	4	5	6	7	8	9	10	>10 (specify)
Plant breeding											
Plant protection											
Soil management & fertilizer											
Crop production practices											
Other											
Postharvest											
Overall commodity											

Adoption Parameters

Before attempting to elicit *parameters* describing the time path of adoption, it is usually necessary to assume a particular type of adoption *process*. Elicitation forms are given below for parameterizing two typical adoption profiles. These curves include the growth phase (during which technologies are taken up) and the decline phase (during which technologies depreciate or become progressively abandoned).

Figure A5.4.2:   *Trapezoidal adoption profile*

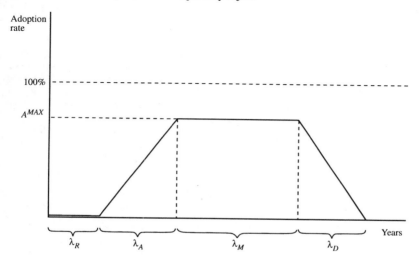

Table A5.4.8: *Sample Data Sheet for Adoption Parameters for the Trapezoidal Adoption Profile*

	Adoption parameters				
Commodity	Ceiling adoption rate, A^{MAX}	Period from initial adoption to maximum adoption, λ_A	Period from maximum adoption to eventual decline, λ_M	Period from the beginning to the end of the decline, λ_D	Total research and adoption lag, $\lambda_T = \lambda_R + \lambda_A + \lambda_M + \lambda_D$
	(%)	(years)	(years)	(years)	(years)

Note: The research lag, λ_R, is obtained from table A5.4.7. The ceiling adoption rate, A^{MAX}, is best measured as the proportion of output produced using the new technology, but it is usually more readily approximated as the maximum area sown to a new crop or cropped area produced with a new technology, or the maximum proportion of farmers adopting a new technology.

See appendix A5.1.2 for details on calculating the trapezoidal adoption profile $A_t, t = 0, \ldots, L_R$ using the data in this table.

Figure A5.4.3: *Logistic adoption profile*

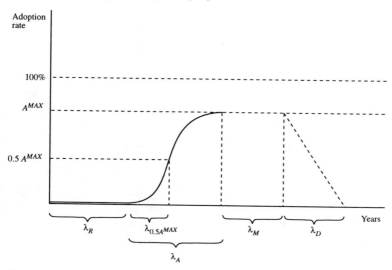

Table A5.4.9: *Sample Data Sheet for Adoption Parameters for the Logistic Adoption Profile*

Commodity	Adoption parameters		
	Ceiling adoption rate, A^{MAX}	Period from initial adoption to maximum adoption, λ_A	Period from initial adoption to attain 50% of maximum adoption, $\lambda_{0.5A^{MAX}}$
	(%)	(years)	(years)

Note: See section 5.3.3 and the references cited therein for details on constructing a logistic adoption curve from these data. The latter part of the adoption profile can be approximated using the λ_M and λ_D parameters from table A5.4.8.

A5.4.5   Research Risk

Mean or Most Likely Effects

Table A5.4.5 is suggested for eliciting three values — lowest, most likely, and highest — to parameterize the potential distribution of yield outcomes for a given research scenario. This information could be used in a number of ways. First, by assuming a particular functional form for the probability distribution — we recommend triangular — an expected value can be deduced (a variance and other moments could be computed as well). For some studies, this expected value may be all that is required: the expected value for the triangular distribution is equal to the simple average of the three elicited values.

In addition, however, the triangular distribution contains information that can be used with the methods described in section 5.3.3 to jointly define the expected value of the yield, given a successful research program, and the probability of achieving success defined in terms of a particular yield outcome or better. Figure A5.4.4 shows the triangular probability density function elicited for a particular research scenario.

Figure A5.4.4:   *Example of a triangular probability density function*

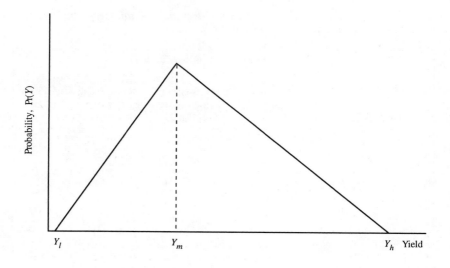

Sensitivity Analysis

The availability of data on distributions of research outcomes is intrinsically valuable because it conveys information on the degree of dispersion around the scientists' estimates of the most likely research outcome — a measure of their confidence — and it is convenient for conducting informal or formal sensitivity analyses. For instance, section 5.4.4 discusses the use of a triangular distribution in a Monte Carlo simulation for sensitivity analysis. Also, some studies might want to take explicit account of research risk in the objective function (section 5.4.5), which can be parameterized using the variance from the probability density. It is important not to confuse the sensitivity analysis, which measures variations in the effects of a *given* program of research, as discussed here, with measures of the effects of variations in research programs. The former holds the research program constant; the latter holds everything else constant and varies research.

A5.4.6 Reconciliation

The purpose of the elicitation is essentially simple: we want an estimate of the time path of research-induced supply shifts (i.e., k_t) for each program alternative, which can be used to compute corresponding benefit streams using the methods described in preceding sections of this appendix. And for both evaluation and priority-setting purposes, estimates of the streams of research costs that correspond directly to the benefit streams (i.e., that are consistent with the underlying k_t estimates) are required.

But estimating these parameters is not easy. It involves combining estimates of underlying parameters. Several hazards arise. Each component is uncertain, and errors in one can corrupt the whole. And scientists might knowingly or inadvertently provide biased estimates. In some cases the biases may be offsetting, but in others they will not be — in particular, scientists seem more likely to overestimate research impacts than to underestimate them, both because they are too optimistic and because they have a stake in a favorable analysis.

Perhaps the best that can be done is to attempt to minimize the hazards by two expedients. First, since scientists compete with one another for resources, peer review at the elicitation stage could provide useful checks on scientists' estimates, and in an ongoing program of research evaluation and priority setting, monitoring actual research performance against initial claims can lead to increased incentives for accuracy. Second, scientists (and others involved in the elicitation) should be pressed to be sure that the various parameter estimates are mutually consistent: is the expected yield gain from a particular program of research consistent with research program expenditures and the R&D (and adoption) lag profiles that have been tabulated? This involves collecting all of the information together at the end of the elicitation and reviewing it. Such a review could involve not only the original sources of the estimates, but also other knowledgeable people, and it could use information available from other sources, such as studies conducted elsewhere or earlier in the same place.

6

Mathematical Programming

The research evaluation methods described in chapter 5 can be used to provide information on research benefits by program, as well as a ranking of program alternatives. However, these methods do not indicate the amount and share of total resources to allocate to each program. In chapter 5 we examined how estimated NPVs can be used in informal decision-making processes. Now we examine ways to use the same information — on the estimated benefits and costs, objectives, and resource constraints — in more formal modeling and analysis of resource allocation decisions.

Optimization subject to constraint is a fundamental part of economics. Results have been derived to characterize the solutions to general classes of problems and to identify the important features of those solutions. Several procedures are available to obtain optimal numerical solutions. The purpose of this chapter is to provide some guidance about the use of some of those procedures for optimizing research program portfolios. Which procedures are most appropriate depends on the characteristics of the optimization problem in terms of (a) the objective function to be maximized (i.e., some function of the costs and benefits of research, and perhaps other impacts), (b) the relationship between changes in research activities and the value of the objective function (i.e., combining the research production function[s] that relate research output to operating expenses and other inputs and the functions that relate research output to its economic impacts), and (c) constraints (on total resources available for research, on particular inputs, and on the research portfolio itself).

Specific situations sometimes satisfy general conditions for optimality, obviating a need for using empirical optimization methods. For instance, the unconstrained maximization of the total anticipated social payoff from

441

research would call for funding all research programs having positive anticipated NPVs. Maximization of the same objective subject to a fixed research
budget would call for choosing the portfolio that maximizes the anticipated
NPV per unit of constraint. This portfolio could be found by ranking programs according to NPV per unit of budget and moving down the list until
the budget was exhausted. But this method for allocating resources to
research only works for a set of discrete alternative investments.

Suppose the size of individual research programs is flexible. If there is a
linear relationship between NPV and program size, the benefits from the total
portfolio will be maximized by allocating *all* resources to the program with the
highest NPV per unit of constraint — a corner solution. An interior solution (i.e.,
a diversified research portfolio) requires either (a) multiple constraints on
inputs to research programs and different input requirements for different
programs (i.e., a linear programming problem), (b) a nonlinear (diminishing-
returns) relationship between the sizes of programs and their NPVs, (c) a
nonlinear relationship between the NPV of a program and its contribution to the
objective function (where multiple objectives are involved), or (d) some
combination of these features. In all of these situations, an explicit optimization
procedure is needed to establish the empirical trade-off among programs where
their marginal contributions to the various relevant objectives are equated.

Mathematical programming is an optimization procedure that can be
applied to such problems.[1] A mathematical-programming model can

- include multiple objectives and be used to quantify the nature of
  trade-offs among objectives (e.g., the economic efficiency sacrificed
  to meet a distributional objective)
- incorporate a research response function that exhibits constant or
  diminishing returns to research so that, for a given objective, the mix
  of research programs can be optimized
- relate the marginal research benefit to the amount of funds going into
  research and their deployment
- examine the implications of changing facility, human resource, and
  financial constraints on research
- identify both short- and long-run priorities by considering changes in
  constraints on resources that may be fixed in the short run but variable
  in the long run

---

1. Several texts are available that document the theory underlying mathematical programming
models, their practical application, and the computer programs that can be used. These include Hazell and
Norton (1986) and Paris (1991). Simulation models have also been proposed to assist with agricultural
research prioritization (Pinstrup-Andersen and Franklin 1977 and Bosch and Shabman 1990). These
models lend themselves to building in risk components and may or may not include an optimization
algorithm.

- provide information on the benefits foregone due to short-run fixities in human resources and facilities
- examine the sensitivity of research priorities to estimated changes in research funding, market conditions, per unit cost reductions due to research, and other assumptions[2]

In this chapter we discuss the use of mathematical-programming models in making decisions about allocating resources to research.[3] We examine issues to consider in model design and suggest possible formulations of a multiple-objective programming model for allocating research resources.

Mathematical programming has its greatest potential for assisting with research resource allocation when it is combined with measures of benefits derived from economic surplus analysis. Hence, a decision to apply a programming procedure in this context implies that adequate resources are also available for implementing the economic surplus approach. Computing the measures of economic surplus changes required for the mathematical-programming models described below is no small task. However, once the economic surplus calculations have been made, a mathematical-programming model offers the possibility of utilizing the information more effectively. Even if formal optimization is not undertaken, thinking through such models can provide additional insights into the problem of allocating resources to research.

This chapter begins with a review of the basics of mathematical-programming models. Then it considers some specific aspects involved in applying those models to agricultural research portfolios. The third main section goes into practical implementation issues, including data, solution procedures, and possible extensions.

6.1 Mathematical-Programming Principles

6.1.1 Basics of Mathematical-Programming Models

Several variants of the basic multiple-objective, mathematical-programming model are available for obtaining a weighted "optimal" solution or a set of feasible solutions that trade off the various objectives. The basic

2. Mathematical programming does assume separability among activities in the model, and the analysis is partial equilibrium like the methods described in chapters 3 to 5.

3. Mathematical programming models have been formulated for agricultural research resource allocation by Russell (1975), de Wit (1988), and Scobie and Jacobsen (1992). Russell applied his model to a set of research projects in the United Kingdom; de Wit applied his to a hypothetical set of data for the CGIAR system. Scobie and Jacobsen provide guidance for allocating research resources across research programs supported by the Australian Wool Corporation.

multiple-objective decision-making model can be represented in its general form as

$$\max z(x) = G\ [\ z_1(x),\ z_2(x),\ \dots\ ,z_k(x)\ ]\tag{6.1a}$$

subject to

$$x \in X \tag{6.1b}$$

$$x \geq 0 \tag{6.1c}$$

where $z(x)$ is the objective function with k objectives, G is the goal operator (which defines the functional form of the objective function being maximized), x is the n-dimensional vector of decision variables (i.e., in this context these will be the research programs to which resources are committed to achieve the stated objectives), and X defines the decision space (in this context, defined by the set of research resources available and any other constraints on the choices of x) so that equation 6.1b is the set of m constraints for the problem. Equation 6.1c is a set of non-negativity conditions that constrain the problem so that the values of the decision variables or activities (e.g., in this context the research resources invested in any program) cannot be negative. Together, equations 6.1b and 6.1c determine the feasible region. Each feasible solution implies a value for each objective $z_i(x)$, $i = 1, 2, \dots, k$.[4]

Basic Solution Approaches

The two basic means of solving this general model are (a) to define and apply a set of decision-makers' preferences or weights before optimization, so as to obtain a unique "optimum" solution, or (b) to generate a set of non-inferior solutions that illustrate the tradeoffs among objectives rather than provide only a single optimum solution (the decision makers must choose then from a, sometimes large, set of possible solutions).[5] In the latter approach, non-inferior solutions are generated without prior specification of preferences by parametric variation (varying by increments) of either the weights on the objective function or constraints on the solution (figure 6.1).[6] This more generally adopted approach, of varying the weights or constraints, amounts to defining empirically the benefit transformation curve or surface which shows how the (maximum) value of the objective function varies with changes in activities (i.e., how the total research benefit varies with changes in combinations of research programs — chapter 2). The first approach

---

4. This formulation of the problem follows Willis and Perlack (1980).

5. A noninferior solution is a feasible solution to the problem, $x \in X$, such that no other feasible solution, $x^* \in X$, exists for which $z_p(x^*) > z_p(x)$ for some $p = 1, 2, \dots, k$, and $z_i(x^*) \geq z_i(x)$ for all $i \neq p$.

6. Cohon and Marks (1973), Cohon (1975), and Willis and Perlack (1980) compare these techniques.

Figure 6.1: *Illustration of a set of noninferior solutions generated by parameterizing weights on the objective functions*

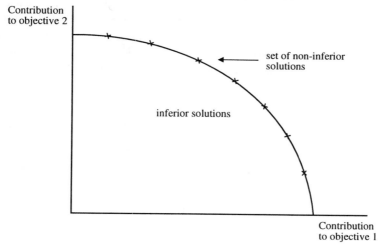

amounts to specifying the slope of a particular indifference curve and the constraints, and then finding a point on the benefit transformation curve.

Goal-programming approach: Following Willis and Perlack (1980), one formulation of the problem, called goal programming, involves specifying weights, w_i, and positive deviations, d_i, and negative deviations, e_i, of the objectives from their targets, T_i. In the case of research resource allocation, the targets might represent the maximum value that would be achieved if all research resources were devoted to satisfying a particular objective.[7]

$$\min \sum_{i=1}^{k} w_i \, (d_i + e_i) \tag{6.2a}$$

subject to

$$x \in X \tag{6.2b}$$

$$x \geq 0 \tag{6.2c}$$

$$z_i(x) - d_i + e_i = T_i \,, \quad i = 1, \ldots, k \tag{6.2d}$$

$$d_i \,, e_i \geq 0 \tag{6.2e}$$

7. Charnes and Cooper (1961) provide an early discussion of the formulation of the goal-programming model and Kornbluth (1973) surveys the subsequent literature. Lee (1972) and Neely, North and Fortson (1977) provide examples of applications.

In goal programming, the solution is constrained to minimize weighted deviations from the goals but is not constrained to achieve the goals. The w_i are the penalties attached to deviating from the targets, and if d_i is nonzero, e_i will be zero, and vice versa. For instance, if there were two objectives, efficiency and equity, one penalty would be attached to any deviations from maximum efficiency benefits and another to any deviations from maximum equity. The solution to the model would minimize the sum of those weighted deviations.

Parametrically varying weights in the objective function: The formulation of the multigoal problem in which G is linear and weights on the objective function are not specified a priori but are parameterized to generate a set of non-inferior solutions can be represented by

$$\max \sum_{i=1}^{k} w_i z_i(x) \tag{6.3a}$$

subject to

$$x \in X \tag{6.3b}$$

$$x \geq 0 \tag{6.3c}$$

where $w_i \geq 0$ for all i and is strictly positive for at least one of the w_i s. The initial w_i s are arbitrarily set and then varied parametrically.

Parametrically varying constraints on the solution: The formulation of the problem in which weights on the objective function are not specified but constraints on the solution are varied by the analyst to generate a set of non-inferior solutions can be represented by

$$\max z_j(x) \tag{6.4a}$$

subject to

$$x \in X \tag{6.4b}$$

$$z_i(x) \geq b_i , i \neq j \tag{6.4c}$$

$$x \geq 0 \tag{6.4d}$$

where b_i are the lower bounds on the k-1 objectives. The lower bounds are set by maximizing equation 6.4a for each of the k objectives individually, subject to equations 6.4b and 6.4c, substituting the values of x for each of the k optimal solutions into $z_i(x)$, and then selecting for each $z_i(x)$ the lowest of its k values to be its b_i. The set of noninferior solutions is then generated by solving equations 6.4a to 6.4d with parametric variation of b_i and substitution of each $z_i(x)$ into equations 6.4a, for all $i \neq j$. In essence, this is goal programming as well, because targets for each goal are being set.

Several comparisons can be made among these three alternatives. First, the approach in which weights are specified a priori can be converted to the approach in which weights are varied parametrically.[8] Second, the formulation in which weights on objectives are varied gives the same noninferior solution set as the formulation in which constraints are varied, as long as the objective space is strictly convex.[9] Third, the formulations vary in degree of quantification of trade-offs and in the ease of presenting results to decision makers. Willis and Perlack (1980) compare these and other criteria for evaluating these approaches. They note that, if the weights were varied six times and if there were four objectives, the set of noninferior solutions would be 216 (and 1,296 for five objectives). They argue that the parameterizing approach is likely to be impractical for more than four objectives. However, it is likely that the 36 solutions generated by only three objectives also provides too much information to be of much help to research decision makers.

Hybrid Programming Approaches

Compromise programming: A hybrid approach can narrow down the noninferior set of solutions. Various hybrid approaches have been suggested in the literature. One is based on a technique called compromise programming.[10] With compromise programming, the ideal point, the coordinates of which are given by the optimum amount for each objective in isolation, is established first (figure 6.2). However, because of conflicting objectives, this ideal point may not be feasible. Compromise programming then defines the best compromise solution as the feasible solution that is closest to the ideal point. Closeness is measured by a weighted sum of deviations from the maximums (ideals) for each individual objective. Closeness for an individual objective is measured by $d_j = z_j^*(x) - z_j(x)$, where $z_j^*(x)$ is the ideal value for objective j.[11]

Compromise programming uses the function

$$L_p = \left[\sum_{j=1}^{k} (w_j d_j)^p \right]^{1/p} \tag{6.5}$$

to measure the distance between each solution and the ideal solution. In this formulation, each w_j weights the importance of the difference between the

8. See Willis and Perlack (1980).

9. Cohon and Marks (1973) and others have used the possibility of inferior solutions as an argument against parameterizing weights in the objective function. While concave portions of the objective space seem unlikely for the objectives described earlier for the model, strict convexity might be violated.

10. See Zeleny (1973), Cohon (1975, 1978), and Romero, Amador and Barco (1987).

11. See Romero, Amador and Barco (1987) for more details. If objectives are in different units, the d_j can be converted to a proportion of the maximum possible deviations from the ideal for each objective. When the jth objective is minimized, $d_j = z_j^*(x) - z_j(x)$.

Figure 6.2: *Trade-off between objectives and illustration of the ideal point and compromise set*

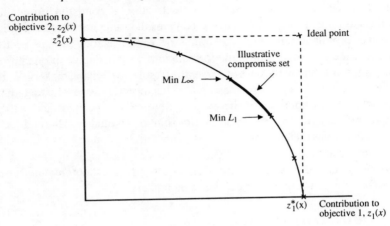

jth objective and its ideal value, and p is a parameter that is set equal to either one or infinity in order to bound the solution. Bounds can be placed on the solution set by first setting $p = 1.0$ such that the following linear programming problem is solved:

$$\min L_1 = \sum_{j=1}^{k} w_j \left[z_j^* (x) - z_j (x) \right] \tag{6.6a}$$

subject to

$$x \in X \tag{6.6b}$$

$$x \geq 0 \tag{6.6c}$$

and then, by setting $p = \infty$, the maximum of the individual deviations is minimized (i.e., only the largest deviation counts and the algorithm minimizes it) to obtain the other bound

$$\min L_\infty = d_\infty \tag{6.7a}$$

subject to

$$w_1 [z_1^*(x) - z_1(x)] \leq d_\infty$$

$$\begin{matrix} \cdot & \cdot & \cdot \\ \cdot & \cdot & \cdot \\ \cdot & \cdot & \cdot \end{matrix} \tag{6.7b}$$

$$w_k [z_k^*(x) - z_k(x)] \leq d_\infty$$

$$x \in X \qquad\qquad (6.7c)$$

$$x \geq 0 \qquad\qquad (6.7d)$$

The compromise programming procedure narrows down the efficient set, but it does so at the cost of requiring the weights on the deviations from the ideal to be specified. Furthermore, the set of efficient solutions could still be large. A filtering technique could be used to remove some of the solutions that are not very different from the other efficient solutions already calculated, but the problem of weighting deviations would remain.[12]

Iterative procedures: A more practical approach to the multiobjective, decision-making problem facing research decision makers may be to combine their opinions about weights on objectives with the generation of a reduced set of solutions and to follow an iterative procedure.[13] First, weights could be elicited from the decision makers for the various objectives using the procedure described in chapter 7, and equation 6.3a could be maximized subject to (6.3b) and (6.3c) to generate an initial solution. At the same time, equation 6.4a could be maximized for each of the k objectives subject to (6.4b) and (6.4c). This would generate the maximum and minimum bounds for each objective. These $k + 1$ solutions would be shown to the decision makers who then would be asked if they would like to change their weights on any objectives, given the trade-offs illustrated by the solutions used to generate the bounds. If they revise their weights, the model is rerun with the new weights and the process is repeated.

An alternative iterative procedure would be to generate the bounds but not to elicit the initial weights. Instead, the k solutions would be shown to the decision makers who would be asked the objective for which they would most like to see the lower bound raised. The model would be rerun after raising that lower bound and at least one of the objectives would achieve a lower maximum than before. This process would be repeated several times until the decision makers were satisfied with the trade-offs made among the objectives. If the process were entirely iterative with no specification of initial weights, it might require a larger number of iterations to arrive at a similar solution than if initial weights were elicited.

The final, and perhaps the recommended, option would be to begin by generating a benchmark solution (e.g., maximize equation 6.3a subject to [6.3b] and [6.3c] with a weight of 1.0 placed on the efficiency objective and zeros placed on other objectives). Then, a weight of say 0.1 could be added to each of the other objectives. These two solutions could be presented to

12. See Steuer and Harris (1980) and Romero, Amador and Barco (1987) for a discussion of a filtering technique.

13. See Candler and Boehlje (1971).

decision makers. Their views could then be solicited on any desired changes in weights. We recommend this option because (a) it is difficult to discuss and evaluate with decision makers more than two or three alternative research portfolios at once, (b) research is a relatively blunt instrument for meeting nonefficiency objectives and, hence, an initial situation with all weight placed on economic efficiency is a reasonable base for comparisons, and (c) in practical experience with eliciting weights in several agricultural research systems, decision makers experimented with different weights in an informal process until nearly all the weight was placed on the efficiency objective (chapter 7). This prior information can be used to provide a useful point of departure for reaching consensus on a research portfolio.

6.1.2   Formulations for Research Resource Allocation

We begin with a simple model in which (a) research resources are allocated across alternative programs under the assumption that increased economic efficiency is the only objective, (b) the research production function is nonlinear, exhibiting diminishing marginal returns (e.g., Scobie and Jacobsen 1992), and (c) there are n research programs and three levels of spending for each program. The model is then modified to incorporate objectives associated with income distribution and risk. Finally, multiperiod optimization is added.

The basic structure of the model is described in figure 6.3. We begin by presenting a single-period, linear-programming model. The research benefit per unit of research input is a discounted sum of economic benefits for several years (although the benefits would accrue over several years, they enter in present value form only once, creating a one–decision-period problem). These discounted totals per unit of research input are allowed to vary with changes in research expenditures so that the research production function exhibits diminishing returns to research inputs.

Maximizing Total Research Benefits

The activities in the model, i.e., the c_{ij}, are research program alternatives, where i = the program and j = level of funding. For example, the activities c_{11}, c_{12}, and c_{13} in figure 6.3 represent aggregate research program 1 under three ranges of financial support. The constraints, R_{ij}, are the maximum funding levels for each program, i, and range of support, j. For example, R_{11}, R_{12}, and R_{13} are the three alternative maximum levels of funding for program 1 ($R_{11} < R_{12} < R_{13}$). This support includes money for facilities and personnel as well as operating costs. In addition, total expenditures on all the research

Figure 6.3: *Single-objective, linear-programming model for allocating resources to agricultural research*

		Research programs										
		Commodity 1			Commodity 2				Commodity *n*			
Equation	Description	c_{11}	c_{12}	c_{13}	c_{21}	c_{22}	c_{23}	. . .	c_{n1}	c_{n2}	c_{n3}	RHS
1	objective function	a_{11}	a_{12}	a_{13}	a_{21}	a_{22}	a_{23}	. . .	a_{n1}	a_{n2}	a_{n3}	MAX
2	total resource limit	1	1	1	1	1	1	. . .	1	1	1	$\leq R$
3	program resource limit	1										$\leq R_{11}$
		1	1									$\leq R_{12}$
		1	1	1								$\leq R_{13}$
					1							$\leq R_{21}$
					1	1						$\leq R_{22}$
					1	1	1					$\leq R_{23}$
								. . .				. . .
									1			$\leq R_{n1}$
									1	1		$\leq R_{n2}$
									1	1	1	$\leq R_{n3}$

programs must be less than R (it is not possible to spend beyond the total research resources on any individual program), and the sum of all maximum individual R_{ij}s must be greater than R (it must be possible to profitably spend up to the total available) — i.e., R is a binding constraint on total research spending so that $\Sigma_i\, c_{ij} \leq R \leq \Sigma_i\, R_{i3}$.

The units for the activities are units of research expenditures (dollars or some other currency). For example, for program c_1, a unit of c_{12} might be a dollar of research expenditure for spending up to the current level of research spending, a unit of c_{11} would be a dollar of research expenditure for the low-expenditure option (say up to 75% of current), and a unit of c_{13} would be a dollar of expenditure for the high-expenditure option (say, up to 125% of current program expenditures). The three levels of support could vary independently by program; the options considered should correspond to the levels of funding assumed when the research benefits were calculated.

The $a_{11}, a_{12}, \ldots, a_{n3}$ represent the contributions to the efficiency objective (discounted economic benefits) associated with the n research programs and their corresponding levels of support. For example, under the low range of research support for program 1, a_{11} represents both the average and marginal products of research in terms of NPV per dollar of research spending, and these average and marginal products are equal within the low range of support. Under the intermediate range of research expenditures (i.e., $R_{11} < c_1 \leq R_{12}$), a_{12} is the marginal product of research measured in NPV per dollar for expenditures between R_{11} and R_{12}. In this range, the marginal product is less than the average product because it is lower than the initial marginal and average product. Because $a_{11} > a_{12} > a_{13}$, the three levels of research benefits per unit of input represent a three-step, research-response function with diminishing marginal returns.[14] The model as formulated requires that successive increases in spending on any research program result in smaller gains to productivity (i.e., it requires that the research production function for each program be concave). Also, if, when questioning scientists, it appears that current levels of research spending are in the range of increasing returns (i.e., $a_{11} < a_{12}$), additional opinions can be solicited from those scientists about the implications of higher spending to obtain information on the diminishing returns portion of the function.

Research support for each commodity cannot exceed the maximum for the highest-cost program for that commodity (i.e., R_{i3}). The program resource limits in figure 6.3 force the model to move up the research production

---

14. While research-response functions may exhibit increasing, constant, or diminishing returns, the assumption of diminishing returns is probably reasonable in most situations because it is a commonly held view that "nature is increasingly niggardly."

function for a commodity, once a specified resource limit is reached (e.g., from c_{11} to c_{12} after R_{11} is reached and from c_{12} to c_{13} after R_{12} is reached). Because $R < (R_{13} + R_{23} + R_{33} + \ldots + R_{n3})$, the research system may not move up to the high level of research spending for some (or even any) of the commodity research programs.

Multiple Objectives

The model in figure 6.3 can be extended to include multiple objectives as illustrated in figure 6.4. For ease of exposition, we assume that the research decision makers identify two objectives: (a) an efficiency objective, to maximize the well-being of all citizens and (b) a distributional objective, to provide additional benefits to a particular group (e.g., small-scale farmers). The $a_{11}, a_{12}, \ldots, a_{n3}$ represent the marginal contributions of changes in research expenditure to the efficiency objective; $b_{11}, b_{12}, \ldots, b_{n3}$ represent the same contributions to the distributional objective. The model contains an objective function with an initial weight of $w_1 = 1.0$ placed on the efficiency objective, $z_1(x)$, and a weight of w_2 placed on the distributional objective, $z_2(x)$. The NPVs for each objective are summed and transferred to the objective function for weighting.

Portfolio Risk

Since the early work on portfolio analysis by Markowitz (1952) and the quadratic programming model suggested by Freund (1956), several different approaches have been suggested for incorporating risk into mathematical-programming models. Many of these procedures are reviewed by Anderson, Dillon and Hardaker (1977), Boussard (1979), and Hazell and Norton (1986).

Over the past 20 years, the two most common approaches for incorporating risk into agricultural applications of mathematical-programming models have been quadratic risk programming, in which a variance-covariance matrix of net returns is incorporated in the model, and the MOTAD approach, in which the *mean of the total absolute deviations* is minimized.[15] Another technique is the focus-loss or safety-first approach that is designed to limit the "risk of ruin" by establishing some maximum admissible loss or minimum income level. Mathematical-programming models for allocating resources to agricultural research can take advantage of this vast literature when a procedure for incorporating risk is selected. In chapter 5 we presented a Monte Carlo approach for deriving measures of dispersion of estimated NPVs for particular research programs (e.g., Scobie and Jacobsen 1992).

15. For risk in a quadratic programming model see Freund (1956) and for risk in a MOTAD linear programming model see Hazell (1971).

Figure 6.4: *Multiple-objective, linear-programming model for allocating resources to agricultural research*

Equation	Description	Objectives		Research programs										RHS
				Commodity 1			Commodity 2			...	Commodity n			
		x_1	x_2	c_{11}	c_{12}	c_{13}	c_{21}	c_{22}	c_{23}	...	c_{n1}	c_{n2}	c_{n3}	
1	objective functions	1	w_2											MAX
2	contributions to objectives	-1		a_{11}	a_{12}	a_{13}	a_{21}	a_{22}	a_{23}	...	a_{n1}	a_{n2}	a_{n3}	= 0
			-1	b_{11}	b_{12}	b_{13}	b_{21}	b_{22}	b_{23}	...	b_{n1}	b_{n2}	b_{n3}	= 0
3	total resource limit			1	1	1	1	1	1		1	1	1	$\leq R$
4	program resource limits			1										$\leq R_{11}$
					1									$\leq R_{12}$
						1								$\leq R_{13}$
							1							$\leq R_{21}$
								1						$\leq R_{22}$
									1					$\leq R_{23}$
										$\vdots$				$\vdots$
											1			$\leq R_{n1}$
												1		$\leq R_{n2}$
													1	$\leq R_{n3}$

454

Production and Income Risk

Production or income risk can be influenced by research in two ways. First, some commodities are inherently riskier than others in terms of yields and prices in a particular location. Therefore, research that in itself does not affect yield or price risk can still influence production or income risk simply by altering the relative amounts of different commodities produced. Second, research itself may be directed at influencing yield or price risk (e.g., it may produce a new pest-management practice that lowers the risk of pest infestation; it may produce a more drought-resistant crop variety; it may suggest a policy change that reduces price risk).

When policymakers speak of a social objective of reducing risk, they usually are referring to a desire to reduce these types of production or income variability and not to the risk associated with the research process itself or with the adoption of research results. Their concern for production or income risk is often derived from a concern for food security. In principle, the ultimate influence of research expenditures on the variability of national agricultural income could be represented by a joint probability distribution that reflects each type of risk.[16] However, in practice, if the public research investment is small relative to total income in the country, as argued above, it may be sufficient, when reduced risk is a social objective, to include in the model the effects of research on production or income risk.

The security goal, particularly as related to the objective of reducing income risk, has been incorporated into numerous mathematical-programming applications, at least for farm-level applications. Other security objectives of research, including sustaining environmental quality, are more difficult to quantify but could also be included.[17] Environmental research benefits are typically multidimensional, and at least some include nonmarket activities, which implies that extensive and relatively costly data gathering and analysis would be required in order to generate the environmental NPVs required for the environmental objective.

The model shown in figure 6.4 could be extended to include a social objective of reducing the income risk associated with the variation in production and price. A variance-covariance matrix could be added, thus converting it to a quadratic programming model. Alternatively, the linear nature of the model could be maintained by converting it to a MOTAD representation[18] in which mean absolute total deviations are incorporated to approxi-

---

16. Finkelshtain and Chalfant (1991, 1993) discuss some issues that arise when dealing with multivariate risk.

17. See, for example, Miller and Byers (1973).

18. See Hazell (1971).

mate the effect of research on the income risk of production. For the portfolio of commodity research programs developed, inclusion of this risk component implies that research will be skewed toward increasing the production of those commodities with lower production and price risk and away from those with higher risk.[19]

One difficulty, however, with incorporating income risk is that the easiest income-risk measures to calculate may capture income risk to producers but not to society as a whole. For example, it is relatively easy to calculate a variance-covariance matrix for producer gross income using historical data. Production and price risk may be negatively correlated, however, so that low production years coincide with high price years, reducing the income risk compared with that implied by production variability alone.

A second complication is that measured variability in income associated with production of any particular commodity must be translated somehow into a measure of research-induced reduction in total risk. This involves paying attention to the effects of research in changing the mix of commodities produced (not necessarily a simple task) and also adjusting, where appropriate, for covariance effects among commodities in the national portfolio. Finally, it must be noted that it is not clear what meaning should be attached to this particular measure of research-induced risk reduction. A more relevant risk measure might be risk as perceived by individual farmers, an entirely different concept than variability of total income to the agricultural sector. Or, the government might be interested in the risk of famine, a concept that may bear little relationship to the variance of gross agricultural income.

Thus, it is much less straightforward to include risk in a mathematical-programming model for allocating resources to research than it is to incorporate the efficiency and distributional objectives — primarily because of conceptual and measurement problems related to the measure of risk and the effect of research on it.

6.2 Mathematical Programming In Practice

Applying a mathematical-programming model for research resource allocation involves four steps: (a) designing the mathematical-programming model, (b) compiling information and calculating the coefficients in the model, (c) running the model, and (d) using the results to develop plans.

19. If the linear programming model were structured around disciplinary programs aimed at one or several commodities, a different approach would be required that would incorporate the effects of specific types of research on risk.

6.2.1   Model Design

Designing a mathematical-programming model of an agricultural research portfolio involves choosing (a) the research programs to include as activities in the model (e.g., commodity- or noncommodity-based research programs, components within research programs, or research projects), (b) the objectives to be incorporated in the model (e.g., economic efficiency, income distribution, security, and research portfolio risk), and (c) the particular procedure to use for weighting the objectives and for generating trade-offs among the objectives.

Research Programs (Activities)

The research program alternatives to be considered must be defined well before the stage of optimization in order to obtain measures of the performance of the alternatives, as discussed in chapter 5. The research programs could be defined according to the broad commodity aggregates (e.g., crops and livestock) or to particular commodity or noncommodity subjects to which the programs of research are directed. The degree of aggregation, or number of potential activities, is not constrained by the procedure itself. For example, Russell (1975) designed a model for selection of research projects; Scobie and Jacobsen (1992) focused on broader program areas defined by the Australian Wool Corporation (AWC) within wool research funded by the AWC.

The real constraints on the choice of activities to be included in the model are (a) the types of decisions the analysis is intended to support and (b) the quality and quantity of meaningful information that can be obtained on the economic effects of the alternatives. It often becomes difficult to get meaningful measures of research benefits and costs as programs are disaggregated (chapter 5). For strategic decisions on agricultural research resource allocation, it may be necessary to structure activities around commodity programs and components within commodity programs (e.g., plant breeding in rice, plant breeding in corn, or sheep nutrition). However, at a practical level, in a NARS or other large research agency, it may be too expensive to compile the information needed to evaluate such highly disaggregated research programs when defining the activities in the model. Consequently, in a typical developing-country NARS, it may be reasonable to structure a model around aggregate commodity research programs. A concern with, say, regional priorities, might be addressed by structuring the same type of model around program components within a limited set of individual commodity programs.

Objectives

In chapter 5 we discussed practical approaches to measuring a research program's contributions to three of these objectives — efficiency (NPV of total domestic economic surplus), distribution (NPV of economic surplus accruing to particular domestic groups), and total portfolio risk (variance of the NPV of total surplus). Here we review those measures and alternatives for use in mathematical-programming models.

Efficiency: The objective of improving the average level of well-being in society can be represented by net total research benefits in terms of net present value, measured using the economic surplus and capital-budgeting techniques described in detail in chapters 4 and 5. Measuring improved economic efficiency provides a yardstick against which the trade-offs associated with attempts to maximize other objectives can be measured. Changes in the net present value of economic surplus due to research can also indicate the efficiency costs associated with alternative research resource allocations, even when efficiency is the only objective.

Distribution: The goal of improving the well-being of particular groups in society may be represented by one or by several objectives, as described in earlier chapters. Examples of distributional objectives include the improved well-being of producers on small farms or of people living in certain regions.[20] Measures of the contributions of alternative research programs to these objectives can be calculated using measures of the net present value of the economic surplus accruing to the particular group(s) as discussed in chapters 4 and 5. These are not the only income-distribution objectives that may be relevant, and where other effects, such as benefits to the urban poor, are to be emphasized, it will be necessary to take a measure of those effects for each research program.

Research portfolio risk: The return from any particular research portfolio will have an expected value and a variance associated with it. The expected return and variance for the complete portfolio depends on the expected value and variance of research benefits (NPV of economic surplus) per unit of research for each research program. It also depends on how the research budget is allocated across programs. As discussed in chapter 2, in most cases, an agricultural research system should be risk neutral and, hence, research portfolio risk can be ignored. However, as discussed in chapter 5, unless the distribution of expected benefits is symmetric around the most likely value (mode), it may be necessary to elicit information on more or less likely values to obtain a good estimate of the mean effect of research. Also,

20. Cohon and Marks (1973) provide an example of a mathematical-programming model in which regional income is traded off against national income.

decision makers might like to know if two research programs or research portfolios with similar expected economic benefits differ widely with respect to the range of possible outcomes, even if they make risk-neutral decisions.[21]

Security: The risk associated with research — variability of returns to the research portfolio — must be distinguished from the risk associated with producing particular commodities. Changes in the research portfolio may affect both these types of risk. If one objective for the research system is to reduce production or income risk, that objective may be included with a weight that reflects the importance of reducing risk. However, the comparative advantage of research as opposed to other policy instruments (e.g., crop insurance, investing in infrastructure such as irrigation) in reducing risk or mitigating its effects should also be considered.

Weighting Objectives

Once the relevant objectives and the quantitative indicators of the contributions of research to attaining these objectives have been defined, procedures for weighting objectives and generating trade-offs among them can be considered. We have discussed measures of the contributions of research to objectives of efficiency, income distribution, and risk. If the decision is made to consider multiple objectives and to apply a set of weights to the objectives prior to the analysis, then these weights would also need to be established (perhaps using the procedures described in chapter 7). However, we recommend an alternative weighting procedure, which is described below.

The problem with trying to define weights in advance is that typically, people do not have a clue as to what a particular set of weights implies for the trade-offs among different objectives. This is the case, even when the contributions to two (or more) objectives are measured in the same units (e.g., NPVs of benefits to different groups). It is even more of a problem when the units are not the same (e.g., one is a measure of income variance and another is the NPV of economic surplus) or even comparable (e.g., one is cardinal, such as the NPV of economic surplus, and one is ordinal, such as a score from one to five representing the "small-farmer" focus of a program). Thus we suggest an empirical approach to eliciting the weights, using the model in which the weights are to be applied.

As discussed earlier, we recommend that for models with multiple objectives, the model be run first with all weight placed on the efficiency objective

---

21. Of course, the decision makers need not be risk neutral from a personal standpoint, even if they should be risk neutral when defining an objective from society's standpoint. That is, when eliciting weights from decision makers, it is not their *personal* preference but their *professional* judgments about preferences that are being sought.

and then be rerun with small weights on other objectives. In the example in figure 6.4, the second run might place a weight of 0.1 on the distributional objective. The two solutions could be presented to decision makers to indicate the opportunity cost associated with placing such a weight on the distributional objective in order to determine whether they would like to see additional solutions with different weights. An alternative way of presenting information that would require more runs would be to maximize each objective individually while placing zero weights on the other objectives. This procedure establishes lower bounds on each objective, as described earlier. The benchmark solution can be reviewed with decision makers and compared with the other solutions. Then weights can be modified or lower bounds raised on the particular objectives as desired to examine the trade-offs among objectives more thoroughly.

6.2.2   Compiling Data and Calculating Coefficients

The mathematical-programming analysis uses as basic data the NPVs computed at three or more levels for each research program in a research evaluation exercise, as described in chapter 5. Some additional data may be required, depending on the other objectives being considered (e.g., a security objective implies a requirement for measures of the contributions of programs to security objectives) and the degree of detail of the set of constraints to be considered (e.g., data will be required on the use of land and labor by individual programs if land and labor are to be included as specific constraints in the analysis).

The a_{ij} and b_{ij} coefficients defined in the models above for each research program, associated with the efficiency and distributional objectives, can be estimated using the economic surplus calculations and capital budgeting procedures described in chapter 5. A single-period model will require a discounted sum of net research benefits (i.e., an NPV) corresponding to each level of research support for each commodity research program. Research benefits per unit of research expenditures are likely to vary with the level of expenditures, reflecting a nonlinear research production function (chapter 2). The NPVs of research benefits corresponding to particular levels of research costs can be incorporated in the mathematical-programming model, and the model can be constructed so that the optimal solution reflects the nonlinear nature of the research production function, as described above.

6.2.3   Running the Model

The steps discussed above permit a benchmark solution and sensitivity analysis to be generated according to weights on multiple objectives.

Components of Research Programs

The model can be redefined for a disaggregated treatment of the components of the most important research programs or regions. As discussed in chapter 5, it is difficult to apply any optimization procedure to some components of research programs because of the inherent difficulties in obtaining a_{ij} and b_{ij} coefficients (measures of contributions to NPVs of economic surplus), particularly for certain areas such as agricultural economics or agroclimatology. However, economic surplus and mathematical-programming models can be applied to some research program components, particularly when only a few commodity programs are involved, as demonstrated by Scobie and Jacobsen (1992). They applied a nonlinear mathematical-programming model to five research program components, defined by five stages in the production and manufacturing process for wool. Their model was nonlinear because it included net revenue functions as polynomials in research spending, incorporated a cost for adjusting research programs away from their current budgets, and added a variance-covariance matrix to account for research portfolio risk.[22]

Resource allocation models need not represent all research program components in a nonlinear framework, and some, such as plant breeding, crop management and protection, and animal nutrition, can be incorporated in models of the types presented earlier in this chapter. One suggestion is to solve a mathematical-programming model, incorporating the components for which economic surplus estimates can be made. Then, priorities for other components (e.g., social science, agroclimatogy, or soil science) can be developed through structured discussion.

Short- and Long-Run Plans

The model can be run with different sets of resource constraints to develop short- and longer-run priorities. Using current resource constraints, the results of the mathematical-programming analysis will lead to short-run research priorities. Relaxing the constraints on human resources and facilities leads to longer-run priorities. Plans for investment in training and facilities can then be developed.

---

22. While it made sense for Scobie and Jacobsen (1992) to include research risk in their model for the Australian Wool Corporation, as discussed in chapter 2, it makes less sense for a public agricultural research system to consider *research* risk (even though they may be concerned about a social objective to reduce *production* risk).

6.3   Conclusion

The above discussion is a brief summary of the use of the mathematical-programming approach as a guide to allocating research resources. Mathematical programming is a potentially useful tool to provide information for allocating research resources. To be meaningfully applied, the model requires an economic surplus model as well as the mathematical-programming analysis. It is perhaps for this reason that unlike the other models described in this book, mathematical-programming models have seldom been applied to assist with agricultural research priority setting at the strategic level. However, as Scobie and Jacobsen (1992) have demonstrated, these models can be practically applied.

From a practical standpoint, it is impossible for research directors to explore all the trade-offs implied when there are several objectives. Nevertheless if sufficient resources are available for research priority setting, a NARS might want to explore the broad options it faces using a procedure that facilitates comparisons of a limited number of alternative research portfolios while readily providing information on the opportunity costs associated with the allocations. As with any research priority-setting procedure, the degree of detail and sophistication should be subject to the criterion that the additional economic benefits associated with the more complete procedure exceed the additional costs of its implementation. However, the marginal costs of incorporating the estimated economic surplus changes into a mathematical-programming model may not be that great. Most of the costs are incurred in the prior step of generating the economic surplus estimates.

7

Scoring and Other Shortcut Approaches

The primary rationale for the research evaluation and priority-setting principles and practices described in this book is to provide information to enable strategic research priorities to be formed and to support resource-allocation decisions that follow from those priorities. A research evaluation study that employs economic surplus measures provides a basis for setting research priorities and making resource-allocation decisions — perhaps using mathematical-programming methods. But this ideal approach is not always feasible. Certain types of research programs (e.g., socioeconomic research or basic research) are not easily amenable to the economic surplus approach, and for such programs some other measures of performance may be required (chapter 5). Moreover, a mathematical-programming model requires a relatively detailed economic-surplus analysis, and in many cases sufficient resources will not be available (chapter 6). In such cases, shortcut procedures might be called upon both to obtain measures of performance (perhaps as approximations of economic surplus) and to assist in setting priorities and making decisions.

Perhaps the most common, formalized approach to making decisions on allocating research resources is to *rank* a set of research program alternatives according to multiple criteria, without appealing to economic surplus and without involving formal optimization.[1] Most of the approaches that have been used combine shortcut procedures for both measuring program performance and making decisions about resource allocations. Often this is done without explicitly identifying the relative importance of the different criteria

1. Chapter 5 (section 5.4) discusses rankings as decision aids and considers the types of decisions that can be addressed by rankings and the types that cannot.

used for making decisions.[2] In recent years, however, relatively formal, structured, weighting procedures called *scoring methods* have become more prevalent.[3]

Scoring methods are viewed as means of reconciling multiple objectives with less information than is required by a mathematical-programming algorithm. In addition, scoring methods can use simple approximations of economic surplus measures when constraints on data or resources for the analysis prohibit a more complete analysis.[4] The term "scoring" has been associated with highly subjective methods that lack rigor. However, even when simple approximations are used, the basic economic principles discussed elsewhere in this book should not be abandoned. These principles concern both measuring the impact of agricultural research and using the measures to set research priorities. In this chapter, we discuss how the elements and results of simplified scoring methods relate to basic principles, and we identify common mistakes that cause those principles to be violated. Steps involved in implementing scoring methods are described as well. In addition, some other "shortcut" methods — including congruence analysis, peer review, and precedence — are reviewed.

This chapter places simple, shortcut methods in the context of economic theory. It is inevitable and obvious that these methods generate less precise, and less informative, estimates than would be obtained using the more demanding methods described in earlier chapters. However, while simplified scoring methods require minimal quantitative skill, their proper application and interpretation does require a more complete understanding of basic economic principles than is sometimes recognized. Unless scoring methods are applied carefully, they will readily produce nonsensical results. One purpose of shortcut methods is to foster the development of an institutionalized "economic way of thinking" about research; but if economic principles are absent from the process, even this purpose will not be served.

The same basic economic principles, concepts, data, and measures are relevant for all serious approaches to research evaluation and priority setting. While each approach may lie at a different point along a spectrum of varying

2. Examples include Binswanger and Ryan (1977), Drilon and Librero (1981), Idachaba (1981), Jahnke and Kirschke (1984), and Norton and Ganoza (1986).

3. Examples include Mahlstede (1971), Williamson (1971), Shumway and McCracken (1975), Paz (1981), Chaparro et al. (1981), Von Oppen and Ryan (1985), Moscoso et al. (1986), Venezian and Edwards (1986), Espinosa, Norton and Gross (1988), Ferreira, Norton and Dabezies (1987), Moscardi (1987), Cessay et al. (1989), Teri, Mugogo and Norton (1990), KARI (1991), Medina Castro (1991, 1993), Palomino and Norton (1992a), Gryseels et al. (1992), and Dey and Norton (1993).

4. Scoring methods can also be (and have been) applied when more complete surplus measures are used to obtain more precise estimates of the contribution of research to a range of objectives. See Lima and Norton (1993), for example.

detail and effort, they all rest on a single theoretical foundation. More elaborate approaches involve more sophisticated ideas and more complete empirical analysis. Simpler, shortcut methods, may be different in practice but ought not to differ in principle.

In keeping with that idea, the main data for well-conceived scoring and other shortcut approaches are essentially the same as the data required for an economic surplus analysis with a balancing of multiple objectives. Indeed the details on data collection and measurement for all of these approaches are provided in chapter 5.

7.1   Scoring

7.1.1   Common Practice versus Basic Principles

Common Practice in Scoring Methods

Many scoring studies make little, if any, appeal to a meaningful conceptual framework, a feature that limits their usefulness for any purpose. Often, they also lack a sound methodological basis, and do not proceed logically; they have usually been conceived and executed in an ad hoc fashion. To focus discussion, and provide a foundation for critical review of common practice, we define a hypothetical scoring study that is comparatively coherent, drawing on elements from the best studies. It should be emphasized that most scoring studies have not involved all of the following steps:

- **Identify objectives**: Several quantifiable objectives, including economic efficiency, distributional, and security objectives, are defined in discussion with the clients of the study. Often research policymakers do not perceive the objectives in this fashion at the outset and, as discussed in chapters 2 and 5, the objectives are commonly derived from a set of broader development goals.
- **Identify program alternatives**: Depending on the institutional context of the study, commodity and noncommodity research programs are usually listed. Often the list is long and includes relatively disaggregated "alternatives." Sometimes alternatives overlap. Often they are not represented quantitatively (i.e., the current funding of programs or alternative amounts of support is not identified).
- **List criteria (grouped by objectives)**: "Criteria" replace objectives as performance measures to be used to assess program alternatives. As we show below, criteria are often incompatible with one another and are poor proxies for achievement of objectives. This need not be the

case, at least to such a great extent. For publicly funded research investments, criteria that relate closely to measures of efficiency or distributional impact could be identified by drawing on the relevant economic theory. Different criteria, corresponding to private objectives, may be used for private research or for producer-funded research organizations.

- **Score programs according to criteria**: Scientists and policymakers are asked to "score" each of the alternative programs. Often, in the scoring process, little or no distinction has been drawn between (a) scoring as a *measure* of contribution to an objective and (b) scoring as a *weight* to be attached to different objectives. As a result, "scores" have been either weights or measures or a hybrid of both. Because there is no formal framework, the analyst must choose units for scores on some arbitrary basis. Often the scores used as measures are ranks (say on a five-point scale from 1 to 5), and the scores used as weights are fractions (from 0 to 1) or percentages (from 0 to 100). Higher scores are usually taken to indicate either a greater contribution to an objective or a contribution to a more important objective, but sometimes the opposite is true. As seen later, unclear or inappropriate definitions of what scores are meant to represent can lead to serious errors.

- **Rank programs according to scores**: Each program alternative (e.g., each commodity program) can be scored according to each criterion and then ranked from highest to lowest. This provides a separate ranking of all programs according to each criterion.

- **Calculate overall scores for program alternatives**: To produce a summary, overall ranking, each program alternative can be scored overall by adding across criteria. The scores on individual criteria might be weighted for aggregation or simply summed. This step might be absent from some studies, which use multiple rankings in decision analysis without reducing them to a summary, overall ranking.

- **Dialogue**: The rankings of program alternatives (either overall or according to individual criteria) are presented to research policymakers and reviewed. The review process is intended to derive implications for resource allocation and, at the same time, to "validate" the results. Thus, in the dialogue, the analyst draws on advice from scientists and policymakers to review the rankings and reevaluate scores, weights, ranks, and implications. How this happens in practice is not always clear.

In summary, problems arise with respect to (a) how objectives are defined and measured, (b) how criteria are defined and what the scores associated with them are supposed to reflect (either a measure of the contribution of research to an objective or a weight reflecting the importance of an objective or elements of both), (c) how scores on criteria are traded off in developing a ranking, (d) how the rankings are validated, and (e) how the results are used to support decisions.

Principles for Scoring

If the economic approach is to be followed when using scoring for evaluating research and for setting priorities, four operational principles are especially pertinent:

Identify meaningful objectives: Setting priorities for agricultural research requires that clear objectives for the research system be identified from discussions with research policymakers (i.e., the research directors, agricultural research boards, or other policymakers who are the "clients" for the work). It is essential that objectives not be confused with *means and measures* of achieving them. For example, increasing production and employment and improving nutrition are means of improving economic and physical well-being. If the research policymakers list means and measures, rather than meaningful objectives, additional work is needed to elicit the fundamental and analytically more meaningful efficiency, distributional, or security objectives.

Distinguish weights from measures: Weights on objectives should reflect the clients' value judgments about the trade-offs among objectives. Determining weights is different from calculating the measures used to assess the research programs' contributions to each objective. Various criteria — such as value of production, probability of research success, and expected adoption rates — can be combined to provide a simple measure of the contribution of research to the efficiency objective. While research policymakers may have views about the relative importance of different objectives, they often have little understanding of how the criteria should be combined to generate meaningful measures of the contributions of research to those objectives.[5] The opinions of scientists, extension workers, and others are needed to specify values for technical criteria, while economic theory provides a guide for how to combine these criteria into a useful measure of the contribution of research to the stated objectives.

In what follows we use "criteria" to refer to performance measures: thus an efficiency criterion is meant to measure the contributions of programs to

---

5. They might not be too good at defining weights, either, as discussed in chapters 5 and 6. Often it is necessary to review the weights in the light of a sensitivity analysis that shows the implications of varying the weights, in order to obtain weights that reflect the preferences of policymakers in relation to trading off the various objectives of the research system.

an efficiency objective. Where possible, we use "scores" to purely reflect weights on objectives. However, we acknowledge that as criteria become increasingly remote from explicit measures of objectives, so too must their corresponding scores stray further from pure measures of weights on the objectives. For instance, the multiplier for area planted to a crop, used as one efficiency criterion, ought to be different from the multiplier on the NPV of research on that crop, used as an additional or, more appropriately, alternative efficiency criterion.

Recognize that research is a blunt instrument: If research policymakers treat research as the only policy instrument available for meeting social objectives, they might select a research portfolio that trades off substantial efficiency for additional equity (or some other objective). If they recognize the presence of other policy instruments, however, they might be less willing to trade off efficiency for, say, equity in selecting a particular research portfolio. Other policies may be more efficient than research at contributing to equity.[6]

Attempt to approximate economic surplus measures: When criteria that relate to the total research benefit and its distribution are being developed, where possible they ought to be combined in ways that correspond to the economic surplus measures described in chapter 5. For instance, an efficiency index that corresponds relatively closely to economic surplus measures may be calculated according to equation 7.1. In this equation, the benchmark or baseline value of production for each commodity ($P_i \times Q_i$ for commodity i) is multiplied (a) by the anticipated proportional reduction in per unit costs, or proportional yield increase, $E(Y_i^{MAX})$, that would follow if the program were fully successful (at the particular funding level in question, usually the current level, and given other factors such as time to complete the research and so on) and the results were fully adopted, (b) by the estimated probability of success, p_i (treating success as an all-or-nothing outcome), and (c) by the proportion of farmers likely to eventually adopt the new technologies, A_i^{MAX}. The result is a gross efficiency index for each commodity research program, G_i:[7]

$$G_i = A_i^{MAX} p_i E(Y_i^{MAX}) P_i Q_i \tag{7.1}$$

6.   In chapter 2 we discussed the fact that research is but one instrument of social policy and is often a high-cost way to attain nonefficiency objectives. In chapter 5 (section 5.4.5), the concepts of opportunity costs and weighting objectives in the presence of multiple policy instruments were related to the discussion of benefit transformation curves, BTCs, and indifference curves, ICs, introduced in chapter 2.

7.   It can be seen that if this efficiency index is divided by the quantity of output, Q_i, the resulting expression corresponds closely to the measure of the per unit research-induced cost saving, k_i, defined in chapter 5 (see box 5.1). The main difference is that the expression for k was time-subscripted, reflecting the time path of adoption and research depreciation, δ_i.

This is a proxy for gross annual research benefits. Many factors are excluded, such as the costs of research and effects of agricultural policies.

A net efficiency index, N_i, can be calculated by dividing the gross efficiency index by the research costs, R_i, that were assumed when questions pertaining to research benefits were asked (e.g., costs of the current research program over the next five years), as in equation 7.2.[8] These net efficiency indexes can be ranked from highest to lowest to provide what is best thought of as an *ordinal* ranking of commodities for the efficiency objective. While the efficiency indexes do provide a rough cardinal ranking as well, their imprecision should be kept in mind — as noted, many factors are not explicitly considered.[9]

$$N_i = \frac{G_i}{R_i} = \frac{A_i^{MAX} p_i \, \mathrm{E}\,(Y_i^{MAX}) \, P_i \, Q_i}{R_i} \tag{7.2}$$

This index is an improvement over the gross efficiency index in that it takes some research costs into account, but there is still no accounting for differences in the timing of flows of benefits and the fact that benefits accrue over many years.[10]

A similar approach will yield indexes of contributions to distributional objectives — for instance the total benefits can be apportioned roughly between consumers and producers using information about elasticities of supply and demand. Thus, an index of producer benefits, $N_{P,i}$, might be derived by multiplying the commodity-specific efficiency indexes by the ratio of the corresponding consumer demand elasticity (in absolute value terms, $\eta_i > 0$) to the sum of the supply-and-demand elasticities ($\eta_i + \varepsilon_i$):[11]

8. An alternative would be to *subtract* the research program costs. The problem is one of scale. The gross index G_i is a one-shot measure of the peak annual flow of research benefits for program i, while the research cost is closer to the present value of costs of the program. In many cases the difference between the two will be a negative number even though the rate of return would be positive, and the difference will be larger for larger programs. Thus the ranking of ($G_i - R_i$) will tend to favor smaller programs (smaller R_i) and could be entirely unrelated to the ranking according to the NPVs or IRRs obtained using the procedures in chapter 5.

9. Expected yield changes, probabilities of research success, and adoption rates together reflect the technical feasibility and usefulness of the research. Elasticities, agricultural policies, and trade patterns are of secondary importance in that they affect the distribution of benefits more than the size of the total benefits.

10. In chapter 5 we discussed the use of the *net present value* per unit of research resources($N_i^* = NPV_i/R_i$) as the conceptually correct criterion for ranking research programs when the total research budget is limited. The use of approximate economic surplus measures rather than the net present value of economic surplus measures to approximate the efficiency benefits of research implies that differences in the timing of research benefits and costs among program alternatives are relatively unimportant. Timing is likely to be unimportant for ranking only if the timing of flows of benefits and costs is similar across research programs or if the discount rate is zero; either of these situations is unlikely.

11. Figure 2.7 and associated text show how the distribution of benefits is determined by the relative sizes of the elasticities of supply and demand. That equation 7.3 provides a reasonable approximation can

$$N_{P,i} = N_i \; \frac{\eta_i}{\eta_i + \varepsilon_i} \tag{7.3}$$

Review and Critique of Previous Scoring Studies

Scoring, as commonly practiced, violates many of the principles for evaluating research and setting priorities identified in the previous chapters of this book.[12] Scoring models have been employed for many years for selecting research projects in private industry.[13] They have also been used in public agricultural research systems for more than 20 years, although most of the examples reported in the literature have occurred in the past 10 years.[14] Early attempts to apply scoring models took place in the mid- to late-1960s in the United States, first in a joint study for the U.S. Department of Agriculture and the state universities and land-grant colleges, and later at the Iowa State and North Carolina State agricultural experiment stations.[15] Subsequent studies have been conducted in Peru, the Dominican Republic, Ecuador, Uruguay, Colombia, Venezuela, Argentina, Kenya, West Africa, The Gambia, Bangladesh, Tanzania, and many other countries.[16]

Most of these studies (including some of our own) have violated, and in some cases grossly violated, several basic principles for research priority setting. While most of the studies established objectives for the research system, some did not. In several cases, weights were elicited from research directors to establish the relative importance of objectives or criteria. Commodity and noncommodity research programs, research program components, or projects were ranked according to each objective or criterion, and these rankings were multiplied by the elicited weights and summed to arrive at overall research rankings.

However, in many cases weights were placed directly on measures that are inappropriate criteria — measures that do not translate usefully into objectives — which made assigning weights effectively meaningless.[17] Several criteria related to the efficiency objective, which have been employed in

be verified from the algebra in section 4.1.1 (equation 4.1).

12. A number of previous studies have discussed the advantages and disadvantages of scoring and how scoring as commonly practiced relates to economic principles. These include Parton, Anderson and Makeham (1984), Fox (1987), Scobie and Jardine (1988), and Norton (1993).

13. See, for example, Moore and Baker (1969) and the literature review by Havlicek and Norton (1981).

14. See the studies cited in footnotes 2 and 3.

15. These studies included Paulsen and Kaldor (1968), Mahlstede (1971), Williamson (1971), and Shumway and McCracken (1975).

16. See the studies cited in footnotes 2 and 3.

17. Examples include Moscoso et al. (1986), Venezian and Edwards (1986), and Gryseels et al. (1992).

previous scoring studies, may partially overlap with one another or with the efficiency indexes defined above. These include, for example, (a) value of production per hectare, (b) number of hectares, (c) yield gap between the country of interest and other countries, (d) foreign exchange earnings, (e) comparative advantage, (f) potential completion of research in a reasonable period of time, (g) likelihood of immediate adoption, and (h) current program capacity. Such criteria provide a less precise approximation to economic surplus than those calculated by combining multiple "criteria" into an appropriate criterion that corresponds to the efficiency objective. Thus, we argue that these other "efficiency criteria" should not be used.

The distributional criteria used in prior studies include (a) the number of people employed in producing a particular commodity, (b) the number of producers, (c) average farm size, (d) the quantity of calories and protein in the diet attributable to consumption of a commodity, (e) contribution to sustainable agriculture, (f) political visibility, and (g) the proportion of a commodity consumed on the farm where it is produced. We argue that these criteria, and others like them, should not be used. Most of them do relate to potentially legitimate distributional objectives; however, as quantitative proxies for the research benefits accruing to particular groups, they are likely to be misleading indicators. For example, if demand for a commodity is inelastic such that the demand for total inputs is reduced when supply increases, then the more people employed in its production, the more will be displaced unless the change in technology is biased in favor of labor. Hence, the number of people employed is a poor proxy for the potential positive benefits of research on employment. As another example, if significant income gains are sacrificed as a result of placing weight on calories or protein as a crude proxy for nutritional benefits, then the malnourished could be harmed more than helped for reasons discussed in chapter 2. The bottom line is that these other proxies for measures of research contributions to objectives are just too crude to be of use — and they will often be downright misleading.

Previous studies have included overlapping criteria that double-count effects. For example, the Technical Advisory Committee (TAC) for the Consultative Group on International Agricultural Research (CGIAR) conducted a study, reported by Gryseels, et al. (1992), that included both value of production and usable land as separate criteria. Clearly these two criteria are highly correlated and both pertain to efficiency. Medina Castro (1991) included value of production, value of trade, and comparative advantage as purportedly independent measures of research contributions to efficiency. The overlapping nature of these criteria is often subtle, but the fact that they are poor proxies for research contributions to efficiency is not.

A separate and equally serious problem with these criteria is that their units are usually incompatible with one other, even for different criteria related to the same objective. Therefore, if weights are attached to them directly in the scoring model, the choice of units for criteria can dominate the weighting and the resulting ranking in unintended ways, as illustrated in appendix A7.1. Several studies have attempted to circumvent this problem by weighting the *rankings* corresponding to the numerical values for the criteria rather than weighting the actual values. However, this procedure introduces a new problem because it eliminates the cardinality of the values within each criterion. And differences across criteria in these cardinal aspects of the data can convey useful information to decision makers when programs are compared.

Although scoring methods are usually implemented when resource constraints preclude a more complete analysis, it is possible to achieve greater consistency with basic principles than has been achieved in the past. Below, we suggest how a scoring model can be constructed and applied so as to achieve as much of this consistency as possible, while economizing on time and other resources. Scoring is not the only shortcut method for informing the priority-setting process when resources for analysis are tight. In many cases it might be preferable to apply some basic priority-setting principles, or guidelines, without calculating economic surplus per se or explicitly weighting even simple surplus measures. Section 7.2 discusses some alternative shortcut procedures that might be preferred to scoring in some settings.

7.1.2 Defining a Simple Scoring Model

Application of a simple scoring procedure involves steps similar to those defined in the beginning of chapter 5 for implementing an economic surplus analysis. In short, it is necessary to (a) define the objectives of the analysis and of the clients, (b) establish weights on the clients' objectives, and (c) identify the program alternatives to be evaluated and compared. Then the contributions of the program alternatives can be assessed and the results used in decision making.

A crucial distinction from the approaches discussed in previous chapters, however, is that in scoring models, the objectives are replaced by "criteria" (that purportedly measure the contributions of research to the objectives) and the weights are replaced by "scores" (that are meant to translate a measure of a criterion into a measure of achievement of an objective). Because the criteria and scores are often ordinal rather than cardinal and because the criteria are proxies, explicit optimization is not possible. Indeed, the use of these approximations means that the result from scoring is, at best, an ordinal ranking. At worst, the ordering will be meaningless.

Specifying Objectives

One of the two major reasons for using a scoring method is to reconcile multiple objectives. Typically, there will be an efficiency objective and several nonefficiency objectives. In most simple scoring models, as we show later, it is unlikely that measures of security objectives will (or should) be included. Two reasons for this are (a) the difficulty of weighting across different units of measures associated with different criteria (e.g., real dollars for efficiency gains versus percentage changes for variability) and (b) the complexity of the calculations associated with measuring meaningful criteria to represent food safety or food security as components of a security objective. The methods discussed in chapters 5 and 6 *may* be helpful for incorporating security objectives related to research risk and income risk in a priority-setting analysis.

As discussed earlier, means or measures of achieving objectives may be specified, and the analyst then has the task of identifying the implied, and operationally meaningful, corresponding objectives. For example, research directors may specify objectives of increasing agricultural productivity, generating foreign exchange, improving nutrition, increasing production of indigenous crops in upland regions, and increasing self-sufficiency. The implied or measurable objectives that are meaningful in an evaluation frame-work could be mapped as shown in table 7.1, for instance. This is not always easy to do in a meaningful way and requires a reasonable depth of under-standing of the economic relationships between research investments and their economic consequences. In other words, it is not appropriate to choose a scoring approach on the grounds that it requires relatively little economic expertise. In many respects, the opposite is true: the requirement for techni-cal economic skills and economic intuition is often greater when informal alternatives replace formal, structured ones.

Table 7.1: *Mapping Stated Objectives into Measurable Objectives*

Stated objectives	Measurable objectives
• Increased agricultural productivity • Increased foreign exchange	• Increased economic and physical well-being for all producers and consumers
• Improved nutrition • Increased production of indigenous upland crops	• Increased economic and physical well-being of the poor, many of whom live in the uplands
• Increased self-sufficiency	• Increased self-reliance

Eliciting Weights and Dealing with Multiple Objectives

Various procedures could be used for eliciting weights for objectives. One method is to collect all of the information required to complete the analysis of the contributions of research to each of the individual objectives, omitting a direct elicitation of weights. Then, the analyst may demonstrate the opportunity costs of using research for nonefficiency objectives by varying the weights on the objectives (and thereby varying the mix of programs in the portfolio). One practical way to proceed is first to choose a research portfolio considering only the efficiency objective. Then, the implications (cost of efficiency benefits foregone) of placing incremental weight on the nonefficiency objectives can be observed by seeing how the decisions change and comparing their efficiency outcomes. However, in the typical scoring context we do not have a proper measure of the research contribution to the efficiency objective. Thus, the efficiency trade-off in a scoring model is strictly qualitative; there is no concrete opportunity cost interpretation.

An alternative method, which can provide a starting point for discussion about alternative research priorities, is to elicit initial weights on all objectives at the beginning of a priority-setting analysis. For instance, research policymakers can be asked to assign 100 points to the efficiency objective that reflects a desire to improve the well-being of the average person in society. Then, they can be asked to give *additional* weight (points) to each distributional objective they have identified. These additional weights place extra emphasis on benefits received by people in the identified group. For example, benefits to low-income producers might receive an additional 20 points, and benefits to people in region X, an additional 5 points. Weight may be given to security objectives as well.

A Delphi procedure can be used to arrive at an initial consensus on the weights. To implement this procedure, the objectives that are identified are listed on a form and each participant is asked to place weights on the objectives. An example of a form (with sample objectives) that can be modified for use in eliciting weights on objectives is given in table 7.2. The answers from all the individuals are averaged and they can each be shown the group average and their own responses and asked if they would like to change any of their weights. The process can be repeated until the participants are "satisfied" with their weights. It may be useful in second or third rounds for the individuals to meet as a group and to endeavor to justify their weights to one another.

In practice, it may make little difference whether weights are elicited directly at the beginning of the priority-setting study or indirectly at the end after trade-offs have been demonstrated. Either way, some adjusting of

Table 7.2: *Sample Questionnaire for Eliciting Weights on Agricultural Research Objectives*

Give 100 points to the objective of raising the average level of well-being in society. Then, if desired, assign additional points (weights) to the other distribution or security objectives that you have identified as being important for public agricultural research.[a]

	Objective	Points	Weights
1.	Improve the average level of well-being for citizens in the nation	100	$\frac{100}{150} = 0.67$
2.	Improve the well-being of producers on small farms in the mountain region.	30	$\frac{30}{150} = 0.20$
3.	Reduce the annual fluctuation in national agricultural income	20	$\frac{20}{150} = 0.13$

[a]It is important to recognize that assigning additional weight to distributional and security objectives is likely to reduce the impact of research on economic growth or the average level of well-being. Each individual in society who is a member of the group identified in objective two is weighted 100 points for being a member of group one plus the points for being a member of group two.

weights occurs at the end of the study after the decision makers are given information about trade-offs. As we show below, even the choice of units for criteria can have major implications for the results of a scoring analysis with a given set of weights. Thus, it is virtually impossible for decision makers to have a sensible prior view of the appropriate weight to put on each criterion, even when they know the weight for each objective. There is little option but to determine weights empirically in the light of the rankings they imply. Unfortunately, this makes the ranking process somewhat circular.

Specifying Commodity and Noncommodity Research Programs

Some aggregation of programs is necessary in order to make the analysis cost-effective. The appropriate aggregation of research programs according to their commodity or disciplinary focus will vary among studies. For example Scobie and Jacobsen's (1992) study was concerned solely with Australian wool research and the disaggregation was according to where research applied in the wool production-processing-marketing chain, in accordance with the Australian Wool Corporation's research program. On the other hand, most NARSs have a long list of commodities on which they are currently (or potentially could be) conducting research. Some commodities are clearly of such minor significance that they would never be high on the list of priorities and can be eliminated from more formal analysis. For example, a 1986 Ecuador study began with a list of 109 commodities that was pared down to 44 for the analysis (Espinosa, Norton and Gross 1988). Some grouping of commodities can also be undertaken. Individual fruits or vegetables or small ruminants are prime candidates for grouping in many countries. But again, it is hard to generalize. It may be inappropriate to aggregate fruits and vegetables when setting research priorities in California, for example, where certain individual horticultural products represent hundreds of millions of dollars in annual output. A possible rationale for grouping commodity programs is whether they are closely related, so that the same researchers could work on them.

In some cases, a relatively homogeneous single commodity may be separated into more than one type of commodity for purposes of analysis. For example, rice research might be differentiated into irrigated rice, upland rice, and swamp rice. This kind of disaggregation may be appropriate if different types of the commodity are produced in different regions or if separate researchers (or research programs) are required for each type. In either of these cases a disaggregated analysis will better reflect the units on which resource allocation decisions are made.

Noncommodity research programs must also be defined. Research systems in developing countries are usually organized in program areas (such as plant protection, plant breeding, animal nutrition, and soil science) in addition to, or as a component of, commodity research programs. While these program areas may correspond to disciplines, usually they do not correspond exactly, and definitions of program areas vary from place to place. It is important to define these research areas in a manner that is meaningful to the scientists who will be responding to requests for information during a priority-setting analysis. It may be necessary to tailor the list of research areas to each region or experiment station. Research directors or program leaders are often logical sources of information when the lists of research areas to be evaluated and prioritized are being developed.

Efficiency Criteria for Commodity Research Programs

In a scoring model, the criteria are meant to indicate the contributions of research to objectives. The efficiency criteria ought to relate meaningfully to economic surplus measures. Several studies have sought approximate economic surplus measures (e.g., Dey and Norton 1993; Palomino and Norton 1992a; Lima and Norton 1993) but others have not (e.g., Venezian and Edwards 1986; Medina Castro 1991; Gryseels et al. 1992). Studies of The Gambia and Tanzania by Cessay et al. (1989) and Teri, Mugogo and Norton (1990) developed simple proxies for economic surplus measures of the contributions of research to the efficiency objective. Studies of Bangladesh, Ecuador, and Venezuela by Dey and Norton (1993), Palomino and Norton (1992a), and Lima and Norton (1993) used explicit economic surplus measures.

The efficiency gains from commodity research programs, as measured by the NPV, depend on the size of the research program (research costs), the size of the industry being affected (value of production), and a number of factors that influence the size of the research-induced cost saving, K. These are discussed below.

- **Size of the research program or research costs** (R): Issues associated with gathering information on research costs are discussed in chapters 3 and 5. We suggest using current costs as a benchmark so that the costs used in interviews with scientists are in the range of their recent experiences. Although it adds some complexity, it is often preferable to ask scientists about the reduction of input costs per unit of production (or yield increase) anticipated under several funding levels — e.g., the current research support and the current funding plus or minus a certain percentage (say, 10% of total costs or 50% of operating costs).

- **Value of production** ($P_0 Q_0$): An average of the past three or four years may be used to smooth out annual variations without introducing marked distortions due to trends in prices or output. For certain commodities, estimates of the value of nonmarket products (e.g., manure or straw) are needed. Also, the value of intermediate products (such as forages that are produced and consumed within agriculture) may be subtracted from the value of the final product and included as separate commodities or, in some cases, the intermediate and final products may be considered together as one commodity research program (e.g., as a combined beef cattle and forage research program).

- **Probability of research success** (p): Recall that, as discussed in chapter 5, this must be defined carefully (it is jointly determined with the definition of a successful research outcome and depends on the assumed value for research costs). In particular, estimates of the cost reductions or yield increases arising from research are best obtained in conjunction with estimates of the probabilities of research success because there is an element of joint determination in the two values.

- **Maximum cost reduction per unit of output or yield increase** (K^{MAX}): For a simplified scoring analysis, a single summary measure is often used, and to facilitate comparisons across programs, the percentage yield or cost changes need to be standardized on a particular period (say, five to 10 years following the initiation of research) and on a common basis in terms of the research programs (say, the current level of research spending). The ability to borrow research results from abroad can be taken into account when establishing the per unit cost reductions or potential yield gains due to research.[18]

- **Likely extent of adoption** (A^{MAX}): Simple scoring models usually incorporate the ceiling rate (anticipated maximum percentage) of adoption, A^{MAX}, and ignore the time dimension.

When commodity programs are being ranked, the above criteria can be combined to provide a rough economic surplus measure of the contribution of research to the efficiency objective. As shown in equations 7.1 and 7.2, these individual criteria are multiplicative rather than additive in their impact on research efficiency — and they are also involved in indexes of the distributional impact of research. Thus, they should not be treated as separate criteria, both because of the potential for double-counting and because their effects are not additive.

Chapter 5 provides details on sources of data and approaches to measuring these criteria, including some discussion of conceptual and measurement issues. Elicitation forms for obtaining information from scientists and others are included in that chapter in appendix A5.3.

Efficiency Criteria for Noncommodity Research Programs or Program Components

When noncommodity programs are important, ranking commodities alone is not sufficient for guiding the allocation of resources to research. However, values for many of the criteria identified above (e.g., per unit cost reduction, adoption rates) are especially difficult to estimate for some cross-commodity or noncommodity research areas (such as socioeconomics and soil science). This problem may be handled in three ways. One option is to abandon formal economic surplus measures altogether and to choose a different set of more qualitative proxies for which each program can be ranked high, medium, or low, rather than utilizing a more specific number.[19] Qualitative proxies may provide inferior measures of changes in economic

---

18. As discussed in some detail in chapter 5, it is important to make sure the information that is gathered on the changes in yields and costs is relative to what costs or yields would have been without the research, rather than relative to current costs or yields. Benchmark information on changes in yields or costs in previous years is particularly valuable (see chapter 5).

19. This alternative has been employed in several studies (e.g., Palomino and Norton 1992a; Dey and Norton 1993). Proxy criteria that have been used are (a) "number and severity of researchable problems" to reflect, in part, per unit cost reductions and probabilities of success, (b) "effects of research on monetary costs" because that factor may influence adoption, (c) research costs, and (d) "complementarity with research in other countries or international centers" on the grounds that in order to maximize efficiency, research in national systems should complement rather than substitute for research abroad.

surplus (or may only roughly correlate with surplus changes) but they can be applied to all research program areas. The drawback of this approach is that it fails to take any advantage of the quantitative information that is readily available for certain research programs.

At the opposite extreme, a second alternative is to use explicit economic surplus measures for all research programs. This approach involves trying to estimate, however poorly, the per unit cost reductions, adoption rates, and so on for noncommodity research areas. In many cases this will be totally infeasible.

A third alternative is to obtain quantitative estimates on criteria for those research programs that can be reasonably quantified, and then to rank the other programs through structured discussion without any scoring. This last alternative, or some variant of it, is probably the most reasonable approach. Quantitative information on projected yield changes, adoption rates, and the like can be obtained for program components (such as genetic improvement, crop or livestock management, crop protection, animal nutrition, and animal health) when information is gathered to prioritize commodity research programs. However, it is extremely difficult to quantify relevant measures of yield changes, adoption rates, and other factors for many noncommodity research areas. It could be misleading to attempt to estimate values for the standard criteria used to calculate expected changes in economic surplus in such cases. Hence, the suggestion is to quantify such effects for certain areas and to rely on discussions among and reviews by scientists and research directors to prioritize the others in relation to them. These discussions can focus on criteria such as the number and severity of researchable problems in each area and the cost of research, but not necessarily using a quantitative approach. The less-formal procedures, peer-group discussion, and rules-of-thumb discussed in section 7.2 may be applicable.

Criteria Related to Distributional Objectives

The same basic criteria related to efficiency can be included in every priority-setting study (i.e., this is basic information needed to estimate total economic surplus). However, this may not be true for criteria related to distributional objectives because those objectives may differ from situation to situation. As shown above (in equation 7.3), however, the distributional effects that relate to shares of total economic surplus generated by research depend directly on the criteria used to define the efficiency index. If distributional criteria are defined as fractions of the efficiency criterion, there is a better chance of consistency with economic theory and a smaller chance of problems arising from the use of different units.

Several criteria have been used as indicators of whether research will contribute to distributional objectives. However, most of the criteria have been crude or misleading proxies for the corresponding economic surplus measures. When a simplified economic surplus model is used in a scoring model (i.e., when detailed distributional effects are not calculated), the total economic surplus can still be roughly apportioned to the relevant groups. For example, if the distributional objective were to help small farmers, the measure already calculated for the efficiency objective for each commodity could be multiplied by an estimate of the share of that commodity grown on farms below some specified size. Clearly this share must vary among commodities to be a useful criterion. If the objective were to help producers in a particular region, the aggregate economic surplus might be apportioned among regions according to their (commodity-specific) shares of production. If the objective were to help low-income consumers, the aggregate economic surplus for each commodity could be allocated according to the share consumed by low-income consumers. Even though the resulting measures of distributional benefits are crude and these shares are sometimes difficult to estimate, rough estimates of them are likely to result in more accurate distributional proxies than are the myriad of other criteria used in many previous studies.

Few of the prior studies have attempted to approximate economic surplus measures of the distributional effects corresponding to the nonefficiency objectives. Lima and Norton (1993) calculated economic surplus measures of distributional effects. Other studies that have used economic surplus to measure efficiency effects used only crude proxies for distributional effects. Indeed, most scoring studies have failed to develop even a plausible proxy for the contribution of research to the efficiency objective. In many cases, the result has been the use of inaccurate and overlapping criteria and double-counting of benefits.[20]

Criteria Related to Security Objectives

Several criteria have been suggested as measures of the contribution of research to security objectives.[21] These criteria relate to objectives of reducing annual income variability, attaining self-sufficiency, and enhancing food

20.   When distributional objectives are disaggregated finely, the use of particular individual characteristics as criteria is liable to involve inaccurate proxies, overlapping criteria, and double-counting. For example, there may be a concern about low-income producers in a particular region, or low-income consumers, rather than simply all low-income people, all people in a particular region, or all consumers. Depending on which single objective or combination of objectives is chosen, a different set of measures may be needed.

21.   For example, Venezian and Edwards (1986), Gryseels et al. (1992), and Dey and Norton (1993).

safety. The implications of incorporating these objectives in an economic analysis of research priorities were discussed briefly in chapters 2 and 5.

Yield, production, price, or income stability: Income variability may be reduced by research that leads to increases in the output of commodities with a relatively stable yield, production, price, or income (Venezian and Edwards 1986). Variability in the value of production of a commodity is sometimes measured by calculating its coefficient of variation (Dey and Norton 1990). Coefficients of variation or other variability measures (perhaps weighted according to the relative importance of the commodity in total income) can be employed to rank commodity research programs according to the potential for research on them to reduce overall income variability by changing the product mix. However, such measures are difficult to incorporate in scoring models because it is not obvious how to trade off coefficients of variation (as measures of risk) against other criteria (such as those that measure contributions to efficiency), even when the relative importance of efficiency and risk are known. As shown below, when weights are placed on objectives, aggregation problems arise because of differences in units of measurement. If yield, production, price, or income variability is a concern in a particular study, we suggest using formal optimization techniques rather than simple scoring.

A separate issue is whether any weight should be attached to research that will reduce yield variability in particular crops by reducing their vulnerability to pests and weather. In some cases a stated research objective is to reduce an individual commodity's production variability. Underlying that stated objective may be a desire to reduce the income variability experienced by individual farmers or a goal of reducing the chance of famine. The relationship between achievement of either of these goals and reducing yield variability is not altogether clear, and the appropriate measure of variability will depend on what fundamental goal is being pursued. Aside from these conceptual and related measurement issues, there is still the difficult (if not intractable) issue of defining the terms of the trade-off between efficiency and variability.

Self-sufficiency: Policymakers often mention self-sufficiency as an objective. A country may prefer to sacrifice some efficiency gains or income to reduce the vulnerability of the food supply to a military conflict or other political trouble elsewhere in the world. Settling on approaches that will achieve this objective is not at all straightforward — even considering more direct interventions than research policy. For instance, if one applies a criterion such as current quantity imported (Venezian and Edwards 1986), so that additional weight is placed on commodities that the country is importing, there is no reason to believe that this emphasis will help the country become more self-sufficient in the aggregate amount of food, even if it becomes more self-sufficient in a particular commodity. Indeed, the empirical evidence and the weight of the literature on the gains from trade suggest that such attempts to become self-sufficient have been counterproductive.

Food safety: As per capita incomes rise and the proportion of the food supply that is processed increases, concerns often arise about food quality (Pingali and Roger 1995). It is difficult to find quantitative measures of research contributions to food safety, and food safety is seldom included in priority-setting studies in developing countries, the place where simple scoring models are most likely to be used. It is possible, however, to calculate the economic benefits associated with food safety by calculating more complete economic surplus measures.

Collecting Information Related to Criteria

It is important to note that the types of data required for a well-conceived scoring model are similar to the types of data required for a corresponding mathematical-programming model. Some scoring procedures use measures of NPVs of economic surpluses and their distribution as data. For simple scoring models, less detail is needed and some parameters required for formal measurement of economic surplus are not needed at all. However, there is a corresponding loss of conceptual rigor and the danger of losing any link to measures of efficiency gains and losses. Chapter 5 spells out the procedures for obtaining and constructing measures of the relevant variables. Appendix A5.4 provides examples of elicitation and data-compilation forms that could be used to develop estimates of technical parameters based on information obtained from scientists, extension workers, research administrators, and others.

7.1.3   Implementing a Scoring Model

Ranking Commodity Research Programs

Scoring models can be developed that incorporate results from the application of economic surplus models, as described in chapters 4 and 5. The studies by Palomino and Norton (1992a), Dey and Norton (1993), and Lima and Norton (1993) each incorporated measures of economic surplus changes due to research, as measures of the contributions to the efficiency objective. Scoring was then used to illustrate the efficiency trade-offs involved when alternative weights were applied to distributional objectives. Scoring might also be used to combine these quantitative measures of economic performance with qualitative measures or ordinal rankings in relation to other criteria — but this is dangerous to do and may not be informative because it is difficult to meaningfully define the terms of the trade-offs between qualitative and quantitative measures. More commonly, scoring has used some type of efficiency index that is related to economic surplus but perhaps only loosely.

Efficiency: Here, we have suggested efficiency indexes that correspond relatively closely to economic surplus measures for ranking commodity research programs when a simplified scoring model is used. Gross and net efficiency indexes, G_i and N_i, respectively, were defined in equations 7.1 and 7.2 as

$$G_i = A_i^{MAX} p_i \, \mathrm{E} \, (Y_i^{MAX}) \, P_i \, Q_i$$

and

$$N_i = \frac{G_i}{R_i}$$

The net efficiency indices can be ranked from highest to lowest to provide an *ordinal* ranking of commodities for the efficiency objective. The G_i and N_i might lead to very different rankings. The N_i at least makes some attempt to factor in the size of the research program and is preferred for that reason. Appendix A7.2 contains templates for computing gross and net efficiency indexes.

Regional distributional objectives: The contributions of each of the commodity research programs to each of the distributional objectives chosen for the study may be best measured as transformations of the efficiency indexes. If the objective were to improve the well-being of people in a particular region, then an efficiency index for each commodity research program for that region could be computed using the values of variables for each commodity in the particular region in equation 7.2. This regional efficiency index would measure the contributions of the research programs to the distributional objective. An approximate measure could be obtained by scaling the aggregate efficiency index by the fraction of total production that is produced in the region of interest.

Other distributional objectives: Above we suggested how a net efficiency index, N_i, could be scaled to derived an index of producer benefits, $N_{P,i}$ – i.e., $N_{P,i} = N_i \eta_i / (\varepsilon_i + \eta_i)$. By the same argument, an index of total consumer benefits, $N_{C,i}$, is given by $N_{C,i} = N_i \varepsilon_i / (\varepsilon_i + \eta_i)$. A particular group of consumers or producers could be targeted by scaling the total producer and consumer benefits by the group's shares of consumption or production of individual commodities. For example, if the distributional objective of helping small farmers were chosen, the N_{C_i} could be multiplied by the share of each commodity produced on small farms to obtain a measure of research contributions to that objective by commodity.[22] Of course, the more detailed this disaggregation, the more information required to disaggregate meaningfully, and the less clear the justification for not doing a complete economic surplus analysis.

Combining criteria: Typically three or four indices of research contribution may be used: one for efficiency and several for distributional objectives. In forming a measure of the weighted contribution of different research programs to the set of objectives, each index could then be multiplied by the average weight for the corresponding objective, using the weights elicited at the start of the exercise (see table 7.2). Then the commodity programs could be ranked from highest to lowest, based on this sum, to arrive at the aggregate ordinal ranking.

Using elicited weights in this way is dangerous. The problem is that the choice of units for criteria can dominate the weighting in unintended (and unanticipated) ways, as illustrated in appendix A7.1. It is difficult to conceive of appropriate weights to be attached to criteria that relate quantitatively, in an unknown way, to an underlying objective. For this reason, a preferable alternative is to begin by placing all the weight on the efficiency objective and then to demonstrate the implications of placing incremental weights on other objectives. The decision makers would then choose the "final" weights in light of that information. Appendix tables A7.2 and A7.3 contain templates for computing weighted rankings to use for this purpose.

Ranking Research Program Components

Analysts conducting strategic priority-setting exercises are often asked to assist with prioritizing research areas only at the regional or experiment-station level, typically as components of commodity research programs. It may be difficult to rank research program components — such as plant breeding, crop management, and soil science — meaningfully for a nation as a whole, if problems and resource bases differ regionally.

An efficiency index for a particular component of a commodity research program can be calculated analogously to the efficiency index for the commodity program as a whole, using the equivalent of equation 7.2, with the exception that several component-specific parameters replace their ag-

---

22. This is tricky. For instance, if it were decided not to adjust for elasticities to obtain a producer share of benefits, an entirely inappropriate ranking could result. This can occur if some commodities are traded (producers obtain all benefits) while some are not traded and demand is very inelastic relative to supply so that the producer share is very small.

gregate counterparts. The proportional yield change attributable to a particular component, c, of the commodity program is equal to the total yield
change attributable to the entire commodity research program multiplied by
the proportion attributed to that component (see appendix table A7.3).[23] The
other parameters — the probability of success, the maximum adoption rate,
and research costs — can be specific to the program component or not. Thus,
for the cth component of the ith commodity research program (where the
subscript, c, denotes the component-specific nature of parameters),

$$N_{i,c} = \frac{A_{i,c}^{MAX} \, P_{i,c} \, E\,(Y_{i,c}^{MAX}) \, P_i \, Q_i}{R_{i,c}} \tag{7.4}$$

In order to achieve internal consistency in the analysis, where net efficiency indices are computed for all components of a commodity research
program, it may be appropriate to compute a net efficiency index for the
commodity research program as a whole. Such an index can be formed as a
weighted average of the indices for its components rather than using equation
7.2 directly. That is, for a program comprising C components,

$$N_i = \sum_{c=1}^{C} \left(\frac{R_{i,c}}{R_i}\right) N_{i,c} \tag{7.5}$$

Consistency is desirable, but the aggregation of components in this way
is likely to ignore important interactions among the components.[24] On the
other hand, the differential information on the disaggregated components has
potential value, too, and should not be wasted. Thus, whether it is better to
use an aggregate index derived from component indexes rather than one
derived directly — or, indeed, to do the converse and derive component
indexes by disaggregating an aggregate index — remains moot. This must
be left to the judgment of the analyst, based on the problem at hand.

Often a ranking of research program components by regions or stations is
desired. Once decisions are made on the distribution of the commodity
research programs among the regions or experiment stations (often outside
the scoring model because simple scoring does not include research spillovers), the efficiency and distributional indices can be apportioned by region
or station to arrive at noncommodity program priorities at the regional or
station level within a country.

23. Recall, as discussed in chapter 5, that when looking at components, we must be especially careful
to be clear about what is being held constant in other components, and the substitution or complementarity
effects between components must be considered.

24. Of course, if there are no interaction effects, there should be no difference between indexes derived
in these alternative ways.

Interpreting and Using Results

Rankings of research programs are usually presented by commodity, sometimes also by research program components within commodity programs or by region and, perhaps, by research program components for each region. Each criterion implies a separate ranking of all programs. Multiple rankings must be reconciled for decisions to be made. As we have seen, the weights on objectives do not carry over as weights on the criteria used to represent those objectives. And choosing appropriate weights is paramount. Using efficiency indexes apportioned across subaggregates as criteria for other (distributional) objectives reduces the potential for totally inappropriate weights. But even when these measures are used, since it is difficult to know what the appropriate weights are (even for sound and consistent measures), we recommend establishing weights or scores empirically, by considering the rankings they imply.

The type of guidance offered by scoring analysis is less complete than often imagined. It might be inferred, for instance, that higher-ranking commodity programs should receive the highest amount of funding and staffing, other factors being equal. Such inferences cannot be drawn from scoring models because these models can only provide an ordinal ranking of the specific alternatives being considered. Indeed, as discussed in chapter 5, ordinal rankings can never dictate decisions about resource allocation. In chapter 5 we argued that even *cardinal* rankings of NPVs are of little use for decision making beyond the all-or-nothing choice to close down programs for which the NPVs are negative or for which the NPVs per unit of research mean they cannot be supported.

When approximations to economic surplus relative to research costs have been used to generate priorities, one may be tempted to use the relative size of the efficiency or weighted indexes as cardinal measures of research priorities. In other words, if the net efficiency index for rice is twice as large as the index for wheat, one might think that rice research should receive twice as many resources — or, perhaps, all of the available resources. This reasoning is incorrect. Particular alternatives would have to be explicitly scored and ranked if a choice were to be made between them. An example of this would be comparing an existing set of programs with a situation in which there was a 10% increase in crop programs, financed by a proportional reduction in all other programs. Scoring models typically do not include any information about the shape of the research production functions for different research programs. Thus, unlike the mathematical-programming approach to optimization, scoring does not allow for any marginal analysis of program changes or optimization within a portfolio of programs.

In addition, rankings derived from using scoring methods can be wrong. The large number of simplifying assumptions incorporated in the analysis, particularly the assumption that the time flows of benefits and costs are the same across programs, means that the results of simple scoring models should not be used as if they represented an accurate cardinal ranking of the performance of research program alternatives. An ordinal ranking of research priorities is provided, nothing more.

At best, the ranking derived from a scoring analysis could be used to make the all-or-nothing decision about which programs to support. This could be done by adding up program costs, moving down the ranking, until the total budget for all programs was exhausted — which amounts to treating the results as if they correspond to cardinal rankings, according to NPVs per unit of research resources. Such a procedure might be justifiable but then the programs must be ranked only according to the net efficiency index, N_i.

7.2   Other Shortcut Procedures

Our analysis suggests that scoring should be used sparingly. The results are unreliable and potentially very misleading. What other approaches are available for evaluating alternatives and guiding decisions about allocating research resources when resources or information constraints preclude an economic surplus analysis? Several options have been developed for circumventing data or other constraints in a shortcut approach to research evaluation and priority setting. These options include rules of thumb, ad hoc or informal procedures drawing on the theoretical results of economic surplus models, and peer review.[25]

7.2.1   Rules of Thumb and Guidelines[26]

Parton, Anderson and Makeham (1984) include precedence and congruence as rules of thumb governing the allocation of research resources. Rules of thumb have been widely used because of their simplicity, low data needs, and low cost. Their primary disadvantage is that they are crude methods that permit a low level of scrutiny and, hence, over time may lead to a certain amount of inflexibility in the allocation of funds.

25.   For example, the Office of Technology Assessment (1991, appendix D) describes the shortcut approaches used to set priorities for academic and basic research by various agencies in the U.K., Germany, France, Japan, The Netherlands, Sweden, and Canada.
26.   This section draws heavily, in some parts verbatim, on a section with a similar title in Scobie and Jardine (1988, pp. 30-33), which in turn draws heavily on Shumway (1977).

Precedence

The precedence model regards the previous year's funding as the base for allocating funds in the next year for each project or research area. Funds are then either increased or decreased. Typically, however, such changes are small. The approach has the advantage of providing long-term continuity in the funding of research projects or areas. Its disadvantage is that research that has reached the limit of its productivity may continue to be funded because of the inbuilt inertia associated with the reliance on past funding practices.

Under a precedence approach, changes in total resources are commonly shared in equal proportion among research activities. Significant changes in the shares of total resources going to programs are likely to occur only when there is a major change in the system and, in effect, the precedence approach is abandoned. Precedence provides no basis for comparing future benefits since decisions are all based on past funding rather than potential performance. This makes it difficult to introduce new areas of research and is liable to result in a suboptimal allocation of research resources.

The fact that funding tends to be allocated to areas with high historical funding levels is not necessarily irrational. If accumulated research skills and experience represent a greater stock of research capital, then the benefits from additional funding may be higher in traditional areas of emphasis than in a program for which historical funding has been limited. On the other hand, there might be marked diminishing returns to further investment in areas that have traditionally been strongly supported. This would suggest that the marginal return to areas in which the accumulated stock of capital knowledge has been very limited may, in fact, be quite high. This dilemma is symptomatic of the imperfect state of understanding of the processes involved in the generation of new knowledge.

Congruence

The congruence or parity model allows more flexibility than the precedence model in the allocation process. It involves the allocation of research funds across research areas in proportion to their contribution to the value of agricultural products.[27] For example, if the value of corn output is twice that of cassava, then corn would receive twice as much research funding. Alter-

---

27. More formally, Boyce and Evenson (1975) defined a congruence index, *CI*, such that

$$CI = 1 - \sum_{i=1}^{n} (S_i - RS_i)^2$$

where S_i = share of each commodity i in total value of output and RS_i = share of total research expenditures spent on commodity i. Perfect congruence between value of production and research expenditure shares would imply $CI = 1$. The greater the mismatch between value of production and research expenditure natively, a congruence ratio can be defined in which the research budget of an area, program, or discipline as a proportion of the total research budget is computed as a ratio of the value produced (added) to the total value of production of the corresponding area or program. For example, if the value of corn output is equal to 20% of the total value of production, congruence would require corn research to receive 20% of total research resources (Boyce and Evenson 1975). In effect, congruence equalizes research-intensity ratios (research spending as a fraction of the value of output or value added) across programs.

The congruence model can be used to compare resource allocations to research by commodity, by factor, by production stage, by region, and among disciplines. It can be applied to each of these dimensions singly or in combination, but then it becomes increasingly complex. The congruence model is a useful starting point in analyzing resource allocations to research and is one of the simplest techniques for allocating research resources. It provides a relatively gross basis for comparison, but its usefulness lies in identifying areas where the ratio is low. Such a low ratio may well be justified, but it might also indicate areas where a reallocation of research resources could be profitable.[28] The role for analysis in a congruence study is in the interpretation of these ratios.

The congruence approach is a distinct improvement over precedence in that it considers two of the determinants of the net payoff to research — the size of the industry and the size of the research program. It argues that funds ought to flow towards programs with relatively low research intensities and from programs with relatively high research intensities. This presumes that an additional dollar of research expenditure would have a higher return if spent on areas with a relatively low ratio of research funding to output value — i.e., it means that moving towards equal research intensities increases the overall research benefit.

To see the relationship between congruence and the scoring approach (and, in turn, the NPV approach), consider the equation for the net efficiency index:

$$N_i = \frac{G_i}{R_i} = A_i^{MAX} p_i \, \mathrm{E} \, (Y_i^{MAX}) \left[\frac{P_i Q_i}{R_i} \right] \tag{7.6}$$

shares, the lower the index. Some versions of congruence go beyond the simple proportionality rules applied between research and the value of production. For instance, Byerlee and Morris (1993) multiplied the value of production by variables representing "expected research progress," "strength of local research effort," and "incidence of poverty." This approach seems to relate more closely to scoring (using a multiplicative objective function with equal weights) or to a modified efficiency index than to congruence as usually understood.

28. For a further discussion of congruence, see Ruttan (1982) and Fox (1987).

The last term, in square brackets, is the inverse of the research intensity ratio, used for congruence. Congruence ignores some key factors that affect the ranking of programs according to N_i (including the probability of research success, likely adoption rates, and likely research-induced productivity gains) as well as the timing and discounting aspects. At best, congruence would yield the same ranking if the combined effects of all the left-out factors were equal among programs. As discussed above, N_is cannot be used beyond ranking for resource allocation. The same restriction applies to using congruence as a rule of thumb to allocate research resources.

Guidelines Implied by the Economic Surplus Model

The congruence rule looks at two aspects of the problem of allocating resources to agricultural research: (a) the baseline value of output and (b) the baseline value of research support. As shown above, several other factors can be considered in addition to the rudimentary information requirements of the congruence approach. These additional considerations might be involved in a formal comparison of alternatives or in a subjective decision-making format.

Box 7.1 qualitatively summarizes the principal determinants of the expected net present value of research that can be used to assess research program alternatives in informal or formal processes.[29]

Peer Review

A number of methods require individuals to compare one proposal either to another proposal or to a group of alternative proposals and to indicate their preference (or sometimes the strength of preference) for the chosen alternative.[30] When more than one individual's opinion is sought, a technique must be chosen for eliciting a group opinion. Group techniques can be used for scoring or for cardinal or ordinal ranking of research projects, program areas, criteria, research needs, or research objectives or for determining the weights to be placed on criteria in research project evaluation.[31]

29. A discussion of the principles that underlie these guidelines is presented in chapters 2, 4, and 5. See also Binswanger and Ryan (1977), Ruttan (1982), Norton and Ganoza (1986), and Lloyd, Harris and Tribe (1990).

30. Shumway (1977) discusses several one-dimensional ranking methods, such as Q-sort, ranking, rating, paired comparisons, dollar metric, standard gamble, and successive comparisons. They are simple and easy to implement, especially when there are few items to be compared. In each, a judge compares the overall subjective worth of one item to one or more other items on one criterion. One-dimensional ranking methods are used to group (Q-sort) or rank projects, program areas, criteria, or objectives.

31. Shumway (1977) and Scobie and Jardine (1988) discuss several of these techniques, including a committee approach, chain of command, the Delphi method, the weighted average method, nominal group technique, and interpretive structural modeling.

Box 7.1: *Guidelines for Agricultural Research Priority Setting*

Market failure: Priorities for public research funding should be in those areas in which there are high social returns and low private returns. Where market failure exists but returns accrue mainly to the private sector, forms of government intervention other than direct funding become appropriate (Lloyd, Harris and Tribe 1990).

Efficiency: Domestic net benefits from research are higher

- the larger the total preresearch value of production of the commodity
- the faster the expected growth of the industry
- the greater the proportional reduction in unit costs induced by research
- the higher the probability of research success
- the higher the ceiling rate of adoption domestically
- the faster the adoption of the research results domestically
- the lower the adoption of research results in other countries
- the sooner the reduction in unit cost is realized
- the lower the rate of research depreciation
- the lower the research cost
- the lower the interest rate
- the lower the opportunity cost of government funds
- the smaller the domestic production as a share of global production of the commodity
- the greater the effect of research on reducing distorting effects of price policies
- the greater the effect of research on reducing distorting effects of externalities

Net domestic research benefits are not affected by many price-distorting policies, although the distribution of benefits tends to be shifted towards those being assisted by the price policy.

Distribution: Research is a relatively blunt tool for meeting distributional objectives, such as income distribution or nutrition, compared with other policy instruments such as taxes and subsidies. Research tends to be both (a) an ineffective and (b) a very costly method for pursuing social policy objectives.

Domestic "producer" benefits are increased as a share of total benefits

- the higher the domestic price elasticity of demand for the commodity
- the lower the price elasticity of supply of the commodity
- the smaller the domestic production as a share of global production of the commodity
- when the technology applies farther down the marketing chain towards farm-level production
- the lower the adoption of research results in other countries
- the faster the adoption of research results domestically relative to other countries.

One of the most widely used approaches to research priority setting is peer review. In this approach, various subjective procedures may be used either by individual judges or in some group decision-making process to rank program or project proposals and to recommend decisions. Peer review is best suited for assessing the scientific merit of proposals because peers are typically best equipped to judge that aspect of a proposal and less well equipped to judge economic merit. For that reason, peer review is most useful for decisions about individual projects rather than broad programs. As such, peer review is a complement to formal economic approaches, which apply at the strategic level and help to define the boundaries within which more detailed project decisions can be made, drawing upon peer reviews. At the same time, an institutionalized peer review program is an important source of insights about technical parameters that feed directly into the measurement of the economic consequences of research.

7.3   Conclusion

Scoring is a way of developing shortcut indicators of the consequences of research and, perhaps, for weighting the estimated contributions of research to various stated objectives in order to derive a summary measure of the effects of research. Occasionally a simplified scoring model can be employed to assist research administrators with priority setting in situations where research resources are being allocated across large numbers of commodity research programs or research areas and where resources are not available to allow a more complete analysis. These simple models are less data-intensive than those that include more complete economic surplus models. With careful selection and manipulation of criteria, the models can, in some circumstances, provide results that may be roughly consistent with models that include more complete measures. More confidence can be placed in the results when the measures derived in the analysis correspond more closely to more complete economic surplus measures.

Simplified scoring procedures must be used with caution. Even careful applications of these models generally use crude measures of the economic consequences of research. As a result, the ranking according to the efficiency criteria used in scoring models may be very different from the ranking according to efficiency as measured in an economic surplus model. Likewise, the distributional criteria used in scoring models may also differ substantially from more complete distributional measures. When multiple objectives are being considered, an overall ranking requires assigning weights, and we have shown that assigning weights is very tricky. Indeed, we have suggested that the most reasonable way to define weights is to use the rankings to do so, and that means that the process of weighting and ranking is circular. Also, use of these models should be tempered by the fact that research tends to be an inefficient policy mechanism for meeting distributional objectives, as discussed earlier. Finally, experience with studying and using scoring models over the past few years has taught us that the simple ad hoc weighting of indicators that make *no* attempt to approximate economic surplus measures provides results that are of little, if any, use in setting research priorities.

Unless attempts are made to calculate at least rough efficiency indices along the lines presented in this chapter, a research system is better advised not to score research programs. It is often better to use informal, but still structured judgments based on an economic way of thinking about research. In a similar vein, precedence and congruence approaches are likely to be poor decision rules. There is really no substitute for the economic surplus model. In the worst of all worlds, when quantitative analysis is ruled out, its qualitative results provide a better guide to allocating research resources than do any simple mechanical rules or shortcut evaluation procedures.

Appendix A7.1: The Problem of Units in Eliciting Weights

Suppose efficiency is weighted 100 and *additional* weights of 60 are given to region X and 40 to small farms, and the weights are rescaled by dividing by their sum (200) so that the rescaled weights total 1.0.

For research on commodity i, the overall score, U_i, is equal to the sum of (a) the efficiency index for the commodity, N_i, multiplied by 0.5 (i.e., 100 / 200), (b) the efficiency index for the commodity in region X, $N_{X,i}$, multiplied by 0.3 (i.e., 60 / 200), and (c) the small farm index for the commodity, SF_i, multiplied by 0.2 (i.e., 40 / 200):

$$U_i = 0.5N_i + 0.3N_{X,i} + 0.2SF_i$$

It might be inferred that this is a scoring rule that puts most weight on efficiency and relatively little weight on the distributional consequences for, say, small farmers. But whether that is so depends entirely on the *units* chosen for the criteria.

To see this, suppose the overall efficiency index (e.g., value of maximum annual research benefits per cost of research over five years, as in equation 7.2) ranges across commodity programs from 10 to 20, and the index of efficiency benefits to region X is a part of overall efficiency benefits that ranges from 5 to 10. And suppose the small-farm index measures the *fraction* of output of a commodity produced by small farms, ranging across commodities from 0.1 to 0.5. In such a situation the ranking will be largely unaffected by the small-farm index. As shown in section 1 of table A7.1, the overall scores in column a indicate that the ranking is program A > B > C. And, in fact this is the ranking implied by efficiency alone, the criterion ostensibly receiving the highest weight. But suppose the small-farm index is instead the *number* of small farmers producing a commodity, ranging from 200 to 10,000. Clearly, with this latter measure, the ranking based on the overall scores in column b will depend only on the small-farm index. Efficiency and regional location will have no *effective* weight.

Under option a for measuring the small-farm criterion, the ranking of programs is A > B > C, and the overall score for the highest-ranked program, A, is about 50% greater than that for the lowest-ranked, C. Under option b, the ranking is reversed (i.e., C > B > A), and the score for the highest ranking, C, is almost 40 times that for the lowest ranking, A.

Two factors have led to this outcome. First, the SF_i criteria were initially much smaller numbers than those for the others, but in the second case they were much larger numbers. Thus, in the second case, they had more effective weight in terms of their influence on the overall ranking. The gross inconsistency of rankings and sensitivity to units may be reduced by normalizing all

Table A7.1: *The Effects of Units in Scoring*

Commodity (i)	Criteria				Overall performance			
			SF$_i$		Overall score		Rank	
	N_i	$N_{x,i}$	(a)	(b)	(a)	(b)	(a)	(b)
(1) *Sensitivity of scoring to units*								
A	20	5	0.1	200	11.52	51.5	1	3
B	15	10	0.3	1,000	10.56	210.5	2	2
C	10	8	0.5	10,000	7.5	2007.4	3	1
(2) *Effects of normalizing criteria*								
A	20/45	5/23	0.1/0.9	200/11,200	0.2097	0.2910	3	3
B	15/45	10/23	0.3/0.9	1,000/11,200	0.3638	0.3150	1	2
C	10/45	8/23	0.5/0.9	10,000/11,000	0.3266	0.3940	2	1
(3) *Effects of using criteria as ordinal ranks rather than cardinal measures*								
A	3	1	1	1	2.0	2.0	2	2
B	2	3	2	2	2.3	2.3	1	1
C	1	2	3	3	1.7	1.7	3	3

criteria to lie on a similar scale, say from 0 to 1. Second, the variance of the measures matters. The variance of the small-farm numbers is much greater than the variances of the other criteria, which were in turn greater than the variance of the small-farm share. In ordinal rankings, components with larger means tend to matter more, everything else equal. That is obvious. But components with larger variances also get greater effective weight (e.g., if all other criteria were equal among programs, then all of the effective weight would be on the farm size criterion in the ranking, regardless of the elicited weights).

Normalizing will reduce (or, at least, conceal) problems arising from gross disparities in units, but it may still lead to inappropriate rankings. To show this, in section 2 of table A7.1, the criteria from section 1 are normalized before the scores are computed. As it turns out, in this case, yet a third ranking is obtained using the normalized criteria when the fraction of output produced on small farms in column a is used as the small-farm index (i.e., B > C > A). When the small-farm number is used instead, normalizing the units does not affect the ranking (i.e., comparing column b in sections 1 and 2 of table A7.1, the ranking is the same). The normalization did succeed in reducing the disparity among the criteria and, thus, the variation among the overall scores (i.e., they all were between 0.2 and 0.4). Thus, using normalized scores might be misunderstood to imply that the alternatives are not very different, even when they differ a lot.

An alternative normalization is to replace the performance measures in sections 1 and 2 of table A7.1 with corresponding rankings from highest (3) to lowest (1) and then computing an overall, weighted score. Section 3 in table A7.1 contains the results from doing so. In section 3 it can be seen that the variance of the performance measures (i.e., the rankings) are equal for all of the criteria. Also, the overall rankings are identical between the two alternative measures of the farm size criterion in columns a and b (since, by chance, the rankings of commodities A < B < C were identical for both the fraction of output produced on small farms and the number of small farms producing the commodity). Now, a fourth overall ranking of commodities is revealed when ranks of criteria are used instead of the cardinal values: B > A > C. Which of these four rankings should be preferred remains unclear.

Table A7.2: *Use of the Scoring Model to Determine Agricultural Research Priorities by Commodity*

Commodity	Value prod. [a]	Yield change [b]	Prob. of success [c]	Adoption rate [d]	Efficiency index [e]	Net efficiency index [f]	Net efficiency rank [g]	Region index [h]	Small-farm index [i]	Weighted index [j]	Weighted rank [k]
Barley											
Cotton											
Maize											
Millet											
Potatoes											
Rice											
Sorghum											
Wheat											

a $P_i Q_i$ = value of production without research for commodity i.

b $E(Y_i^{MAX})$ = maximum proportional reduction in per unit cost or proportional yield increase presuming the research is successful.

c p_i = probability of research success.

d A_i^{MAX} = maximum proportion of farmers likely to adopt the new technology.

e $G_i = A_i^{MAX} p_i E(Y_i^{MAX}) P_i Q_i$ = gross efficiency index = (adoption rate) × (probability of success) × (proportionate yield change) × (value of production).

f $N_i = G_i/R_i$ = net efficiency index = (gross efficiency index) / (research cost or number of scientists).

g Priority rank based on size of N_i.

h Regional index = N_i × fraction of production produced in the priority region.

i Small-farm index = N_i × share of the commodity produced on small farms.

j Weighted index = (weight on efficiency objective × net efficiency index) + (weight on regional objective × regional index) + (weight on small-farm objective × small-farm index).

k Weighted rank = priority rank based on weighted index.

Table A7.3: *Disaggregating the Scoring Model to Include Both Commodities and Research Program Areas*

Commodity	Value of prod. [a]	Total yield change [b]	Yield change by program [c]				Probability of success by program [d]				Adoption rate of program [e]				Efficiency index [f]				Net effic. Index [g]	Small-farm index [h]	Wt'd index [i]
			PB	CP	CM	OT	PB	CP	CM	OT	PB	CP	CM	OT	PB	CP	CM	OT			
Barley																					
Cotton																					
Maize																					
Millet																					
Potatoes																					
Rice																					
Sorghum																					
Wheat																					

a $P_i Q_i$ = value of production without research for commodity i.

b $E(Y_i^{MAX})$ = maximum proportional yield change due to research presuming the research is successful.

c Proportional yield change due to plant breeding (PB), crop protection (CP), crop management (CM), and other (OT), calculated by multiplying the total yield change due to research by the proportion attributable to each program area.

d Probability of obtaining the yield change.

e Maximum proportion of farmers that will adopt the research results.

f Gross efficiency index for each research program area = (value of prod.) × (yield change by program) × (prob. of success by program) × (maximum adoption rate by program).

g Net efficiency index = sum of program area gross efficiency indexes / research cost (or number of scientists).

h Small-farm index = (Net efficiency index) × (percent small farmers/100). A small farm index could also be developed for each program area.

i Weighted index = (Net efficiency index × corresponding weight) + (Small-farm index × corresponding weight). A weighted index could also be developed for each program area.

Part IV

Overview and Assessment

8

Assessment and Conclusion

Research resource allocation questions can take several forms. What is the appropriate total amount to spend on agricultural research and, relatedly, how should it be financed (i.e., by whom and through what mechanism)? Given the total resources for research, how much should be allocated to different commodity programs and noncommodity programs and to disciplinary (and other) components within programs? Choices about the regional focus and problem orientation of research programs may be involved as well. Another set of questions concern the input mix used in research. How should the budget be allocated between physical capital-investment programs, human resources, and other operating expenses? Some of these questions are rather open-ended, but more specific questions lend themselves to more concrete answers. For instance, what are the implications of a 10% increase (or decrease) in the overall budget? Should all programs grow or be cut in proportion, or should some fare better than others? Or, is it time to cut out some programs, or certain components of programs, altogether and invest the money elsewhere? Some questions concern marginal decisions while others relate to all-or-nothing decisions, requiring different types of information.

This book has presented and evaluated various procedures for evaluating research and setting priorities.[1] These are procedures that can be used to help

---

1. The discussion in this book is confined to *economic* evaluation procedures. There are many other procedures that have been proposed and advocated for research evaluation and priority setting. Some such procedures measure research "inputs" (e.g., scientists' time, resources, organizational structures, and procedures), intermediate "outputs" (e.g., publications, new varieties, or experiments conducted or completed), or components that influence economic effects (e.g., adoption rate). These methods rarely attempt to establish a systematic causal relationship between the costs and benefits of research, and as a result, they are most unlikely to yield any meaningful indications of the economic effects of research. Because they are

answer the kinds of questions listed above. Earlier chapters describe the theory underlying these procedures and also provided some guidance on applying them. Our key premise is that any procedure used should draw on a consistent conceptual framework and yet be tailored to the characteristics of the individual research system. The procedures discussed here have been examined for their consistency with economic theory, ease of implementation, and appropriateness for the job at hand. In this chapter we briefly recap the earlier discussions and review the advantages and disadvantages of the various alternatives.

8.1   Conceptual Framework Revisited

Agricultural research involves the investment of scarce resources in the production of knowledge to increase future agricultural productivity and, thereby, to contribute to a range of economic and social objectives. The main goal of agricultural research is usually enhanced economic efficiency. There are good reasons for this being the exclusive goal, but equity and security may also be important secondary goals. These three goals may be described, respectively, as increased total income, improved income distribution, and reduced income variability. They are multidimensional, particularly equity and security. They can include such objectives as greater well-being for low-income groups, conservation of natural resources, and increased national self-reliance.

Most "other" objectives are really efficiency or distributional objectives. For instance, concern with "sustainability" or, more concretely, natural resource conservation may reflect either a concern that efficiency requires accounting properly for changes in the stocks of natural resources or a distributional concern about intergenerational equity, or concerns about both efficiency and distribution. The effects of research on some of these objectives are difficult to measure, but most are amenable to economic analysis.

Contributions of research to economic efficiency and the distribution of benefits can be measured as the net present value of research-induced changes in economic surplus. The size of these economic gains depends on the size of the research-induced shift in the product supply curve, the nature of the shift, elasticities of supply and demand, the pattern of trade in the commodity, and market distortions. The major determinants of net research benefits are the value of production, probability of research success, size and

not systematic, they offer little prospect of establishing the link between changes in the quantity of resources going into research, their deployment, and likely benefits. Therefore, they are not useful for informing allocation decisions. In this book we focus on methods and measures that are less likely to be vulnerable to this criticism.

timing of per unit cost reductions or yield increases if the research is successful, the discount rate, and the cost of the research.

Measurement of research benefits is complicated because (a) benefits are spread geographically and vertically in markets for goods and services, (b) research can affect product quality, (c) some research is not commodity oriented (and some commodity-oriented research leads to disembodied technical changes), (d) some research is aimed at modifying institutions, (e) some research generates externalities, and (f) research may be relatively basic or very applied. Although these factors present measurement difficulties, research evaluation and priority-setting methods should attempt to use measures that approximate changes in economic surplus.

The contributions of research to security objectives may involve calculating how research reduces the variability of agricultural income. Such calculations, however, are difficult, and agricultural research is a blunt instrument compared with other policy tools for achieving security objectives. Agricultural research is a blunt instrument for achieving distributional objectives as well, even though it does have distributional consequences. Policymakers usually have multiple policy tools at their disposal, and the least-cost solution for meeting societal objectives might not involve research or might best be achieved using some combination of research and other policies. Hence, an important role for economists involved in research priority-setting analysis is to inform decision makers about the costs of income foregone as a result of biasing the research portfolio in the pursuit of nonefficiency objectives.

We recommend incorporating measures of economic surplus changes in any procedure for evaluating agricultural research. The presence of multiple objectives complicates the evaluation and priority-setting process but does not require that we abandon economic principles. Since the comparative advantage of research is primarily in meeting the efficiency objective, great care is needed when an attempt is made to weight alternative objectives in research evaluation or priority setting.

8.2   Deciding on the Method and Degree of Detail

Several factors influence the choice of a method and the degree of detail for a research evaluation or priority-setting analysis. The most important of these is the type of question to be answered and the purpose of the analysis as dictated by the problem at hand. Some are operational considerations, such as the data available, the financial and other resources available for the analysis, and the skills of the analyst. Finally, there is the completeness and consistency of the procedures in relation to the conceptual economic framework described in chapter 2. Each procedure has its advantages and disadvantages and no one approach is best for every situation. In some cases, alternative procedures can be combined.

The degree of detail such as analytical sophistication or commodity coverage can be increased over time as the procedures become more fully integrated into the decision-making processes of a particular research system. Indeed, one of the major advantages of institutionalizing an economic approach to allocating research resources is that it supports a progressive accumulation of data, analytical experience, and the ability of policymakers and others to make effective use of the information. Thus, over time, the costs of decision making fall and the decisions get better. Sporadic ad hoc reviews do not generate capital resources in the form of human capital and data and so are less able to take advantage of prior investments.

8.2.1 Methods for Ex Post Evaluation of Research Programs

Assessments of previous research are frequently desired by research directors (a) to justify research budgets and (b) as a guide to areas of likely future research payoffs. These assessments can be made in the aggregate or for specific research programs. While we are treating the evaluation of research that has been done as an "ex post" analysis, some of the effects might not yet be realized, calling for the use of methods described under the heading "ex ante" assessment in section 8.2.2 and elsewhere.

Aggregate Research Programs

Econometric approaches are generally best for ex post evaluations of *aggregate* agricultural research programs if the quantity and quality of the data allow the use of statistical methods. Such evaluations can reveal the productivity or efficiency benefits of agricultural research and the effects of research on the structure of production. A knowledgeable analyst with good data can use the results of a production-function, cost-function, or profit-function model to statistically test the size and significance of estimated research impacts. The effects of research on economies of size or the input bias of research can also sometimes be examined econometrically. Often a production-function approach is best for such analysis, if multicollinearity problems are not severe. However, in some cases, other approaches (i.e., productivity, cost, or profit functions) may be preferred, depending on the data available and other factors.

Countries with adequate data for conducting an econometric analysis are still primarily those with statistical reporting services that were established long ago. Although the number of countries with this capability continues to grow, many African nations and several Asian and Latin American countries are excluded from this group. There is little point in proceeding with an econometric analysis unless 25 to 30 years of data are available on quantities (and, perhaps, also prices) of outputs and inputs, along with data on research and extension expenditures going back a further 20 years or so. It is sometimes possible to proceed with shorter time series if they can be combined with cross-sectional (i.e., regional or provincial) data.

Research Programs for Individual Commodities

An econometric approach that enables estimation (or derivation) of supply functions is usually preferred for the ex post evaluation of individual commodity research programs. In this approach, coefficients on research variables can be employed to estimate shifts in supply curves. These shifts (the "*K*-factor" from the equations in chapters 4 and 5), as well as the supply elasticities generated in the estimation, can be incorporated in economic surplus models. This permits the distributional and efficiency effects to be estimated statistically.

Such approaches include the direct estimation of single-equation supply models and the estimation of production, cost, and profit functions from which supply functions can be derived. Which of these approaches is chosen depends on the characteristics of the problem at hand — especially the availability of data and the degree of commodity interdependence. As with aggregate analysis, this set of approaches is recommended only in situations for which adequate historical data are available. Adjustments can be made to the estimated shifts in the supply curve, based on scientists' opinions or experimental data, before they are used in an economic surplus analysis. Still, the econometrically estimated relationships between previous research expenditures and supply shifts provide useful standards for comparison as a benchmark.

Implementing this combination of methods requires that the supply models be estimated first. Estimated coefficients on the research variables can be used to calculate economic surplus effects and rates of return to research and to gain quantitative insights into the distributional consequences of research (and these may help to justify research budgets). When adequate time-series data are not available, an economic surplus approach can be used that relies on experimental data and the opinions of scientists and extension workers to estimate the per unit cost changes (or yield improvements) and adoption rates for the key technologies that have been developed over the relevant time period.

The degree of detail to include in the economic surplus model depends on the purpose of the analysis, available information on factors such as agricultural policies and agroecological zones, the detail of the analysis (e.g., the number of commodity research programs involved), and the resources available. The estimated distributional effects of research are particularly sensitive to the degree of detail in the model. As spatially disaggregated market-related and scientific data become increasingly available in many countries, the potential for accounting for the distribution of benefits across regions increases. Likewise, with the development of computerized research evaluation programs such as *Dream©* (see chapter 5), the effort required to do the analysis has been greatly reduced. The major constraints are the availability of information and the time needed to collect and construct the data sets required and to interpret and present the results in ways that are meaningful for decision makers.

Noncommodity Research Programs

Noncommodity research programs might focus on a disciplinary area of work (e.g., genetics), on a problem that involves multiple commodities (e.g., pest management), on natural resources and their management (e.g., soil science), or on particular factor markets (e.g., farm labor). The ex post evaluation of disciplinary research program areas relies almost exclusively on direct application of economic surplus methods. If the purpose of the analysis is to evaluate the effects of several disciplinary programs, one approach is to apportion the benefits estimated for each commodity research program to the several disciplines involved, and then to sum the benefits across commodities for each discipline.

The benefits of certain program areas that are wholly or partially noncommodity focused (e.g., parts of natural resource management, agricultural economics, agroecology, and soil science) may be difficult to measure in an economic surplus model. Some noncommodity research areas are difficult to evaluate because they affect multiple commodities, which implies a need for joint estimation of benefits. However, other noncommodity programs that focus on (or have their primary effects in) a market for a particular factor used in the production of several commodities can be analyzed in the context of the single market for that factor, using vertically disaggregated market models. Certain components of these programs can be evaluated; others are the subject of current research into designing appropriate research-evaluation procedures.

8.2.2 Methods for Ex Ante Research Evaluation

Ex ante research evaluation and priority-setting analyses that relate to research yet to be done can use results from econometric analyses to provide a benchmark for the magnitude of supply-curve shifts in economic surplus models. However, the general purpose of these analyses is to assist with priority setting and resource allocation across a large set of individual commodities and disciplinary research program areas for research yet to be done. In most cases this calls for an economic surplus model to be used without econometric analysis.

An economic surplus model can incorporate the geographical spread of research results across regions in the country, the complexity of pricing and other agricultural policies, the division of commodity research programs into their technology types (or research program areas), and the effects of research at various stages in the marketing chain. Many research systems will use a simpler economic surplus method in which market and policy differences are taken into account and effects are disaggregated among horizontally (but not vertically) related markets. In this type of analysis, certain distributional effects can be calculated (e.g., research benefits accruing to small farms, to producers, to consumers, and to government) but other effects usually cannot (e.g., research benefits to processors).

8.2.3 Setting Priorities

As discussed in chapter 5, the economic surplus or net present value measures may be broad indicators of research priorities, but usually some additional work is required before they can be used for allocating research resources. Unless the additional work is done, the typical measures (i.e., the present value of gross or net research benefits or the corresponding internal rates of return) provide at best only an ordinal ranking of research program areas. But they ought not to be used even in this way, because typically they have not taken suitable account of the scales of the programs, which can affect the program rankings. For example, the rice program in an Asian country would be expected to have a much larger total NPV than almost any other program simply because of its size, even though some smaller programs might be much more productive in terms of benefits per unit of research. Programs could be ranked more meaningfully according to NPV per unit of constraint, such as per scientist or per research dollar. Even still, the ranking does not provide much information about priorities.

The proper use of the outcome from an economic surplus analysis of ex ante research benefits is as data for an optimization process that can accommodate the system's objectives, the constraints, and perhaps, the effects of different scales of research programs on their marginal benefits. Chapter 5 discusses some relatively informal approaches for using the results of economic surplus analysis to establish the *marginal* effects of research program alternatives in order to consider specific allocations of research resources. Chapter 6 shows how to use the same, or similar, information in more formal optimization approaches using mathematical-programming models.

In chapter 7, we illustrate that scoring methods can provide a shortcut approximation to the same problem but that the quality of the approximation rests on how closely the criteria in the scoring model approximate reasonable proxies for measures of performance against program objectives. Moreover, the process involved in applying scoring methods does not correspond closely to the actual constrained optimization problem being faced (i.e., scoring at best ranks current programs; it typically does not compare alternative allocations of resources and does not consider the resource constraints). Hence, scoring is not as good a complement to economic surplus as mathematical-programming methods are. Indeed, as we showed in chapter 7, the results of scoring can be worthless in decision making. The research program rankings from scoring models are strictly ordinal, with no implications for optimal decisions about resource allocation. Sometimes, because the units in scoring procedures are incompatible with economic surplus measures, the rankings from scoring models are wrong.

In some cases, a simple variant of economic surplus can be used to arrive at a first approximation of research priorities and then a more detailed analysis can be applied to the highest-priority commodities (i.e., those with the highest NPV per unit of constraint). At the other end of the spectrum, a relatively complete variant of the economic surplus model, including an explicit consideration of alternative funding levels for programs, could be applied. The results could be embedded in a mathematical-programming model to explore the opportunity cost of placing alternative weights on objectives and to provide information on research resource allocation, given the constraints on finances, human resources, and facilities facing the research system.

In summary, the appropriate research evaluation or priority-setting procedure (or degree of detail) for a particular situation depends on the purpose of the analysis and the resources available. All procedures involve subjective judgments, particularly in ex ante analysis, but by organizing the information in a manner consistent with the conceptual economic framework presented in chapter 2, the odds of providing accurate and transparent assessments of research contributions to objectives are increased.

8.2.4   Selecting Projects or Experiments

The research evaluation and priority-setting procedures described in this book are designed for assessing research programs at a strategic level. They are less applicable at the project level, both because of the costs involved relative to the benefits of evaluating a large number of potential projects and because priorities at the project level are usually influenced primarily by technical questions (as opposed to economic ones).[2] Of course, some individual projects (particularly large ones) may warrant quantitative evaluation. In general, however, although the methods could be applied to individual research projects or experiments, in most cases the information yielded is unlikely to justify the costs. Excessive use of formalized procedures for research evaluation and priority setting could even stifle ingenuity, serendipity, and scientific entrepreneurship.

Once decisions have been made on targets for numbers and types of scientists and supporting resources for each program, planning projects and tasks within program areas is typically accomplished through a system of technical committees using peer review and specific criteria. Producer input on these committees can be very useful. The social relevance and technical merit of the projects and tasks proposed by scientists are influenced by the extent to which the scientists are made aware of research system objectives and are provided with incentives and rewards based on performance as measured against appropriate criteria.

Micromanagement of scientists can be counterproductive. But delegation of authority for detailed decisions does not mean that those making them ought to be free to ignore their economic implications. On the contrary, it may be especially important for senior management in a scientific agency to ensure that researchers are acquainted with the agency's objectives, and the economic arguments related to how they are achieved, in order to ensure that decentralized decisions are made well. An understanding of simple efficiency indexes (such as equations 7.1 and 7.2) and the guidelines laid out in box 7.1 may be sufficient for these purposes.

8.3   Areas for Future Model Development and Application

The methods for research evaluation and priority setting are deficient in some areas, and these are potentially fruitful areas for further model development or for refined application in research evaluation analyses. Most research evaluation and priority-setting analyses are undertaken in the presence of multiple social objectives. Research directors are aware of these multiple objectives, would often like to know the potential contributions of research to each of the objectives, and must decide on the weights to place on the objectives when allocating research resources. We have argued that agricultural research can contribute to the achievement of a wide variety of

2.   As Anderson and Hardaker (1992) point out, for a research project manager costs are largely fixed, so the task of increasing efficiency is reduced to that of improving the efficiency of research.

objectives, but that it is a blunt, costly, and often ineffective instrument for achieving nonefficiency objectives compared with other policy instruments. Additional research is needed to demonstrate to policymakers the opportunity costs of achieving their multiple objectives through various combinations of research, tax and subsidy, and other policies.[3] If practical procedures for this type of analysis can be further developed, it may reduce the tendency to naively choose among research alternatives as if research were the only (or best) means of achieving the objectives.

Further research is also needed on how best to incorporate risk and uncertainty in research evaluation and priority setting. Agricultural production is risky. The research process itself is also risky. In addition, the analysis of benefits from research involves a number of uncertain parameters: the impact and adoption of research results is uncertain, the natural, economic, political environments in which agricultural commodities are produced are uncertain, and it is difficult to measure the weights that different policymakers place on stable income from agriculture (the degree of risk aversion) or on food security. In chapters 5 and 7, we suggest ways of incorporating the riskiness of research into the evaluation process, but the approaches so described are rudimentary and in need of further refinement. Anderson (1991) reviews some of the simple approaches that have been employed to incorporate risk in research planning studies, but concludes that the "role of risk in such decisionmaking is a sadly neglected field" (p. 127).

In order to measure the benefits from agricultural research in the presence of environmental externalities and to accommodate concerns about natural resource conservation, additional research and application of these methods are needed. We suggested a simple conceptual model in chapter 4, but that model needs considerable elaboration and application in concrete situations. The opportunity cost of using research versus other policy instruments for achieving goals related to natural resource conservation cannot be fully assessed without applying economic models that incorporate research investments. We have argued that "sustainability" is best understood in relation to more fundamental concerns with efficiency and equity. Thus, incorporating environmental issues in research-benefit studies is likely to involve further development of the economic surplus approach.

A few studies have attempted to evaluate research that influences product quality, but more work is required on that topic as well — particularly as the demand for product quality can be expected to rise with increasing incomes (Senauer, Asp and Kinsey 1991). Changes in product quality can occur at the primary or processing levels and can be aimed at reducing the cost of

---

3. In this regard, there may be a role for elaboration of the mathematical-programming approach discussed in chapter 6.

producing the product at a specified quality. Per unit cost reductions are usually modeled as downward shifts in supply curves. Previous work has represented changes in quality by shifts in demand curves as if tastes and preferences change (Unnevehr 1986; Voon and Edwards 1991a, 1992). The issue is complicated because of the potential substitution effects that reduce demand for lower-quality products as higher-quality products are made available through research. Models are needed that represent changes in quality in a way that is conceptually defensible yet implementable.

A few studies have attempted to conceptualize and empirically measure the impact of social science research in agriculture (e.g., Norton and Schuh 1981; Lindner 1987); however, little progress has been made. Measuring the effects of research aimed at evaluating institutions (e.g., price policies) is particularly challenging because (a) studies are often directed at a particular institutional change and (b) even if an institutional change occurs, it is often nearly impossible to ascertain the contribution of research compared with political or other factors in influencing the change. Also, social science research is directed at such diverse topics, most of which do not directly shift product supply curves, that aggregate evaluation is extremely difficult. However, it may be possible to evaluate particular categories of social science research using tools that place a value on the new information coming from such research.

There is a strong need for additional study of the general-equilibrium effects of research. The implications of focusing only on the partial-equilibrium economic surplus measurement of research benefits were briefly mentioned in chapters 2 and 4. Elaboration and application of the approach suggested by Martin and Alston (1992, 1994) offers some promise for practical, empirical research evaluations, at least for ex post analysis.

Finally, additional work is needed on means for linking the results of research evaluation and priority-setting studies to the development of plans for investing in human resources and facilities, and to decisions on operating budgets. Some research directors have been more successful than others in translating the results of these studies into such plans, decisions, and actions. We need more information on how to maximize the chances that follow-up to research evaluation and priority setting occurs.

8.4   Conclusion

The demand for improved methods for evaluating and setting priorities for agricultural research has grown in recent years. Research evaluation and priority-setting procedures must be rigorous yet cost effective. The key to successful research evaluation and priority setting is not simply the method chosen, but how that chosen method is implemented. We suggest that for many situations, a partial-equilibrium framework based on the concept of economic surplus is the soundest and most practical conceptual framework. The methods discussed in this book can be made consistent with this concept at various levels of approximation. Some general-equilibrium effects can, and in some instances should, be included as well.

The application of theoretically consistent measures can yield information that is useful in decision making. Perhaps the major benefit from a process of research program review, evaluation, and priority setting is that the participants gain a clearer view of what they are trying to achieve — and how best to get there. Scientists and policymakers will make better decisions as they develop an economic way of thinking about research investment choices. It is especially important that they develop an economic way of thinking that has at its foundations a theoretically consistent and defensible economic structure. This implies institutionalizing a process of evaluation (which does not imply evaluating everything in sight) in order to develop information and incentives that enhance the chance that the invisible hand will do its job in allocating scarce scientific resources. Such an outcome will be less likely with one-off evaluation or priority-setting exercises in which research system personnel are not actively involved. These considerations reinforce the value of a consistent, economically sound approach.

This is not a book of rules of thumb for making *allocation* decisions about research resources. It is not a black box, nor is it a gratuitous complication of the intuitive. Rather, it is an attempt to establish a defensible link between research and its objectives. It is necessary to apply the principles expounded here explicitly to a particular problem in order to make meaningful progress. The methods might seem demanding, but the problems are inherently difficult. We believe that the effort is worthwhile in many cases, but usually a real effort is necessary. If the applied work is not done with care, one runs the risk of spurious attribution of the past, actual, and future potential impact of research, which is of questionable value for defending budgets and of no use for economizing on scarce scientific, human, and natural resources.

By no means do we countenance the wholesale adoption of highly sophisticated, mechanical approaches to evaluation and priority setting. On the other hand, it is all too easy to let an application of these procedures and processes slip from the simple to the simplistic. While resource constraints, in practice, often necessitate the use of simplifying assumptions and procedures, the fundamental principles developed throughout this book, particularly in chapter 2, should not be forsaken.

An overriding consideration is that the benefits from any research evaluation or priority-setting study depend on how the results are used by the client. Whatever the method chosen, research directors, councils, or boards must find the results of the analysis *useful* for making decisions on budgets, facilities, and people. Thus, the analyst conducting the research evaluation or priority-setting analysis can view his or her services (and models) as a bridge between the raw data pertaining to the economic context and the technological opportunities, and the information needed by those making decisions on strategic priorities or research budgets.

References

Adams, J. "Fundamental Stocks of Knowledge and Productivity Growth." *Journal of Political Economy* Vol. 98, No. 4 (August 1990): 673–702.

Adusei, E. "Evaluation of the Importance and Magnitude of Agricultural Maintenance Research in the United States." Unpublished Ph.D. Thesis, Virginia Polytechnic Institute and State University, Blacksburg, Virginia, 1988.

Adusei, E.O. and G.W. Norton. "The Magnitude of Agricultural Maintenance Research in the USA." *Journal of Production Agriculture* Vol. 3, No. 1 (January-March 1990): 1–6.

Akino, M. and Y. Hayami. "Efficiency and Equity in Public Research: Rice Breeding in Japan's Economic Development." *American Journal of Agricultural Economics* Vol. 57, No. 1 (February 1975): 1–10.

Allen, R.C. and W.E. Diewert. "Direct Versus Implicit Superlative Index Number Formulae." *Review of Economics and Statistics* Vol. 63, No. 3 (August 1981): 430–5.

Alston, J.M. "An Analysis of Growth of U.S. Farmland Prices, 1963–82." *American Journal of Agricultural Economics* Vol. 68, No. 1 (February 1986): 1–9.

Alston, J.M. "Research Benefits in a Multimarket Setting: A Review." *Review of Marketing and Agricultural Economics* Vol. 59, No. 1 (April 1991): 23–52.

Alston, J.M. and J.A. Chalfant. "Consumer Demand Analysis According to GARP." *North Eastern Journal of Agricultural and Resource Economics* Vol. 21, No. 2 (October 1992): 127–39.

Alston, J.M. and J.W. Freebairn. "Producer Price Equalization." *Review of Marketing and Agricultural Economics* Vol. 56, No. 3 (December 1988): 306–39.

Alston, J.M. and B.H. Hurd. "Some Neglected Social Costs of Government Spending in Farms Programs." *American Journal of Agricultural Economics* Vol. 72, No. 1 (February 1990): 149–56.

Alston, J.M. and D.M. Larson. *Precision vs Bias in Choosing Welfare Measures.* Department of Agricultural Economics Working Paper No. 92–14. Davis: University of California, Davis, 1992.

Alston, J.M. and D.M. Larson. "Hicksian vs Marshallian Welfare Measures: Why

Do We Do What We Do?" *American Journal of Agricultural Economics* Vol. 75, No. 3 (August 1993): 764–9.

Alston, J.M. and W.J. Martin. "Reversal of Fortune: Immiserizing Technological Change in Agriculture." Invited paper presented at the International Agricultural Trade Research Consortium Annual Meeting, St. Petersburg, Florida, December 1992.

Alston, J.M. and W.J. Martin. "A Comment on Border Price Changes and Domestic Welfare in the Presence of Distortions." *Oxford Economic Papers* (forthcoming 1995).

Alston, J.M. and J.D. Mullen. "Economic Effects of Research into Traded Goods: The Case of Australian Wool." *Journal of Agricultural Economics* Vol. 43, No. 2 (May 1992): 268–78.

Alston, J.M. and P.G. Pardey. "Technical Change, Constraints and Incentives: The Damaging Consequences of Getting Policies Wrong." Invited paper presented at the Conference on *Agricultural Technology: Current Policy Issues for the International Community and The World Bank*, organized by the Agriculture and Rural Development Department of The World Bank, October 1991.

Alston, J.M. and P.G. Pardey. "Market Distortions and Technological Progress in Agriculture." *Technological Forecasting and Social Change* Vol. 43, No. 3/4 (May/June 1993): 301–19.

Alston, J.M. and P.G. Pardey. "Distortions in Prices and Agricultural Research Investments." In J.R. Anderson, ed., *Agricultural Technology: Current Policy Issues for the International Community.* Wallingford: CAB International, 1994.

Alston, J.M. and G.M. Scobie. "Distribution of Research Gains in Multistage Production Systems: Comment." *American Journal of Agricultural Economics*

Vol. 65, No. 2 (May 1983): 353–6.

Alston, J.M. and V.H. Smith. "Some Economic Implications of Minimum Pricing: The Case of Wine Grapes in Australia—Comment." *Review of Marketing and Agricultural Economics* Vol. 51, No. 2 (August 1983): 179–85.

Alston, J.M. and M.K. Wohlgenant. "Measuring Research Benefits Using Linear Elasticity Equilibrium Displacement Models." In J.D. Mullen and J.M. Alston. *The Returns to the Australian Wool Industry from Investment in R&D (appendix 2).* Rural & Resource Economics Report No. 10. Sydney: New South Wales Department of Agriculture & Fisheries, Division of Rural and Resource Economics, 1990.

Alston, J.M., J.R. Anderson and P.G. Pardey. "Perceived Productivity, Foregone Future Farm Fruitfulness, and Rural Research Resource Rationalization." Invited plenary paper for theme VII *National and International Research and Technology Transfer* Twelfth International Conference of Agricultural Economists, Harare, August 1994. Mimeo.

Alston, J.M., J.A. Chalfant and P.G. Pardey. *Structural Adjustment in OECD Agriculture: Government Policies and Technical Change.* Center for International Food and Agricultural Policy Working Paper WP93–3. St. Paul: University of Minnesota, June 1993.

Alston, J.M., G.W. Edwards and J.W. Freebairn. *The Effects of Protection Policies on the Benefits from Research.* Economics Branch Working Paper. Melbourne: Department of Agriculture, Victoria, 1986.

Alston, J.M., G.W. Edwards and J.W. Freebairn. "Market Distortions and Benefits from Research." *American Journal of Agricultural Economics* Vol. 70, No. 2

(May 1988): 281–8.

Alston, J.M., P.G. Pardey and H.O. Carter, eds. *Valuing UC Agricultural Research and Extension*. Agricultural Issues Center Publication No. VR-1. Davis: University of California, March 1994.

Alston, J.M., J.W. Freebairn and J.J. Quilkey. "A Model of Supply in the Australian Orange Growing Industry." *Australian Journal of Agricultural Economics* Vol. 24, No. 3 (December 1980): 248–67.

American Agricultural Economics Association (AAEA). *Measurement of U.S. Agricultural Productivity: A Review of Current Statistics and Proposals for Change*. ESCS Technical Bulletin No. 1614. Washington, DC: U.S. Department of Agriculture, 1980.

Anania, G. and A.F. McCalla. "Assessing the Impact of Agricultural Technology Improvements in Developing Countries in the Presence of Policy Distortions." Invited paper presented at the International Agricultural Trade Research Consortium Annual Meeting, St. Petersburg, Florida, December 1991.

Anderson, J.E. and J.P. Neary. "Trade Reform with Quotas, Partial Rent Retention and Tariffs." *Econometrica* Vol. 60, No. 1 (January 1992): 57–76.

Anderson, J.R. "Agricultural Research in a Variable and Unpredictable World." In P.G. Pardey, J. Roseboom and J.R. Anderson, eds., *Agricultural Research Policy: International Quantitative Perspectives*. Cambridge: Cambridge University Press, 1991.

Anderson, J.R. "Research Priority Setting in Agriculture: Problems in Ex-ante Analysis." In D.R. Lee, S. Kearl and N. Uphoff, eds., *Assessing the Impact of International Agricultural Research for Sustainable Development*. Ithaca: Cornell International Institute for Food, Ag-

riculture and Development, 1992.

Anderson, J.R. and J.L. Dillon. *Risk Analysis in Dryland Farming Systems*. Farm Systems Management Series No. 2. Rome: Food and Agriculture Organization, 1992.

Anderson, J.R. and J.B. Hardaker. "Efficacy and Efficiency in Agricultural Research: A Systems View." *Agricultural Systems* Vol. 40, Nos. 1–3 (1992): 105–23.

Anderson, J.R. and P.B.R. Hazell, eds. *Variability in Grain Yields: Implications for Agricultural Research and Policy in Developing Countries*. Baltimore: Johns Hopkins University Press, 1989.

Anderson, J.R., J.L. Dillon and J.B. Hardaker. *Agricultural Decision Analysis*. Ames: Iowa State University Press, 1977.

Anderson, J.R., P.G. Pardey and J. Roseboom. "Sustaining Growth in Agriculture: A Quantitative Review of Agricultural Research Investments." *Agricultural Economics* Vol. 10, No. 2 (April 1994): 107–23.

Antle, J.M. "Infrastructure and Aggregate Agricultural Productivity: International Evidence." *Economic Development and Cultural Change* Vol. 31, No. 3 (April 1983): 609–19.

Antle, J.M. "The Structure of U.S. Agricultural Technology, 1910–78." *American Journal of Agricultural Economics* Vol. 66, No. 4 (November 1984): 414–21.

Antle, J.M. and S.M. Capalbo. "An Introduction to Recent Developments in Production Theory and Productivity Measurement." In S.M. Capalbo and J.M. Antle, eds., *Agricultural Productivity: Measurement and Explanation*. Washington, DC: Resources for the Future, 1988.

Antle, J.M. and T. McGuckin. "Technological Innovation, Agricultural Productivity, and Environmental Quality." In G.A. Carlson, D. Zilberman and J.A. Miranowski, eds., *Agricultural and Environmental Resource Economics.* New York: Oxford University Press, 1993.

Antony, G. "User's Guide to Program CBR: Calculation of the Costs and Benefits of PNG Export-Crop Research: Version 3.2." Department of Agricultural Economics and Business Management, University of New England, Armidale, Australia, June 1989. Mimeo.

Apland, J., R.N. Barnes and F. Justus. "The Farm Lease: An Analysis of Owner-Tenant and Landlord Preferences under Risk." *American Journal of Agricultural Economics* Vol. 66, No. 3 (August 1984): 376–84.

Archibald, S.O. "Incorporating Externalities into Agricultural Productivity Analysis." In S.M. Capalbo and J.M. Antle, eds., *Agricultural Productivity: Measurement and Explanation* Washington, DC: Resources for the Future, 1988.

Arndt, T.M., D.G. Dalrymple and V.W. Ruttan, eds. *Resource Allocation and Productivity in National and International Agricultural Research.* Minneapolis: University of Minnesota Press, 1977.

Arrow, K.J. "The Economic Implications of Learning by Doing." *Review of Economic Studies* Vol. 29, No. 80 (June 1962): 155–73.

Arrow, K.J. *Social Choice and Individual Values.* New York: John Wiley, 1963.

Arrow, K.J. and R.C. Lind. "Uncertainty and the Evaluation of Public Investment Decisions." *American Economic Review* Vol. 60, No. 3 (June 1970): 364–78.

Arrow, K.J. and R.C. Lind. "Uncertainty and the Evaluation of Public Investment Decisions: Reply." *American Economic Review* Vol. 62, No. 1 (March 1972): 171–2.

Ayer, H.W. and G.E. Schuh. "Social Rates of Return and Other Aspects of Agricultural Research: The Case of Cotton Research in São Paulo, Brazil." *American Journal of Agricultural Economics* Vol. 54, No. 4., Pt. I (November 1972): 557–69.

Ayer, H.W. and G.E. Schuh. "Social Rates of Return and Other Aspects of Agricultural Research: The Case of Cotton Research in São Paulo, Brazil: Reply." *American Journal of Agricultural Economics* Vol. 56, No. 4 (November 1974): 842–4.

Baker, N.R. and J.R. Freeland. "Recent Advances in R&D Benefit Measurement and Project Selection Methods." *Management Science* Vol. 21, No. 10 (June 1975): 1164–75.

Baker, N.R. and W.H. Pound. "R&D Project Selection: Where We Stand." *IEEE Transactions on Engineering Management* Vol. EM-11 (December 1964): 124–34.

Baker, N.R., W.E. Souder, C.R. Shumway, P.M. Maher and A.H. Rubenstein. "A Budget Allocation Model for Large Hierarchical R&D Organizations." *Management Science* Vol. 23, No. 1 (September 1976): 59–70.

Ball, V.E. "Output, Input, and Productivity Measurement in U.S. Agriculture." *American Journal of Agricultural Economics* Vol. 67, No. 3 (August 1985): 475–86.

Ball, V.E. "Modeling Supply Response in a Multiproduct Framework." *American Journal of Agricultural Economics* Vol. 70, No. 4 (November 1988): 813–25.

Ball, V.E. and R. Chambers. "An Economic Analysis of Technology in the Meat Products Industry." *American Journal of Agricultural Economics* Vol. 64, No. 4 (November 1982): 699–709.

Ballard, C.L., J.B. Shoven and J. Whalley.

"General Equilibrium Computations of the Marginal Welfare Costs of Taxes in the United States." *American Economic Review* Vol. 75, No. 1 (March 1985): 128–38.

Bantilan, M.C.S. and J.M. Lantican, eds. *Setting Research Priorities for Philippine Agriculture.* Quezon City, Philippines: Bureau of Agricultural Research, 1994.

Barnett, W.A. and Y.W. Lee. "The Global Properties of the Minfex Larent, Generalized Leontief, and Translog Flexible Functional Forms." *Econometrica* Vol. 53, No. 6 (November 1985): 1421–37.

Barten, P. "Maximum Likelihood Estimation of a Complete System of Demand Equations." *European Economic Review* Vol. 1, No. 1 (Fall 1969): 7–73.

Baumol, W.J. "Williamson's The Economic Institutions of Capitalism." *Rand Journal of Economics* Vol. 17, No. 2 (Summer 1986): 279–86.

Beach, D.E. and J.M. Alston. "Market Distortions and the Benefits from Research into New Uses for Agricultural Commodities: Ethanol from Corn." Paper presented at CPI session on Policy Economics of New Industrial Uses of Agricultural Materials, Western Economics Association International Annual Meeting, Lake Tahoe, June 1993.

Beattie, B.R. and C.R. Taylor. *The Economics of Production.* New York: John Wiley and Sons, 1985.

Belsley, D.A., E. Kuh and R.E. Welsch. *Regression Diagnostics: Identifying Influential Data and Sources of Collinearity.* New York: John Wiley and Sons, 1980.

Bengsten, D.N. "A Price Index for Deflating State Agricultural Experiment Station Research Expenditures." *Journal of Agricultural Economics Research* Vol, 41, No. 4 (Fall 1989): 12–20. 1989a.

Bengsten, D.N. "Price Indexes for Deflating Public Forestry Research Expenditures." *Forest Science* Vol. 35, No. 3 (September 1989): 756–74. 1989b.

Berndt, E.R. *Practice of Econometrics: Classic and Contemporary.* New York: Addison Wesley, 1991.

Berndt, E.R. and M. Khaled. "Parametric Productivity Measurement and Choice among Flexible Functional Forms." *Journal of Political Economy* Vol. 87, No. 6 (December 1979): 1220–45.

Bernhart, K. and R.K. Perrin. "On Predicting Supply Shifts from New Technology: Diethylstilbestrol." Department of Economics and Business, North Carolina State University, 1989. Mimeo.

Bernstein, J.I. "The Structure of Canadian Inter-Industry R&D Spillovers, and the Rates of Return to R&D." *Journal of Industrial Economics* Vol. 37, No. 3 (March 1989): 315–28.

Bernstein, J.I. and M.I. Nadiri. "Interindustry R&D Spillovers, Rates of Return, and Production in High-Tech Industries." *American Economic Review* Vol. 78, No. 2 (May 1988): 429–34.

Bernstein, J.I. and M.I. Nadiri. "Research and Development and Intra-Industry Spillovers: An Empirical Application of Dynamic Duality." *Review of Economic Studies* Vol. 56, No. 2 (April 1989): 249–69.

Bhagwati, J. "Immiserizing Growth: A Geometrical Note." *Review of Economic Studies* Vol. 25, No. 68 (June 1958): 201–5.

Bhagwati, J. "Distortions and Immiserizing Growth: A Generalization." *Review of Economic Studies* Vol. 35, No. 104 (October 1968): 481–5.

Bieri, J., A. de Janvry and A. Schmitz. "Agricultural Technology and the Distribution of Welfare Gains." *American Journal of Agricultural Economics* Vol.

54, No. 5 (December 1972): 801–8.

Binswanger, H.P. "A Cost Function Approach to the Measurement of Elasticities of Factor Demand and Elasticities of Substitution." *American Journal of Agricultural Economics* Vol. 56, No. 2 (May 1974): 377–86. 1974a.

Binswanger, H.P. "The Measurement of Technical Change Biases with Many Factors of Production." *American Economic Review* Vol. 64, No. 6 (December 1974): 964–76. 1974b.

Binswanger, H.P. *The Use of Duality between Production, Profit, and Cost Functions in Applied Econometric Research: A Didactic Note.* Economics Program Occasional Paper No. 10. Hyderabad, India: International Crops Research Institute for the Semi-Arid Tropics, July 1975.

Binswanger, H.P. "Measuring the Impact of Economic Factors on the Direction of Technical Change." In T.M. Arndt, D.G. Dalrymple and V.W. Ruttan, eds., *Resource Allocation and Productivity in National and International Agricultural Research.* Minneapolis: University of Minnesota, 1977.

Binswanger, H.P. "Income Distribution Effects of Technical Change: Some Analytical Issues." *South East Asian Economic Review* Vol. 1, No. 3 (December 1980): 179–218.

Binswanger, H.P. and J.G. Ryan. "Efficiency and Equity Issues in Ex-ante Allocation of Research Resources." *Indian Journal of Agricultural Economics* Vol. 32, No. 3 (July/September 1977): 217–31.

Binswanger, H.P., M.C. Yang, A. Bowers and Y. Mundlak. "On the Determinants of Cross-Country Aggregate Agricultural Supply." *Journal of Econometrics* Vol. 36, No. 1 (September/October 1987): 111–31.

Birdsall, N. and A. Steer. "Act Now on Global Warming—But Don't Cook the Books." *Finance and Development* Vol. 30, No. 1 (March 1993): 6–8.

Blackorby, C. and R.R. Russell. "Will the Real Elasticity of Substitution Please Stand Up? (A Comparison of the Allen/Uzawa and Morishima Elasticities)." *American Economic Review* Vol. 79, No. 4 (September 1989): 882–8.

Blackorby, C., C.A.K. Lovell and M.C. Thursby. "Extended Hicks Neutral Technological Change." *Economic Journal* Vol. 86, No. 344 (December 1976): 845–52.

Bockstael, N.E. and I.E. Strand. "The Effect of Common Sources of Regression Error on Benefit Estimates." *Land Economics* Vol. 63, No. 1 (February 1987): 11–20.

Boisvert, R.N. *The Translog Production Function: Its Properties, Its Several Interpretations and Estimation Problems.* Department of Agricultural Economics Research Series No. 82–28. Ithaca, N.Y.: Cornell University, September 1982.

Bosch, D.J. and L.A. Shabman. "Simulation Modeling to Set Priorities for Research on Oyster Production." *American Journal of Agricultural Economics* Vol. 72, No. 2 (May 1990): 371–81.

Bottomley, J.A. and R.B. Contant. *Methods for Setting Priorities among Different Lines of Agricultural Research.* ISNAR Staff Notes No. 88–38. The Hague: International Service for National Agricultural Research, December 1988.

Bouchet, F.C. "An Analysis of the Sources of Growth in French Agriculture, 1960–1987." Unpublished Ph.D. Thesis, Virginia Polytechnic Institute and State University, Blacksburg, 1987.

Bouchet, F.C., D. Orden and G.W. Norton. "Sources of Growth in French Agriculture." *American Journal of Agricultural Economics* Vol. 71, No. 2 (May 1989): 280–93.

Boulding, K.E. *Economics as a Science.* New York: McGraw Hill, 1970.

Boussard, J.-M. "Risk and Uncertainty in Programming Models: A Review." In J.A. Roumasset, J.-M. Boussard and I. Singh, eds., *Risk, Uncertainty, and Agricultural Development.* New York: Agricultural Development Council, 1979.

Boyce, J.K. and R.E. Evenson. *Agricultural Research and Extension Programs.* New York: Agricultural Development Council, 1975.

Bredahl, M.E. and W.L. Peterson. "The Productivity and Allocation of Research at U.S. Agricultural Experiment Stations." *American Journal of Agricultural Economics* Vol. 58, No. 4 (November 1976): 684–92.

Bredahl, M.E., W. Myers and K.J. Collins. "The Elasticity of Foreign Demand for U.S. Agricultural Products: The Importance of the Price Transmission Elasticity." *American Journal of Agricultural Economics* Vol. 61, No. 1 (February 1979): 58–63.

Brennan, J.P. "Measuring the Contribution of New Varieties to Increasing Wheat Yields." *Review of Marketing and Agricultural Economics* Vol. 52, No. 3 (December 1984): 175–95.

Brennan, J.P. *Impact of Wheat Varieties from CIMMYT on Australian Wheat Production.* Agricultural Economics Bulletin No.5. Sydney: Department of Agriculture New South Wales, September 1986.

Brinegar, G.K. "Discussion—A Framework for Establishing Research Priorities." *Journal of Farm Economics* Vol. 48, No. 5 (December 1966): 1638–40.

Brown, W.G. and B.R. Beattie. "Improving Estimates of Economic Parameters by Use of Ridge Regression with Production Function Applications." *American Journal of Agricultural Economics* Vol. 57, No. 1 (February 1975): 21–32.

Browning, E.K. "The Marginal Cost of Public Funds." *Journal of Political Economy* Vol. 84, No. 2 (April 1976): 283–98.

Browning, E.K. "The Marginal Cost of Raising Tax Revenue." In P. Cagan, ed., *Essays in Contemporary Economic Problems, 1986: The Impact of the Reagan Program.* Washington, DC: American Enterprise Institute, 1986.

Browning, E.K. "On the Marginal Welfare Cost of Taxation." *American Economic Review* Vol. 77, No. 1 (March 1987): 11–23.

Bruno, M. "Domestic Resource Costs and Effective Protection: Clarification and Synthesis." *Journal of Political Economy* Vol. 80, No. 1 (January/February 1972): 16–33.

Burniaux, J. and D. van der Mensbrugghe. *Trade Policies in a Global Context: Technical Specification of the Rural/ Urban-North/South (RUNS) Applied General Equilibrium Model.* Technical Paper No. 48. Paris: Organization for Economic Cooperation and Development, Development Centre, 1991.

Burt, O.R. and V.E. Worthington. "Wheat Acreage Supply Response in the United States." *Western Journal of Agricultural Economics* Vol. 13, No. 1 (July 1988): 100–11.

Buse, R.C. "Total Elasticities—A Predictive Device." *Journal of Farm Economics* Vol. 15, No. 4 (November 1958): 881–91.

Byerlee, D. *Comparative Advantage and Policy Incentives for Wheat Production in Ecuador.* CIMMYT Economics Program Working Paper No. 01/85. Mexico: Centro Internacional de Mejoramiento de Maíz y Trigo, 1985.

Byerlee, D. and E.H. de Polanco. "Farmers' Stepwise Adoption of Technological Packages: Evidence from the Mexican Altiplano." *American Journal of Agricultural Economics* Vol. 68, No. 3 (August 1986): 519–27.

Byerlee, D. and S. Franzel. *Institutionalizing the Role of the Economist in National Agricultural Research Institutes.* CIMMYT Economics Program Working Paper 93–02. Mexico: Centro Internacional de Mejoramiento de Maíz y Trigo, 1993.

Byerlee, D. and M. Morris. "Research for Marginal Environments. Are We Underinvested?" *Food Policy* Vol. 18, No. 5 (October 1993): 381–93.

Byerlee, D., M. Igbal and K.S. Fisher. "Quantifying and Valuing the Joint Production of Grain and Fodder from Maize Fields: Evidence from Northern Pakistan." *Experimental Agriculture* Vol. 25, No. 4 (October 1989): 435–45.

Candler, W. and M. Boehlje. "Use of Linear Programming in Capital Budgeting with Multiple Goals." *American Journal of Agricultural Economics* Vol. 53, No. 2 (May 1971): 325–30.

Capalbo, S.M. and J.M. Antle, eds. *Agricultural Productivity: Measurement and Explanation.* Washington, DC: Resources for the Future, 1988.

Capalbo, S., M. Denny, A. Hoque and C.E. Overton. *Methodologies for Comparisons of Agricultural Output, Input, and Productivity: A Review and Synthesis.* Agriculture and Trade Analysis Division Staff Report No. AGES 9122. Washington, DC: U.S. Department of Agriculture, April 1991.

Carew, R., P. Chen and V. Stevens. "Evaluating Publicly Funded Research in Canadian Agriculture: A Profit Function Approach." *Canadian Journal of Agri-*cultural Economics* Vol. 40, No. 4 (December 1992): 547–60.

Carter, C.A. and W.H. Gardiner, eds. *Elasticities in International Agricultural Trade.* Boulder, Colorado: Westview Press, 1988.

Cassells, J.M. "The Nature of Statistical Supply Curves." *Journal of Farm Economics* Vol. 15, No. 2 (April 1933): 378–87.

de Castro, J.P.R. and G.E. Schuh. "An Empirical Test of an Economic Model for Establishing Research Priorities: A Brazil Case Study." In T.M. Arndt, D.G. Dalrymple and V.W. Ruttan, eds., *Resource Allocation and Productivity in National and International Agricultural Research.* Minneapolis: University of Minnesota Press, 1977.

Caves, D. and L. Christensen. "Global Properties of Flexible Functional Forms." *American Economic Review* Vol. 70, No. 3 (June 1980): 422–32.

Cessay, S., E. Gilbert, B. Mills, J. Rowe and G.W. Norton. *Analysis of Agricultural Research Priorities in the Gambia.* ACIAR/ISNAR Project Paper No. 16. Canberra and The Hague: Australian Centre for International Agricultural Research and International Service for National Agricultural Research, November 1989.

Cetron, M.J., J. Martino and L.A. Roepeke. "The Selection of R&D Program Content—Survey of Quantitative Methods." *IEEE Transactions on Engineering Management* Vol. EM-14 (March 1967): 1–13.

CGIAR/TAC. *TAC Review of CGIAR Priorities and Future Strategies.* Rome: TAC Secretariat, Food and Agriculture Organization, December 1986.

Chalfant, J.A. "Choosing Among Flexible Functional Forms: An Application of the Generalized Box-Cox and the Fourier Flexible Forms to U.S. Agriculture." Unpublished Ph.D. Thesis. Raleigh: North Carolina State University, 1983.

Chalfant, J.A. "Comparisons of Alternative Functional Forms with Application to Agricultural Input Data." *American Journal of Agricultural Economics* Vol. 66, No. 2 (May 1984): 216–20.

Chalfant, J.A. and N.E. Wallace. "Bayesian Analysis and Regularity Conditions on Flexible Functional Forms: Application to the U.S. Motor Carrier Industry." In W. Griffiths, H. Lüetkepohl and M.E. Bock, eds., *Readings in Econometric Theory and Practice*. Amsterdam: Elsevier, 1992.

Chalfant, J.A. and B. Zhang. "Variations on Invariance or Some Unpleasant Nonparametric Arithmetic." Department of Agricultural Economics, University of California, Davis, 1994. Mimeo.

Chambers, R.G. *Applied Production Analysis: A Dual Approach.* Cambridge: Cambridge University Press, 1988.

Chambers, R.G. and R. Lopez. "Public Investment and Real-Price Supports." *Journal of Public Economics* Vol. 52, No. 1 (August 1993): 73–82.

Chang, C.C., B.A. McCarl, J. Mjelde and J. Richardson. "Sectoral Implications of Farm Program Modifications." *American Journal of Agricultural Economics* Vol. 74, No. 1 (February 1992): 38–49.

Chaparro, F., G. Montes, R. Torres, A. Balzaca and H. Jaramillo. "Research Priorities and Resource Allocation in Agriculture: The Case of Colombia." In D. Daniels and B. Nestel, eds., *Resource Allocation to Agricultural Research.* Ottawa: International Development Research Centre, 1981.

Charnes, A. and W.W. Cooper. *Management Models and Industrial Application of Linear Programming. Volume 1.*

New York: John Wiley and Sons, 1961.

Chavas, J.-P. and T.L. Cox. "A Nonparametric Analysis of Agricultural Technology." *American Journal of Agricultural Economics* Vol. 70, No. 2 (May 1988): 303–10.

Chavas, J.-P. and T.L. Cox. "A Nonparametric Analysis of the Influence of Research on Agricultural Productivity." *American Journal of Agricultural Economics* Vol. 74, No. 3 (August 1992): 583–91.

Chavas, J.-P. and S.R. Johnson. "Supply Dynamics: The Case of U.S. Broilers and Turkeys." *American Journal of Agricultural Economics* Vol. 64, No. 3 (August 1982): 558–64.

Chipman, J.S. and J.C. Moore. "The New Welfare Economics, 1939–1974." *International Economic Review* Vol. 19, No. 3 (October 1978): 581–84.

Chipman, J.S. and J.C. Moore. "Compensating Variation, Consumer's Surplus, and Welfare." *American Economic Review* Vol. 70, No. 5 (December 1980): 933–49.

Christensen, L.R., D.W. Jorgenson and L.J. Lau. "Conjugate Duality and the Transcendental Logarithmic Production Function." *Econometrica* Vol. 39, No. 4 (July 1971): 255–56.

Christensen, L.R., D.W. Jorgenson and L.J. Lau. "Transcendental Logarithmic Production Frontiers." *Review of Economics and Statistics* Vol. 55, No. 1 (February 1973): 28–45.

CIMMYT. *The Adoption of Agricultural Technology: A Guide for Survey Design.* Mexico: Economics Program, Centro Internacional de Mejoramiento de Maíz y Trigo, 1993.

Cline, P.L. "Sources of Productivity Change in United States Agriculture." Unpublished Ph.D. Thesis, Oklahoma State University, Stillwater, 1975.

Cline, W.R. *The Economics of Global Warming.* Washington, DC: Institute for International Economics, 1992.

Coble, K.H., C.C. Chang, B.A. McCarl and B.R. Eddelmann. "Assessing Economic Implications of New Technology: The Case of Cornstarch-Based Biodegradable Plastics." *Review of Agricultural Economics* Vol. 14, No. 1 (January 1992): 33–43.

Cochrane, W.W. "Some Nonconformist Thoughts on Welfare Economics and Commodity Stabilization Policy." *American Journal of Agricultural Economics* Vol. 62, No. 3 (August 1980): 508–11.

Cohon, J.L. "A Review and Evaluation of Multiobjective Programming Techniques." *Water Resources Research* Vol. 11, No. 2 (April 1975): 208–20.

Cohon, J.L. *Multiobjective Progamming and Planning.* New York: Academic Press, 1978.

Cohon, J.L. and D.H. Marks. "Multi-Objective Screening Models and Water Resource Investment." *Water Resources Research* Vol. 9, No. 4 (August 1973): 826–36.

Colman, D. "A Review of the Arts of Supply Response Analysis." *Review of Marketing and Agricultural Economics* Vol. 51, No. 3 (December 1983): 201–30.

Constantine, J.H., J.M. Alston and V.H. Smith. "Economic Impacts of the California One-Variety Cotton Law." *Journal of Political Economy* (forthcoming 1995).

Cooke, S.C. and W.B. Sundquist. "The Incidence of Benefits from U.S. Soybean Productivity Gains in a Context of World Trade." *American Journal of Agricultural Economics* Vol. 75, No. 1 (February 1993): 169–80.

Corden, W.M. *Trade Policy and Economic Welfare.* Oxford: Oxford University Press, 1974.

Cornes, R. *Duality and Modern Economics.* Cambridge: Cambridge University Press, 1992.

Cox, T.L. and J.-P. Chavas. "A Nonparametric Analysis of Productivity: The Case of U.S. Agriculture." *European Review of Agricultural Economics* Vol. 17, No. 4 (1990): 449–64.

Craig, B.J. and P.G. Pardey. *Patterns of Agricultural Development in the United States.* Department of Agricultural and Applied Economics Staff Paper P90–72. St. Paul: University of Minnesota, December 1990.

Craig, B.J., P.G. Pardey and K.W. Deininger. "Capital Services in U.S. Agriculture." Department of Agricultural and Applied Economics, University of Minnesota, St. Paul, 1993. Mimeo.

Craig, B.J., P.G. Pardey and J. Roseboom. *International Agricultural Productivity Patterns.* Center for International Food and Agricultural Policy Working Paper WP94–1. St Paul: University of Minnesota, February 1994.

Crosson, P. and J.R. Anderson. *Concerns for Sustainability: Integration of Natural Resource and Environmental Issues in the Research Agendas of NARS.* ISNAR Research Report No. 4. The Hague: International Service for National Agricultural Research, October 1993.

Currie, J.M., J.A. Murphy and A. Schmitz. "The Concept of Economic Surplus and Its Use in Economic Analysis." *Economic Journal* Vol. 81, No. 324 (December 1971): 741–99.

Dalrymple, D.G. "The Excess Burden of Taxation and Public Agricultural Research." In R.G. Echeverría, ed., *Methods of Diagnosing Research System Constraints and Assessing the Impact of Agricultural Research. Volume II, As-*

sesssing the Impact of Agricultural Research. The Hague: International Service for National Agricultural Research, 1990.

David, C.C. and K. Otsuka, eds. *Modern Rice Technology and Income Distribution in Asia.* Boulder: Lynne Rienner Publishers, 1994.

Davidson, B.R. and B.R. Martin. "The Relationship between Yields on Farms and in Experiments." *Australian Journal of Agricultural Economics* Vol. 9, No. 2 (December 1965): 129–40.

Davidson, B.R., B.R. Martin and R.G. Mauldon. "The Application of Experimental Research to Farm Production." *Journal of Farm Economics* Vol. 49, No. 4 (November 1967): 900–07.

Davis, H.T. *The Theory of Econometrics.* Bloomington: Principia Press, 1941.

Davis, J.S. "Stability of the Research Production Coefficient for U.S. Agriculture." Unpublished Ph.D. Thesis, University of Minnesota, St. Paul, 1979.

Davis, J.S. "The Relationship between the Economic Surplus and Production Function Approaches for Estimating Ex Post Returns to Agricultural Research." *Review of Marketing and Agricultural Economics* Vol. 49, No. 2 (August 1981): 95–105.

Davis, J.S. *Spillover Effects of Agricultural Research: Importance for Research Policy and Incorporation in Research Evaluation Models.* ACIAR/ISNAR Project Paper No. 32. Canberra and The Hague: Australian Centre for International Agricultural Research and International Service for National Agricultural Research, February 1991.

Davis, J.S. and M.C.S. Bantilan. *Import Replacement and Export Enhancement as Objectives of Agricultural Research Policy: Interpretation and Measurement.* ACIAR/ISNAR Project Paper No.

22. Canberra and The Hague: Australian Centre for International Agricultural Research and International Service for National Agricultural Research, October 1990.

Davis, J.S., P. Oram and J.G. Ryan. *Assessment of Agricultural Research Priorities: An International Perspective.* Canberra and Washington, DC: Australian Centre for International Agricultural Research and International Food Policy Research Institute, 1987.

Deaton, A.S. and J. Muellbauer. "An Almost Ideal Demand System." *American Economic Review* Vol. 70, No. 3 (June 1980): 312–26. 1980a.

Deaton, A.S. and J. Muellbauer. *Economics and Consumer Behavior.* Cambridge: Cambridge University Press. 1980b.

Denison, E.F. "Measurement of Labor Input: Some Questions of Definition and the Adequacy of Data." In *Output, Input and Productivity Measurement.* Princeton: The National Bureau of Economic Research, Princeton University, 1961.

Denison, E.F. "Some Major Issues in Productivity Analysis: An Examination of Estimates by Jorgenson and Griliches." *Survey of Current Business* Vol. 49, No. 5 (May 1969): 1–27.

Denny, M. and M. Fuss. "The Use of Discrete Variables in Superlative Index Number Comparisons." *International Economic Review* Vol. 24, No. 2 (June 1983): 419–21.

Dey, M. and G.W. Norton. *Analysis of Agricultural Research Priorities in Bangladesh.* ISNAR Discussion Paper No. 93–07. The Hague: International Service for National Agricultural Research, March 1993.

Diewert, W.E. "An Application of the Shephard Duality Theorem: Generalized Leontief Production Function." *Journal of Political Economy* Vol. 79, No. 3

(May-June 1971): 481–507.

Diewert, W.E. "Functional Forms for Profit and Transformation Functions." *Journal of Economic Theory* Vol. 6, No. 3 (June 1973): 284–316.

Diewert, W.E. "Applications of Duality Theory." In M. Intrilligator and D.A. Kendrick, eds., *Frontiers of Quantitative Economics. Volume II.* Amsterdam: North-Holland, 1974.

Diewert, W.E. "Exact and Superlative Index Numbers." *Journal of Econometrics* Vol. 4, No. 2 (May 1976): 115–45.

Diewert, W.E. "The Comparative Statistics of Industry Long-Run Equilibrium." *Canadian Journal of Economics* Vol. 14, No. 1 (February 1981): 78–92.

Diewert, W.E. *The Early History of Price Index Research.* Working Paper No. 2713. Cambridge: National Bureau of Economic Research, 1988a.

Diewert, W.E. "Test Approaches to International Comparisons." In W. Eichorn, ed., *Measurement in Economics.* Heidelberg: Physica Verlag, 1988b.

Dillon, J.L. and J.R. Anderson. *The Analysis of Response in Crop and Livestock Production.* Third edition. Oxford: Pergamon Press, 1990.

Dixon, P., B. Parmenter, J. Sutton and D. Vincent. *ORANI: A Multisectoral Model of the Australian Economy.* Amsterdam: North-Holland, 1982.

Dorfman, J.H. and D. Heien. "The Effects of Uncertainty and Adjustment Costs on Investment in the Almond Industry." *Review of Economics and Statistics* Vol. 71, No. 2 (May 1989): 263–74.

Drechsler, L. "Weighting of Index Numbers in Multilateral International Comparisons." *Review of Income and Wealth* Vol. 19, No.1 (March 1973): 17–35.

Drilon, J.D. and A.R. Librero. "Defining Research Priorities for Agriculture and Natural Resources in the Philippines."

In D. Daniels and B. Nestel, eds., *Resource Allocation to Agricultural Research.* Ottawa: International Development Research Center, 1981.

Duncan, R.C. "Evaluating Returns to Research in Pasture Improvement." *Australian Journal of Agricultural Economics* Vol. 16, No. 3 (December 1972): 153–68.

Duncan, R.C. and C. Tisdell. "Research and Technical Progress: The Returns to the Producers." *Economic Record* Vol. 47, No. 117 (March 1971): 124–9.

Dyer, P.T., G.M. Scobie and S.R. Davis. *The Payoff to Investment in a Recombinant DNA Research Facility at Ruakura: A Monte Carlo Simulation Study.* Economics Division Discussion Paper 1/84. Hamilton, New Zealand: Ministry of Agriculture and Fisheries, February 1984.

Echeverría, R.G. "Assessing the Impact of Agricultural Research." In R.G. Echeverría, ed., *Methods for Diagnosing Research System Constraints and Assessing the Impact of Agricultural Research. Volume II, Assessing the Impact of Agricultural Research.* The Hague: International Service for National Agricultural Research, 1990.

Echeverría, R.G., G. Ferreira and M. Dabezies. *Returns to Investment in the Generation and Transfer of Rice Technology in Uruguay.* ISNAR Working Paper No. 30. The Hague: International Service for National Agricultural Research, 1989.

Edwards, G.W. and J.W. Freebairn. *Measuring a Country's Gains From Research: Theory and Application to Rural Research in Australia.* A Report to the Commonwealth Council for Rural Research and Extension. Canberra: Australian Government Publishing Service, 1981.

Edwards, G.W. and J.W. Freebairn. "The Social Benefits from an Increase in Productivity in a Part of an Industry." *Review of Marketing and Agricultural Economics* Vol. 50, No. 2 (August 1982): 193–210.

Edwards, G.W. and J.W. Freebairn. "The Gains from Research into Tradeable Commodities." *American Journal of Agricultural Economics* Vol. 66, No. 1 (February 1984): 41–49.

Ehui, S.K. and D.S.C. Spencer. "Measuring the Sustainability and Economic Viability of Tropical Farming Systems: A Model for sub-Saharan Africa." *Agricultural Economics* Vol. 19, No. 4 (December 1993): 279–96.

Eichorn, W. "Fisher's Tests Revisited." *Econometrica* Vol. 44, No. 2 (March 1976): 247–56.

Eichorn, W. and J. Voeller. *Theory of the Price Index.* Berlin: Springer Verlag, 1976.

Espinosa, P., G.W. Norton and H.D. Gross. *Metodología para Determinar Prioridades de Investigación Agropecuaria.* Serie Technica, Doc. No. 1. Quito, Ecuador: Instituto Nacional de Investigación Agropecharia, 1988.

Evenson, R.E. "The Contribution of Agricultural Research to Production." *Journal of Farm Economics* Vol. 49, No. 5 (December 1967): 1415–25.

Evenson, R.E. "The Contribution of Agricultural Research and Extension to Agricultural Production." Unpublished Ph.D. Thesis, University of Chigaco, Chicago, 1968.

Evenson, R.E. *A Century of Productivity Change in U.S. Agriculture: An Analysis of the Role of Invention, Research, and Extension.* Economic Growth Center Discussion Paper No. 276. Yale: Yale University, August 1978.

Evenson, R.E. "A Century of Agricultural Research, Invention, Extension and Productivity Change in U.S. Agriculture: An Historical Decomposition Analysis." In A.A. Araji, ed., *Research and Extension Productivity in Agriculture.* Moscow: Department of Agricultural Economics, University of Idaho, 1980.

Evenson, R.E. "Research, Extension, and U.S Agricultural Productivity: A Statistical Decomposition Analysis." In S.M. Capalbo and J.M. Antle, eds., *Agricultural Productivity: Measurement and Explanation.* Washington, DC: Resources for the Future, 1988.

Evenson, R.E. "Spillover Benefits of Agricultural Research: Evidence from U.S. Experience." *American Journal of Agricultural Economics* Vol. 71, No. 2 (May 1989): 447–52.

Evenson, R.E. "Priority Setting: Ex Ante Project Evaluation and Ex Post Evaluation: A Comparative Perspective." Paper prepared for the Rice Research Prioritization Workshop, International Rice Research Institute, Los Baños, Philippines, 13–15 August 1991.

Evenson, R.E. "Notes on the Measurement of the Economic Consequences of Agricultural Research Investment." In D.R. Lee, S. Kearl and N. Uphoff, eds., *Assessing the Impact of International Agricultural Research for Sustainable Development.* Ithaca: Cornell International Institute for Food, Agriculture and Development, 1992.

Evenson, R.E. and H.P. Binswanger. "Technology Transfer and Research Resource Allocation." In H.P. Binswanger, V.W. Ruttan et al., *Induced Innovation: Technology, Institutions, and Development.* Baltimore: Johns Hopkins University Press, 1978.

Evenson, R.E. and Y. Kislev. *Agricultural Research and Productivity.* New Haven: Yale University Press, 1975.

Evenson, R.E. and J. Putnam. "Intellectual Property Management." In G.J. Persley, ed., *Agricultural Biotechnology: Opportunities for International Development.* Wallingford: CAB International, 1990.

Färe, R., S. Grosskopf, M. Norris and Z. Zhang. "Productivity Growth, Technical Progress, and Efficiency Change in Industrialized Countries." *American Economic Review* Vol. 84, No. 1 (March 1994): 66–83.

Fawson, C. and C.R. Shumway. "A Nonparametric Investigation of Agricultural Production Behavior for U.S. Subregions." *American Journal of Agricultural Economics* Vol. 70, No. 2 (May 1988): 311–17.

Feder, G. and D.L. Umali. "The Adoption of Agricultural Innovations: A Review." *Technological Forecasting and Social Change* Vol. 43, Nos. 3/4 (May/June 1993): 215–39.

Feder, G., R.E. Just and D. Zilberman. "Adoption of Agricultural Innovations in Developing Countries: A Survey." *Economic Develoment and Cultural Change* Vol. 33, No. 2 (January 1985): 255–98.

Ferguson, C.E. *The Neoclassical Theory of Production and Distribution.* Cambridge: Cambridge University Press, 1975.

Ferreira, G., G.W. Norton and M. Dabezies. *Definición de Prioridades de Investigación Agropecuaria.* Montevideo, Uruguay: Centro de Investigaciones Agrícolas Alberto Boerger, 1987.

Findlay, C.C. and R.L. Jones. "The Marginal Cost of Australian Income Taxation." *Economic Record* Vol. 58, No. 162 (September 1982): 253–66.

Finkelshtain, I. and J.A. Chalfant. "Marketed Surplus under Risk: Do Peasants Agree with Sandmo?" *American Journal of Agricultural Economics* Vol. 73, No. 3 (August 1991): 557–67.

Finkelshtain, I. and J.A. Chalfant. "Portfolio Choices in the Presence of Other Risks." *Management Science* Vol. 39, No. 8 (August 1993): 925–36.

Fishel, W.L. "Uncertainty in Public Research Administration and Scientists' Subjective Probability Estimates about Changing the State of Knowledge." Unpublished Ph.D. Thesis, North Carolina State University, Raleigh, 1970.

Fishel, W.L., ed. *Resource Allocation in Agricultural Research.* Minneapolis: University of Minnesota Press, 1971.

Fisher, B. "Rational Expectations in Agricultural Research and Policy Analysis." *American Journal of Agricultural Economics* Vol. 64, No. 2 (May 1982): 260–65.

Fisher, I. *The Making of Index Numbers.* Boston: Houghton Mifflin, 1922.

Flacco, P.R. and D.M. Larson. "Nonparametric Measures of Scale and Technical Change for Competitive Firms under Uncertainty." *American Journal of Agricultural Economics* Vol. 74, No. 1 (February 1992): 173–76.

Flores-Moya, P., R.E. Evenson and Y. Hayami. "Social Returns to Rice Research in the Philippines: Domestic Benefits and Foreign Spillover." *Economic Development and Cultural Change* Vol. 26, No. 3 (April 1978): 591–607.

Food and Agriculture Organization (FAO). *Agricultural Protection: Domestic Policy in International Trade.* Rome: Food and Agricultural Organization, 1973.

Fox, G. "Is the United States Really Underinvesting in Agricultural Research?" *American Journal of Agricultural Economics* Vol. 67, No. 4 (November 1985): 806–12.

Fox, G. "Models of Resource Allocation in Public Agricultural Research: A Survey." *Journal of Agricultural Economics* Vol. 38, No. 3 (September 1987): 449–62.

Fox, G., G. Brinkman, and N. Brown-Andison. "An Economic Analysis of the Returns to the Animal Productivity Research Program of Agriculture Canada from 1968 to 1984". Intercambia Limited, Guelph, Ontario, March 1987. Unpublished report.

Fox, G., B. Roberts and G.L. Brinkman. "The Returns to Canadian Federal Dairy Cattle Research: 1968–83." Department of Agricultural Economics and Business Working Paper No. 98–20. Guelph, Ontario: University of Guelph, October 1989.

Freebairn, J.W. "Evaluating the Level and Distribution of Benefits from Dairy Industry Research." *Australian Journal of Agricultural Economics* Vol. 36, No. 2 (August 1992): 141–65.

Freebairn, J.W., J.S. Davis and G.W. Edwards. "Distribution of Research Gains in Multistage Production Systems." *American Journal of Agricultural Economics* Vol. 64, No. 1 (February 1982): 39–46.

Freebairn, J.W., J.S. Davis and G.W. Edwards. "Distribution of Research Gains in Multistage Production Systems: Reply." *American Journal of Agricultural Economics* Vol. 65, No. 2 (May 1983): 357–59.

French, B.C. and J.L. Matthews. "A Supply Response Model for Perennial Crops." *American Journal of Agricultural Economics* Vol. 53, No. 3 (August 1974): 478–90.

Freund, R.J. "The Introduction of Risk into a Programming Model." *Econometrica* Vol. 24, No. 3 (July 1956): 253–63.

Friedman, M. *Price Theory.* Chicago: Aldine Publishing Company, 1976.

Frisch, R. "A Complete Scheme for Computing All Direct and Cross Demand Elasticities in a Model with Many Sectors." *Econometrica* Vol. 27, No. 2 (April 1959): 177–96.

Fulginiti, L.E. and R.K. Perrin. *Prices and Productivity in Agriculture.* Department of Agricultural Economics Journal Paper No. J-14462. Ames: Iowa State University, 1992.

Fulginiti, L.E. and R.K. Perrin. "The Theory and Measurement of Production Response under Quotas." *Review of Economics and Statistics* Vol. 75, No. 1 (February 1993): 97–106.

Fullerton, D. "Reconciling Recent Estimates of the Marginal Welfare Cost of Taxation." *American Economic Review* Vol. 81, No. 1 (March 1991): 302–8.

Fuss, M., D. McFadden and Y. Mundlak. "A Survey of Functional Forms in the Economic Analysis of Production." In M. Fuss and D. McFadden, eds., *Production Economics: A Dual Approach to Theory and Applications.* Amsterdam: North-Holland, 1978.

Gallant, A.R. "Unbiased Determination of Production Technologies" *Journal of Econometrics* Vol. 20, No. 2 (November 1982): 285–323.

Gardner, B.L. "The Farm-Retail Price Spread in a Competitive Food Industry." *American Journal of Agricultural Economics* Vol. 57, No. 3 (August 1975): 399–409.

Gardner, B.L. "Futures Prices in Supply Analysis." *American Journal of Agricultural Economics* Vol. 58, No. 1 (February 1976): 81–9.

Gardner, B.L. "Efficient Redistribution through Commodity Markets." *American Journal of Agricultural Economics* Vol. 65, No. 2 (May 1983): 225–34.

Gardner, B.L. *The Economics of Agricultural Policies.* New York: MacMillan, 1987.

Gardner, B.L. *Price Supports and Optimal Agricultural Research Spending*. Department of Agricultural and Resource Economics Working Paper No. 88–1. College Park: University of Maryland, January (revised June) 1988.

Gardner, B.L. "How the Data We Make Can Unmake Us: Annals of Factology." *American Journal of Agricultural Economics* Vol. 74, No. 5 (December 1992): 1066–75.

Geigel, J. and W.B. Sundquist. *A Review and Evaluation of Weather-Crop Yield Models*. Department of Agricultural and Applied Economics Staff Paper P84–5. St. Paul: University of Minnesota, February 1984.

Gijsbers, G. *Methods and Procedures for the Development of INFORM*. The Hague: International Service for National Agricultural Research, March 1991.

Godyn, D.L., J.P. Brennan and B.G. Johnston. "The Gains from Research into Tradeable Commodities: A Comment." Department of Agriculture, New South Wales, Sydney, February 1987. Mimeo.

Goodwin, B.K. and D.A. Sumner. "Market Supply Parameters under Mandatory Production Quotas." Department of Economics and Business, North Carolina State University, October 1990. Mimeo.

de Gorter, H. and G.W. Norton. "A Critical Appraisal of Analyzing the Gains from Research with Market Distortions." Department of Agricultural Economics, Cornell University, Ithaca, April 1990. Mimeo.

de Gorter, H., D.J. Nielson and G.C. Rausser. "Productive and Predatory Public Policies: Research Expenditures and Producer Subsidies in Agriculture." *American Journal of Agricultural Economics* Vol. 74, No. 1 (February 1992): 27–37.

Graham-Tomasi, T. "Sustainability: Concepts and Implications for Agricultural Research Policy." In P.G. Pardey, J. Roseboom and J.R. Anderson, eds., *Agricultural Research Policy: International Quantitative Perspectives*. Cambridge: Cambridge University Press, 1991.

Greig, I.D. "Agricultural Research Management and the Ex Ante Evaluation of Research Proposals: A Review." *Review of Marketing and Agricultural Economics* Vol. 49, No. 2 (August 1981): 73–94.

Griliches, Z. "Specification Bias in Estimates of Production Functions." *Journal of Farm Economics* Vol. 39, No. 1 (February 1957): 8–20. 1957a.

Griliches, Z. "Hybrid Corn: An Exploration in the Economics of Technological Change." *Econometrica* Vol. 25, No. 4 (October 1957): 501–22. 1957b.

Griliches, Z. "Research Costs and Social Returns: Hybrid Corn and Related Innovations." *Journal of Political Economy* Vol. 66, No. 5 (October 1958): 419–31.

Griliches, Z. "Measuring Inputs in Agriculture: A Critical Survey." *Journal of Farm Economics* Vol. 42, No. 5 (December 1960): 1411–27.

Griliches, Z. "Estimates of the Aggregate Agricultural Production Function from Cross-Sectional Data." *Journal of Farm Economics*. Vol. 45, No. 2 (May 1963): 419–28. 1963a.

Griliches, Z. "The Sources of Measured Productivity Growth: United States Agriculture, 1940–60." *Journal of Political Economy* Vol. 71, No. 4 (August 1963): 331–46. 1963b.

Griliches, Z. "Capital Stock in Investment Functions: Some Problems of Concept and Measurement." In C. Christ, et al., eds., *Measurement in Economics: Studies in Mathematical Economics and*

Econometrics in Memory of Yehuda Grunfeld. Stanford: Stanford University Press, 1963c.

Griliches, Z. "Research Expenditures, Education and the Aggregate Agricultural Production Function." *American Economic Review* Vol. 54, No. 6 (December 1964): 961–74.

Griliches, Z. "Distributed Lags: A Survey." *Econometrica* Vol. 35, No. 1 (January 1967): 16–47.

Griliches, Z. "Issues in Assessing the Contribution of Research and Development to Productivity Growth." *Bell Journal of Economics* Vol. 10, No. 1 (Spring 1979): 92–116.

Griliches, Z., ed. *R&D, Patents, and Productivity*. Chicago: University of Chicago Press, 1984.

Griliches, Z. "Productivity, R&D, and Basic Research at the Firm Level in the 1970s." *American Economic Review* Vol. 76, No. 1 (March 1986): 141–54. 1986a.

Griliches, Z. "Economic Data Issues." In Z. Griliches and M.D. Intriligator, eds., *Handbook of Econometrics. Volume 3.* Amsterdam: North-Holland, 1986. 1986b.

Griliches, Z. "Patent Statistics as Economic Indicators." *Journal of Economic Literature* Vol. 28, No. 4 (December 1990): 1661–707.

Griliches, Z. "The Search for R&D Spillovers." *Scandinavian Journal of Economics* Vol. 94 (Supplement 1992): 29–47.

Griliches, Z. "Productivity, R&D, and the Data Constraint." *American Economic Review* Vol. 84, No. 1 (March 1994): 1–23.

Gruen, F.H. "Agriculture and Technical Change." *Journal of Farm Economics* Vol. 43, No. 4 (November 1961): 838–58.

Gryseels, G., C.T. de Wit, A. McCalla, J. Monyo, A. Kassam, E. Craswell and M. Collinson. "Setting Agricultural Research Priorities for the CGIAR." *Agricultural Systems* Vol. 40, No. 1 (1992): 59–103.

Hanoch, G. and M. Rothschild. "Testing the Assumptions of Production Theory: A Nonparametric Approach." *Journal of Political Economy* Vol. 80, No. 2 (March-April 1972): 256–75.

Haque, E.A.K., G. Fox and G.L. Brinkman. "Product Market Distortions and the Returns to Federal Laying-Hen Research in Canada." *Canadian Journal of Agricultural Economics* Vol. 37, No. 1 (March 1989): 29–46.

Harberger, A.C. "Three Basic Postulates for Applied Welfare Economics: An Interpretive Essay." *Journal of Economic Literature* Vol. 9, No. 3 (September 1971): 785–97.

Harberger, A.C. *Project Appraisal: Collected Papers*. Chicago: University of Chicago Press, 1976.

Harberger, A.C. "On the Use of Distributional Weights in Social Cost-Benefit Analysis." *Journal of Political Economy* Vol. 86, No. 2, Pt. 2 (April 1978): S87–S119.

Hart, O. "On the Optimality of Equilibrium When the Market Structure Is Incomplete." *Journal of Economic Theory* Vol. 11, No. 3 (December 1975): 418–43.

Hatanaka, M. and T.D. Wallace. "Multicollinearity and the Estimation of Low-Order Moments in Stable Lag Functions." In J. Kmenta and J. Ramsay, eds., *Evaluation of Econometric Models.* San Diego: Academic Press, 1980.

Hausman, J.A. "Exact Consumer's Surplus and Dead-Weight Loss." *American Economic Review* Vol. 71, No. 4 (September 1981): 662–76.

Havlicek Jr., J.G. and G.W. Norton. *A Review of Research Project Evaluation and Selection Methods: A Report to BARD.* Department of Agricultural Economics Staff Paper SP-13–81. Blacksburg: Virginia Polytechnic Institute and State University, November 1981.

Hayami, Y. and R.W. Herdt. "Market Price Effects of Technological Change on Income Distribution in Semisubsistence Agriculture." *American Journal of Agricultural Economics* Vol. 59, No. 2 (May 1977): 245–56.

Hayes, K. and S. Porter-Hudak. "Deadweight Loss: Theoretical Size Relationships and the Precision of Measurement." *Journal of Business Economics and Statistics* Vol. 5, No. 1 (January 1987): 47–52.

Hazell, P.B.R. "A Linear Alternative to Quadratic and Semi-Variance Programming for Farm Planning under Uncertainty." *American Journal of Agricultural Economics* Vol. 53, No. 1 (February 1971): 53–62.

Hazell, P.B.R. and R.D. Norton. *Mathematical Programming for Economic Analysis in Agriculture.* New York: Macmillan, 1986.

Hazell, P.B.R. and C. Ramasamy. *Green Revolution Reconsidered: The Impact of the High-Yielding Rice Varieties in South-India.* Baltimore: Johns Hopkins University Press, 1991.

Heady, E.O. and J.L. Dillon. *Agricultural Production Functions.* Ames: Iowa Sate University Press, 1961.

Heim, M.N. and L.L. Blakeslee. "Biological Adaptation and Research Impacts on Wheat Yields in Washington." Paper presented at annual meeting of the American Agricultural Economics Association, Reno, 1986.

Herdt, R.W. and C. Capule. *Adoption Spread, and Production Impact of Modern Rice Varieties in Asia.* Los Baños: International Rice Research Institute, 1983.

Herendeen, J.B. "A Framework for Establishing Research Priorities: Comment." *Journal of Farm Economics* Vol. 49, No. 3 (August 1967): 741–3.

Hertel, T.W. "Factor Market Incidence of Agricultural Trade Liberalization: Some Additional Results." *Australian Journal of Agricultural Economics* Vol. 35, No. 1 (April 1991): 77–107.

Hertford, R. and A. Schmitz. "Measuring Economic Returns to Agricultural Research." In T.M. Arndt, D.G. Dalrymple and V.W. Ruttan, eds., *Resource Allocation and Productivity in National and International Agricultural Research.* Minneapolis: University of Minnesota Press, 1977.

Hicks, J.R. *Value and Capital: An Inquiry into Some Fundamental Principles of Economic Theory.* Second ed. Oxford: Clarendon Press, 1946.

Hicks, J.R. *The Theory of Wages.* New York: P. Smith, 1948.

Higgs, P.J. *Adaptation and Survival in Australian Agriculture: A Computable General Equilibrium Analysis of the Impact of Economic Shocks Originating Outside the Agricultural Sector.* Melbourne: Oxford University Press, 1986.

Holloway, G.J. "Distribution of Research Gains in Multistage Production Systems: Further Results." *American Journal of Agricultural Economics* Vol. 71, No. 2 (May 1989): 338–43.

Horner, F.B. "Elasticity of the Demand for Exports of a Single Country." *Review of Economics and Statistics* Vol. 34, No. 4 (November 1952): 326–42.

Horton, D., P. Ballantyne, W. Peterson, B. Uribe, D. Gapasin and K. Sheridan, eds. *Monitoring and Evaluating Agricultural Research.* Wallingford, U.K.: CAB

International, 1993.

Hotelling, H. "Edgeworth's Taxation Paradox and the Nature of Demand and Supply Functions." *Journal of Political Economy* Vol. 40, No. 5 (October 1932): 577–616.

Hout, M.-F., G. Fox and G.L. Brinkman. "The Returns to Swine Research in Canada." *North Central Journal of Agricultural Economics* Vol. 11, No. 2 (July 1989): 189–201.

Hu, F. and J.M. Antle. "Agricultural Policy and Productivity: International Evidence." *Review of Agricultural Economics* Vol. 15, No. 3 (September 1993): 495–505.

Hueth, D.L. and R.E. Just. "Applied General Equilibrium Welfare Analysis: Discussion." *American Journal of Agricultural Economics* Vol. 73, No. 5 (December 1991): 1517–19.

Huffman, W.E. "Decision-Making: The Role of Education." *American Journal of Agricultural Economics* Vol. 56, No. 1 (February 1974): 85–97.

Huffman, W.E. "Assessing Returns to Agricultural Extension." *American Journal of Agricultural Economics* Vol. 60, No. 5 (December 1978): 969–75.

Huffman, W.E. and R.E. Evenson. "Supply and Demand Functions for Multiproduct U.S. Cash Grain Farms: Biases Caused by Research and Other Policies." *American Journal of Agricultural Economics* Vol. 71, No. 3 (August 1989): 761–73.

Huffman, W.E. and R.E. Evenson. "Contributions of Public and Private Science and Technology to US Agricultural Productivity." *American Journal of Agricultural Economics* Vol. 74, No. 3 (August 1992): 752–6.

Huffman, W.E. and R.E. Evenson. *Science for Agriculture: A Long-Term Perspective.* Ames: Iowa State University Press, 1993.

Huffman, W.E. and J.A. Miranowski. "An Economic Analysis of Expenditures on Agricultural Experiment Station Research." *American Journal of Agricultural Economics* Vol. 63, No. 1 (February 1981): 104–18.

Hulten, C.R. "Divisia Index Numbers." *Econometrica* Vol. 41, No. 6 (November 1973): 1017–25.

Hulten, C.R. "Growth Accounting with Intermediate Inputs." *Review of Economic Studies* Vol. 45, No. 3 (October 1978): 511–8.

Hulten, C.R. "Growth Accounting When Technical Change Is Embodied in Capital." *American Economic Review* Vol. 82, No. 2 (September 1992): 964–80.

Idachaba, F.S. "Agricultural Research Allocation Priorities: The Nigerian Experience." In D. Daniels and B. Nestel, eds. *Resource Allocation to Agricultural Research.* Ottawa: International Development Research Centre, 1981.

Industries Assistance Commission (IAC). *Financing Agricultural Research.* Canberra: Australian Government Publishing Service, June 1976.

Jaffe, A.B. "Technological Opportunity and Spillovers of R&D: Evidence from Firms' Patents, Profits, and Market Value." *American Economic Review* Vol. 76, No. 5 (December 1986): 984–99.

Jaffe, A.B. "Characterizing the 'Technological Position' of Firms, with Application to Quantifying Technological Opportunity and Research Spillovers." *Research Policy* Vol. 18, No. 2 (April 1989): 87–97.

Jahnke, H.E. and D. Kirschke. "Quantitative Indicators for Priorities in International Agricultural Research." Background Working Paper commissioned by FAO for TAC/CGIAR. Food and Agriculture

Organization, Rome, September 1984. Mimeo.

Jain, H.K. *Organization and Structure in National Agricultural Research Systems.* ISNAR Working Paper No. 21. The Hague: International Service for National Agricultural Research, 1989.

Jarrett, F.G. and R.K. Lindner. "Research Benefits Revisited." *Review of Marketing and Agricultural Economics* Vol. 45, No. 4 (December 1977): 167–78.

Jarvis, L.S. "Cattle as Capital Goods and Ranchers as Portfolio Managers: An Application to the Argentine Cattle Sector." *Journal of Political Economy.* Vol. 82, No. 3 (May/June 1974): 489–520.

Johnson, G.L. "Discussion: Economic Implications of Agricultural Experiments." *Journal of Farm Economics* Vol. 39, No. 1 (February 1957): 390–7.

Johnson, H.G. *International Trade and Economic Growth.* London: George Allen and Unwin, 1958.

Johnson, H.G. "The Possibility of Income Losses from Increased Efficiency or Factor Accumulation in the Presence of Tariffs." *Economic Journal* Vol. 77, No. 305 (March 1967): 151–4.

Johnson, P.R. "The Social Cost of the Tobacco Program." *Journal of Farm Economics* Vol. 47, No. 2 (May 1965): 242–55.

Johnson, P.R. "The Elasticity of Foreign Demand for U.S. Agricultural Products." *American Journal of Agricultural Economics* Vol. 59, No. 4 (November 1977): 735–6.

Johnson, S.R., Z.A. Hassan and R.D. Green. *Demand Systems Estimation: Methods and Practice.* Ames: Iowa State University Press, 1984.

Jorgenson, D.W. "The Embodiment Hypothesis." *Journal of Political Economy* Vol. 74 (February 1966): 1–17.

Jorgenson, D.W. "The Economic Theory of Replacement and Depreciation." In W. Sellekaerts, ed., *Economics and Econometric Theory, Essays in Honor of Jan Tinbergen.* London: Macmillan, 1974.

Jorgenson, D.W. and Z. Griliches. "The Explanation of Productivity Change." *Review of Economic Studies* Vol. 34, No. 99 (July 1967): 249–83.

Josling, T. and S. Tangerman. "Measuring Levels of Protection in Agriculture: A Survey of Approaches and Results." Paper presented at the Twentieth Conference of the International Association of Agricultural Economists, Buenos Aires, Argentina, 24–31 August 1988.

Just, R.E. "American Agricultural Supply." Paper presented at the International Association of Agricultural Economics Meetings, Tokyo, Japan, 1991.

Just, R.E. "Discovering Production and Supply Relationships: Present Status and Future Opportunities." *Review of Marketing and Agricultural Economics* Vol. 61, No. 1 (April 1993): 11–40.

Just, R.E. and J.M. Antle. "Interactions between Agricultural and Environmental Policies." *American Economic Review* Vol. 80, No. 2 (May 1990): 197–202.

Just, R.E. and D.L. Hueth. "Welfare Measures in a Multimarket Framework." *American Economic Review* Vol. 69, No. 5 (December 1979): 947–54.

Just, R.E., D.L. Hueth and A. Schmitz. *Applied Welfare Economics and Public Policy.* Englewood Cliffs, New Jersey: Prentice-Hall, Inc., 1982.

Kaldor, D. "A Framework for Establishing Research Priorities: Reply." *Journal of Farm Economics* Vol. 49, No. 3 (August 1967): 743–45.

Kamien, M.I. and N.L. Schwartz. *Market Structure and Innovation.* Cambridge: Cambridge University Press, 1982.

Karagiannis, G. and W.H. Furtan. "Production Structure and Decomposition of Biased Technical Change: An Example from Canadian Agriculture." *Review of Agricultural Economics* Vol. 15, No. 1 (January 1993): 21–37.

KARI. *Kenya's Agricultural Research Priorities to the Year 2000.* Nairobi: Kenya Agricultural Research Institute, May 1991.

Karp, L.S. "Dynamic Games in International Trade." Unpublished Ph.D. Thesis. University of California, Davis, 1982.

Kennedy, C. and A.P. Thirwall. "Surveys in Applied Economics—Technical Progress." *Economic Journal* Vol. 82, No. 325 (March 1972): 11–72.

Khaldi, N. "Education and Allocative Efficiency in U.S. Agriculture." *American Journal of Agricultural Economics* Vol. 57, No. 4 (November 1975): 650–57.

Kim, C.S., G. Schaible, J. Hamilton and K. Barney. "Economic Impacts on Consumers, Growers, and Processors Resulting from Mechanical Tomato Harvesting in California—Revisited." *Journal of Agricultural Economics Research* Vol. 39, No. 2 (Spring 1987): 39–45.

Klein, K.K. and W.H. Furtan, eds. *Economics of Agricultural Research in Canada.* Alberta, Canada: The University of Calgary Press, 1985.

Kling, C.L. "The Reliability of Estimates of Environmental Benefits from Recreation Demand Models." *American Journal of Agricultural Economics* Vol. 70, No. 4 (November 1988): 892–901.

Kling, C.L. "Estimating the Precision of Welfare Measures." *Journal of Environmental Economics and Management* Vol. 21, No. 3 (November 1991): 244–59.

Kling, C.L. "Some Results on the Variance of Welfare Estimates from Recreation Demand Models." *Land Economics* Vol.

68, No. 3 (August 1992): 318–28.

Kmenta, J. and R. Gilbert. "Small Sample Properties of Alternative Estimators of Seemingly Unrelated Regressions." *Journal of American Statistical Association* Vol. 63, No. 324 (December 1986): 1180–2000.

Kohli, U. *Technology, Duality and Foreign Trade: The GNP Function Approach to Modeling Imports and Exports.* Ann Arbor: University of Michigan Press, 1991.

Kornbluth, J. "A Survey of Goal Programming." *Omega* Vol. 1, No. 2 (April 1973): 193–205.

Krueger, A.O. "Government Failures in Development." *Journal of Economic Perspectives* Vol. 4, No. 3 (Summer 1990): 9–23.

Krueger, A.O., M. Schiff and A. Valdés. "Agricultural Incentives in Developing Countries: Measuring the Effects of Sectoral and Economywide Policies." *World Bank Economic Review* Vol. 2, No. 3 (September 1988): 255–71.

Krueger, A.O., M. Schiff and A. Valdés, eds. *The Political Economy of Agricultural Pricing Policy. Volume I, Latin America.* Baltimore: Johns Hopkins University Press, 1991.

Lau, L.J. "A Characterization of the Normalized Restricted Profit Function." *Journal of Economic Theory* Vol. 12, No. 1 (February 1976): 131–63.

Lau, L.J. "On Exact Index Numbers." *Review of Economics and Statistics* Vol. 61, No. 1 (February 1979): 73–82.

Lau, L.J. and P.A. Yotopoulos. "Profit, Supply, and Factor Demand Functions." *American Journal of Agricultural Economics* Vol. 54, No. 1 (February 1971): 11–18.

Lau, L.J. and P.A. Yotopoulos. "The Meta-Production Function Approach to Technological Change in World Agriculture." *Journal of Development Economics* Vol. 31, No. 2 (October 1989): 241–69.

Lee, S.M. *Goal Programming for Decision Analysis*. Philadelphia: Auerbach, 1972.

Leiby, J.D. and G.D. Adams. "The Returns to Agricultural Research in Maine: The Case of a Small Northeastern Experiment Station." *Northeastern Journal of Agricultural and Resource Economics* Vol. 20, No. 1 (April 1991): 1–14.

Lekvall, P. and C. Wahlbin. "A Study of Some Assumptions Underlying Innovation Diffusion Functions." *Swedish Journal of Economics* Vol. 75, No. 4 (December 1973): 362–77.

Lemieux, C.M. and M.K. Wohlgenant. "Ex Ante Evaluation of the Economic Impact of Agricultural Biotechnology: The Case of Porcine Somatotropin." *American Journal of Agricultural Economics* Vol. 71, No. 4 (November 1989): 903–14.

Lichtenberg, E., D.P. Parker and D. Zilberman. "Marginal Analysis of Welfare Costs of Environmental Policies: The Case of Pesticide Regulation." *American Journal of Agricultural Economics* Vol. 70, No. 4 (November 1988): 868–74.

Lim, H. and C.R. Shumway. "Separability in State-Level Agricultural Technology." *American Journal of Agricultural Economics* Vol. 74, No. 1 (February 1992): 120–31.

Lima, M. and G.W. Norton. "Determinación de Prioridades de Investigación Agropecuaria en Venezuela." Fondo Nacional de Investigaciones Agropecuarias and International Service for National Agricultural Research, Maracay, Venezuela and The Hague, September, 1993. Mimeo.

Lindner, R.K. "Adoption as a Decision Theoretic Process." Unpublished Ph.D.

Thesis, University of Minnesota, St. Paul, 1981.

Lindner, R.K. "Toward a Framework for Evaluating Agricultural Economics Research." *Australian Journal of Agricultural Economics* Vol. 31, No. 2 (August 1987): 95–111.

Lindner, R.K. and F.G. Jarrett. "Supply Shifts and the Size of Research Benefits." *American Journal of Agricultural Economics* Vol. 60, No. 1 (February 1978): 48–58.

Lindner, R.K. and F.G. Jarrett. "Supply Shifts and the Size of Research Benefits: Reply." *American Journal of Agricultural Economics* Vol. 62, No. 4 (November 1980): 841–44.

Lindner, R.K., P.G. Pardey and F.G. Jarrett. "Distance to Information Source and the Time Lag to Early Adoption of Trace Element Fertilizers." *Australian Journal of Agricultural Economics* Vol. 26, No. 2 (August 1982): 98–113.

Lipton, M.L. "Accelerated Resource Degradation by Third World Agriculture: Created in the Commons, in the West, or in Bed." In S.A. Vosti, T. Reardon and W. von Urff, eds., *Agricultural Sustainability, Growth and Poverty Alleviation: Issues and Policies*. Washington, DC: International Food Policy Research Institute, 1991.

Lipton, M.L. with R. Longhurst. *New Seeds and Poor People*. Baltimore: Johns Hopkins University Press, 1989.

Little, I.M.D. *A Critique of Welfare Economics*. Oxford: Oxford University Press, 1960.

Little, I.M.D. and J.A. Mirrlees. *Project Appraisal and Planning for the Developing Countries*. London: Heineman Educational Books, 1974.

Lloyd, A.G., M. Harris and D.E. Tribe. *Australian Agricultural Research: Some Policy Issues*. Melbourne: Crawford Fund for International Agricultural Research, 1990.

Lloyd, P. and A. Schweinberger. "Trade Expenditure Functions and the Gains from Trade." *Journal of International Economics* Vol. 24, No. 3 (May 1988): 257–97.

Lopez, R.E. "The Structure of Production and the Derived Demand for Inputs in Canadian Agriculture." *American Journal of Agricultural Economics* Vol. 62, No. 1 (February 1980): 38–45.

Lopez, R.E. "Estimating Substitution and Expansion Effects Using a Profit Function Approach." *American Journal of Agricultural Economics* Vol. 66, No. 3 (August 1984): 358–67.

Lopez, R.E. "Supply Response and Investment in the Canadian Food Processing Industry." *American Journal of Agricultural Economics* Vol. 67, No. 1 (February 1985): 40–8. 1985a.

Lopez, R.E. "Structural Implications of a Class of Flexible Functional Forms for Profit Functions." *International Economic Review* Vol. 26, No. 3 (October 1985): 593–601. 1985b.

Lucas, R.E. "Adjustment Cost and the Theory of Supply." *Journal of Political Economy* Vol. 75, No. 4 (August 1967): 321–34.

Lynam, J.K. and P.G. Jones. "Benefits of Technical Change as Measured by Supply Shifts: An Integration of Theory and Practice." Centro Internacional de Agricultura Tropical, Colombia, February 1984. Mimeo.

Lyu, S.-J. L., F.C. White and Y.-C. Lu. "Estimating Effects of Agricultural Research and Extension Expenditures on Productivity: A Translog Production Function Approach." *Southern Journal of Agricultural Economics* Vol. 16, No. 2 (December 1984): 1–8.

Macagno, L.F. "The Nature and Distribution of Gains from Quality Improving Research in a Multimarket Framework: The Case of Barley." Unpublished Ph.D. Thesis, University of Minnesota, St. Paul, September 1990.

Maddala, G.S. *Econometrics.* New York: McGraw Hill, 1977.

Mahlstede, J.P. "Long-Range Planning at the Iowa Agricultural and Home Economics Experiment Stations." In W.L. Fishel, ed., *Resource Allocation in Agricultural Research.* Minneapolis: University of Minnesota Press, 1971.

Mansfield, E. "Basic Research and Productivity Increase in Manufacturing." *American Economic Review* Vol. 70, No. 5 (December 1980): 863–73.

Mansfield, E. "Price Indexes for R and D Inputs, 1969–1983." *Management Science* Vol. 33, No. 1 (January 1987): 124–9.

Maredia, M.K. *The Economics of the International Transfer of Wheat Varieties.* Unpublished Ph.D. Thesis, Michigan State University, East Lansing, 1993.

Markowitz, H.M. "Portfolio Selection." *Journal of Finance* Vol. 7 (March 1952): 77–91.

Marschak, J. and W.H. Andrews. "Random Simultaneous Equations and the Theory of Production." *Econometrica* Vol. 12, No. 3 (July-October 1944): 143–206.

Marshall, A. *Principles of Economics.* London: Macmillan, 1890.

Martin, M.A. and J. Havlicek, Jr. "Some Welfare Implications of the Adoption of Mechanical Cotton Harvesters in the United States." *American Journal of Agricultural Economics* Vol. 59, No. 4 (November 1977): 737–44.

Martin, W.J. and J.M. Alston. *An Exact Approach for Evaluating the Benefits from Technological Change.* Policy Research Working Paper Series No. WPS 1024. Washington, DC: International

Economics Department, World Bank, November 1992.

Martin, W.J. and J.M. Alston. "Trade Distortions and the Global and Domestic Impacts of Technological Change in Agriculture." Invited paper presented at the International Trade Research Consortium Meeting, Calabria, Italy, June 1993.

Martin, W.J. and J.M. Alston. "A Dual Approach to Evaluating Research Benefits in the Presence of Trade Distortions." *American Journal of Agricultural Economics* Vol. 76, No. 1 (February 1994): 26–35.

Mayshar, J. "On Measures of Excess Burden and Their Application." *Journal of Public Economics* Vol. 43, No. 3 (December 1990): 263–89.

McCalla, A.F. and J.G. Ryan. "Setting Agricultural Research Priorities: Lessons from the CGIAR Study." *American Journal of Agricultural Economics* Vol. 74, No. 5 (December 1992): 1095–100.

McCloskey, D.N. *The Rhetoric of Economics.* Madison: University of Wisconsin Press, 1985.

McElroy, M.B. "Additive General Error Models for Production, Cost, and Derived Demand or Share Systems." *Journal of Political Economy* Vol. 95, No. 4 (August 1987): 737–57.

McFadden, D. "Factor Substitutability in the Economic Analysis of Production." Unpublished Ph.D. Thesis, University of Minnesota, Minneapolis, 1962.

McKay, L., D. Lawrence and C. Vlastuin. "Production Flexibility and Technical Change in Australia's Wheat-Sheep Zone." *Review of Marketing and Agricultural Economics* Vol. 50, No. 1 (April 1982): 9–26.

McKay, L., D. Lawrence and C. Vlastuin. "Profit, Output Supply, and Input Demand Functions for Multi-Product Firms: The Case of Australian Agriculture." *International Economic Review* Vol. 24, No. 2 (June 1983): 323–39.

McKenzie, G.W. *Measuring Economic Welfare: New Methods.* Cambridge: Cambridge University Press, 1983.

McKenzie, G.W. and I.F. Pearce. "Welfare Measurement—A Synthesis." *American Economic Review* Vol. 72, No. 4 (September 1982): 669–82.

McNally, M.M. "Strategic Trade Interaction in the International Wheat Market." Unpublished Ph.D. Thesis, University of California, Davis, 1993.

Medina Castro, H. "Prioridades de Investigación Agropecuaria en Costa Rica Bajo Differentes Escenarios." San José, Costa Rica: Instituto Interamericano de Cooperación para la Agricultura, November 1991.

Medina Castro, H. "Prioridades de Investigación Agropecuaria en Los Países de America Central." San José, Costa Rica: Instituto Interamericano de Cooperación para la Agricultura, June 1993.

Mellor, J.W. and B.F. Johnston. "The World Food Equation: Interrelations among Development, Employment and Food Consumption." *Journal of Economic Literature* Vol. 22, No. 2 (June 1984): 531–74.

de Melo, J. and S. Robinson. "Trade Policy and Resource Allocation in the Presence of Product Differentiation." *Review of Economics and Statistics* Vol. 63, No. 2 (May 1981): 169–77.

Miedema, A.K. "The Retail-Farm Price Ratio, the Farmer's Share and Technical Change." *American Journal of Agricultural Economics* Vol. 58, No. 4 (November 1976): 750–56.

Mikesell, R.F. "Project Evaluation and Sustainable Development." In R. Goodland, H. Daly and S. El Serafy, eds.,

Environmentally Sustainable Economic Development: Building on Bruntland. World Bank Environmental Working Paper 46. Washington, DC: World Bank, July 1991.

Miller, G.Y., J.M. Rosenblatt and L.J. Hushak. "The Effects of Supply Shifts on Producers' Surplus." *American Journal of Agricultural Economics* Vol. 70, No. 4 (November 1988): 886–91.

Miller, W.L. and D.M. Byers. "Development and Display of Multiple Objective Project Impacts." *Water Resources Research* Vol. 9, No. 1 (February 1973): 11–20.

Minasian, J.R. "Research and Development, Production Functions, and Rates of Return." *American Economic Review* Vol. 59, No. 2 (May 1969): 80–5.

Mishan, E.J. *Elements of Cost-Benefit Analysis.* London: George Allen and Unwin Ltd, 1972.

Mishan, E.J. *Cost-Benefit Analysis: An Introduction.* New York: Praeger Publishers, 1976.

Mishan, E.J. *Introduction to Normative Economics.* New York: Oxford University Press, 1981.

Mishan, E.J. *What Political Economy Is All About—An Exposition and Critique.* Cambridge: Cambridge University Press, 1982.

Monke, E.A. and S.R. Pearson. *The Policy Analysis Matrix for Agricultural Development.* Ithaca: Cornell University Press, 1989.

Moore, J.R. and N.R. Baker. "Computational Analysis of Scoring Models for R&D Project Selection." *Management Science* Vol. 16, No. 4 (December 1969): B212–32.

Moscardi, E.R. "Allocating Resources for Agricultural Research and Extension in Argentina: Experiences of I.N.T.A." Paper presented at the conference on Allocating Resources for Developing Country Agricultural Research, Bellagio, Italy, 6–10 July 1987.

Moscoso, W., A. Coutu, D. Bandy and G.W. Norton. *Contenido Técnico de la Investigación del Instituto Dominicana de Investigaciones Agropecuarias.* Report prepared for ISNAR. Dominican Republic: Instituto Superior de Agricultura, June 1986.

Mullen, J.D. and J.M. Alston. *The Returns to the Australian Wool Industry from Investment in R&D.* Division of Rural & Resource Economics Report No. 10. Sydney: New South Wales Department of Agriculture & Fisheries, 1990.

Mullen, J.D. and J.M. Alston. "The Impact on the Australian Lamb Industry of Producing Larger Leaner Lamb." *Australian Journal of Agricultural Economics* Vol. 62, No. 1 (April 1994): 43–61.

Mullen, J.D., J.M. Alston and M.K. Wohlgenant. "The Impact of Farm and Processing Research in the Australian Wool Industry." *Australian Journal of Agricultural Economics* Vol. 33, No. 1 (April 1989): 32–47.

Mullen, J.D., T.L. Cox and W.E. Foster. "Measuring Productivity Growth in Australian Broadacre Agriculture." Paper presented to the Annual Conference of the Australian Agricultural Economics Society. Canberra, February 1992. Mimeo.

Mullen, J.D., M.K. Wohlgenant and D.E. Farris. "Input Substitution and the Distribution of Surplus Gains from Lower U.S. Beef Processing Costs." *American Journal of Agricultural Economics* Vol. 70, No. 2 (May 1988): 245–54.

Mundlak, Y. "Elasticities of Substitution and The Theory of Derived Demand." *Reviw of Economic Studies* Vol. 35, No. 2 (April 1968): 225–36.

Murphy, J.A., W.H. Furtan and A. Schmitz.

"The Gains from Agricultural Research under Distorted Trade." *Journal of Public Economics* Vol. 51, No. 2 (June 1993): 161–72.

Musalem, A.R. "Social Rates of Return and Other Aspects of Agricultural Research: The Case of Cotton Research in Sao Paulo, Brazil: Comment." *American Journal of Agricultural Economics* Vol. 56, No. 4 (November 1974): 837–39.

Muth, R.F. "The Derived Demand Curve for a Productive Factor and the Industry Supply Curve." *Oxford Economic Papers* Vol. 16, No. 2 (July 1964): 221–34.

Nagy, J. "The Pakistan Agricultural Development Model: An Economic Evaluation of Agricultural Research and Extension Expenditures." Unpublished Ph.D. Thesis, University of Minnesota, St. Paul, 1984.

Neely, W.P., R.M. North and J.E. Fortson. "An Operational Approach to Multiple Objective Decision-Making for Public Water Resources Projects Using Integer Goal Progamming." *American Journal of Agricultural Economics* Vol. 59, No. 1 (February 1977): 198–203.

Nelson, R.R. and S.G. Winter. *An Evolutionary Theory of Economic Change.* Cambridge, MA: Harvard University Press, 1982.

Nerlove, M. "Estimates of the Elasticity of Supply of Selected Agricultural Commodities." *Journal of Farm Economics* Vol. 38, No. 2 (May 1956): 496–509.

Nerlove, M. "Returns to Scale in Electricity Supply." In C.F. Christ, et al., eds., *Measurement in Economics: Studies in Mathematical Economics and Econometrics.* Stanford: Stanford University Press, 1963.

Nguyen, D. "Intersectoral Distributional Implications of Agricultural Technical Progress in an Open Economy: An Extension." *American Journal of Agricultural Economics* Vol. 59, No. 2 (May 1977): 307–74.

North, D.C. "Government and the Cost of Exchange in History." *Journal of Economic History* Vol. 44, No. 2 (June 1984): 255–64.

North, D.C. "Institutions, Transactions Costs, and Economic Growth." *Economic Inquiry* Vol. 25, No. 3 (July 1987): 419–28.

Norton, G.W. "Scoring Methods." In D. Horton, P.G. Ballantyne, W. Peterson, B. Uribe, D. Gapasin and K. Sheridan, eds., *Monitoring and Evaluating Agricultural Research: A Sourcebook.* Wallingford, U.K.: CAB International, 1993.

Norton, G.W. and J.S. Davis. "Evaluating Returns to Agricultural Research: A Review." *American Journal of Agricultural Economics* Vol. 63, No. 4 (November 1981): 683–99.

Norton, G.W. and V.G. Ganoza. "Guidelines for Allocations of Resources to Agricultural Research and Extension in Peru." Paper prepared for INIPA and USAID. Lima, Peru, February 1986. Mimeo.

Norton, G.W. and P.G. Pardey. *Priority Setting Mechanisms for National Agricultural Research Systems: Present Experience and Future Needs.* ISNAR Working Paper No.7. The Hague: International Service for National Agricultural Research, November 1987.

Norton, G.W. and G.E. Schuh. "Evaluating Returns to Social Science Research: Issues and Possible Methods." In G.W. Norton, W.L. Fishel, A.A. Paulsen and W.B. Sundquist, eds. *Evaluation of Agricultural Research.* Minnesota Agricultural Experiment Station Miscellaneous Publication 8–1981, St. Paul: University of Minnesota, April 1981.

Norton, G.W., J.D. Coffey and E.B. Frye. "Estimating Returns to Agricultural Research, Extension, and Teaching at the State Level." *Southern Journal of Agricultural Economics* Vol. 16, No. 1 (July 1984): 121–28.

Norton, G.W., V.G. Ganoza and C. Pomareda. "Potential Benefits of Agricultural Research and Extension in Peru." *American Journal of Agricultural Economics* Vol. 69, No. 2 (May 1987): 247–57.

Norton, G.W., P.G. Pardey, and J.M. Alston. "Economic Issues in Agricultural Research Priority Setting." *American Journal of Agricultural Economics* Vol. 74, No. 5 (December 1992): 1089–94.

Norton, G.W., W.L. Fishel, A.A. Paulsen and W.B. Sundquist, eds. *Evaluation of Agricultural Research*. Minnesota Agricultural Experiment Station Miscellaneous Publication 8–1981. St. Paul: University of Minnesota, April 1981.

OECD. *The Measurement of Scientific and Technical Activities—"Frascati Manual" 1980*. Paris: Organization for Economic Cooperation and Development, 1981.

OECD. *National Policies and Agricultural Trade*. Paris: Organization for Economic Cooperation and Development, 1987.

OECD. *Environmental Policy Benefits: Monetary Valuation*. Paris: Organization for Economic Cooperation and Development, 1989.

Oehmke, J.F. *A Multiple Objective Explanation of Government Research and Target Price Policy*. Staff Paper 88–5. East Lansing: Department of Agricultural Economics, Michigan State University, January 1988a.

Oehmke, J.F. "The Calculation of Returns to Research in Distorted Markets." *Agricultural Economics* Vol. 2, No. 4 (December 1988): 291–302. 1988b.

Oehmke, J.F. "The Calculation of Returns to Research in Distorted Markets: Reply." *Agricultural Economics* Vol. 5, No. 1 (January 1991): 83–8.

Oehmke, J.F. and X. Yao. "A Policy Preference Function for Government Intervention in the U.S. Wheat Market." *American Journal of Agricultural Economics* Vol. 72, No. 3 (August 1990): 631–40.

Office of Technology Assessment (OTA). *Federally Funded Research: Decisions for a Decade*. Washington, DC: Congress of the United States, May 1991.

Ohta, M. "A Note on the Duality Between Production and Cost Functions: Rate of Returns to Scale and Rate of Technical Progress." *Economic Studies Quarterly* Vol. 25, No. 3 (December 1994): 63–5.

Oskam, A. "Productivity Measurement, Incorporating Environmental Effects of Agricultural Production." In K. Burger et al., eds., *Agricultural Economics and Policy: International Challenges for the Nineties*. Amsterdam: Elsevier, 1991.

Otto, D.M. "An Economic Assessment of Research and Extension Investments in Corn, Wheat, Soybean, and Sorghum." Unpublished Ph.D. Thesis, Virginia Polytechnic Institute and State University, Blacksburg, Virginia, 1981.

Pachico, D., J.K. Lynam and P.G. Jones. "The Distribution of Benefits from Technical Change among Classes of Consumers and Producers: An Ex-Ante Analysis of Beans in Brazil." *Research Policy* Vol. 16, No. 5 (October 1987): 279–85.

Pakes, A. and Z. Griliches. "Patents and R&D at the Firm Level: A First Report." *Economics Letters* Vol. 5, No. 4 (April 1980): 377–81.

Palomino, J. and G.W. Norton. "Determinación de Prioridades de Investigación en Ecuador." Unpublished Report. Quito, Ecuador: INIAP/FUNDAGRO/

ISNAR, July 1992a.

Palomino, J. and G.W. Norton. "Evalua-icón de Investigación Agropecuarias en Ecuador: El Case de Maíz." Quito, Ecuador: INIAP/FUNDAGRO/ISNAR, November 1992. Unpublished Report. (1992b).

Pardey, P.G. "The Diffusion of Trace Element Technology: An Economic Analysis." Unpublished M.Sc. Thesis, University of Adelaide, Adelaide, 1978.

Pardey, P.G. "Public Sector Production of Agricultural Knowledge." Unpublished Ph.D. Thesis, University of Minnesota, St. Paul, 1986.

Pardey, P.G. "The Agricultural Knowledge Production Function: An Empirical Look." *Review of Economics and Statistics* Vol. 71, No. 33 (August 1989): 453–61.

Pardey, P.G. and B. Craig. "Causal Relationships between Public Sector Agricultural Research Expenditures and Output." *American Journal of Agricultural Economics* Vol. 71, No. 1 (February 1989): 9–19.

Pardey, P.G. and J. Roseboom. *ISNAR Agricultural Research Indicator Series: A Global Database on National Agricultural Research Systems.* Cambridge: Cambridge University Press, 1989.

Pardey, P.G. and S. Wood. "Targeting Research by Agricultural Environments." In J.R. Anderson, ed., *Agricultural Technology: Current Policy Issues for the International Community.* Wallingford, U.K.: CAB International, 1994.

Pardey, P.G., B.J. Craig and M.L. Hallaway. "U.S. Agricultural Research Deflators: 1890–1985." *Research Policy* Vol. 18, No. 5 (October 1989): 289–96.

Pardey, P.G., J. Roseboom and J.R. Anderson, eds. *Agricultural Research Policy: International Quantitative Perspectives.* Cambridge: Cambridge University Press, 1991.

Pardey, P.G., J. Roseboom and B.J. Craig. "A Yardstick for International Comparisons: An Application to National Agricultural Research Expenditures." *Economic Development and Cultural Change* Vol. 40, No. 2 (January 1992): 333–49.

Pardey, P.G., R.K. Lindner, E. Abdurachman, S. Wood, S. Fan, W.M. Eveleens, B. Zhang and J.M. Alston. *The Economic Returns to Indonesian Rice and Soybean Research.* Unpublished AARD/ISNAR Report. Jakarta and The Hague: Agency for Agricultural Research and Development and International Service for National Agricultural Research, November 1992.

Paris, Q. *An Economic Interpretation of Linear Programming.* Ames: Iowa State University Press, 1991.

Parton, K.A., J.R. Anderson and J.P. Makeham. *Evaluation Methods for Australian Wool Production Research.* Agricultural Economics Bulletin No. 29. Armidale, Australia: University of New England, 1984.

Paulsen, A. and D.R. Kaldor. "Evaluation and Planning of Research in the Experiment Station." *American Journal of Agricultural Economics* Vol. 50, No. 5 (December 1968): 1149–62.

Paz, L.J. "A Methodology for Establishing Priorities for Research on Agricultural Products." in D. Daniels and B. Nestel, eds. *Resource Allocation to Agricultural Research.* Ottawa, Canada: International Development Research Center, 1981.

Pearce, D., E. Barbier and A. Markandya. *Sustainable Development: Economics and Environment in the Third World.* Aldershot: Edward Elgar, 1990.

Pearl, R. *Studies in Human Biology.* Baltimore: Williams and Wilkins, 1924.

Perrin, R.K. "Asset Replacement Principles." *American Journal of Agricultural Economics* Vo. 54, No. 1 (February 1972): 60–7.

Perrin, R.K. "The Impact of Component Pricing of Soybeans and Milk." *American Journal of Agricultural Economics* Vol. 62, No. 3 (August 1980): 445–55.

Perrin, R.K. "Equilibrium Displacement Models." EB641 Class Notes. Department of Economics and Business, North Carolina State University, 1981. Mimeo.

Perrin, R.K. "Ex-Ante Evaluation of Experimental Technology." Department of Agricultural and Resource Economics, North Carolina State University, 1992. Mimeo.

Perrin, R.K. and G.M. Scobie. "Market Intervention Policies for Increasing the Consumption of Nutrients by Low Income Households." *American Journal of Agricultural Economics* Vol. 63, No. 1 (February 1981): 73–82.

Persley, G.J., ed. *Agricultural Biotechnology: Opportunities for International Development.* Wallingford, U.K.: CAB International, 1990.

Peterson, W.L. "Return to Poultry Research in the United States." *Journal of Farm Economics* Vol. 49, No. 3 (August 1967): 656–70.

Peterson, W.L. "International Farm Prices and the Social Cost of Cheap Food Policies." *American Journal of Agricultural Economics* Vol. 61, No. 1 (February 1979): 12–21.

Peterson, W.L. "Land Quality and Prices." *American Journal of Agricultural Economics* Vol. 68, No. 4 (November 1986): 812–9.

Peterson, W.L. and Y. Hayami. "Technical Change in Agriculture." In L.R. Martin, ed., *A Survey of Agricultural Economics Literature. Volume 1.* Minneapolis: University of Minnesota Press, 1977.

Phlips, L. *Applied Consumption Analysis.* Amsterdam: North-Holland, 1974.

Pingali, P. and P. Roger, eds. *Impact of Pesticides on the Rice Environment and Human Health.* Boston: Kluwer Academic Publishers, 1995.

Pinstrup-Andersen, P. "Decision-Making on Food and Agricultural Research Policy: The Distribution of Benefits New Agricultural Technology among Consumer Income Strata." *Agricultural Administration* Vol. 4, No. 1 (January 1977): 13–28.

Pinstrup-Andersen, P. "A Methodological Note on the Measurement of the Nutrition Impact of Agricultural Research." Paper prepared for workshop on *Methodological Problems in Measuring Research Impact.* CGIAR Secretariat, World Bank, Washington, DC, April 1984.

Pinstrup-Andersen, P. and D. Franklin. "A Systems Approach to Agricultural Research Resource Allocation in Developing Countries." In T.M. Arndt, D.G. Dalrymple and V.W. Ruttan, eds., *Resource Allocation and Productivity in National and International Research.* Minneapolis: University of Minnesota Press, 1977.

Pinstrup-Andersen, P., N. Ruiz de Londoño and E. Hoover. "The Impact of Increasing Food Supply on Human Nutrition: Implications for Commodity Priorities in Agricultural Research." *American Journal of Agricultural Economics* Vol. 58, No. 2 (May 1976): 131–42.

Pomareda, C. "A Spatial Equilibrum Model for the Central American Agricultural Sector." Guatemala: ECID, 1978

Pope. R.D. "To Dual or Not to Dual?" *Western Journal of Agricultural Economics* Vol. 7, No. 2 (December 1982): 337–52.

Pray, C.E. and C.F. Neumeyer. "Problems

of Omitting Private Investments in Research When Measuring the Impact of Public Research." In R.G. Echeverría, ed., *Methods for Diagnosing Research System Constraints and Assessing the Impact of Agricultural Research. Volume II, Assessing the Impact of Agricultural Research.* The Hague: International Service for National Agricultural Research, 1990.

Prescott, E.C. and M. Visscher. "Organization Capital." *Journal of Political Economy* Vol. 88, No. 3 (July 1980): 446–61.

Rao, D.S.P. *Intercountry Comparison of Agricultural Output and Productivity.* FAO Economic and Social Development Paper No. 112. Rome: Food and Agriculture Organization, 1993.

Ravenscraft, D. and F.M. Scherer. "The Lag Structure of Returns to Research and Development." *Applied Economics* Vol. 14, No. 6 (December 1982): 603–20.

Ray, A. *Cost-Benefit Analysis: Issues and Methodologies.* Baltimore: Johns Hopkins University Press, 1986.

Ray, S. "A Translog Cost Function Analysis of U.S. Agriculture, 1939–77." *American Journal of Agricultural Economics* Vol. 64, No. 3 (August 1982): 490–98.

Richter, M.K. "Invariance Axioms and Economic Indexes." *Econometrica* Vol. 34, No. 4 (December 1966): 739–55.

Robinson, S. *Multisectoral Models of Developing Countries: A Survey.* Department of Agricultural and Resource Economics Working Paper No. 401. Berkeley: University of California at Berkeley, 1986.

Roe, T.L. and P.G. Pardey. "Economic Policy and Investment in Rural Public Goods: A Political Economy Perspective." In P.G. Pardey, J. Roseboom and J.R. Anderson, eds., *Agricultural Research Policy: International Quantitative Perspectives.* Cambridge: Cambridge University Press, 1991.

Romano, L. "Economic Evaluation of the Colombian Agricultural Research System." Unpublished Ph.D. Thesis, Oklahoma State University, Stillwater, 1987.

Romero, C., F. Amador and A. Barco. "Multiple Objectives in Agricultural Planning: A Compromise Programming Application." *American Journal of Agricultural Economics* Vol. 69, No. 1 (February 1987): 78–86.

Rose, R.N. "Supply Shifts and Research Benefits: A Comment." *American Journal of Agricultural Economics* Vol. 62, No. 4 (November 1980): 834–44.

Roseboom, J. and P.G. Pardey. *Statistical Brief on the National Agricultural Research System of Kenya.* Statistical Brief No. 5. The Hague: International Service for National Agricultural Research, November 1993.

Rosenberg, N. *Perspective on Technology.* Cambridge: Cambridge University Press, 1976.

Ruble. W. "Improving the Computation of Simultaneous Stochastic Linear Equation Estimates." Unpublished Ph.D. Thesis, Michigan State University, East Lansing, 1968.

Runge, C.F. and R.J. Myers. "Shifting Foundations of Agricultural Policy Analysis: Welfare Economics When Risk Markets Are Incomplete." *American Journal of Agricultural Economics* Vol. 67, No. 5 (December 1985): 1010–16.

Russell, D.G. "Resource Allocation in Agricultural Research Using Socio-Economic Evaluation and Mathematical Models." *Canadian Journal of Agricultural Economics* Vol. 23, No. 2 (July 1975): 29–52.

Ruttan, V.W. "The Green Revolution:

Seven Generalizations." *International Development Review* Vol. 19, No. 4 (August 1977): 13–16.

Ruttan, V.W. *Agricultural Research Policy.* Minneapolis: University of Minnesota Press, 1982.

Ruttan, V.W. "Why Foreign Economic Assistance?" *Economic Development and Cultural Change* Vol. 37, No. 2 (January 1989): 411–24.

Ruttan, V.W. "Constraints on the Design of Sustainable Systems of Agricultural Production." *Ecological Economics* Vol. 10 (1994): 209–19.

Ruttan, V.W. and Y. Hayami. "Technology Transfer and Development." *Technology and Culture* Vol. 14, No. 2 (April 1973): 119–51.

Ryan, J.G. and J.S. Davis. *A Decision Support System to Assist Agricultural Research Priority Setting: Experience at ACIAR and Possible Adaptations for the TAC/CGIAR.* ACIAR/ISNAR Project Paper No. 17. Canberra: Australian Centre for International Agricultural Research, March 1990.

Sakong, Y. and D.J. Hayes. "Testing the Stability of Preferences: A Nonparametric Approach." *American Journal of Agricultural Economics* Vol. 75, No. 2 (May 1993): 269–77.

Samuelson, P.A. "Prices of Factors and Goods in General Equilibrium." *Review of Economic Studies* Vol. 21 (1953/54): 1–20.

Sarhangi, R.F., J. Logan, R.C. Duncan and P. Hagan. "Who Benefits from Agricultural Research: Comment." *Review of Marketing and Agricultural Economics* Vol. 45, No. 4 (December 1977): 179–85.

Sarles, M. "USAID Experiments with the Private Sector in Agricultural Research in Latin America." In R.G. Echeverría, ed., *Methods for Diagnosing Research*

System Constraints and Assessing the Impact of Agricultural Research. Volume I, Diagnosing Research System Constraints. The Hague: International Service for National Agricultural Research, 1990.

Schimmelpfennig, D. and C. Thirtle. "Cointegration, and Causality: Exploring the Relationship Between Agricultural R&D and Productivity." *Journal of Agricultural Economics* Vol. 45, No. 2 (May 1994): 220–31.

Schmitz, A. and D. Seckler. "Mechanized Agriculture and Social Welfare: The Case of the Tomato Harvester." *American Journal of Agricultural Economics* Vol. 52, No. 4 (November 1970): 569–77.

Schuh, G.E. and H. Tollini. *Costs and Benefits of Agricultural Research: The State of the Arts.* World Bank Staff Working Paper No. 360. Washington, DC: The World Bank, October 1979.

Schultz, T.W. *The Economic Organization of Agriculture.* New York: McGraw-Hill, 1953. 1953a.

Schultz, T.W. "Gauging the Relevant Income Elasticity." In T.W. Schultz, *The Economic Organization of Agriculture.* New York: McGraw-Hill, 1953. 1953b.

Schultz, T.W. "Reflections on Agricultural Production, Output and Supply." *Journal of Farm Economics* Vol. 38, No. 3 (August 1956): 748–62.

Schultz, T.W. "The Value of the Ability to Deal with Disequilibria." *Journal of Economic Literature* Vol. 13, No. 3 (September 1975): 827–46.

Schultz, T.W. "Uneven Prospects for Gains from Agricultural Research Related to Economic Policy." In T.M. Arndt, D.G. Dalrymple, and V.W. Ruttan, eds., *Resource Allocation and Productivity in National and International Agricultural Research.* Minneapolis: University of

Minnesota Press, 1977.

Schultz, T.W. "On Economics and Politics of Agriculture." In T.W. Schultz, ed., *Distortions in Agricultural Incentives.* Bloomington: Indiana University Press, 1978.

Schultz, T.W. "The Economics of Agricultural Research." In C.K. Eicher and J.M. Staatz, eds., *Agricultural Development in the Third World* (Second edition). Baltimore: Johns Hopkins University Press, 1990.

Scobie, G.M. "Who Benefits from Agricultural Research?" *Review of Marketing and Agricultural Economics* Vol. 44, No. 4 (December 1976): 197–202.

Scobie, G.M. "The Demand for Agricultural Research: A Colombian Illustration." *American Journal of Agricultural Economics* Vol. 61, No. 3 (August 1979): 540–45. 1979a.

Scobie, G.M. *Investment in International Agricultural Research: Some Economic Dimensions.* World Bank Staff Working Paper No. 361. Washington, DC: The World Bank, October 1979b.

Scobie, G.M. "On Estimating Money Flexibility: A Note." *American Economist* Vol. 24, No. 1 (Spring 1980): 76–8.

Scobie, G.M. *Investment in Agricultural Research: Some Economic Principles.* CIMMYT Working Paper 08/84. Mexico: Centro Internacional de Mejoramiento de Maíz y Trigo, August 1984.

Scobie, G.M. and W.M. Eveleens. *The Return to Investment in Agricultural Research in New Zealand: 1926–27 to 1983–84.* Economics Division Research Report 1/87. Hamilton, New Zealand: Ministry of Agriculture and Fisheries , October 1987.

Scobie, G.M. and V. Jacobsen. *Allocation of R&D Funds in the Australian Wool Industry.* Hamilton, New Zealand: Department of Economics, University of Waikato, 1992.

Scobie, G.M. and V. Jardine. *Investing in Wool Research and Development: Allocating Research Budgets.* Hamilton, New Zealand: Scobie Economic Research, February 1988.

Scobie, G.M. and R.T. Posada. *The Impact of High-Yielding Rice Varieties in Latin America—with Special Emphasis on Colombia.* Series JE-01. Cali, Colombia: Centro Internacional de Agricultura Tropical, April 1977.

Scobie, G.M. and R.T. Posada. "The Impact of Technical Change on Income Distribution: The Case of Rice in Colombia." *American Journal of Agricultural Economics* Vol. 60, No. 1 (February 1978): 85–92.

Scobie, G.M., J.D. Mullen and J.M. Alston. "The Returns to Investment in Research on Australian Wool Production." *Australian Journal of Agricultural Economics* Vol. 35, No. 2 (August 1991): 179–95.

Seaton, M.L. "Interactions between Basic and Applied Research: The Example of Multiple Disease Resistant Potato Cultivar Development." Unpublished M.S. Thesis, Virginia Polytechnic Institute and State University, Blacksburg, Virginia, 1986.

Senauer, B., E. Asp and J. Kinsey. *Food Trends and the Changing Consumer.* St. Paul: Eagan Press, 1991.

Shephard, R. *Cost and Production Functions.* Princeton: Princeton University Press, 1953.

Shumway, C.R. "Allocation of Scarce Resources to Agricultural Research: Review of Methodology." *American Journal of Agricultural Economics* Vol. 55, No. 4 (November 1973): 557–66.

Shumway, C.R. "Models and Methods Used to Allocate Resources in Agricultural Research: A Critical Review." In

T.M. Arndt, D.G. Dalrymple and V.W. Ruttan, eds., *Resource Allocation and Productivity in National and International Research*. Minneapolis: University of Minnesota Press, 1977.

Shumway, C.R. "Supply, Demand, and Technology in Multi-Product Industry: Texas Field Crops." *American Journal of Agricultural Economics* Vol. 65, No. 4 (November 1983): 748–60.

Shumway, C.R. "The Statistical Base for Agricultural Productivity Research: A Review and Critique." In S.M. Capalbo and J.M. Antle, eds., *Agricultural Productivity: Measurement and Explanation*. Washington, DC: Resources for the Future, 1988.

Shumway, C.R. and R.J. McCracken. "Use of Scoring Models in Evaluating Research Programs." *American Journal of Agricultural Economics* Vol. 57, No. 4 (November 1975): 714–8.

Shumway, C.R., R.S. Saez and P.E. Gottret. "Multiproduct Supply and Input Demand in U.S. Agriculture." *American Journal of Agricultural Economics* Vol. 70, No. 2 (May 1988): 330–7.

Sidhu, S. and C. Banante. "Estimating Farm Land Input Demand and Wheat Supply in the Indian Punjab Using a Translog Profit Function." *American Journal of Agricultural Economics* Vol. 63, No. 2 (May 1981): 237–46.

Silver, J.L. and T.D. Wallace. "The Lag Relationship between Wholesale and Consumer Prices: An Application of the Hatanaka-Wallace Procedure." *Journal of Econometrics* Vol. 12, No. 3 (April 1980): 375–87.

Smith, V.K. "Estimating Recreation Demand Using the Properties of the Implied Consumer Surplus." *Land Economics* Vol. 66, No. 2 (May 1990): 111–20.

Smith, B.L., G.W. Norton and J. Havlicek Jr. "Impacts of Public Research Expenditures on Agricultural Value Added in the U.S. and the Northeast." *Journal of the Northeastern Agricultural Economics Council* Vol. 12, No. 2 (Fall 1983): 109–14.

Solow, R.M. "Technical Change and the Aggregate Production Function." *Review of Economics and Statistics* Vol. 39, No. 3 (August 1957): 312–20.

Solow, R.M. "On a Family of Distributed Lags." *Econometrica* Vol. 28, No. 2 (April 1960): 393–406.

Souder, W.E. "A Scoring Methodology for Assessing the Suitability of Management Science Models." *Management Science* Vol. 18, No. 10 (June 1972): 526–43.

Sprow, F.B. "Evaluation of Research Expenditures Using Triangular Distribution Functions and Monte Carlo Methods." *Industrial and Engineering Chemistry* Vol. 59, No. 7 (July 1967): 35–8.

Squire, L. and H.G. van der Tak. *Economic Analysis of Projects*. Baltimore: Johns Hopkins University Press, 1975.

Squires, D. "Long-Run Profit Functions for Multiproduct Firms." *American Journal of Agricultural Economics* Vol. 69, No. 3 (August 1987): 558–69.

Srinivasan, T.N. and J.N. Bhagwati. "Shadow Prices for Project Selection in the Presence of Distortions: Effective Rates of Protection and Domestic Resource Costs." *Journal of Political Economy* Vol. 86, No. 1 (February 1978): 97–116.

Stallings, J.L. "Weather Indexes." *Journal of Farm Economics* Vol. 42, No. 1 (February 1960): 180–6.

Star, S. "Accounting for the Growth of Output." *American Economic Review* Vol. 64, No. 1 (March 1974): 123–35.

Steuer, R.E. and F.W. Harris. "Inter-Set

Point Generation and Filtering in Decision and Criterion Space." *Computing and Operations Research* Vol. 7 (1980): 41–53.

Stevenson, R. "Measuring Technological Bias." *American Economic Review* Vol. 70, No. 1 (March 1980): 162–73.

Stiglitz, J.E. "The Inefficiency of the Stock Market Equilibrium." *Review of Economic Studies* Vol. 49, No. 2 (April 1982): 241–61.

Stiglitz, J.E. "Information and Economic Analysis: A Perspective." *Economic Journal* Vol. 95 (Supplement 1985): 21–41.

Stranahan, H.A. and J.S. Shonkweiler. "Evaluating Returns to Post Harvest Research in the Florida Citrus-Processing Subsector." *American Journal of Agricultural Economics* Vol. 68, No. 1 (February 1986): 88–94.

Summers, L.H. "Summers on Sustainable Growth." *The Economist* 30 May 1992, p. 71.

Sumner, D.A. and J.M. Alston. *Effects of the Tobacco Program: An Analysis of Decontrol.* Washington, DC: American Enterprise Institute for Public Policy Research, 1986.

Sundquist, W.B., ed. *Evaluating Agricultural Research and Productivity.* Minnesota Agricultural Experiment Station Miscellaneous Publication 52–1987. St. Paul: University of Minnesota, 1987.

Sundquist, W.B., ed. *The Economic Impacts of Agricultural Research.* Proceedings of a workshop sponsored by the Agricultural Research Institute, Washington, DC, May 1991.

Swallow, B.M., G.W. Norton, T.B. Brumback Jr. and J.R. Buss. *Agricultural Research Depreciation and the Importance of Maintenance Research.* Agricultural Economics Report No. 5. Blacksburg: Department of Agricultural Economics, Virginia Polytechnic Institute and State University, November 1985.

Swanson, E.R. "Problems of Applying Experimental Results to Commercial Practice." *Journal of Farm Economics* Vol. 39, No. 1 (February 1957): 382–9.

Teri, J., S.E. Mugogo and G.W. Norton. "Analysis of Agricultural Research Priorities in Tanzania." The Hague: International Service for National Agricultural Research, July 1990. Mimeo.

Thirtle, C.G. and V.W. Ruttan. *The Role of Demand and Supply in the Generation and Diffusion of Technical Change.* Chur, Switzerland: Harwood Academic Publishers, 1987.

Thompson, G.D. "Choice of Flexible Functional Forms: Review and Appraisal." *Western Journal of Agricultural Economics* Vol. 13, No. 2 (December 1988): 169–83.

Thurman, W. "Applied General Equilibrium Welfare Analysis." *American Journal of Agricultural Economics* Vol. 73, No. 5 (December 1991): 1508–16. 1991a.

Thurman, W. "On the Welfare Significance and Nonsignificance of General Equilibrium Demand and Supply Curves." Department of Agricultural and Resource Economics, North Carolina State University, Raleigh, 1991. Mimeo, 1991b.

Timmer, C.P. "On Measuring Technical Efficiency." *Food Research Institute Studies in Agricultural Economics, Trade, and Development* Vol. 9, No. 2 (1970): 99–171.

Tower, E. *Effective Protection, Domestic Resource Costs, and Shadow Prices: A General Equilibrium Perspective.* World Bank Staff Working Paper No. 664. Washington, DC: World Bank, September 1984.

Tower, E. and G. Pursell. *On Shadow Pricing.* World Bank Staff Working Paper No. 792. Washington, DC: World Bank, January 1986.

Traxler, G. and D. Byerlee. "A Joint-Product Analysis of the Adoption of Modern Cereal Varieties in Developing Countries." *American Journal of Agricultural Economics* Vol. 75, No. 4. (November 1993): 981–9.

Traxler, G. and D. Byerlee. "National and International Research in the Post-Green Revolution: Complement or Substitute Investments?" Paper presented at the annual meeting of the American Agricultural Economics Association, San Diego, CA, August 1994.

Trigo, E.J. *Agricultural Research Organization in the Developing World: Diversity and Evolution.* ISNAR Working Paper No. 4. The Hague: International Service for National Agricultural Research, 1986.

Tripp, R., ed. *Planned Change in Farming Systems: Progress in On-farm Research.* Chichester: John Wiley, 1991.

Tsakok, I. *Agricultural Price Policy—A Practioner's Guide to Partial-Equilibrium Analysis.* Ithaca: Cornell University Press, 1990.

Tweeten, L. "The Demand for U.S. Farm Output." *Food Research Institute Studies* Vol. 7, No. 3 (1967): 343–69.

Tweeten, L. "The Elasticity of Foreign Demand for U.S. Agricultural Products: Comment." *American Journal of Agricultural Economics* Vol. 59, No. 4 (November 1977): 737–8.

Tyers, R. and K. Anderson. *Disarray in World Food Markets: A Quantitative Assessment.* Cambridge: Cambridge University Press, 1992.

Ulrich, A., W.H. Furtan and A. Schmitz. "Public and Private Returns from Joint Venture Research: An Example from Agriculture." *Quarterly Journal of Economics* Vol. 101, No. 10 (February 1986): 101–29.

Ulrich, A., W.H. Furtan and A. Schmitz. "The Cost of a Licensing System Regulation: An Example from Canadian Prairie Agriculture." *Journal of Political Economy* Vol. 95, No. 1 (February 1987): 160–78.

UNESCO. *Manual for Statistics on Scientific and Technology Activities.* Paris: Division of Statistics on Science and Technology, UNESCO, June 1984.

Unnevehr, L.J. "Consumer Demand for Rice Grain Quality and Returns to Research for Quality Improvement in Southeast Asia." *American Journal of Agricultural Economics* Vol. 68, No. 3 (August 1986): 634–41.

Unnevehr, L.J. "Assessing the Impact on Improving the Quality of Food Commodities." In R.G. Echeverría, ed., *Methods for Diagnosing Research Constraints and Assessing the Impact of Agricultural Research. Volume II, Assessing the Impact of Agricultural Research.* The Hague: International Service for National Agricultural Research, 1990.

USDA. *Estimates of Producer and Consumer Subsidy Equivalents: Government Intervention in Agriculture.* ATAD Staff Report No. AGES 880127. Washington, DC: U.S. Department of Agriculture, April 1988.

Uzawa, H. "Duality Principles in the Theory of Cost and Production." *International Economic Review* Vol. 5, No. 1 (January 1964): 216–20.

Vanzetti, D. "Trade Games: Noncooperative Strategies in the International Wheat Market." Unpublished Ph.D. Thesis, La-Trobe University, 1989.

Varian, H.R. *Microeconomic Analysis.* New York: Norton, 1978.

Varian, H.R. "The Nonparametric Approach

to Production Analysis." *Econometrica* Vol. 52, No. 3 (May 1984): 579–97.

Varian, H.R. *Microeconomic Analysis.* 3rd Edition. New York: Norton, 1992.

Venezian, E. and G. Edwards. "A Model for Setting Agricultural Research Priorities in the West Africa Region." Unpublished report submitted to the World Bank, Washington, DC, June 1986. Mimeo.

Von Oppen, M. and J.G. Ryan. "Research Resource Allocation—Determining Regional Priorities." *Food Policy* Vol. 10, No. 3 (August 1985): 253–64.

Voon, J.P. "Measuring Research Benefits from a Reduction of Pale, Soft and Exudative Pork in Australia." *Journal of Agricultural Economics* Vol. 42, No. 2 (May 1991): 180–84.

Voon, J.P. and G.W. Edwards. "Research Payoff from Quality Improvement: The Case of Backfat Depth in Pigs." *Journal of Agricultural Economics* Vol. 42, No. 1 (January 1991): 66–76. 1991a.

Voon, J.P. and G.W. Edwards. "The Calculation of Returns to Research in Distorted Markets: Comment." *Agricultural Economics* Vol. 5, No. 1 (January 1991): 75–82. 1991b.

Voon, J.P. and G.W. Edwards. "The Calculation of Research Benefits with Linear and Nonlinear Specifications of Demand and Supply Functions." *American Journal of Agricultural Economics* Vol. 73, No. 2 (May 1991): 415–20. 1991c.

Voon, J.P. and G.W. Edwards. "Research Payoff from Quality Improvement: The Case of Protein in Australian Wheat." *American Journal of Agricultural Economics* Vol. 74, No. 3 (August 1992): 565–72.

Vousden, N. *The Economics of Trade Protection.* Cambridge: Cambridge University Press, 1990.

Wall, C.A. and B.S. Fisher. "Supply Response and the Theory of Production and Profit Functions." *Review of Marketing and Agricultural Economics* Vol. 56, No. 3 (December 1988): 383–404.

Weaver, R.D. "Multiple Input, Multiple Output Production Choices and Technology in the U.S. Wheat Region." *American Journal of Agricultural Economics* Vol. 65, No. 1 (February 1983): 45–56.

Weber, A. and M. Sievers. *Instability in World Food Production: Statistical Analysis, Graphical Presentation, and Interpretation.* Kiel, Germany: Wissenschaftsverlag Vauk, 1985.

Weinberg, G.M. *An Introduction to General Systems Thinking.* New York: Wiley, 1975.

Welch, F. "Education in Production." *Journal of Political Economy* Vol. 78, No. 1 (January/February 1970): 35–59.

White, H. "Using Least Squares to Approximate Unknown Regression Functions." *International Economic Review* Vol. 21, No. 1 (February 1980): 149–70.

Williamson, J.C. "The Joint Department of Agriculture and State Experiment Stations Study of Research Needs." In W.L. Fishel, ed., *Resource Allocation in Agricultural Research.* Minneapolis: University of Minnesota Press, 1971.

Williamson, O.E. *The Economic Institutions of Capitalism.* New York: Free Press, 1985.

Willig, R.O. "Consumer's Surplus without Apology." *American Economic Review* Vol. 66, No. 4 (September 1976): 589–97.

Willis, C.E. and R.D. Perlack. "A Comparison of Generating Techniques and Goal Programming for Public Investment, Multiple Objective Decision Making." *American Journal of Agricultural Economics* Vol. 62, No. 1 (February 1980): 66–74.

Wingate-Hill, R. and G.R. Davis. "Assessment of Research and Development

Projects." *Journal of the Australian Institute of Agricultural Science* Vol. 42, No. 4 (December 1976): 231–37.

Wise, W.S. and E. Fell. "Supply Shifts and the Size of Research Benefits: Comment." *American Journal of Agricultural Economics* Vol. 62, No. 4 (November 1980): 838–40.

de Wit, C.T. "The Use of Interactive Multiple Goal Programming in the Resource Allocation Process of the CGIAR System." Paper prepared for TAC/CGIAR, Rome, January 1988. Mimeo.

Wohlgenant, M.K. *The Retail-Farm Price Ratio in a Competitive Food Industry with Several Marketing Inputs.* Department of Economics and Business Working Paper No. 12. Raleigh: North Carolina State University, 1982.

Wohlgenant, M.K. "Demand for Farm Output in a Complete System of Demand Functions." *American Journal of Agricultural Economics* Vol. 71, No. 2 (May 1989): 241–52.

Wohlgenant, M.K. "Distribution of Gains from Research and Promotion in Multi-Stage Production Systems: The Case of the U.S. Beef and Pork Industries." *American Journal of Agricultural Economics* Vol. 75, No. 3 (August 1993): 642–51.

Wood, S. and P.G. Pardey. *Agroecological Dimensions of Evaluating and Prioritizing Research from a Regional Perspective: Latin America and Caribbean.* ISNAR Discussion Paper No. 93–15. The Hague: International Service for National Agricultural Research, June 1993.

Yotopoulos, P.A. "From Stock to Flow Capital Inputs for Agricultural Production Functions: A Microanalytical Approach." *Journal of Farm Economics* Vol. 49, No. 2 (May 1967): 476–91.

Yotopoulos, P.A. and J.B. Nugent. *Economics of Development—Empirical Investigations.* New York: Harper & Row, 1976.

Young, D.L., R.R. Mittelhammer, A. Rostamizadeh and D.W. Holland. *Duality Theory and Applied Production Economics Research: A Pedagogical Treatise.* College of Agriculture and Home Economics Research Bulletin No. EB 1473. Pullman: Washington State University, (revised) September 1987.

Zachariah, O.E.R., G. Fox and G.L. Brinkman. "Product Market Distortions and the Returns to Broiler Chicken Research in Canada." *Journal of Agricultural Economics* Vol. 40, No. 1 (January 1989): 40–51.

Zeleny, M. "Compromise Progamming." In J.L. Cochrane and M. Zeleni, eds., *Multiple Criteria Decision Making.* Colombia: University of South Carolina Press, 1973.

Zentner, R.P. "Analysis of Public Wheat Research Expenditures in Canada." Unpublished Ph.D. Thesis, University of Minnesota, St. Paul, 1982.

Zentner, R.P. "Returns to Public Investment in Canadian Wheat and Rapeseed Research." In K.K. Klein and W.H. Furtan, eds., *Economics of Agricultural Research in Canada.* Alberta: The University of Calgary Press, 1985.

Zentner, R.P. and W.L. Peterson. "An Economic Evaluation of Public Wheat Research and Extension Expenditures in Canada." *Canadian Journal of Agricultural Economics* Vol. 32, No. 2 (July 1984): 327–53.

Zhang, B., P.G. Pardey, S. Fan and J.M. Alston. "Economics of Technical Change and Productivity Growth in Indonesian Rice and Soybean Production." Department of Agricultural Economics, University of California, Davis, June 1993. Mimeo.

Author Index

A

B

Subject Index

Food Systems and Agrarian Change

Edited by Frederick H. Buttel, Billie R. DeWalt,
and Per Pinstrup-Andersen